FREE access to

InfoTrac® College Edition, **an extensive online library of top journals and periodicals.**

This innovative, energizing text shows students how to apply critical thinking, theory, and research to everyday classroom practice.

Offering an unprecedented linkage between educational research, theory, *and how they can be applied in the classroom,* this exciting book guides students in using their observational skills as a way of checking research and theory against demonstrated classroom results. In every chapter the authors give students real-life examples of how teachers have applied their own classroom research to address classroom issues/problems...and how they employ critical thinking and decision-making to test theory in real situations and make it their own.

While offering reviewer-praised, comprehensive coverage of learning theory and a structural organization familiar to educational psychology instructors, this book's innovation and success with your students also lies in its impressive ability to *demonstrate* how effective, reflective teachers make daily classroom decisions based on conscious use of theory and research.

"**D**efinitely, this is the text for the year 2000.... The first educational psychology text that parallels the outcomes for Phase I of the education bachelor's degree in content, educational 'language,' and flow of the material.... All aspects of the book are excellent...it is a compliment to the field of educational psychology."

—Ruth Doyle, Casper College

Linked to a wonderful array of online and multimedia technology and resources. Turn the page to begin your quick PREVIEW

Shows your students how to actively use their own classroom research to make practical teaching decisions

Action Research

Model Educational Television

M s. Alicia B is a middle school science teacher. She has taught for fifteen years and has become increasingly concerned that the students, while learning concepts, don't seem to be able to recall information meaningfully. She recently learned about a program in which school-aged students explored the environment via a scientific inquiry method and a study using concept mapping and other structuring strategies. She wondered which strategy would facilitate her students' learning and might create a little fun in the classroom besides. She is trying a "mini-experiment."

She has decided to teach her morning and afternoon classes differently: the morning classes would utilize the scientific inquiry method exclusively and the remaining classes would be taught to integrate concept mapping into their study of the environment. With the insightful learning groups, Ms. B. used a series of guided questions and structured lab exercises. These lab exercises required that the student employ naturalistic observations of their neighborhood stream and pond area. Ms. B knew that the "upper portion" of the stream appeared viable, alive, whereas the lower portion and the pond areas were beginning to become stagnant as a result of pesticide runoff. Ms. B. structured the students' labs so that they would measure the clarity and odor of the water, as well as making a timed sampling of evidence of aquatic life, at ten different sections of the stream and pond, moving from the top portion to the bottom. At each station, she had the students make "predictions" (hypotheses) about what they thought they would find, and in class the predictions and the observations were compared and discussed in class.

Ms. B. supplemented the afternoon classes' inquiry with structuring strategies. First, she utilized advance organizers at the start of each subunit and integrated mediators throughout the lesson. She also challenged students to derive their own mnemonics and instructed them on how to construct concept maps. She then guided them in the application of the steps when constructing maps relative

Action Research boxes throughout this book demonstrate how teachers can conduct their own classroom research and arrive at hypotheses that they then apply to issues or problems in the classroom. In this "Action Research" box from Chapter 7, "Cognitive Learning Theories," a middle school teacher experiments with concept mapping and other structuring strategies to see if she can improve her students' abilities to recall information meaningfully. Praised by reviewers, "Action Research" boxes demonstrate to students that classroom research is not only viable, but that the resulting knowledge makes them better classroom decision makers and more effective teachers.

"I really like the connections to the classroom, the Action Research, the Reflections from the Field, Teacher Tool Box, and Class Illustrations. These are all very practical components that assist the instructor in bringing theories to life within a classroom.... This is a very user-friendly and usable text."

—Warren Shillingburg, Community College of Southern Nevada

llustrates the teacher's decision-making process with realistic, thought-provoking cases...and video clips!

CLASS ILLUSTRATION
Stand and Deliver

The movie *Stand and Deliver* is a powerful presentation of the potential impact of self-efficacy. Throughout the movie, the teacher, Jaime Escalante, "fights" with the students' beliefs in their inability to perform at the advanced placement level. Through his efforts, the students slowly come to believe that they can pass the A.P. exam. The second component in Bandura's theory suggests that not only must one believe one can perform the activity, but that one needs to believe the activity will lead to the desired outcome. Having successfully passed the A.P. examination, the students in Mr. Escalante's class receive word that all of their passing scores are being discounted because ETS had suspicion of cheating, even though no cheating had occurred. The [...] Mr. Escalante) are not only devastated, but the students dem[...] ness to try again. They know they can do the work, but wh[...] never rewarded?

FREE *Stand and Deliver* VIDEO to adopting instructors!

CLASS ILLUSTRATION

Imagine the case of Sister Alice's fourth grade math class. As we observe the class, we note that one student is at the board, struggling to complete a problem. Sister Alice continues to press the student to try harder, to remember what he has learned, and to see the task as "easy," as simple. The student, out of a sense of frustration, announces that he can't do it. It's too hard. He is not as smart as everyone else in the class. The student almost pleads for Sister to help him. "Show me how to do it!"

This classroom presentation clearly demonstrates one student's attributional profile in relationship to that particular problem. The student clearly believes that his own low ability (being the dumbest in the class) makes this problem (task difficulty) beyond his reach. Since both ability and task difficulty are stable, uncontrollable conditions, the student loses all motivation to continue trying at the task and surrenders.

"Class Illustrations" integrated within each chapter encourage students to think about theory in practical terms, and gain a more developed feel for the multiple demands and decisions being made by the teacher.

Stand and Deliver...A powerful film filled with many illustrations of the concepts discussed in this book

Throughout this book, the authors offer interesting examples from the classroom experiences of Jaime Escalante, a teacher whose powerful story is told in the film, *Stand and Deliver*. Now being offered FREE to adopting instructors, this video gives you a wonderful opportunity to enhance your lectures visually by showing topic-specific clips from the film.

"Highly recommended.... An excellent book... Practical examples make the text very interesting. Content is full of current events. Both organization and accuracy are excellent."

—Mahadev Rathnam, The George Washington University

Clear, engaging presentation of major learning theories...

Praised for their accuracy, richness, and clarity, the theory chapters in this book offer a solid foundation for the realities of teaching practice. In Chapter 6, "Learning Theories: Behaviorism," and Chapter 7, "Cognitive Learning Theories," the chapter opening vignettes introduce theoretical coverage with intriguing classroom scenarios, so students quickly see how theory relates to real-world teaching practice.

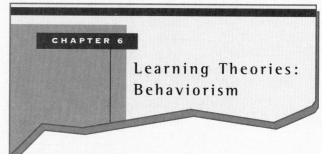

CHAPTER 6

Learning Theories: Behaviorism

Theory to Practice

sections in each chapter offer classroom scenarios showing how individual teachers employ theories or concepts discussed in the chapter. They often describe choice points at which these teachers make critical decisions and are followed by case illustrations which require the student to make decisions.

T he teacher stands before his class with an inquiring look, a raised baton, a bucket of ice cubes, and a ship's captain's uniform. He distributes sheet music for the "Main Theme from Titanic. The sounds of excerpts of the work fill the practice room. He points to a nearby student with an oboe poised at the ready and asks, "Who has the melody?" She looks puzzled and cannot answer. He waits a moment, then moves on to a student holding a flute in her lap. He asks again, "Who has the melody?" The flutist looks at the music for a second and then responds, "The string section." The teacher smiles broadly and replies, "Good!" A third student, a percussionist, has little trouble answering the question and receives

THEORY TO PRACTICE

A Look at Teacher as Decision Maker, Addressing Students' Unique Needs

Recall the initial scene described in this chapter. Mrs. Simon was confronted with the reality of teaching students with a variety of special needs and exceptionalities. Many of the students in her class spoke only Spanish. Some of her students appeared almost gifted whereas others were clearly over their heads academically. But perhaps her biggest challenge was in addressing the unique needs of two of the students. These were two males who made their grand appearance well after the bell and attempted to threaten Mrs. Simon if she recorded them as tardy. Certainly, these students had unique social-emotional needs, and their presence in her class would clearly be a challenge.

Perhaps Mrs. Simon questioned why some of these students were her responsibility or perhaps she understood that increasingly exceptional students were being helped to learn in environments that are minimally restrictive. Regardless of her reaction, Mrs. Simon, like all teachers, needed to understand the legislation that has formed th...

of the school, classroom, and the ing these illustrations, try to appl order to

1. Identify the probable exceptio
2. Suggest the next steps that sho
3. Recommend at least three strat

As you review the scenario, c research on learning disabilities as tions provided in the teacher tool the chapter provide insight and d concerned about helping these st

Case Illustration 1:
Boxtown Junior High

Your School
Boxtown Junior High School is growing, suburban area. The population comes from m...

T he music teacher's smiles and praise were certainly sincere personal gestures, but they were also tools of an effective teacher-designed behavior to increase the likelihood of both participation and thoughtful answers in his classroom. learning about melody was evident. But why? Do learning and performance need to re in a payoff? Do learners need incentives? If so, what kinds of incentives are necessary? learners need goals to work towards? Should teachers help students control and monit their behavior? Should teachers consider what their students are thinking about in learning?

The music teacher clearly realized the need to have a clear understanding of "What" he was about to teach. Further, as discussed in previous sections, an effective teacher has t consider the unique cognitive, social-emotional, cultural, and individual characteristics the "Who" they are about to teach. With both the "What" and "Who" of teaching identified, you, we, and the music teacher can begin to consider the "How" of our teaching. Identifying this "How" is a way for us to understand the theories that explain learning process.

Remember that in Chapter 1 you learned that theories are reasoned explanations for various phenomena in education. As you work through this chapter and the next, you will come to understand more about the phenomena of human learning. You will come to understand various reasoned explanations of human learning and their applications in classroom settings. These theories are often prescriptive, meaning that they can offer instructional suggestions, regardless of developmental level, subject area or the social context of the class. An understanding of learning theories is crucial to teachers, especially to new teachers.

"**W**ell written....Clear, it covers the major theories that are applicable to educational psychology."

—*Christopher Rand, Atlantic-Cape Community College*

...combined with many ways to analyze, think critically, and apply

Content Maps near the beginning of every chapter help students identify relationships between the various concepts about to be presented. These "Maps" are especially useful for integrating the complex relationships found among the separate concepts embedded within the theories of human development and learning presented throughout the text.

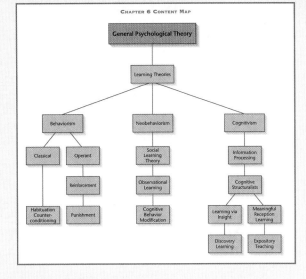

You Make the Call boxes present intriguing situations, issues or ideas related to chapter material, asking students to form an opinion, answer a question, or make a decision.

YOU MAKE THE CALL

WORKING WITH AND WITHOUT ROUTINES

Perhaps you have experienced classrooms that employed a set of routine procedures to facilitate administrative duties such as roll taking or homework collection. As you review the two scenarios listed below, begin to think of the conditions that may invite student misbehavior and how these may be reduced by effective routines.

Teacher A: Teacher A enjoys interacting and being personal with her fourth grade class. She starts each class by walking from desk to desk greeting her students and individually collecting their homework.

Teacher B: Teacher begins each class with the following instructions: "Take a deep breath, let it out slowly and with your eyes closed remind yourselves to become focused, active learners, respectful of each other. Now slowly open your eyes and begin the day!" Following this exercise, she asks the students who are aisle captains for that week to please collect the homework. While the captains are collecting the work, she asks the class if there were any questions about the problems they did for homework.

Teacher Tool Box sections throughout every chapter provide many practical classroom suggestions related to chapter topics.

Teacher Tool Box

Developing Class Cohesiveness

1. Structure class time to allow for student-to-student communications and interaction.

2. Encourage pro-social behaviors such as sharing, assisting, etc.

3. Reduce competition and Subgroups by
   - periodically changing academic work group compositions,
   - employing a grading system that recognizes individual achievement and group progress,
   - reducing evaluation procedures that pit one student against another.

4. Provide learning exercises that require students to share information and resources in order to be successful.

5. Recognize individual students' special talents and encourage them to share these talents with others in the class as would be the case with peer tutors.

6. Promote activities that encourage student sharing on a personal level to facilitate the development of personal relationships.

"I like the 'You Make the Call' and the 'Teacher Tool Box' features as a way of highlighting key issues, principles, and theories. I have reviewed many textbooks on educational psychology and this one is as well written as any I've seen. It 'speaks to me' as the learner...Easy to read, always close to the basic principle at hand with clear examples and interesting scenarios.**"**

—*Donald W. Kobabe, Pepperdine University*

Insights from the people who are "on the front line" ...the classroom teachers

Reflections from the Field

Much more than just general comments about teaching, these *Reflections* sections found in every chapter offer the practical suggestions, sage advice, and many ways that teachers have succeeded in their classrooms. Each of the *Reflections from the Field* sections quote a range of teachers, who describe classroom practices or ideas related to the chapter topic. For example, in this **Reflections** section from Chapter 2, "Developmental Theory: Cognitive Development," these teachers offer their class-tested ideas for teaching children to understand abstract concepts.

Reflections from the Field

1. I recommend teaching elementary students about fractions by having them work with familiar objects they enjoy such as cutting up pizza slices.

   —*Heidi (first grade teacher), Pottstown, PA*

2. To teach junior high students about abstractions such as how to balance an equation, I have them first experience the concept I'm teaching. For example, they first make observations of what their partner does when trying to . balance herself on a line of tape I've put on the floor. Then we discuss these observations and use them in explaining what is involved in balancing an equation.

   —*Jerry (middle school science teacher), West Chester, PA*

3. I found that teaching abstract concepts to my eighth graders was the most difficult aspect of my student teaching. One idea that worked well was to have my students act out the concepts. For instance, they had a lot of trouble understanding irony. So I asked them to get into groups and make up an ironic skit for the rest of the class. You could see as the skits were performed that lightbulbs started to go on.

   —*Jack (senior high social studies teacher), Phoenixville, PA*

4. Piaget's ideas are not only useful when it comes to teaching academics. When teaching my elementary students about classroom rules, I find that it's essential to use concrete demonstrations of what I mean. When teaching them about appropriate noise levels, I either play a tape for them that features various noise levels or have groups of students model these noise levels.

   —*Toby (third grade teacher), Philadelphia, PA*

5. You've got to tie what you're teaching to examples that are familiar to the kids. I learned from my co-operating teacher how to do this. In teaching the myth "Echo and Narcissus," I had the students first write about a conflict they had experienced in their own lives. Then we looked for conflicts as we read the myths. Next, my students wrote about how their personal conflicts

Field Experience Questions

These incisive questions relating to chapter topics guide students in their field observations of classroom teachers, help make field observations more targeted *and* productive, and encourage students to begin formulating their own teaching strategies.

• Field Experience Questions

As you begin your development as a teacher, it is helpful to learn from those with experience. Observing "experts" and questioning them about their own decision-making models is an excellent way to formulate your own reflective teaching model. Below are a series of field experience questions, related to the topics covered within this chapter. Use them to guide your classroom observations.

1. As you observed the class, could you identify evidence of the teacher's planning? (For instance, did he arrange class materials prior to class? Did he appear to have a goal and a developed set of strategies?)

2. As you observed the class, did you observe any times when the teacher was sensitive to student feedback (verbal or nonverbal) and attempted to adjust his strategies to better address the students' needs?

3. How would changing the composition of the class, in terms of the types of students involved, affect the "what" and the "how" of that particular lesson?

4. In discussion with the teacher, what data (theory, research, or personal experience) did he use as a basis for his initial planning and decision making?

5. In discussion with the teacher, how did he experience the interplay between the WHAT, the WHO, and the HOW of his teaching?

"**T**he content coverage is both accessible and comprehensive, offering the student a firm foundation on which to build. The organization is splendid...**"** *—Carl L. Denti, Dutchess Community College*

Highlighting the unique demands of culturally diverse populations

The authors include stellar coverage of the diversity issues your students will encounter in their classrooms. Chapter 5, "Student Diversity," offers in-depth discussion of cultural, racial, and ethnic diversity, as well as linguistic diversity, varied learning styles, gender roles, and how socioeconomic status affects achievement.

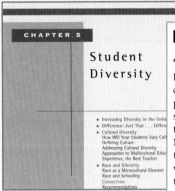

CULTURAL DIVERSITY

♦ How Will Your Students Vary Culturally?

In an early scene from the movie *Stand and Deliver,* teacher Escalante is coaxing a student to attempt a response to a math question. The camera pans the faces of the other students, who are anxiously waiting. The student finally responds correctly. The teacher praises him and moves to the front of the room. He faces his students, most of whom were of Mexican and South American ancestry and tells them that their ancestors, the Mayans, were unique in their contemplation of the absence of value or "zero." He tells them that math is part of their heritage—"its in their blood".

What happened here? Why did the teacher feel it was necessary to make those statements? Mr. Escalant~
cle for enhancing not only instr
motivati~ ~~ well. He use~

	Principles of Multicultural Education
Principle No. 1	Multicultural education should take into consideration students' backgrounds and experiences or "what the students bring to class."
Principle No. 2	Multicultural education should facilitate intercultural dialogue between student~
Principle No. 3	Multicultural education should be a long-term, ongoing process, not a short-ter implemented effectively overnight.
Principle No. 4	Multicultural education, in the end, should be "integrative, comprehensive, and (Appleton, 1983; p. 211). It should be incorporated into the entire curriculum.
Principle No. 5	Multicultural education should yield changes in instructional choices as well as
Principle No. 6	Multicultural education should not be limited to cognitive objectives and activities, but should extend to affective and psychomotor learning in the classroom also.
Principle No. 7	Multicultural education should facilitate student learning and achievement. All areas and all levels of achievement should be served by the process.
Principle No. 8	Multicultural educators should incorporate resources (e.g., written materials, guest speakers) in class that explore pluralism and are drawn from the students' local communities.
Principle No. 9	Multicultural education should address, not avoid, social problems in our national history and culture and encourage exploration and understanding of issues such as oppression and inequality.
Principle No. 10	Multicultural education should be promulgated by educators who show "care, understanding, and sensitivity" to their students, realizing that such concerns greatly influence motivation (Appleton, 1983; p. 216).

YOU MAKE THE CALL

RELUCTANCE TO FACE DIVERSITY

Take a look at the list of "excuses." Think carefully about which ones may reflect any reluctance you might have about facing diversity. It's natural to be reluctant, but it's necessary to confront our feelings. Then, it's necessary to start thinking about how the excuses can be eliminated.

"**G**REAT JOB!!...The content, applicability, and tables are excellent... The coverage of urban settings and culturally diverse populations fit into the student profiles our education majors would be reaching." *—Marylou Curcio Szabo, St, John's University*

Connected to the best of the Web...teaching and learning resources, late-breaking research, and more

The HomeRoom...Wadsworth's Education Resource Center

http://education.wadsworth.com

Features password-protected instructor's materials for this text, plus links to a variety of education-related sites, journals and publications, conference sites, and grants/funding information.

Connections boxes...linking every chapter to the Web

Enriching your students' understanding of the topics discussed in every chapter, these *Connections* offer site addresses and descriptions of Web sites that provide teacher forums, new research, teaching tools, and much more.

Connections

The good news in terms of effective teaching of diverse populations is that there is a growing literature of research findings and practical teaching suggestions. There are also more teachers willing to talk about the benefits as well as difficulties they face in their classrooms. Using the Internet, go to the Global Classroom Exchange website at <http://ePALS.com>; solicit comments from practicing teachers about multicultural classroom teaching.

Connections

While the current chapter provided you with theory and research that should help guide your decisions and your critical thinking about classroom management, it is the experience of applying the theory and research that will prove most fruitful.

There are a number of teacher forums found on the Internet, where teachers can exchange information, ideas, and even problems. Go to <http://www.pacificnet.net/~mandel/ClassroomManagement.html > and review the topics presented within the forum. What is the current concern? Latest approach? Suggested programs?

The latest online technologies give you and your students the teaching edge

FREE access to
InfoTrac® College Edition,

an extensive online library featuring hundreds of scholarly and popular publications.

Every new copy of this book includes a *FREE* four-month sub-scription to *InfoTrac College Edition*—a world-class, online library giving you and your students access to late-breaking news and research articles (full text, not abstracts). Available 24 hours a day, seven days a week, *InfoTrac College Edition* is updated daily with articles going back as far as four years. Access through a simple interface quickly and seamlessly provides the answers you need—and even the capability to print complete articles whenever you wish!

A Wadsworth/Thomson Learning exclusive! *Available to North American college and university students only. Journals subject to change.*

Thomson Learning Web Tutor™ 2.0...takes your course
beyond classroom boundaries to online teaching and tutoring

Rich with content for the educational psychology course, this online resource gives instructors and students a virtual environment filled with study, course management, and communication tools. With **Web Tutor** you can provide virtual office hours, post your syllabi, set up threaded discussions, and track student progress. You can also customize **Web Tutor's** content in any way you choose, from uploading images and other resources, to adding Web links and creating your own practice materials. For your students, WebTutor offers real-time access to many study tools, including flashcards (with audio), practice quizzes, online tutorials, and Web links.

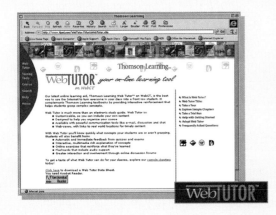

Available on WebCT
and Blackboard:

* Thomson Learning Web Tutor on WebCT: 0-534-55706-6.
* Thomson Learning Web Tutor on WebCT packaged with this text: 0-534-70230-9
* Thomson Learning Web Tutor on Blackboard: 0-534-55717-1
* Thomson Learning Web Tutor on Blackboard, packaged with this text: 0-534-70221-X

Connected, correlated, easy to use... an outstanding system of linked resources!

Instructor's Edition...featuring Supplement Correlation Guide!

At the center of this book's linked system of instructor resources, this information-packed *Instructor's Edition* supplement helps you effectively utilize all the resources available with this text. Following this PREVIEW, you'll find a key teaching resource, the Supplement Correlation Guide. This essential guide links each chapter's outline topic by topic to instructional ideas and corresponding supplement resources. At a glance, you'll see which specific videos, test questions, Web resources, and learning activities are appropriate for each key chapter topic.

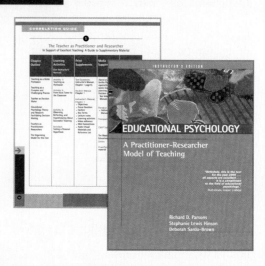

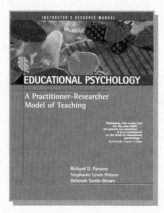

Instructor's Resource Manual with Test Items... Comprehensive!

This extensive manual supports both this text and your own classroom strategies with chapter objectives, focus questions, chapter outlines, key terms, lecture notes, learning activities, reference vignettes from the film *Stand and Deliver,* Web addresses, handout masters, video references, and a comprehensive test bank. 0-534-55703-1

ExamView®...No other computerized testing software compares!

Helps you create and customize tests in minutes. Test appears on screen just as it will print. You can easily edit and import your own questions and graphics, change test layout, and move questions—all in a WYSIWYG mode. Also offers flexible delivery and the ability to test and grade online. Windows/Macintosh: 0-534-55707-4

PowerPoint Presentation Tool...For engaging lectures!
0-534-55716-3

ExamView® and ExamView Pro® are trademarks of FSCreations, Inc. Windows is a registered trademark of the Microsoft Corporation used herein under license. Macintosh and Power Macintosh are registered trademarks of Apple Computer, Inc. Used herein under license.

Videos, transparencies...variety, excellence, and lecture-launching power!

CNN Today videos: Educational Psychology

Launch your lectures with riveting footage from CNN, the world's leading 24-hour global news television network. Organized by topics covered in a typical educational psychology course, this video is divided into exciting clips, each several minutes long. They're perfect for illustrating key topics and concepts—and for sparking class discussion. Volume I: 0-534-55708-2. Volume II: 0-534-55710-4. *Free to qualified adopters.*

The Wadsworth Education Video Library

This wonderful collection is being continually updated to give you the most current videos available. Please contact your local representative for a full list of selections and policy by adoption size.

Transparency Acetates... illustrations from the text!

A set of 40 full-color acetates featuring tables, photographs, illustrations, and other visual material. 0-534-55705-8

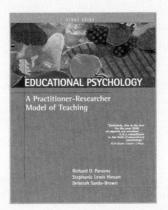

Also available: Study Guide...for your students' convenience, order it packaged with this text.

Correlated chapter-by-chapter *with Educational Psychology: A Practitioner-Researcher Model of Teaching,* this carefully prepared *Study Guide* reinforces the concepts presented in the text through use of chapter summaries, important terms and concepts, practice texts, focus questions, activities, and Web addresses for each chapter. Stand-alone: 0-534-55702-3. Packaged with the text: 0-534-69985-5

1

The Teacher as Practitioner and Researcher
In Support of Excellent Teaching: A Guide to Supplementary Material

Chapter Outline	Learning Activities (See Instructor's Manual)	Print Supplements	Media Supplements	Web "Connections"
Teaching as a Noble Profession Teaching as a Complex and Challenging Process Teacher as Decision Maker Educational Psychology Theory and Research: Facilitating Decision Making Teachers as Practitioners-Researchers The Organizing Model for this Text	Activity 1: Teaching as Profession Activity 2: From Ivory Tower to the Classroom Activity 3: Observing, Reflecting, and Hypothesizing About Successful Teaching Activity4: Testing a Personal Hypothesis	Test Questions: Instructor's Manual, Chapter 1 page15 Student Manual Chapter 1 Instructor's Manual, Chapter 1 • Objectives • Focus Question • Outline • Key Terms • Lecture notes • Learning activities • Video reference • Web Connections • Audio Visual Materials and Reference List	*Stand and Deliver* (entire film, especially opening scene-Teacher planning and Decision making) See Instructor's Manual, Chapter1 Handout Masters • Instructor's Manual, Chapter1 Transparency Packet CNN® Today Video The Wadsworth Education Video Library PowerPoint lecture material	*HomeRoom* *http://education. wadsworth.com* "Connections" in text, Chapter 1 Web "Connections" See Instructor's Manual, Chapter 1. *InfoTrac® College Edition* Thomson Learning Web Tutor™

2

Developmental Theory: Cognitive Development
In Support of Excellent Teaching: A Guide to Supplementary Material

Chapter Outline	Learning Activities (See Instructor's Manual)	Print Supplements	Media Supplements	Web "Connections"
What Is Development? Principles of Development Piaget's Theory of Cognitive Development Basic Cognitive Concepts. Piaget's Stages of Cognitive Development Adolescent Social Cognition: The Work of Elkind The Alternative Perspective of Vygotsky The Work of the Constructivist and the Neo-Piagetians Language Reflecting and Affecting Cognition Language Development Teaching and Language	**Activity 1:** Strategies for different stages of cognitive development **Activity 2:** Teaching a class in transition **Activity 4:** Adolescent Egocentricism **Activity 3:** Zone of proximal development	Test Questions: Instructor's Manual, Chapter 2: page 42 Student Manual, Chapter 2 Instructor's Manual, Chapter 2 • Objectives • Focus Question • Outline • Key Terms • Lecture notes • Learning activities • Video reference • Web "Connections" • Audio Visual Materials and Reference List	Handout Masters • Instructor's Manual, Chapter 2 Transparency Packet *Stand and Deliver* (2 scenes: Assimilation and Zone of proximal development): See Instructor's Manual, Chapter 2. CNN® Today Video The Wadsworth Education Video Library PowerPoint Lecture Material	*The HomeRoom* http://education. wadsworth.com "Connections" in text, Chapter 2 Web "Connections" See Instructor's Manual, Chapter 2. *InfoTrac® College Edition* Thomson Learning Web Tutor™

3

Developmental Theory: Moral and Psychosocial Development
In Support of Excellent Teaching: A Guide to Supplementary Material

Chapter Outline	Learning Activities (See Instructor's Manual)	Print Supplements	Media Supplements	Web "Connections"

Moral Development
  Piaget
  Kohlberg
  Glligan
	Activity 2:
	Confronting moral dilemmas
		Test Questions:
		Instructor's Manual, Chapter 3: page 65
		
		Student Manual, Chapter 3
			Handout Masters
			 • Instructor's Manual, Chapter 3
			
			Transparency Packet
			
			Stand and Deliver (3 scenes: Adolescent psycho-social development; Ego integrity; Imaginal audience):
			  See Instructor's Manual Chapter 3.
				The HomeRoom
				http://education.
				wadsworth.com
				
				"Connections" in text, Chapter 3
				
				Web "Connections"
				  See Instructor's Manual, Chapter 3.
				
				InfoTrac® College Edition

Psychosocial Development
  Erickson
  Marcia
	Activity 3:
	Psychosocial Development
		Instructor's Manual, Chapter 3
		 • Objectives
		 • Focus Question
		 • Outline
		 • Key Terms
		 • Lecture notes
		 • Learning activities
		 • Video reference
		 • Web "Connections"
		 • Audio Visual Materials and Reference List
			CNN® Today Video
			
			The Wadsworth Education Video Library
			
			PowerPoint Lecture Material
				Thomson Learning Web Tutor™

Other Psychological Issues
  Self-concept
  Teen pregnancy
  Eating disorders
  AIDS
  Child Abuse
  Divorce
  Suicide
	Activity 4:
	Reflecting a personal crisis and projecting a future one
	
	Activity 1:
	Students confronting emotional issues			

4

Exceptionalities: Addressing Students' Unique Needs
In Support of Excellent Teaching: A Guide to Supplementary Material

Chapter Outline	Learning Activities (See Instructor's Manual)	Print Supplements	Media Supplements	Web "Connections"
Responding to the Educational Needs of Exceptional Students	Activity 2: IEP	Test Questions: Instructor's Manual, Chapter 4: page 92	Handout Masters • Instructor's Manual, Chapter 4	*The HomeRoom* http://education. wadsworth.com
Full Inclusion versus a Continuum of Service	Activity 4: Assessing teacher expectations	Student Manual, Chapter 4	Transparency Packet	"Connections" in text, Chapter 4
Including Children with Exceptional Intelligence	Activity 1: Inclusion impact on 'normal' students	Instructor's Manual, Chapter 4 • Objectives • Focus Question	*Stand and Deliver* (1 scene: Externalized behavioral/emotional disorder): See Instructor's Manual, Chapter 4.	Web "Connections" See Instructor's Manual, Chapter 4.
Mental Retardation		• Outline • Key Terms • Lecture notes • Learning activities	CNN® Today Video	*InfoTrac® College Edition*
Gifted and Talented Students	Activity 3: From the eye of the child	• Video reference • Web "Connections" • Audio Visual Materials and Reference List	The Wadsworth Education Video Library	Thomson Learning Web Tutor™
Specific Learning Disabilities			PowerPoint Lecture Material	
Students with Physical Challenges and Chronic Health Problems				
Sensory Impairment				
Students with Communicative Disorders				
Students with Emotional/Behavioral Disorders.				

5

Student Diversity

In Support of Excellent Teaching: A Guide to Supplementary Material

Chapter Outline	Learning Activities (See Instructor's Manual)	Print Supplements	Media Supplements	Web "Connections"
Increasing Diversity	Activity 2: Classroom observation-Individual differences	Test Questions: Instructor's Manual, Chapter 5: page 118	Handout Masters • Instructor's Manual, Chapter 5	*The HomeRoom* *http://education. wadsworth.com*
Difference is just that!		Student Manual, Chapter 5	Transparency Packet	"Connections" in text, Chapter 5
Cultural Diversity		Instructor's Manual, Chapter 5 • Objectives	*Stand and Deliver* (the entire movie: The culturally sensitive classroom)	Web "Connections" See Instructor's Manual, Chapter 5.
Race and Ethnicity		• Focus Question • Outline	See Instructor's Manual, Chapter 5.	*InfoTrac® College Edition*
Linguistic Diversity		• Key Terms • Lecture notes • Learning activities	CNN® Today Video	
Learning Styles	Activity 4: Preferred learning styles	• Video reference • Web "Connections" • Audio Visual Materials and Reference List	The Wadsworth Education Video Library	Thomson Learning Web Tutor™
Gender Role	Activity 1: Gender Models		PowerPoint Lecture Material	
Socioeonomic Status				
Embracing Diversity	Activity 3: Preparing my own classroom			

6

Learning Theories: Behaviorism
In Support of Excellent Teaching: A Guide to Supplementary Material

Chapter Outline	Learning Activities (See Instructor's Manual)	Print Supplements	Media Supplements	Web "Connections"
What Is Learning? An Overview of learning theories		Test Questions: Instructor's Manual, Chapter 6: page 139	Handout Masters • Instructor's Manual, Chapter 6	*The HomeRoom* http://education. wadsworth.com
How Do Behaviorist Explain How We learn?	**Activity 1:** Applied Behavior Analysis **Activity 3:** Observation of Conditioned Stimuli	Student Manual, Chapter 6 Instructor's Manual, Chapter 6 • Objectives • Focus Question • Outline • Key Terms • Lecture notes • Learning activities	Transparency Packet *Stand and Deliver* (2 scenes: Cues/prompts/ rein- forcement and Observational learn- ing): See Instructor's Manual Chapter 6.	"Connections" in text, Chapter 6 Web "Connections" See Instructor's Manual, Chapter 6. *InfoTrac® College Edition*
Focusing on Operant Conditioning	**Activity 2:** Modifyng a student's attention seeking behavior	• Video reference • Web "Connections" • Audio Visual Materials and Reference List	CNN® Today Video The Wadsworth Education Video Library	Thomson Learning Web Tutor™
Neobehaviorist Learning Theory	**Activity4:** Social Learning and modeling		PowerPoint Lecture Material	

7

Cognitive Learning Theories
In Support of Excellent Teaching: A Guide to Supplementary Material

Chapter Outline	Learning Activities (See Instructor's Manual)	Print Supplements	Media Supplements	Web "Connections"
Foundations of Cognitive Learning theories	**Activity 1:** Applying Information Processing Model	Test Questions: Instructor's Manual, Chapter 7: page 161	Handout Masters • Instructor's Manual, Chapter 7	*The HomeRoom* *http://education. wadsworth.com*
Contemporary Cognitive theories		Student Manual, Chapter 7	Transparency Packet *Stand and Deliver* (1 scene: Information processing model): See Instructor's Manual, Chapter 7.	"Connections" in text, Chapter 7 Web "Connections" See Instructor's Manual, Chapter 7.
	Activity 2: Advanced Organizers	Instructor's Manual, Chapter 7 • Objectives		*InfoTrac® College Edition*
	Activity 3: Discovery versus Meaningful Reception Learning	• Focus Question • Outline • Key Terms	CNN® Today Video	
Factors affecting rote and meaningful verbal learning		• Lecture notes • Learning activities • Video reference	The Wadsworth Education Video Library	Thomson Learning Web Tutor™
	Activity 4: The Role of Elaboration	• Web "Connections" • Audio Visual Materials and Reference List	PowerPoint Lecture Material	

8

Motivation in the Classroom
In Support of Excellent Teaching: A Guide to Supplementary Material

Chapter Outline	Learning Activities (See Instructor's Manual)	Print Supplements	Media Supplements	Web "Connections"
What Is Motivation?		Test Questions: Instructor's Manual, Chapter 8: page 184	Handout Masters • Instructor's Manual, Chapter 8	*The HomeRoom* *http://education. wadsworth.com*
The Motivation-Learning Connection	**Activity 4:** Giving teacher feedback	Student Manual, Chapter 8	Transparency Packet	"Connections" in text, Chapter 8
Understanding Motivation		Instructor's Manual, Chapter 8 • Objectives • Focus Question • Outline • Key Terms • Lecture notes • Learning activities • Video reference • Web "Connections" • Audio Visual Materials and Reference List	*Stand and Deliver* (theme of the movie is motivation: Value x expectancy; Maslows need hierarchy; Locus of control) See Instructor's Manual, Chapter 8.	*Web "Connections"* See Instructor's Manual, Chapter 8.
Value: An Essential Motivational Ingredient	**Activity 2:** Maslow's Hierarchy-Bread before Bach			*InfoTrac® College Edition*
Expectancy: A Second Motivational Ingredient	**Activity 1:** Identifying the Locus of Causality		CNN® Today Video The Wadsworth Education Video Library	Thomson Learning Web Tutor™
The Classroom: Impacting Student Motivation	**Activity 3:** Goal Structure and Class Motivation		PowerPoint Lecture Material	

9

Classroom Ecology and Management

In Support of Excellent Teaching: A Guide to Supplementary Material

Chapter Outline	Learning Activities (See Instructor's Manual)	Print Supplements	Media Supplements	Web "Connections"
The Classroom: A Complex Environmental Setting	Activity 1: Analyzing a class-room	Test Questions: Instructor's Manual, Chapter 9: page 205	Handout Masters • Instructor's Manual, Chapter 9	*The HomeRoom* http://education. wadsworth.com
		Student Manual, Chapter 9	Transparency Packet	"Connections" in text, Chapter 9
Creating a Positive Physical Environment	Activity 3: Developing a plan— creating a positive physical environment	Instructor's Manual, Chapter 9 • Objectives • Focus Question • Outline • Key Terms	*Stand and Deliver* (3 scenes: Action zone, Social environment-entitavity, physical environment-materials) See Instructor's Manual, Chapter 9.	Web "Connections" See Instructor's Manual, Chapter 9. *InfoTrac® College Edition*
Creating a Positive Social Environment	Activity 2: Creating a sense of cohesion	• Lecture notes • Learning activities • Video reference	CNN® Today Video	Thomson Learning Web Tutor™
	Activity 4: Modeling a Learning Community	• Web "Connections" • Audio Visual Materials and Reference List	The Wadsworth Education Video Library PowerPoint Lecture Material	

10

Classroom Management
In Support of Excellent Teaching: A Guide to Supplementary Material

Chapter Outline	Learning Activities (See Instructor's Manual)	Print Supplements	Media Supplements	Web "Connections"
Student or Classroom Management?	**Activity 3:** Classroom Management or Student Discipline	Test Questions: Instructor's Manual, Chapter 10: page 228 Student Manual, Chapter 10	Handout Masters • Instructor's Manual, Chapter 10 Transparency Packet	*The HomeRoom* *http://education. wadsworth.com* "Connections" in text, Chapter 10
Prevention	**Activity 2:** Inclusion **Activity 4:** Developing a Plan	Instructor's Manual, Chapter 10 • Objectives • Focus Question • Outline • Key Terms	*Stand and Deliver* (2 scenes-Rules and consequences, Soft reprimand) See Instructor's Manual, Chapter 10.	Web "Connections" See Instructor's Manual, Chapter 10. *InfoTrac® College Edition*
Intervention	**Activity 1:** Reflecting and Remembering	• Lecture notes • Learning activities • Video reference • Web "Connections"	CNN® Today Video The Wadsworth Education Video Library	Thomson Learning Web Tutor™
Remediation		• Audio Visual Materials and Reference List	PowerPoint Lecture Material	

11

Planning: Essential to Instruction
In Support of Excellent Teaching: A Guide to Supplementary Material

Chapter Outline	Learning Activities (See Instructor's Manual)	Print Supplements	Media Supplements	Web "Connections"
Purpose of Planning		Test Questions: Instructor's Manual, Chapter 11: page 254	Handout Masters • Instructor's Manual, Chapter 11	*The HomeRoom* http://education. wadsworth.com
Classroom Planning: Reflecting the Mission of the Educational System	**Activity 1:** Reviewing the curriculum-mission connection	Student Manual, Chapter 11	Transparency Packet	"Connections" in text, Chapter 11
Factors Affecting Planning		Instructor's Manual, Chapter 11 • Objectives • Focus Question • Outline • Key Terms	*Stand and Deliver* (2 scenes-Planning flexibility and Lesson plan) See Instructor's Manual, Chapter 11.	Web "Connections" See Instructor's Manual, Chapter 11. *InfoTrac® College Edition*
Instructional Objectives	**Activity 2:** Writing an Instructional Objective	• Lecture • Learning activities • Video reference • Web "Connections"	CNN® Today Video The Wadsworth Education Video Library	Thomson Learning Web Tutor™
Domains and Taxonomies of Objectives		• Audio Visual Materials and Reference List	PowerPoint Lecture Material	
Gagne's Outcomes of Instruction				
Effective Planning and Teaching	**Activity 3:** Giving shape to the next lesson			
	Activity 4: Planning for special needs			

12

Learner: Centered Instruction
In Support of Excellent Teaching: A Guide to Supplementary Material

Chapter Outline	Learning Activities (See Instructor's Manual)	Print Supplements	Media Supplements	Web "Connections"
What Is Metacognition?		Test Questions: Instructor's Manual, Chapter 12: page 272	Handout Masters • Instructor's Manual, Chapter 12	*The HomeRoom* *http://education. wadsworth.com*
Teachers Role in Training Metacognition	Activity 1: It sounds good but...	Student Manual, Chapter 12	Transparency Packet	"Connections" in text, Chapter 12
	Activity 2: It's IDEAL	Instructor's Manual, Chapter 12 • Objectives	*Stand and Deliver* (1 scene- Constructivistic approach to the classroom)	Web "Connections" See Instructor's Manual, Chapter 12.
	Activity 3: Teaching metacognition	• Focus Question • Outline • Key Terms	See Instructor's Manual, Chapter 12.	*InfoTrac® College Edition*
Constructivism: The "New" Movement		• Lecture notes • Learning activities	CNN® Today Video	
	Activity 4: Creating a Constructivistic classroom	• Video reference • Web "Connections" • Audio Visual Materials and Reference List	The Wadsworth Education Video Library	Thomson Learning Web Tutor™
			PowerPoint Lecture Material	

13

Classroom Assessment
In Support of Excellent Teaching: A Guide to Supplementary Material

Chapter Outline	Learning Activities (See Instructor's Manual)	Print Supplements	Media Supplements	Web "Connections"
What Is classroom assessment?		Test Questions: Instructor's Manual, Chapter 13: page 293	Handout Masters • Instructor's Manual, Chapter 13	*The HomeRoom* *http://education. wadsworth.com*
Why Plan for Assessment?	Activity 1: Assessment Plan	Student Manual, Chapter 13	Transparency Packet	"Connections" in text, Chapter 13
What Are the Different Kinds of Traditional Assessment?		Instructor's Manual, Chapter 13 • Objectives • Focus Question • Outline • Key Terms	*Stand and Deliver* (1 scene-Test validity and individual differences and test measures) See Instructor's Manual, Chapter 13.	Web "Connections" See Instructor's Manual, Chapter 13. *InfoTrac® College Edition*
How Do Teacher-made Tests Facilitate Assessment?		• Lecture notes • Learning activities • Video reference • Web "Connections" • Audio Visual Materials and Reference List	CNN® Today Video The Wadsworth Education Video Library	Thomson Learning Web Tutor™
How Do Standardized Tests Facilitate Assessment?	Activity 3: Scoring Rubric–Chocolate chip cookies		PowerPoint Lecture Material	
Basic Considerations and Concepts in Assessment.	Activity 4: Table of Specifications			
New Developments: Authentic Assessment	Activity 2: Developing a Portfolio			

www.wadsworth.com

wadsworth.com is the World Wide Web site for Wadsworth and is your direct source to dozens of online resources.

At *wadsworth.com* you can find out about dozens of online resources. *thomson.com* helps you find out about supplements, demonstration software, and student resources. You can also send email to many of our authors and preview new publications and exciting new technologies.

wadsworth.com
Changing the way the world learns®

EDUCATIONAL PSYCHOLOGY

A Practitioner-Researcher Model of Teaching

Richard D. Parsons

Stephanie Lewis Hinson

Deborah Sardo-Brown

West Chester University

Wadsworth
Thomson Learning™

Australia • Canada • Mexico • Singapore • Spain • United Kingdom • United States

Education Editor: *Dianne Lindsay*
Assistant Editor: *Tangelique Williams*
Editorial Assistant: *Keynia Johnson*
Marketing Manager: *Becky Tollerson*
Project Editor: *Trudy Brown*
Print Buyer: *April Reynolds*
Permissions Editor: *Joohee Lee*
Text Designer: *Lisa Delgado*
Cover Designer: *Lisa Delgado*
Production Services: *Thompson Steele, Inc.*
Photo Researcher, Copy Editor, Illustrator, and Compositor: *Thompson Steele, Inc.*
Cover Printer: *Transcontinental Printing*
Printer: *Transcontinental Printing*

Printed in Canada
1 2 3 4 5 6 7 04 03 02 01 00

> For permission to use material from this text, contact us by
> Web: http://www.thomsonrights.com
> Fax: 1-800-730-2215
> Phone: 1-800-730-2214

For more information, contact
Wadsworth/Thomson Learning
10 Davis Drive
Belmont, CA 94002-3098   USA
http://www.wadsworth.com

International Headquarters
Thomson Learning
International Division
290 Harbor Drive, 2nd Floor
Stamford, CT 06902-7477
USA

UK/Europe/Middle East/South Africa
Thomson Learning
Berkshire House
168-173 High Holborn
London WC1V 7AA
United Kingdom

Asia
Thomson Learning
60 Albert Street, #15-01
Albert Complex
Singapore 189969

Canada
Nelson Thomson Learning
1120 Birchmount Road
Toronto, Ontario M1K 5G4
Canada

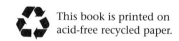 This book is printed on acid-free recycled paper.

Library of Congress Cataloging-in-Publication Data
Parsons, Richard D.
    Educational psychology: a practitioner-researcher model of teaching / Richard D. Parsons, Stephanie Lewis Hinson & Deborah Sardo-Brown.—1st ed.
        p. cm.
Includes bibliographical references and index.
ISBN 0-534-55701-5   ISBN 0-534-55709-0
1. Educational psychology. 2. Child development. 3. Effective teaching. I. Hinson, Stephanie Lewis. II. Sardo-Brown, Deborah. III. Title.
LB1051 H533 2001

                                                          00-024140

BRIEF CONTENTS

CONTENTS

SECTION I ♦ Considering the Uniqueness of "Who" We Teach

The focus of this section is on the identification of the special resources, limitations and instructional opportunities to be encountered as a function of the student's normative level of cognitive, psychosocial and moral development, and individual social, cultural and personal variations.

SECTION II ◆ The How of Teaching: Learning Theory and Instructional Practice

Section II focuses on the presentation of various theories of learning and their implications for teacher decision making.

SECTION III * The How of Teaching: Considering Issues of Motivation and Management

The focus of Section III is on the presentation of various theories of motivation and management as they impact teacher instructional decision making and classroom instructional practice.

Chapter 8 * Motivation in the Classroom 280

SECTION IV ♦ Putting It All Together: Planning-Doing-Assessing

Throughout the previous sections, reference was made to the importance of research—theory and findings as they form one's instructional approach. Further, the reader was introduced to the concept that the way one instructs needs to be formed and shaped by the mutually influencing and interactive nature of "what" is being taught, "why" it is being taught, and to "whom" it is being taught. The final section will highlight this dynamic process and provide the student with integrated models of instructional planning and delivery.

Chapter 11 ♦ Planning: Essential to Instruction 386

Having written numerous prefaces for other textbooks and having read more than our share of prefaces during our years as students, we are very aware of how easy it is to skip a preface in order to jump into the "meat of the text." ***Warning! Caution! Beware!*** Challenging material ahead! (We hope that got your attention.)

While it is obvious that *Educational Psychology: A Practitioner-Researcher Model of Teaching* is a textbook that you may be reading as part of your professional preparation for teaching, counseling, or psychology, what might not be as obvious is that it is also an invitation and a challenge. It is an *invitation* and a *challenge* to you to reconsider your view of the complexity of the teaching-learning process, the intricacy of the role and function of the classroom teacher, and the "professionalism" of teaching. It is an invitation to be a *critical thinker* both now as a student and later as a practitioner.

TEACHING—ART FROM SCIENCE

While perhaps always an art, teaching is also a professional practice based on science. As evidenced by the quantity and increasing quality of educational psychology research, our understanding of the factors affecting human growth and development and the educational process is expanding at near exponential rates. Those of you seeking to enter this profession are challenged not only to become familiar with the science and research of the teaching-learning process, but also to become knowledgeable, critical consumers who can integrate good theory and good research into your own classroom practices.

Educational Psychology: A Practitioner-Researcher Model of Teaching reflects our belief that teachers of the twenty-first century will not only need to understand the principles and findings that reflect the current state of their profession, but they will also need to value and employ an ongoing *critical thinking, decision-making, hypotheses-testing approach* to their teaching practices. In preparing this text, we tried very hard to (a) provide clear, concise presentations of the classic theories and current research; (b) demonstrate the connection between theory/research and the day-to-day decisions made by the classroom teacher; and (c) provide a consistent and coherent model for integrating the massive amount of information required by one in training to become a teacher.

ORIENTATION OF THIS TEXT

Educational Psychology: A Practitioner-Researcher Model of Teaching provides an introduction to the many areas of theory and research (e.g., motivation, memory, cognitive development) that comprise the essential informational base for the practice of teaching. However, this is not intended to be a passive text, one to read, memorize, and soon forget. Teaching is DECISION MAKING! Teaching is decision making based on the critical reflection of well-developed theories, research, and professional experiences. Teaching is active and reflective—and we intend the text and your reading of it to be active and reflective. Beyond the presentation of essential information, the text is designed to help you (a) understand and value the research-practice connection; (b) identify the many decisions a teacher is called upon to make and the many options from which to choose; and (c) begin to develop and apply your own critical thinking and decision-making skills as a professional educator in training.

UNIQUE FEATURES OF THIS TEXT

To accomplish the above goals, *Educational Psychology: A Practitioner-Researcher Model of Teaching* offers not only the more common textbook features, such as case illustrations, personal exercises, and additional resource listings, but also the following unique features. You will find that this text:

1. Provides you with examples of classroom teachers' *action research projects* relevant to chapter-specific topics. Our belief is that teachers need to integrate a researcher's observational skills and hypothesis-testing approach into their classroom teaching. Our text will encourage you to begin that process.

2. Invites you to actively engage—through observations, reflections, and dialogue—with the people who are "on the front line" as classroom teachers. Within each chapter you will be invited to visit the classroom and observe teaching in action (see *field experience questions*). Further, each chapter we will provide you with the opportunity and direction for making *Connections* via the Internet with the latest, most up-to-date information in educational psychology and in the world of the teacher.

3. Highlights the unique demands and special considerations for those working in *urban education settings* and/or with *culturally diverse populations.*

4. Suggests *field experience questions* to assist the reader to "see" the science of educational psychology and the process of professional decision making take form in the art of classroom teaching.

5. Provides integrating case illustrations. Each chapter provides multiple examples and case illustrations of the theory and concepts discussed.

To assist you further to gain a more developed feel for the multiple demands and multiple decisions being made by the classroom teacher we have included examples from a movie entitled *Stand and Deliver* (Warner Brothers). The movie is the dramatic presentation of the experience of one teacher, Jaime Escalante. We have selected this particular illustration because it provides a wonderful visual presentation of a number of concepts discussed within the chapters and provides an interesting learning supplement. We are not suggesting that this is the best, or only, example of the use of these principles. Nor are we suggesting that the portrayal of this teacher be seen as a model of teaching. The case simply provides additional illustrations and visual resources for highlighting the concepts, theory, or research under discussion within a specific chapter. Further, it is hoped that its appearance across chapters will help to highlight the number and types of decisions any one teacher will be required to make and the breadth of the theory and research needed as a base to adequately make those decisions. Each of the case illustrations employed is intended to illustrate the decision-making process and the need for a practitioner-researcher approach to teaching.

TEXT FORMAT AND CHAPTER STRUCTURE

Since a primary goal of this text is to demonstrate teaching as a critical thinking, decision-making, hypothesis-testing process, the material within each chapter has been arranged in the following manner:

1. A clear presentation the major theories, concepts, and research that serve as a foundation for good teaching practices;

2. Multiple illustrations of the utilization of those theories, concepts, and research in the practice of teaching;

3. The provision of the opportunity to reflect on specific classroom situations and to develop hypotheses about what is happening and what needs to happen; and

4. Directives to assist the reader in drawing upon the current pool of theory and research in order to develop a plan to guide the teacher's practical decision making in an illustrative classroom setting.

THE PLAN OF THE BOOK

In the introductory chapter you are challenged to view teaching as a noble profession that is both an art and a science, and to see the process of teaching as a *critical-thinking, decision-making process based in research and practice*. In this chapter, you will be asked to reflect on your own experiences and biases as they form your attitudes about teaching and teachers. Further, the chapter highlights the changing nature of the teaching profession and the increasing demands placed upon those serving the profession. In Section I, we will highlight how the unique characteristics of the students you are teaching (the *who*) must influence the decisions you make about the *how* of your teaching. In this section, you will be introduced to the importance of understanding the unique resources, limitations, and instructional opportunities to be encountered as a function of the students' normative level of cognitive, psychosocial, and moral development and their individual social, cultural, and personal variations.

"The How of Teaching: Learning Theory and Instructional Practice" is the next section of the text. The chapters in this section offer a look at the current theories and research into the processes governing learning. The chapters in this section highlight the implication these theories and research findings have for a teacher's instructional decision making.

In addition to understanding the process of learning, the effective teacher needs to master the subtleties of motivation and management as vehicles of instructional practice. The next section, "The How of Teaching: Considering Issues of Motivation and Management," offers a look at the current theory and research on motivating and managing today's students. Implications for instructional decision making and classroom practice are presented.

Throughout the previous sections, reference is made to the importance of research, theory, and findings as they form one's instructional approach. Key to each chapter is the premise that the way one instructs (the *how* of teaching) needs to be formed and shaped by the mutually influencing and interactive nature of *what* is being taught and to *whom* it is being taught.

The final section of the text, "Putting It All Together: Planning–Doing–Assessing," highlights the importance of knowing *what* one is attempting to achieve and *why*, PRIOR to venturing into the process of achieving it. The material in this chapter "puts it all together" by demonstrating how instructional practices are reflections of the teacher's considerations of the interactive and mutually influencing connection between *what* a teacher hopes to achieve, with the *who* the teacher hopes to achieve it, and *how* it will be achieved. Further, the chapter on assessment will assist you in developing reliable and valid assessment procedures as well as direct you on the use of such assessment as the data from which to continue the reflective process as a researcher-practitioner.

PROFESSIONAL RESPONSIBILITY

As you begin your own professional development, we invite you to not only become the best you can be, but to serve as a challenge and a support for all of your colleagues in the profession of teaching. Each of us in the teaching profession needs to challenge our models, our strategies, and our beliefs about the teaching-learning process if we are to continue to improve in knowledge and skill. This text and this class are only your first step into this ongoing process of professional development. As you read this text and as you develop as a teacher, you will be enriched by many experiences. We invite you to share those insights and experiences with us. We also invite you to respond to our text. Help us grow through your feedback. Were there points that you found particularly helpful? Were there points that seemed less than clear or less than helpful? Do you have suggestions which may benefit future readers? Do you have your own Action Research or Reflections from the Field that you would like to share? Please send your letters to:

Drs. Parsons, Hinson, & Sardo-Brown
c/o *Educational Psychology: A Practitioner-Researcher Model
    of Teaching*
Wadsworth/Thomson Learning
10 Davis Drive
Belmont, CA 94002

REVIEWERS

Julius Gregg Adams
SUNY College at Fredonia

William Bart
University of Minnesota

David A. Bergin
University of Toledo

Janet Byrne
Roane State Community College

Martha Carr
University of Georgia

Carl L. Denti
Dutchess Community College

Ruth Doyle
Casper College

John Durnin
Villanova University

Daniel Fasko
Morehead State University

Kathleen V. Fox
Salisbury State University

Don Hamachek
Michigan State University

David P. Hanson
James Madison University

Robert L. Hohn
University of Kansas

James A. Jacobs
Indiana State University

Donald W. Kobabe
Pepperdine University

Gail Lawson
Rhode Island College

James Mahler
California Lutheran University

Carla Mathison
San Diego State University

Nancy Billings Meyer
Northeast Iowa Community College

Ludwig Mosberg
University of Delaware

Morris C. Peterkin
North Carolina A&T State University

Judith Puncochar
University of Minnesota

Christopher L. Rand
Atlantic Cape Community College

Mahadev Rathnam
The George Washington University

Steven M. Ross
University of Memphis

Margaret A. Schimmoeller
Randolph-Macon Woman's College

Warren Shillingburg
Community College of Southern Nevada

Margaret Smith-Dietzer
Ball State University

Marylou Curcio Szabo
St. John's University

Bette Sue Talley
Briarwood Christian School

James M. Webb
Kent State University

Mary M. Wellman
Rhode Island College

Charles K. West
University of Illinois, Urbana-Champaign

EDUCATIONAL PSYCHOLOGY

A Practitioner-Researcher Model of Teaching

The Teacher as Practitioner and Researcher

T he first day of class . . . very exciting for most people and even more exciting for someone like Richard Farland, who, after spending his last four years as an undergraduate at the local university, now finds himself about to step from the role of student to the role of teacher. It is certainly a big, somewhat risky step for him to take, but a step he has taken with pride and much anticipation.

Entering school that first day, Mr. Farland imagined his class filled with students eager to learn. He recognized the awesome responsibility he was accepting—becoming a major influence on these developing lives. However, entering his classroom he soon realized that there was much more in store for him than he ever could have imagined.

The classroom was certainly energized on this first day of class and the students were eager, but learning computers may not have been their primary focus. Students, excited about reuniting after a summer break, seemed more intent on sharing stories of summer love than on learning computers.

The classroom is a place of energy. It can be a place of excitement and wonderment, and it has been a place where lives are formed. But classrooms with such energy, excitement, and impact don't just happen. They are the creation of skillful teachers and the reflective decisions those teachers make.

Classrooms are places where much is happening, and a there are many ways to respond from which a teacher must choose. W. Doyle (1989), for example, estimated that elementary school teachers have over 500 exchanges with students in a single day. When 20 or more individuals, all with their own specific needs, idiosyncrasies, and personal distractions, have gathered in a relatively small space for an extended period of time, the multifarious pulls and tugs on a teacher can be quite challenging. In the film *Stand and Deliver* (Warner Brothers), the teacher depicted, Mr. Jaime Escalante, provides an excellent, though dramatized, view of life in the classroom and the numerous points of decision making that confront every teacher. Within the first few minutes of the film, we see Mr. Escalante (1) find out which students do not speak English and request them to move to the front of the room; (2) start his second class, dressed in a short order cook's hat and apron, distributing apples to members of his class; and (3) decide to approach a resistant student (later identified as "finger man") quietly and softly, and confront him about his lack of preparation for class, instead of making a classroom scene.

The examples cited above represent only a few of the types of decisions that teachers must confront in the course of their duties. Further, the specific choices made by Mr. Escalante were only some of the options available. Presumably, he made each decision with the hope of facilitating learning in his classroom. Were they good decisions? Only time will tell. Were they conscious and reflective decisions? Only the teacher can tell. Were they representative of the types of decisions all teachers will be called upon to make? Absolutely!

Teaching is both a noble profession and a challenging, complex process, a process with no clear-cut formulas or recipes to follow. It requires a teacher who knows how to plan and how to adjust that plan to maximize the potential for learning in the class. If you are in the early stages of your own professional development, the thought of entering a classroom such as Mr. Farland's may be both exciting and anxiety provoking. It is exciting because of its challenge and the clear evidence it provides for the need and value of good teachers. It is anxiety provoking because there is so much to do and so many decisions to make. You may feel ill prepared to make those decisions and have many questions on how to decide which ones will be correct. This chapter will help you answer these questions.

✦ Chapter Objectives

As previously suggested, there are few if any clear-cut "how to's" in teaching, but there is a history of experience of successful teachers, as well as scientific information gathered through educational research that can serve as the foundation and guide for professional decision making. The current chapter will introduce you to that information. In addition to this information base of what we know about the teaching-learning process, this chapter will introduce you to a process of self-awareness, observation, reflection, and correction, which, if adopted as part of your professional decision-making style, will guide you to more effective teaching.

After reading this chapter you should be able to do the following:

1 Define teaching;

2 Explain the primary differences between "expert" and "novice" teachers;

3 Describe the "artistic" and "scientific" components to teaching;

4 Explain one model for conceptualizing the various interactive components of the teaching-learning process;

5 Describe your own personal assumptions about the teaching-learning process;

6 Explain the relationship between teachers' theories of teaching and their decisions about their own teaching;

7 Describe three traditional methods employed in contemporary educational psychology research;

8 Describe the process of reflective teaching.

CHAPTER 1 CONTENT MAP

5

TEACHING: A NOBLE PROFESSION

Before proceeding, take a moment to reflect on the title of this section, "Teaching: A Noble Profession." Does that phrase resonate with your experience? Does it reflect your own career choice?

In a country that provides free, compulsory education, we risk becoming desensitized to the value of education in general and to the noble role of the professional educator in particular. Education can make a difference, and effective teachers can truly change lives! Research (as reviewed in Brophy & Good, 1986) demonstrates the significant role teachers, at all levels, play in student achievement. Teachers are more than parent substitutes; they are, as Feiman-Nemser and Floden (1986) noted, thinking professionals who have important effects on student learning.

Perhaps you have encountered a teacher who has made a significant impact on your life, a teacher who excited you about your possibilities, a teacher who modeled the values you would like to model for your students, a teacher who gave direction to your own personal development. If you have, then you certainly can identify with the statement that "teaching is a noble profession!"

Teachers change lives. ◆

YOU MAKE THE CALL

A NOBLE TEACHER

Perhaps, before you get too far into the theory, the research, and the concepts of educational psychology and effective teaching, it would be worthwhile to "reconnect" with your own experience as a student of an effective teacher.

Take a moment to l upon your experience as a student. Which teacher (or teachers) comes to mind as being a positive, meaningful part of that experience? Why that teacher? What did he or she do that made the experience positive for you? How has he or she impacted your life? What would you like to take from this teacher to pass on to your students?

Now that you have identified the "difference" this teacher made in your life—why not tell him or her!

◆ The Many Roles of a Teacher

Many outside of the profession may simply assume that all a person needs to become an effective teacher is "content expertise." While it would be foolish to suggest that content expertise or subject knowledge is not essential, it is imperative to remember that content knowledge, alone, is NOT sufficient. We are sure you can reflect on teachers who were truly brilliant in their fields, but were extremely poor at conveying that knowledge and helping you to understand.

Teaching is a complex process, and the teacher must wear a variety of hats and play multiple roles while trying to increase students' knowl-

Far left, teacher as instructional expert; above, as manager; left, as counselor ◆

edge and understanding of the content under study. A simple reflection upon your own experience as a student will help you begin to identify the "many hats" of the classroom teacher. The role most typically associated with a teacher is that of **instructional expert.** In that role, the teacher is *responsible* for planning activities that facilitate learning. The teacher is responsible for guiding students in learning activities and evaluating the outcomes of their experience. This role requires that a teacher possess not only subject expertise but *pedagogical content knowledge* (Shulman, 1986). **Pedagogical content knowledge** is knowledge about the effective ways to present information to learners, which in turn requires an awareness of what makes topics difficult or easy to learn for students of different ages and backgrounds. As noted by Jetton and Alexander (1997), this type of knowledge does not automatically accompany content expertise.

Beyond these instructional responsibilities, a teacher also takes on the role of **manager.** A teacher needs to bring order and structure to the classroom to foster the learning process. This task of managing the learning environment places the teacher in the various roles of "task master," "social psychologist," and even "environmental engineer," a point that will be discussed in greater detail in Section III. Finally, a role that is taking on increasing significance is that of **teacher-as-counselor.** Professional educators understand the "reality" that teaching involves the whole person and not just the "head." Students bring various

instructional expert the role a teacher assumes when he/she employs behaviors targeted to inducing learning

pedagogical content knowledge knowledge about the effective ways to present information to learners along with an awareness of what makes topics difficult or easy to learn for students of different ages and background

manager a role assumed by teacher in which he/she employs behaviors which help bring order and structure to the classroom environment as a way of fostering the learning process

teacher-as-counselor one of the roles a teacher may embrace; assisting students with their personal concerns and problems through availability, approachability, listening, and problem solving

developmental issues to the classroom as well as additional emotional or societal stressors. To facilitate learning, a teacher must be aware of these stressors and be available to assist students directly or to make appropriate referral to other professionals when necessary.

YOU MAKE THE CALL

THE CHANGING NEEDS OF OUR STUDENTS

Bennett (1993) observed a number of the changes that have concerned teachers and impacted their roles within the classroom. Consider the following. How might each of the changes impact traditional procedures and processes (such as homework assignments, scheduling parent-teacher meetings, etc.) employed by teachers or change the various roles (instructional, managerial, counseling, etc.) played by the classroom teacher?

1. Changes in the "traditional" family structure: single-parent families, endemic homelessness, working mothers, etc.;

2. Cultural Diversity: increasing proportions of Latinos, Native Americans, Asian Americans, and African Americans;

3. Inclusion: incorporation of children with special needs into regular classroom settings;

4. Increasing demands for teacher accountability and continued professional development.

TEACHING: A COMPLEX AND CHALLENGING PROCESS

Although there are numerous definitions of teaching, most, if not all, include three specific attributes: (1) teaching as an *action* or series of behaviors; (2) teaching as *interpersonal*, involving a relationship and dynamic between teacher and student(s); and (3) teaching as a process which is *intentional*, that is, it is done with a purpose (Anderson & Burns, 1989). With these three components as guides, Anderson and Burns (1989) present the following definition of teaching.

> Teaching is an interpersonal, interactive activity, typically involving verbal communication, which is undertaken for the purpose of helping one or more students learn or change the ways in which they can or will behave (p. 8).

◆ Teaching as Action

Central to the definition of teaching is the concept of teaching as action. *Teaching is what one DOES in an attempt to induce or facilitate learning.* The recognition that teaching is more than mastery of subject matter, that it involves processes for delivery and transformation, will change the way we think about the teaching profession (Breuer, 1993).

Teaching—an interpersonal process ◆

Thus, an effective teacher is one who transforms content to induce or facilitate learning. But what are these actions?

Cruickshank (1987) found that in addition to being enthusiastic, warm, and supportive, effective teachers could be identified by the following features or "actions." Effective teachers demonstrated the ability to

1. *Organize classrooms* by structuring their curriculum, setting high goals, and communicating these features to students. Effective teachers involve students in the planning and organization of the class.

2. *Manage by setting and maintaining clear rules*. Effective teachers consistently apply rules and reward successful adherence to the rules. While consistent in establishing routines, they understand what is typical in the classroom and allow for flexibility.

3. *Employ didactic teaching*. Effective teachers employ elaborate systems of knowledge for understanding problems in teaching and knowing how to transform content into curriculum. While much attention can be given to becoming "content experts," teaching is still the process of translating this content into procedures that stimulate the understanding in our students.

◆ Teaching as Art and Science

Knowing what an effective teacher does will not reveal how a person becomes an effective teacher. How does someone come to organize and manage a class or transform content into curriculum? Eisener (1982) suggested that every successful teaching encounter could be analyzed both in terms of the science of instructional planning and delivery and the art of creating a conducive environment in which learning occurs.

Artistry

Rubin (1985) observed that teaching is an art, in that it involves processes and procedures that are so complex that it is impossible to reduce them to systematic investigation or formulation. Flinders (1989), in an analysis of teaching behaviors, suggests that a number of the types of behaviors enacted reflect the true artistry of teaching, such as employing communication that goes beyond speaking and writing. Teachers communicate through body language, the use of space, voice intonation, and eye contact—all ways of making a subtle impact on the child and conveying a message of caring for students (Flinders, 1989). Furthermore, teachers demonstrate a sensitivity to students' needs and a capacity to adapt to the emotional context of the classroom. For example, research (e.g., Pintrich & Schunk, 1996) suggests that students should learn to set personal goals that are moderately difficult. However, this same "science" fails to direct the teacher on how to approach the process or even how to know what is moderately difficult. The teacher as artist is able to apply that research sensitively and critically with an eye to the unique and diverse needs and abilities of each student. Finally, the teacher, as artist, often employs humor, individual contact, and opportunities for recognition and empowerment of students as means of building cooperation.

Effective teaching—true artistry based in science ◆

This artistry is dramatically presented every day in our classrooms. The effective teacher has the knack of simply knowing when to close the space between himself and a resistant student as a method of management. This teacher knows how to change the tone and inflection of his voice to gain the attention of the class. Also, he certainly will demonstrate sensitivity and awareness of his students and their emotional needs, often making adjustments to class routines and requirements in response to these needs. This effective classroom teacher is certainly an artist. His skillful humor, individual contact, and recognition, and ongoing empowerment fit the definition highlighted by Flinders (1989).

Science

Clearly, there is artistry in successful teaching, but artistry emanates from knowledge and skill. In one study, Livingston and Borko (1989) compared expert and novice teachers in three areas: (1) planning, (2) student interaction during lessons, and (3) post-lesson reflection. These authors reported an important difference between the ways experts and novices think about their teaching. Expert teachers have larger, better-integrated stores of facts, principles, and experiences to draw upon as they engage in planning, interactive teaching, and reflection. Effective teachers don't simply "stab in the dark." they make decisions based on a thorough understanding of human behavior, child development, and the learning processes. Research suggests that in their instructional planning and delivery, expert teachers: (a) understand and apply psychological theory and principles to their classrooms; (b) understand the instructional process; and (c) demonstrate an adaptability, blending technology and research findings to the unique characteristics of individual students and their particular classroom settings (e.g., Berlinger, 1986; Carter, Sabers, Cushing, et al., 1987; Carter, Cushing, Sabers, et al., 1988). Thus, expert teachers seem to *employ educational research as the scientific basis for the art of their teaching* (Berliner, 1987). It is their comfort with this knowledge base, along with their familiarity with their classrooms and material, that allows them to employ this knowledge with skill and dexterity (Rubin, 1985).

Teaching has its artistry, but it is an art that can be studied, analyzed, and understood (Breuer, 1993). Once understood, effective action can be taught, incorporated, practiced, and, perhaps become so automatic for the effective teacher that it once again appears as an art (Breuer, 1993). Once this occurs, we may have what Gage (1985) described as the scientific basis for the art of teaching.

YOU MAKE THE CALL

CREATIVELY EMPLOYING THE SCIENCE OF TEACHING

As noted in text, effective teachers understand theory and research but also have the facility to adapt it to their unique content, classroom, and students. Throughout this book, you will find explanations of educational theory and research. For example, in Chapter 7 you will be introduced to the concept of reinforcement. The effective teacher understands this concept but has also developed a natural manner of incorporating reinforcement into the daily routine. As a way of understanding the transformation of theory into practice, of science into artistry, interview elementary, middle, and high school teachers and identify the specific ways they have assimilated the concept of reinforcement into their own routines and teaching processes.

You could select other concepts and theories from the later chapters of the text and similarly find how the teachers you know employ those concepts.

TEACHER AS DECISION MAKER

It would be nice if there was a clear set of "how to's" to guide teaching decisions. But, as with most human endeavors, teaching is not cut and dry, nor is there a single, simple direction for effective teaching. This being the case, each teacher has to engage in an ongoing series of **decision making**. As a teacher, you will be engaged in many planning decisions, such as deciding what you want to teach, when you wish to teach it, and how you will go about the teaching process. You will make decisions about your classroom arrangement and decisions about if and how to respond to any one particular child at any one particular time. Each time a teacher is confronted with a decision, she can choose from a variety of possible actions or responses. Each of these responses will have its consequences, a point to be considered before making a decision. If we return to Mr. Farland we can more fully understand this process. When confronted with two students sharing pictures of their summer vacations and stories of their latest romances, Mr. Farland slowly moves in their direction while asking the other students to please

decision making the constant found within a teacher's day; selecting from options at any one moment with the intent of facilitating student learning

Illustration by Alex Raffi © 2000

Decisions that facilatate learning ◆

take their seats. He leans over and quietly asks them to put the pictures away and to take their seats now that "class is ready to begin." Why? What would have happened if he allowed them to talk a bit longer? Or what would have happened if he had simply yelled from the front of the class to put the pictures away and take a seat using a tone loud enough for all to hear? Or consider the teacher who in midst of taking roll at the beginning of class notices a student who strolls in late to class without his materials. Does she chastise the student upon entry, directing him to leave and go to the discipline office for his tardiness? Or does she ignore the student? Perhaps, she completes the roll and then after assigning seat work to the class, walks over to the student to ask why he is late and to remind him of the need to bring his materials to class. How might each of these responses, these *teacher decisions*, impact the learning process of that student and the others within that class?

There are many possible options from which she could have selected her actions. This will be true of all the decisions she will be called upon to make. There will be many options and alternatives from which to choose. But which should you choose? How will you know which actions will best facilitate learning? What will you base your decision upon? What will you use to guide your decision making? The answers to these questions can be found in and be part of your personal theory of teaching.

◆ Personal Theory Guiding Decision Making

Many teachers fail to devote much time, thought, or energy to the examination and development of their own view, their own model or theory of teaching (Glaser, 1988). Many teachers simply employ the same methodology that they experienced as students, without truly reflecting on the effectiveness of these methods. One's own experiences with the teaching-learning process can contribute to the development of a model of teaching, but they are not the only sources, nor necessarily the best sources of data to develop an effective teaching model. Teachers need a stronger theoretical base if they are to teach a far broader range of students and to take them farther than ever before, as modern society demands (Glaser, 1988).

Theory and research, Yikes!

The terms *theory* and *research* need not be overwhelming nor overly aversive. As a beginning, the "theory" referred to here can be simply the teacher's set of beliefs or assumptions about what needs to be done.

We all use such personal theories to guide our decision making. For example, you may have a set of assumptions or beliefs on how to make a "great first impression" which will guide your decisions to prepare for a date or job interview. You may feel it is important to initiate and assert yourself in these situations, while another person's decisions may be guided by a different theory, which suggests that first impressions are most favorable when the individual takes a more subtle, laid-back approach. Regardless of which theory a person operates from, each will employ a cluster of assumptions and beliefs to decide how to make a positive first impression.

We have sets of assumptions or "theories" that guide our choices and decisions in every aspect of life. It is most likely that you currently have a set of assumptions, beliefs, or theories about what constitutes effective teaching and what decisions one must make to be an effective teacher. Your own experiences as students have given you opportunities to develop assumptions about what is or is not effective teaching. These assumptions may serve as your current theoretical base for your decision making. As noted above, some teachers simply teach the way they were taught, without reflection (e.g., Feinman-Nemser & Floden,1986; Huling-Austin, 1994). Assuming that this may be true for you, consider the implications. How have thousands of hours of formal teaching-learning experience shaped your assumptions and theory about the teaching-learning process?

YOU MAKE THE CALL

PLACING YOURSELF IN MR. FARLAND'S SHOES

There is a good chance that your own experience as students has introduced you to a variety of teacher styles and actions. Using that experience as a reference point, how would you have responded to

1. Mr. Farland's class with its initial noise and chaos?

2. To a student asking, "Hey—are you the teacher?"

3. To the students who were sharing pictures of their summer vacations?

How might your actions differ from those of one of your classmates or colleagues? What differences may have resulted?

✦ Testing Personal Theories

While we are all theorists, we may not be aware of the assumptions we use to guide our decision making. Furthermore, we may not be aware of how to test the accuracy of our assumptions as a guide for making appropriate adjustments. If we are to be effective in our decision making and to select actions that truly facilitate learning, we must first become aware of our assumptions and be able to assess their validity.

For example, if you compared your assumptions regarding effective teaching to research on effective teaching, you may find that when subjected to systematic study some of your positions are confirmed, while others are relegated to myths. Perhaps you went to a school where underachievers in a particular grade were retained one year. Such a common sense approach to underachievement, although intuitively appealing, is not supported by systematic investigation. Doyle (1989) found that the practice of retention failed to increase achievement and often negatively impacted the students' motivation and self-esteem.

Other similar common sense approaches may prove less than "sensible" when reviewed in light of what we know about theory and research governing human learning. Would grouping students according to common abilities help or hinder motivation? Achievement? Self-Esteem? Common sense may suggest that being with similar students is beneficial, but research reports it often has destructive effects (Slavin, 1987). Consider the issue of in-class questioning. It may seem reasonable that a teacher should employ a random procedure when calling on students in class. Such a procedures appears to ensure that all students will eventually be called upon and no one student will be a central focus or be wholly ignored. It might also be assumed that such a random approach will keep all the children on their toes! However, research shows that such random questioning is not as effective with first grade students as is an orderly system of questioning.

As you proceed through the text, many of your personal beliefs and theories about the teaching-learning process may find support, while others may be proven inaccurate. This awareness will help you develop a more accurate guide for your professional decision making.

YOU MAKE THE CALL

IDENTIFYING PERSONAL BELIEFS TO BE TESTED

For each of the following, jot down your belief about the actions to be taken or the best way for a teacher to proceed. As you go through the text, look for research to support or challenge your belief.

- Discipline through punishment;

- The use of reward in class;

- Giving students choices;

- Setting high expectations;

- Learning: Teacher directed? Student directed?

- Adjusting teaching approaches to meet individual student needs;

- Including children with special needs in regular classes.

EDUCATIONAL PSYCHOLOGY THEORY AND RESEARCH: FACILITATING TEACHER DECISION MAKING

As previously suggested, personal experience with the teaching-learning process is an important source of data in formulating strategies for teaching. They are, however, data that need to be systematically examined for accuracy. One source against which a teacher can test these experiences is the informational base provided by the theory and research found within the field of educational psychology.

Educational psychology is concerned with the development, evaluation, and application of theories and principles of human learning and instruction that can enhance lifelong learning (Wittrock & Farley, 1989). The classroom practitioner, the teacher as artist may question the need for so much research and theory. In addressing the need and value of theory, Breuer (1993) noted:

> The world didn't need Isaac Newton to know that apples fall off trees. It did need Newton to give us a general theory that explains why apples fall off trees. Knowing why apples fall off trees has allowed us to go to the moon and to see television images of the planets. Knowing why leads to other discoveries, new applications of psycho-educational research and further refinements (p. 17, quoted with permission of MIT Press).

Breuer (1993) suggests that educational theory and research play an analogous role in education. Being familiar with the research and theory describing the teaching-learning process positions teachers to "discover" new applications and improvements in instructional techniques.

Professional educators strive to identify the various elements that can create an effective teaching strategy or methodology. Having clear answers to the many complex questions presented daily to teachers is essential for effective teaching. What do we know about the processes of learning and development? What role does motivation play in the teaching-learning process? What techniques are best for which students? Which strategies are best for which courses? How much should a teacher be involved in the learning process? Finding answers to these and the thousands of other practical concerns is the focus of educational psychology and psychoeducational research. While the developing body of knowledge is far from perfect (as is true in other professions such as psychology and medicine), a great deal about the connection between teaching and learning and the factors influencing this process has been accumulating and continues to grow.

◆ Methods of Educational Research

Research in the broadest sense of that term is *simply a systematic process for collecting information.* Quite often, this research supports everyday experience or common sense conclusions, while at other times it fails to offer that support and in fact may challenge the wisdom of the "common sense." Thus, in addition to our experience, our intuition, and our common sense, our professional decisions must also be based on our critical review and understanding of theory and research. But as with all things, we need to approach theory and research with a knowledgeable and critical eye. Thus, understanding the value and limitations of research methodology is essential for the effective teacher.

There are many different kinds of research studies conducted on the teaching-learning process. As you proceed through your professional training, you will learn more about research design and statistics and the various ways to conduct education research. Let us take a brief look at three types of education research methods: (a) descriptive, (b) correlational, and (c) experimental.

Descriptive Research

descriptive research research which employs systematic observation and recording of data without manipulation of the observed phenomenon

Descriptive research is often the method used in natural settings such as classrooms. These studies are designed to collect detailed information about specific situations or events. The descriptive researcher employs surveys, questionnaires, and observational coding procedures to systematically describe the phenomena being observed. A descriptive study may include records of classroom activities, actual classroom dialogue, or records of student-teacher interactions. For example, a researcher may be interested in describing the interactions a teacher employs during a particular class period. That researcher may first define the types of interaction she wishes to categorize (e.g., ask questions, provide answers, correct a student, approach a student, and touch a student) and then either directly observe the teacher's class or videotape the class for later analysis. If one were to observe a teacher whom we experienced as effective, we would most likely note that she uses humor, often modifies the tone and volume of her voice, and tends to move about the class. These observations may lead the researcher to begin to wonder if there is any relationship between these actions and the actions of her students. Considering the relationships between two variables is the topic of correlational studies.

Correlational Research

correlational research research which identifies apparent relationships between variables or factors

Whereas descriptive research attempts to describe an event, **correlational research** extends the type of questions asked from "what occurred?" to "what is the relationship between two or more things observed?" For example, a researcher may want to know if there is any type of relationship between the amount of homework assigned and the eventual academic achievement of the students. Thus, the researcher may collect data that depict varying amounts of homework assigned to students, along with the grades for those same students. Using various statistical techniques, the researcher will attempt to identify the possible relationship between these two variables (i.e., amount of homework and academic achievement).

positive correlation a relationship between two variables in which change in one variable is marked by change in the other variable in the same direction; as one increases, the other increases

negative correlation a relationship between two variables in which change in one variable is marked by change in the opposite direction for the other variable; as one increases, the other decreases

The researcher may find that the variables are related, in that the more one variable (for example, homework) is present, the more the other (in this case, achievement) variable is present. This would be considered a **positive correlation.** On the other hand, the researcher may find that the two variables are related but in an inverse fashion. That is the more of one variable, the less of the other. This would be a **negative correlation.** It is important to remember that correlational research focuses on possible relationships between variables but DOES NOT address the issue of causation.

Consider the situation where a researcher discovers a relationship between the frequency of a teacher's use of aggressive language and the frequency of aggressive language exhibited by the students. While these two phenomena may be correlated, the cause is not clear. The teacher's aggressive comments may cause student aggressive language, or the student's aggression may cause the teacher's response. The two events, however, may even be caused by a third unobserved event. Perhaps some painful event experienced by both the teacher and the students, for example the recent death of a well liked faculty member, may be causing both the teacher's and the students' aggressive response.

Correlational research may find that variables have either no relationship at all and thus have a zero correlation, or they can be related in a way which suggests that when one variable is present, the other variable is also present (i.e., a positive correlation) or that when one is present, the other is not (this would be a negative correlation). The type and degree of relationship is generally expressed as a statistic known as a **correlation coefficient.** This correlation coefficient can range from −1.00 (a perfect negative correlation), through .00 (no correlation), to +1.00 (a perfect positive correlation). The farther the correlation is from zero, whether in a positive or negative direction, the stronger the relationship between the variables. But no matter how strong that relationship is, even if it were represented by a perfect correlation (i.e., +1.00 or −1.00), it would still not indicate cause and effect. To answer causative questions a researcher needs to conduct a well controlled, valid experiment—something that is often difficult in educational research.

correlation coefficient a number, ranging between −1.00 and +1.00 which indicates the size and direction of a relationship between variables

Experimental Research

Experimental research involves the active and deliberate manipulation of a variable in order to observe changes in another variable. For example, assume that a teacher wanted to investigate the effects of employing a particular teaching strategy on the academic achievement of her students. The teacher may believe that using audiovisual presentation of material is more effective than traditional lecturing. To test this hypothesis, the teacher divided her class into separate groups, using a table of random numbers to assign students to two groups. She then presented her lesson to both groups, with one group receiving audiovisual material plus a lecture whereas the other group received a lecture only. She then compared the group scores on her unit test. In this situation, the researcher is not just observing, but is attempting to affect what was observed (student achievement) by manipulating one of the characteristics of the classroom (the audiovisual material).

experimental research research method in which variables are manipulated in order to observe and record effects

The variable selected by the researcher to manipulate (i.e., the audiovisual material) is called the **independent variable,** or the treatment. Various changes measured (e.g., achievement as recorded by unit test scores), which resulted from the manipulation of the independent variable are called **dependent variables.** For this researcher to be able to conclude that the changes observed were in fact "caused" by the independent variable, she would have to demonstrate that there were no other changes that could have accounted for the results. Thus, in our example, if the researcher simply observed another class whose teacher

independent variable the variable in an experiment which is manipulated and being tested for its impact on other variables

dependent variable the variable in an experiment which changes as a result of the independent variable; the effect, in a study of cause and effect

used audiovisuals and contrasted that class's performance to her own class, any differences could have been created by many other things other than the presence or absence of the audiovisual presentation. Could you think of other possible differences that could have accounted for the different levels of achievement? (Hint: a different teacher? different "classroom"? other factors?).

In considering this simple example, it becomes obvious how difficult experimental research is to implement in a classroom setting. So many factors need to be controlled in order to allow for the manipulation of only the independent variable.

◆ Statistics: A Language of Research

Educational research often presents its findings using statistical analysis. As you review educational research, you will become aware that the data described are often discussed using terminology such as "significant differences" or stating "these data are significant." When used statistically the word **"significant"** refers to the degree to which these findings are due to "nonchance" occurrence. It is not an automatic signal that the findings are greatly important or have meaning. A significant finding is simply one in which "chance" has been ruled out. Thus, "significance" really refers to the belief that the data have occurred as a result of the manipulation of the independent variable and not by chance alone. Since chance can never be completely ruled out in any study, researchers have established a standard upon which to judge whether findings are statistically significant or not. Traditionally, there are two levels of significance employed: the .05 level and the .01 level. When the results of a study are stated to be significant at the .05 level, this means that the results are expected to occur by chance alone only 5 of 100 times. Similarly, if the results are significant at the .01 level, there is only 1 chance in 100 that they are the result of chance alone. Thus, significance refers to statistical probability and not necessarily to the absolute essentialness or value of the information to the classroom teacher.

significance (statistically) an indication that the results are not likely a chance occurrence

┃TEACHERS AS PRACTITIONERS-RESEARCHERS

Breuer (1993) has noted that for a revision in education to take place, greater interaction between research findings and professional practice must occur. Teachers need to employ research as part of their own ongoing approach to the classroom, in their own style and thus need to formulate their own model of teaching. While educational theory and research serve as meaningful information and data to guide instructional decisions, they do not always provide absolute, hard and fast rules to follow. Teachers must use research and theory as a foundation or structure to guide their decisions, but those decisions must be professional judgments based upon knowledge, experience, and constructive reflection about teachers' own situations and the effectiveness of their theory. This **practitioner-researcher** model is actively employed by

practitioner-researcher role of teachers in that they must use research and theory as a foundation or structure to guide their decisions, but those decisions must be professional judgments based upon knowledge, experience, and constructive reflection about their own situations and the effectiveness of their theory

other professionals. It is safe to assume that you would not feel comfortable being treated by a physician who was not aware of the latest research on your condition. Similarly, you might find it discomforting to find that your physician rigidly applied the same approaches to everyone, without considering the patient's previous history or individual conditions.

Good and Brophy (1990) suggest that research findings should be used as a basis for personal elaboration. That is, rather than looking for answers or specific guidelines for how to teach, teachers should employ research as the impetus for thoughtful action. This would be pre-planned action and action that occurs spontaneously within the classroom. To be successful, a teacher must be both a practitioner and a researcher. Teachers need to investigate in greater depth the effects of their own experiments with various instructional and management practices.

◆ Reflective Teaching

As theoretical practitioners (or, if you prefer, practical theorists) teachers need not only to interact in the moment with students, but also need to reflect, inquire, and critique their own interactions (Brandt, 1988). Thus, to be effective, a teacher will need to be an active participant and an observer of that process. As an observer, the teacher needs to process and interpret all the information presented within the classroom and to employ that information, along with the more classic theory and research, as a base for planning and decision making.

This ability to interpret classroom activity to make instructional and management decisions is a characteristic of "expert" teachers. (Berliner, 1987, 1988; Borko & Shavelson, 1990; Carter et al., 1987; Leinhardt & Greeno, 1986; Peterson & Comeaux, 1987). Consider the case of Louise Meyers, a high school algebra teacher. Ms. Meyers had just spent the previous week introducing a process for solving algebraic equations. However, it was clear that while her students were paying attention, taking notes, and attempting the homework problems, many were simply not "getting it"! Even though her lessons for the upcoming week had been planned, she decided to modify that plan and schedule a class trip to a nearby business where the students could see algebra in action. She felt that seeing the real world application of algebra would help her students embrace the value of algebra, which in turn would help them grasp the concepts she would be presenting.

Connections

Although it may be somewhat of a cliché, the truth remains that we are certainly immersed in the "information age." The ability to dialogue with colleagues, tap the most current research, and be informed about trends and issues within one's profession is often no more than a mouse click away. Throughout the remaining chapters you will be invited to surf the Net and make connections. The exercises found within the "Connections" section may ask you to engage in dialogue with a teacher, review the most recent research on a particular topic, or even just find out what is hot within the profession. Staying connected will be essential if you are to remain a critically thinking research-practitioner and in turn effectively impact your students.

Throughout the chapter and the remainder of the text, we will try to demonstrate that teaching is a profession that blends art and science. Visit the following Web site: <http://www.nbpts.org>. This is the Web site for the National Board of Professional Teaching Standards. Read the five propositions of accomplished teaching that were developed by the National Board (1997). Along with your classmates, discuss your reactions and the implications that these standards hold for your continued education and training.

This process of developing lessons and plans with thoughtful consideration of educational theory and research, along with the analysis of the effect of that plan on the students' learning, and then adjusting accordingly, has been called *reflective teaching* (Schon, 1983; Cruickshank, 1987). The **reflective teacher** is one who knows what she is doing, and why she decided to do it, and who reviews the effect of what she has done. The reflective teacher employs educational psychology and research in formulating hypotheses about effective classroom strategies, which can then be employed, evaluated, and revised. Often, the reflective teacher employs systematic approaches to gathering data about the classroom and the effect of the decisions she has implemented. Under these conditions of systematic observation, the reflective teacher, steps into the realm of *action researcher!*

reflective teacher teachers who are thoughtful and inventive, who review situations, analyzing what they did and why along with the impact of that decision in order to improve future decision making

✦ Action Research

As suggested above, effective teachers are reflective teachers. They use research and theory to hypothesize about effective strategies, which they employ, evaluate, and revise. In their quest to assess the effectiveness of their strategies, most teachers who attempt to be reflective employ observations that are nonsystematic. The observations they make and the data they collect are often anecdotal and subjective. To be an effective teacher it is important to learn to make systematic classroom observations in which you will take measurements of frequency, duration, magnitude, or latency of specific behaviors and events (Moore, 1992). Being more systematic about your observations and data collection helps transform your reflection into **action research** (Casanova, 1989; Cochran-Smith & Lytle, 1990; Hovda & Kyle, 1984; Parsons & Brown, in press; Sardo-Brown, 1990).

action research research which stems from a practical problem and is planned and implemented by the person most likely to be affected by the findings; it involves systematic observation, data collection, and incorporation of results into planning and practice

Because action research is conducted by a classroom teacher, it serves as a vehicle through which the teacher can investigate issues of interest and then incorporate the results into his own planning and future teaching. Action research stems from a practical problem and is planned and implemented by the person most likely to be affected by the findings—the teacher (Parsons & Brown, in press; Sardo-Brown, 1994).

Action research can take many forms and employ a wide range of methodologies. To be meaningful and important to the teacher, the key to a worthwhile teacher-initiated investigation lies not in the methodology used or the types of data collected, but in the questions researched (Spaulding, 1992). Throughout the following chapters, examples of action research will appear. It will become apparent that action research is not intended to meet the rigors of publication or theory building. Rather, it is designed to help the teacher document the effectiveness of a particular program or procedure employed within her classroom. Yet, even with this purpose in mind, this informal classroom-based research should be coherent and systematic, and should provide valuable information for the teacher (Parsons & Brown, in press).

THE ORGANIZING MODEL FOR THIS TEXT

The field of educational psychology provides an extensive informational base from which you can begin to form your teaching decisions. Organizing that material for your planning and decision making can be overwhelming, unless you have an overriding organizing model. We have organized this text along three dimensions: the WHO that is being taught, the HOW through which the teaching may occur, and the WHAT that is to be achieved. As a classroom teacher, you certainly will be concerned with the question of WHAT you will be teaching. Certainly, as you prepare for your own first day in the classroom, you will give a lot of time and energy to deciding what—of all the many pieces of information you could convey—will be the focus of your first few days of class. Deciding WHAT you are teaching and WHAT you are attempting to achieve is clearly fundamental. It is an essential ingredient to the teaching-learning process. Deciding on the WHAT of your teaching is only part of the equation, however, and it is a part than can only be addressed with an eye toward the next two components, the HOW and the WHO.

Knowing that I am teaching computer science, mathematics, or English composition stimulates thoughts about HOW to teach that material. These decisions regard the sequencing of topics, manner of

Action Research

An Integrated Approach to Teaching Map Reading Skills

A s noted in this chapter, action research is both an important way to promote the reform of schools and a way for increasing the effectiveness of a classroom teacher. Action research provides the teacher with an opportunity to address practical problems in the classroom. Throughout the upcoming chapters, you will be introduced to specific examples of classroom teachers-turned-researchers, through their application of action research. As an example, the following excerpt is of one teacher's concern regarding her utilization of classroom time.

Utilization of Classroom Time

Nancy, a veteran third grade teacher, wanted to know if teaching map-reading skills through a 10-week integrated social studies curriculum would improve students' place location skills. Nancy hypothesized that employing an integrated approach, in which she used math, language arts, and science to convey map skills, in addition to social studies, might prove more effective in teaching map skills than simply using social studies alone. Her interest in this issue stemmed from reading journal articles that indicated that American students' knowledge of geography was very poor. To test her assumptions, Nancy compared the scores on a geographic location test for two classes, one having the integrated social studies approach, and the other not having this exposure. Nancy found that the scores were significantly higher for those students taught with the integrated social studies approach. Therefore, she feels encouraged that her initial hunch about the value of an integrated approach was supported. Nancy is now investigating the ideal amount of time to spend each day on map reading skills with third graders.

presentation, types of materials to be employed, and the manner in which to present the material. For example, consider a teacher who is going to teach American history. It can be assumed that the methods and techniques employed in teaching this content area may differ from that which would be useful in teaching another subject matter such as art or physical education. Thus, the WHAT helps give shape to the HOW.

While knowing that the WHAT will help set the stage for the HOW, decisions about both the WHAT and HOW of teaching will have to take into consideration the unique characteristics and needs of the particular students you teach. Again, if we consider teaching American history, we can probably appreciate the fact that the types of information and levels of knowledge conveyed, along with strategies and methods employed, will differ depending upon whether this is a class for fifth graders, tenth graders, or college history majors. Being aware of the unique characteristics, individual talents, and limitations of the students you teach is another component to be considered in your decision-making process. In the upcoming chapters, we will highlight the importance of teacher decision making that takes into consideration the multiple, interactive influence of these three interrelated variables (see Figure 1.1).

WHAT is the content of teaching? Teachers need to have mastery over their content area, knowing not only the basic concepts of the material but the sequence and prioritization of the content to be presented. Teachers also need to plan and decide on the level of complexity with which this material will be taught (see Chapter 11).

WHO are the active participants in this process? As a teacher, you must be aware not only of the general developmental abilities and limitations of your students, but also their individual differences. In addition to knowing the characteristics students bring to the learning environment, you must be aware of your own expectations, attitudes, and style, and the way these effect the learning process.

HOW will I approach the teaching process? As a teacher, you must become aware of the explicit set of teaching strategies, classroom management and behaviors you employ. The "how" involves learning theories, teaching methods of classroom management, and student motivation.

A FINAL NOTE

A major focus of this text is to help you make explicit the various theories, assumptions, and beliefs that dictate your decisions regarding the teaching-learning process. Further, as we proceed through the upcoming chapters, we invite you to test your "beliefs," your "assumptions," your "theories" against the theories and research that serve as the informational base for the practice of teaching.

As you proceed through this text and through your careers as educators, we encourage you to always remember that while there is much

Figure 1.1
The Teaching-Learning Process: An Integration of "Who," "What," and "How."

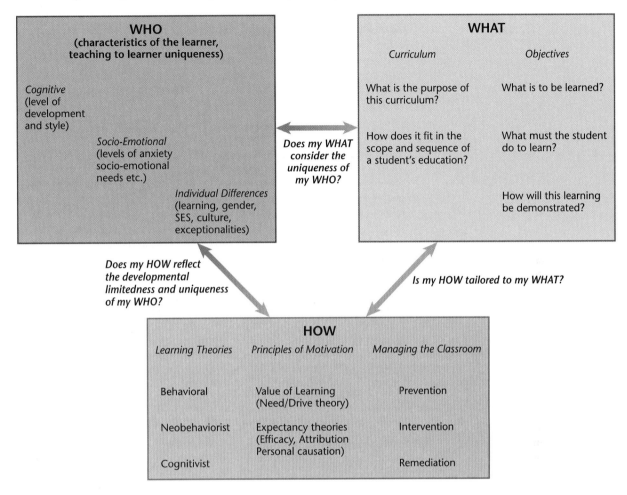

science and research to teaching, teaching remains a human endeavor. Teachers have the potential for influencing students in ways that can be far reaching and long lasting. Thus, while being concerned with your proficiency and professionalism as a teacher, never lose sight of the awesome responsibility you have assumed. Always continue to value and prize your students, since students know which teachers care, and caring makes a difference within the classroom (Purkey & Novak, 1984).

Reflections from the Field

1 When I first graduated, I thought teaching—what a blast. Summers off, major holidays . . . working with kids, half decent pay . . . not bad. I was two weeks into my first assignment teaching third grade, and I was ready for retirement. There is so much to do, so many demands, so many things you need to balance—to juggle—it can be exhausting. But, you know what . . . I love it!

—Joan L. (elementary school teacher in her first year), West Chester, PA

2 Throughout my undergraduate studies, I was constantly pushing to just go do it. I always questioned why did I have to have all these theories and research courses. Thank goodness the university knew better. I am amazed how many times when I have had a problem with a particular lesson or if I found one of my students really struggling—I would return to my educational psychology textbook (it's kind of tattered now) or go to the library and check out a journal . . . for ideas. I know theory has to be translated—but it sure gives you a frame of reference.

—Harvey H. (middle school math teacher), Pittsburgh, PA

3 One thing I have truly come to appreciate—after 27 years of teaching—is that my responsibilities go well beyond the classroom. I am a representative of my profession, and I find it really important to involve myself in attending school board meetings, providing my "expertise" (even though it is limited) to curriculum discussions and being a constant reminder to the district that we have a mission and a consumer to whom we must be true. Teaching is not just doing . . . it is being . . . being a professional!

—Althea S. (high school English teacher), Newark, NJ

4 There are people who would die laughing if they knew that I was into action research, but I really am. I really like to take notes on the impact of a particular strategy or the use of a specific technique, and then I try to hypothesize how I can improve it. One of the things I did this year was to treat my third period history class a little different from my fifth period. For the third period, I used the first two class periods for just doing team-building exercises. The kids thought I was a bit strange, since this is an American History class, but my hypothesis was that if I could get them to feel connected as a class, a group, then when I established classroom rules, or encouraged active participation, it should go easier. So far, so good. The students made (with my guidance) the classroom rules—and the energy in this class and their level of involvement is noticeably more than in my fifth period.

—Al M. (high school social studies teacher), Boston, MA

5 My advice for those entering the profession . . . is stay connected. Teaching can be an isolating experience. It is hard and sometimes frustrating. But you are not alone. I found it very renewing to go on to the Internet . . . there are various chat rooms or resources with great ideas . . . just search "education" and you will be surprised!

Tina A. (middle school math teacher), Washington, DC

THEORY TO PRACTICE

One Teacher's Application of Educational Psychology in His Decision Making

The first teacher we will highlight in this section, demonstrating the translation of theory into practice, is Jaime Escalante, a teacher whose experience has been depicted in the film, *Stand and Deliver* (Warner Bros.). While subsequent chapters will investigate the decision making of other classroom teachers, we have chosen to use Mr. Escalante as our first illustration, first because he has proven to be an effective classroom teacher, employing many of the principles discussed within this and upcoming chapters. Secondly, we provide this as a case illustration and encourage you to review the film because as only Hollywood can do, it provides a wonderful, moving view of the many challenges, disappointments, victories, and joys experienced by a classroom teacher.

The scene selected for this particular chapter is one depicting Mr. Escalante's second day in the classroom. After an introduction to a class that he didn't know he would be teaching, Mr. Escalante enters the room on this second day, dressed in a short order cook's hat and apron! Standing in front of class, he pulls out a meat cleaver and dramatically slices an apple in half! *Hat, apron, cleaver, certainly this was something he thought about. Clearly, this was a choice, a decision he made, but why?* As you proceed through this text, see if you can find the answer (hint: see Chapters 8, 12).

As the scene unfolds, you will see numerous points at which Mr. Escalante makes critical decisions to facilitate the teaching-learning process. They are decisions that reflect his awareness of the need to consider both the WHAT and the WHO of his class, as he struggled to find the HOW. As you proceed through the text, consider each of the decisions highlighted below, and see if you can find the theoretical and/or research base for each. While there may be many theories or research studies supporting any one of the actions, we have suggested at least one chapter where you may begin to find the answers.

Decisions

1. As he stood in front of the class dressed in his short order cooks outfit, one student yelled out, "You look like Julia Child." Mr. Escalante chooses to ignore the comment. Why? (See Chapter 10.)

2. He distributes apples, all with pieces missing, some with 25 percent missing, some with 50 percent and some with 75 percent. Apples with percentages missing, why? (See Chapter 2.)

3. He asks one student, a soft-spoken girl with glasses sitting in the last seat of the class, "What's you got?" She responds, "It's missing 25 percent." Escalante walks slowly back to her seat, bends down, looks her in the eye and asks her again. After she repeats her answer, he picks up the apple, looks at it and says loudly enough for the class to hear: "Right, missing 25 percent" and then he adds: "Is it true that intelligent people make better lovers?" This one interaction represents numerous critical decisions. Walking close to the student and bending down, eye to eye, was certainly one decision. (See Chapter 10.) Repeating her response, loudly enough for the class to hear was another decision. His comment regarding intelligence and lovers is clearly a decision but based on what? (See Chapters 3, 8, 9, and 10.)

You, as Teacher, as Decision Maker, Applying Educational Theory and Research to Practice

Below you will find two illustrations of classroom situations. Your task is to imagine that you have been hired to teach a class in twelfth-grade literature. As you review the description of the school and student population, ask yourself the following:

1. What might I select as the content for my course? What literature? What genre? Which authors?

2. How would I structure my class? How much freedom do I give to the students for selecting their own readings, projects, and dates for completing assignments.

3. How would I attempt to teach the class? Lecture? Discussion? Small groups? Cooperative learning?

4. How would I approach homework? Research projects? Student presentations?

5. Should I make different decisions regarding what I would teach and how I would teach for each of the classes? How might my perceptions and expectations about the students I would be teaching (the WHO) influence my decisions regarding the WHAT and the HOW?

Case Illustration 1:
St. Thomas High School for Boys

St. Thomas High School is a private Catholic school for boys located in the upper-middle-class town of Sleighton, Massachusetts. St. Thomas is a residential school, located on 125 acres. Boys come from all over the world to attend St. Thomas because of its reputation for excellence. Although there are many nationalities and cultures represented within the student body, each boy has gained entrance by passing very rigid entrance exams, and each boy has mastery of the English language.

There is a college atmosphere at the campus, and the students have permission to return to their rooms or go anywhere on campus, if they are not scheduled to be in class. The school has all the latest technological resources available, and teachers are encouraged to employ technology and multimedia in every class.

You have twelve students in your class. Ten of your students are American-born citizens (eight Caucasian, two African-American); one student is from Ghana, and one is from Pakistan. Each of your students has attended St. Thomas for the past three years, starting in ninth grade.

Case Illustration 2:
Ewal High School

Ewal High is located in the very conservative, rural community of Ewal, Iowa. Ewal is a small rural setting where agriculture is the major industry and most of students are extensively involved in working on their families' farms, both before and after school. The school has a total of 450 students (45 percent male; 55 percent female). The students have all lived in Ewal all of their lives, and with the exception of one family all of the students' parents attended Ewal High School.

All of the students at Ewal take the same courses. The curriculum is very structured, with much attention given to the development of "traditional family values." Upon graduation, most of the students from Ewal stay and work on the family farm or become employed at the granary. Less than 2 percent of the students go on to college and those that do typically major in agricultural sciences or animal husbandry.

You have twelve students in your class, five boys and seven girls, all Caucasian. Having been born and raised in Ewal, all of the students know each other very well. Two of your students have been identified as having learning disabilities, which interfere with their ability to read and comprehend written material. One of the students in your class has been diagnosed as having an Attention Deficit Disorder and is currently on medication.

SUMMARY

Teaching: A Noble Profession

Research demonstrates the significant role teachers, at all levels, play in student achievement. A teacher's most typical role is that of *instructional expert*. In that role, the teacher is responsible for planning activities to facilitate learning. The teacher is responsible for guiding students in learning activities and evaluating them. Beyond these instructional responsibilities, a teacher also takes on the role of *manager*. A teacher needs to bring order and structure to the environment to facilitate the learning process. Finally, a role that is taking on increasing significance it that of *"teacher as counselor."* Professional educators understand the "reality" that teaching involves the whole person and not just the "head." Students bring various developmental issues to the classroom as well as emotional or societal stressors. To facilitate learning, a teacher must be aware of these stressors and be available to assist students directly or make appropriate referral to other professionals when needed.

Teaching: A Complex and Challenging Process

Central to the definition of teaching is the concept of teaching as action. *Teaching is what one DOES in an attempt to induce or facilitate learning.* Effective teachers demonstrate the ability to (1) *organize classrooms;* (2) *manage by setting and maintaining clear rules,* and (3) *employ didactic teaching*, which is an elaborate system of knowledge for understanding problems in teaching and knowing how to transform content into curriculum.

Teaching has its artistry, but it is an art that can be studied, analyzed, and understood. Once the science of teaching has been understood, effective action can be taught, incorporated, practiced, and perhaps become so automatic for the effective teacher that it once again appears as an art.

Teacher As Decision Maker

As a teacher, you will be engaged in many planning decisions, such as deciding what you want to teach, when you wish to teach it, and how you will go about the teaching process. The decisions you make may occur before your actual teaching, as with planning your curriculum and learning activities at the beginning of the year, or they may involve "spontaneous" decisions to adjust your presentation on any one day or at any one time. Teachers will make decisions about "what" they are going to teach, but such decisions are not made in isolation. To decide "what" one will teach requires the teacher to consider the unique characteristics of the students (i.e., the "who") to be taught. These two factors of "what" and "who" will shape and guide decisions of "how" to teach it.

Teachers need a stronger theoretical base if they are to teach a far broader range of students and take them farther than ever before, as modern society demands. While many teachers employ their own personal theories to guide their decision making, these theories need to be tested against experience and educational research.

Educational Psychology: Facilitating Decision Making

As suggested, a teacher's personal experience with the teaching-learning process is an important source of data to be considered as she formulates her strategies for teaching. They are, however, data that need to be systematically examined for accuracy. One source against which a teacher can test these experiences is the informational base provided within the field of educational psychology.

Educational psychology is the field of psychology concerned with the development, evaluation, and application of theories and principles of human learning and instruction that can enhance lifelong learning.

Teachers must be familiar with the research and theory describing the teaching-learning process, since it is this research that provides a scientific basis for the improvement of instruction. There are many different kinds of research studies—descriptive, correlational and experimental—on the teaching-learning process.

Teacher as Practitioner-Researcher

Although educational theory and research provide meaningful information and data to guide instructional decisions, they do not always give absolute, hard and fast rules to follow. Teachers must use research and theory as a foundation or structure to guide their decisions, but those decisions must be professional judgments based upon knowledge, experience, and constructive reflection about their own situations and the effectiveness of their theory. As practitioner-researchers, teachers need not only to interact with students in the moment, but also to reflect, to inquire, and to critique their own interactions. As an observer, the teacher needs to process and interpret all the information presented within the classroom and to employ that information, along with the more classic theory and research, as a base for planning and decision making. This process begins by developing lessons and plans with thoughtful consideration of the educational theory and research. It then analyzes the effect of that plan on the students' learning and adjusts accordingly. This is *reflective teaching.*

Often, the reflective teacher employs systematic approaches to gathering data about the classroom and the effect of the decisions she has implemented. As a systematic observer, the reflective teacher steps into the realm of *action researcher!*

◆ Field Experience Questions

As you begin your development as a teacher, it is helpful to learn from those with experience. Observing "experts" and questioning them about their own decision-making models is an excellent way to formulate your own reflective teaching model. Below are a series of field experience questions, related to the topics covered within this chapter. Use them to guide your classroom observations.

1. As you observed the class, could you identify evidence of the teacher's planning? (For instance, did he arrange class materials prior to class? Did he appear to have a goal and a developed set of strategies?)

2. As you observed the class, did you observe any times when the teacher was sensitive to student feedback (verbal or nonverbal) and attempted to adjust his strategies to better address the students' needs?

3. How would changing the composition of the class, in terms of the types of students involved, affect the "what" and the "how" of that particular lesson?

4. In discussion with the teacher, what data (theory, research, or personal experience) did he use as a basis for his initial planning and decision making?

5. In discussion with the teacher, how did he experience the interplay between the WHAT, the WHO, and the HOW of his teaching?

◆ Key Terms

action research
correlation coefficient
correlational research
decision making
dependent variable
descriptive research

experimental research
independent variable
instructional expert
manager role
negative correlation
pedagogical content knowledge

positive correlation
practitioner-researcher
reflective teaching
significance (statistically)
teacher-as-counselor

◆ Additional Resources

As you continue to develop professionally, it is important that you remain current in the theory and research in educational psychology. Therefore, you should become familiar with references in which you will find information of research and application.

The Educational Resources Information Center (ERIC)

Established by the Office of Education, ERIC provides information on papers presented at educational conferences, federally funded studies, and other information on education. Abstracts in ERIC appear in a monthly publication titled *Resources in Education.* These abstracts can be accessed by subject area or author.

Psychological Abstracts

Each month, the American Psychological Association publishes abstracts of articles appearing in more than 500 journals in psychology and related areas. Articles are indexed by subject.

Specific Journals in Education and Psychology

While there are many excellent journals in the areas of education and psychology, a few of the more popular journals are as follows: *Action in Teacher Education, American Educational Research Journal, Child Development, Educational Leadership, Elementary School Journal, High School Journal, Journal of Educational Psychology, Journal of Educational Research, Middle School Journal, Phi Delta Kappan, Psychology in the Schools, Review of Research in Education.*

Resources on the Internet

The Internet is a great resource for teachers, with professional organizations, universities, and other teachers exchanging the latest on research and practice. A search of the Net under the term "education" will reveal a vast array of Web sites. For example, consider reviewing <http://www.yahoo.com/Education/K_12>, which is a wonderful K-12 resource index. Also, as you proceed through the upcoming chapters, you will be directed to other internet *connections.*

Developmental Theory: Cognitive Development

A s a group of high school students wait for the beginning of their math class, they energetically and quite noisily discuss what they did over the weekend. Suddenly, their math teacher, Mr. Nuygen, chops a pear into quarters with a kitchen knife. As Mr. Nuygen eats one of the quarters, he announces, "I still have 75 percent left for my lunch." As the students all turn to watch their teacher, they realize that some of their peers also have pears of different sizes on top of their desks. Next, Mr. Nuygen asks a student in the front row who is seated at a desk with a pear, "How much do you have?" She responds, "Half." After acknowledging this response as correct, he asks another student seated toward the back of the class, "What do you have?" As she feels and touches her pear, which has been pared down to approximately three-fourths its original size, she says quietly, "Missing 25 percent." Mr. Nuygen then tells the class that they will be studying the multiplication of percentages and fractions. The scene ends with Mr. Nuygen relating 25 percent, 50 percent, and 75 percent of the pears back to information covered in the textbook.

W hile the approach employed by this math teacher was certainly creative and attention getting, it was also a good illustration of a teacher whose lesson planning took into consideration the developmental characteristics of his students. Specifically, Mr. Nuygen developed a lesson plan that reflected his understanding of the nature of cognitive development. In teaching an abstract concept, such as percentages, to students who are just developing their abilities to think abstractly, the use of concrete props, such as pears, is an excellent way to structure a lesson, a point that Mr. Nuygen most certainly understood.

To be effective, a teacher needs to consider "whom" he is teaching, as he plans the "what" and "how." One aspect of knowing your students is to understand the nature of their cognitive development and the implications a student's level of cognitive development has for a specific lesson plan. Understanding cognitive development allows classroom teachers to plan instruction in a way that takes the cognitive limitations of their students into account. It is vital that teachers set challenging, yet realistic, expectations for their students based on what they know about their students' cognitive development.

This chapter will introduce you to (1) the concept of cognitive development, (2) theories that describe and explain the process of cognitive development, and the implications that such a process holds for the classroom teacher. While much attention will be given to the theory of Jean Piaget, it is important to note that, like all theories, Piaget's has its limitations and its critics, and as such alternative theories of cognitive development will be presented as well. In addition to this look at the broad topic of cognitive development, attention will be given to social cognition and language development.

◆ Chapter Objectives

After reading this chapter you should be able to do the following:

1 Explain what is meant by development;

2 Articulate two reasons why classroom teachers need to be informed about research on child development;

3 Identify Piaget's four cognitive processes and, using these processes, outline how development occurs;

4 List and describe the key features of each of Piaget's four stages of cognitive development;

5 Critique Piaget's stage theory by citing recent research done that pertains to each of Piaget's stages;

6 Discuss two classroom implications that emerge from Piaget's theory for teaching pre-operational and concrete operational thinkers;

7 Explain how Elkind's concept of adolescent egocentrism, compared to Piaget's work, expands our view of adolescent cognition;

8 Compare and contrast Vygotsky's theory with Piaget's with regard to how cognitive development occurs;

9 Apply three principles of Vygotsky's work to the teaching of children;

10 Delineate how the constructivists and the Neo-Piagetians add to the work of Piaget in helping us understand how cognitive development occurs;

11 Compare and contrast the three major theories of language acquisition;

12 Outline the major milestones of language development from birth through age six;

13 Identify the key elements of the phonics approach;

14 Formulate a plan for incorporating the whole language approach into your own teaching.

CHAPTER 2 CONTENT MAP

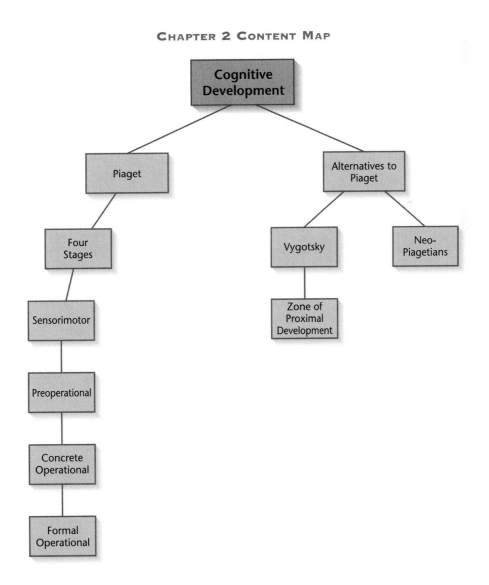

WHAT IS DEVELOPMENT?

development orderly, adaptive changes we go through from conception to death

Development refers to growth, adaptation, and change that occur over the course of a lifetime. Through the process of development, we have all changed significantly in many different ways. While changes in one's physical make-up (physical development) may be the most apparent form of development, people also develop in their ability to form and use language (language development), interact with others (social development), and process information and make meaning from experiences (cognitive development).

WHY IS UNDERSTANDING DEVELOPMENT IMPORTANT TO CLASSROOM TEACHERS?

You may be wondering, "Why is understanding human development so important to the classroom teacher?" Well, if you assume that teachers are simply experts in some content area, for example chemistry, language arts, social studies, etc., who act as depositories of information, data bases if you will, waiting to tapped by their students, and then perhaps this knowledge of development is not important. Surprisingly, this view of the teacher as content specialist is not that unusual. Many people assume that all it takes to be an effective teacher is to know content well.

While content knowledge is important, a critical part of effective teaching concerns how that content is communicated to students. Teaching is not a passive activity. It is a series of actions delivered with the intention of inducing or facilitating learning. As such, the teacher needs to be both "expert" in the content specialty, as well as "expert" in the way to deliver that information to an audience in such a way that it induces or facilitates learning. Thus, knowing the "how" of teaching is as important as knowing the "what" of teaching. Further, knowing the "how" is highly determined by the specific characteristics, needs, resources, and limitations of the audience to whom we wish to deliver the material.

Similar to an advertising firm telling its employees that they must first understand the needs of their clients before beginning a project, it is imperative that teachers understand the developmental needs of their students prior to making plans for instruction.

This means that the strategies a teacher decides to employ for teaching should match the physical, cognitive, and social development of the students. Thus, truly understanding the "who" of our classroom is an essential element to be combined with the "what" of our content, before effective decisions around the "how" could ever be made.

While there are many dimensions to human development, the focus of this chapter is on the major research on one piece of the devel-

The strategies a teacher decides to employ for teaching should match the physical, cognitive, and social development of the students. ◆

opmental pie, cognitive development. While the major theorist who has contributed to modern-day thought regarding children's cognitive development is Jean Piaget, we will also consider some recently espoused alternatives to Piagetian theory.

PIAGET'S THEORY OF COGNITIVE DEVELOPMENT

Swiss psychologist Jean Piaget is well known for his theory, which describes how humans gather and organize information and how this process changes developmentally. Piaget used a clinical-descriptive method to collect his research data. The method involved asking children carefully selected questions and recording their responses, along with meticulous observations of children's behavior. Although he frequently observed small numbers of children, his observations were longitudinal in nature, that is, following the development of these same children over a period of years. While much of his early work was based on systematic observations of his own three children, a large part of his later work was based on statistical findings (Piaget, 1964, 1969).

BASIC COGNITIVE CONCEPTS

Piaget's conceptualization of cognitive development was greatly influenced by his early work as a biologist. From this early work, Piaget came to believe that behavior and biological acts are acts of adaptation to the demands of the physical environment. Piaget believed that these acts were the organism's attempt to organize the environment in some significant manner and thus facilitate adaptation to that environment. These principles of adaptation and organization became cornerstones for his view of cognitive development.

Piaget's conceptualization of cognitive development was greatly influenced by his early work as a biologist. ◆

To understand this process of adaptation, Piaget identified four concepts, which he used to explain how and why cognitive development occurs. These include *schema, assimilation, accommodation,* and *equilibration.*

◆ Schema

schema mental network for organizing concepts and information

Piaget used the term **schema** (plural is *schemata*) to refer to the cognitive structures by which individuals intellectually adapt to and organize their environment. Based on his interests in biology, Piaget postulated that the mind has mental structures or schemata, just as the body has physical structures. Piaget suggested that when an organism encounters stimulation or a new experience, it is motivated to adapt to that experience and relies on its structures to assist in that adaptation. Thus, just as the human body is "organized" into various structures such as the stomach, kidneys, etc., which assist in ongoing adaptation, so too does the mind have structures or ways of organizing experiences, which facilitate adaptation to these experiences.

These mental structures, or schemata, were, for Piaget, the structures that allow each of us to "understand" or create meaning out of our experiences and thus facilitate our cognitive adaptation to those experiences. For example, a child who for the first time perceives a glowing metal object, which she picks up, only to experience a painful burning sensation, will attempt to adapt to this experience by creating a cognitive structure, which connects the visual experience—the action—and the resulting pain into an organizational pattern. This schema could prove useful in directing the child to adapt to its environment, should it experience a similar glowing object in the future.

Perhaps a useful analogy would be to view schemata as analogous to index cards in a file. These cards or schemata are used to identify and process stimuli. Thus, a child who experiences the pleasure of sucking on a pacifier will identify the visual stimulus of the pacifier as something that should be placed within the mouth and sucked. It is as if the index card had a picture of the pacifier on the tab and the directions of what to do (i.e., suck) or even anticipate (i.e., pleasure) written on the card itself.

At birth, there are very few index cards or schemata. This would intuitively make sense if we remember the schemata exist to organize our experiences. Thus, at birth experience, and thus schemata, is just beginning. As the child grows older, encountering more stimuli and experiences, more cards are needed to contain the information.

Piaget suggested that as we attempt to organize our new experiences into schemata we employ two separate cognitive processes, assimilation and accommodation.

◆ Assimilation

Most of us have either experienced first hand or certainly could imagine a toddler who proudly identified the family dog as a "bow-wow." The recognition of the dog, the joyful glee, and the verbalized "bow-wow" are all part of the toddler's schema for dog. Imagine that same toddler now encountering a small deer or Shetland pony. The animals perceptually are very similar to the family hound in that they possess four legs, tails, long ears, fur, etc. Because the deer or the pony are new experiences for the toddler, she will most likely attempt to cognitively adapt to these experiences by making some meaning out of them. If you can relate to this scenario, then you, like Piaget, have most likely noted that the first attempt to adapt is for the toddler to simply group these new experiences with that of the previous "dog" experience and respond with the same glee and verbalized "bow-wow." It appears that the toddler has simply added additional information to the "bow-wow" index card.

This process of integrating new perceptual, motor, or conceptual material or experiences into an existing schemata is termed **assimilation.** Teachers often facilitate the students' use of assimilation by connecting the new material to the students' existing knowledge. Thus, after watching a nature film, a child may discover new animals to add to existing groups of animals she has already stored in memory.

> **assimilation** Piaget's term for the process of making sense of experiences and perceptions by fitting them into previously established cognitive structures (schemata)

As this child develops, her ability to record finer and more detailed characteristics of experiences will help her differentiate between experiences (e.g., "Hey that 'bow-wow' has a different head and makes different sounds and look at those funny feet!"). With this discrimination of experiences, the ability to assimilate data into existing structures becomes harder to do.

◆ Accommodation

When this process of assimilation is not possible because there are no schemata into which to fit new data or the characteristics of incoming data do not match the characteristics of an available schema, a new schema will have to be developed in order to adapt to these new and unique experiences. This process of creating a new schema Piaget termed **accommodation.** Consider the following case scenario:

> **accommodation** according to Piaget it is the process of creating new schema

---

CLASS ILLUSTRATION

Mrs. Straka is a social studies teacher. She asks her sixth graders: "What is modern-day Africa like?" In so doing, Mrs. Straka is trying to tap into her students' pre-existing schema for the continent of Africa. That is, she is asking them to access those index cards that may hold this information, so that they will assimilate the new information she is about to provide. Perhaps to her surprise one of her students yells out: "All of Africa is a dark, scary jungle filled with wild animals." After class, Mrs. Straka says quietly to herself that the unit on Africa is going to take a lot of work.

What Mrs. Straka was noting was that even though a schema existed for understanding Africa, in this social studies class that schema would have to be modified. Thus, the students would not simply be able to assimilate the new information into the existing schema, but rather would have to modify that schema to accept the new information. Mrs. Straka is correct in suggesting this is going to take a lot of

This student is developing a schema in the process of accommodation to allow for the fact that parts of Africa are jungle and other parts are urban and industrialized. ◆

equilibration achieving a proper balance between assimilation and accommodation

cognitive disequilibrium a discrepancy between what is perceived and what is understood

work, not because the students are slow, but because adjusting or creating a schema in a process of accommodation takes a lot of work.

Thus, as an individual increases her experience and ability to differentiate, she begins to develop schemata that are increasingly more differentiated, complex, and numerous. Our toddler, for example, will not only begin to differentiate dogs from deer or ponies but will also begin to develop ways of organizing a variety of animals in schemata we may call domestic animals, barnyard animals, hoofed creatures, etc. Students in Mrs. Straka's class will begin to develop schemata that allow for the fact that while some parts of Africa are jungle and filled with wild animals, other parts are urban and industrialized.

◆ Equilibration

Although assimilation and accomodation are both critical cognitive processes, Piaget stated that achieving a proper balance between assimilation and accommodation is even more critical. He asks us to consider the consequences if a child always assimilated new information. As Piaget points out, this child's schema would consist of just a few large index cards resulting in difficulty with discrimination. He also asks that we ponder the opposite scenario. That is, what would happen if the child always accommodated? Piaget says that most new things would be seen as different and therefore generalities would go undetected. Thus, Piaget hypothesized that a self-regulatory process called **equilibration** operated in all children and adults. This equilibrium is a state of balance between assimilation and accommodation.

Disequilibrium is a state of cognitive conflict. It occurs when an individual's experience fails to match expectations. For example, consider any trick performed by a magician. As a member of the audience, you may find yourself surprised by the appearance of a rabbit from a previously empty hat, or the disappearance of a magician who had been placed, shackled, in a closed trunk. The surprise is a result of our cognitive conflict, our disequilibrium. In addition to surprise or amazement, we will also most likely attempt to make sense out of what we just encountered by hypothesizing how the tricks were accomplished. This need to make sense out of cognitive confusion is a result of our own need to return to cognitive balance or equilibrium.

Piaget believed that one of the most effective methods for motivating a child was to set up a state of **cognitive disequilibrium** in which the child is thrown into "cognitive conflict" when he expects something to happen a certain way and it does not. Under these conditions, the child, just like the audience of the magic trick, will attempt to come to an understanding of the situation that has caused the conflict and thus assimilate new experiences into existing schemata or create new schemata to incorporate the new experience.

Consider another teaching episode below from the classroom of Mr. Nuygen, the teacher we described in the opening scene of this chapter:

CLASS ILLUSTRATION

As Mr. Nuygen begins a new chapter, he has his math students recite, "Division by zero is undefined." He encourages the students over and over to repeat the phrase "Division by zero is undefined." He asks them to say it again and again, louder and louder. After his students are quite comfortable in the mode of recitation, he asks, "Why?" The silence that follows may be the sound of cognitive conflict.

As you read this, you too may find that his question momentarily places you in a state of disequilibrium. If so, perhaps just like the students in Mr. Nuygen's class you may find yourself motivated to learn more in order to return to equilibrium. This process of motivating students will be discussed more extensively in Chapter 8.

PIAGET'S STAGES OF COGNITIVE DEVELOPMENT

According to Piaget, cognitive development unfolds as the child passes through four distinct and qualitatively different stages: the sensorimotor, pre-operational, concrete operation, and formal operation stages (Table 2.1).

Piaget made several assumptions about how these stages unfold. First, he held that they represent an invariant sequence of development. That is, all children pass through these stages in the same order and cannot skip a stage. Second, Piaget assumed that each stage is qualitatively different from the next. Therefore, the child must learn a set of schemata at one stage in order to be able to pass to the next stage. Third, although Piaget proposed that maturational readiness, or biological programming, played an important role in determining when a child would move to the next stage, he acknowledged that culture and the environment could accelerate or retard growth. Thus, the ages represented in Table 2.1 should be thought of as age norms, which approximate the age corresponding to each Piagetian stage, and not as absolute points for stage development.

The fact that Piaget assumed the environment played a role in fostering or hindering cognitive development is of special significance for the classroom teacher. The types of learning experiences a classroom teacher plans can dramatically facilitate students' cognitive growth.

Teacher Tool Box
Employing Understanding of Cognitive Adaptation

◆ In your lesson plans, reserve some time to address students' pre-existing schemata with regard to the content you teach. For instance, you may have students either write down or discuss what they think of when you mention a certain term. At this juncture in the textbook, we might ask you to think about what the term *sensorimotor* brings to mind. In this way, you can help students relate new information to something already familiar to them. You are also in an excellent position, by the way, to address any incorrect pre-existing beliefs that students may have.

◆ Make students consciously aware of the processes of assimilation and accommodation by using the KWL method. That is, in three separate columns have students write down what they know about a topic (K), what they would like to find out about this same topic (W), and at the end of a lesson or unit, what they have learned (L), about this topic. Then have students compare the three columns to increase their awareness of how they may have assimilated or accommodated while learning something new.

◆ When you write your lesson plans, try to think of ways to create a sense of cognitive disequilibrium in your students. Instead of just presenting content to them, perhaps you could first present a perplexing problem or have them do an experiment, the outcome of which is a surprise. For instance, when teaching about the properties of metals, you could heat a metal rod and have students observe that the first time it is heated it bends downward. However, the second time you heat it, it bends upward. At this point, you have aroused students' sense of cognitive disequilibrium, and they will want to know the reason for this perplexing phenomenon. You can then offer an explanation tied to the properties of metals.

Table 2.1   The Four Periods of Intellectual Development

The Cognitive Periods and Approximate Ages

1. The sensorimotor period (birth to 18–24 months),

2. The preoperational period (2 to 7 years),

3. The concrete operational period (7 to 11 years),

4. The formal operational period (over 11 years).

Note: This is a "stage invariant" theory, meaning that the order of the stages does not vary; everyone passes through these stages in this sequence. It is not an "age invariant" theory, meaning that a child's age may vary in any one of the periods.

Source: From J. F. Travers, S. N. Elliott, and T. R. Kratochwill in *Educational Psychology: Effective Teaching, Effective Learning.* Copyright © 1993 by The McGraw-Hill Companies. Reprinted by permission.

✦ The Sensorimotor Stage

sensorimotor stage Piaget's first stage of intellectual development, in which the child moves from the reflexive activities of reaching, grasping, and sucking to more highly organized forms of activity

Piaget labeled the earliest stage of cognitive development **sensorimotor.** The name, sensorimotor, depicts the two modes (sensory and motor actions) through which an infant adapts to and organizes experiences. At the start of this period, an infant has only a few simple reflexes, such as sucking and grasping, which help fulfill biological needs and assist in coming to "know" the world.

With increased development, intentional behavior emerges, in which infants try to solve simple problems. For example, having experienced the movement of a mobile hanging above the crib, the infant may begin to kick and move as a motoric response "intended" to provide the visual stimulation of the moving mobile. Later within this stage, an interesting and very significant event takes place. The infant begins to understand that there is a difference between him/herself and the rest of the world and that the sensory experiences received are in fact suggestive of the existence of some form of "objects" or "events" that exist outside of themselves.

object permanence Piaget's term for children's understanding that objects continue to exist apart from the children's perception of them

This development of **object permanence** expands the infant's view of the world beyond that which is immediately and directly experienced. Thus, the infant may begin to search for objects that are out of sight. Whereas a five-month-old will not typically search for a rattle that has dropped out of his crib, a seven-month-old may look for the rattle, if only for a brief period. Between eight and twelve months, infants will search for familiar objects that are hidden, say under a blanket, and are delighted when they find such objects. This is why infants of this age begin enjoying the game of peek-a-boo. During this period, the infant develops object permanence, the realization that objects exist even if they are out of sight.

The development of object permanence forms the basis for using symbols to represent objects in our minds so that we can think about

MY NEPHEW'S NOT IMPRESSED

Imagine that one of your classmates approaches you with the following concern. He states that he was babysitting his infant nephew and playing with his favorite teddy bear. As he played with the bear, he placed a towel over the bear and then secretively slid the bear from under the towel and hid it behind his back. When he removed the towel, his nephew wasn't even surprised! In fact, his nephew almost acted as if he didn't care to look for the bear. Now your friend is concerned because his girlfriend's niece, who is a couple of months older, loves to play hide and seek. She is always surprised when the toy has "disappeared." With your understanding of this stage of cognitive development and the concept of object permanence, what would you tell your friend?

them, even when we are not experiencing them. By the end of the sensorimotor period, full object permanence has evolved, in which children actively search for objects they believe are hidden, although they may not have seen these objects placed in a particular spot. At this point, children are able to use mental combinations to imagine where such objects may be located. And as might be expected, this ability to "recreate" experiences with mental representations forms a basis for the engagement in pretend play, something that becomes evident by the end of this period.

Another milestone of the sensorimotor period is the development of the beginnings of problem-solving ability. While at first this is based largely on trial and error, by the end of the period, approaches to problem solving are planned. For instance, young infants who want an object may reach for it several times but soon give up. A few months later, they may use another object to help them reach the initial object. By age two, they may very well ask that a stool be moved to help them obtain the desired object.

It is important to note that the sensorimotor way of thinking about the world never disappears in an individual but is rather subsumed as the individual progresses into more advanced stages of cognitive development. That means that although an individual is at the concrete operational stage of cognitive development, her thinking, in some cases, may have elements of an earlier stage, such as sensorimotor. Consider the scene with which we opened the chapter. Mr. Nuygen distributed pears to members of his high school class and used them as props for a discussion of fractions. When Mr. Nuygen asked: "How much do you have?" one student in the scene responded on a concrete basis by feeling and touching how much pear was left.

Although Piaget's description of the sequence of cognitive abilities in the sensorimotor period was accurate, recent research indicates that he underestimated the onset of object performance thought now to occur at about four months of age (Meltzoff, 1988). However, it does appear that Piaget correctly described the sequence by which development in the first two years of life takes place.

◆ The Preoperational Stage

In contrast to the sensorimotor period, the child's thinking in the next stage does not occur through actions, but rather functions in a representational and conceptual framework. That is, the child is now able to employ mental symbols to re-create or represent previous or current experiences. Piaget termed this the **preoperational stage** because the child has not yet mastered the ability to completely mentally manipulate these symbols.

The Use of Symbolic Function

The major development during the preoperational period is the ability to represent objects and events or to use **symbolic function.** You will recall that toward the end of the sensorimotor period, children became capable of engaging in activities that involve mental representation such as pretending. Between the ages of two and seven, these mental abilities come to unfold fully as advances in language development and imagination enable the child to think and play in new ways. Whereas the two-year-old is likely to put a cup on a saucer and pretend to drink, the four-year-old can engage in symbolic or pretend play and transform the cup and saucer into nearly anything (Lowe, 1975). In the blink of an eye, the child may turn a cup and a saucer, which she had been using to play tea party, into an imaginary hat or spaceship. Or consider the child who plays with a block of wood and pretends it is a car by assigning to it the characteristics of a car. By six or seven, the objects of pretend play may exist solely in the child's mind (Hinson, 1988; Rubin et al., 1983).

In addition to symbolic function, the preoperational period is characterized by several unique features.

Egocentrism

Piaget described the preoperational child's thinking as egocentric. That is, preoperational children cannot put themselves in others' shoes or see someone else's perspective. Consider the four-year-old who can label his own right hand and left hand, but cannot identify the right and left hands of a friend. Or ponder the case of the five-year-old who buys his mother his favorite toy for her birthday. Piaget emphasized that **egocentrism** has nothing to do with selfishness, but merely reflects the qualitative limitations in thinking apparent during the preoperational stage. As the child gets older, egocentrism wanes. By age six, children exhibit less egocentrism than at age three.

Centration

Another characteristic of preoperational thought is **centration** or concentration on only one aspect of an object or activity, usually the aspect

preoperational stage the second stage in Piaget's theory of cognitive development, in which the lack of logical operations forces children to make decisions based on their perceptions

symbolic function emerges during preoperations; the ability to represent objects and events

egocentrism the tendency of young children to assume that everyone views the world in the same way they do and that they are, quite literally, the center of everything

centration the tendency to focus on one perceptual aspect of an event to the exclusion of others that is perceptually dominant. For instance, a child of four or five is presented with two rows of objects in which one row contains nine objects and a second, but longer row, contains seven objects. The preoperational child will typically select the longer row as having more objects, even though the child knows that nine is more than seven. Or consider the child who sees a cereal bowl the parent has placed on the table for a midnight snack, but assumes it must be morning because that is when cereal is eaten. By age six or seven, cognition begins to assume a more appropriate position with respect to perceptual judgments.

Inability to Reverse Operations

A third feature of preoperational thought is inability to reverse one's thinking. Understanding subtraction is a prime example of this feature. Preschoolers may have learned that $1 + 1 = 2$, but cannot comprehend that $2 - 1 = 1$. Or ponder the case of the preoperational child who is presented with two identical glasses, both short and fat in shape. Then water from one of the glasses is poured into a tall, thin glass. The child is then asked if the glasses contain the same amount of water. In order to answer correctly, the child would have to be mentally able to reverse the operation of pouring the water from the original short, fat glass into

A preoperational child is presented with two identical beakers, both short and fat in shape. When liquid from one of the beakers is poured into a tall, thin beaker, the peoperational child, unable to reverse operations, typically believes that the tall, thin beaker contains more liquid. ◆

the tall, thin one. But preoperational children typically respond that the tall, thin glass contains more water.

The latter illustration shows that preoperational children are not yet ready to engage in **conservation** or to conceptualize that the quantity or amount of matter stays the same despite changes in an irrelevant dimension. Table 2.2 depicts the different types of conservation and when children are typically capable of each.

conservation a Piagetian term for the realization that certain properties of an object (i.e., weight and length) remain the same regardless of changes in its other properties (i.e., shape and position)

Animism

animism Piaget's term for a child's tendency to attribute life to inert objects

A fourth feature of the preoperational child is **animism.** An animistic thinker attributes human characteristics to inanimate objects. For instance, consider the preoperational child who is asked the question "where do boats go at night?" and responds "to bed." Or ponder the drawings of a preoperational child, which feature a face drawn on a sun or a moon. Piaget believed that this tendency decreased by age six or seven as the child became more cognizant of his or her own personality.

Transductive Reasoning

transductive reasoning feature of preoperations in which the child neither reasons deductively or inductively

Finally, the preoperational child exhibits a fifth characteristic known as **transductive reasoning.** That is, he or she reasons neither deductively or inductively. Deduction is reasoning from general to specific. If we acknowledge that all men are mortal and Socrates was a man, then Socrates has to be mortal. Inductive reasoning, in contrast, involves establishing generalizations from specific instances. However, according to Piaget, the thinking of preoperational children is somewhere in between, moving from particular to particular without touching on the general. The following example of transductive reasoning was reported by Piaget (1952): When his daughter failed to take a nap one afternoon, she said, "I haven't had my nap, so it isn't afternoon." At this age, chil-

Table 2.2   Types of Conservation

Conservation of . . .	Example	Approximate Age
1. Number	Which has more?	6–7 years
2. Liquids	Which has more?	7–8 years
3. Length	Are they the same length?	7–8 years
4. Substance	Are they the same?	7–8 years
5. Area	Which has more?	7–8 years
6. Weight	Will they weigh the same?	9–10 years
7. Volume	Will they displace the same amount of water?	11–12 years

Source: From J. F. Travers, S. N. Elliott, and T. R. Kratochwill in *Educational Psychology: Effective Teaching, Effective Learning.* Copyright © 1993 by The McGraw-Hill Companies. Reprinted by permission.

dren often reason from particular to particular, thinking if A causes B, then B must cause A. In the same vein, when asked why it gets dark at night the preoperational child will most likely respond, "Because that's when I go to sleep." Piaget observed that this form of reasoning begins to decline around age six to be replaced with inductive reasoning.

Piaget seemed to be very accurate with his description of advances in thinking that occur in what he termed the five-to-seven shift at ages five to seven. As noted above, children during this time evidence a decrease in the characteristics of preoperations and begin to take on the features of concrete operational thought. Recently, research has been conducted in biology that corroborates Piaget's conclusion. That is, physiological changes in our neurons, called **myelinization**, may contribute to the rapid cognitive growth evident between the ages of five and seven (Lemire et al., 1975). Although Piaget seems to have accurately described the cognitive advances which occur between the ages of five and seven, he probably underestimated what children can do during preoperations (Bee, 1992). That is, preoperational children can be taught to decenter and to be less egocentric, even though they do not spontaneously exhibit internal rules for doing so.

myelinization physiological changes in neurons that contribute to rapid cognitive growth

concrete operational stage the third of Piaget's four major stages, characterized by children's ability to think logically, but only about concrete problems and objects

◆ The Concrete Operational Stage

In contrast to preoperations, the child in **concrete operations** now engages in logical thought to solve concrete problems. At this stage of development, a child's "logic" is directed by cognitive activity rather than dominated by immediate experience, as was the case with preoperational thought.

Decentering

A child in the concrete operational stage is able not only to imagine things independent of their immediate experience, but now is capable of employing all of the perceptual features of an experience (i.e., decenter) in order to derive logical solutions to concrete problems. Consider the research of Piaget and Inhelder (1963), in which young children were shown a large three-dimensional exhibit of three mountains of different shapes, sizes, and colors (see Figure 2.1). After viewing the exhibit from all sides, the children were seated on one side of the table that held the exhibit, with a doll seated on the other side. Next, the children were asked to choose which one of a series of photos depicted the scene that the doll was viewing. Although children at six and seven years of age realized that the doll's view would be different from their own, it was not until the ages of seven and nine that children were able to decenter, or focus on multiple aspects of a situation.

Teacher Tool Box
Preoperational Thinkers

A number of implications for teaching preoperational thinkers follow from the research of Piaget:

◆ Take egocentrism into account when planning activities. For instance, participation in "Simon Says" games shows children they cannot always be the winner. Rotating special classroom duties also shows children they must take turns.

◆ Provide opportunities for children to represent their observations, such as putting things in order and drawing the sequence of shapes that once appeared on the blackboard.

◆ Allow children to learn through active exploration and interaction with adults, peers, and materials. To promote reading, children may work with the teacher to make a short story book in which they illustrate their own stories. Then, the children can take this book home and read it aloud to their parents.

◆ Use concrete props and visual aids when teaching. For instance, provide students with cut-out letters to build words or let children add or subtract with counting sticks or colored chips.

◆ Utilize a wide variety of experiences to teach a concept, such as field trips, storytellers, art projects, and musical performances. During late preoperations, children can even act out concepts with each other.

Figure 2.1

Piaget's Three Mountains

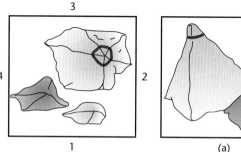
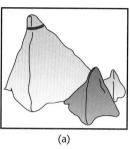
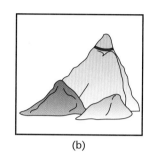
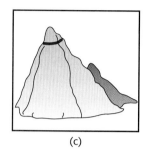

(a) Replications of Piaget's three-mountains experiment are used to measure the ability to imagine a different point of view. The child is first shown a display model of three mountains, and then is shown ten drawings of various views of the mountains. The child is asked to select the drawing that most accurately portrays the point of view of a doll seated at various positions around the table. For instance, if a child were sitting in position 1 looking at the three-mountain display (here shown in an overhead view) and asked how the display would look from sitting-position 4, which picture—(a), (b), or (c)—should the child select? Preoperational children often wrongly select their own view (b) rather than correctly choosing (a).

Source: From *Developing Person Through the Lifespan*, Fourth ed., by Berger. © 1998 by Worth Publishers, Inc. Used with permission.

During this period children improve in their abilities to distinguish reality from fantasy. In one study Skeen, Brown, and Osborn (1982) presented children three different versions of episodes from *Star Trek*. One of the versions was an animated version and the other two were television versions. While early concrete operational children were sure the animated version was not real, they were not sure if the television versions were real. By the late concrete operational stage, all of the children were positive that none of the versions of *Star Trek* was real.

The concrete operational child is capable of several important advances in thought compared to preoperations. Table 2.3 illustrates some of the major developmental milestones that occur during the concrete operational stage.

Reversibility

Piaget proposed that the most important of these was reversibility. A concrete operational child understands that a model of an airplane, which had formerly been a ball of clay, can be changed back into a ball of clay. She can also understand that while eight checkers added to six checkers makes fourteen checkers, six checkers taken away from fourteen checkers leaves eight checkers.

Conservation

The fact that the child in the concrete operational stage of development is able to decenter and to reverse operations facilitates the ability to develop conservation skills. A child is able to solve conservation of

Table 2.3   Concrete Operational Milestones

Milestone	*Age*
Becomes proficient in the art of persuasion	11 or 12 years
Understands play on words	8 years
Comprehends a metaphor	10 or 11 years
Begins to estimate accurately how much time is needed to study	8 or 9 years
Classifies according to categories and subcategories	8 years
Successfully plays board games that require turn-taking	8 years

number problems around the age of six, area and mass problems around seven or eight, and volume problems by eleven or twelve. Additional types of conservation problems along with approximate ages of development are listed in Table 2.2.

Classification

Other significant changes in problem-solving ability can be seen in the concrete operational child's ability to engage in **classification**. Before the age of seven children typically form classifications of objects along one dimension. That is, children can classify according to color or shape. Thus, presented with a group of white and black circles, squares, and triangles, a child may classify them into two groups, all the white and all the black designs together. Prior to the concrete operational stage, most children do not possess the concept of class inclusion, the idea that a particular person or object may belong to more than one class.

classification grouping objects into categories

Take the case of the child who has brothers and sisters, and assumes that all brothers and sisters belong to the category "child." Before the onset of concrete operations, this youngster will believe that because adults are not children, they cannot be brothers or sisters. Or consider the following "typical" class inclusion task. A child is presented with twenty brown wooden beads and two white wooden beads. After agreeing that the beads are all wooden and that twenty are brown and two are white, he is asked, "Are there more wooden beads or brown beads?" (Piaget, 1952a). It is only around the age of eight that children can answer this question correctly because now they can consider differences as well as similarities in classification and are able to reason about the relationships between classes and subclasses.

Seriation

Seriation is the ability to mentally arrange a series of elements according to increasing or decreasing size, volume, weight, or some other

seriation arranging objects in sequential order according to one aspect, such as size, weight, or volume

dimension. While the ability to seriate is in evidence with children four years old or younger, their forms of seriation tend to be gross and developed through trial and error. For instance, the child is able to construct a logical series that A < B < C and so on. Before concrete operations, the child is likely to be fixated on the observation that both A and B are small since A is smaller than B and B is smaller than C. Thus, the fact that B is larger than A is overlooked. A child in the concrete operational stage begins to employ strategies such as searching for the smallest stick, then the next, etc., to develop the solution to seriation problems (Wadsworth, 1996).

Shortcomings of Piaget's Presentation

While Piaget seemed to be correct about the sequence of development during concrete operations, he attributed the advances in cognition that appear during this time to the processes of organization and adaption. He emphasized that children work largely on their own, like little scientists. Missing in his writings are considerations of how both peers and culture influence the advancing cognitive development of the child, concerns spoken to by other psychologists, such as Vygotsky (1978). Recent research also indicates that the upper limits of concrete operations may extend far above age eleven. That is, recent estimates indicate that upwards of 75% of children are still primarily concrete thinkers at ages twelve, thirteen, and fourteen (Shayer, 1978). Furthermore, up to 40 percent of those in the twelfth grade are thought to be primarily concrete thinkers. Consider teaching the concept of irony to an eighth grade English class. Imagine that the teacher reads the definition of irony to the class. According to the above data, few eighth graders will be able to understand such an abstract concept. Even many high school students will be confused. Therefore, it is incumbent upon teachers to find concrete methods of teaching such concepts. One teacher we recently observed had her students break into small groups and with her guidance, develop an ironic skit, which they performed for the class. Only then did the light bulb go on for this teacher's concrete thinkers. Or similarly, recall the scene with which we opened this chapter, depicting the teacher introducing the concepts of percentages. You will recall that the teacher provides the senior high school students with very concrete, familiar props to help them understand percentages. The various pears placed throughout the classroom were meant to convey various percentages: 25 percent, 50 percent, and 75 percent.

Teacher Tool Box
Teaching to the Concrete Operational Stage

Additional implications for teaching concrete thinkers are listed below:

- Use concept-building techniques when presenting abstract concepts. Teachers should provide plenty of concrete, familiar examples first before offering an abstract explanation.
- Use hands-on teaching methods that incorporate a multisensory approach. That is, in addition to talking about a concept provide visual examples, allow students to feel and manipulate what they are learning about, even provide the opportunity for them to dance, sing, or act out the concept.
- Have students work together in pairs, triads, or teams in which they can explain difficult concepts to each other in language with which they feel comfortable.
- Introduce a difficult topic by having students first engage in an activity related to that topic which they enjoy and are successful.
- Ask students to justify their answers, even when they are correct. This will force them to verbalize their thinking and allow the teacher the opportunity to detect any logical fallacies.
- Ask students divergent thinking questions for which there is more than one right answer. This will encourage them to begin to develop hypotheses.

Mr. Nuygen's use of concrete props and the use of role plays described above are wonderful illustrations of using developmentally appropriate teaching strategies. These approaches afforded even the concrete operational students the opportunity to directly experience the "abstract" mathematical concept they were learning about. The teachers who selected these approaches recognized that not all of their students were yet formal operational thinkers, and even students who are formal thinkers benefit from references to concrete, familiar examples.

◆ The Formal Operational Stage

With the onset of Piaget's fourth stage of cognitive development, **formal operations,** comes the ability to solve abstract problems. The development of formal operations provides the ability to reason and construct logic useful for all classes of problems. Although the type of problem solved may have been resolved by those at earlier stages of cognitive development, the manner in which it was approached was significantly different.

formal operational stage
Piaget's final stage of cognitive development, characterized by children's increasing ability to employ logical thought processes

Consider the early classic experiments reported by Inhelder and Piaget (1958). In these experiments, the children were asked to balance a balance scale with weights that could be hooked onto the scale's arms. While this task was completely beyond the ability of preoperational children, by the early stage of concrete operations children realized the scale could be balanced by putting the same amount of weight on both arms. However, they did not realize that the distance of the weights from the center of the scale is also an important factor. By age ten, children did discover that the further from the fulcrum a given weight is, the more force it exerts. However, concrete operational children discovered this by trial and error. It was not until about age thirteen or fourteen that some children were able to hypothesize a general law that there is an inverse relationship between a weight's proximity to the fulcrum and the force it exerts.

Even with such a concrete problem as this, the difference in approach clearly distinguishes a concrete operations thinker from one operating from the formal operational stage of cognitive development. But beyond the approach to problem solving, the formal operational stage is different from concrete thought in that it is not limited to solving tangible concrete problems. The formal operational thinker is not bound to content and available experience. Rather, this individual is now free to conjecture, to hypothesize, and to deal in the "what if."

During this stage of development, thinking has a number of unique structural properties, those of being hypothetical, analogical, and deductive.

Hypothetical Reasoning

Hypothetical reasoning transcends perception and memory and deals with things not in the realm of direct experience. Consider the concrete operational child who is asked "What would happen if there was no sun?" and responds "It would be dark." The formal operational child, in contrast, is able to hypothesize about a number of different consequences that would result if there was no sun such as the destruction or radical

hypothetical reasoning the ability to formulate many alternative hypotheses in dealing with a problem and to check data against each of the hypotheses to make an appropriate decision

transformation of plant, animal, and human life. Further, an individual with formal operational thought can and will entertain hypotheses that are thought to be untrue. For instance, if a logical argument is prefixed by the statement "Suppose coal is white," a concrete operational child will invariably say that is not possible and therefore the question cannot be answered. However, a formal operational child will readily accept the assumption of the argument and go on to reason about its logic.

This ability to hypothesize and generate possibilities is evidenced even in the way the formal operational thinker approaches the issue of AIDS when compared to children in the concrete or preoperational stage. Notice that teaching ideas for a developmentally based AIDS/HIV education program (see Table 2.4) need to take into account the students' stage of cognitive development.

Analogical Reasoning

analogical reasoning
heuristic in which one limits the search for solutions to situations that are similiar to the one on hand

Analogical reasoning, in which children can fully explain why an analogy works and how each part of the analogy is connected to the other, also emerges in formal operations. Consider the following analogy: "Dog is to hair as bird is to feathers." The heart of the analogy is the

Table 2.4 Developmentally Based AIDS/HIV Education

	Younger Children (5–7)	*Intermediate Children (8–10)*	*Older Children (11 +)*
Fear	Vague fears; need reassurance from authority figures about their non-vulnerability	Concrete fears; need strategies for excluding potential causes; need concrete information about noncauses	Healthy fear; need specifics of biological mechanisms, underlying causes, and preventive behavior
Cause	Unconcerned with cause	Preoccupied with discrete causes; need list of noncauses; not concerned with details of mode of transmission	Understand body systems; detailed biological explanations of various causes and mechanisms of transmission helpful
Prevention	Unconcerned with prevention	Beginning concept of prevention; introduce notion of prevention across many illnesses including AIDS; broad categories of preventive behavior	Understand prevention; need detailed biological explanations of preventive behavior and conditions under which it operates and which affect use

Source: Adapted with permission from M. E. Walsh and R. Bibace, *Developmentally-based AIDS/HIV Education* in *Journal of School Health, 60:* 256–261, 1990. Copyright © 1990, American School Health Association, Kent, OH 44240.

relationship between dog-hair and bird-feathers. Understanding these relationships is only possible through reflective thinking and not observation. When using analogies in teaching, it is vital to use them in developmentally appropriate ways. That is, when working with concrete thinkers a teacher needs to make sure that she fully explains the analogy and has students explain the analogy themselves. She should also describe where the analogy breaks down (Mastrilli, 1995).

Deductive Reasoning

Deductive reasoning is reasoning from generalities to specifics. The type of reasoning contained in a syllogism is deductive reasoning. If given the statements "All women are mortal" and "Joan of Arc was a woman," the formal operational child is able to deduce the logical conclusion "Therefore, Joan of Arc was mortal." Or consider the child who correctly responds to the following complex if-then statement: "If all animals have four legs, and if this table has four legs, then is this table an animal?" The child who correctly responds reasons that although both tables and animals have four legs, a table cannot be an animal because it is not a living creature.

deductive reasoning drawing conclusions by applying rules or principles; logically moving from a general rule or principle to a specific solution

Reflective Abilities

In addition to the above described abilities, formal operational thinkers possess a sophisticated set of reflective abilities. For instance, they are able to systematically generate all possible solutions to a problem or engage in combinatorial reasoning. For example, consider the child who is presented with five glasses or jars, each of which contains a colorless liquid (see Figure 2.2). Four of the five jars look exactly the same, but the fifth jar contains an eyedropper in addition to the colorless liquid. This fifth container, labeled "G" contains potassium iodide. Water oxidizes potassium iodide in an acid mixture, turning the water yellow. Water (2) is neutral and thiosulfate is a bleach (4). The child is given two glasses, one containing water and the other containing sulfuric acid and oxygenated water (1 + 3). The experimenter places several drops of potassium iodide (G) into each of the two glasses and the reaction is noted. Then the child is asked to reproduce the yellow color by using the five original containers in any way that she wishes. The only combinations which will produce the yellow color are 1 + 3 + G or 1 + 3 + G + 2. As there are twenty-five possible combinations of two or more of the liquids, the problem cannot be solved through observation. The formal operational thinker realizes she must systematically test all possible combinations or use combinatorial logic to solve the problem (Wadsworth, 1989).

The Gradual Emergence of Formal Operational Thinking

It is essential for classroom teachers to understand that the various aspects of formal operational thinking emerge gradually, not all at once.

Figure 2.2
The Colorless Chemical Liquid Problem

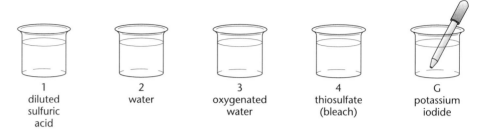

1	2	3	4	G
diluted sulfuric acid	water	oxygenated water	thiosulfate (bleach)	potassium iodide

Source: From *Piaget's Theory of Cognitive and Affective Development* by J. Barry Wadsworth. Copyright © 1996, 1989. Reprinted with permission.

In fact, the Arlin Test of Formal Reasoning (1980) is one measure designed to ascertain to what degree students are concrete or formal operational thinkers. This assessment tool is used by guidance counselors and teachers who know that the gradual emergence of formal operational thought can be particularly deceiving with regard to a student's performance across subject areas. Although a given student may be using formal operational reasoning to solve a problem raised in social studies class, this same student may not yet be employing formal operations to solve a problem in geometry. Thus, the onset of formal operations is task-dependent; while primarily formal operational with regard to academic problem solving, the same student may respond in concrete operational ways when attempting to solve a problem under the hood of a car. Recent estimates, in fact, indicate that only one in three teens routinely use formal logic (Santrock, 1992). Furthermore, about 40 to 60 percent of college students fail formal operational problems that involve content unfamiliar to them (Keating, 1979). Recent research has confirmed the tendency of subjects to pass certain formal operational reasoning tasks and fail others, a phenomenon known as horizontal decalage (Niaz, 1991). This is why the use of teaching strategies that build on the students' own experience is a wise idea, even with seemingly very mature students.

Although a given student may be using formal operational reasoning to solve a problem raised in social studies class, this same student may not yet be employing formal operations to solve a problem in geometry. ◆

Shortcomings of Piaget's Presentation

Although Piaget was correct about pinpointing the onset of formal operations in the early teen years, recent research indicates that concrete thinkers can be taught abstract reasoning (Hawkins, Pea, Glick, & Scribner, 1984). However, these effects appear to be transitory.

In addition, Piaget may have neglected to consider a fifth stage of cognitive development. Researchers such as Arlin (1977) postulate that great thinkers such as Einstein and Piaget operate at a fifth stage of cognitive development in which they are able to reconceptualize existing knowledge and generate unique ways of thinking about the world.

ADOLESCENT SOCIAL COGNITION: THE WORK OF ELKIND

An interesting extension of the analysis of cognitive development, as it impacts one's view of oneself and of others, has been discussed in the work of David Elkind (1967, 1968, 1981). Elkind suggests that an adolescent's thought patterns tend to be characterized by adolescent egocentrism (Elkind, 1981). By this, Elkind referred to the tendency of adolescents to assume that everyone else in the world views the world as they do and are thus focused on the same concerns.

Elkind suggests that this **adolescent egocentrism** has two unique and interesting facets; one is called the personal fable and the other the imaginary audience.

adolescent egocentrism
assumption that everyone else shares one's thoughts, feelings, and concerns

◆ Personal Fable

The personal fable is the self-generated, often romanticized story of one's personal destiny. The adolescent may develop an image of him- or herself that portends a destiny, a life story as a great hero, rock star, or the great reformer of the world's evils. As the central character in this story of destiny, the adolescent acts out a drama never before lived or a story so unique that no one else could possibly understand it. One of the potential dangerous twists to this personal fable is the notion that with this unique destiny, the adolescent is invincible and that despite the recognition that bad things happen to others, they will not happen to him. Consider the teen who believes that while her friends may get pregnant, it will never happen to her. Or the adolescent who truly believes that while smoking may cause lung cancer in others, it will not affect him. Many teens may believe that even if they drink and drive, somehow they will be spared the dire consequences. The notion of the personal fable may also help to explain why adolescents often believe that no one understands their academic difficulties, especially adults.

The belief that one is so unique as to be misunderstood by all others is difficult to penetrate. However, the use of peer mediators, counselors, and tutors often bridges the gap in this projected sense of being misunderstood (Selman, Newberger, & Jacquette, 1977).

◆ Imaginary Audience

Adolescent egocentrism, as previously noted, implies that the adolescent assumes that others are focused upon and concerned about the same issues which he personally feels are so important. Following upon this process it is easy to understand that since the adolescent is often his own most important concern, then he will anticipate that "he" is also the most important concern to those around him. As adolescents appear to constantly scrutinize themselves for subtle changes in physical appearance, adequacy of choices, etc., so too do they feel they are being scrutinized by all those around them. Clearly, this is not true, especially if those who surround the adolescent are also self-absorbed in adolescent egocentrism. This audience is truly imaginary.

This concept of the imaginary audience may help to explain why some teens are mortified about the prospect of making a presentation or speech to the class. The anxiety experienced by believing one is under such scrutiny is real and can interfere with the acquisition and demonstration of learning. Teachers would do well to be sensitive to this issue and attempt to reduce the potential negative impact of adolescent egocentrism. In such cases, it may be useful to suggest practicing in front of a mirror or using a tape recorder before actually giving the presentation. Providing encouragement and positive feedback for even small improvements may also be helpful. Another strategy is to have students work in dyads as they do presentations in which both partners take the "stage" together.

THE ALTERNATIVE PERSPECTIVE OF VYGOTSKY

The value of Piaget's theory lies in the direction it has given to our understanding of cognitive development and in the additional research and theorizing it has stimulated.

◆ Vygotsky's Views of Knowledge Construction

Piaget, as noted above, was very interested in the way knowledge was formed or constructed. Piaget clearly focused our attention on the inner working of the individual as she actively constructed her knowledge through the various stages of cognitive development. One of the criticisms of Piaget's theory was that he seemed to de-emphasize the significance of social and cultural factors in cognitive development. An alternative to Piaget's approach that values the rich array of social and cultural variables which impact cognitive development was offered by Lev Semanovich Vygotsky (Vygotsky, 1978; Vygotsky, 1993).

Although Vygotsky critiqued Piagetian theory more than sixty years ago, his perspective is just beginning to gain popularity today. One of Vygotsky's key constructs for explaining how children learn was called the **zone of proximal development.** Vygotsky believed that children are often at a cognitive level where they can solve problems independently. He termed this level as the zone of actual development. In contrast, he believed that there are times when a child can solve problems with support, and this he identified as the zone of proximal development. From this perspective, he posited that learning takes place when

zone of proximal development Vygotsky's description for the difference between an individual's current level of development and his or her potential level of development

the child is working in her zone of proximal development. Tasks within this zone are ones that the child is not yet capable of doing herself, but can be accomplished if she is given assistance by a peer or teacher. Consider the scenario presented in Figure 2.3. For this particular child, reading words with single vowels is too easy. However, reading words with multiple syllables and consonant blends is too hard. Following Vygotsky's lead, the area in which learning will take place, the child's zone of proximal development, is somewhere in between these two. That is, learning is most likely to take place if the child is given the opportunity to read words with two vowels together and at the same time have access to peer or teacher assistance.

Connected to the idea of the zone of proximal development is Vygotsky's view of language. While Piaget saw the phenomenon of self-talk in children as a form of egocentric speech, Vygotsky viewed this **private speech** as guiding the child's development. Private speech is a mechanism emphasized by Vygotsky that helps turn shared knowledge

private speech   children's self-talk, which guides their thinking and action; eventually these verbalizations are internalized as silent inner speech

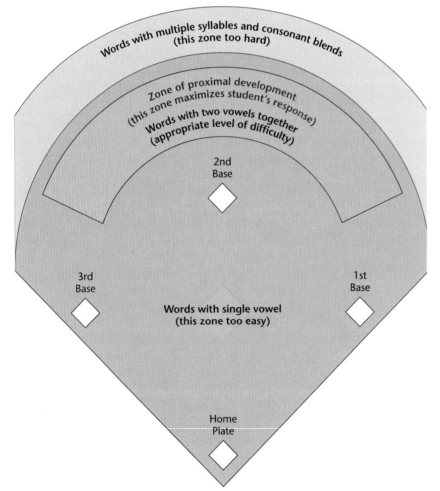

Figure 2.3
Vygotsky's Zone of Proximal Development
The zone of proximal development is that zone which, if stimulated by you, will bring a learner's response to the next level of refinement.

Source: Adapted with permission from Addison-Wesley from *Educational Psychology: A Contemporary Approach* by Borich and Tombari, 2nd Edition, p. 55.

into personal knowledge. That is, young children are observed to frequently talk to themselves when they face difficult tasks, repeating helpful advice that was previously offered to them (Berk & Garvin, 1984). Later, although private speech becomes silent, it is still very important. In fact, recent studies indicate that children who employ private speech learn complex tasks much more effectively than other children (Bivens & Berk, 1990). Vygotsky argued that children use the speech of others by incorporating it with their own speech in order to solve problems. Thus, dialogue and discussion are critical means by which a child learns (Karpov & Bransford, 1995; Kozulin & Presseisen, 1995). Vygotsky also believed that scaffolding plays a critical part in the learning process. **Scaffolding** refers to the support given to the child early on in the learning process. This support becomes diminished in the later stages of learning by having the child take on more responsibility for learning as she is able.

scaffolding support for learning and problem solving; the support could be clues, questions, prompts, breaking a problem down into steps, and anything else that helps a learner become more successful

---

YOU MAKE THE CALL

READING COMPREHENSION AND SCAFFOLDING

In the classroom, a teacher encourages her students to use signal words such as *who*, *what*, *why*, *when*, and *where* as they reflect on the meaning of a reading passage. How would this pattern aid in the learning process? How would this pattern reflect an example of scaffolding?

◆ Vygotsky's Sociocultural Perspective

Vygotsky also believed that in order to understand how a child views the world, a teacher must first understand something about the culture of the child's home and peer group.

Included in this cultural knowledge are language, shared beliefs, and ways of interacting with people. While Piaget believed that cognitive development took place as the individual child progressed through stages, Vygotsky proposed that the stages delineated by Piaget are not necessarily natural for all children, because to a certain extent they are indicative of the types of activities valued in a child's culture (Rogoff & Chavajay, 1995). Furthermore, Vygotsky believed that children learn not as solitary actors in the world, but by using ways of acting and thinking provided by their culture (Kozulin & Presseisen, 1995). Vygotsky also emphasized that a child masters tasks that are deemed to be culturally important primarily through interacting with others. Be cognizant of Vygotsky's ideas as you work with diverse student populations. Consider the following teacher as she tries to link her students' cultural backgrounds to the importance of the academic subject at hand.

CLASS ILLUSTRATION

Mrs. Sanchez works in a school populated predominately with Chinese-American students. She begins to introduce the concept of thermodynamics and the chemistry of violent chemical reactions. Mrs. Sanchez notices that many of her students appear uninterested in the topic. She then mentions to them that from the perspective of their cultural backgrounds, they should find this topic quite fascinating. Mrs. Sanchez proceeds to share with her class that it was the Chinese who are credited for being the first to develop fireworks and that understanding fireworks is directly related to principles of thermodynamics and the chemistry of violent chemical reactions.

constructivism a growing movement in education that places primary importance on direct experience and students' active construction of mental structures, and that de-emphasizes lecturing and "telling" as instructional tools

The importance of being sensitive to your students' cultural heritage and experience is a point that will be discussed further in Chapter 5.

THE WORK OF THE CONSTRUCTIVISTS AND THE NEO-PIAGETIANS

Building on the work of Piaget, for example, the **constructivists** posit that children actively construct knowledge by continually assimilating and accommodating information (Anderson, 1989). According to constructivist theories, cognitive development occurs as children actively build systems of meaning through their experiences and interactions (Brooks, 1990; Leinhardt, 1992).

◆ Bronfenbrenner's Ecological Systems Theory

One example of a constructivist theory is Bronfenbrenner's (1989) ecological systems theory. According to Bronfenbrenner, the child experiences cognitive development in the context of a complex system of relationships including parent-child interaction (the "microsystem"), the extended family, school and neighborhood (the "mesosystem"), and the general society and culture (the "exosystem"). Changes at any of these levels have the potential to influence cognitive development. An immediate implication of such a systems theory is the need to provide programs that impact these various relationships in order to maximize their positive influence on a child's cognitive development Such prevention and intervention programs would include parent-child communication, child abuse detection, coping with divorce, and social skills training.

Teacher Tool Box
Vygotsky: Implications for Practice

◆ Use cooperative learning groups comprised of members of varying abilities. This makes sense since students would have the opportunity to converse with their peers about academic material.

◆ Provide peer tutoring opportunities to afford students the chance to interact with a peer at a more advanced level of cognition who could provide the student assistance as she works in the zone of proximal development.

◆ Use dynamic assessment techniques to test not only the lower level of the zone of proximal development but the higher level as well. In this procedure, the teacher provides the child with hints and prompts at different levels of complexity during the assessment process (Cronbach, 1990; Spector, 1992). In order to ascertain how much the child benefits from certain types of assistance, notations are made about the child's ability before and after the hints as well as about the hints and prompts that were most useful.

◆ Develop an instructional plan aimed at each child's zone of proximal development. When assisting the child in working in this zone, the teacher needs to provide scaffolding in such a way that the teacher's intervention is graduated (Greenfield, 1984).

Imagine the scenario from the household of an impoverished student. The student is asked by her very tired mother to please turn out the light, thus interfering with the student's attempt at completing her homework. This example fits with Bronfenbrenner's work. The sociocultural setting of this household, one in which the parents worked in shifts and were physically exhausted when they arrived home, could, in fact, have a profound effect on their daughter's cognitive development. Although somewhat similar to Vygotsky's view that cognitive development occurs in a rich social and cultural context, Bronfenbrenner's theory is much more encompassing with regard to defining the level of interactions and does not address the role of language in cognitive development as does Vygotsky. That said, Bronfenbrenner's work should also be kept in mind by teachers as they work with diverse student populations.

♦ Information-Processing Theories

Neo-Piagetian updated research on Piagetian stages as applicable to transition from concrete to formal operations

Neo-Piagetian theories have been hypothesized recently to help explain some of the limitations of Piagetian theory (Pascual-Leone, 1987). Another example of this research is reflected in the work of Robbie Case (1984, 1985). As an information-processing theorist (covered in greater depth in Chapter 8), Case is in basic agreement with Piaget's description of what children know at different ages. However, the information-processing theorists challenge the Piagetian notion about how children's thinking changes. Instead of proposing that changes in thinking are driven by assimilation and accommodation, theorists such as Case argue that children of different ages vary with regard to how much memory space they require to process basic operations such as reaching for a toy. Case suggests that as children mature they develop more effective strategies for remembering and are better able to monitor what they are remembering. They begin to think about their thinking as a way of making their processes more efficient. This process of metacognition will be discussed in greater detail in Chapter 12.

Siegler, another information-processing theorist, believes that a child experiences changes in cognitive growth in part because of its acquisition of increasingly powerful rules or procedures. He also argues that children can be taught to discover deficiencies in their own thinking and to apply new logical principles (Siegler, 1983, 1985). Consider the way a child learns to attach an "ed" sound to verbs to indicate that an action has occurred in the past. Early on in development, the child would use his or her memory space to clearly perceive words and endings they hear. With greater experience in listening, more memory space would be available so that he or she could begin to notice that similar meanings were expressed by words that sometimes ended with an "ed" sound and sometimes did not (e.g.,

Connections

When contemplating the use of the whole language approach, there are many sources of information. Using the Internet, access either a sample book list, a fact sheet on the whole language approach, or information on whole language conferences at the whole language site <http://www.lycos.co>.

walk or walked). With repeated practice, the child would encode the "ed" sound as a separate unit. After being reminded of cases in which it is and is not appropriate to add the "ed," the child would then be able to make the connection between the "ed" sound and the action occurring in the past. The child could then construct a new strategy based on the following rule: "Whenever you want to indicate that an action has occurred in the past, attach an 'ed' to the ending of the word describing the action" (Siegler, 1986).

LANGUAGE REFLECTING AND AFFECTING COGNITION

Language development and cognitive development are closely intertwined. Often, insight into a student's language development provides important information about cognition. Understanding students' language development is important because by modeling appropriate speech patterns teachers can facilitate cognitive development. In addition, knowledge about the milestones of language development aids teachers in diagnosing a variety of learning problems such as learning disabilities (we will return to this topic in Chapter 4).

◆ How Do We Acquire Language?

Three different theories attempt to explain how language acquisition occurs. The biological theorists posit that humans are genetically pre-wired to learn language. The cognitive theorists argue that language emerges from existing cognitive structures according to the child's needs. The social learning theorists contend that language comes about primarily as a result of adult modeling and the child's imitation of adult speech. Let's take a more detailed look at each of these theoretical perspectives.

Biological Explanations

Eric Lenneberg (1967) believes that language development occurs in accordance with a biological schedule and parallels cognitive and motor development. He thinks that it is no accident that the ability to walk, stand, and manifest general muscle coordination appear at approximately the same times as the appearance of certain language characteristics. Lenneberg further contends that the spurts evident in children's language development are biologically programmed. For instance, between the ages of fourteen and thirty months there is a rapid increase in vocabulary, which occurs for every normal child in the world. By age four, youngsters also learn the rules of language without instruction.

In a similar vein, Noam Chomsky (1957) thinks that all humans have an innate knowledge of language, which he referred to as the language acquisition device (LAD). Recent biological research, which pinpoints Broca's area of the brain as holding control over speech functions,

psycholinguistics the combined study of psychology and linguistics; refers most often to Chomsky's work on language development

corroborates Chomsky's LAD idea (Reuter-Lorenz & Gazzaniga, 1991). Chomsky's theory of **psycholinguistics** states that children learn language by acquiring a grammar that can generate an infinite number of sentences in their native language. He believes that although all children possess competence for learning language, older children vary in their ability to use language because of differences in opportunity to speak, listen, write, and read.

Cognitive Explanations

In contrast to this biological approach, cognitive theorists such as Piaget postulated that language, rather than being biologically programmed, develops in accordance with existing cognitive structures and differs according to the stage of cognitive development. For instance, in the case of the preoperational child, Piaget noted that both **egocentric speech** and **socialized speech** are outgrowths of cognition. In egocentric speech, children do not care to whom they speak or if anyone is listening to them. Egocentric speech consists of repetition of words that contain no social content, a monologue in which children talk to themselves as if they were thinking out loud, and a collective monologue in which children talk in front of others who are not listening to the speaker. Piaget also observed that socialized speech occurs during the preoperational stage as children criticize each other, ask questions, give answers, and make commands. According to Piaget, egocentrism in languages declines rapidly between the ages of seven and eight, and it is during this period that children engage in more socialized speech. He argues this results primarily because of changing cognitive structures.

egocentric speech speech characteristic of the preoperational child

socialized speech speech characterized by marked decline in egocentrism

Social Learning Explanations

Unlike biological and cognitive theorists, the **social learning** perspective hypothesizes that a child's speech results from modeling, imitation, reinforcement, and feedback (Bandura, 1977, 1986). Albert Bandura proposed that children first listen to others speak, then try it out for themselves. Their attempts at speech are frequently followed by praise or corrective feedback, which in turn generates more trying out. We will return to this process of modeling and learning through observation in Chapter 6.

social learning theory a theory of learning that places heavy emphasis on parent modeling and the child's imitation of adult behavior; used to explain the acquisition of language and complex behaviors

LANGUAGE DEVELOPMENT

Before uttering their first word, infants communicate through many modes, including crying, smiling, and body movements. Although most children speak their first word by the first year, it is not until between one and two years of age that children use words to convey meaning. During this period the child also uses intonation to communicate meaning for the first time.

By about eighteen months of age, children enter the two-word stage in which they employ two words together in a quasi-sentence fashion such as "Play at" or "More light." In fact, by twenty months a child's vocabulary is usually about fifty words (Nelson, 1981). In this **telegraphic speech** stage, the words that carry the most meaning are included, while nonessentials are left out (R. Brown, 1973). Sometime during the "twos," children begin to add plurals and endings for words, such as "ed" and "ing." Grammatical rules tend to become overgeneralized during this period. For instance, the child may utter, "He goed home." By age three, children learn to use sentences more strategically to form both questions and negative statements. For instance, "He hit him" may be changed into "He didn't hit him" or "Did he hit him?" (R. Brown, 1973).

In addition to acquiring grammar, children also make remarkable advances in learning vocabulary during the preschool years. Every six months, between the ages of two and four, vocabulary doubles. Children's command of words numbers about 2,000 by the age of four. Often at this time, they enjoy making up words and tend to assume that others know the meaning of these new words. By age five or six, most children have successfully mastered the basics of their language. It seems that the time before puberty, particularly the preschool years, is a sensitive period for language acquisition and growth. Thus, extremely positive or extremely negative conditions in the critical period before puberty can greatly aid or hamper language development (Anglin, 1993).

telegraphic speech children's speech using only essential words, as in a telegram

◆ **Vocabulary and Meaning**

By age six, a child's vocabulary typically includes from 8,000 to 14,000 words. In fact, the period roughly between the ages of five and seven has been referred to as a critical period of language development in which children are very receptive to picking up the vocabulary of a second language (Berger, 1986). By age eleven, the child's vocabulary has expanded by at least another 5,000 words. However, it is vital for teachers to understand that despite possessing a fairly sophisticated vocabulary, that the vocabulary may NOT be reflective of sophisticated conceptualizations. For example, students in the elementary years may appropriately employ words such as "justice" without fully understanding its meaning. Or these same children may not comprehend the meaning of a metaphor such as "The prison guard was hard as a rock." The preoperational child will typically envision the guard as a rock upon hearing this statement, whereas a child in concrete or formal operations will go beyond the literal interpretation. Other illustrations of the close tie between cognition and language can be found in the limited facility elementary-aged children have for understanding sarcastic remarks or satire (Gardner, 1982).

Syntax

Word order, or basic **syntax**, is usually mastered early in a child's development. While more complex forms of syntax such as the passive voice ("The ball was thrown by Mary") are understood by early elementary children, they are not used by them until later. The more complicated

syntax the set of rules that one uses (often unconsciously) to put words together in sentences

forms of syntax emerge during the elementary years. During this period, complex grammatical structures such as conjunctions, clauses, and qualifiers come into play.

Pragmatics

pragmatics the study within psycholinguistics of how one uses language in social situations; emphasizes functional use of language rather than its mechanics

It is also during the elementary years that children learn how to use language to communicate appropriately. Their use of **pragmatics**, such as applying the rules of turn-taking, is not in full force until the later elementary years. As they become less egocentric, their conversations provide evidence that they have in fact listened to each other. It is not until the later elementary years, for instance, that children become really proficient in the art of persuading a peer to do something he or she did not initially want to do. By adolescence, they become very interested in understanding the perspectives and motivations of other speakers (Dorval & Eckerman, 1984).

Metalinguistic Awareness

metalinguistic awareness knowledge about language and the ability to think about one's own knowledge of language

By age five or six a child develops the ability to think about language and how it works. This ability is termed **metalinguistic awareness** (Keil, 1979). Children are now ready to study the rules that govern language explicitly. This opens the door to a wide range of teaching strategies designed to facilitate even more sophisticated metalinguistic abilities.

TEACHING AND LANGUAGE

The next section will review research and ideas for practice related to the teaching of language from both the **phonics** and whole language perspectives.

phonics approach approach to reading instruction that urges students to sound out words they read

◆ Key Elements of the Phonics Approach

phonological awareness one's awareness of phonemes as related to reading comprehension

Recent research suggests that teachers do need to incorporate **phonological awareness** (i.e., hearing distinct sounds or phonemes within a spoken word) into their teaching because it is an essential part of successful reading. Students who have difficulty identifying the specific phonemes in a word tend to have more trouble reading than their peers (Foorman, Francis, Fletcher, et al., 1998). To facilitate phonological awareness, teachers can ask students to go home and look for pictures or objects that begin or end with the sound of the week, have students select from a varied group of pictures those that do not begin with the sound of the week, and provide oral models of rhyming words, eventually asking students to create their own rhymes (Bradley & Bryant, 1991).

Along with sound recognition, teachers should ascertain if students can distinguish individual letters of the alphabet in both upper and lower case form, as this skill is another important prerequisite to suc-

Sucessful reading entails word decoding skills in which students identify the sounds associated with the word's letters and blend them together to identify what the word is. ◆

cessful reading. Teachers can promote this skill by asking students to practice writing the letters, drawing the letters in sand, making the letters with their bodies, and reading alphabet books that depict the letters in the context of a story. In addition, recent studies also suggest that successful reading entails **word decoding** skills in which students identify the sounds associated with the word's letters and blend them together to identify what the word is. In order to strengthen word decoding skills teachers can have students practice sounding out unfamiliar words, teach rules for spelling that apply in most cases, have students pick out patterns in words that are spelled and pronounced in a

word decoding ability to identify the sounds associated with the word's letters and blend them together to identify what the word is

Action Research

Whole Language

A s we discussed in Chapter 1, as decision makers teachers frequently conduct their own action research. While action research helps teachers to act as critical thinkers as they better reflect on their own practice, it also provides them with direct data on how well a given intervention is working in their classroom. One such action research study, which pertains to a topic discussed in this chapter, whole language, is described below.

Mrs. McElmore wanted to know how a thematic, nonbasal reading program she developed would affect middle level students' skill mastery and interest in reading (Sardo-Brown, 1990). After teaching her newly developed reading program to twenty-three students over an eight-week period, she compared student scores on a teacher-developed skill mastery test to scores from the previous semester and compared scores on a pre- and post-test reading inventory. She also read student journal entries. Mrs. McElmore found that both skill mastery and interest in reading increased. Mrs. McElmore plans to continue to modify her whole language approach to teaching reading to include a greater number of authentic tasks that incorporate a variety of subject areas.

Teacher Tool Box

Key Elements of the Whole Language Approach

- Read quality literature to children so that they will in turn read on their own;
- Repeatedly read appealing rhymes, songs, poems, and stories;
- Engage in sustained silent reading (the teacher too!);
- Assign small groups of children to read the same books followed by reading conferences;
- Establish an individualized reading program that is carefully monitored;
- Make oral language available to children in written format by scripting or tape recording it;
- Use the writing process of rehearse, draft, revise, edit, publish, and receive responses;
- Model the writing process to students often;
- Provide opportunities for students to share their writing with an audience such as through published book projects;
- Provide students with reading and writing assignments in a variety of content areas so that they are able to see connections between content areas as they read and write.

whole language approach a philosophical approach to teaching and learning that stresses learning through authentic, real-life tasks; emphasizes using language to learn, integrating learning across skills and subjects, and respecting the language abilities of student and teacher

similar way, and teach students how to spell the words they read (Adams, 1990; Reuter & Cooter, 1999).

◆ Teaching Elements of the Whole Language Approach

Another approach for facilitating language development in young children is called the **whole language approach.** Proponents of this method contend that the best way to learn language is in the context of its use (Goodman & Goodman, 1990). They argue that children are most likely to develop control over the processes of language when they have a real purpose for using language. That is, writing assignments need to be linked to authentic or real-life tasks. In addition, whole language supporters argue that the curriculum should be integrated so that writing, listening, speaking, and reading skills are developed together. The curriculum should also be integrated so that subjects are not taught in isolation from each other. Instead, the connections between subjects such as science and social studies should surface in the course of completing an authentic task.

Recent evidence indicates that students with learning disabilities also profit from the whole language approach (Dudley-Marling, 1995), although other studies suggest that students with learning disabilities need direct instruction in hearing sounds and building phonemic knowledge before learning how to read provided in the phonics approach (Chall, 1991). In essence, students with learning disabilities need many types of instruction; they can benefit from the whole language approach if appropriate supplemental teaching is provided (Mather, 1991).

An overview of the elements of a whole language approach recently adopted by one school district is presented in the tool box (Robbins, 1990).

Reflections from the Field

1 I recommend teaching elementary students about fractions by having them work with familiar objects they enjoy such as cutting up pizza slices.

—Heidi (first grade teacher), Pottstown, PA

2 To teach junior high students about abstractions such as how to balance an equation, I have them first experience the concept I'm teaching. For example, they first make observations of what their partner does when trying to balance herself on a line of tape I've put on the floor. Then we discuss these observations and use them in explaining what is involved in balancing an equation.

—Jerry (middle school science teacher), West Chester, PA

3 I found that teaching abstract concepts to my eighth graders was the most difficult aspect of my student teaching. One idea that worked well was to have my students act out the concepts. For instance, they had a lot of trouble understanding irony. So I asked them to get into groups and make up an ironic skit for the rest of the class. You could see as the skits were performed that lightbulbs started to go on.

—Jack (senior high social studies teacher), Phoenixville, PA

4 Piaget's ideas are not only useful when it comes to teaching academics. When teaching my elementary students about classroom rules, I find that it's essential to use concrete demonstrations of what I mean. When teaching them about appropriate noise levels, I either play a tape for them that features various noise levels or have groups of students model these noise levels.

—Toby (third grade teacher), Philadelphia, PA

5 You've got to tie what you're teaching to examples that are familiar to the kids. I learned from my co-operating teacher how to do this. In teaching the myth "Echo and Narcissus," I had the students first write about a conflict they had experienced in their own lives. Then we looked for conflicts as we read the myths. Next, my students wrote about how their personal conflicts were resolved. As we read the myth we also looked for resolutions to conflicts.

—Jackie (middle school student teacher), Upper Darby, PA

THEORY TO PRACTICE

A Look at Teacher as Decision Maker

Let's return to our initial scene in which Mr. Nuygen attempts to teach his students about fractions. In reviewing the scene without our knowledge of cognitive development, one would surely think Mr. Nuygen is not teaching "content." However, with our understanding of the theories presented within this chapter the "method to his madness" will clearly emerge.

Along with the fact that Mr. Nuygen gets his students' attention by using a knife to cut a pear, he has also cut up several pears, each into different portions and placed these on the desks of selected students. Pointing to the students who have the pears, he asks, "What do you have?" Mr. Nuygen's appreciation for Piaget's theory of cognitive development is obvious. His decisions to use these props reflects his appreciation of the need to blend his course content with the unique cognitive characteristics of the students in his class. He is allowing the "who" of his classroom to interact with the "what" of his material so that together they give form to the "how" of his lesson.

Clearly, teachers need to plan lessons that employ methods congruent with their students' cognition. In the above scene, Mr. Nuygen realizes that because some of his students are primarily concrete operational thinkers and some are in transition from concrete to formal operations, using a concrete reference point to begin instruction is essential. Thus, teachers need to understand the Piagetian stages of cognitive development reviewed in this chapter in order to create and implement lesson plans that will work for their students.

Another facet of cognition, social cognition, becomes especially important for teachers to keep in mind as they interact with middle and senior high school students. Teachers who are sensitive to their students' beliefs in the personal fable and imaginary audience, for instance, operate with such knowledge in mind.

Teachers, such as Mr. Nuygen, who call upon the knowledge base described in this chapter as they critically think about instructional issues will most likely use the following strategies to help their students learn. As you reflect on your own experience of being a student or do field observations this semester in actual classrooms, look for evidence of each of the following.

1. Developmentally appropriate plans, which take into account the cognitive limitations of students;
2. Sensitivity when dealing with manifestations of the personal fable and imaginary audience;
3. Scaffolding strategy to facilitate student learning;
4. Consideration of factors described in ecological systems theory when assessing why students behave as they do;
5. Authentic activities in which students see real-world applications and the connection between one subject area and another.

You, as Teacher, as Decision Maker

In the following case presentations, you will be provided with the description of a number of salient characteristics of the school, the classroom, and the students. In reviewing these illustrations, try to apply your knowledge of cognitive development in order to

1. Identify if instruction is developmentally appropriate;
2. Determine how Vygotsky's ideas could be employed to facilitate student learning;
3. Explain from a constructivist and Neo-Piagetian point of view why learning may be difficult; and
4. Suggest two specific ways the whole language approach could be used help students learn.

Case Illustration 1:
Tyndall Elementary

The School

Tyndall Elementary School is located a few minutes from a navy base. The majority of the student population comes from middle and lower income households. The neighborhood surrounding the school is well kept, but a short distance away many families live in low-income housing.

Your Class

Your class is a self-contained second grade. There are twenty-seven children in your class, sixteen boys and eleven girls. The racial composition of your class, similar to the community at large, is 92 percent white, 7 percent African American, and 1 percent Asian American. About 35 percent of your students qualify for federally provided lunch programs. While some of the children walk to school, others are bused from several miles away as part of a desegregation plan.

Your Students

Your students are learning about maps and globes. After students read a story, the teacher stops to ask them where the main characters live. He then uses both a map and a globe to help students see how far away these cities are from where they live. Although some students seem to understand the concept of long distances, others seem to struggle.

Guides for Reflection

In reviewing the above features, consider how each of the following may provide insight and direction for a teacher concerned about using research on cognitive development to help his students learn.

Piaget's theory
Vygotsky's work
Constructivist theory
Neo-Piagetian theory
The whole language approach

Case Illustration 2:
Augusta Middle School

Your School

The Augusta Middle School is located in a rural community composed of students from upper, middle, and lower socioeconomic households. The school's constituencies and teachers are both largely conservative in orientation. Many members of the community still gather at the mainstreet diner to discuss local and current events.

Your Class

You are teaching eighth grade language arts. In March, you begin a unit on mythology by having students read the myth "Echo and Narcissus," the major theme of which is conflict. Your primary teaching format is to introduce the story first, have students read the remainder of it at home, and then discuss the story the next day.

Your Students

Although the students have been generally attentive throughout the school year, you begin to see their interest wane. After giving the weekly quiz, it becomes apparent to your that your students are not keeping up with the assigned reading.

Guides for Reflection

In reviewing the above feature, consider how each of the following may provide insight and direction for a teacher concerned about how to use research on cognitive development to help their students learn:

Piaget's theory
Vygotsky's work
Constructivist theory
Neo-Piagetian theory
The whole language approach

SUMMARY

What Is Development?

Development refers to growth, adaptation, and change that occurs over the course of a lifetime.

Piaget's Theory of Cognitive Development

The principles of adaptation and organization became cornerstones for Piaget's view of cognitive development.

To understand the process of adaptation, Piaget identified four concepts, which he used to explain how and why cognitive development occurs. These include schema, assimilation, accommodation, and equilibration.

According to Piaget, cognitive development unfolds as the child passes through four distinct and qualitatively different stages; the sensorimotor, pre-operational, concrete operational, and formal operational stages.

Adolescent Social Cognition: The Work of Elkind

David Elkind suggests that adolescents' thought patterns tend to be characterized by adolescent egocentrism. By this, Elkind refers to the tendency of adolescents to assume that all other people view the world as they do and are thus focused on the same concerns as they are at any one time.

Elkind suggests that this adolescent egocentrism has two unique and interesting facets; one is called the personal fable and the other one is called the imaginary audience.

1. The *personal fable* is the self-generated, often romanticized story of one's personal destiny;
2. The *imaginary audience* refers to the adolescent tendency to feel always in the spotlight.

The Alternative Perspective of Vygotsky

Vygotsky believed that children often are at a cognitive level where they can solve problems independently. He termed this level as the *zone of actual development*. In contrast, he believed that there are times when a child can solve problems with support, and this he identified as the *zone of proximal development*.

Vygotsky viewed a child's private speech as guiding the child's development. Private speech is a mechanism emphasized by Vygotsky, which helps turn shared knowledge into personal knowledge.

The Work of the Constructivists and the Neo-Piagetians

The *constructivists* posit that children actively construct knowledge by continually assimilating and accommodating information. According to constructivist theories, cognitive development occurs as children actively build systems of meaning through their experiences and interactions.

Language Reflecting and Affecting Cognition

There are three different theories that attempt to explain how language acquisition occurs.

1. The *biological theories* posit that humans are genetically pre-wired to learn language;
2. The *cognitive theorists* argue that language emerges from existing cognitive structures and according to the child's needs;
3. The *social learning theorists* contend that language comes about primarily as a result of adult modeling and a child's imitation of adult speech.

Teaching and Language

Research suggests that teachers do need to incorporate phonological awareness (i.e., hearing distinct sounds or phonemes within a spoken word) into their teaching because it is an essential part of successful reading.

Another approach for facilitating language development in young children that is gaining in popularity is called the whole language approach. Proponents of this method contend that the best way to learn language is in the context of its use.

◆ Field Experience Questions

You will gather a variety of different types of data about teachers and students as you observe classrooms. This can be accomplished by writing down detailed field notes of what you observe, asking teachers and students interview questions, and recording the frequency and nature of certain types of behaviors. Below are a series of field experience questions, related to topics covered in this chapter, that you can try to answer based on classroom observations:

Piagetian Theory

1. Based on your observations, how would you characterize the stage of Piagetian cognitive development of most of the learners?
2. Give at least two illustrations from the classroom that support this.
3. Were the teaching techniques appropriate for this stage? Why or why not?
4. What additional teaching techniques, based on Piagetian theory, should be employed for these children?

Vygotsky's Theory

1. Shadow a student for a day. Based on Vygotsky's theory identify if the child is working in his or her zone of proximal development with regard to the attainment of one skill.
2. If the child is working in the zone of proximal development, explain how Vygotsky's principles are being used to provide support to the child. If these principles are not being employed, how would you suggest they could be in this setting?
3. If the child is not working in his or her zone of proximal development, try to identify what that zone is. Hint: Try to delineate what tasks are too easy for the child and what tasks are too difficult. Then identify what the child could do with appropriate assistance.

Whole Language

1. Based on the content from this chapter, look for evidence that the whole language approach is being used.
2. If it is being used, describe the key features you have observed related to those discussed in this chapter.
3. If it is not being used, formulate a plan to incorporate it into this classroom.

◆ Key Terms

accommodation	classification	development
adolescent egocentrism	cognitive disequilibrium	egocentric speech
analogical reasoning	concrete operational stage	egocentrism
animism	conservation	equilibration
assimilation	constructivism	formal operational stage
centration	deductive reasoning	hypothetical reasoning

metalinguistic awareness
myelinization
neo-Piagetian
object permanence
phonics approach
phonological awareness
pragmatics
preoperational stage

private speech
psycholinguistics
scaffolding
schema
sensorimotor stage
seriation
socialized speech
social learning theory

symbolic function
syntax
telegraphic speech
transductive reasoning
whole language approach
word decoding
zone of proximal development

◆ Additional Resources

Anderson, P. S., & Lapp, D. (1988). *Language skills in elementary education* (4th ed.). New York: Macmillan.

Anselmo, S. (1987). *Early childhood development: Prenatal through age eight.* Columbus, Ohio: Merrill.

Bergin, D. A. (1998). Continuities between motivation research and whole language philosophy of instruction. *Journal of Literacy Research, 30,* 321–356.

Cowan, P. A. (1978). *Piaget with feeling.* New York: Holt, Rinehart and Winston.

Elkind, D. (1981). *The hurried child.* Reading, MA: Addison-Wesley.

Flavell, J. (1985). *Cognitive development.* Englewood Cliffs, NJ: Prentice-Hall.

Ginsburg, H., & Opper, S. (1988). *Piaget's theory of intellectual development.* Englewood Cliffs, NJ: Prentice-Hall.

Goodman, K. (1986). *What's whole in whole language.* Portsmouth, NH: Heinemann.

Needels, M., & Knapp, M. (1994). Teaching writing to children who are underserved. *Journal of Educational Psychology, 86(3),* 339–349.

Rothman, R. (1990, Jan. 10). Balance between phonics and whole language urged. *Education Week,* 8–10.

Tittnich, E., Bloom, L., Schomberg, R., & Szekeres, S. (eds.). (1990). *Facilitating children's language: Handbook for child-related professionals.* New York: The Hayworth Press.

Developmental Theory: Moral and Psychosocial Development

A s we observe Mrs. Fry's class struggle with a difficult physics problem, our attention is drawn to one female student, gazing out the window, apparently longing to be somewhere else. After a few more moments of unsuccessful attempts at resolving the problem, Mrs. Fry announces: "Okay, we'll have to stay late again." At this, the student who was staring out the window gets up to leave class. Mrs. Fry asks, "Where are you going?"

The student responds, "It's none of your business," and proceeds to run out of the classroom and down the hall. Mrs. Fry runs after her and asks what the problem is.

The student replies: "It's all too much. Keeping up with school, my job, my boyfriend. Look at my hair. It's never right. I hate my life."

Mrs. Fry responds, "Let's give it one more try."

W hile this scene, adapted from the movie *Stand and Deliver*, is quite dramatic, it clearly highlights a reality many of us have experienced in our own personal lives. Our emotional and social needs affect our academic achievement. Consider how often your own attitude about a subject, a teacher, or even the class members have affected how well you did in that subject. Similarly, were there times when a personal issue or concern interfered with your ability to achieve or perform within a class?

The psychosocial needs and characteristics of our students play an important role in their academic performance and achievement. These unique characteristics of our students must be understood if one is to be an effective teacher, who not only understands the unique characteristics of the WHO of each student, but employs that understanding to make decisions about the WHAT and the HOW of the class. To be an effective teacher, you will need to reach beyond the content or WHAT of your course; and even beyond knowing the unique cognitive characteristics of the WHO within your class. You must also consider the unique influence your students' moral and psychosocial levels of development will have on your class and teaching. As we saw in Chapter 2, you need to consider the cognitive characteristics of WHO you are teaching as you plan for the WHAT and the HOW of your class. In this chapter, we urge you to think critically about the moral and psychosocial features of your students. These features must be considered if teachers are to treat students in a sensitive, caring manner. It is encumbent upon all teachers to understand that this a vital part of their professional responsibility.

In this chapter, we will review theory and research concerning students' moral and psychosocial development. We will consider major theories of moral development and discuss ways in which teachers can facilitate moral behavior and curb cheating and aggression. We will also focus on the psychosocial development of students by reviewing the theories of Erik Erikson and James Marcia. Finally, we will discuss psychosocial issues facing our students, including the development of self-concept, teen pregnancy, eating disorders, AIDS, divorce, child abuse, and suicide.

◆ Chapter Objectives

After reading this chapter you should be able to do the following:

1 Compare and contrast the three major theories of moral development presented, including Piaget's theory, Kohlberg's theory, and Gilligan's theory;

2 Explain how teachers can facilitate moral behavior in their students by incorporating the use of the four-component Lickona model into their curriculum;

3 Provide three guidelines you can use as a classroom teacher to help prevent cheating by your students;

4 Explain how classroom teachers can curb aggressive behaviors in their students;

5 Delineate Erikson's eight-stage theory of psychosocial development by describing the psychosocial crisis faced by the individual at each stage;

6 Explain how each of the first five stages of Erikson's theory are related to how the individual's cognitive development unfolds as specified by Piaget;

7 For the initiative versus guilt, industry versus inferiority, and identity versus confusion stages, formulate a plan for how to address the healthy psychosocial development of students you may teach;

8 Explain how your own psychosocial development as a classroom teacher may affect the way in which you view your professional responsibilities;

9 Discuss how a student's self-concept changes over time and why the academic self-concept is so important;

10 Describe recent data relevant to teen pregnancy and eating disorders, and what classroom teachers should be aware of relative to each of these problems;

11 Discuss the major misconceptions students hold about AIDS;

12 Delineate the four major types of child abuse and explain the legal responsibilities of classroom teachers regarding child abuse;

13 Differentiate how children typically respond to divorce, based on their cognitive stage of development;

14 Discuss the warning signals teachers should look for in students contemplating suicide.

CHAPTER 3 CONTENT MAP

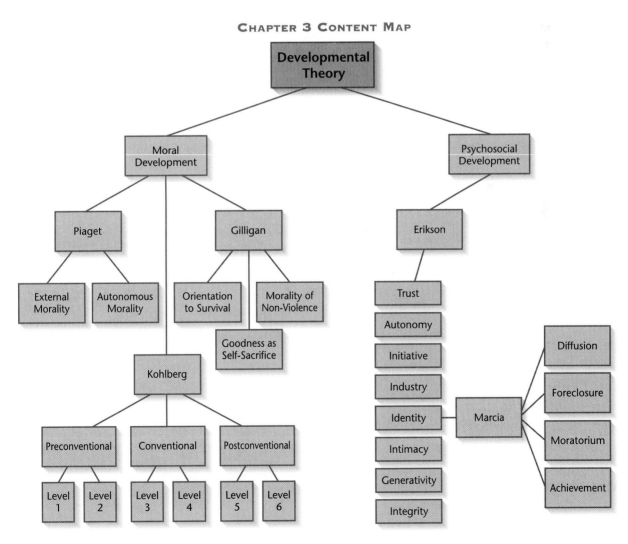

MORAL DEVELOPMENT

On first reflection, you may question the reason you, as a future science or math or health educator, need to understand the moral development of your students. After all, you are not trying to teach religion. And isn't a child's moral development a parent's responsibility?

moral reasoning the thinking processes involved in judgments about questions of right and wrong

You will quickly find that as a classroom teacher you are confronted with hundreds of issues pertaining to your students' **moral reasoning** each day. These may range from decisions they make about whether to cheat on a test to whether to be tolerant toward a classmate who is being picked on by others. A student's moral reasoning may also play a part in a decision to give help to someone in a cooperative learning group or even to treat with respect a prized possession brought from home by a peer. In fact, the mere acts of following class rules or saying "Excuse me" when passing another in the aisle or "God bless you" after someone sneezes—all these acts communicate something about a student's values! Beyond the influence a student's moral reasoning may have on how she behaves within your class, a student's view of "right and wrong" along with her orientation to what is important, or to be valued, can affect her approach to your class and class material. For example, a student's moral reasoning can play a significant role in how she arrives at judgments about various aspects of curriculum content such as assessing the merit of the North and the South in the Civil War or the complex argument for and against dropping the atomic bomb on Japan. Every day, your students make hundreds of comments and decisions that involve moral reasoning. Knowing how and when to respond requires that the effective teacher understand the theory and principles underlying the process of moral development.

A student's moral reasoning may also play a part in a decision to give help to someone in a cooperative learning group. ◆

◆ Piaget's Work

You'll recall Jean Piaget's theory of cognitive development from Chapter 2. Piaget also posed a theory of moral development, which essentially divided the way that children think about moral issues into two stages. The first stage, called **external morality** or **moral realism**, was used to describe children younger than ten years of age (Piaget, 1965). In this stage, children tend to view rules as inflexible and not open to negotiation. They also view rules as based in a constrained relationship. That is, rules are set by adults, and the adults who made the rules must be obeyed. From this perspective, children under ten would judge the badness of an act solely by considering the consequences. For example, a child in the external morality stage of development would conclude that a little girl who spilled a jar of ink that ruined her mother's expensive drawing should be severely punished regardless of whether the act was accidental or intentional. The consequence, which in this case was the destruction of a costly drawing, would dictate the level of badness and not the person's intent or mental state.

> **external morality** or **moral realism** stage of development wherein children see rules as absolute

Consider the preschooler who refuses to share a toy. When asked to share she responds, "No, I had it first." For this student, it appears that the "rule" of "first come first served" should apply regardless of the circumstances. Such inflexibility is a characteristic of this stage of external morality.

Piaget described the child's moral reasoning as shifting to **autonomous reality** or **morality of cooperation**, beginning at some point late concrete operational stage. With this development, a child begins to perceive rules as more flexible and subject to renegotiation. Children, operating from this autonomous reality, view rules as developed cooperatively by people who are equals instead of solely by authority figures. "Badness" is now determined by considering not just the consequences but the actor's intentions. In other words, punishments are no longer perceived as automatic and inflexibly tied to an action.

> **autonomous morality** or **morality of cooperation** stages of development wherein children realize that people make rules and people can change them

YOU MAKE THE CALL

A third-grade teacher reminds her students not to touch the animal cages containing hamsters in the back of the room. Later in the day, one third grader named Pete hears one of the hamsters whimpering in pain. He moves closer to the cage during free reading time and actually touches it to try to find out what is wrong. One of his peers named Tim screams: "I'm going to tell on you, Pete. That's against the rules." However, a tutor visiting from the eighth grade reminds Tim that Pete approached the cage with the intention of helping the animal.

It would appear that Pete and Tim are operating from a different level of moral development and reasoning. How do you think Piaget would explain or describe this difference?

◆ Kohlberg's Stages

Like Piaget, Lawrence Kohlberg believed that children's movement from one stage of moral reasoning to another is governed by transformations in the child's cognitive structures. However, Kohlberg believed that while a person's cognitive stage is a prerequisite for how the individual reasons about moral issues, the cognitive stage does not guarantee that the individual will ascend to the latter stages of moral reasoning.

Kohlberg's theory of moral development is more extensive than Piaget's because he describes the moral reasoning of children from four years old through adulthood. He proposes three levels of moral development, including preconventional (four to ten years), conventional (ten to thirteen years), and postconventional (thirteen years and older). Encompassed in each of these three levels are two specific moral stages (see Table 3.1).

Kohlberg's data about moral development were derived from children's and adults' responses to moral dilemmas or hypothetical situations (Kohlberg, 1963). His subjects were asked what they would do in the same situation and why. One of the classic hypothetical vignettes concerned the case of Heinz whose wife was dying of cancer. Heinz learns that there is a drug available that may help his wife, but he cannot afford to buy it. Heinz's dilemma is whether or not to steal the drug to save his dying wife. During the course of Kohlberg's research, he found that his subjects responded to these scenarios in very different ways. From these varying responses, Kohlberg generated the following stages of moral development.

Level I: Preconventional Morality

preconventional morality
rules of conduct of children (birth–9 years) who do not yet understand the conventions of society; level I of Kohlberg's theory of moral reasoning

Moral reasoning in the **preconventional level** of development is characterized by a focus on the consequence experienced by the person as a result of his/her actions. Morality at this stage is determined by the consequences of an action rather than by the inherent goodness or badness of the act. This level consists of two stages: (1) punishment-obedience and (2) market exchange. Individuals reasoning in the punishment-obedience stage would say that if Heinz was caught stealing the drug, then he was wrong. However, if Heinz was not caught stealing, then he was right.

In the market-exchange stage, individuals are still driven by the consequences of an action when making decisions about morality, but are also focused on the idea of reciprocity. That is, they reason that an act is moral if the consequence of obeying a rule results in their obtaining something positive. A child reasoning at this hedonistic stage may argue that Heinz was right in stealing the drug if he left a note promising to do a favor for the druggist. A child in the market-exchange stage may also reason that Heinz is right in stealing the drug because Heinz will feel better if his wife is not sick. Some researchers estimate that approximately 15 to 20 percent of adolescents reason primarily at

Table 3.1   Kohlberg's Stages of Moral Development

Level and Stage	Description
Level 1: Preconventional Reasoning	The ethics of egocentricity. Typical of children up to about age ten. Called pre-conventional because young children don't really comprehend the rules set down by others. The consequences of the act determine if it is good or bad.
Stage 1: Punishment-Obedience	The ethics of "What's in it for me?"
Stage 2: Market Exchange	Obeying rules and exchanging favors are judged in terms of benefit to the person.
Level II: Conventional Ethics	The ethics of others. Typical of ten to twenty year olds. The name comes from conformity to the rules and conventions of society.
Stage 3: Interpersonal Harmony	Sometimes called "Nice girl/good boy." Ethical decisions are based on what pleases, helps, or is approved of by others.
Stage 4: Law and Order	The ethics of order. Right is doing one's duty, obeying the law, and maintaining an orderly society.
Level III: Postconventional Ethics	The ethics of principle. Rarely reached before age twenty and only by a small segment of the population. Focuses on the principles underlying society's rules.
Stage 5: Social Contract	Rules are based on principles of justice and common good and are mutually agreed upon by members of society.
Stage 6: Universal Principles	Rarely encountered in life. Ethics determined by individual's conscience guided by the abstract principles of justice and equality.

Source: From *Essays on Moral Development: The Psychology of Moral Development (Vol. II)* by Lawrence Kohlberg. Copyright © 1984 by Lawrence Kohlberg. Reprinted by permission of HarperCollins Publishers, Inc.

stage 1 or 2 (Turiel, 1973). Consider the scenario in which a junior high school teacher begins passing out a history test. As he does, someone from class pulls the fire alarm. While we maybe able to understand the possible dangers of such an action or even the level of inconsideration exhibited, it is most likely that the perpetrator would simply conclude that since it was "fun" and "I didn't get caught," "it was okay!"

Mrs. Rosemont, a ninth grade English teacher, has assigned each of her students a partner to help students catch up if they are absent. One of Mrs. Rosemont's rules is that each class member must help her assigned partner by informing them what assignments need to be done in the event a student is absent. When Nina is informed by her mother that her partner Wendy has called her to catch up on assignments, Nina resists calling her back. She wonders: "How do I have time to call her tonight and study for my algebra test and practice my cheerleading?" Early that evening Nina thinks to herself: "Why should I call Wendy? She'll never tell the teacher that I haven't helped her." However, as the evening goes on, Nina begins to think: "Well, maybe I should call Wendy because I may want her to do a favor for me soon."

Review the quotes from above and identify where you think stage 1 and stage 2 moral reasoning are occurring.

Level II: Conventional Morality

As the child develops through Level I, we see increasing "concern" or "consideration" for the impact of one's decision on another. From this increasing concern for others, an individual would conclude that Heinz should have left the druggist a promissory note. As egocentrism continues to decline, the child increasingly views moral issues from the perspective of others. Rather than viewing morality in terms of immediate concrete consequences, the individual now makes moral decisions by considering factors of a less concrete and more social nature, such as the approval of others, family loyalty, obedience to the law, and social order. Individuals operating at the **conventional levels** have internalized the rules or, if you will, the "conventions" of society. This level of moral reasoning consists of two stages: (1) interpersonal harmony and (2) law and order.

conventional morality rules of conduct of older children (9–young adulthood) based on the conventions of society; level II of Kohlberg's theory of moral reasoning

Initially, the rules of society to which individuals seek to adhere are those imposed by their parents or other adult authority figures. The key feature of the interpersonal harmony stage involves loyalty and gaining the approval of others, who may include family, peers, and teachers. An individual at this stage may well say that Heinz was wrong to steal because the druggist would be mad at him. However, using the same reasoning process, another individual at this stage may think Heinz was right in stealing because he gained his dying wife's approval.

As development continues, the individual moves from concerns of pleasing others to a more generalized orientation to following codified societal rules and laws. Individuals in the law and order stage base moral decisions upon whether or not they are congruent with codified law. An individual in this stage may argue that Heinz was wrong to steal because stealing is against the law. Or a student engaged in play may become quite upset when someone breaks the rules, exclaiming: "That's not the way you play," and perhaps terminating the game, with a loud and definitive "I QUIT!"

Approximately 80 percent of the adult population is estimated to be operating at Level II when it comes to reasoning about moral issues.

YOU MAKE THE CALL

Let's think back to the earlier situation with Nina and her partner Wendy. Later that same evening, as Nina continues to debate as to whether to call Wendy, she thinks: "Maybe I better help her because her friends won't like me if word gets around that I didn't." Nina also recalls how her teacher set up the rule that all class members must help their partners in the event they are absent.

"What choice do I have?" she wonders. "It's the rule."

After you review the above quotes, decide where stage 3 and stage 4 moral reasoning are occurring.

Level III: Postconventional Morality

The final level of Kohlberg's development model is the **postconventional level** of morality. At this level, individuals move beyond the issues of pleasing or following the concrete rules and begin to focus on the principles that underlie these rules. Comparatively few people reach Kohlberg's third level of moral reasoning. In fact, it is not until the early twenties that individuals reason on this basis—if at all. This level is made up of two stages: (1) social contract and (2) universal principles. In the social contract stage, an individual conceptualizes rules as mutually agreed upon and based on principles of justice and the common good. That is, rules are not deemed moral because they are codified law; rather they are moral because they reflect the common good. Thus, while an individual operating at Level II (i.e., conventional morality) may adhere to specific laws of our land as the basis for decision making, one reasoning at Level III would be directed less by the specific laws and more by the underlying principles of our Constitution such as life, liberty, and the dignity of the individual. Someone reasoning in stage 5 may very well contend that Heinz was right for stealing because his wife's right to life was more important than a law against stealing. However, someone else in this stage may argue Heinz was wrong because in stealing he deprived the druggist of his right to make a living and, therefore, his dignity.

In stage 6, an individual reasons about moral issues by referring to universal, abstract principles that transcend society's laws. In fact, the specific laws have validity only to the degree that they are in accord with these abstract principles. Kohlberg said that such an individual made decisions based on a well developed set of internalized ethical principles. One example of this is found in the "Golden Rule." Because Kohlberg discovered that so few people operate at this stage, he focused more on stage 5 in his later work (Kohlberg, 1984).

postconventional morality rules of conduct of adults who recognize the societal need for mutual agreement and the application of consistent principles in making judgments; level III of Kohlberg's theory of moral reasoning

---

YOU MAKE THE CALL

Let's return to the earlier scenario involving Nina. Nina's older sister, who happened to stop in because of her semester break at college, offers Nina some advice about how to approach Wendy. "Look, Nina, I think Wendy has a perfect right to do as well as possible in her studies and in this case, you could help. And just think about it; wouldn't you want Wendy to call you back if you had been the one who was absent?"

After reviewing the tips offered by Nina's sister above, explain where you see both stage 5 and stage 6 moral reasoning occurring.

◆ An Alternative to Kohlberg

Gilligan's ethics of caring refers to part of Gilligan's stage theory describing female moral development

Recent research on the moral development of females has cast doubt on the generalizability of Kohlberg's data, which were collected on male subjects. Whereas Kohlberg found that his subjects' moral decisions were based upon a morality of justice, Gilligan has found that the moral decisions of females are based on an **ethics of caring** (Gilligan, 1977, 1982). While Gilligan and Kohlberg agree that the initial stage of moral reasoning is based on self-interests, Gilligan contends that females move from self-interests to a focus on specific individuals and relationships. Gilligan found that the highest level of morality is based on the principles of responsibility and care for all people. Clearly, Gilligan's version contrasts with Kohlberg's emphasis on universal principles that involve justice. She contends that females define morality more in terms of the quality of relationships, whereas males tend to define morality in terms of maintaining justice. For example, let's return to the situation in which two students are study buddies, each responsible to catch the other one up in the event of an absence. According to Gilligan's theory, male students would justify their decision as to whether or not to help their partner very differently from female students. That is, a male student might reason, "I shouldn't interfere with someone else's right to learn." A female student may decide, "I really should be concerned about the needs of my partner." Gilligan's three levels of moral reasoning are summarized in Table 3.2.

◆ From Moral Reasoning to Moral Behavior: The Lickona Model

Understanding our students' moral reasoning will certainly assist us in both understanding their decisions and perhaps in preparing them to make decisions. For example, in Chapter 10 we will discuss the issue of classroom management. Clearly, the setting and enforcement of classroom rules will be different depending on whether your students are in the preconventional, conventional, or postconventional levels of moral reasoning. However, beyond understanding our students' level of moral reasoning and attempting to set up our curriculum and rules accordingly, is there more a teacher can do to link moral reasoning to moral behavior? One recently developed model provides direction for teachers

Table 3.2 Gilligan's Theory of Moral Development for Women

Levels and Descriptions

Level I: Orientation to Individual Survival
Here, decisions center on the self, and concerns are pragmatic.

First Transition: From Selfishness to Responsibility
As attachment to others appears; self-interest is redefined in light of "what one should do."

Level II: Goodness as Self-Sacrifice
A sense of responsibility for others appears (the traditional view of women as care-takers). Goodness is equated with self-sacrifice and concern for others.

Second Transition: From Goodness to Truth
Women begin to include concern for self with their concern for others. Is it possible to be responsible to one's self as well as to others? The answer requires knowl-edge, hence the shift from goodness to truth. Recognizing one's needs is not being selfish but rather being honest and fair.

Level III: The Morality of Nonviolence
Resolution of the conflict between concern for self and concern for others results in a guiding principle of nonviolence. Harmony and compassion govern all moral action involving self and others. Level III defines both femininity and adulthood.

Source: From J. F. Travers, S. N. Elliott, and T. R. Kratochwill in *Educational Psychology: Effective Teaching, Effective Learning.* Copyright © 1993 by The McGraw-Hill Companies. Reprinted by permission.

seeking recommendations as to how to promote moral behavior among their students (Lickona, 1983).

The **Lickona model** proposes a four-component program designed to facilitate moral behavior. The four components include self-esteem, cooperative learning, moral reflection, and participatory decision mak-ing. Lickona has collected data that demonstrate that the systematic use of this model produces an increase in moral behavior among students. Let's consider the implementation of this model in the classroom.

Lickona (1983) defines **self-esteem** as a student's sense of mastery or competence. He contends that showing students that you respect their uniqueness as individuals is a powerful way to raise self-esteem. Higher self-esteem, writes Lickona, leads to the greater liklihood of moral behaviors. Two suggestions follow for how to promote self-esteem in your students. First, it may be of value to learn at least one unique thing about each one of your students early in the school year. Many teachers do this by having students complete an interest inventory or a hobby list during the first few weeks of school. Imagine how impressed you would be if your college professor demonstrated that she knew some-thing unique about you! Lickona recommends that throughout the school year teachers refer to student interests and hobbies, making an effort to connect these to academic content as much as possible. Second, Lickona suggests that teachers consistently find a way to recog-nize the selected moral behaviors that students already engage in. For

Lickona model model of character education encompassing self-esteem cooperative learning, moral reflecting, and participatory decision making

self-esteem the value each of us places on our own characteristics, abilities, and behaviors

instance, if a student has helped another student find a misplaced belonging, Lickona says that the teacher should take the time to write a brief note of encouragement for engaging in that moral behavior. Lickona has collected research data that indicate that such practices actually yield an increase in the frequency of the targeted behavior.

YOU MAKE THE CALL

Think about your own K through 12 teachers. What efforts did they make to learn something unique and personal about you? Did they perhaps give you a survey or interest inventory to ascertain how you preferred to spend your leisure time or learn what your favorite hobbies were? Did they use show and tell activities as a way of learning something special about you? Did they inquire about the movies and literature you liked, either in a survey or via informal conversation? Did your teachers ask you what job you thought you might like to do later in life?

How did your teachers use information about you to help you to learn? Did they utilize such knowledge to motivate you to do well in a subject you were struggling with? Did they use such information as a conversation starter to get to know you better? Did they make attempts to integrate such information into their teaching? Using this information, how could teachers encourage moral behavior on the part of their students?

cooperative learning arrangement in which students work in mixed-ability groups and are rewarded on the basis of the success of the group

Likewise, Lickona contends that **cooperative learning** (see Chapter 8) is also linked with promoting moral behavior, especially helping or prosocial behavior. He defines cooperative learning as students learning from and with each other. Lickona recommends that in classes unfamiliar with cooperative learning approaches teachers should start out by having students work in diads or teams. For instance, third graders studying units of measurement may break into diads to record observations about each other such as how high they are able to jump next to the school building or how far they are able to jump on a sidewalk. After working together, these dyads of students would then return to the classroom where they would share their observations. In this way, they have begun to learn how to work together as a team. Another strategy that Lickona suggests is helpful in promoting prosocial behavior is to use an affirmation exercise in which students publicly affirm how someone else in the class helped them that day or week. He cautions that such a practice may involve several weeks to model and teach to students, since many students are not in the habit of saying something positive about their peers. A modification of this practice involves the use of "proud whips" in which students briefly share with the rest of the class something they are proud of doing. These exercises afford students the opportunity of learning how to give and receive compliments, an important social skill.

moral reflection a process in Lickona's model that focuses on consideration of the cognitive aspects of moral development

Providing opportunities for **moral reflection,** the third component of the Lickona model, is also a critical part of promoting moral reflection. Lickona defines moral reflection as the chance to read, write, think, and debate about moral issues. These issues may involve such things as whether cheating or stealing are ever justified and may spring up naturally in the course of classroom life such as when a class has been incubating chicken eggs. Moral reflection might involve having students consider the implications of one of these eggs not hatching. Students could also engage in moral reflection centered around any number of content issues. For example, a fifth grade teacher whose district curriculum guide required her to cover the Middle Ages turned her entire classroom into a scriptorium in which her students had the opportunity to mimic the work of the monks. In this setting, she also provided her students with the chance to read, write, and reflect upon some of the moral issues considered by the monks.

Two caveats, however, are in order when implementing the moral reflection component of the Lickona model. First, individual teachers need to know their school district guidelines very well. Some districts, for instance, prohibit teachers from discussing issues such as abortion due to the wishes of the constituency of that district. Second, moral reflection may often lead students into discussions that involve religion. You should be aware of the recent guidelines issued by the U.S. Department of Education regarding religious expression in public schools (see Table 3.3).

The final component of the Lickona model is **participatory decision making**, which means allowing students to participate in making decisions which affect the quality of classroom life. He contends that the more students are able to help make these decisions, the more students will exhibit moral behaviors as they begin to feel a sense of ownership in the rules that govern how the classroom works. These decisions may pertain to what to do about cases of stolen lunch money or the fact that too little help is being offered during cleanup time. Or they may involve the regulation of classroom noise levels or the fact that a student is being bullied by her peers. Lickona suggests that holding class meetings in which students brainstorm a number of solutions related to these issues may be a useful first step in instilling a sense of ownership in the decision-making process. Lickona tells the story of a substitute teacher who was given a six-week long-term substitute position with a group of seventh graders renowned for their bad behavior. Soon after meeting these students, she held a class meeting in which class members generated a list of rules they believed were needed to help the classroom run smoothly. Although there was disagreement about which rules were the most important, the class finally agreed upon one primary rule as follows: "We all need to care about each other." From then on, whenever there was a classroom management problem the teacher cleverly referred students to this rule. Although some management problems persisted, this substitute began to notice a dramatic difference

Teacher Tool Box
Setting Up Classroom Rules with Moral Development Stages in Mind

◆ For students at the preconventional level, you may find it helpful to explain what they "get back" or "what's in it for them" when explaining why they need to abide by classroom rules.

◆ For students at the conventional level, role playing that involves peers may be a helpful way to convey the importance of adhering to classroom rules. You may also want to appeal to what the popular role models in the school or community think about certain rules as a way of convincing students of their importance.

◆ With postconventional students, try asking them to generate their own classroom rules based upon the "Golden Rule" principle.

participatory decision making a process in Lickona's model that holds students accountable for decisions that influence the quality of classroom life

Table 3.3 Guidelines Regarding Religion in the Public Schools

Students Can Express Views; Schools Can't

Religious expression in public schools? A new directive from the U.S. Department of Education advises what's allowed, and what's not.

Student prayer, religious discussion
Students may read their Bibles or other scriptures, say grace before meals, and pray before tests to the same extent they may engage in comparable nondisruptive activities. In informal settings, such as cafeterias and hallways, students may pray and discuss their religious views with each other; students may also speak to, and attempt to persuade, their peers about religious topics. And students may participate in before- or after-school events with religious content.

Graduation prayer and baccalaureates
School officials may not mandate or organize prayer at graduation, nor organize religious baccalaureate ceremonies.

Equal Access Act
Religious and secular student activities have the same access to public school facilities.

Official neutrality on religious activity
Teachers and administrators are prohibited from participating in religious activities with students and discouraging activity because of its religious content.

Teaching about religion and values
Public schools may teach about religion, including the Bible or other scripture, Comparative religion, the Bible as literature and the role of religion in U.S. history and in other countries. Schools may not observe holidays as religious events but may play an active role in teaching civic values.

Assignments
Students may express their religious beliefs in homework, artwork, and other written and oral assignments free of discrimination based on the religious content of their submissions.

Religious literature
Students may distribute religious literature to their schoolmates.

Religious excuses
Schools enjoy substantial discretion to excuse individual students from lessons that are objectionable to the student or parents. Outsiders cannot teach religion on school premises during the school day.

Student garb
Students may wear yarmulkes and head scarves and display religious messages on clothes to the same extent that they are permitted to display other messages.

Source: From the U.S. Department of Education.

---

constructivist classroom
view that emphasizes the active role of the learner in building understanding and making sense of information

in terms of how often behavioral problems arose. This concept of participatory decision making involves the creation of a **constructivist classroom** in which students actively participate in the construction of classroom rules (Castle & Rogers, 1993/1994). While this process is critical to undertake at the start of the school year, it is useful to repeat before embarking on new classroom formats such as cooperative learning. This process involves students' formulating as many rules as they possibly can to govern classroom life or a particular activity. Students then review the rules in small groups and decide which of these rules could be combined to create a shorter list. The class then meets to brainstorm a short list of working rules. This short list is then used to guide classroom activities. We will return to this idea in Chapter 10, on classroom management.

◆ Cheating Behavior

Recent surveys based on self-report data indicate that 75 percent of the brightest high school students have cheated in school (*Philadelphia Inquirer*, 1997). In a recent survey conducted by *Who's Who Among American High School Students,* 80 percent of high-achieving high school students admitted having cheated at least once. Half of these same students did not believe cheating was necessarily wrong, and 95 percent of the cheaters said they had never been caught. Research on cheating suggests that cheating depends more on the situation students find themselves in than on the general honesty of that individual (Burton, 1963). In fact, other studies which have surveyed students to uncover the causes of cheating behavior indicate that the pressure to succeed (see Chapter 8, regarding Failure Avoidance) and students' estimates of the likelihood of getting caught are two of the most significant factors related to cheating behavior (Schab, 1980). Therefore, there are several measures that classroom teachers can undertake to minimize cheating.

Research on cheating suggests that cheating depends more on the situation students find themselves in than on the general honesty of the individual. ◆

One caution pertaining to the issue of cheating is illustrated in the film *Stand and Deliver*. Each of the eighteen students in the advanced placement class successfully passed the advanced placement test in calculus. However, because these students came from a poor, inner city school, where such success is not typically found, and because they made similar types of errors, the Educational Testing Service assumed that the only explanation for their passing scores must have been cheating, when in fact, no cheating occurred. The impact on these students could have been devastating if it had not been for their teacher, who continued to believe in them and helped them to continue to believe in themselves. When you teach, be careful not to assume a student has cheated because of your own preconceived notions.

◆ Violence and Aggression

Even suburban and rural schools are seeing an increase in violence and aggressive behavior among

Teacher Tool Box
How to Minimize Cheating

◆ While it is important to keep work interesting and challenging, do not assign work that is beyond the capacity of your students.

◆ Address the issue directly with your class, and explain to them the measures that you use to monitor cheating in the classroom. These may include careful monitoring during test time, alternate forms of tests, and the moving of desks. It will also be critical to clearly spell out the consequences of cheating and to consistently follow through with these when cheating does occur.

◆ If a student does cheat, try to find out the reasons for it and, if possible, help the student overcome the need to do it. Interventions that may be helpful include providing the student with extra help, de-emphasizing competition, and reducing student anxiety (which is discussed in detail in Chapter 10).

If students do become entangled in a physical struggle, your response should be in accordance with the policies and procedures of your district and should maximize the saftey of all involved. ◆

their students (Begley, 1999). While there are many factors related to this development, two of the most important are (1) the increasing amount of aggression viewed on television, and (2) the violence experienced and observed in the home or community in which the student lives, including the widespread availability of guns. In addition, research also indicates that aggressive children who are rejected by peers often persist in their aggressive tendencies (Kupersmidt, Coie, & Dodge, 1990). Teachers need to be aware of steps they can take to prevent the demonstration of aggression within their classroom (see Teacher Tool Box) as well as their duties and responsibilities when aggression occurs.

While preventative measures are clearly more desirable than intervention strategies, the reality is that aggression will most likely not be completely prevented, and as a teacher you will be exposed to student aggression. For example, students may engage in fighting in the play yard or even within the classroom. Many physical altercations among students occur when teachers are absent from the classroom. Teachers are legally responsible for the welfare of students within their class, therefore, it is important not to leave a class unsupervised.

If students do become entangled in a physical struggle, your response should be in accordance with the policies and procedures of your district and should maximize the safety of all involved. For a teacher to become physically involved in wrestling with students, for example, is not only unwise for someone untrained in the use of restraint techniques, but it is most likely inap-

Teacher Tool Box
Steps for Preventing Aggression

◆ Make the consequences of aggressive and violent behaviors clear to your students and be sure to follow up on these immediately and consistently.

◆ Try to model nonviolent ways of resolving conflict such as discussing problems vis-à-vis peer mediation. This is further discussed in the classroom management chapter of this textbook (Chapter 10) in the section about Gordon's no-lose method of conflict resolution. Many schools already have included conflict negotiation skills as part of their curriculum (Lantieri, 1995).

◆ Stress with children that the violence and aggression observed on television is not real and does not reflect the way that most members of our society resolve conflict.

◆ Provide ample opportunities for students to work together on classroom projects. These provide an excellent opportunity to teach communication skills, prosocial or helping behaviors, and conflict negotiation skills.

propriate given school districts' concerns over abuse and litigation. When confronted with student violence, it is important to call for help and not insert yourself in the middle of the fray.

PSYCHOSOCIAL DEVELOPMENT

In addition to understanding students' value structure and the moral bases upon which they make decisions, the effective teacher will begin to understand how a child sees him or herself and how this sense of self develops. Erik Erikson is one theorist who provides insight into the important role one's social environment plays on the formation of a self-concept and one's psychological development.

◆ Erikson's Work

Erikson, in his theory of **psychosocial development**, highlighted the importance of relationships with others in the formation of one's own identity. Erikson investigated the manner in which an individual's personality evolved in the context of changing interactions and relationships with others through the process of psychosocial development. Table 3.4 illustrates how the stages of Erik Erikson's theory of psychosocial development fit together with the stage theories of Piaget and Kohlberg. You will notice this table also incorporates Freud's psychosexual stages as a reference point, although we will not consider them in this text.

Erikson believed that personality develops through eight stages or critical periods of life. Further, he suggested that at each stage of life an individual is confronted by a crisis (Erikson, 1950). Erikson assumed

psychosocial development describing the relation of the individual's emotional needs to the social environment

Table 3.4   Summary of Four Stage Theories of Development

Kohlberg	Piaget	Erikson	Freud	Age
Self-accepted morality	Formal operations	Integrity vs. despair		60
		Generativity vs. stagnation	Genital	40
				20
		Intimacy vs. isolation		18
		Identity		16
		vs.		14
		role confusion		12
Conventional morality	Concrete operations	Industry vs. inferiority	Latency	10 / 8 / 6
	Preoperational	Initiative vs. guilt	Phallic	4
Premoral		Autonomy vs. shame	Anal	2
	Sensorimotor	Trust vs. mistrust	Oral	Birth

Source: J. Santrock, *Lifespan Development, Third Edition.* © 1989 by The McGraw-Hill Companies. Reproduced with the permission of the publisher.

Teacher Tool Box
Addressing Trust Issues in the Classroom

♦ When working with students who have profound mistrust issues, it will be especially important to set and consistently enforce safety rules in the classroom. These may pertain to stealing as well as emotional insults and physical threats.
♦ Have a routine for starting the beginning of the day and the end of the day. These routines represent something predictable the student can trust to occur.
♦ With new students, especially, institute a buddy system in which students are paired with at least one other partner or several other partners in a base group with whom they can develop a trusting relationship.

trust versus mistrust stage of Erikson's psychosocial theory pertaining to the first year of life

autonomy versus shame and doubt independence autonomy versus shame and doubt marks stage 2 of Erikson's theory of psychosocial development

In the autonomy vs. shame and doubt stage, the push toward independence and self-governance can clearly be seen in one of the primary tasks of this period—toilet training. ♦

that personality develops in accordance to one's ability to interact with the environment and to resolve the conflicts/crises experienced. The manner in which the crises are resolved will have a lasting effect on the person's view of him- or herself and the surrounding world. Below is a brief description of each of these stages.

Stage 1: Trust versus Mistrust (Birth to One Year)

The first psychological challenge faced involves developing a sense of trust in others. For the infant, this sense of trust develops if she is predictably cared for when she cries and is warmly treated by her primary caregivers. If an infant, instead, is cared for in unpredictable ways such as not being fed, diapered, or comforted when necessary, Erikson believed this infant would develop basic mistrust of others, which would lead to fear and suspicion. Sometimes a child's mistrust of teachers and school can be traced back to a general mistrust developed during infancy. One implication for practice is for teachers to develop predictable, consistent routines. Further, for students experiencing a general mistrust, it may be necessary to treat them especially with warmth and caring concern. Although a lifetime of mistrust is difficult to overturn, students must believe that teachers are genuinely concerned with their best interests and that classrooms are safe and loving places.

Stage 2: Autonomy versus Shame and Doubt (Ages One to Three)

In the second psychosocial stage, children want to do things on their own or act autonomously. Yet this need to become autonomous must be balanced by the reality of safety issues. For instance, while Erikson thought it was healthy to allow two-year-olds to explore their world about them, this exploration must be done in a constrained way such that the child does not enter the street and is hit by a car. Therefore, Erikson called for a delicate interplay between freedom and restraint. Interestingly, the child also has a conflicting need to let go of the parent but still hold on. This conflict emerges again in adolescence.

This push toward independence and self-governance can be clearly seen in one of the primary tasks in this period, toilet training. Because the goal of this stage is to instill a sense of self-control without a loss of self-esteem, Erikson believed that parental reactions were critical. For instance, he cautioned against using toilet training measures that were too harsh. He believed that the child's personality would become overly rigid as a result. However, the use of too lackadaisical toilet training may result in an overly self-indulgent personality. A parent who supports a child's effort to care for his or her own needs by assisting with easily removable clothing and perhaps providing the child's own smaller potty would assist the child in being an autonomous person.

Several educational implications follow. First, when you must impose restrictions, never humiliate a child either physically or verbally. Second, provide young children with adequate opportunities to do things for themselves, even if it means the task may be messier or take more time than when an adult does it. Third, set up discipline in which the same consequence is administered consistently each time a rule is broken. This gives a sense of a secure and ordered world. Children need clearly stated boundaries to protect them from physical harm and to help them develop a sense of self-control.

Stage 3: Initiative versus Guilt (Ages Four to Five)

As an outgrowth of the autonomy stage, Erikson wrote that children will want to explore and investigate when faced with new challenges. He termed this the development of a sense of initiative. In this period, children begin to ask many questions about their world. The ever-present questions of "why" and "what" seem to engulf a child at this stage as do the inquisitive behaviors that often accompany taking initiative. For example, many of your parents may have a number of quite insightful and perhaps amusing stories about your own efforts to take the initiative, be it in regards to selecting your own clothes, cutting your (or your little brother's or sister's) hair, or even making your own breakfast. While such questioning and experimenting can be quite tiring for the adults in a child's life, they should be welcomed and encouraged as steps of essential growth. For instance, children may ask questions about and want to help with work underway in the kitchen. In situations in which a child is discouraged from taking the initiative, Erikson believed that the child would develop a sense of guilt regarding her natural tendency to explore and investigate, which would carry over into later years. Because preschool children are faced with so many new challenges such as learning to read, dressing themselves, and adjusting to school, learning that it is acceptable to take the initiative is critical to a child's development.

A number of implications follow for teachers. First, praise children you work with for taking the initiative, and use peers who do so as a model for other children who seem to be hesitant. A second implication involves the use of a developmentally appropriate curriculum in which students have the chance to develop the necessary muscular coordination needed to manipulate the toys and objects they are using (Calvert, 1986). A third implication is to provide this age group with plenty of opportunities to play. Recent research shows that play aids in cognitive development because through play a child learns how objects work (such as the fact that toy cars have wheels). Play also facilitates social skills by lessening egocentrism and instilling a will-

initiative versus guilt the quality of undertaking, planning, and attacking a new task; characterizes stage 3 of Erikson's theory of psychosocial development

Teacher Tool Box
Addressing Autonomy Issues in the Classroom

- For students in this stage, provide safe areas for physical as well as social exploration so that children can practice being autonomous. You will want to make sure that children cannot hurt themselves in these areas.
- Be careful not to punish children in this stage in situations where they could not have possibly foreseen the consequences. For instance, often children who act autonomously may, in fact, end up falling and ripping their clothes or knocking something over through no fault of their own. Punishing them in these cases would discourage autonomous behavior in the future.

ingness to share. In addition, play serves as a source of emotional release, providing an imaginary escape world for the child.

Stage 4: Industry versus Inferiority (Ages Six to Eleven)

industry versus inferiority an eagerness to produce; typifies stage 4 of Erikson's theory of psychosocial development

The major psychological task in Erikson's fourth psychosocial stage is the development of a sense of competence or industry. While previously children were primarily interested in trying new things, as they grow and move into this stage of development, which lasts throughout the elementary school years, they will want to not only try but succeed and gain recognition for producing things, hence the term *industry*. In the Western world, children are faced with the challenges of producing academic work related to reading, writing, and mathematical skills. During this same period, in preliterate societies, children had to master hunting and fishing. However, the basic principle is the same. While "trying" was important during the initiative stage, now the focus is on "doing it correctly."

Erikson worried that some children may leave the elementary years without this sense of industry, feeling that they are a failure at everything. The "everything" is not limited to academic achievement but includes such things as competence in a hobby, playing sports, maintaining a positive relationship with teachers, and developing friendships. In fact, recent research has documented the importance of developing positive peer relationships. That is, peer rejection tends to carry over from elementary to high school and may contribute to later academic difficulties as well as to adjustment problems later in life (Kupersmidt, Coie, & Dodge, 1990). Research has shown that social skills training as well as attention to social problem solving can be helpful in terms of developing student competence in forming friendships and developing social skills (Compas, 1987). A myriad of additional implications for classroom practice follow.

Teacher Tool Box
Addressing Initiative Issues in the Classroom

- For children in the initiative stage, provide plenty of opportunities for dramatic play. Some favorite dramatic play situations among children include domestic scenes between spouses or parents and children, trauma situations such as injuries to a pet, or "sudden threat" scenes in which two children pair up as the "defenders."
- Provide the opportunity for students to simply "try" new things, be they new ethnic foods or ways to approach a problem. Place emphasis on trying more than on succeeding or failing.
- Have your students make up questions to ask you or a guest speaker about topics you discuss. This will encourage them to take the initiative to find out why in the future.

Stage 5: Identity versus Role Confusion (Ages Twelve to Eighteen)

identity versus confusion a sense of well being, a feeling of knowing where one is going, and an inner assuredness of anticipated recognition from those who count

For middle school and high school teachers, in particular, Erikson's fifth stage of psychosocial development, is at times painfully obvious. While each stage and the particular way a person resolves the crises at hand have implications for psychological development and sense of self, it is in this stage that the questions of identity truly emerge. In this stage, adolescents struggle to resolve the question of "Who am I?" That is, as they move increasingly from their parents to peers as a point of reference, they need to understand how they are both alike and at the same time uniquely different from everyone else. Consider the scene we described at the beginning of this chapter.

CLASS ILLUSTRATION

As we observe Mrs. Fry's class struggle with a difficult physics problem, our attention is drawn to one female student, gazing out the window, apparently longing to be somewhere else. After a few more moments of unsuccessful attempts at resolving the problem, Mrs. Fry announces: "Okay, we'll have to stay late again."

At this, the student who was staring out the window gets up to leave class. Mrs. Fry asks, "Where are you going?"

Many issues related to the development of this student's identity are unfolding in this scene, including how to balance what she wants out of life with demands apparently made by others, including her boyfriend and boss at her job. Beginning to identify and integrate the many unique aspects of her personality including the "her" that is a student, the "her" that has needs to develop special loving relationships, and the " her" that needs to earn spending money, etc., is certainly a challenging task for this student. What advice would you give her?

A significant part of this search for personal identity concerns physical appearance including clothing, make-up, ways of walking, and ways of dressing (e.g., shirts buttoned at top only). By the way, along with this search for ideal physical appearance is the advent of the personal fable and imaginary audience which we discussed in Chapter 2. Another piece of this identity crisis concerns sexual identity. That is, the adolescent searches for comfortable expressions of sexuality through friendships and dating. Adolescents often say that the main reason they continue coming to school is to be with their friends or close to someone they have a crush on. Erikson would say that giving such reasons for coming to school is healthy, in that it represents a comfortable expression of sexuality and need for establishing identity via friendship.

In addition, adolescents strive to find or clarify their own personalities. That's why they are often observed to imitate the attitudes and actions of others they admire. Throughout adolescence, students tend to emulate the appearance and behavior of media figures they admire as well as those in their immediate clique. Still another aspect of the identity

Teacher Tool Box
Addressing Industry Issues in the Classroom

- Be sure to direct children to academic tasks that are challenging yet within their range of ability, so that children are not "set up" for failure.
- Congratulate children for their successes, even if they are small ones. This can be accomplished by teachers providing both verbal and written feedback as well as having peers write compliments to each other for work well done.
- Take photographs of your students and post them on a "brag board." Periodically, add special pieces of information next to the photos, such as the child's favorite hobby or what she is most proud of about herself.
- Have students share their expertise by having them do presentations on a hobby or particular skill they may have developed. This activity could also incorporate bringing something unique from home into class and explaining it.
- Have students from diverse cultural backgrounds bring something from their home into the classroom to enhance their sense of self-esteem.
- Have students write journal entries in which they share something they have accomplished.
- Encourage students to engage in self-competition whereby they get in the habit of setting reasonable goals for themselves instead of being focused on "How can I beat everyone else?"
- Recognize a wide variety of talents and gifts in your students. As Gardner notes, these gifts may not only be represented in reading, writing, and math achievements, but could include musical, bodily-kinesthetic, spatial, interpersonal, and intrapersonal talents.

An important aspect of identity pertains to one's cultural and ethnic identity. Teachers need to be particularly sensitive to this as they work with diverse student populations. ◆

issue pertains to one's cultural and ethnic identity (see the discussion in Chapter 5). Be particularly sensitive to this as you work with diverse student populations.

Resolving this question of "who am I" can be overwhelming, especially when we include the additional task of attempting to wrestle with not only "Who am I?" but "Who will I become?" Consider the following classroom scene:

CLASS ILLUSTRATION

After class, one of Mr. Wise's students approaches him and explains why he will not be able to continue to participate in the after-school preparation for the AP calculus exam. The student explains: "My step dad offered me a job working on a construction crew on the weekends. I'll be making time and a half. In two years, I'll be making more money than most teachers." When Mr. Wise reminds the student that he will have lots of options in the future if he attends college, the student says, "I'll be able to buy nice things for myself and my girlfriend." Mr. Wise responds, "But eventually college grads make much more money than those who only graduate from high school."

In this scene, we see that often, as adolescents begin to struggle with identity issues involving choice of occupation, they approach these issues from a short-term perspective. This is in part reflective of the fact that so many teens, even in the high school years, are moving from concrete to formal operational thinking. As such, they will need your guidance to ensure that they explore a wide range of options. Think about the difference that teachers make in the life of students by steering them to go to college, despite the short-term sacrifices. Has one of your teachers similarly affected your life? Your life choices? The way you were or are seeing yourself?

The pressure of making life choices can be quite disruptive at a time when individuals are not completely clear about who they are or what they may become. While it certainly can be argued that this challenge is forced upon the adolescent by the practice of tracking students according to achievement and intelligence test scores as well as intense societal pressure to "line up one's ducks" as early as possible, as recent as several decades ago adolescents did not have the flexibility to make occupational decisions as they do today. Often, youngsters were ex-pected just to work in the family business or go to work early to support the family. Yet the very blessing of flexibility is seen by some as a curse because there exists a mind-boggling array of options from which adolescents can choose. Do you remember how you felt as you wrestled with the issue of what to do with your life? What college to attend? What to major in? Maybe you are still trying to decide.

Erikson said that those who leave adolescence with these issues resolved have achieved a sense of identity. Those who remain locked in doubt and insecurity, however, experience identity confusion. While we could argue that in today's society adolescence is really extended into the early if not mid-twenties, the issues related to the development of one's identity are nonetheless important to recognize in the students you teach, for they may very significantly affect their motivation to attend to academic tasks.

◆ Marcia's Identity Status Theory

As you might expect, the way in which adolescents go about resolving this crisis of identity varies. James Marcia (1966, 1980), in fact, found that there are four primary ways or statuses that describe how adolescents do this. These styles or statuses are listed below.

Identity diffusion is the failure to commit oneself to choices that must be made as part of the development of identity, such as a decision about what work one will do. Marcia thought that adolescents in this status repressed the issue of resolving their identity in an effort to deny that they had such overwhelming decisions to make. Some adolescents in this category are thought to develop a negative identity in whch they adopt values completely opposite of those they were raised with. For instance, consider the teen who comes from a very religious family and goes off to join a Satanic cult. Other teens with a negative identity may become antisocial and engage in criminal activities.

Identity foreclosure is resolving the identity crisis too quickly by adopting the identity of an authority figure known to the teen without engaging in adequate deliberation as to whether the decisions made are appropriate. Consider the case of the adolescent who decides in her early teen years to become a teacher because her mother and several

Marcia's identity statuses theory descriptive of four ways in which adolescents resolve the issue of identity

identity diffusion when the adolescent has not made any firm commitments to any ideology, occupation, or interpersonal relationship and is not currently thinking about such commitments

identity foreclosure when the adolescent selects a convenient set of beliefs and goals without carefully considering the alternatives an example would be accepting one's parents' choice of life-style and career without considering other options

identity moratorium when the adolescent considers alternative choices, experiences different roles, but has made no final decision regarding his or her identity

identity achievement when the adolescent has a strong sense of commitment to life choices after careful consideration of options

intimacy versus isolation the state of having a close psychological relationship with another person; stage 6 of Erikson's theory of psychosocial development

generativity versus stagnation characterized by either a sense of productivity or self-absorption; stage 7 of Erikson's psychosocial theory

integrity versus despair a sense of understanding how one fits into one's culture and the acceptance that one's place is unique and unalterable; stage 8 in Erikson's theory of psychosocial development

aunts and uncles are teachers, without giving careful thought as to whether this career path fits her and without exploring other options.

Identity moratorium is delay in making critical decisions related to the development of one's identity. While moratorium is sometimes used as an excuse to avoid the hard work involved in resolving one's identity issues, it is often thought to be psychologically healthy as the adolescent goes through a period of exploration of several possible options before coming to a decision. How many of you have considered several different majors or still may be keeping your options open?

Identity achievement is success in committing oneself to choices about one's identity and following through on that commitment. Students in this category still struggle with decisions related to identity, but they do so in a timely, well-focused fashion. They are thought to have the highest levels of self-esteem of the four statuses.

Consider the case of Mr. Wise's student whose stepfather has offered him a job in construction. Marcia would have us ponder to what extent his decision to become part of a construction crew is one that he made after considering many options. From what we are told above, it would appear that such a decision would best be described as identity foreclosure or taking on a career role by adapting the identity of an authority figure close to the adolescent, in this case, his step dad.

CLASS ILLUSTRATION

Mrs. Granberg, a social studies teacher, and her husband stop at a local produce stand. The owner approaches them, asking, "Did you find everything you needed?" Mrs. Granberg replies, "Yes." However, looking at her sales receipt, she exclaims "Except for one thing." At this remark, the cashier takes a break and walks over to Mrs. Granberg. The cashier turns out to be one of Mrs. Granberg's star students, Domenica. All three exchange a hearty laugh. Then, in a very serious tone Mrs. Granberg remarks, "You should get another cashier. She could be the first one in your family to graduate and go on to college." (Earlier in the week Domenica had told Mrs. Granberg she would not be returning to school because she had to work at her father's produce stand.) Her father replies, "We are not well off. She's needed here. This is a family business. She'd probably not finish college anyway." Mrs. Granberg interjects: "She wants to go to law school. You should let her make her own choices." Domenica's father angrily retorts, "School is a waste of time" and then laments that Mrs. Granberg has some nerve to come into his place of business and tell him how to raise his own daughter.

In the above scene, we observe how identity foreclosure may often occur, especially among females. That is, some parents put so much pressure on their children to adopt the family's professional identity that the child does the easiest thing and accepts this identity. However, recall from Marcia's theory that this is indeed not a healthy way to go about establishing one's identity. As in the scene above, there is no room for the individual to explore a variety of options. Notice through Mrs. Granberg's example just how influential a teacher can be. Numerous implications follow for the educator as described in the Teacher Tool Box.

Stage 6: Intimacy versus Isolation (Ages Eighteen to Thirty-five)

Although learning should be a lifelong process, typically the students you will teach are not old enough to grapple with the crises presented in Erikson's last three psychosocial stages. However, recent qualitative studies describing the nature of both novice and second-career teachers' planning (Sardo-Brown, 1996) indicate that it may be useful for classroom teachers to identify which psychosocial stage they are in, as it may be related to the way in which they perceive their role as teacher and subsequently interact with students. The major crisis in Erikson's sixth stage is the development of a true and intimate relationship. Erikson cited that individuals in this stage should be able to care for others without losing their self-identity. He feared that those who never know this intimacy will develop a sense of isolation and tend to avoid relationships with others and make commitments.

Stage 7: Generativity versus Stagnation (Thirty-five to Sixty-five)

Erikson conceived individuals in middle age who were psychologically healthy as focused on the care and well-being of the next generation, without being overly self-concerned. He argued that if a sense of generativity, which he defined as creativity or productivity, was not present, the individual would experience stagnation and become overly self-preoccupied.

Stage 8: Integrity versus Despair (Over Sixty-five)

In the last stage of life, Erikson observed that individuals who have managed to adapt to the triumphs and tragedies of life are able to review their lives with a sense of satisfaction and acceptance. Others will be absorbed with despairing over missed

Teacher Tool Box
Addressing Identity Issues in the Classroom

- Provide plenty of opportunities for adolescents to explore identity issues as they relate to understanding who they are as individuals. Activities that involve making a collage about themselves or writing their autobiography would fit this bill.
- Allow chances for students to discuss their ethnic backgrounds, as this is an important component of understanding one's identity. Try to tie such information into academic topics such as the ethnic backgound of a mathematician or scientist or ethnicities written about in great pieces of literature or studied in history.
- Coordinate activities designed to promote awareness of a variety of career opportunities with your school's guidance counselor. This may involve asking parents of your students to come in and speak about their careers or inviting resource persons from the local community to speak. Try to choose speakers who represent a diversity of gender and ethnic backgrounds, so that your students, regardless of their gender or ethnicity, will be open to many career options.
- Try to enhance your students' self-esteem by encouraging your students to substitute self-statements that are positive in place of negative self-statements.
- In an effort to facilitate the development of identity, provide ample opportunity for students to work together on academic projects. This may at first involve students working in dyads and later in three-member cooperative learning groups. More will be said in the motivation chapter about how to set up such instructional formats.
- Have students research how what they are currently learning will prepare them for a variety of careers.
- To promote more awareness as to who students are as unique individuals, have them become adept at evaluating their own strengths and weaknesses. One way to develop this skill is to teach students how to complete self-assessments of their own work, a method that is often employed in portfolio assessment.
- Stress the skill of communication. This serves several purposes related to the development of identity. First, by learning how to listen to others effectively, students learn that their problems and concerns are not unique. Second, being able to effectively communicate with others increases social contact, which in turn is vital as adolescents "try on" many identities until they arrive at one that feels comfortable.
- Be sensitive to the unique identity issues faced by students who come from impoverished backgrounds as they may be the only individuals in their family who have striven to do well academically.

opportunities, age, and failure. The healthy resolution to the seven preceding crises was thought to be a prerequisite to achieving a sense of integrity at the end of one's life.

Recent research that has followed novice teachers longitudinally (Aitken, 1993; Sardo-Brown, 1994; Sorenson, 1991) demonstrates that a critical factor affecting how teachers plan for instruction and perceive their students is a new marriage. Clearly, this event is directly linked to the resolution of Erikson's intimacy versus isolation stage as one picks a mate for life. As one novice teacher observed, "I feel more comfortable as their teacher now; I'm a Mrs." Another newly married novice teacher commented that she tended not to become so obsessive about her teaching, since she had someone to distract her attention from it in the evenings. This is not to say that one needs to get married to become an effective teacher but simply to show how a teacher's psychosocial development may affect teaching. Or consider the case of second-career teachers who may be in the generativity stage. A longitudinal case study of one such teacher discovered that instead of being concerned about students liking him, as is typical during the student teaching experience, he was more concerned with planning opportunities that ensured the next generation would be well taken care of, such as visiting student homes to offer them extra encouragement and tutoring (Sardo-Brown, 1996). Does this ring a bell? Remember Mrs. Granberg's visit to the produce stand?

YOU MAKE THE CALL

Try to recall each of the following times in your own life: a time when you were afraid to make the first move or take the initiative; a time when you felt like a failure at everything; a time when you had no idea what decision to make about where to go to college or what to major in. How did each of these decision points get resolved? What advice could you offer your own students based on these experiences?

OTHER PSYCHOSOCIAL ISSUES

While understanding the major theoretical frameworks for psychosocial development is important for classroom teachers, it is also essential to have a sense of the contemporary issues related to psychosocial development that affect today's students. In this section we will first review current research on the development of self-concept. Next, we will consider problems such as teen pregnancy, eating disorders, AIDS, child abuse, divorce, and suicide.

◆ The Development of Self-Concept

self-concept the way in which an individual perceives or thinks about him- or herself

An issue closely related to the theoretical frameworks already described in this chapter is the development of a child's **self-concept.** Recent theorists have described self-concept as "the total of people's perceptions about their physical, social, and academic competence" (Pintrich & Schunk, 1996). Unfortunately, while children typically enter school with positive views about themselves as learners, these conceptions tend to become less positive with the passage of time (Frey & Ruble, 1987; Stipek, 1993). Research has indicated that after parents, teachers wield the greatest influence over a child's evaluations of self-concept (D. Phillips, 1990). While parents and teachers are especially important factors that influence self-concept in the early years, peers and friends also play a powerful role as the child progresses through upper elementary and secondary grades (Berk, 1994).

The relationship between general self-concept and academic achievement is weak (Walberg, 1984). The reason researchers believe this is the case is that self-concept comprises three parts: academic, social, and physical (Marsh, 1989). While social and physical self-concept are unrelated to academic achievement, academic self-concept is linked with school performance (Harter & Connell, 1984; House, 1997; Marsh & Yeung, 1997; McLean, 1997).

In fact, the strongest correlations exist between specific academic self-concepts and corresponding subject-area performance. For instance, researchers have found that over time students differentiate between and among their performances in different subject areas (Marsh, 1992; Marsh & Shavelson, 1985). Students may state, "I'm really good in English" or "I'm not so hot at math."

Such data has led to research designed to discover how to modify students' academic self-concept. Efforts have been most successful when self-concept intervention is implemented along with concerted attempts to improve student performance (Marsh, 1992). This is largely the case because students use both external information (e.g., how their performance compares with others in the same subject) and internal information (e.g., how their own performance varies across subject areas) in forming academic self-concept. The tool box provides some suggestions as to how teachers can positively influence academic self-concept.

◆ Teen Pregnancy

Recent estimates indicate that approximately 75 percent of American youth have sexual intercourse by the age of nineteen (Guttmacher Institute, 1994) and that upwards of 50 percent of females have intercourse before age fifteen (Sonenstein, Pleck, & Ku, 1991). One noteworthy result of such behavior is teen pregnancy; more than one million teens become pregnant each year. Of this number, 30,000 are younger than 15 years old (DeRidder, 1993).

The reasons for this phenomenon are quite complex. One important factor underlying such alarming rates of teen pregnancy is that adolescents have little

Teacher Tool Box
Ideas for Influencing Self-Concept

◆ Design learning activities that are perceived by students to be worthwhile.
◆ Help students to be successful at completing these worthwhile activities.
◆ Communicate positive teacher expectations that all students can do well.
◆ Offer students the opportunity to participate in making classroom decisions.
◆ In terms of assessment, stress that there are many ways to succeed.
◆ Put an emphasis on individual student effort, not ability.

information or incorrect information about birth control (Zabin & Clark, 1981). Another reason uncovered in research studies is the feeling that a contraceptive may spoil the spontaneity and pleasure of sex (Zelnik & Shah, 1983). Still another factor relates to Elkind's notion of personal fable or the cognition "It won't happen to me" (see Chapter 2 discussion). In addition, some adults fear that providing students with information about birth control will lead to promiscuity.

However, research does not confirm this; rather the major consequence of such education seems to be a decrease in unwanted pregnancies (Brooks-Gunn & Furstenberg, 1989; Wingert, 1998). It should be mentioned that abstinence education is receiving increased attention. The most effective of these programs provide basic information about the risks of unprotected intercourse and address the impact of social influences on teen sexual behavior (Natale, 1995).

anorexia nervosa an eating disorder in which individuals (primarily females) starve themselves to maintain a slim figure; the illness causes a distortion in one's perceptions of body image

bulimia eating disorder characterized by overeating, then getting rid of the food by self-inducing vomiting or laxatives

AIDS a fatal virus-caused illness resulting in a breakdown of the immune system; currently, no cure exists

◆ Eating Disorders

Students in early and middle adolescence tend to be very concerned about their bodies as they begin and progress through puberty. This concern is heightened by what Elkind called the belief in the imaginary audience (see discussion in Chapter 2). Recent research indicates that more than 40 percent of adolescents report feeling fat or wanting to lose weight (Childress et al., 1993). When these concerns become excessive, one result is the onset of eating disorders.

Anorexia is self-imposed starvation in which the individual refuses to eat or eats practically nothing. Anorexic students usually appear pale and have brittle fingernails. They develop dark hairs all over their body since they have little fat to insulate their bodies; consequently they are easily chilled. **Bulimia**, or binge eating, occurs when individuals binge on food and then purge themselves by vomiting or using laxatives in order not to gain weight. While bulimics tend to maintain average body weight, their digestive systems can become permanently damaged. The treatment of these eating disorders often requires the help of medical and psychiatric professionals (Harris, 1991). As such, the role of classroom teachers is that of referral agent when symptoms are evident.

Connections

Use the Internet to find helpful resources on some of the many contemporary psychosocial issues we have identified in this chapter. With regard to the topic of child abuse, consult the following Web site for information and resources for helping children understand what abuse is and what they can do if they are in an abusive situation: http://www.multnomah.lib.or.us/mccf/pre1.html. Consult the Web site http://www.divorcewizards.com/teachers.html for books and tapes which focus on how teachers can help children going through divorce.

◆ AIDS

As of 1995, about 14 percent of all **AIDS** cases occurred in the twenty- to twenty-four-year-old age group with only 2 percent occurring in those thirteen to nineteen years. However, it is very likely that most of the infections in the early twenties age group were contracted during adolescence (CDC, 1995). Research has found that most cases of adolescent HIV infection result from intimate sexual contact or intravenous drug usage. Many students believe that AIDS can be contracted via casual touching, sharing food, or by being spit upon, all of which are fallacies. For the virus to be transmitted, people must exchange bodily fluids without the fluids coming in contact with the air first (Seifert & Hoffnung, 1991). Thus, the Task Force on Pediatric AIDS of the American Psychological Association (1989) recommends that education about AIDS commence in the early grades. Recent research indicates that such educational efforts should be designed with the developmental characteristics of students in mind. In other words, an effective AIDS curriculum for college students might not be effective for a junior high school population (Serovich & Greene, 1997).

◆ Child Abuse

Child abuse is just one of the myriad of psychosocial issues some of your students will be confronting. In fact, recent research indicates that one in every six Americans has suffered from some form of child abuse (Kohn, 1987). Table 3.5 depicts the four major types of child abuse including categories of physical, sexual, and emotional abuse and neglect. You will need to familiarize yourself with both the physical and behavioral indicators of abuse because teachers in all fifty sates are legally required to report any suspicion of child abuse, much like the responsibility of a physician. Teachers are protected from lawsuits involving charges of libel and slander, since making such reports is one of their professional responsibilities. It is important for you to become familiar with the policies and procedures governing such reporting in your school district. Make sure that when you teach you inquire with someone in your district as to how to make such reports. Often, teachers are asked to make such reports to the building principal or school nurse. In other cases, teachers are encouraged to directly report their suspicions to a social services agency. It is not a bad idea to follow up on your reporting and make sure the appropriate investigation took place as social service agencies are typically overworked and understaffed.

   If a child does confide a scenario of abuse to you, you should remember the guidelines listed in the tool box.

child abuse the deliberate physical sexual or emotional injury of a helpless child

◆ Divorce

Another frequently encountered psychosocial issue for the classroom teacher is that of students coping with divorce. At least four out of every ten marriages fail in the United States, which makes the odds high that every year you will teach a number of students whose families have either undergone divorce or are in the process of doing so. Similar to child abuse, the psychological impact of divorce is often powerful enough to affect a student's academic life. Research

Teacher Tool Box
Guidelines for Dealing with Child Abuse

- ◆ Believe the child.
- ◆ Tell them that you are glad they confided in you, although you are sorry about what has happened to them.
- ◆ Try not to communicate feelings of horror, repugnance, or fright.
- ◆ Reassure the child that it is okay to talk.
- ◆ Tell the child that the abuse is not her fault.
- ◆ Let the child tell her story at her own pace.
- ◆ Tell the child that you must report what they have told you in order to help everyone involved.
- ◆ Do not tell the child that you will keep what she has confided in you a secret. Remember, from a legal standpoint you must make a report.

Action Research

An Advisor–Advisee Program

A ction research, as we've stated before, affords the classroom teacher the opportunity to determine how well a recommended strategy or program is working in the classroom or school. One program that has been suggested as a means to address issues related to students' moral and psychosocial development is called the advisor-advisee program (George, 1987). While most popular at the middle school level, it is beginning to catch on in other grade levels as well. Typically, schools with advisor-advisee programs arrange for students to spend one period per day discussing a wide range of psychological issues with their teachers and peers, including issues related to the development of self-awareness, values, communication skills, pressure encountered in academics and sporting activities, and peer pressure as it is related to drug and alcohol abuse as well as sex. In the school studied below, a different activity related to these issues is planned each day of the week. These activities include a discussion of hypothetical cases of teen alcohol and drug abuse, study skills, intramurals or noncompetitive sports, special interest classes designed around student hobbies, and community service projects. As such, this advisor-advisee program addressed a number of the issues we have covered in this chapter related to Erikson's fifth stage, identity versus role diffusion, as well as Marcia's identity status theory.

In the following action research study, Jean, a middle school science teacher, seeks to determine how the teachers and students at her school perceive their advisor-advisee program (Sardo-Brown & Shetlar, 1994). She wishes to survey teachers and students to find out if there are aspects of the program that could be improved and, if so, how. Jean administers a questionnaire about the advisor-advisee program to all of the teachers and students in her school. Of the teachers surveyed, 87 percent return completed questionnaires as do 88 percent of the students. While the middle school teachers who responded to the survey overwhelmingly approved of the advisor-advisee program, they suggested several changes. These changes included the elimination of the use of hypothetical scenarios of drug and alcohol abuse because they believed the students found them difficult to relate to, the removal of students who disrupted the advisor-advisee period, and the use of better-planned activities. Teachers also called for better in-service training for themselves along with the chance to visit other schools with successful programs. In addition, they expressed a desire to determine which students would be assigned to which teacher for the advisor-advisee period.

The responding middle school students also made a number of suggestions. While the majority of students said they liked the program, similar to the teachers, they wanted both the use of the hypothetical drug and alcohol abuse cases and disruptive peers eliminated from the advisor-advisee period. Other student ideas for change included the following: (1) allow students to select the teacher they will be placed with; (2) give students more choice as to the intramural activities to select from; and (3) address student concerns about such issues as homework, interaction between the sexes, and what to do in leisure time. Further, students thought teachers needed to be more sensitive to differences between older and younger students, as older students preferred more emphasis on how to cope with academic pressures while the younger students were more interested in activities such as holiday celebrations.

From these data, Jean and her school have discovered a number of ways to improve their advisor-advisee program. As you can see from the student responses, in particular, middle school students have a tremendous desire to to obtain advice from teachers about the myriad of moral and psychosocial issues discussed in this chapter. The message of this research is that these issues cannot be separated from academic content. By addressing such issues, teachers make the curriculum relevant to students' lives and subsequently motivate students to learn.

Table 3.5   Indicators of Child Abuse

Type of Abuse	Physical Indicators	Behavioral Indicators
Physical	Unexplained bruises and welts ◆ on face, lips, or mouth ◆ on torso, back, buttocks, or thighs ◆ in various stages of healing ◆ clustered or forming patterns ◆ shaped like recognizable object (e.g., belt buckle) ◆ appearing regularly after absences, weekends, or vacation periods Unexplained burns ◆ by cigars or cigarettes, especially on soles, palms, back, or buttocks ◆ by immersion in hot liquid, especially on hands, feet, buttocks, or genitalia ◆ shaped in a recognizable form (e.g., electric range coils, electric iron) ◆ by rope on arms, legs, neck, or torso Unexplained fractures ◆ of skull, nose, or facial bones ◆ in various stages of healing ◆ in multiple locations Unexplained lacerations or abrasions ◆ on mouth, lips, gums, or eyes ◆ on external genitalia	Wary of adult contacts Apprehensive when other children cry Extreme aggressiveness or extreme withdrawal Fear of parents Fear of going home Reporting of injury by parents or others
Sexual	Difficulty in walking or sitting Torn, stained, or bloody underclothes Pain or itching in genital area Bruises or bleeding in external genitalia, vaginal, or anal areas Venereal disease symptoms, especially in pre-teens Pregnancy	Unwillingness to change clothing or to participate in physical education classes Withdrawal, fantasy, or infantile behavior Bizarre, sophisticated, or unusual sexual behavior or knowledge Poor peer relationships Chronic delinquency Reporting of sexual assaults
Emotional	Speech disorders Lag in physical development Severe allergies, asthma, or ulcers Alcohol or drug abuse	Habit disorders (e.g., thumb sucking, lip biting, rocking) Antisocial or destructive conduct Psychoneurotic traits (e.g., hysteria, obsessions, compulsions, phobias, hypochondria) Behavior extremes of compliance or aggression Inappropriate adult or infantile behavior Mental and emotional developmental lags Suicide threats or attempts
Neglect	Consistent hunger Poor hygiene Inappropriate dress Unattended physical problems or medical needs Alcohol or drug abuse	Begging or stealing food Early arrivals and late departures Constant fatigue or listlessness Chronic delinquency, especially thefts Reporting of no caretaker at home

Source: Adapted from *The Educator's Role in the Prevention and Treatment of Child Abuse and Neglect.* Washington, DC: U.S. Department of Health and Human Services, 1984.

has shown that teachers often become a central figure in the lives of children in such situations, particularly several months after a separation has occurred (Kelly & Wallerstein, 1977). It is important to understand that your students' reactions to divorce will vary, depending on their developmental stage. Remember Piagetian theory (see Chapter 2)? Well, the students' stage of cognitive development significantly determines how they will react to any number of stressors, including divorce. Table 3.6 summarizes the typical reactions to expect according to the child's age.

Table 3.6   How Your Child Responds to Divorce

3 1/2 to 5 YEARS OLD

Children of this age think in terms of themselves and their own immediate needs. They believe the world revolves around them. Because of their sense of "power" that results from the manner in which they perceive the world, they frequently blame themselves for the divorce.

   Example: "If I were good, Mommy and Daddy would not fight."

Since they live in the present (here and now) they are likely to say, "I want everyone to stay here—I don't want to go anywhere and I don't want Mommy/Daddy to go."

They may regress in their behavior. They may wet the bed, have trouble sleeping, turn more to security blankets, and have toilet training problems. They may also withdraw, or detach themselves from the absent parent in order to protect themselves from the emotional pain of loss.

   Example: They may be upset when they return from seeing their nonresidential parent because they are subjected to the experience of separation once more. HOWEVER, this is preferable to the children who suppress or deaden their feelings because of no contact at all with the nonresidential parent.

5 & 6 YEARS OLD

This age group also deals mainly with the present. However, they do speculate about the immediate future; i.e., "What will happen next?" Parents therefore need to be precise about answering questions regarding "What happens now?"

   Example: "Mom/Dad will pick you up at 10:00 o'clock after *Sesame Street* and will bring you home at 5:00 o'clock after *Mr. Rogers*."

This age group is able to vocalize their feelings, and frequently communicate relief when matters are settled. They may regress in their behavior in ways similar to the younger child.

6–10 YEARS OLD

Children at this age can think ahead (foresee) as well as think back (remember). They want to undertake more responsibility for the family and may make an effort to bring everyone back together. They are fully aware of their extreme anger and are able to demonstrate it and express it verbally.

(continued)

Example: They may be demanding, dictatorial, and may scold either or both parents.

This age group may feel fearful, powerless, and unsure of their place in the world. School performance may drop; there may be petty stealing (usually in an attempt to bring back what is lost). Children need love and support form parents and significant others. Typical questions they may voice are, "Will I still have my friends? Will I have a bed?"

Their separation fears may increase:

Example: They may not want to attend school because they fear Mom/Dad will also be gone when they return home. In addition, there may be stomachaches or headaches symptomatic of separation anxiety.

ADOLESCENTS/TEENAGERS

Children at this age are perfectionists and want their parents to be flawless. They may see their "over idealized" parents as not meeting their needs. Therefore, they must begin to come to terms with the conflict between the idealized and more realistic parental figures. This can be extremely painful. They are sharply aware of the reality of divorce and may not wish to be involved in their parents' arguments. They may try to deal with this by becoming more connected with their peer group. They worry about money in terms of specific use.

Example: "Will there be money to buy a car? Will I still be able to go to college?"

At this age their own sexuality is heightened and they may feel more stress regarding their parents' sexuality.

Example: If Mom/Dad have a relationship with a new girl/boyfriend, they can experience a conflict in loyalty and feel a need to take sides.

There may be an increase in harmful or inappropriate behavior if the father is no longer there to set limits for them, or if they sense feelings of uncertainty, fear and powerlessness in the residential mother. For example, they may drive the car too fast or become involved in petty thefts.

In all these age groups listed, many of these reactions will be reduced significantly or disappear completely within a year.

Several important implications for the classroom teacher with regard to working with students whose parents have divorced or are in the process of divorce are listed in the tool box on the next page.

◆ Suicide

The suicide rate among youth has tripled in the last thirty years. In fact, according to recent estimates a teenager attempts suicide every seventy-eight seconds somewhere in the United States. And every ninety minutes, one succeeds. Suicide is the second leading cause of death among adolescents, and while accidents are the leading cause of death, many of

Teacher Tool Box
Guidelines for Helping Students Who Have Experienced Divorce

◆ Encourage your school to set up a divorce support group if it does not already have one.

◆ Avoid making comments that presuppose that all of your students live in two-parent households. Instead, refer to your students' primary caregiver or guardian instead of father and mother.

◆ Maintain as much consistency and stability in the student's schedule as possible. The school environment may very well be the most stable factor in the child's life for a while.

◆ Take every opportunity to reassure the student that he or she is worthwhile.

◆ Employ the use of whole class discussions related to the topic of divorce. In this way, children of divorce will come to see that they are not the only ones grappling with this issue and children who have not experienced divorce will become sensitized to the needs of their peers who have.

◆ Provide opportunities for students to express their feelings about divorce in a variety of ways including writing in journals, drawing, dramatic play, painting, or molding clay.

◆ Provide opportunities for the student to be successful in controlling his or her life. For instance, make sure learning equipment and materials are matched to the child's ability. Allow the child to make as many academic choices as he or she can handle.

◆ Prepare the student for end-of-school-year separation by arranging for a visit to the new classroom or school ahead of time.

◆ Act as a referral agent to your school's guidance counselor or school psychologist. Signs that may signal additional help include extreme sadness, fear, anger, guilt, loneliness, and a preoccupation with death and disease.

these may be suicides in disguise. In addition, recent studies have found that more than half of all teenagers have contemplated suicide (Bolger et al., 1989).

The most common reasons why your students may consider suicide include the following: (1) loss of someone close, including the death of a family member, a friend moving away, a divorce, or loss of a pet; (2) breaking up with a girlfriend or boyfriend; (3) loneliness; (4) family problems including situations in which the child has been abused, threatened, or abandoned; and (5) pressure or feelings of failure that occur in relation to school, sports, or peer pressure surrounding drugs, alcohol, or sex. The key warning signs that you should be alert to as a classroom teacher are listed below (Halmi, 1987):

1. Expression of suicidal thoughts or preoccupation with death;

2. Depression over a broken love relationship;

3. Giving away prized possessions;

4. Abuse of alcohol or drugs;

5. Marked personality changes such as a withdrawn child becoming gregarious or vice versa

6. Change in eating or sleeping habits;

7. A sense of hopelessness.

Many schools, in response to the marked increase in teen and child suicide, are starting suicide-awareness programs, which seek to dispel myths about suicide and to encourage discussion of emotional conflict through **psychodrama**, in which students act out potentially troublesome situations and discuss ways to solve them (Parsons, 1994; 1996). Educators who favor this approach contend that the benefits of such programs are twofold. First, there is a benefit to those students who are considering suicide as they learn coping and problem-solving skills. Second, by addressing the typical warning signs of suicide, these programs make other students more apt to recognize the problems of their peers. Table 3.7 describes the recommended steps to use upon rendering psychological first aid to a student contemplating suicide. As useful as this information is, however, remember that

psychodrama technique in which students act out potentially troublesome situations and discuss ways to resolve them

you should consult other professionals in your school or district for help such as guidance counselors, social workers, and school psychologists instead of trying to handle such a problem alone.

Table 3.7	Recommendations for Working with Suicidal Youth

Step 1: Listen
The first thing a person in a mental crisis needs is someone who will listen and really hear. Every effort should be made to understand the feelings behind the words.

Step 2: Evaluate the seriousness of the youngster's thoughts and feelings
If the person has made clear self-destructive plans, the problem is apt to be more acute than when his thinking is less definite.

Step 3: Evaluate the intensity or severity of the emotional disturbance
It is possible that the youngster may be extremely upset, but not suicidal. If a person has been depressed and then becomes agitated and moves about restlessly, it is usually cause for alarm.

Step 4: Take every complaint and feeling the student expresses seriously
Do not dismiss or undervalue what the person is saying. In some instances, the person may express his difficulty in a low key, but beneath his seeming calm may be profoundly distressed feelings. All suicidal talk should be taken seriously.

Step 5: Do not be afraid to ask directly if the individual has entertained thoughts of suicide
Suicide may be suggested, but not openly mentioned, in the crisis period. Experience shows that harm is rarely done by inquiring directly into such thoughts at an appropriate time. As a matter of fact, the individual frequently welcomes the query and is glad to have the opportunity to open up.

Step 6: Do not be misled by the youngster's comments that he is past his emotional crisis
Often the youth will feel initial relief after talking of suicide, but the same thinking will recur later. Follow-up is crucial.

Step 7: Be affirmative but supportive
Strong, stable guideposts are essential in the life of a distressed individual. Provide emotional strength by giving the impression that you know what you are doing, and that everything possible will be done to prevent the young person from taking his life.

Step 8: Evaluate the resources available
The individual may have both inner psychological resources, including various mechanisms for rationalization and intellectualization, which can be strengthened and supported, and outer resources in the environment such as ministers, relatives, and friends, whom one can contact. If these are absent, the problem is much more serious. Continuing observation and support are vital.

Step 9: Act specifically
Do something tangible; that is, give the youngster something definite to hang on to, such as arranging to see him later or subsequently contacting another person. Nothing is more frustrating to the person than to feel as though he has received nothing from the meeting.

Reflections from the Field

1 I use something called "proud whips" to affirm students' prosocial behaviors. At the end of class, I'll take two or three minutes and go around the classroom, asking students to share something good they've done for someone else that they are especially proud of. This takes awhile to launch, but you'd be surprised the kinds of things students are doing, once they get in the habit.

—Kelly (middle school language arts teacher), Quakertown, PA

2 Our team has begun a program in which we invite guest speakers from the community to visit and discuss how what we are teaching can be used on the job. The unique twist to our program is that we try hard to make sure these guest speakers are representative of our student population, which is 90 percent African American and 10 percent Latino American.

—David (senior high math teacher), Chester, PA

3 In the foyer of our school is a bulletin board called "Random Acts of Kindness." Each week, several students are honored here for something kind they did for someone else in the school. The idea is catching on, and now our school is honoring staff, faculty, and administrators for these random acts of kindness.

—Emily (middle school guidance counselor), Panama City, FL

4 Some of our middle school students participate in a new program in which they spend part of the school day at a job site. At this job site, they learn about how to apply content from their academic classes to the real world. The hope is that this may help motivate these kids to stay in school. It fits in well with Erikson's identity vs. confusion stage in that it may even help them to narrow down a career choice.

—Cindy (middle school science teacher), Wichita, KS

5 Our school has activity clubs, which meet during the last period of the day. Students sign up for the club they are interested in. In this way, students are able to affirm their sense of identity by participating in something unique and by identifying with others who have similar interests.

—Jim (middle school social studies teacher), West Chester, PA

THEORY TO PRACTICE

A Look at Teacher as Decision Maker

We began this chapter by introducing a scene from a physics class. You'll recall that in this scene one of Mrs. Fry's students walks out of class, lamenting that her life is falling apart. Her problems include a boyfriend and a boss who apparently fail to understand her commitment to school. She also has uncooperative hair. In this scene, we are provided with a brief glimpse into some of the factors, besides a student's cognitive stage, that affect learning.

Clearly, teachers need to understand these factors, which pertain to the emotional and social characteristics of students, very well. Teachers should have a firm grasp of the stages of moral development, which depict students' capabilities with regard to moral reasoning. Because all well managed classrooms are based around a set of rules, teachers are also well served by familiarity with the Lickona model, which speaks to the issue of how to facilitate moral behavior in students. As cheating and aggression are common problems in today's schools, teachers also need to be kept abreast of recent research on these topics. Another piece of the developmental pie, psychosocial development, is an essential part of a teacher's knowledge base as well. As teachers plan their lessons, students are well served if their teachers critically think about how to facilitate healthy psychosocial development, as conveyed in Erikson's eight-stage theory. Teachers of adolescents, in particular, can glean even more descriptive information about their students' quest for identity by studying Marcia's identity status theory. Finally, teachers at all grade levels are confronted with a myriad of psychosocial issues as they teach their students. Issues such as the development of the self-concept, teen pregnancy, eating disorders, AIDS, child abuse, divorce, and suicide can obviously impact a student's academic motivation and performance in dramatic ways.

Teachers who are able to address the needs of the whole student (cognitive, social, and emotional) are more likely to facilitate student learning. As you review both your own experiences as a student and contemplate what you may be observing as part of your field experience assignment this semester, think about the following:

1. Efforts made by teachers to address issues related to values, especially issues raised by the students themselves;
2. Methods used to prevent cheating;
3. Illustrations of how the teacher tries to foster a healthy sense of industry in students;
4. Opportunities the teacher has to aid students as they try to resolve identity issues and methods employed to do so;
5. Examples of how students' sexual identity and related issues affect their academic life;
6. Efforts that this school could be making to address a variety of psychosocial issues affecting the student population, such as teen pregnancy, eating disorders, AIDS, divorce, child abuse, and suicide.

You, as Teacher, as Decision Maker

In the following illustrations, you will be provided with descriptions of a number of salient characteristics of the school, the classroom, and the students. In reviewing these illustrations you are to apply your knowledge of moral and psychosocial theories in order to

1. Identify which of the research findings can be utilized to help solve the problem posed and
2. Brainstorm how to use this research in the stated setting to address the problem posed.

Case Illustration 1:
Rosedale Middle School

Your School

Rosedale Middle School is located in a small, rural community. Most families in the community are involved in farming. The community is a combination of middle and lower socioeconomic households. Recently, a new Wal-Mart store brought hundreds of jobs to the area, but led to the closing of several family-run businesses on Main Street.

Your Class

As a substitute teacher, you are assigned to teach five periods of eighth grade American history for a two-week period. The make-up of your class reflects the community in general. All of your twenty-seven students are white. Thirteen are male and fourteen female. You have a range of ability levels represented in the five sections you teach with one section identified as "honors," three as "average," and another as "below average."

Your Student

After your third day with the students, a usually quiet boy stays behind after school to talk to you. He tells you that he and most of his classmates support a local paramilitary group. He explains that his family is also involved with this group's activities. Then he asks you where you stand in regard to this paramilitary group.

Guides for Reflection

In reviewing the features, consider how each of the following may provide insight and direction for a teacher confronting this or similar issues.

Kohlberg's stages of moral development,
The Lickona model,
Erikson's psychosocial stages,
Marcia's identity status theory.

Case Illustration 2:
Fairless Hills Elementary

Your School
Fairless Hills Elementary School is located in a major metropolitan area. Over half of the families in this community are recent immigrants from Southeast Asia. Most of the remaining households are made up of blue collar workers who work in a nearby auto manufacturing plant.

Your Class
Your class is a group of thirty-one second graders. You already have been told that most class members read below grade level. In addition, you quickly observe that several students do not seem to understand English.

Your Student
At recess time, you notice that one of your Asian students is crying. She explains to you that some of her classmates are making fun of her because of the way she speaks and writes.

Guides for Reflection
In reviewing these features, consider how each of the following may provide insight and direction for the teacher concerned with how to deal with this and similar scenarios.

> Kohlberg's stages of moral development,
> The Lickona model,
> Erikson's psychosocial stages.

SUMMARY

Moral Development

Every day, your students will make decisions that involve issues of moral reasoning. Knowing how and when to respond requires that the effective teacher understand the theory and principles underlying the process of moral development.

Piaget posed a theory of moral development that essentially divided the way that children think about moral issues into two stages. *External morality,* or *moral realism,* is a stage in which children tend to view rules as inflexible and not open to negotiation. In the second phase, *autonomous reality* or *morality, of cooperation,* a child begins to perceive rules as more flexible and subject to renegotiation.

Kohlberg's theory of moral development is more extensive, describing moral reasoning from childhood through adulthood. He proposes three levels of moral development including:

1. *Preconventional* (four to ten years) where moral reasoning is characterized by a focus on the consequence experienced by the person as a result of his/her actions;

2. *Conventional* (ten to thirteen years), where individuals have internalized the rules or, if you will, the "conventions" of society, and;

3. *Postconventional* (thirteen years and older), where individuals move beyond the issues of pleasing or following the concrete rules and begin to focus on the principles that underlie these rules.

Whereas Kohlberg found that his subjects' moral decisions were based upon a morality of justice, Carol Gilligan has found that the moral decisions of females are based on an ethics of caring. While Gilligan and Kohlberg agree that the initial stage of moral reasoning is based on self-interests, Gilligan contends that females move from self-interests to a focus on specific individuals and relationships. Gilligan found that the highest level of morality is based on the principles of responsibility and care for all people.

Psychosocial Development

Erikson, in his theory of psychosocial development highlighted the importance of relationships with others in the formation of one's own identity. Erikson believed that personality develops through eight stages or critical periods of life. Further, he suggested that at each stage of life an individual is confronted by a crisis. Erikson assumed that personality develops in accordance with one's ability to interact with the environment and to resolve the conflicts/crises experienced. The stages he listed included the following:

Stage 1: Trust versus mistrust (birth to one year);
Stage 2: Autonomy versus shame and doubt (ages one to three)
Stage 3: Initiative versus guilt (ages four to five);
Stage 4: Industry versus inferiority (ages six to eleven);
Stage 5: Identity versus role confusion (ages twelve to eighteen);
Stage 6: Intimacy versus isolation (ages eighteen to thirty-five);
Stage 7: Generativity versus stagnation (ages thirty-five to sixty-five);
Stage 8: Integrity versus despair (over sixty-five).

Other Psychosocial Issues

While understanding the major theoretical frameworks for psychosocial development is important for classroom teachers, it is also essential to have a sense of the contemporary issues related to psychosocial development that affect today's students. Teachers must understand the psychological and legal implications of working with children who are experiencing teen preg-

nancy, eating disorders, AIDS, child abuse, divorce, and thoughts of suicide.

◆ Field Experience Questions

As we discussed in the last chapter, you can conduct action research even if you are not yet teaching by keeping systematic records of what goes on in classrooms you visit. Below are a series of field experience questions related to topics covered in this chapter. You can try to answer them based on classroom observations:

Moral Reasoning (Kohlberg and Gilligan) and Moral Behavior (Lickona)

Based on your observations, what stage or stages of Kohlberg's moral reasoning are being used by most of the students?

1. How do you think the stage(s) of moral reasoning being used are related to the Piagetian stage(s) of the students you are observing? Explain.

2. How do you think the stage(s) of moral reasoning being used may be related to the Erikson identity crises prevalent in the students you are observing?

3. How does the classroom teacher address the issue of values? Try to find examples of how she deals with such behaviors as cheating, respect for others' property, honesty, tolerance, or helping others.

Erikson's Stages

Based on your observations, which of Erikson's identity crises are most children struggling with?

1. Try to identify instructional approaches used by the classroom teacher to foster healthy psychosocial development for the respective Erikson stage. For example, if students are in identity vs. role confusion, are they provided the opportunity to encounter a variety of career models such as guest speakers who share their career paths with students?

2. If you do not see any evidence of an effort being made to address the Erikson stage of psychosocial development, how would you suggest the classroom teacher should attempt to do so?

◆ Key Terms

AIDS
anorexia
autonomous morality or morality of cooperation
autonomy versus shame and doubt
bulimia
child abuse
constructivist classroom
conventional morality
cooperative learning
external morality or moral realism
generativity versus stagnation

Gilligan's ethics of caring
identity achievement
identity diffusion
identity foreclosure
identity moratorium
identity versus confusion
industry versus inferiority
initiative versus guilt
integrity versus despair
intimacy versus isolation
Lickona model
Marcia's identity statuses

moral reasoning
moral reflection
participatory decision making
postconventional morality
preconventional morality
psychodrama
psychosocial development
self-concept
self-esteem
trust versus mistrust

◆ Additional Resources

Bee, H. (1992). *The developing child* (6th ed.). New York: HarperCollins.

Dacey, J., & Kenny, M. (1994). *Adolescents today*. Dubuque, Iowa: W. C. Brown.

James, M. (1986). *Advisor-advisee programs: Why, what, and how*. Columbus, OH: National Middle School Association.

Lickona, T. (1985). *Raising good children*. New York: Bantam.

Turiel, E. (1983). *The development of social knowledge: Morality and convention*. Cambridge: Cambridge University Press.

Van Hoose, J. (1991, Fall). The ultimate goal: Advisor-advisee across the school day. *Midpoints (2)*, 1.

Wiles, J., & Bondi, J. (1984). *The essential middle school*. Tampa, FL: Wiles, Bondi, and Associates, Inc.

Exceptionalities: Addressing Students' Unique Needs

quick perusal of her classroom was all it took for Mrs. Simon, a language arts teacher, to know her students had unique needs.

As she read her class roster, she noticed several students had been newly included because of a school mandate to incorporate those with learning disabilities into regular classes. Further, as she reviewed the list of names, she remembered that while some of her students were labeled "gifted" others were clearly over their heads, academically. As Mrs. Simon gazed up, she noticed that a student, who was profoundly hearing impaired, was accompanied by an aide who signed for him during the class. But perhaps her biggest challenge was in addressing the unique needs of two of the students. Two males who were known as gang leaders made their grand appearance well after the bell and attempted to threaten Mrs. Simon if she recorded them as tardy. Certainly, these students had unique social-emotional needs, and their presence in her class would clearly be a challenge.

Mrs. Simon's class, like most of our classes, included students with unique talents and special needs. And while we are given specific information to indicate that several of her students were classified as "exceptional," the two males who strolled into her class and attempted to intimidate the teacher also presented some very challenging and unique social-emotional needs. As you review the scene, you may be tempted to assume that such variation of students can only happen in a textbook, but such is not the case. Teachers are increasingly being called upon to incorporate and include students with special intellectual, physical, and social-emotional needs in their classroom. Of course, before the teacher can do this effectively he or she must understand the nature of these exceptionalities.

Teachers for the twenty-first century will be required to adapt the "What" and "How" of the class in response to the unique needs or special demands of the students "Who" compose that class. And while it is certainly true that each student is special and presents distinctive challenges and opportunities, some have been identified as exceptional because they require special education or supportive services in order to reach their potential. Understanding the unique demands and resources of those categorized as having an exceptionality is essential if their teachers are to effectively create lesson plans, deliver instruction, and assess student performance.

✦ Chapter Objectives

After completing this chapter the reader should be able to

1 Explain how legislation such as PL 94-142 and IDEA have changed the way in which the public schools provide services to exceptional students;

2 Compare and contrast the three contemporary theories of intelligence, including the theories proposed by Guilford, Gardner, and Sternberg;

3 Describe the psychological and behavioral characteristics of students with mental retardation;

4 Delineate the major educational, social, and emotional characteristics of students who are gifted;

5 Explain the criteria used for determining if a child has a learning disability;

6 Describe the major characteristics of neurological disorders including cerebral palsy, epilepsy, and spina bifida;

7 Delineate the major characteristics of chronic diseases such as asthma, diabetes, cancer, and AIDS;

8 Describe the major characteristics of visual and hearing impairment;

9 Distinguish the major characteristics of a speech disorder as compared to a language disorder;

10 Discuss the major psychological and behavioral characteristics of students who have an emotional/behavioral disorder;

11 Adapt teaching methods to meet the unique needs of students identified as exceptional.

CHAPTER 4 CONTENT MAP

RESPONDING TO THE EDUCATIONAL NEEDS OF EXCEPTIONAL STUDENTS

Before we begin our discussion, it may be useful to consider the following questions as they reflect your own elementary and secondary school experiences. Can you recall any children in your classes who required braces, or aids for hearing or vision? Were there any children who attended your school and participated in extracurricular activities who were identified as mentally retarded or as children with severe learning disabilities? Did you know any children who needed to take medication because of seizures or attention deficits?

It is quite likely that most of you could respond "yes" to some of these questions. This was not always the case! Ask the same question of individuals who attended elementary or high school prior to 1970, and you may find that they shared very little of your experiences. Prior to the mid-1970s most children with exceptional educational needs were simply ignored or placed in special settings away from the mainstream of education.

✦ The Role of Legislation

PL 94-142 the education for all handicapped children act, which contains a mandatory provision stating that to receive funds under the act, every school system in the nation must make provision for a free, appropriate public education for every child between the ages of three and eighteen (now extended to ages three to twenty-one) regardless of how, or how seriously, he or she may be disabled

IDEA Individuals with Disabilities Education Act extending rights of disabled beyond PL 94-142

It is vital for classroom teachers to understand that the way in which public schools serve the needs of exceptional students is rooted heavily in legislation. A landmark piece of legislation that revolutionized the treatment of exceptional students in public schools was the Education for All Handicapped Children Act or **Public Law 94-142.** This was the first federal law mandating a free, appropriate education for children with disabilities. Its basic provisions are described in Table 4.1.

In 1990, **IDEA,** or the Individuals with Disabilities Education Act amended PL 94-142. Several important alterations to PL 94-142 occurred as a result of IDEA. The first major change is one involving terminology. That is, the term "handicapped" has been changed to "with disabilities" to mark the distinction between limitations imposed by society (handicaps) and the inability to do certain things (disabilities). Thus, a student who is blind may be visually disabled and unable to "read" visually presented material. However, being without vision does not need to be a handicap to that students' progression through school or through a career unless limitations, such as providing only printed text in school, are imposed by society. And additional change in the wording of the law is that the term "children" has been replaced with "individual" to refer to provision of a free and appropriate public education for persons between the ages of three and twenty-one years.

FULL INCLUSION VERSUS A CONTINUUM OF SERVICES

least restrictive environment (LRE) placing children with disabilities in as normal a setting as possible

As we mentioned in Table 4.1, PL 94-142 has mandated that students with disabilities be placed in the **least restrictive environment (LRE).** The intent of this aspect of the law is that each child should be in a setting that is as normal and in as much of the mainstream of education as possible. This idea assumes that there is a continuum of special education services

Table 4.1 Major Provisions of IDEA (PL 94-142)

Each state and locality must have a plan to ensure	
Identification	Extensive efforts must be made to screen and identify all children and youths with disabilities.
Full service, at no cost	Every student with a disability must be assured an appropriate public education at no cost to the parents or guardians.
Due process	The student's and parents' rights to information and informed consent must be assured before the student is evaluated, labeled, or placed, and they have a right to an impartial due process hearing if they disagree with the school's decisions.
Parent/guardian surrogate consultation	The student's parents or guardian must be consulted about the student's evaluation and placement and the educational plan; if the parents or guardian are unknown or unavailable, a surrogate parent to act for the student must be found.
LRE	The student must be educated in the least restrictive environment that is consistent with his or her educational needs and, insofar as possible, with students without disabilities.
IEP	A written individualized education program must be prepared for each student with a disability. The program must state present levels of functioning, long- and short-term goals, services to be provided, plans for initiating and evaluating the services, and needed transition services (from school to work or continued education) for students at an appropriate age (usually by age fourteen or sixteen).
Nondiscriminatory evaluation	The student must be evaluated in all areas of suspected disability and in a way that is not biased by the student's language or cultural characteristics or disabilities. Evaluation must be by a multidisciplinary team, and no single evaluation procedure may be used as the sole criterion for placement or planning.
Confidentiality	The results of evaluation and placement must be kept confidential, though the student's parents or guardian may have access to the records.
Personnel development, in-service	Training must be provided for teachers and other professional personnel, including in-service training for regular teachers, in meeting the needs of students with disabilities.

Detailed federal rules and regulations govern the implementation of each of these major provisions. The definitions of some of these provision—LRE and nondiscriminatory evaluations, for example—are still being clarified by federal officials and court decisions

Source: From D. Hallahan and J. M. Kaufman, *Exceptional Children: Introduction to Special Education,* Sixth Edition. Copyright © 1994 by Allyn & Bacon. Reprinted by permission.

available, with residential institutions (the most restrictive) on one end of the continuum and regular education classes (least restrictive) on the other. In the middle of this continuum is the use of mainstreaming in which exceptional students spend part of the school day integrated with students in general education classes. The latter arrangement is probably very familiar to most of you from your own days as a student.

Regular Education Initiative (REI) an attempt to restructure special education so that the regular classroom would serve as the primary setting for special education services a regular education initiative also attempts to include all special needs students (i.e., economically disadvantaged and non-English-speaking) in one basic program rather than establish separate programs for each type of need

Advocates of what has been termed the **Regular Education Initiative (REI)** argue for the elimination of special education all together. They argue for a single educational system in which all students are viewed as special and entitled to the same quality education. Advocates of REI believe that mainstreaming should be replaced with a concept called full inclusion. That is, instead of spending part of the day in general education classes, exceptional students now would spend the entire day in general education classes, or be fully included. While some proponents insist on the total elimination of special education, others acknowledge the need for special education teachers, speech therapists, physical therapists, and so forth, to serve a role in public schools. However, the notion of full inclusion specifies that these professionals would now carry out their duties in the general education classroom, working collaboratively with the general education teacher to meet the needs of exceptional students. The basic components of most full inclusion models are listed below (Laski, 1991; Sailor, 1991; Stainback & Stainback, 1992):

1. All students would attend the school to which they would go to if they had no disability;

2. No student should be rejected from a school site because of type or extent of the disability presented;

3. No self-contained classes should operate at the school site; instead placements should be age- and grade-appropriate;

4. Cooperative learning and peer instructional methods should receive significant use in fully inclusive general education classrooms;

5. Special education support should be provided in the context of the general education classroom and in other integrated environments.

◆ The Argument for Full Inclusion

full inclusion the belief that all students with disabilities should be educated in regular classrooms in their neighborhood schools

Those who argue for **full inclusion** contend that there are serious problems with the concept and implementation of mainstreaming. These are summarized below:

1. A disproportionate number of students currently placed in special education are African American, Native American, Latino American, or from lower socioeconomic groups;

2. The curriculum of pull-out programs is poorly integrated with the curriculum of general education classes;

3. Pulling students in and out of general education classes creates an environment in which the exceptional students tend not to feel that they are full-fledged members of the school community;

4. The criteria for entrance into special education are often vague and inconsistently applied;

5. Special education has become a dumping ground into which students are placed who may, in fact, not be disabled but rather difficult to teach.

There is much debate about how to interpret the issues raised above. Those who think we should continue to mainstream and not move toward full inclusion fear that many general education teachers neither desire nor have the skills necessary to work with all categories of exceptionality. One recent survey of teachers confirms this notion (Sardo-Brown & Hinson, 1995). Advocates of keeping a mainstreaming arrangement are also concerned that adequate supportive personnel will not be provided to general education teachers in a full inclusion arrangement, including special educators, aides, and necessary medical support staff. They further fear that some districts may seize upon the notion of full inclusion to save money. Some teachers also worry that full inclusion may compromise the kind of instruction students without exceptional needs receive. And some recent research has called into question whether all students who are newly included actually benefit from placement in an inclusion setting (Zigmond et al., 1995). For all of these reasons, we will look at the unique characteristics and educational needs of students with various disabilities. The teacher tool boxes consider implications for teaching under each exceptionality.

INCLUDING CHILDREN WITH EXCEPTIONAL INTELLIGENCE

When discussing the issue of inclusion and the education of children with special needs, one topic jumps to the forefront of controversy. The concept of intelligence is widely discussed and yet quite often misunderstood. Whether there is one or many types of intelligence and whether intelligence can accurately be measured are but a few of the questions that confront educators today.

◆ Intelligence: A Singular Trait or Multiple Dimensions?

Researchers define intelligence as the capacity to acquire knowledge, the ability to think and reason in the abstract, and the capability for solving problems (Sternberg, 1986). Early researchers believed intelligence was a general or unitary trait because scores on diverse measures of intelligence including verbal ability, numerical competence, and abstract reasoning were all highly correlated (Spearman, 1927). Those taking such a g-factor approach to intelligence might assume that an individual who was identified by these tests as having high intelligence would prove successful on all types of tasks. Similarly, those scoring at the lower end of these test may be presumed to do poorly in all types of tasks. Critics of such a general intelligence position suggest that there are multiple forms of mental abilities, not just one (Thurstone, 1938). A number of contemporary researchers (e.g., Guilford's structure of intellect, Gardner's theory of multiple intelligences, and Sternberg's triarchic theory of intelligence) support the notion of multiple intelligence, and their models are discussed below.

Researchers define intelligence as the capacity to acquire knowledge, the ability to think and reason in the abstract, and the capacity for solving problems. Pictured here is Albert Einstein, widely believed to be one of the most intelligent people who ever lived. ◆

Guilford's Structure of Intellect

J. P. Guilford (1967, 1988) proposed that intelligence depends on what we are thinking (the contents), our mental operations (the process of thinking), and the products or end results of these operations. He developed a **Structure of Intellect** model that describes intelligence as the intersection of five cognitive operations, four content areas, and six products (see Figure 4.1).

Guilford's structure of intellect stipulates that intelligence depends on what we are thinking (i.e., contents), our mental operations (or process of thinking); and the products or end results of these operations.

Guilford's model leads us to conclude that any time one is engaged in a mental operation he or she would be employing some process or operation on some specific content to derive some final product. For example, the student in Escalante's class, when asked to derive the sum of a positive one plus a negative one, would have to employ convergent operations (since there is one right answer) with symbolic content (algebraic numbers) to achieve a unit (ZERO).

YOU MAKE THE CALL

Looking for the one or many right answers, Goodlad (1984) suggested that, using Guilford's model as a backdrop, it becomes clear that schools focus heavily on memorizing facts and definitions while spending far less time on divergent thinking, the search for relationships, and evaluation. Review your own experience in high school and college. Was the focus on content? Finding the one right answer? Or were you encouraged to find alternative answers or solutions? Were you assisted in identifying relationships between events—rather than simply reviewing the facts of the events?

Figure 4.1
Guilford's Structure of Intellect Model

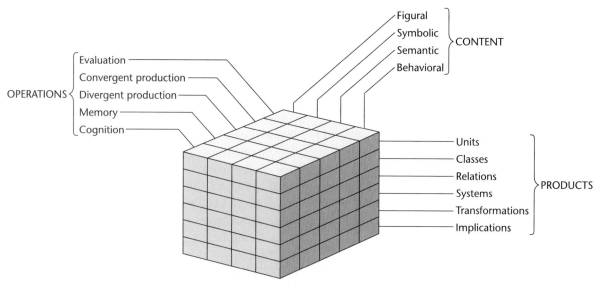

Source: Educational Psychology, 3rd Edition, Windows on Classrooms by Eggen/Kauchack, © 1993. Reprinted by permission of Prentice-Hall, Inc., Upper Saddle River, NJ.

Gardner: Multiple Intelligences

Like Guilford, Howard Gardner (1983) believed that definitions of intelligence were too narrow and should encompass aspects of intelligence outside of school. He argues for the notion of **multiple intelligences** and proposes eight relatively independent types of intelligence (see Table 4.2).

Gardner makes several important assumptions about these intelligences. First, he contends that most of us can develop each intelligence to an adequate level through environmental enrichment. In other words, Gardner believes that the nature of your strengths across the eight intelligences can be attributable to a combination of genetic endowment and environmental experiences. Second, Gardner believes that for most of us, our abilities across the eight intelligences lie on a continuum. That is, many people may be very strong in one or two or three areas, but not have a particular strength in any of the other areas. On the other hand, some people may have strengths in five or six areas or perhaps in all of them. Third, Gardner maintains that there are multiple ways to demonstrate proficiency in one intelligence. For instance, someone may be very skilled at telling a story aloud, but may be undeveloped with regard to reading comprehension (both are reflective of linguistic intelligence).

Fourth, Gardner cautions that although the intelligences are relatively independent entities on paper, in everyday life they work together in complex ways. For example, when it comes to the task of cooking, many intelligences come into play. One must be able to read and comprehend a written recipe (linguistic) as well as be able to perform basic mathematical operations such as combining fractions (logical-mathematical). In addition, one must be able to prepare a meal

Gardner's multiple intelligences theory specifying eight different intelligences that presume a broadened definition of intelligence

Howard Gardner has proposed eight independent types of intelligences. ◆

Table 4.2   The Eight Intelligences

1. Linguistic intelligence is the capacity to use language, your native language, and perhaps other languages, to express what's on your mind and to understand other people. Poets really specialize in linguistic intelligence, but any kind of writer, orator, speaker, lawyer, or a person for whom language is an important stock in trade highlights linguistic intelligence.

2. People with a highly developed logical-mathematical intelligence understand the underlying principles of some kind of a causal system, the way a scientist or a logician does; or can manipulate numbers, quantities, and operations, the way a mathematician does.

3. Spatial intelligence refers to the ability to represent the spatial world internally in your mind—the way a sailor or airplane pilot navigates the large spatial world, or the way a chess player or sculptor represents a more circumscribed spatial world. Spatial intelligence can be used in the arts or in the sciences. If you are spatially intelligent and oriented toward the arts, you are more likely to become a painter or a sculptor or an architect than, say, a musician or a writer. Similarly, certain sciences like anatomy or topology emphasize spatial intelligence.

4. Bodily kinesthetic intelligence is the capacity to use your whole body or parts of your body—your hand, your fingers, your arms—to solve a problem, make something, or put on some kind of a production. The most evident examples are people in athletics or the performing arts, particularly dance or acting.

(continued)

Table 4.2   The Eight Intelligences *(Continued)*

5. Musical intelligence is the capacity to think in music, to be able to hear patterns, recognize them, remember them, and perhaps manipulate them. People who have a strong musical intelligence don't just remember music easily—they can't get it out of their minds, it's so omnipresent. Now, some people will say, "Yes, music is important, but it's a talent, not an intelligence." And I say, "Fine, let's call it a talent." But, then we have to leave the word *intelligent* out of *all* discussions of human abilities. You know, Mozart was damned smart!

6. Interpersonal intelligence is understanding other people. It's an ability we all need, but is at a premium if you are a teacher, clinician, salesperson, or politician. Anybody who deals with other people has to be skilled in the interpersonal sphere.

7. Intrapersonal intelligence refers to having an understanding of yourself, of knowing who you are, what you can do, what you want to do, how you react to things, which things to avoid, and which things to gravitate toward. We are drawn to people who have a good understanding of themselves because those people tend not to screw up. They tend to know what they can do. They tend to know what they can't do. And they tend to know where to go if they need help.

8. Naturalist intelligence designates the human ability to discriminate among living things (plants, animals) as well as sensitivity to other features of the natural world (clouds, rock configurations). This ability was clearly of value in our evolutionary past as hunters, gatherers, and farmers; it continues to be central in such roles as botanist or chef. I also speculate that much of our consumer society exploits the naturalist intelligences, which can be mobilized in the discrimination among cars, sneakers, kinds of makeup, and the like. The kind of pattern recognition valued in certain of the sciences may also draw upon naturalist intelligence.

Source: Kathy Checkly. "The First Seven and the Eighth: A Conversation with Howard Gardner." *Educational Leadership 55,* 1, p. 12. Used by permission of the Association for Supervision and Curriculum Development. Copyright © 1997 by ASCD. All rights reserved.

that appeals to other people's preferences (interpersonal) as well as one's own likes and dislikes (intrapersonal).

Gardner defines intelligence as the human ability to solve problems or to make something that is valued in one or more cultures. In order for an ability to be labeled an intelligence, Gardner maintains that it must meet three additional criteria. First, there must be a particular representation in the brain for that ability. Second, some populations should be especially good in an intelligence. That is, Gardner contends that these intelligences are reflective of the diversity of skills found in our modern, technological society. Whereas some of us tend to be highly skilled at spatial tasks (such as artists or architects), others of us are adept at verbal tasks (such as journalists or ministers). Third, according to Gardner there should be an evolutionary history of the intelligence observed in animals other than human beings.

This conceptualization has intuitive appeal because often individuals skilled in one area, such as getting along with others on the interper-

---

YOU MAKE THE CALL

GARDNER'S EIGHT INTELLIGENCES

After reviewing Table 4.2, attempt to place names of people with whom you have some familiarity in each of the types of intelligence. For example, would you consider Michael Jordon, the professional basketball player, as giving clear evidence of bodily-kinesthetic intelligence? How about Maya Angelou, the poet, could we assume she excels in linguistic intelligence? Can you identify others? How about yourself?

---

sonal dimension, experience greater occupational success than do their peers who may have scored higher on a traditional measure of intelligence. Further, teachers can use Gardner's theory as a base from which to appreciate the varied talents and special abilities their students may bring to the classroom. Even the two students described in the opening scene of this chapter could be said to possess interpersonal intelligence because of their ability to organize and maintain gang loyalty.

The Teacher Tool Box includes a list of implications for classroom teachers which stem from Gardner's theory of multiple intelligences.

Sternberg's triarchic theory of intelligence three-part theory of intelligence including componential, experiential, and contextual types of intelligence

Intelligence, a Triarchic Theory and Process Model

Still another proponent of multiple intelligences, Robert Sternberg (1988, 1990), proposes a three-part **(triarchic) theory.** Sternberg identified three kinds of intelligence which he termed componential (i.e., the processes that underlie behavior), experiential (i.e., the ability to relate to novel tasks or new ideas in one's environment), and contextual (i.e., reflected in one's ability to adapt, select, or shape one's environment). As contrasted to the other theories which emphasized the content and construct of intelligence, Sternberg's theory focuses on the way people gather and use information. For Sternberg, intelligence is "purposive adaptation to, selection of, and shaping of real-world environment relevant to one's life and abilities" (Sternberg, 1989, p. 65).

Sternberg's model includes processing components, the link between intelligence and the environment, and a mechanism for modifying intelligence through experience (see Figure 4.2).

Componential intelligence consists of three parts: a metacomponent, a performance component, and a knowledge-acquisition component. Sternberg (1986) claims that these components interact when we engage in any complex process such as writing a term paper. The metacomponents are processes that

Teacher Tool Box

Using Gardner's Multiple Intelligence Theory in the Classroom

1. Get to know each student well enough to have a good sense of his or her strengths and undeveloped abilities.

2. Design activities geared to developing children's abilities in each of the eight areas described by Gardner.

3. Provide the opportunity for students to participate in activities and assignments based on Gardner's eight intelligences. For instance, besides having students write what they know (linguistic), allow them to draw pictures (spatial), construct a time line or graph (logical-mathematical), role-play or re-enact (bodily-kinesthetic), or teach other students (interpersonal).

4. Assess student performance in ways conducive to multiple intelligence theory by using many different assessment means besides the traditional paper-and-pencil ones. For instance, permit students to show you what they know in a videotaped performance or via an independent research project in which they put together their own diorama.

Figure 4.2
Sternberg's Triarchic Theory of Intelligence

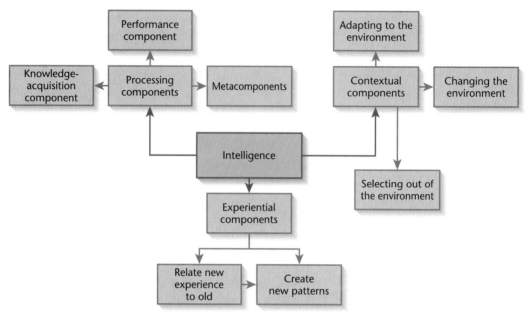

Source: Educational Psychology, 3rd Edition, Windows on Classrooms by Eggen/Kauchack, © 1993. Reprinted by permission of Prentice-Hall, Inc., Upper Saddle River, NJ.

identify problems, plan, establish goals, and monitor performance. Thus, in attempting to write a term paper, metacomponents decide on a topic for the paper, plan the paper, and evaluate progress on the paper. The knowledge acquisition component includes the processes by which new learning occurs. Thus, it is the knowledge-acquisition components that research the paper and combine facts into integrated ideas. The actual writing of the

Sternberg labeled the process of adapting, selecting, and changing one's environment as contextual intelligence. Consider a student adapting to her college professor's expectations for a term paper by reorganizing her ideas to fit with the structure required. ◆

paper is done by the performance components. The performance components are the processes that are used to carry out the task and execute plans.

For Sternberg, another important aspect of intelligence concerns how people use the environment to accomplish their goals. He believes this is done by adapting to the environment, changing it, or selecting out of it. These processes of adapting, selecting, and changing one's environment he labeled contextual intelligence. Consider the example with the term paper. A student might adapt to her college professor's expectations for a particular term paper by reorganizing her ideas to fit with the structure required by the professor. If this same student is still unsure about what the professor wants the term paper to look like, she may consult some of her peers who have previously done well in this professor's course. In doing so, she would be changing her environment. And if this same student sees she will not do well writing term papers for this particular professor, she may select out of the environment by dropping the class.

The final part of Sternberg's triarchic theory of intelligence describes how intelligence is modified through experience, that is experiential intelligence. For Sternberg, intelligent behavior is characterized by the ability to cope effectively with novel experiences and to solve problems efficiently and automatically. This view of intelligence means that students should be provided with many experiences that are novel situations in which they are required to relate new experiences to old ones.

These recent notions of multiple intelligences and multiple components of intelligence challenge the ways teachers and parents view how students can exhibit intelligent behavior (Bransford, Goldman, & Vye, 1991). Not only do we need to allow for and support student variability and strengths in the academic areas, but in others areas such as music, body-kinesthetics, interpersonal, etc. Further, if Sternberg is correct and intelligence should be viewed as consisting of subcomponents, which can be improved upon with further education, then the role of the classroom teacher in relation to "intelligence" is changed. For example, he argues that if solving analogies is an important subcomponent of intelligence, schools should train students, through experience, how to become proficient in solving analogies (Detterman & Sternberg, 1982).

◆ Assessing Intelligence

While the work of Sternberg has certainly aroused interest within the academic community, it has yet to have a widespread impact on the way intelligence is typically assessed in our schools. The tests, to be described, focus on assessing intelligence as content and specific abilities. It is important for teachers to understand these traditional measures, since many of the definitions of exceptional categories reviewed in this chapter are strongly linked to these tests.

Stanford-Binet and the IQ

Standardized intelligence tests originated in the early 1900s with the work of Alfred Binet. Originally, Binet and his partner Theodore Simon used tasks on their intelligence test that differentiated students at each grade level. Initially, they described performance as a mental age; for instance, a child who succeeded on tasks that had been demonstrated to be passable by most nine-year-old children, was described as having the mental age of nine years. However, there were problems applying this method with older populations.

When the Simon-Binet test came to the United States it was translated by Lewis Terman at Stanford University. This revised form became known as the **Stanford-Binet test**, and with the revision the concept of Intelligence Quotient (IQ) was added. The formulation was a relatively simple. Divide the mental age (M.A.), as defined by the number of items on the test successfully passed, by the person's actual Chronological Age (C.A). This ratio formed the basis for the ratio intelligence quotient and the multiplication by 100 removed the decimals from the final product.

Stanford-Binet test an individually administered standardized test of intelligence composed of verbal and performance subtests; correlates well with school success and teachers' evaluation of intelligence

$$IQ = \frac{M.A. \text{ (mental age)}}{C.A. \text{ (chronological age)}} \times 100$$

For instance, if a child who was six years old successfully completed all the tasks that were typically completed by those who were eight, that child would have a mental age of eight years and her IQ would be 133. This would be calculated as follows: (8/6 = 1.33 × 100 = 133).

The Stanford-Binet test is an individually administered intelligence test that consists of subtests. While earlier versions emphasized verbal tasks, the most recent edition is more diverse and includes performance items that do not require verbal skills. In 1986, it was revised and renormed using 5,000 children in forty-seven states, grades three through twelve, stratified by economic status, race, geographic region, and community size (Thorndike, Hagen, & Sattler, 1986).

The Wechsler Scales

Wechsler test an individually administered intelligence test with 13 subtests, of which 6 are verbal and 7 are performance oriented

The most popular intelligence test used today, however, is the **Wechsler test.** There are three versions in use: one is for the preschool-primary population, one for elementary students, and another designed for adults. The scale employed for most school aged students is known as the WISC-III (the Wechsler Intelligence Scale for Children, Third Edition).

The Wechsler test, regardless of which version, is designed in two parts, verbal and performance. The verbal tests all require a question to be posed orally and the student to respond verbally. The performance subtests all require the student to visually process some test material and respond with a motoric response. The test is individually administered and consists of thirteen subtests, six of which are verbal and seven of which are performance. Understanding the specific types of abilities tapped by each of the subtests can help a trained clinician draw important conclusions about the relative strengths and weaknesses of a student. For example, even a gross comparison of the verbal and performance sections can yield valuable information. Consider a student who performed much higher on the performance than on the verbal subtests. That student may be giving evidence of a language problem related to poor reading or cultural differences (Kaplan & Saccuzzo, 1993). Similarly, a student who shows significantly poorer abilities in the performance subtests may be demonstrating problems with visual processing or motor functioning. While the interpretation of the specific scales and the student profile requires specialized training, the information gathered may prove useful for the classroom teacher as he or she attempts to adapt teaching methods and materials to tap the child's strengths.

Interpreting IQ Scores

On the Wechsler intelligence test, the average score is 100. Fifty percent of the general population will score above 100 and fifty percent will score below 100. About 68 percent of the population will score between 85 and 115. Only about 16 percent of the population will receive scores below 85, whereas only about 16 percent of the population will receive scores above 115 (see Figure 4.3). The correlation between scores on the Wechsler test and school achievement has been reported to be fairly strong, .65 (Sattler, 1988). However, previous research (e.g., McClelland, 1973; Jencks et al., 1972; Sattler, 1988) called into question the degree to which an individual's IQ score is correlated with success in later life, since other factors such as motivation, years of formal education, emotional intelligence, etc., cloud the issue.

As you will see, however, the intelligence and the intelligence test play significant roles in defining a number of exceptionalities, including mental retardation, giftedness, and specific learning disabilities.

Figure 4.3

Theoretical Distribution of IQ Scores Based on a Normal Curve

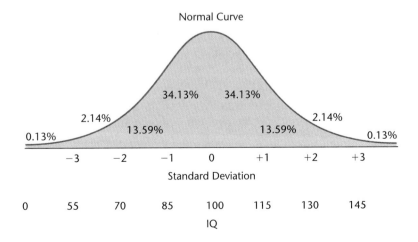

MENTAL RETARDATION

At one time, the diagnosis of mental retardation was based solely on an estimate of an individual's intellectual functioning or IQ score. Quite often, the scores selected to define retardation varied from school district to school district. With this approach, an individual who scored below a cutoff such as 70 might be identified as retarded in school district A but would not be labeled as such in school district B, which used a 67 IQ as the cutoff point. However, the use of IQ score as the only criterion upon which to classify students is inadequate. Today, we also consider the individual's adaptive skills or abilities related to coping with one's environment. That is, although some students may do poorly on an IQ test, they may still be streetwise or able to cope with everyday issues such as maintaining an after—school job or using the bus or subway system—or even organize and lead a gang!

Perhaps the most widely accepted definition of mental retardation is that provided by the American Association of Mental Retardation (AAMR).

> Mental retardation refers to substantial limitations in present functioning. It is characterized by significantly subaverage intellectual functioning, existing concurrently with related limitations in two or more of the following applicable adaptive skills areas: communication, self-care, home living, social skills, community use, self-direction, health and safety, functional academics, leisure and work. Mental retardation manifests before age 18. (AAMR Ad Hoc Committee on Terminology and Classification, 1992, p. 5)

In its new definition of mental retardation, the American Association for Mental Retardation posits that the functioning of nearly all persons with mental retardation can be improved with appropriate education (AAMR Ad Hoc Committee on Terminology and Classification, 1992). In fact, they contend that persons with mild mental retardation can improve to the point where they are no longer classified as retarded. Education programs aimed at facilitating the development of school-readiness skills (e.g., ability to follow directions, sit still, etc.), self-help skills (e.g., dressing, caring for bodily needs, etc.), community living (e.g., budgeting, maintaining a living space, etc.), and vocational skills (e.g., performing work tasks, being on time, etc.) can assist some retarded students to function more independently. Thus, mental retardation is no longer viewed as a condition that is static and unchangeable.

For many years, the AAMR classified persons with mental retardation according to severity, using terminology keyed to a person's performance on a standardized test of intelligence. For instance, **mild mental retardation** is from approximately 50–55 to 70, and **severe retardation** is from 20–25 to 35–40. While most school systems still use these classifications, in 1992 the AAMR suggested a departure from the classification system to one in which students were classified according to how much support they needed to function as competently as possible. Table 4.3 depicts these newly described levels of support for persons with mental retardation.

mild retardation a classification used to specify an individual whose IQ test score is between 55 and 69

severe retardation a classification used to specify an individual whose IQ test score is between approximately 25 and 40

◆ Causes of Retardation

A number of specific organic (biological/physical) causes of mental retardation have been identified. One such cause is the presence of an extra chromosome (#23), which results in **Down syndrome.** Individuals identified with Down syndrome can vary in intelligence from low normal to severely retarded. It should be noted that with the increased use of early identification genetic screening and intensive preschool intervention programming, more children today with Down syndrome are, in fact, functioning in the mildly retarded range.

In addition to such chromosomal anomalies and inherited diseases (e.g., phenylketonuria or Tay Sachs), retardation can be the result of maternal infection with rubella, herpes simplex, or syphilis during pregnancy; maternal drug or alcohol use during pregnancy; maternal and fetal blood type incompatibility (Rh factor); and any trauma at birth that may significantly deplete oxygen supply to the child's brain. In fact, recent investigations have concluded that up to 50 percent of mental retardation cases could be prevented through better prenatal care, preventing accidents, and providing preschool services and parent training for young children deemed at risk (Hardman, Drew, & Egan, 1996; Smith & Luckasson, 1995).

Down syndrome a condition resulting from a chromosomal abnormality; characterized by mental retardation and such physical signs as slanted-appearing eyes, flattened features, shortness, tendency toward obesity; the three major types of Down syndrome are *trisomy 21, mosaicism,* and *translocation*

◆ Implications for the Classroom Teacher

In reviewing various causes of retardation, one may be tempted to conclude that this is strictly a medical problem and not something with which a teacher needs to concern herself. Clearly, a number of the causes for retardation are biological and fall outside of the educational arena.

Table 4.3	AAMR Classification Scheme for Mental Retardation Based on Levels of Support
Intermittent	Supports on an "as needed basis." Characterized by episodic nature, person not always needing the support(s), or short-term supports needed during life-span transitions (e.g., job loss or an acute medical crisis). Intermittent supports may be high or low intensity when provided.
Limited	An intensity of supports characterized by consistency over time, time-limited but not of an intermittent nature, may require fewer staff members and less cost than more intense levels of support (e.g., time-limited employment training or transitional supports provided during the school-to-adult period).
Extensive	Supports characterized by regular involvement (e.g., daily) in at least some environments (such as work or home) and not time-limited (e.g., long-term home living support).
Pervasive	Supports characterized by their constancy, high intensity, provided across environments; potential life-sustaining nature. Pervasive supports typically involve more staff members and intrusiveness than do extensive or time-limited supports.

Source: From AAMR Ad Hoc Committee on Terminology and Classification (1992). *Mental retardation: Definition, classification, and systems of support.* Copyright © 1992 by American Association on Mental Retardation. Reprinted with permission.

Action Research

Students with Mental Retardation

A s we discussed in Chapter 1, in acting as decision makers and critical thinkers, teachers frequently conduct their own action research. While action research helps teachers to better reflect on their own practice, it also provides direct data on how well a given intervention is working in the classroom. One such action research study, which pertains to a topic discussed in this chapter, working with students who are mentally retarded, is described below.

Mary wanted to know if educable mentally handicapped students would increase their initiation of both verbal and nonverbal communication as a result of being involved in cooperative learning. Mary audiotaped and videotaped students before, during, and after cooperative learning. Both during and after cooperative learning, students showed an increase in initiating both verbal and nonverbal behaviors when compared to before the cooperative learning treatment. Mary is now studying the effects of using cooperative learning on the self-esteem of these same students.

Further, it is highly likely that as a regular classroom teacher you will not experience a severely retarded child in your classroom. However, as suggested by the AAMR's definition and findings, the functioning of children identified as retarded can be improved by early, intensive intervention and education. You will therefore most likely encounter and work with students identified as mildly retarded. It is important, therefore, to recognize and understand the various unique psychological and behavioral characteristics of a mildly retarded child so that you can develop appropriate educational environments and tasks to facilitate development. These characteristics include the following.

The child with mental retardation may exhibit attention problems (Brooks & McCauley, 1984). First, they often pay attention to wrong things or have difficulty allocating their attention properly. Second, students with mental retardation have difficulty remembering, especially with regard to those tasks that require complicated or deeper levels of processing, compared to their nondisabled peers (E. E. Schultz, 1983). Third, students with mental retardation have difficulty with self-regulation, the ability to regulate and monitor their own behavior. For instance, when given a list of words to remember, most people use a strategy to help them remember the list. However, those with mental retardation are less likely than their nondisabled peers to use self-regulatory strategies. Fourth, delayed or deviant language development is present in nearly all cases of mental retardation. Fifth, students with mental retardation often suffer from a variety of social problems such as trouble making friends, and they tend to have poor self-concepts. Often, these difficulties are intertwined with delayed language skills and the fact that they do not know how to strike up friend-ships with others. In addition, some of their typi-cal characteristics, such as inattention, also pose problems as they attempt to interact with others. Sixth, students with mental retardation tend to lag behind their peers in terms of academic achieve-ment. Finally, because of the long history of academic failure they have usually endured, they are at risk for developing learned helplessness, or a feeling that they have little control over what happens to them and that they are primarily controlled by other people and events.

Having considered the typical psychological and behavioral characteristics of students with mental retardation, we are now ready to contem-plate how best to facilitate the learning of these students in the classroom. The Teacher Tool Box provides a number of suggestions for those work-ing with students with mild retardation. You should be aware that **transition programming**, or preparing the retarded student to function and work in the community, is becoming increasingly popular. As such, an **ITP**, or **individualized transi-tion plan**, may be part of a student's IEP or indi-vidualized education plan (Hallahan & Kauffman, 1997).

For those working with students with severe mental retardation the tool box on page 130 pro-vides a number of guidelines to be considered.

Learning to structure the classroom environ-ment, learning tasks, and even teaching style to maximize the educa-tional benefits accrued by students with exceptional intellectual and social-emotional needs is NOT restricted to those working with retarda-tion. Another population, gifted students, while not considered a dis-ability, certainly presents unique educational challenges and opportuni-ties for the classroom teacher.

Teacher Tool Box

Teaching Students with Mild Retardation

1. In early elementary education, focus on teach-ing students with mild retardation readiness skills. These readiness skills include the follow-ing: sit still and pay attention to the teacher; discriminate auditory and visual stimuli; follow directions; develop language; increase gross and fine motor coordination, such as helping them to hold a ball or cut with a pair of scis-sors; develop self-help skills, such as tying shoes, buttoning, zipping, interacting appropri-ately with same-aged peers.

2. Model appropriate social behaviors by using a tightly sequenced and structured set of activi-ties, such as those available in the ACCEPTS cur-riculum or A Curriculum for Children's Effective Peer and Teacher Skills (Walker et al., 1985).

3. In later elementary years, place the focus on teaching functional academics, or skills neces-sary for the individual to function indepen-dently. For instance, reading is often taught in a way to enable the individual to read the news-paper, read labels at the store, make change, fill out a job application, or read the phone book.

4. As children get older, teach them the basics involved in community and vocational living skills.

transition programs for secondary students accommodations to help secondary students with learning disabilities make the transfer to adulthood and the world of work; these students often require additional support and assistance to make this transfer

individualized transition plan (ITP) a plan designed to prepare the mentally retarded student to function and work in the community

gifted a category in special education that defines individuals who give evidence of high-performance capability in certain areas

GIFTED AND TALENTED STUDENTS

Because giftedness is not considered a disability and is not addressed in IDEA, or any other federal law or regulation, the unique educational needs of **gifted** students often go unattended and overlooked. In the past, students who were viewed as "bright" or "gifted" may have simply been advanced to a higher grade. Perhaps you were one of the students who "skipped" a grade?

However, as we gain more knowledge about the characteristics of these students and modify our definitions of giftedness, we begin to see the need to develop approaches to facilitating the development of the gifted student which go beyond the simple "passing on" method.

Teacher Tool Box

Teaching Students with Severe Retardation

1. Use age-appropriate curriculum materials. "Babying" this population has been shown to be educationally harmful (Bates, Renzaglia, & Wehman, 1981).

2. Planned activities need to be as practical as possible, focusing on how this population can take care of themselves, such as on dressing skills.

3. Have students actually experience the settings in which they are learning to apply their skills, such as visiting a local store in order to practice the skill of making change and buying food.

4. Services offered by speech, physical, and occupational therapists for students with severe mental retardation should be integrated into authentic, real-life situations as much as possible.

5. Students with severe mental retardation should interact with their same-aged nondisabled peers as they are often an excellent source of modeling. One idea is to have nondisabled peers tutor students with severe mental retardation.

6. Involve the families of students with severe mental retardation in their education as much as possible, either through frequent conferences or by having parents work as an aide in the classroom.

7. Use applied behavior analysis (Chapter 10) to teach skills to this population. This involves the teacher setting objectives for the child, that are then broken into specific skills the child has to learn. The teacher then plans an intervention designed to increase the needed skills or decrease inappropriate behavior. The child's progress is then monitored every day so that both the teacher and student have immediate feedback about progress.

revolving door model model which proposes to include more students, up to 15 percent, in gifted programs

◆ Defining Giftedness

The traditional definition of giftedness has been based on general intelligence as measured by an individually administered intelligence test. Children have traditionally been labeled gifted if they fall in the top 3 percent of scores on these tests. However, there have been recent calls to expand the definition of giftedness beyond IQ test performance. For example, the Council of State Directors of Programs for the Gifted (1991) reviewed twenty-six state programs for gifted students and concluded that the definitions used included general intellectual ability, specific academic aptitude, creative thinking, advanced ability in the fine and performing arts, and leadership ability. Recent research has identified three characteristics that are predictive of remarkable achievements later in life (Renzulli & Reis, 1991). These characteristics are becoming widely accepted criteria for identification of the gifted:

1. High ability, including high intelligence;

2. High creativity, or the ability to formulate new ideas and apply them to the solution of problems;

3. High task commitment, or a high level of motivation and the ability to see a project through to its completion.

With this expanded definition of giftedness, many authors argue for including in gifted programs, not only 3 to 5 percent of the school-aged population who exceed the IQ cut-off, but as much as 15 percent of the school-aged population (Renzulli & Reiss, 1991). These authors argue for a **revolving door model** in which more students could participate in gifted programs to facilitate the development of their "giftedness."

◆ Implications for the Classroom Teacher

Despite the growing debate as to how inclusive gifted programs should be, there is quite an extensive literature available on the characteristics of the gifted population. Much of this research was based on the work of Lewis Terman's longitudinal studies of the gifted, which followed students over time who were labeled "gifted" as a result of their superior scores on standardized tests of intelligence. With regard to physical characteristics, this research has shown that as a group gifted students are taller, heavier, stronger, more energetic, and healthier than their nongifted peers (Terman & Oden, 1959). One caveat is in order here; because there is a sizable correlation between IQ and socioeconomic status, it may be that the apparent physical superiority identified in these studies is due to nonintellectual factors.

In terms of educational characteristics, gifted children tend to be far ahead of other, same-aged peers in academic achievement. Most learn to read easily and before entering school. Gifted students tend to be highly verbal and also manifest significant differences in cognitive processing abilities. That is, they can manipulate information in short-term memory and access information in long-term memory faster than same-aged peers. They are also able to sequence unordered information more rapidly than others. Research also indicates that most gifted students enjoy school and love learning (Gallagher, 1985). Frequently, gifted students are younger than their classmates because of their superior academic performance.

With regard to social and emotional characteristics, many gifted students are leaders in their schools, and most are happy and well accepted by their peers. Recent research also indicates that they tend to see themselves very positively (Coleman & Fultz, 1985). Most studies also show gifted people to be superior to average individuals in concern for ethical and moral issues and in moral behavior (Gallagher, 1985). In fact, at an earlier age than most, gifted children tend to be focused on abstract concepts such as good and evil, morality and justice (Gailbraith, 1985). Most gifted children are also emotionally stable and are less prone to neurotic and psychotic disorders than other children (Janos & Robinson, 1985). However, recent research has indicated that those students on the extreme end of giftedness (those with an IQ score of 180 and above) seem to experience adjustment problems, including being teased by their peers because they are perceived as smart, feeling different from others, and feeling overwhelmed by the number of things they can do with their lives (Keogh & MacMillan, 1996).

Often, the recognition of a gifted student may be distorted or blocked because that child exhibits characteristics not typically associated with giftedness. One segment of the gifted population that may be overlooked includes gifted students with disabilities. Many teachers assume that if a child lacks the ability to speak or to be physically active, the child could not possibly be of superior intellect. However, Whitmore and Maker (1985) estimate that about 2 percent of children with disabilities are, in fact, gifted. Another group of students who are underrepresented in the ranks of the gifted are minority students. Because children from minority cultural groups may be viewed negatively or because the strengths and abilities valued in their culture may be in conflict with the majority, teachers may often overlook minority students as candidates for giftedness. Sometimes, the lack of basic necessities and opportunities for learning may mask creativity. Recent estimates indicate that while African-American students comprise about 16 percent of the total school-aged population, they make up only about 8 percent of those enrolled in gifted programs. However, the largest group of neglected gifted students are females (Callahan, 1991). One reason may be that historically they have lagged behind males with regard to performance on standardized achievement and aptitude measures. Additional factors that may bias classroom teachers are the host of cultural and social expectations for female students. Be especially sensitive to these issues as you work with diverse student populations.

In a scenario described in Chapter 3, Mrs. Granberg confronts a father who has withdrawn his daughter from school so that she can work in the family produce stand. Domenica, the student, is bright, gifted, and wants to become a lawyer. It would appear that being female and poor somehow impaired the recognition of her giftedness by her parents and school administrators. In such cases, a gifted student might have received a restriction on her education, when enrichment was needed.

Now that you know a little about the characteristics of gifted students, what does the research literature say about how best to teach them? There are many ways to answer this question. However, research suggests that enrichment and acceleration programs are about equally beneficial to the gifted population (Fox, 1979). **Enrichment programs** provide additional educational opportunities for gifted students while they remain enrolled in their current grade level. These may include before- and after-school programs, summer institutes, independent research projects, courses taken at local colleges, advanced classes taken with experts in a certain field, or special-interests clubs. There is also some evidence that gifted students do best when paired with other gifted students (Mitchell, 1984). However, Renzulli (1986) has severely criticized some of these programs. He and others argue that enrichment programs should target particular projects or activities to which gifted students bring superiority in terms of intellect, creativity, and task commitment. In such a program, students are given the chance as individuals or in a small group to tackle real-life problems such as those encountered by geologists, pollsters, politicians, and editors. The teacher's role is to provide students with the tools necessary to solve such problems and to assist them in communicating their findings to authentic audiences. This has also become known as the schoolwide enrichment model because students remain in the program as long as they have the ability, creativity, and motivation to continue with these activities.

Of course, **acceleration programs** involve moving gifted students ahead in one or more areas of the curriculum, beyond same-aged peers. This may mean skipping grades or attending classes with students from higher grades. Acceleration is typically used with the highly gifted or those scoring over 145 on an individually administered intelligence test. Research on acceleration, contrary to popular belief, does not indicate that there are negative social effects for gifted students, although acceleration has not been shown to be beneficial in all cases (Jones & Southern, 1991).

With the advent of full inclusion, it will become essential that all teachers feel comfortable working with the gifted. In the Teacher Tool Box is a list of specific teaching suggestions to help you facilitate the learning of the gifted students you teach.

enrichment program an educational program that provides richer and more varied content through strategies that supplement or go beyond normal grade level work

acceleration program educating gifted students by placing them in grade levels ahead of their peers in one or more academic subjects

SPECIFIC LEARNING DISABILITIES

Before we begin our discussion, consider the following case illustration. Cynthia was a nineteen-year-old college sophomore. On the first day of class, she approached her professor and asked if she could tape record the class. This was not an unusual request, and she was immediately granted permission.

Throughout the first weeks of class, Cynthia was an active participant in class, asking and answering questions, demonstrating a good grasp of the material and in general presenting as a bright, active learner. At the beginning of one class, the professor handed out a printed exercise sheet and asked each student to take a minute to "quietly read the sheet and answer the questions." As the students began the task, Cynthia approached the professor's desk to explain that she was unable to read the sheet and would need the professor to assist her. To say that the professor was shocked was a bit of an understatement. She could not read the sheet? How could that be? She was apparently bright and capable and in college!

Despite her obvious intelligence, motivation, and high level of academic achievement, Cynthia was unable to read printed material. Cynthia had a learning disability. Cynthia was dyslexic.

◆ Defining Specific Learning Disabilities

While children with specific **learning disabilities** comprise nearly half of all handicapped children, this disability remains widely misunderstood. Just as students with learning disabilities were integrated into Mrs. Simon's class in the initial scene of this chapter, you too will most probably be teaching classes in which students with learning disabilities are included. There are four major criteria to consider that must be present for a diagnosis in this category (U.S. Department of Education, 1977). The first involves a discrepancy between IQ and achievement. This means that the child is not achieving up to potential as measured by a standardized intelligence test. The traditional way of measuring this discrepancy was to compare the mental age obtained from an intelligence test to the grade-equivalent taken from a standardized achievement test. In the past, a difference of two years or more was often enough to indicate a learning disability. However, two years below

Teacher Tool Box

Teaching the Gifted

1. Involve gifted students in planning their own curriculum by having them generate their own learning goals and assignments when appropriate.

2. Focus gifted students on divergent thinking and problem-solving activities rather than on frequent tests of factual information.

3. Allow gifted students to use computers to master material independently.

4. Permit gifted students to do independent research, either in the library or by providing community resources and experts.

5. Afford gifted students the opportunity to work periodically with other gifted students on abstract problem-solving tasks.

6. Use the KWL method to identify what gifted students already know (K) and what they want to learn (W). At the end of an independent research project or problem-solving session with other gifted students, have them record what they have learned (L).

7. Plan assignments for gifted students that involve the higher levels of thinking in Bloom's taxonomy, such as analysis, synthesis, and evaluation. For instance, have them critique the ideas of others, synthesize original solutions, and judge the quality of these solutions.

8. Use learning centers in the classroom, which gifted students can visit to explore their own interests when these are not included as a regular part of the curriculum.

9. Employ contracts with gifted students to help facilitate self-directed learning.

learning disability problem with acquisition and use of language; may show up as difficulty with reading, writing, reasoning, and math

expected grade level is not equally serious at all points in a child's education. Therefore, special formulas have been developed to take into account this differential weighting across grade levels. However, because some of these formulas are statistically flawed and because of additional theoretical issues, you should know that there is a growing argument to abandon the use of the IQ-achievement discrepancy as a criterion for identifying learning disabilities (Fletcher, 1992; Siegel, 1989).

Three additional criteria must be present in order to use the term *learning disability*. These include the following: (1) learning problems in reading, writing, math, or speaking; (2) learning problems not due to mental retardation, visual or hearing impairments, environmental disadvantages, or an emotional disturbance; and (3) learning problems due to a central nervous system dysfunction (NJCLD, 1988, p. 1; Hammill, 1990, p. 77). In other words, the root cause of a learning disability is based in brain physiology.

◆ Dyslexia

dyslexia learning disability characterized by difficulty in reading, spelling, confusion between right and left, and the tendency to reverse letters in writing and speech

We opened this section with a look into one student's experience of **dyslexia**. Dyslexia is a complex of neurological disabilities that inhibit symbol recognition and the orderly processing and assimilation of language. Just imagine the difficulty you might have in school if rather than processing the symbols *C A T* in a way that elicited images of your favorite feline, your brain received * & # one time and perhaps *T A C* another.

It is important to note that dyslexia occurs on a continuum, meaning that one case may be very different from, and not as severe as, another case. Recent estimates indicate that dyslexia affects between 10 and 20 percent of the population (Griffin, 1992).

Implications for the Classroom Teacher

Identification is the first step for a teacher who is working with a student who has a specific learning disability. Clearly, the sooner the child is identified, the sooner the child can be assisted to work with the learning disability, thus reducing the chances of continued failure, frustration, and crippling psychological consequences.

The following list summarizes these major features, but a few cautions are in order. First, dyslexia should never be diagnosed before age seven because many of the following characteristics, such as reversals, may be developmentally normal before this time. Second, while the teacher may be one of the first to see the signs of dyslexia, she is not expected to be the definitive diagnostician. The official diagnosis must be made by a psychologist who is specially trained in the diagnosis of learning disabilities. The classroom teacher, however, can serve as an excellent referral agent for such testing. With these caveats in mind, here are the characteristics to be watching for (Hallahan & Kauffman, 1994):

1. Reading skills that are far behind those of peers, without apparent explanation;

2. Frequent reversals of letters or entire words (such as *b* for *d* or *was* for *saw*);

3. Illegible handwriting;

4. Confusion between left and right and no apparent preference for using one hand over the other;

5. Having other family members who were poor readers without apparent explanation;

6. Appearing clumsy and immature when compared to same-aged peers;

7. Reversals in speech well past infancy including *aminals* for *animals;*

8. Confusion about differentiating concepts such as "up" and "down" or "yesterday" and "tomorrow";

9. Bizarre spelling errors;

10. Serious difficulty in learning or remembering printed words or symbols;

11. Problems with organization and managing simple tasks or following simple instructions;

12. Learning to talk later than peers.

So now that you know about the major features of dyslexia, how do you best help a dyslexic student in your class? What, if anything, could the professor do to assist Cynthia? Of course, the answer to that question depends on the type and severity of the dyslexia.

Teacher Tool Box

Working with Dyslexia

1. Reading remediation is often very helpful. Recent research indicates that the phonics approach is especially useful with dyslexics (Chall, 1991).

2. The use of compensatory aids such as computers, which allow the student with dyslexia to express her ideas without having to worry about mechanical issues such as spelling and handwriting.

3. The use of books on tape as well as film strips and video to supplement printed material.

4. The use of typed handouts with large print instead of handwritten materials.

5. Having other students share class notes by using carbon paper.

6. For dyslexics who have scotopic sensitivity syndrome (about 50 percent of dyslexics do), use tinted eyeglasses or overhead transparencies. With this population of dyslexics, there is difficulty filtering out certain wavelengths of light (a perceptual not a visual problem). With the use of tinted overheads or eyeglasses, for many dyslexics the printed words on a page appear normal instead of jumping around or washing off the page.

◆ Attention Deficit Disorder

Although less frequent in our population than dyslexia, **attention deficit disorder (ADD)** is probably one of the most commonly discussed learning disabilities among classroom teachers. Estimated to affect from between 3 and 5 percent of the school-aged population, this disability is also heavily rooted in brain physiology. Recent studies have indicated that the frontal lobe region of children with attention deficit disorder is smaller than in children who do not have this disability (Hynd, 1992). Attention deficit disorder is defined as "abnormalities in neurological function, in particular, a disturbance in brain neurochemistry involving a class of brain neurochemicals termed neurotransmitters." As with dyslexia, this is a chronic disorder, which can extend into adulthood.

It should be emphasized that there is more than one type of attention deficit disorder. That is, while schools probably devote most of their efforts to students with attention deficit disorder who also have the hyperactivity component (called ADHD), this disorder can occur

attention deficit disorder (ADD) medical condition characterized by attention problems and impulsivity; may exist with or without hyperactivity

without the hyperactivity feature (termed undifferentiated attention deficit disorder). In the latter type, the most significant characteristic is inattentiveness (Shaywitz, 1987). Because the hyperactivity component is not present, many psychologists worry that this form of the disorder may be currently underdiagnosed. Often, these children are seen as simply quiet or passive.

The diagnosis of attention deficit disorder must be made in a multi-model assessment approach (Shaywitz & Shaywitz, 1991). This means that a team of people, headed by a physician, should be involved in providing input. Other members of the team should include a psychologist, teachers, and parents. At least eight of the following set of characteristics should be observed for a period of least six months to diagnose the most frequently encountered form of the disorder, **attention deficit hyperactivity disorder (ADHD).** The characteristics designated by the American Psychiatric Association are as follows:

attention deficit hyper-activity disorder (ADHD)
current term for disruptive behavior marked by overactivity, excessive difficulty sustaining attention, or impulsiveness

1. Often fidgets with hands or feet or squirms in seat;
2. Has difficulty remaining seated when asked to do so;
3. Is easily distracted by extraneous stimuli;
4. Often blurts out answers to questions before they have been completed;
5. Has difficulty waiting for his turn in a game or in group situations;
6. Has difficulty following through with instructions from others; may fail to finish chores;
7. Has difficulty sustaining attention in tasks or play activities;
8. Often shifts from one uncompleted activity to another;
9. Has difficulty playing quietly;
10. Often talks excessively;
11. Often interrupts others, for example, butts into other children's games;
12. Often does not seem to listen to what is being said to him or her;
13. Often loses things necessary for tasks at school or home, such as toys or pencils;
14. Often engages in physically dangerous activities without considering the possible consequences, such as running out into the street without looking; in addition, recent research shows that females, especially, may daydream a lot and appear withdrawn (Shaywitz & Shaywitz, 1991).

Implications for the Classroom Teacher

As with all specific learning disabilities, a key implication is for classroom teachers to be sensitive to the early warning signs, so that early identification and intervention can be implemented. Treatment for ADHD may involve the prescription of medication, such as Ritalin, along with the development of specific behavioral management programs.

But beyond serving as a source for early identification, what else can the regular classroom teacher do to facilitate the education and development of a student with an attention deficit disorder? The Teacher Tool Box includes a number of practical steps you can employ to modify the behavior of a student who has been diagnosed with attention deficit disorder (Ignersall, 1988).

STUDENTS WITH PHYSICAL CHALLENGES AND CHRONIC HEALTH PROBLEMS

For some children, the ability to participate fully in the learning activities of a regular classroom may be somewhat inhibited by their physical condition. Without appropriate modification of the classroom environment and learning activities, their physical condition may directly or indirectly restrict their ability to learn. The physical challenges to be discussed will include neurological disabilities and chronic diseases.

◆ Neurological Disabilities

Damage to or deterioration of the central nervous system is one of the most common causes of physical disabilities in children. This damage may range from the nearly undetectable to that which is profound enough to reduce the child's physical or cognitive functioning to a very low level. A child with brain damage may show a variety of symptoms, including mental retardation, learning problems, perceptual problems, lack of coordination, distractibility, emotional or behavioral disorders, and communication disorders. Some of the most commonly encountered types of neurological impairments include cerebral palsy, epilepsy, and spina bifida (Hallahan & Kauffman, 1994).

Cerebral Palsy

Cerebral palsy is part of a syndrome that includes motor dysfunction, psychological dysfunction, seizures, or emotional or behavioral disorders, which result from brain damage. Whereas some students with cerebral palsy manifest only one aspect of brain damage, such as motor dysfunction, others may show a

Teacher Tool Box
Working with ADD and ADHD

1. Arrange the learning environment properly. This may include the following ideas: seating the student near the teacher's desk or with his back to the rest of the class to eliminate distracting stimuli, surrounding the student with good role models; avoiding sitting the student near the heater, door, air conditioner, or high traffic areas as these may be especially distracting; preparing the student ahead of time for any change in schedule; and setting up a "stimuli-reduced" area, but allowing all students access to this area so that the student with attention deficit disorder will not feel different.

2. Give instructions very carefully. For instance, maintain eye contact with the student while giving a verbal instruction, make directions clear and concise, simplify complex directions, avoid multiple instructions, and make sure the child understands the instructions before starting the task. Be aware that students with attention deficit disorder may need more help for a longer period of time than other children. Having the child keep a daily assignment notebook can also be helpful. Such a notebook should be signed by parents and teachers to signify completion of assignments.

3. Monitor students closely as they perform assignments. Only one task should be given at a time, and student progress on this task should be monitored frequently with positive feedback from the teacher. Make sure that when you test, you allow enough time and are testing for knowledge and not attention span. As these children are easily frustrated, try to minimize stress and pressure.

4. Use immediate consequences for students' behavior. Enforce pre-established consequences consistently with these students. However, make sure the consequence fits the offense, and avoid public ridicule and criticism. Never publicly reminding these students to take their medicine. Try to provide more rewards than punishments by praising immediately after appropriate behavior. Teach the child to reward him- or herself by encouraging positive self-talk such as "You did very well remaining in your seat today."

5. Use social skills training, as many students with attention deficit disorder have difficulty getting along with peers.

cerebral palsy condition involving a range of motor or coordination difficulties due to brain damage

hypoxia damage to the brain which stems from a loss of oxygen

Recent research has shown that cerebral palsy is a complex, multidisabling condition. ◆

epilepsy disorder marked by seizures and caused by abnormal electrical discharges in the brain

combination of symptoms. The usual definition of cerebral palsy is a condition characterized by paralysis, weakness, incoordination, and/or other motor problems due to damage to a child's brain before it has matured (Batshaw & Perret, 1986). A myriad of factors are related to causing such brain damage including maternal infections, chronic diseases, physical trauma, and maternal exposure to X-rays or to toxic substances. Complications during the birth process as well as premature birth, **hypoxia,** high fever, poisoning, and hemorrhaging may also cause brain damage.

Recent research has shown that cerebral palsy is a complex, multidisabling condition (Kirk, Gallagher, & Anastasiow, 1993). A high proportion of children with cerebral palsy also have hearing impairments, visual impairments, perceptual disorders, speech defects, behavior disorders, mental retardation, facial contortions, or some combination of these. While some students with cerebral palsy have above-average intellectual capacity and a few test in the gifted range, the average tested intelligence of students with cerebral palsy is lower than average for the general population (Batshaw & Perret, 1986). Special equipment and procedures must be provided for these students because of their physical disabilities. In addition, a variety of special education services are often needed to accommodate the other disabilities listed above. Continuous assessment of the child's capabilities is especially important in this population.

Epilepsy

Persons with **epilepsy** often have recurrent seizures in which there is an abnormal discharge of electrical energy in certain brain cells. This discharge spreads to nearby cells sometimes resulting in loss of consciousness, involuntary movements, or abnormal sensory phenomena. Most seizures occur before the individual is six years old and more often in children with developmental disabilities such as mental retardation and cerebral palsy. The most common causes of seizures are damage to the brain, which stems from loss of oxygen (hypoxia), low blood sugar (hypoglycemia), infections, or physical trauma. Seizures may take many forms. They can last only a few seconds or for several minutes. They may occur as often as every few minutes or as little as only once a year. They may result in major convulsive movements or only in minor motor symptoms such as eye blinks. Seizures may be controlled completely by drugs, or they may be controlled only partially.

About half of all children with seizure disorders have average or higher than average intelligence. Among those without mental retardation who have seizures, however, there is a disproportionate incidence of learning disabilities (Westbrook, Silver, Coupey et al., 1991). While some of the learning and behavior problems observed among students with seizures stem from brain damage, some of these problems are believed to result as side effects of anticonvulsant medication or from mismanagement by parents and teachers. Brief seizures may require the teacher to repeat instructions or allow the child extra time to respond. Children with seizures also experience a higher frequency of emotional and behavioral problems than do other children (Hoare, 1986). However, it may well be that the stress of dealing with seizures, medications, and adverse environmental conditions is more likely to cause these problems. Recent research has shown that many such problems can be overcome if the student is educated about seizures and given appropriate work assignments (Freeman, Jacobs, Vining et al., 1984).

Teachers should deal with seizures by following the medical guidelines listed in Table 4.4. In addition to these guidelines, teachers should record the length of the seizure and the type of activity the child was engaged in before the seizure occurred, for this information will help the physician who is treating the child. Physicians, in turn, should inform the child's teacher about the medication the child is using as well as its side effects.

Spina Bifida

Spina bifida is a congenital defect that results from failure of the bony spinal column to close completely during fetal development. The defect may occur from the head to the lower end of the spine. Damage to the nerves, paralysis, and/or lack of function or sensation below the site of the defect may occur. This condition is called myelomeningocele and is often accompanied by paralysis of the legs and of the anal and bladder sphincters. Although some children with this condition can walk independently, others need braces, and some require wheelchairs (Hallahan & Kauffman, 1994). It is important for classroom teachers to recognize

spina bifida congenital defect resulting from failure of bony spinal column to completely close

---

Table 4.4   **First Aid for Epileptic Seizures**

A major epileptic seizure is often dramatic and frightening. It lasts only a few minutes, however, and does not require expert care. These simple procedures should be followed:

- REMAIN CALM. You cannot stop a seizure once it has started. Let the seizure run its course. Do not try to revive the child.
- If the child is upright, ease him to the floor and loosen his clothing.
- Try to prevent the child from striking his head or body against any hard, sharp, or hot objects; but do not otherwise interfere with his movement.
- Turn the child's face to the side so that saliva can flow out of his mouth.
- DO NOT INSERT ANYTHING BETWEEN THE CHILD'S TEETH.
- Do not be alarmed if the child seems to stop breathing momentarily.
- After the movements stop and the child is relaxed, allow him to sleep or rest if he wishes.
- It isn't generally necessary to call a doctor unless the attack is followed almost immediately by another seizure or the seizure lasts more than ten minutes.
- Notify the child's parents or guardians that a seizure has occurred.
- After a seizure, many people can carry on as before. If, after resting, the child seems groggy, confused, or weak, it may be a good idea to accompany him home.

Courtesy of Epilepsy Foundation, Landover, Maryland.

asthma characterized by difficulty breathing from narrowing of small airways in the lungs

that spina bifida is often accompanied by excessive pressure of the cerebrospinal fluid, or hydrocephalus, which may lead to an enlarged head, attention disorders, learning disabilities, or mental retardation.

Students with spina bifida may need to be positioned periodically during the school day because of the risk of getting burns, pressure sores, and abrasions resulting from lack of sensation in certain areas of the skin. Deficiencies in sensation below the myelomeningocele may also result in problems with spatial judgment, sense of direction, organization of motor skills, and body image and awareness. Some children with spina bifida may also be more likely to fracture bones in the lower extremities. Others will experience lack of bladder and bowel control, which may require periodic catheterization (Hallahan & Kauffman, 1994).

Implications for the Classroom Teacher

Neurological conditions, such as those discussed, present unique challenges for both the student and the teacher. The list of suggestions in the toolbox pertains to instructional adaptations that you may need to make for students with neurological conditions (Hallahan & Kauffman, 1994).

◆ Chronic Diseases

In addition to these common neurological impairments, classroom teachers will also work with students who suffer from chronic diseases. Among the most frequently encountered of these are asthma, diabetes mellitus, and cancer (Lammers, 1991). Although not as common, we will consider a fourth chronic disease, acquired immune deficiency syndrome or AIDS.

Asthma

Asthma is estimated to afflict about 5 percent of the U.S. population, with over half of new cases diagnosed before the age of seventeen. In fact, asthma is the leading cause of disability and disease in the school-aged population. Persons with asthma experience difficulty breathing brought about by a narrowing of small airways in the lungs, known as bronchi. When an asthmatic attack occurs, these bronchi become blocked, resulting in shortness of breath, chest tightening, wheezing, and coughing. Asthmatic attacks can be triggered by environmental irritants present in the school building or playground such as pollens,

Teacher Tool Box

Working with Neurologically Impaired Students

1. To help students complete written assignments, you may want to try some of the following stabilization techniques: writing on a pad of paper rather than loose sheets, using masking tape or a clipboard to secure loose papers, placing a rubber strip on the back of a ruler or using a magnetic ruler to prevent slipping when drawing or measuring lines, using adhesive-backed Velcro to attach items to a desk or wheelchair laptray.

2. You may also want to employ the following guidelines regarding materials for written assignments: using pens and pencils that require less pressure, such as felt tips and soft lead pencils; using an electronic typewriter, word processor, or computer; using typing aids such as a pointer stick attached to a head or mouthpiece to strike the keys; and line spacers that hold written materials while typing, audiotaping assignments, lectures, and other activities that require extensive writing.

3. To facilitate communication, use speech synthesizers, which voice the responses that students with severe speech impairments type on the computer. Communication boards, charts, pictures, symbols, numbers, or words also allow students to indicate their response to specific items.

4. To facilitate reading, use devices such as book holders; reading stands that adjust to reclining, sitting, and standing positions; electric-powered page turners; and talking books, which enable students who cannot hold a book to enjoy recorded novels, textbooks, and magazines.

mold spores, animal dander, aerosol sprays, chemicals, or strong odors (Daniele, 1988).

Classroom teachers should be alert to the signs of an asthmatic attack, such as wheezing, shortness of breath, and excessive coughing after exercise. The student should be encouraged to sit down, relax, and catch his breath. He should also be told to focus on his breathing and breathe deeply; the teacher can model this process and ask the student to follow along. It can also be helpful to have the student sip warm water. When these techniques are not effective, the teacher should seek medical help (Daniele, 1988).

Diabetes Mellitus

Over 7 million people in the United States are estimated to have diabetes. Of those, 5 to 10 percent have diabetes mellitus, the kind most common in children. **Diabetes mellitus** impairs the body's ability to use glucose to obtain energy. In order for the cells to adequately absorb glucose, the insulin hormone must be present. However, in children with type I diabetes, the pancreas produces little or no insulin. The sugar that cannot be used for energy turns into stored fats, which in turn release chemicals that may become poisonous as they build up in the blood. Without proper treatment a diabetic can fall into a coma and require hospitalization.

diabetes mellitus impairs body's ability to use glucose to obtain energy

Thus, a child with type I diabetes must take steps to keep glucose levels in the blood close to normal (Olefsky, 1988). This is done by controlling levels of food, insulin, and exercise. Snacks and meals must be eaten at regularly scheduled times to keep glucose and insulin levels in balance. Children should be given advanced notice before undertaking exercise so that they can make appropriate adjustments. In addition, diabetic children take one or more shots of insulin each day. They may also need to have their blood tested for sugar, using a finger prick, several times each day.

Teachers of students who suffer from diabetes mellitus should keep an emergency supply of fruit juice, sugar cubes, or Lifesavers on hand. The teacher should also keep in mind that food makes glucose levels rise while exercise and insulin make glucose levels fall. Therefore, a child who has eaten too little food, exercised vigorously without eating, or taken too much insulin may experience hypoglycemia or a drop in glucose levels. The major symptoms of **hypoglycemia** include confusion, drowsiness, pale complexion, perspiration, headache, lack of coordination, dizziness, trembling, and sudden hunger. If the child exhibits these symptoms, the teacher should provide sugar immediately. If the child does not improve in 10 or 15 minutes, medical help should be sought (Olefsky, 1988).

hypoglycemia low blood sugar

Cancer

Although **cancer** in children is rare, it is the chief cause of death from disease in children aged four to ten (Lammers, 1991). Cancer refers to a variety of diseases that involve the disorderly and uncontrolled growth of cells in the body. The common cancer warning signs for children are

cancer characterized by disorderly and uncontrolled growth of cells in the body

nausea, weight loss, double vision, swelling, stumbling, nosebleeds, drowsiness, and listlessness. Cancers that occur in children tend to grow more quickly than in adults. The most common forms of cancer that affect children are cancers of the blood, bone, brain, nervous system, and kidney.

leukemia most frequent form of cancer in children

The most frequent form of cancer in children is **leukemia**, a cancer of the blood-forming tissues. White blood cells, which usually protect the body from disease, are not able to function properly, and the child gets sick and bleeds easily. Cancers of the nervous system are the second most common cancers in children. These cancers, known as **neuroblastomas**, are most commonly found in the adrenal glands located above the kidneys. Another form of childhood cancer you may encounter is a form of bone cancer called **osteogenic sarcoma**. It usually develops in the forearm or lower leg. The limb swells and the child may have difficulty using the arm or leg. Still another of the common childhood cancers are **brain tumors**. Typically, brain tumors cause symptoms very early in the disease such as blurred or double vision, dizziness, difficulty walking or handling objects, and unexplained nausea. As a classroom teacher, you may also teach students who suffer from **lymphomas**, or cancers that involve the lymph nodes. These lymphomas may cause swelling of the lymph nodes in the neck, armpit, and groin. They are often accompanied by a general weakness and fever.

neuroblastoma second most common cancer in children; found in adrenal glands

osteogenic sarcoma form of childhood cancer located in the bone

brain tumor symptoms include blurred or double vision, dizziness, difficulty walking, and nausea

lymphoma cancers which involve the lymph nodes

AIDS

AIDS acquired immunodeficiency syndrome which interferes with the body's immune system leading to chronic and fatal infections

The virus that causes acquired immunodeficiency syndrome (**AIDS**) interferes with the body's immune system, leaving the individual vulnerable to chronic and often fatal infections. As we indicated in Chapter 3, the disease can be transmitted through intimate sexual contact with an AIDS patient or carrier of the virus, through transfusions of the blood from patients or carriers, through other exchanges of blood as in the cases of transmissions in which an infected individual bites someone else, and from contaminated hypodermic needles.

Recent research suggests that central nervous system involvement is a prominent clinical finding in children with HIV (Rudigier et al., 1990). Because of this, teachers can expect to see global developmental delay, loss of previously achieved milestones, cognitive disorders, motor function abnormalities, spasticity, sensory impairment, and acquired microencephaly in students who are HIV infected. In addition, it is expected that the virus will become the leading infectious cause of mental retardation and developmental disability in children (Rudigier et al., 1990).

Both the U.S. Surgeon General and the National Academy of Sciences have called for widespread educational programs to prevent an epidemic of AIDS. As a classroom teacher, you should know that such education is controversial because it involves sex education and because fear of the disease has created pressure to exclude infected

Connections

The Internet can provide many useful resources relative to the topics covered in this chapter. Try searching for additional information on learning disabilities and giftedness by consulting the Council for Exceptional Children Web site at <http://www.cec.sped.org/>. The following Web site contains valuable information about dyslexia: <www.interdys.org>

children and adults from the classroom. As children born with AIDS continue to survive longer, we will see an increasing need for special educational services to accommodate the variety of cognitive, behavioral, and neurological conditions that accompany AIDS. Some of these considerations may include psychotic behavior, mental retardation, seizures, and neurological impairments similar to cerebral palsy. Teachers should be aware that "there is no serious concern regarding HIV infection in the setting of usual developmental services" (Rudigier et al., 1990, p. 28). In fact, most states now have policies concerning the education of children with AIDS in regular classrooms (Katsiyannis, 1992).

SENSORY IMPAIRMENTS

As full inclusion becomes increasingly popular, you will encounter more students who suffer from a variety of sensory impairments. The most common of these are hearing and vision problems. It is important to remember that you as the teacher can do a variety of things to facilitate the learning of these students.

◆ Hearing Impairment

Because educators are primarily concerned with how much the hearing loss is likely to affect the child's ability to speak and develop language, they categorize hearing loss on the basis of spoken language abilities. From this standpoint, **hearing impairment** is defined as a generic term indicating a hearing disability that may range from mild to profound, including the subsets of deaf and hard of hearing. A **deaf** person is defined as one whose hearing disability precludes successful processing of linguistic information through audition, with or without a hearing aid. A **hard of hearing** person is one who, with the use of a hearing aid, has residual hearing sufficient to enable successful processing of linguistic information through audition (Brill, MacNeil, & Newman, 1986). Educators are concerned with the age of onset of hearing loss because the earlier the hearing loss occurs in a child's life, the more difficulty the child will have in developing the language of the hearing society. Thus, the term **congenitally deaf** is used to describe those who were born deaf, while the **adventitiously deaf** are those who acquired deafness some time after birth.

It is important for classroom teachers to understand some of the typical psychological and behavioral characteristics that result from a hearing impairment. The most affected area of development for the hearing impaired is the comprehension and production of the English language. Teachers report that 23 percent of students who are hearing impaired have unintelligible speech, 22 percent have speech that is barely intelligible, and 10 percent are unwilling to speak in public. Of course, those students with less severe hearing loss are more likely to possess intelligible speech (Wolk & Schildroth, 1986). There is much disagreement, though, as to whether children with hearing impairments

hearing impairment having a hearing loss significant enough to require special education or training; term includes both deaf and hard-of-hearing persons

deaf hearing that is impaired enough so that other channels or senses, usually sight, are used to communicate

hard of hearing a term describing those individuals with sufficient hearing potential (with hearing aids) to process linguistic information through audition

congenitally deaf refers to those who were born deaf

adventitiously deaf those who acquire deafness sometime after birth

American Sign Language (ASL) a manual language, used by people who are deaf, to communicate a true language with its own grammar

oral approach approach for aiding the deaf which includes hearing aids and speech reading

manual approach approach in which finger spelling is used to aid the deaf, or representing letters of the alphabet by finger positions

visual impairment a difficulty in clearly distinguishing forms or discriminating details by sight at a specified distance, resulting in the need for special methods and materials

are cognitively deficit. We cannot assume that a deficiency in spoken language is synonymous with a deficiency in cognition nor that persons who are deaf cannot speak, because if they use **American Sign Language (ASL)**, they are using a true language with its own rules of grammar. Furthermore, any assessment of intelligence should involve a performance test, rather than a verbal test, which is also administered in sign for a fair assessment of intelligence.

However, we do know that most children who are hearing impaired have extreme deficits in academic achievement, particularly in the area of reading. Recent studies have shown that the growth in reading achievement for students who are deaf is about one-third of that experienced by hearing students (Allen, 1986; Wolk & Allen, 1984). Frequently, students who are hearing impaired graduate from high school able to read only at the fourth or fifth grade level. Interestingly, students who are hearing impaired who have parents who are hearing impaired are more likely to be better readers. Lane (1992) hypothesizes that this may be because these parents are more likely to use American Sign Language and ASL aids students with hearing impairments in learning how to read. In addition to academic difficulties, children with hearing impairment are also at heightened risk for social maladjustment. Because these children often face difficulty finding others with whom they can communicate, children who are deaf are at risk for loneliness (Charlson, Strong, & Gold, 1992). Even in mainstream settings, children who are deaf often have difficulty finding others they can communicate with, due to the low incidence of this disability (Stinson & Whitmire, 1992). Currently, the majority of educators favor the use of both **oral** and **manual methods** for students who are hearing impaired (Hallahan & Kauffman, 1997).

See the tool box for several specific teaching techniques to try when using lecture and discussion formats. These approaches should help teachers such as Mrs. Simon in our initial scenario to facilitate the learning of students with hearing impairments.

◆ Visual Impairment

As with the case of hearing impairments, there is an educational definition of **visual impairments**, which stresses the method of reading instruction. For educational purposes, individuals who are blind are so severely impaired they must learn to read either by using **Braille** (a system of raised dots by which blind people read with their fingertips) or aural methods such as audiotapes or records. Those individuals who can read print with the use of magnifying devices or large-print

Teacher Tool Box

Teaching Students with Hearing Impairments

1. Position yourself so that your face is illuminated, even when showing slides or filmstrips;
2. Use an overhead projector to convey major points of emphasis so that you are able to face your students as you speak;
3. Provide lecture notes or outlines;
4. Avoid moving around the room or turning your back to students;
5. Shorten and simplify directions;
6. Repeat main points;
7. Repeat questions and answers given by other students;
8. Provide summaries throughout the lecture or discussion;
9. Use nonverbal cues such as facial expression, body movements, or gestures;
10. Signal changes in topics within a lecture or discussion;
11. Require students to raise hands to reduce confusion and noise when several students are talking at once;
12. Monitor student comprehension of instruction often.

books are referred to as having low vision. The major signs indicative of a vision problem are summarized in Table 4.5.

There are several psychological and behavioral characteristics unique to students with visual impairments. Although lack of vision is not believed to significantly alter the ability to use and understand language, children with visual impairments do develop somewhat differently when compared to sighted children (Warren, 1984). For instance, sighted children tend more to use language that refers to activities in their visual experience involving other people and objects, whereas students with visual impairments use language that is more self-centered. Comparing the intellectual ability of sighted students with those who are visually impaired is problematic because finding comparable intelligence tests is nearly impossible. While verbal IQ tests continue to be used, there is a growing argument to employ intelligence tests that measure spatial and tactile abilities as these abilities have a direct bearing on how students with visual impairments are able to navigate their environment and read Braille. While studies comparing the academic achievements of students who are visually impaired with those who are sighted must be interpreted with caution, some studies do suggest that children with low vision and those who are blind are behind their sighted peers (Rapp & Rapp, 1992). However, their academic achievement is not nearly as impaired as that of students who are hearing impaired.

Individuals who are blind are so severely impaired they must learn to read either by using Braille or aural methods such as audiotapes or records. ◆

Braille a system in which raised dots are used to allow blind people to "read" with their fingertips; consists of a quadrangular cell containing from one to six dots whose arrangement denotes different letters and symbols

---

Table 4.5   Signs Indicating Possible Eye Problems

BEHAVIOR
- ◆ Rubs eyes excessively;
- ◆ Shuts or covers one eye, tilts head, or thrusts head forward;
- ◆ Has difficulty in reading or in other work requiring close use of the eyes;
- ◆ Blinks more than usual or is irritable when doing close work;
- ◆ Holds books close to eyes;
- ◆ Is unable to see distant things clearly;
- ◆ Squints eyelids together or frowns.

APPEARANCE
- ◆ Crossed eyes;
- ◆ Red-rimmed, encrusted, or swollen eyelids;
- ◆ Inflamed or watery eyes;
- ◆ Recurring sties.

COMPLAINTS
- ◆ Eyes itch, burn, or feel scratchy;
- ◆ Cannot see well;
- ◆ Dizziness, headaches, or nausea following close eye work;
- ◆ Blurred or double vision.

Source: From D. Hallahan and J. M. Kaufman, *Exceptional Children: Introduction to Special Education,* Sixth Edition. Copyright © 1994 by Allyn & Bacon. Reprinted by permission.

Another unique behavioral characteristic of those who are visually impaired relates to mobility or skill in moving about one's environment. Mobility seems to depend a great deal upon spatial ability. While some students with visual impairments tend to use a sequential route to navigate their environment, others employ a map depicting the general relation of various points in the environment. The latter method, known as cognitive mapping, seems to be more effective because of its flexibility.

Now that we have considered some of the typical psychological and behavioral characteristics that accompany visual impairment, let's focus on modifications necessary to maximize the education of these students. First, we must consider the use of Braille. Although only 10 percent of those who are visually impaired are estimated to use Braille, there is a growing group of advocates in favor of this strategy (Mauler, 1991). They argue that technological devices such as tape recorders and computers cannot replace Braille, especially when taking notes for a class, reading a speech, or skimming a text. Many are also arguing that students with low vision be taught to use Braille so that they will be well prepared when their vision does worsen (Holbrook & Koenig, 1992). Second, large-print books and magnifying devices can be used to train students to best use what visual abilities they do have (Collins & Barraga, 1980). Third, developing good listening skills is essential for students who are visually impaired, especially with the advent of more recorded material (Swallow & Conner, 1982). It is not true that students who are blind spontaneously compensate through better listening skills. These must be taught. Fourth, mobility training involving the use of canes, guide dogs, human guides, and electronic devices is still another educational consideration since it enhances everyday living skills. Fifth, technological aids can be employed including the **Optacon** (a hand-held scanner that converts print to tactile letters that are felt on the index finger), the **VersaBraille** (which records Braille onto cassettes and plays them back), and the **Descriptive Video Service** (which makes television more accessible for the visually impaired).

The Teacher Tool Box includes several more specific teaching suggestions you will find helpful when working with students who are visually impaired. These all involve making adaptions to instructional, materials, approaches, or the classroom environment.

Teacher Tool Box

Teaching Students with Visual Impairments

1. Consider using the following list of tactile and raised materials;
   a. In geography: Braille atlases, molded plastic relief maps, relief globes;
   b. In math: abacus, raised clockfaces, geometric shapes, Braille rulers, talking calculators
   c. In writing: raised checkbooks, signature guides;
   d. Other areas: Braille or large-type answer sheets, sports-field kit, which includes raised drawings of various sports playing fields, and audible goal indicators used as warning devices.
2. When using written materials use typed, rather than handwritten materials; use materials that provide high contrast such as black lettering on nongloss white paper; arrange written materials on a page so that they are not crowded; use only one side of the paper; keep chalkboards clean; and write with only white or yellow to highlight the contrast.
3. Provide a notebook that contains vital information displayed in the classroom, such as assignments, bulletin board announcements, classroom rules, word lists, and pictures.
4. Provide first-hand experiences, such as concrete materials and hands-on learning, to enrich the learning of students who are visually impaired.
5. Transfer instructional materials to tape recordings.
6. Provide an orientation to the physical arrangement of your classroom and school, and keep students who are visually impaired informed of any changes to their physical surroundings.
7. Make sure appropriate lighting is available. Natural lighting should come from behind or to the side of the student, and a lamp should be used to illuminate the workplace, if appropriate.

STUDENTS WITH COMMUNICATIVE DISORDERS

It is important to recognize that some of your students will have speech and language problems that are unrelated to cognitive disability or sensory handicaps. **Communicative disorders** are relatively prevalent compared to the other categories of exceptionality, with federal estimates of over one million children receiving services for these disorders in 1990—more than one-fourth of all those in special education (Hallahan & Kauffman, 1994).

While the terms *language*, *speech*, and *communication* are often used to mean the same thing, each of these terms has a very specific meaning teachers need to keep in mind. Table 4.6 describes the definitions of speech and language disorders as well communicative variations put forth by the American Speech-Language-Hearing Association.

Optacon a device used to enable persons who are blind to "read"; consists of a camera that converts print into an image of letters, which are then produced by way of vibration onto the finger

VersaBraille a device used to record Braille onto tape cassettes that are played back on a reading board; the VersaBraille ii Plus is a laptop computer on which a person can type Braille that can be converted into print copies

Descriptive Video Service provides audio narrative of key visual elements; available for several public television programs; for use of people with visual impairment

communicative disorder an impairment in the ability to use speech or language to communicate

---

Table 4.6   Definitions of the American Speech-Language-Hearing Association

COMMUNICATIVE DISORDERS

A. A SPEECH DISORDER is an impairment of voice, articulation of speech sounds, and/or fluency. These impairments are observed in the transmission and use of the oral symbol system.

   1. A VOICE DISORDER is defined as the absence or abnormal production of voice quality, pitch, loudness, resonance, and/or duration.

   2. An ARTICULATION DISORDER is defined as the abnormal production of speech sounds.

   3. A FLUENCY DISORDER is defined as the abnormal flow of verbal expression, characterized by impaired rate and rhythm that may be accompanied by struggle behavior.

B. A LANGUAGE DISORDER is the impairment or deviant development of comprehension and/or use of a spoken, written, and/or other symbol system. The disorder may involve (1)the form of language (phonologic, morphologic, and syntactic systems), (2) the content of language (semantic system), and/or (3) the function of language in communication (pragmatic system) in any combination.

   1. Form of Language
      a. PHONOLOGY is the sound system of a language and the linguistic rules that govern the sound combinations.
      b. MORPHOLOGY is the linguistic rule system that governs the structure of words and the construction of word forms from the basic elements of meaning.
      c. SYNTAX is the linguistic rule governing the order and combination of words to form sentences, and the relationships among the elements within a sentence.
   2. Content of Language
      a. SEMANTICS is the psycholinguistic system that patterns the content of an utterance—the intent and meanings of words and sentences.
   3. Function of Language
      a. PRAGMATICS is the sociolinguistic system that patterns the use of language in communication, which may be expressed motorically, vocally, or verbally.

(continued)

Table 4.6 Definitions of the American Speech-Language-Hearing Association *(Continued)*

COMMUNICATIVE VARIATIONS

A. COMMUNICATIVE DIFFERENCE/DIALECT is a variation of a symbol system used by a group of individuals that reflects and is determined by shared regional, social, or cultural/ethnic factors. Variations or alterations in the use of a symbol system may be indicative of primary language interferences. A regional, social, or cultural/ethnic variation of a symbol system should not be considered a disorder of speech or language.

B. AUGMENTATIVE COMMUNICATION is a system used to supplement the communicative skills of individuals for whom speech is temporarily or permanently inadequate to meet communicative needs. Both prosthetic devices and/or non-prosthetic techniques may be designed for individual use as an augmentative communication system.

Source: © American Speech-Language-Hearing Association. Reprinted by permission.

◆ Language Disorders

Language disorders are classified according to the following criteria or subsystems of language: **phonology** (sounds), **morphology** (word forms), **syntax** (word order and sentence structure), **semantics** (word and sentence meaning), and **pragmatics** (social use of language). Although difficulty with one of these dimensions is nearly always accompanied by trouble in another one, some children have particular difficulty with one of these areas. A second method of classification is by comparison to the normal developmental schedule and sequence (Leonard, 1986). Some children with language disorders follow the same sequence of development as most other children, but achieve each language milestone at a later age. Now that we've considered how language disorders are classified, let's focus on some of the most common ones you'll encounter in the classroom. Some students will have an absence of verbal language. They may make noises, but they will communicate as infants and toddlers do, using prelinguistic communication. Another type of language disorder you may see is the child who can make speech sounds with no difficulty and acquire an extensive oral vocabulary. The way they use words, though, is very different, in that some of them will repeat in a parrotlike form what they have heard while others will speak jargon or nonsense words that fail to meet the demands of social situations. Still other children with language disorders will be language delayed. And still others will experience interrupted language development due to an illness or an accident that has damaged the brain, sometimes called acquired aphasia.

◆ Speech Disorders

Grouped under the category of **speech disorders** are a number of specific problems. Voice disorders involve characteristics of pitch, loudness,

---

language disorder a lag in the ability to understand and express ideas that puts linguistic skill behind an individual's development in other areas, such as motor, cognitive, or social development

phonology the study of the sound system of a language and the structure of those sounds

morphology the study within psycholinguistics of word formation; of how adding or deleting parts of words changes their meaning

syntax word order and sentence structure

semantics the study of the meanings attached to words

pragmatics refers to the social use of language

speech disorder oral communication that involves abnormal use of the vocal apparatus, is unintelligible, or so inferior that it draws attention to itself and causes anxiety, feelings of inadequacy, or inappropriate behavior in the speaker

and quality that may harm the larynx, hamper communication, or stand in marked contrast to what is customary for a given sex, age, and cultural background. Some of these voice disorders may stem from a dysfunction in the oral and nasal air passageways, which may be caused by conditions such as cleft palate or nerve damage (Love, 1992). Other students with speech disorders suffer from articulation disorders, which involve errors in producing words. Here, word sounds may be omitted, substituted, distorted, or added. One example of this is lisping or the substitution or distortion of the sound "s." Still other children you will work with have a disorder of fluency. This involves interruptions in the flow of speech that are so frequent that they keep the speaker from being understood. The most frequent form of this problem is **stuttering** which affects about 1 percent of the population (Andrews et al., 1983). While this is usually detectable between ages two and five, many children quickly outgrow stuttering; however, early diagnosis and intervention is critical. Still other speech disorders involve abnormalities of the mouth and face such as those of the tongue, lips, nasal passages, ears, teeth, gums, and palate. The most common of these problems is **cleft lip** or a split in the upper part of the oral cavity or upper part of the lip. Other speech disorders are associated with neurological damage to muscles that control breathing, the larynx, throat, tongue, jaw, or lips. These may result in difficulty articulating speech sounds or in selecting or sequencing speech.

Now that we've described the most frequently observed problems students have with regard to language and speech disorders, it's time to consider how to help these students in the classroom as described in the Teacher Tool Box.

stuttering speech characterized by abnormal hesitations, prolongations, and repetitions; may be accompanied by grimaces, gestures, or other bodily movements indicative of a struggle to speak, anxiety, blocking of speech, or avoidance of speech

cleft lip condition in which there is a rift or split in the upper part of the oral cavity or the upper lip

STUDENTS WITH EMOTIONAL/BEHAVIORAL DISORDERS

It is certainly not unusual for a child to act in ways that disrupt the classroom as in the opening scene of this chapter. Such disruptions are often quite typical, even normal and are easily managed by good classroom management (see Chapter 10). However, children who display serious and persistent age-inappropriate behaviors that result in social conflict, personal unhappiness, and school failure may be classified as behaviorally disordered students (Kirk & Gallagher, 1989). A quick perusal of the You Make the Call may clarify this distinction.

Teacher Tool Box

Techniques for Working with Students with Communicative Disorders

1. Provide appropriate language models for students by reading stories to them, making audiotapes of content available, and showing videotapes related to what you are teaching.

2. Plan how you will positively reinforce students' attempts at appropriate language so that you can shape successive approximations of the final language behavior. Once again, using models of appropriate language will be helpful.

3. Ensure that all students have opportunities to use listening and language skills. In one format of cooperative learning, each student in a four-person group receives a number, one through four. After posing a question, the teacher asks students to put their heads together to be certain that each person in the group knows the answer and can explain it. The teacher then calls one number, indicating that students with only this number may raise their hands to answer. This structure facilitates the participation of all group members.

4. Offer scaffolding to assist students in being active participants in language. Scaffolding consists of procedures such as prompts, questions, and restatements. These prompts communicate that more information is needed and the type of information that is required. Giving students a chance to paraphrase their understanding of a concept or pointing to a visual cue as a student formulates an answer are further examples of scaffolding.

5. Encourage nondisabled classmates to talk to those with communication disorders as much as possible and reinforce them for doing so.

WHEN AGGRESSION GOES BEYOND NORMAL BOUNDARIES

Tony and Edward, two ninth grade students, got into a bit of a shouting match when Tony accidentally bumped Edward in the hall during the change of class. While there was some initial pushing and name calling, the situation was quickly quelled when Mr. Hanson, the disciplinarian, approached. The incident is not that unusual and is probably encountered daily by most high school teachers. And while Tony was a bit annoyed, he was able to compose himself and begin to move to his next class. For Edward, moving on was not an easy task. As Tony began to walk toward class, Edward grabbed the large metal fire extinguisher off the wall and began to run toward Tony in an attempt to hit him in the head. It took a number of teachers to wrestle Edward to the ground. All the while he was cursing, spitting, and attempting to bite whoever was close by.

Anger, under some circumstances, is a normal human emotion. Most ninth grade students have developed the ability to control their anger and to release it in acceptable ways. For some, like Edward, anger is an uncontrollable emotion and their anger response can prove extremely harmful to themselves and others.

◆ Defining Emotional/Behavioral Disorders

While there has been much debate about the terminology to use in a definition of students with **emotional or behavioral disorders,** the following three criteria seem to be common across all definitions. These include behavior that goes to the extreme, a problem that is chronic or does not quickly disappear, and behavior that is unacceptable due to social and cultural norms. What follows is the federal definition of "seriously emotionally disturbed" contained in IDEA (Bower, 1981).

(I) One or more of the following characteristics over a long period of time, which adversely affects academic performance:

a. An inability to learn that cannot be explained by intellectual, sensory, or health factors;
b. An inability to build or maintain satisfactory relationships with peers and teachers;
c. Inappropriate types of behavior or feelings under normal circumstances;
d. A general pervasive mood of unhappiness or depression;
e. A tendency to develop physical symptoms or fears associated with personal or school problems.

(II) The term also includes children who are **schizophrenic** or **autistic,** but does not include those who are socially maladjusted unless it is determined that they are seriously emotionally disturbed.

However, a second definition proposed by the National Mental Health and Special Education Coalition in 1990 may be soon be incor-

emotional or behavioral disorder a handicapping condition in which people have difficulty controlling their feelings and behavior

schizophrenia characterized by psychotic behavior manifested by loss of contact with reality, bizarre thought processes, and inappropriate actions

autism a disorder characterized by extreme withdrawal, self-stimulation, cognitive deficits, language disorders, and onset before the age of thirty months

porated into the federal definition. Its key components are as follows:

(I) Behavioral or emotional responses so different from appropriate age, cultural, or ethnic norms that they adversely affect educational performance including academic, social, vocational, and personal skills. Such a disability

a. is more than a temporary, expected response to stressful events;
b. is consistently exhibited in two different settings, at least one of which is school-related; and
c. is unresponsive to direct intervention in general education, or the child's condition is such that general education interventions would be insufficient.

(II) Emotional and behavioral disorders can co-exist with other disabilities.

(III) This category may include those with schizophrenic, anxiety, and affective disorders as well as other sustained disorders of conduct or adjustment which adversely adversely affect educational performance.

The latter definition is, of course, more inclusive of the full range of emotional and behavioral disorders that teachers encounter. It also acknowledges that disorders of emotion and behavior can either occur separately or in combination, and that youth can have multiple disabilities.

Although data published by the U.S. Department of Education show that only about 1 percent of school children in the United States are "seriously emotionally disturbed," recent research studies have indicated that at least 6 to 10 percent of school-aged youths suffer from persistent emotional/behavioral problems (Brandenburg, Friedman, & Silver, 1990; Kaufman, 1993). The causes of emotional or behavioral disorders are not clearly understood but have been identified as involving biological disorders and diseases, pathological family relationships, negative cultural influences, and undesirable experiences at school. It is safe to assume that it is usually several of these factors, not only one, that are contributing causes to the given behavior.

Teacher Tool Box

Working with Children Exhibiting Emotional/Behavioral Disorders

1. For students with conduct disorders, emphasize classroom rules and use positive reinforcement when these rules are followed. Demonstrate and model these rules to allow plenty of time for students to practice them until they are mastered. Try to remove as many distractions as possible from these students; you could even ask several peers around them to ignore their disruptive behaviors and attend to positive behaviors. Avoid using sarcasm, ridicule, or force with these students.

2. For students with either emotional and behavioral disorders, use a step-by-step process to manage student behaviors such as the one listed below (Lewis & Doorlag, 1990):
   a. State the behavioral expectations for all students in the class;
   b. Determine whether students who meet these expectations are receiving reinforcement so they will continue to meet the expectations;
   c. If there are students who do not meet the expectations, determine whether they understand the expectations and whether they have the needed skills to perform the behaviors;
   d. For students who use inappropriate behaviors, identify a specific behavior to change;
   e. Decide how you will observe and gather information on this behavior;
   f. After reviewing the information you have gathered, determine whether the behavior needs to be increased, decreased, or learned;
   g. Choose a positive, strategy; not punishing,
   h. While using the strategy, collect information on the student's behavior;
   i. Review the information to decide if the strategy should be continued, modified, or stopped;
   j. When the student performs the behavior at the desired level, continue to monitor the behavior and turn to step "d" if there are other behaviors at issue.

3. Try using the Premack principle or contracting with students in order to increase the frequency of a desired behavior.

4. Combine the use of punishment, such as time out, with the use of positive reinforcement to affect a decrease in the frequency of a behavior.

Given the complexity of behavioral/emotional disorders, you may be wondering what the classroom teacher could do besides be a source of early identification. Several ideas for practice are listed in the tool box on page 151.

◆ Implications for the Classroom Teacher

Classroom teachers are neither trained nor expected to serve as therapists for students with severe behavioral or emotional problems. However, the classroom teacher can serve as an excellent early-identification source. As such, it is important that the classroom teacher learn to recognize student behaviors that are excessive and may indicate the need for special assistance.

While there are a number of specific diagnostic categories of emotional and behavioral disorder as identified by the American Psychiatric Association, a discussion of these and the defining criteria are well beyond the scope of this chapter. One approach to conceptualizing these disorders was presented by Drabman and Patterson (1981) and involved responses that were externalized and those that were internalized. This model can be a useful framework from which to present a number of the behaviors that should alert the classroom teacher.

Externalized

externalizing dimension dimension of emotional/behavior disorder characterized by aggressive, acting-out behavior

conduct disorder a disorder characterized by overt, aggressive, disruptive behavior or covert antisocial acts such as stealing, lying, and fire setting; may include both overt and covert acts

The child who appears to exhibit an **externalized dimension** of an emotional/behavioral disorder is characterized by aggressive, acting-out behavior. Students identified as having a **conduct disorder**, for example, fall within this category and exhibit aggressive, hostile, destructive behaviors. These students may consistently engage in hitting, fighting, teasing, yelling, or simply refusing to comply with requests. It is not unusual for these children to exhibit destructiveness and vandalism. When combined with school failure, aggressive, antisocial behavior in childhood is correlated strongly with future social adjustment and mental health problems, especially for males.

Internalized

internalizing dimension dimension of emotional/behavior disorder characterized by immaturity, anxiety, and depression

While the overt aggression and hostility exhibited by the child externalizing an emotional disorder will certainly draw adult attention and emphasize the special needs of that child, the child who internalizes emotional problems, while drawing less attention, is equally in need of special assistance. Students fitting into this **internalized dimension** often appear immature, anxious, withdrawn, and even depressed.

Reflections from the Field

1 We have found it helpful to use photo albums with sticky backings and plastic cover sheets to help students with physical disabilities hold onto their instructional materials.

—Ron (fourth grade teacher), Coatesville, PA

2 As a guidance counselor, I designed a program in which all of our middle schoolers now carry a multisubject notebook so they have one place to put all of their papers and assignments. While this has especially helped our students with learning disabilities, it aids all of our students and does not single out those with special needs.

—Karen (middle school guidance counselor), Wilmington, DE

3 I've found it useful to teach our kids with communication disorders how to use language in social situations. For instance, how to begin and end a conversation, give information, make a request, and take turns. This is what they need in the real world.

—Suzanne (second grade teacher), Boyertown, PA

4 After much positive reinforcement and shaping, I make an effort to use the work of newly included students as a model for the rest of the class to follow. I have even been able to do this with some of the work done by students with mental retardation. This helps the other kids see that their new classmates are capable after all.

—Linda (junior high special education teacher), Downingtown, PA

5 With gifted students, I've found the Jigsaw method of cooperative learning to work well. This method requires students to become experts on a given topic and then return to their own group and teach others about the topic.

—Rick (senior high math teacher), West Chester, PA

THEORY TO PRACTICE

A Look at Teacher as Decision Maker, Addressing Students' Unique Needs

Recall the initial scene described in this chapter. Mrs. Simon was confronted with the reality of teaching students with a variety of special needs and exceptionalities. Many of the students in her class spoke only Spanish. Some of her students appeared almost gifted whereas others were clearly over their heads academically. But perhaps her biggest challenge was in addressing the unique needs of two of the students. These were two males who made their grand appearance well after the bell and attempted to threaten Mrs. Simon if she recorded them as tardy. Certainly, these students had unique social-emotional needs, and their presence in her class would clearly be a challenge.

Perhaps Mrs. Simon questioned why some of these students were her responsibility or perhaps she understood that increasingly exceptional students were being helped to learn in environments that are minimally restrictive. Regardless of her reaction, Mrs. Simon, like all teachers, needed to understand the legislation that has formed the basis for how schools deal with such issues, including Public Law 94-142, the Individuals with Disabilities Education Act (IDEA), and the Americans with Disabilities Act (ADA), and the implications this legislation has for the classroom teacher. In addition to understanding her responsibilities, Mrs. Simon would also need to understand the unique learning characteristics of these exceptional students so that she could adapt this classroom environment and its learning activities to maximize their learning.

We could envision Mrs. Simon critically thinking and reflecting as to how to make adjustments to her classroom and her teaching style as a way to accommodate the unique needs of her students. For those with learning disabilities she could divide their work up into smaller, more manageable pieces, providing frequent feedback as they worked. She could encourage the gifted students to reach beyond the standard curriculum with enrichment activities and independent research. For the student who is hearing impaired, she could be sure to use nonverbal cues and gestures to signal important points during class discussion. And for the students who threatened and challenged her authority, she could employ clear structure and cues for appropriate behavior and implement strategies of assertive discipline (see Chapter 10).

You, as Teacher, as Decision Maker, Addressing Your Students' Unique Needs

In the following case presentations, you are provided with a description of a number of salient characteristics of the school, classroom, and the students. In reviewing these illustrations, try to apply your knowledge in order to

1. Identify the probable exceptionality present,
2. Suggest the next steps that should be taken, and
3. Recommend at least three strategies that will help.

As you review the scenario, consider how the research on learning disabilities as well as the suggestions provided in the teacher tool boxes throughout the chapter provide insight and direction for a teacher concerned about helping these students learn.

Case Illustration 1:
Boxtown Junior High

Your School

Boxtown Junior High School is located in a small, but growing, suburban area. The majority of the school population comes from middle and upper-middle income families. Recently, the community has debated about whether to build a new junior high school building or add on to the current building to accommodate its growing student body.

Your Class

Your class is a self-contained fifth grade class with twenty-one male and eight female students. The students are heterogeneously grouped; you have been informed that most class members are reading at or above grade level.

Your Student

One student, although you are sure she is "smart as a whip," is of special concern to you. She has the handwriting of a first grader, makes bizarre spelling errors, and reverses letters while copying and reading aloud. The principal assures you that this child does not require further testing because the discrepancy between her IQ score and achievement is only about 1.5 years. However, each day you observe that this student seems to be getting more and more frustrated with academic assignments.

Case Illustration 2:
Carleton Elementary

In reviewing the next scenario, consider how the information provided on students with physical challenges may provide insight and direction for a teacher concerned with helping a special student.

Your School

The Carleton Elementary Intermediate Unit is a facility designed for students with severe physical challenges. It is part of a growing district that has recently experienced some financial difficulties.

Your Class

You are teaching a self-contained class of eight students who have a variety of physical challenges. These challenges include cerebral palsy, epilepsy, and head traumas. Two classroom aides are available to assist students throughout the school day in your classroom.

Your Student

One of your students has been diagnosed with cerebral palsy. Although he requires much physical assistance, you have noticed that his academic work is head and shoulders above what other students in the intermediate unit are doing. In fact, you have observed that he is unusually creative and extremely persistent in completing academic tasks. However, you are concerned that he is becoming bored in your classroom.

SUMMARY

Responding to the Educational Needs of Exceptional Students

The way in which public schools serve the needs of exceptional students is rooted heavily in legislation. The landmark legislation that revolutionized the treatment of exceptional students in public schools was the Education for All Handicapped Children Act, Public Law 94-142. This was the first federal law mandating a free, appropriate education for children with disabilities.

Full Inclusion versus a Continuum of Service

PL 94-142 has mandated that students with disabilities be placed in the least restrictive environment (LRE). The intent of this aspect of the law is that each child should be in a setting that is as normal and in as much of the mainstream of education as possible.

More recently the movement has been to full inclusion, the basic components of which are

1. Students would attend the school to which they would go to if they had no disability.

2. No student should be rejected from a school site because of type or extent of the disability presented.

3. No self-contained classes should operate at the school site; instead placements should be age and grade appropriate.

4. Cooperative learning and peer instructional methods should receive significant use in fully inclusive general education classrooms.

5. Special education support should be provided in the context of the general education classroom and in other integrated environments.

Including Children with Exceptional Intelligence

Researchers define intelligence as the capacity to acquire knowledge, the ability to think and reason in the abstract, and the capability for solving problems. Early researchers believed intelligence was a general or unitary trait because scores on diverse measures of intelligence including verbal ability, numerical competence, and abstract reasoning were all highly correlated. A number of contemporary theories (e.g., Guilford's structure of intellect, Gardner's theory of multiple intelligences and Sternberg's triarchic theory of intelligence) support the notion of multiple intelligence.

Mental Retardation

Perhaps the most widely accepted definition of mental retardation is that provided by the American Association of Mental Retardation (AAMR).

> Mental retardation refers to substantial limitations in present functioning. It is characterized by significantly subaverage intellectual functioning, existing concurrently with related limitations in two or more of the following applicable adaptive skills areas: communication, self-care, home living, social skills, community use, self-direction, health and safety, functional academics, leisure and work. Mental retardation manifests before age 18. (AAMR Ad Hoc Committee on Terminology and Classification, 1992, p. 5)

A number of specific organic (i.e., biological/physical) causes of mental retardation have been identified. These include chromosomal anomalies, inherited diseases, the result of maternal infection with rubella, herpes simplex, or syphilis during pregnancy; maternal drug or alcohol use during pregnancy; maternal and fetal blood type incompatibility (Rh factor), and any trauma at birth that may significantly deplete oxygen supply to the child's brain.

Gifted and Talented Students

Children have traditionally been labeled gifted if they fall in the top 3 percent of scores on intelligence tests. However, there have been recent calls to expand the definition of giftedness beyond IQ test performance.

Recent research has identified three characteristics that are predictive of remarkable achievements later in life. These characteristics are becoming widely accepted criteria for identification of the gifted:

1. High ability, including high intelligence;
2. High creativity or the ability to formulate new ideas and apply them to the solution of problems;
3. High task commitment or a high level of motivation and the ability to see a project through to its completion.

Specific Learning Disabilities

There are four major criteria to consider that must be present for a diagnosis in this category (U.S. Department of Education, 1977):

1. A discrepancy between IQ and achievement;
2. Learning problems in reading, writing, math, or speaking;
3. Learning problems that are not due to mental retardation, visual or hearing impairments, environmental disadvantages, or an emotional disturbance;
4. Learning problems that are due to a central nervous system dysfunction.

Students with Physical Challenges and Chronic Health Problems

Damage to or deterioration of the central nervous system is one of the most common causes of physical disabilities such as cerebral palsy, epilepsy, and spina bifida. In addition to these neurological impairments, classroom teachers will also work with students who suffer from chronic diseases. Among the most frequently encountered are asthma, diabetes mellitus, and cancer (Lammers, 1991). Although not as common, a fourth chronic disease, acquired immune deficiency syndrome, or AIDS, needs to be considered.

Sensory Impairment

The most common of these are hearing and vision impairments. It is important to remember that you as the teacher can do a variety of things to help facilitate the learning of these students.

Hearing Impairment

Hearing impairment is defined as a generic term indicating a hearing disability that may range from mild to profound, including the subsets of deaf and hard of hearing. A deaf person is defined as one whose hearing disability precludes successful processing of linguistic information through audition, with or without a hearing aid. A hard of hearing person is one who, with the use of a hearing aid, has residual hearing sufficient to enable successful processing of linguistic information through audition.

Visual Impairment

For educational purposes, individuals who are blind are so severely impaired they must learn to read either by using Braille (a system of raised dots by which blind people read with their fingertips) or aural methods such as audiotapes or records. Those individuals who can read print with the use of magnifying devices or large-print books are referred to as having low vision.

Students with Communicative Disorders

Communicative disorders involve disorder in the use of language, speech, or communication.

Language is the communication of ideas from an arbitrary system of symbols used according to certain rules, which determine meaning. Thus, language could encompass the use of a spoken, written, or some other symbol system.

Speech is the forming and sequencing the sounds of oral language. However, it is important to recognize that American Sign Language does not involve speech sounds but is instead a manual language.

Communication refers to any process that transmits information such as language, speech, telephone, or computer. Augmentative communication is a supplemental aid for people with disabilities, which helps them communicate despite the presence of a physical impairment.

Students with Emotional/Behavioral Disorders

Children who display serious and persistent age-inappropriate behaviors that result in social conflict, personal unhappiness, and school failure may be classified as behaviorally disordered students.

The federal definition of "seriously emotionally disturbed" contained in IDEA, suggests:

(I) One or more of the following characteristics over a long period of time, which adversely affects academic performance:

    a. An inability to learn that cannot be explained by intellectual, sensory, or health factors;

    b. An inability to build or maintain satisfactory relationships with peers and teachers;

    c. Inappropriate types of behavior or feelings under normal circumstances;

    d. A general pervasive mood of unhappiness or depression;

    e. A tendency to develop physical symptoms or fears associated with personal or school problems.

(II) The term also includes children who are schizophrenic or autistic, but does not include those who are socially maladjusted unless it is determined that they are seriously emotionally disturbed.

However, a second definition proposed by the National Mental Health and Special Education Coalition in 1990 may be soon be incorporated into the federal definition. Its key components are as follows:

(I) Behavioral or emotional responses so different from appropriate age, cultural, or ethnic norms that they adversely affect educational performance including academic, social, vocational, and personal skills. Such a disability:

    a. is more than a temporary, expected response to stressful events;

    b. is consistently exhibited in two different settings, at least one of which is school-related; and

    c. is unresponsive to direct intervention in general education, or the child's condition is such that general education interventions would be insufficient.

(II) Emotional and behavioral disorders can co-exist with other disabilities.

(III) This category may include those with schizophrenic, anxiety, and affective disorders as well as other sustained disorders of conduct or adjustment which adversely affect educational performance.

◆ Field Experience Questions

If you are not yet teaching, another way that you can conduct action research is to collect a variety of different types of data about teachers and students as you observe classrooms. This could be accomplished by writing down detailed field notes of what you have observed, asking teachers and students interview questions, and recording the frequency and nature of certain behaviors. Below are a series of field experience questions related to topics covered in this chapter, that you can try to answer based on classroom observations.

Regular Education Initiative and Inclusion

Based on your observations, to what extent is the Regular Education Initiative (REI) being implemented?

1. Are any learners with disabilities included in the regular classroom for the entire school day? If so, learners with what types of disabilities are included? Is a special education teacher, in this case, also working in the regular classroom?

2. If learners with disabilities are not included in the regular classroom, ask why they are not. Are there plans to include them in the future?

Students Who Are Gifted and Talented

Try to make a record of the students you believe meet the criteria for giftedness. After repeated observations, check with the teacher to see if you were correct.

1. Does your teacher treat gifted students differently from nongifted students? If so, how?

2. Do the gifted students you observe seem to be benefiting from the type of instruction provided for them? Why or why not?

Students with Learning Disabilities

Shadow a student diagnosed with attention deficit disorder or dyslexia for a day. Try to answer the following questions.

1. What interventions are being used to facilitate the learning of this student? Are they consistent with those recommended in this chapter? If not, why not? How would you suggest modifying the education provided to the student?

2. How does the student you shadow seem to get along with other students in the classroom?

3. Does this student seem to be working up to potential? How can you tell?

◆ Key Terms

acceleration program
adventitiously deaf
AIDS
American Sign Language (ASL)
asthma
attention deficit disorder (ADD)
attention deficit hyperactivity
    disorder (ADHD)
autism
Braille
brain tumor
cancer
cerebral palsy
cleft lip
communicative disorder
conduct disorder
congenitally deaf
deaf
Descriptive Video Service
diabetes mellitus
Down syndrome
dyslexia
emotional/behavioral disorder
enrichment program

epilepsy
externalizing dimension
full inclusion
Gardner's multiple intelligences
gifted
Guilford's structure of intellect
hard of hearing
hearing impairment
hypoglycemia
hypoxia
IDEA
individualized transition plan
    (ITP)
internalizing dimension
language disorder
learning disability
least restrictive environment
leukemia
lymphoma
manual approach
mild retardation
morphology
neuroblastoma
Optacon

oral approach
osteogenic sarcoma
phonology
PL 94-142
pragmatics
Regular Education Initiative (REI)
revolving door model
schizophrenia
semantics
severe retardation
speech disorder
spina bifida
Stanford-Binet test
Sternberg's triarchic theory of
    intelligence
stuttering
syntax
transition programs for secondary
    students
VersaBraille
visual impairment
Wechsler test

◆ Additional Resources

Featherstone, H. (1980). *Life with a disabled child.* New York: Basic Books.

Hallahan, D. P. (1992). Some thoughts on why the prevalence of learning disabilities has increased. *Journal of Learning Disabilities, 25(8),* 523–528.

Hallahan, D., & Kauffman, J. (1997). *Exceptional Children.* (7th ed.). Needham Heights, MA: Allyn & Bacon.

Luckasson, R., Coulter, P., Pollaway, E., et al. (1992). *Mental retardation: Definition, classification, and systems of supports.* Washington, DC: American Association of Mental Retardation.

Lynch, E. W., & Stein, R. (1982). Perspectives on parent participation in special education. *Exceptional Education Quarterly, 3(2),* 56–63.

Martin, S. S., Brady, M. P., & Kortarba, J. A. (1992). Families with chronically ill children: The unsinkable family. *Remedial and Special Education, 13(2),* 6–15.

Mims, A., Harper, C., Armstrong, S. W., & Savage, S. (1991). Effective instruction in homework for students with disabilities. *Teaching Exceptional Children, 24(1),* 42–47.

Vaughn, S., Bos, C., Harrell, J., & Lasky, B. (1988). Parent participation in the initial placement/IEP conference 10 years after mandated involvement. *Journal of Learning Disabilities, 21(2),* 82–89.

Student Diversity

1 n one of the opening scenes of the hit 1988 movie *Stand and Deliver*, the camera pans the campus outside of the high school. We see students walking to class, standing around, conversing with friends, standing in groups, standing alone. We see students with dark complexions, light complexions, tall students, short students, well-dressed students, not-so-well dressed students, smiling students, and students who are expressionless. As the scene shifts to the hallways and main office, we see further examples of variations and diversity. The camera moves next to Mr. Escalante's first classroom, where he looks out over a sea of students walking and standing, dark and light, well-dressed and not . . .

The scene depicted is different from those previously used to open our chapters. As you read it, you may have asked yourself, "Where's the action?" "Is there something important going on in this scene?" Actually, there is a lot of "action" in this scene and quite a bit of extremely important information for teachers.

In the previous chapters, we have discussed theory and research about students, teachers, and the teaching-learning process. Often this research presents findings that emphasize "commonalities" and "generalizations." While these are important, they can lead us to the conclusions that every classroom, every school, every teaching-learning experience is the same. A quick look at the students in Jaime Escalante's school will demonstrate that this is not the case. Of all the characteristics students may share, the one that serves as the focus for this chapter is their "uniqueness." Each student is certainly unique. Each class will be awash in diversity. As humans, we share much in common, and we have much that is unique, a point beautifully depicted in the following poem by Maya Angelou.

Human Family

I note the obvious differences
in the human family.
Some of us are serious,
some thrive on comedy.

Some declare their lives are lived
as true profundity,
and others claim they really live
the real reality.

The variety of our skin tones
can confuse, bemuse, delight,
brown and pink and beige and purple,
tan and blue and white.

I've sailed upon the seven seas
and stopped in every land,
I've seen the wonders of the world,
not yet one common man.

I know ten thousand women
called Jane and Mary Jane,
but I've not seen any two
who really were the same.

Mirror twins are different
although their features jibe,
and lovers think quite different thoughts
while lying side by side.

We love and lose in China,
we weep on England's moors,
and laugh and moan in Guinea,
and thrive on Spanish shores.

We seek success in Finland
are born and die in Maine.
In minor ways we differ,
in major we're the same.

I note the obvious differences
between each sort and type,
but we are more alike, my friends,
then we are unalike.

We are more alike, my friends,
than we are unalike.

We are more alike, my friends
than we are unalike.

Source: From *I Shall Not Be Moved* by Maya Angelou. Copyright © 1990 by Maya Angelou. Reprinted by permission of Random House, Inc.

Any effective teacher will tell you that children vary. They vary from each other and from the teacher. What's more, they may not vary in singular ways, but in any number of ways. The students may vary in terms of culture, learning style, language, gender, and socioeconomic status. This chapter will introduce you to individual variations you will encounter in your classrooms and will encourage you to view such diversity positively.

◆ Chapter Objectives

After reading this chapter you should be able to

1 Discuss the role of culture in shaping similarities and differences among individuals.

2 View race as an element of microcultural diversity.

3 Consider the educational implications of differences in students' cognitive styles.

4 Realize the complexities of teaching in a multilingual classroom.

5 Describe the sources of many gender differences.

6 Discuss the relationship between socioeconomic status and student achievement.

CHAPTER 5 CONTENT MAP

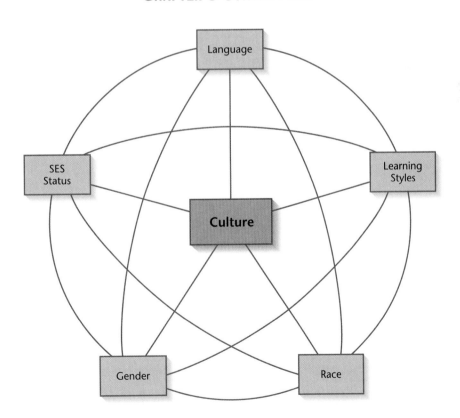

INCREASING DIVERSITY IN THE UNITED STATES

diversity ways in which students differ from each other and differ from their teacher

Let's back up a little—a previous statement needs reiteration: *You will encounter diversity in your classrooms.* Regardless of where you plan to teach, you will encounter student **diversity** in the ways described above. By all accounts, the demographics of the United States in general and in public schools in particular are changing (McNergney, 1988).

We can predict with some certainty that greater diversity will continue well into the next century. Population demographers have reported that in 1990, 20 million people in the United States were foreign born (Nieto, 1996); by 1992 almost one in every two districts had a more than 50% minority population (Nieto, 1996). Minority populations will continue to increase to nearly 50 million in 2026, while the Euro-Caucasian student population will decrease from 71% to 66% (Garcia, 1994). It has been estimated that by the turn of the century, at least six million students will have limited language proficiency in English (Garcia, 1994). At the same time, we see increased socioeconomic diversity and almost 40% of people living below the poverty line in the United States are children (Reed & Sutter, 1990).

DIFFERENCE: JUST THAT . . . DIFFERENCE!

As you look across your classroom, you will most likely be struck by the variations and differences presented by your students. Your class will most likely have boys and girls, some blonde, others dark, some of European lineage, others perhaps native to America, Asia, or Africa. Your students will represent many groups, and your class will reflect diversity. But the level of difference doesn't end with these groupings. Although it may be possible for you to group or cluster your students according to gender or ethnicity, you must be sensitive to the fact that no student can be adequately classified or described in one way only. The groups to which your students belong—the categories or variations identified—overlap! Two male, middle-class students in your class may share gender and socioeconomic groups, but they may bring dissimilar experiences to your classroom because of cultural, learning style, and language variations. Three of your students may be "brown-skinned" but may not represent the same cultural heritage (e.g., African-American, Caribbean-American, African immigrant), the same socioeconomic group, gender, learning styles, or language usage.

Regardless of where you plan to teach, you will encounter student diversity. The demographics of the United States and of public schools are changing. ◆

This chapter offers you a choice: You can choose to see student variation and diversity as a problem or an obstacle between you and your teaching career. Or you can choose to honor and celebrate diversity and see it not just as a

challenge, but as a resource to enrich both the content you teach and the methods you use. We hope you will choose the latter. The challenge for you will be to refrain from seeing differences as deficiencies, but to see them instead for what they are—differences!

CULTURAL DIVERSITY

◆ How Will Your Students Vary Culturally?

In an early scene from the movie *Stand and Deliver,* teacher Escalante is coaxing a student to attempt a response to a math question. The camera pans the faces of the other students, who are anxiously waiting. The student finally responds correctly. The teacher praises him and moves to the front of the room. He faces his students, most of whom are of Mexican and South American ancestry and tells them that their ancestors, the Mayans, were unique in their contemplation of the absence of value or "zero." He tells them that math is part of their heritage—"it's in their blood."

What happened here? Why did the teacher feel it was necessary to make those statements? Mr. Escalante was using a very intriguing vehicle for enhancing not only instruction, but his students' self-esteem and motivation as well. He used "cultural heritage." Students will vary from each other and from teachers culturally.

◆ Defining Culture

"Culture" is a broad and encompassing concept. Often, we equate culture with race or ethnic identity, but that is not always the case. The truth is that *within* racial or ethnic groups there can be cultural variations. Group membership can include racial identifications, but regardless of race it can vary further in terms of assumptions, values, language, religion, behavior, and symbols (O'Connor, 1988; Banks & Banks, 1989). Our membership in "teacher" groups (e.g., elementary or urban) or "student" groups (e.g., as juniors or low-achievers) or "age" groups (e.g., preschoolers or middle-aged adults) or "language" groups (e.g., American English users or Ebonics users) often transcends race and ensures distinctive, yet overlapping diversity in classrooms. Yes, culture is a broad and encompassing term that refers to

> characteristic[s] of [an] individual's society, or of some subgroups within this society . . . [it] includes values, beliefs, notions about acceptable and unacceptable behavior, and other socially constructed ideas that members of the culture are taught are "true" (Garcia, 1994; p. 51).

In short, culture governs how we think and feel, how we behave, and how we live—and it is born largely of socialization. We often recognize national cultures—we share American citizenship and, therefore, American cultural group membership. Or we may have friends or relatives elsewhere in the world who share a national (e.g., Venezuelan, Japanese, Ethiopian) culture. In fact, you may remember when you studied countries and national cultures around the world in elementary school where everyone dressed and ate food and sang songs representative of a

culture socialized influences that govern how we think, feel, behave, and live

particular part of the globe. But within shared national cultures, there may be additional group memberships and additional cultural elements. Even as Americans, our families may worship, dress, and enjoy food and music differently from other American families.

We are familiar with some elements of culture. Saville-Troike (cf. Taylor, 1988) lists several familiar cultural elements like religion, food, holidays and celebrations, dress, history and traditions, and art and music. We are less familiar with the fact that cultural diversity can manifest in our views of the life cycle (e.g., important life stages, periods, transitions), decorum and discipline (e.g., behavior at home and in public), health and hygiene (e.g., explanations of illness and death), values (e.g., important traits and attributes), work and play (e.g., behaviors considered "play" and "work"), and time and space (e.g., importance of punctuality) (cf. Taylor, 1988; p. 4). All could be elements of a shared national culture or of additional family cultures. Each element represents a varying and overlapping group or "world" to which our students—and we ourselves—belong (Davidson & Phelan, 1993).

So, with all of the groups and worlds and memberships and cultures, why do we even bother trying to incorporate "culture" into our instruction. Looking back at the movie scene that started this section, why did Mr. Escalante utilize the cultural element (i.e., heritage) in class? We need to keep in mind that our students' memberships in cultural groups significantly influence their lives both inside and outside of school (O'Connor, 1988; Phelan, Davidson, & Cao Yu, 1993). Therefore, like Mr. Escalante, we bother because honoring cultural diversity enhances classroom teaching and learning. We can have rich and distinctive classrooms via diversity, and cultural roots are wonderful sources of motivation for our students (Dunne, 1988). Effective teaching today is being defined more and more in terms of how we address diversity in general and cultural diversity in particular.

◆ Addressing Cultural Diversity

Assimilation and amalgamation theories. How do we address cultural diversity? Historically, educators and society have dealt with cultural diversity in one of three ways. Many educators adopted what Gordon described as the "Assimilation/Anglo" approach or the "Cultural Deficit" model (cf. Davidson & Phelan, 1993; p. 9). According to the **assimilation theory**, all students must conform to the rules of the Anglo-American group culture, regardless of their family culture or of the rules of other groups to which they belong; "Anglo" culture is superior to all others; differences are threatening and are rejected. Proponents of this view often equate "differences" from the shared national culture with student deficiencies—citing cultural differences as a significant reason why some children don't do well in school. In fact,

---

Teacher Tool Box

Teachers need to identify and accept elements beyond the traditional, Anglo cultural elements predominant in most schools. Exercise your critical thinking skills by asking yourself the following questions.

◆ What are the expectations for children in the student's family culture?

◆ What are the methods of discipline?

◆ What are the accepted forms of greeting in the student's family culture?

◆ How are feelings expressed?

◆ How is humor displayed?

---

assimilation theory all students must conform to the rules of the Anglo American group culture regardless of family culture or to the rules of the groups to which they belong

research has shown that the learning environments of culturally diverse homes are rich and stimulating (Davidson & Phelan, 1993).

Some educators adopted an "Amalgamation" approach to cultural diversity (Davidson & Phelan, 1993). The **amalgamation theory** is the "melting pot" approach in which elements of individual cultures are blended to become a "new," synthesized American culture (Davidson & Phelan, 1993). Cultural differences are ignored. Through the years, many of us have been comforted by the melting pot view of our society's institutions. But, it too has encouraged the loss of individual identity—a loss that has taken its toll on both self esteem and achievement.

Cultural pluralism. Currently, educators are encouraged to take a multicultural view, or "cultural pluralism," in which we attempt to address the elements of both shared national culture and individual and/or family culture together (Davidson & Phelan, 1993; Janzen, 1994). This is the "multiple group memberships" view described earlier in this section. Diversity is not feared or criticized or ignored; it is valued, even celebrated. Adler (cf. Janzen, 1994) noted that in **cultural pluralism:** "Every culture has its own internal coherence, integrity, and logic; No culture is inherently better of worse than another; and All persons are to some extent culturally bound" (p. 10). The effective teacher holds this view of diversity and incorporates beliefs about **multicultural education** as described in Figure 5.1.

amalgamation theory elements of individual culture are blended to become a new, synthesized culture

cultural pluralism education attempts to address both shared national culture and/or individual/family culture

multicultural education education in which a range of cultural perspectives are presented to students

Figure 5.1
Principles of Multicultural Education

	Principles of Multicultural Education
Principle No. 1	Multicultural education should take into consideration students' backgrounds and experiences or "what the students bring to class."
Principle No. 2	Multicultural education should facilitate intercultural dialogue between students, not polarize them.
Principle No. 3	Multicultural education should be a long-term, ongoing process, not a short-term event. It cannot be implemented effectively overnight.
Principle No. 4	Multicultural education, in the end, should be "integrative, comprehensive, and conceptual" (Appleton, 1983; p. 211). It should be incorporated into the entire curriculum.
Principle No. 5	Multicultural education should yield changes in instructional choices as well as in the curriculum.
Principle No. 6	Multicultural education should not be limited to cognitive objectives and activities, but should extend to affective and psychomotor learning in the classroom also.
Principle No. 7	Multicultural education should facilitate student learning and achievement. All areas and all levels of achievement should be served by the process.
Principle No. 8	Multicultural educators should incorporate resources (e.g., written materials, guest speakers) in class that explore pluralism and are drawn from the students' local communities.
Principle No. 9	Multicultural education should address, not avoid, social problems in our national history and culture and encourage exploration and understanding of issues such as oppression and inequality.
Principle No. 10	Multicultural education should be promulgated by educators who show "care, understanding, and sensitivity" to their students, realizing that such concerns greatly influence motivation (Appleton, 1983; p. 216).

Source: Adapted from Appleton, N. (1983). *Cultural Pluralism.* New York: Longman.

✦ Approaches to Multicultural Education

The effective teacher may choose between different approaches for addressing cultural diversity in the classroom. Some choices are better than others; each can be used in combination with others. First, there is the **human relations approach** in which the development of positive self-concept and student interrelationships are emphasized (York, 1992). Students learn about both similarities and differences between people and how to build interpersonal skills. If a teacher were to adopt this approach, he might encourage his students to learn about the similarities and differences between them and to avoid hurting each other's feelings. Second, there is the **single group study approach** to diversity (York, 1992). This approach is based on the idea that to embrace diversity, we first understand ourselves. Students are encouraged to explore their own cultural elements and sources. In Mr. Escalante's class, we might see a study of the evolution of the Mayan people.

human relations approach teaching model in which the development of positive self concept and student interests are emphasized

single group study approach teaching model emphasizing self exploration of cultural elements and sources

The single study approach is probably one of the most familiar and popular, but its use in some classrooms has been criticized for its seeming treatment of "cultural differences as entertainment" (Ladson-Billings, 1994; York, 1992). The earlier description of classes where diversity is examined exclusively through listening to music, eating ethnic foods, and wearing native costumes or where study of diverse people occurs only once or twice a year or on special "days" or during special months of the year are examples of the "culture as entertainment" single study approach (Ladson-Billings, 1994; York, 1992).

transformative multicultural education model teaching model which focuses on the value of diversity

In a third approach, the **transformative multicultural education model**, multicultural education is not viewed exclusively as entertainment nor is it trivialized by "days" or "months" (Ladson-Billings, 1994; York, 1992). In this approach, a range of cultural perspectives are presented to students. Students learn about contributions and characteristics of many different cultures through multicultural literature, multilinguistic experiences, and diverse resource persons. Teachers model that "difference is good" (Boutte & McCormick, 1992). Mr. Escalante's incorporation of the contributions of the Mayans to mathematics was an example of this approach.

antibias education model teaching model stressing the inequalities of society and problem-solving strategies; also called "antibias curriculum" and "bicultural education models"

Additionally, diversity may be addressed through **Antibias Education**, **Antibias Curricula** and/or **Bicultural Education** models (York, 1992; Thomson, 1993; Sherman & Thompson, 1994). Teachers using the former approach instruct students on the inequalities in society, the existence and effects of discrimination and injustice. If students are taught problem-solving skills and critical thinking and are encouraged to seek change in the social structure themselves, they are involved in the antibias approach to cultural diversity (York, 1992). In the latter approach, students are taught "switching" or the ability to traverse "worlds." They develop the ability to maintain pride in their family culture and, at the same time, adapt to the larger, shared culture. The bicultural student learns to live successfully in two (or more) worlds (York, 1992). The student learns that cultures and people are not inferior or superior, but simply vary (Thomson, 1993).

A teacher's attempts to work with linguistically diverse students was an example of this approach. Some students can make smooth transitions between worlds or cultures, or they manage the transitions with limited difficulty. Other students have a very difficult time traversing worlds; for them, switching is difficult or impossible (Phelan, Davidson, & Cao Yu, 1994).

Effective teachers look for ways to make the transition as smooth as possible. James Vazquez (1990) summed up several recommendations for teaching culturally diverse students in his three-step procedure. More attention has been paid to addressing multiculturalism via curriculum content than via instructional process (Garcia, 1994), but Vazquez (1990) goes beyond mere curriculum content changes:

Step 1. The teacher observes/identifies student trait. In Table 5.1 on page 171, we can examine some cultural characteristics of learners.

Step 2. The trait is passed through a "filter" of three questions to identify which aspect of teaching (content, context, mode) should be affected.

   a. Content: Does any aspect of the trait suggest the kind of material I should be teaching?

   b. Context: Does any aspect of the trait suggest the physical or psychological setting I should create in the classroom?

   c. Mode: Does any aspect of the trait suggest the manner in which I should be teaching?

Step 3. Teacher verbalizes/writes out the new instructional strategy (Vazquez, 1990; p. 303). A sample lesson plan appears in Figure 5.2.

◆ Experience, the Best Teacher

As teachers, even before we attempt to address diversity in our classrooms, we need to understand our own feelings about diversity and we need to "know our students." We need to learn about their cultural elements and groups and worlds to be able to utilize the recommendations presented in this chapter. Still, the best way to learn about cultural elements is to experience them. As Orlando Taylor (1988) notes, "The lack of reading matter in various cultures is, in some ways, a blessing since knowledge of other cultures is better acquired by experience than by study" (p. 3).

It's an interesting point, imploring us to keep an open mind about cultural diversity and to do our own research. Education students who sought multiple cross-cultural experiences showed less bias towards minority students than students with no experience or a single

Teacher Tool Box

Communication is key in effective multicultural teaching. We can help every student move successfully between cultures—the school culture and family culture—if we remove barriers to communication. Stereotypical language is a barrier to effective teaching. Avoid stereotypical qualifiers, unnecessary racial identifications, negative implications of color symbolism, and language with questionable racial or ethnic connotations. Additionally, we need to steer clear of violations of cultural rules about communication (Taylor, 1988). Improve communication and avoid pitfalls by considering these reminders:

◆ Note rules for attentiveness during discussions and conversation;

◆ Be informed about the rules for personal space during conversations;

◆ Find out about the rules for turn-taking during conversations; and,

◆ Be aware of the rules for entering ongoing conversations (Taylor, 1988).

Figure 5.2

Multicultural Lesson Plan

Multicultural Lesson Plan

Subject: Reading, Social Studies, and Language Arts   Grade Levels: 4-6

Topic: Delaware

Advanced organizer: Maya Angelou's poem, "The Human Family."

Objectives:
  1. Students will understand which ethnic groups have influenced the development of Delaware.
  2. Students will discuss how ethnic traditions have become a part of urban life.
  3. Students will be more aware of ethnic places, names and landmarks in Delaware.

Procedures:
Present the students with definitions of ethnic groups. Divide the class into several groups representing some of the following groups: Quakers, African Americans, Native Americans, Swedes, Italians, and Poles. (The teacher may wish to identify other ethnic groups in the school.) Research materials on the ethnic groups. The following questions should be answered by each group:
  1. What traditions did ethnic groups bring to Delaware? Where did these traditions come from?
  2. How do the traditions of different ethnic groups become a part of urban living?
  3. Why is it important that different ethnic groups keep some of the customs of their native land?
  4. Does sharing ethnic customs and traditions bring people closer together? If so, how? If not, why?
  5. Which landmarks, parks, agencies, streets, etc., in Delaware are named after persons belonging to various ethnic groups?
  6. Which ethnic groups were responsible for the early development of Delaware? What did these groups contribute to its development?

Activities:
Students will prepare reports relating to the information they have gathered. Reports will be shared through cooperative group presentations to the class. Whole class and small groups discussion will explore findings further.

Materials:
Reference material (e.g., books, videos, artifacts, photographs) will be housed in the classroom. Other resources will be available from the school and public library and via field trips to local sites.

---

multicultural exposure (Grottkau & Nickolai-Mays, 1989). Ignorance (and bias) can result in misinterpreted behavior—and ineffective teaching (Dunne, 1988).

RACE AND ETHNICITY

◆ Race as a Microcultural Element

Race. Does the mere mention of the term make you uncomfortable? You are not alone. Many teachers—many people in general in our society—are reluctant to acknowledge the possibility of racial differences in school. But race is another element of microcultural diversity and should be examined as we will all the other elements in this chapter.

Table 5.1 Learning Styles, Cultural Patterns, and Instructional Strategies

Cultural Patterns of Racial/Ethnic and Sex Groups	*Suggested Instructional Strategies*
CHILD-ADULT RELATIONS	
1. Does the child obey the adult because of his/her role as adult or must respect be earned?	
Low-income Urban Black Respect is earned by adult relating to child as an individual. Child responds to shame and to avoidance of physical punishment. Child may openly confront adult if respect is not earned.	Teacher needs to earn respect by relating to students personally.
Traditional Native American Leaders chosen by community and will stay as long as community accepts them. Older adults seen as wise.	Teacher can gain respect if he/she demonstrates acceptable behavior. Older teachers may easily gain more respect.
Traditional Mexican American Respect is given to adult if adult demonstrates approved values such as contributing to community.	Same as above
Middle-class White Respect is earned. Boys allowed more open disagreement; girls not encouraged to be aggressive and disagreement more passive and hidden. Child responds to guilt, withdrawal of love, and external rewards.	Teacher may need to encourage children away from external awards such as grades in order to be self-directed.
2. Does the child seek a relationship with the adult which is friendly and personal or formal and task-oriented?	
Traditional Mexican American Child seeks friendly and personal adult relationships.	Teacher needs to arrange instructional time so that he/she can work with students in a small group and in individualized situations where personal feelings and experiences can be shared. Since assistance to others is given freely without asking for it and is highly valued, teacher needs to be sensitive to need for help. Older students also need to experience working in a more formal and task-oriented situation.
Middle-class White Child functions in relationship which is somewhat formal and task-oriented.	Child can try working independently of teacher, interactions with teacher can focus on task at hand. Child working alone should not be perceived as rejecting teacher or other children.
3. Is the child encouraged to disagree or challenge the adult on ideas or is disagreement seen as disrespectful?	
Traditional Native American Respect shown to adult does not allow disagreement. Adult perceived as wise, particularly if old.	Teacher should avoid placing student in a position which encourages him/her to disagree. Teacher who perceives self as equal to students may find student doesn't share that opinion. Student may be unsure how to act in this situation.
Middle-class White Child is encouraged to challenge adult on opinions.	Teacher can play "devil's advocate" to stimulate independent thinking.
CHILD-CHILD RELATIONS	
4. How do boys and girls interact with each other?	
Traditional Mexican American Physical contact and discussion of sex are not sanctioned between adolescent boys and girls.	Human relations and physical education activities which encourage physical contact between boys and girls should be avoided so that girls are not placed in a position where school encourages them to violate their self-respect.

(continued)

Table 5.1 Learning Styles, Cultural Patterns, and Instructional Strategies *(Continued)*

Cultural Patterns of Racial/Ethnic and Sex Groups	*Suggested Instructional Strategies*
5. Does the child work well with children who are older, younger, and/or the same age?	
Low-income Urban Black Children are frequently partially cared for by older siblings. After about age six, children relate mostly to peers.	Cross-age tutoring and multi-age classrooms can be used effectively.
6. Does the child work well independently or cooperatively with other students?	
Low-income Urban Black and traditional Mexican American Children are encouraged to help siblings, particularly younger ones. Families tend to be large and may include cousins. Competition discouraged. Peer groups tend to be strong and give members support.	Small group situations where students cooperate, tutoring and paired learning are encouraged. Where peer group are strong, it may be helpful to maintain existing peer group as instructional group in classroom. Students may need more practice working by themselves.
Traditional Native Americans Individual competition or demonstrating achievement in front of a group is discouraged. Competition appropriate in sports with teams.	Same as above.
Middle-class White Male Working independently is highly valued.	Students can learn when working by themselves and may need skill development in working cooperatively.
Traditional Female Girls are not encouraged to problem-solve independently. Friendliness and ability to get along with others valued, so conflict and disagreement are frequently hidden.	Female students may need skill development in facing independent tasks and in reducing test anxiety.
7. How is status achieved?	
Traditional Mexican American Working for the benefit of family and community and assisting others are highly valued.	Small group situations where students can cooperate. Tutoring and paired learning are encouraged. If competition with others is used, even those who excel may not want to participate in outshining their peers. Students need practice working in competitive situations, such as timed tests, so that they can also do well in these situations.
Low-income Urban Black Rivalry and competition are discouraged in augmented families and working for benefit of family is emphasized. Status is also given for one's communicative style.	Teacher should avoid embarrassing student in front of peers. Direct confrontation better handled privately with students.
Traditional Native American Person should be developed in many spheres of life including spiritual, bodily, and artistic ability, not only marketable skills. Dignity in front of peers highly valued.	Teacher should develop program to facilitate holistic development.
Middle-class White Male Achievement and being the best highly valued in academic and athletic areas.	Students will respond to competitive situations where they can excel. If they perceive they cannot compete, they may give up. Relying on competition is questionable since only those who feel comfortable in succeeding may respond. Status for working cooperatively needs to be encouraged.
Traditional Female Physical appearance and friendliness valued. Academic achievement negatively valued as girls approach adolescence since this is seem as unfeminine, particularly in science and math. Approval from males is often negatively related to academic success.	Female students need to overcome fear of rejection for excellence. They may need opportunities to compete only with other females. They also need to be encouraged to use their abilities when working with male students.

(continued)

Cultural Patterns of Racial/Ethnic and Sex Groups	*Suggested Instructional Strategies*
8. Does the student become more involved in the task or social surroundings?	
Traditional Female, Traditional Mexican American and Low-income Urban Black Child is sensitive to feelings of others. "Soul" (empathetic understanding), the ability to participate in the feelings of others or the capacity to interject one's own emotions into a situation to be able to analyze subjectively all the nuances of feelings in that situation, is valued among low-income blacks.	Teacher needs to allow time for students to relate to each other before working together. Tasks may not be completed successfully unless human relations have been attended to.

COGNITIVE STYLE

9. Is the child more analytic or global in problem solving? *Analytic:* Field independent, gives attention to parts and details; abstract thinking, spatial ability, and analytic problem solving skills; inductive thinking or forming generalizations. *Global:* Field sensitive or field dependent, gives attention to the whole contextual field; holistic thinking.	
Traditional Native American, Traditional Mexican American, Traditional Female, and Low-income Urban Black Global style. Holistic thinking is encouraged. Ways of knowing can include subjective and intuitive approaches. Artistic as well as intellectual pursuits are encouraged. Analytic areas such as math and science are discouraged for females.	Uses personalized and holistic approaches. Concepts presented in humanized story forms ("S" is a snake); analogies instead of dictionary definitions. May need to develop analytic style.
Middle-class White Male Analytic style. Encouraged from young age to think abstractly. Emotions should not enter into thinking, thought should be logical, empirical.	Learns well from graphs, charts, formulas. May need to develop holistic approach to conceptual style.

Source: Howard (1987). *Learning to Persist/Persisting to Learn.* Reprinted with permission from Mid-Atlantic Center Publications.

Valli (1995) cites two oft-repeated statements: "Teachers should be colorblind" and "If you don't see the color, you don't see the child" (p. 121). These statements, as described by Valli, illustrate the "schizophrenia" many of us have about addressing race in our classrooms. We want to treat all of our students fairly, but we think that means we should ignore their race and treat all students the same. As Ladson-Billings (1994) notes, "The notion of equity as sameness only makes sense when all students are exactly the same" (p. 33). Identical twins are rarely—if ever—exactly the same in all aspects of their lives, so why should we expect to treat diverse students in our classrooms identically! Ignoring race means that we may be ignoring an important aspect of our students' cultural makeups—and you now know the significance of incorporating cultural variations in class from the recommendations presented previously in this chapter.

Nonetheless, there is often great fear and anxiety about race among teachers, especially white teachers and new teachers (Ladson-Billings, 1994; Valli, 1995). The reasons given are that discussions of race are "messy," may be "demoralizing to my students," make the teacher feel "guilty." Some believe that race is just "too dangerous" a subject to broach (Nietlo, 1996; p. 308). Many teachers are apprehensive about appearing discriminatory or fear being labeled racists if they attempt to address racial differences in attitude, behavior, values, or achievement in school, but typically that is not the case. Most teachers do not discriminate intentionally; they just fail to address differences adequately—if at all (Ladson-Billings, 1994). Let's address some of the differences anyway.

◆ Race and Schooling

Differences in achievement. The differences in achievement between racial groups in schools in the United States are well-documented: whites perform better than most racial minorities (Nietlo, 1996; Singham, 1998). What we remain uncertain about is why this is the case. There is no lack of possible explanations. Singham (1998) describes three major categories—although none has been endorsed decisively in the research literature. The *genetic model* is the model that has gotten the most publicity in recent years. In this model, differences between racial groups are attributed to long-term evolution and genetic predisposition. It is a flawed model, however, because there is little, if any, conclusive evidence attesting to this rationale (Singham, 1998).

The *socioeconomic model* assigns the differences in achievement to the pervasive and long-lasting affects of a history of institutional racism in our society (Singham, 1998). Despite the fact that all races have known some form of discrimination, people of color in particular have been discriminated against institutionally for many years. Nietlo (1996) defines institutional racism as "the harmful policies and practices within institutions aimed at certain groups of people by other groups of people" (p. 37); it is about people with power discriminating against those with little or no power in society. As groups, through institutions, people with power who are discriminating can have a significant negative impact on the education—and lives—of students of color. Even so, the socioeconomic model has its flaws as well. Ladson-Billings (1994) maintains that the socioeconomic model condemns students of color, African-American students in particular, to relive the past and not move beyond it. It leaves students and their teachers resigned to the status quo.

A third explanation for academic discrepancies between races is the *sociopathological model* in which, as proponents of the model maintain, cultural diversity is to blame. Proponents suggest that, since all discriminatory barriers have been removed with the legal victories of the Civil Rights Movement, persistent differences in achievement must be due to so-called cultural deficiencies (Singham, 1998). This explanation is problematic because it undermines diverse cultures and, therefore, the students' self-esteem. It also *assumes* that no further discrimination exists in our society when we know that it does exist in the choice of curricula and instructional materials; student sorting policies; and the relationships between schools, students, and their families (Nietlo, 1996).

> ### Connections
>
> The good news in terms of effective teaching of diverse populations is that there is a growing literature of research findings and practical teaching suggestions. There are also more teachers willing to talk about the benefits as well as difficulties they face in their classrooms. Using the Internet, go to the Global Classroom Exchange Web site at <http://www.ePALS.com>; solicit comments from practicing teachers about multicultural classroom teaching.

There are other possible explanations as well. Fordham (1988) suggests that, for some people of color, individual achievement is viewed as less desirable than the success of the group, so individuals are reluctant to "stand out." Steele (1992) proposes that achievement presents a "stereotype threat" to racially diverse students, which depresses performance; a self-fulfilling prophecy perpetuates the discrepancies. Ogbu (1991) maintains that some minorities (i.e., African-Americans, Native Americans, Latinos) see little benefit in and have little expectation of succeeding in the dominant culture (i.e., white culture); this mindset might also depress achievement. The fact is, we are just not sure why the gaps persist. We do know, however, that teacher expectations can be a contributing factor.

You Make The Call

Think critically about this scene: A student teacher who has volunteered to participate in a special group of student teachers interested in teaching in diverse settings is talking in the student teaching practicum seminar. She tells the group about her inconsistent disciplinary methods. When the white children in her class misbehave, she sternly reprimands them because, she believes, they know the rules and they know what they are supposed to do. When the seven African-American students misbehave, however, she gives them another chance. In her own words, she allows them to "get away with murder" because she feels sorry for them and wants them to know that she "cares" (Ladson-Billing, 1996; p. 20).

♦ What's going on here?

♦ Was this teacher right to expect different "acceptable" behaviors from students from different racial groups?

♦ What's the likely effect of her choices on her students? Her effectiveness?

♦ Is this teacher a racist?

♦ Is this a true story?

Teacher expectations. What happened in the scene above is that a well-meaning, pre-service teacher allowed her lowered expectations for the behavior of students from one racial group to influence her instructional decision making to the likely detriment of the African-American students and non-African-American students in her class as well. And, yes, this is a true story (cf. Ladson-Billings, 1996).

Bias in teachers' expectations of students is not a new area of research: its existence is well-documented (Good & Brophy, 1974). As you will study in Chapter 8: Motivation in the Classroom, teachers' expectations influence their instructional choices, which in turn impact student attitudes and, subsequently, student achievement. In a classic study of bias in teachers' expectations, Rosenthal and Jacobsen (cf. Nietlo, 1994) found that teachers who were told that certain students were "intellectual bloomers"—although the students were not—responded quite favorably to the students' work—more so than was warranted.

Teachers' perceived choices for effective instruction were narrowed by their biased perceptions of race. Teachers' expectations may contribute to biased students' attitudes as well. ◆

There is a substantial body of research that suggests that teachers' differing expectations for students correlate with student race (Carter & Goodwin, 1994; Ladson-Billings, 1994; Nietlo, 1996; McCabe, 1996; Graybill, 1997; Lipman, 1997). Simpson and Erickson (1983) found differential treatment of white and black elementary students by their white and black teachers: White teachers were more critical of black students in general and of black male students in particular than were their black counterparts. Lipman (1997) observed that teachers' perceived choices for effective instructional alternatives were narrowed by their biased perceptions about racial differences in the classroom. Teachers are less likely to be creative and innovative when there are racially diverse children in class. Some researchers believe that there is an over-representation of minorities in special education classes and an under-representation of them in gifted classes because of the differences in culture between minority students and their teachers and due to teachers' biased expectations (Meier & Brown, 1994; Graybill, 1997). School principals have noted lowered expectations for poor children and children of color as well (Crosby & Owens, 1991).

Teachers' expectations may contribute to biased attitudes in students also, although it must be noted that students come to school with a multitude of prior experiences as well. Nonetheless, Hall (1981) noted that students' races were a correlating factor in the students' perceived likability by others in class. In a simultaneously fascinating yet tragic finding, teacher Marc Elrich (1994) reported that when he asked his suburban Maryland sixth graders "How many of you think that black people are bad?" 24 of the 29 students responded affirmatively. *All but two of his students, however, were Black or Hispanic!* When we hold biased expectations of students, we undermine their self-esteem and their achievement. Singham concludes: "What the academic achievement gap may really be telling us is that, while the symptoms of the education system's ills are more clearly visible in the black community than in the white, there are fundamental problems with the way education is delivered to all students" (Singham, 1998; p. 15).

So what can we as teachers do? Or more to the point, what do effective teachers of racially and ethnically diverse students do?

◆ Recommendations

Why can't we just teach racially and ethnically diverse students to be more like white students? Remember in our look at cultural differences we examined assimilation and amalgamation theories and concluded that they are each flawed because they undermine individual and group self-concept and, subsequently, achievement. A similar case against race/ethnic assimilation or amalgamation can be made here. A better solution includes getting to know your students well.

The effective teacher of racially and ethnically diverse students knows her students through interaction and exploration. Again, experience is key. Getting to know first hand students' families and the communities from which they come is important. The effective teacher becomes aware of characteristic distinctions between members of racial groups and finds ways to incorporate them into instruction (Vasquez, 1990).

There are differing contexts for learning preferred by various racial groups who may be represented in our classrooms. For instance, some African Americans, Native Americans, and Latino Americans prefer to work with the support of other students, and they derive meaning from tasks based on the setting and situation and prior experiences that surround the assignment (Brown & McGraw-Zoubi, 1995; Vasquez, 1990; Morales-Jones, 1990). Asian Americans and European Americans may prefer to derive meaning from verbal or written messages without regard to the contextual elements of the assignment, and they may value individual rather than socially-mediated efforts. Additional differences like these—which may examine the relationship between culture and learning style preferences—are examined further later in this chapter. Keep in mind that these differences are qualitative, but when we ignore them, the effects can be pervasive (Vasquez, 1990; Morales-Jones, 1990; Carter & Goodwin, 1994; Brown & McGraw-Zoubi, 1995). Keep in mind, also, that these descriptions of characteristics should be treated as reminders to teachers to incorporate a variety of teaching strategies

Teacher Tool Box

Winfield (cf. Ladson-Billings, 1994) and Ladson-Billings (1994) distinguished between six teacher beliefs and behavior patterns:

Tutors: Believe all students can improve and that it is the teacher's responsibility to help them.

General Contractors: Believe that improvement is possible, but that additional personnel are needed.

Custodians: Don't believe that much can be done to help some children and do not seek others to assist; they help students maintain the status quo.

Referral Agents: Don't believe that all students can succeed, and they shift responsibility for maintenance of the status quo to additional personnel.

Conductors: Believe all students can succeed, assume responsibility for their students' successes and setbacks, and seek excellence from all.

Coaches: Believe all students are capable of excellence, but share responsibility with parents, communities, and the students themselves (pp. 21–24).

into their repertoires and *not as concrete predictors* for all members of all groups; there will be many, many exceptions (Carter & Goodwin, 1994).

Effective teachers also examine their own attitudes and beliefs about racial diversity and racial differences and conclude that it is necessary to set challenging expectations for all students in the classroom (Carter & Goodwin, 1994; Cochran-Smith, 1995; Irvine & Foster, 1996). They are more likely to hold themselves responsible and accountable for the success of all students in their classrooms (Ladson-Billings, 1994).

Think for a minute: Which pattern would you think is most effective? Although the tutor might be helpful in the short run, successful teachers of racially and ethnically diverse students reflect the characteristics of the latter two patterns. Effective teachers' views of themselves and the depth of their commitment to increased achievement in all students as well as their unbiased view of their students' differences is what is distinguishing.

LINGUISTIC DIVERSITY

At the beginning of the school year, the teacher first addresses her class and notices puzzled expressions on some of the students' faces as assignment instructions are given. She quickly surmises that the students speak little if any English. She tells them, in Korean, to sit near the front so they can be helped.

◆ How Will Your Students Vary Linguistically?

linguistic diversity ways in which students may differ relative to their language usage

One cultural element that may vary in your class is "language." Don't be fooled. Many of you will encounter **linguistic diversity** in your classes, regardless of where you plan to teach. Be reminded of the demographics on ethnicity and English proficiency reported at the beginning of this chapter. Your class will have linguistic diversity, and you, like the teacher in the scene just described, will have to realize that you need to be sensitive to this linguistic diversity and adjust accordingly.

Effective teachers examine their own attitudes and beliefs about diversity and set challenging expectations for all students. They hold themselves responsible and accountable for all students' success. ◆

What do I know about culture, communication, and language?

Directions: Circle **A** for each statement with which you agree or **D** for each statement with which you disagree.

A   D   1. One's culture and one's race are usually one and the same.
A   D   2. Culture consists primarily of a group's arts, music, dances, food, language, and dress.
A   D   3. Cultural groups are generally mutually exclusive of one another.
A   D   4. Cultural traits tend to have a genetic base.
A   D   5. In general, people who speak the same language are members of the same culture group.
A   D   6. People are often unaware of some of the rules of their culture.
A   D   7. Culture is expressed exclusively by one's verbal behavior.
A   D   8. The only significant components of one's communication system are pronunciation rules, vocabulary, and grammatical rules.
A   D   9. Standard English is the correct way to speak at all times.
A   D 10. There are universal norms for acceptable communicative behavior within the United States.
A   D 11. If a student violates the school's cultural or communicative norms, it is usually an act of defiance.
A   D 12. In general, speaking a nonstandard dialect suggests low cognitive development.
A   D 13. Standard English has more and better structures than other varieties of English.
A   D 14. Most standardized tests are based on rules of English used by all linguistic groups.
A   D 15. Standard English is white English
A   D 16. In general, students from poor families do not communicate as well as those from middle class families.
A   D 17. In general, black students do not communicate as well as white students.
A   D 18. Parents who do not speak standard English should avoid talking to their children to prevent them from developing poor speech habits.
A   D 19. If a child is to learn standard English, he/she must unlearn any other variety of English that he/she speaks.
A   D 20. Black American English is by definition a nonstandard variety of English.

Figure 5.3

What do I know about culture, communication, and language?

Source: From Orlando Taylor, *Cross cultural communication: An essential dimension of effective education* (1988). Used by permission of Mid-Atlantic Center Publications.

But before we consider ways to "adjust" or to address linguistic diversity, ask yourselves: What am I bringing to my linguistically diverse classroom? What attitudes, perceptions, and **biases** do I have? Get a quick gauge of what you might be bringing by taking a few minutes to respond to the statements of the survey by Dr. Orlando Taylor of Howard University (1988) shown in Figure 5.3.

biases the tendency to favor one group over another

YOU MAKE THE CALL

Take the Taylor survey and review your responses critically. If you are sensitive to issues of linguistic and cultural diversity, if you are knowledgeable about language variations and do not adhere to certain myths concerning the relationship between language and culture, you should disagree with each of the 20 statements in the Taylor survey. Each represents a myth or misperceptions or instances of misinformation concerning linguistic diversity (Taylor, 1988). If you were not aware that these were myths and misperceptions you owe it to yourself and your future students to learn more.

Knowledge and an open mind can help dispel myths, so let's try to come to an understanding about linguistic diversity.

dialectal language language of a particular cultural or family group

◆ Dispelling Myths

Student language can vary. Students may use American English or a cultural or familial or American **dialectal language**. They may enter school using variations like these (Taylor, 1988, p. 8).:

◆ "He just kept a-begging and a-crying and a-wanting to go out" (Appalachian English);

◆ "He be scared, but I be brave" (black English);

◆ "She's a good cook, your mother" (New York City nonstandard English); and

◆ "I mon' rest" (Southern American English)

Various students can and will use these conventions and others. But what do we know about language variations like these? What's more, what do we know about standard American English?

standard language language of the marketplace within a shared national culture

Standard American English is a vehicle for shared communication across cultural groups in the United States. As is true of any **standard language**, it is the language of the marketplace and, typically, is part of our shared national culture. Much of this chapter deals with dispelling myths surrounding diversity, and we need to dispel a few here. First, standard English transcends race, ethnicity, and region: it is neither "White English" nor "Northern English" (Taylor, 1988, p. 8). American English is not in danger of being "lost," nor is it the only language of value in the United States (Wiley, 1997). It is a larger context for communication and within this larger communication context are cultural and familial and regional variations.

YOU MAKE THE CALL

Exercise your critical thinking skills: Imagine that in your classroom there are several students who use cultural or dialectal variations of American English. Your instructional leader tells *you* to address the diversity yourself—no resource help in this hypothetical scenario!—and help the students the best you can. Should you try to change their language? Why? Why not? What do your classmates think?

These variations are not tied necessarily to intelligence, cultural inferiority, or academic achievement. Unfortunately, however, some children are referred to special education programming simply because they are linguistically diverse—not because they have disorders that interfere with their learning (Olson, 1992). They are not speaking "slang." Slang is transient, faddish, and includes few consistent language conventions. Think back to the developmental components of language described in an earlier chapter. Cultural or family languages all have phonological, semantic, syntactical, and pragmatic components also. They are, in fact, just as complex, just as rule-governed as standard American English. (You'll notice that the variations above transcend race and ethnicity, and region of the country.)

◆ Facilitating American English

So, why encourage standard language use in students? Why not just leave well enough alone? Some people do feel that the teaching of standard American English is injurious to students' self-esteem and that teachers should leave well enough alone indeed. But remember standard American English allows people to communicate with each other across groups or "worlds." Also, it is the language of the marketplace, which means that most jobs, business transactions, and financial concerns utilize it. Therefore, if we believe philosophically in preparing students to become productive citizens in society, we must offer dialectal users the opportunity to learn standard American English.

What's important is *how* and *why* we want to facilitate language change in children. Attempting change "to make students smarter," "to teach them 'good' English," "to correct cultural deprivation or disadvantage," or "to replicate Anglo culture" are not reasons that will facilitate change. These reasons will cause students to resist the teacher's efforts. Attempting change to provide students with a tool for communicating across cultures in general and in the marketplace in particular is a reason that is least threatening. We need to let students know explicitly that family or cultural language can be preserved, but that we are teaching an additional communicative tool.

◆ Characteristics of Linguistic Diversity in Students

Your class may contain a variety of linguistically diverse students (Soto, 1991). It may include

- *Linguistic minority students* who speak the language of a racial or ethnic minority group (e.g., Spanish or Vietnamese);
- *Linguistic majority students* who speak the shared language of the primary culture (e.g., standard American English);
- *Limited English proficient students* who are linguistically diverse and who have limited ESOL skills (i.e., English as a second language);
- *Non-English proficient students* who do not use the standard language in any form, only cultural or family language;
- *English only students* who speak only English; and,
- *Fluent English proficient students* who are capable of "code switching" smoothly between standard and cultural languages. (Snow in Soto, 1991).

YOU MAKE THE CALL

If you've had a chance to see *Stand and Deliver* and you've seen the scene described at the beginning of this section, you'll remember that Mr. Escalante has students who typify each of these characteristics. Which of the above characteristics of student language users need language learning assistance? Why?

In reflecting on the above, *You Make the Call,* did you identify all but the last student category? Actually, diversity would be important for each of the above categories except the last; the fluent English proficient student is diverse already. It may appear easy to conclude that linguistic minority students and limited English proficient students need to learn additional language tools, but what about the linguistic majority and English-only students? The question should be: Are they linguistically diverse?

In a pluralistic society and world, we need linguistically diverse students. Singular proficiency may not be enough to be successful in the American and the world marketplaces. Have you ever heard the old story about the car company that was puzzled and disappointed when their newly released automobile, the Nova, was not selling in Spanish-speaking countries (Lewis, 1988)? It finally occurred to an auto executive to look into the language of the region, upon which it was discovered that the car's name, "Nova," translated into "won't go." We can't blame the citizens for avoiding a car titled "Won't go"!

◆ General Recommendations

Teaching English as a tool for cultural, nonswitching language users requires skill and sensitivity. First, we must realize our own biases and accept diversity (Taylor, 1988; Lockhart, 1991; Soto, 1991; Hlvana, 1994). It contributes to our effectiveness when we reflect on our own definitions of standard and varied language and when we hold positive attitudes concerning diversity. It also facilitates our understanding of language diversity and helps us help our students when we learn everything we can about their culture (Canney et al., 1999).

Second, we can emphasize comprehension in our classrooms. If you can understand the student and the student can understand you, then achievement can continue (Taylor, 1988; Soto, 1991; Krashen, 1997). Increased student achievement should be our overall instructional goal, regardless of linguistic diversity issues. At the same time, however, we can seek ways to provide monolingual and limited proficiency students with an additional communicative tool. The question of the best way to introduce and develop standard language as a nonthreatening tool remains just that—a question. The third recommendation, therefore, calls for addressing linguistic diversity and to explore ways to teach standard language from a cultural perspective.

"Immersion" and Transitional Methods

Traditionally, we believed an **"immersion" approach** was the best way to move children to standard language usage. You may be familiar with foreign language classes in which, from the moment you first enter the class, the instructor uses nothing but the language to be learned. All instruction is in the language to be learned. It becomes, then, a "sink or swim" proposition. Some children swim; they thrive under these conditions; they learn the language with few problems. Other students, however, sink; they do not learn the language and suffer inside and outside

immersion approach
teaching model for addressing language diversity by placing students in classrooms where all instruction and verbal socialization are in the language to be learned

transitional approach
teaching model for addressing language diversity by allowing students to learn and socialize initially in the students' cultural or familial language and moving students gradually to standard language usage

of class. Similarly, linguistically diverse students can sink or swim in language learning.

Some students placed in immersion settings may face barriers to classroom learning, and their self-esteem may suffer also. Preschoolers taught English via an immersion strategy may be disrupted intellectually, developmentally, and socially (Rodriguez, 1991; Pyle, 1996). The resulting loss of cultural language correlated positively with "alienation, high suicide rates, loss of labor market productivity, high dropout rates, [and] crime" (Rodriguez, 1991; p. 5).

Transitional or balanced bilingual strategies for adding standard language as a shared communicative tool are being examined. These approaches start with the language the student brings to the classroom and build on family and cultural language to promote standard language usage.

Several years ago, a Massachusetts teacher, Gary Simpkins, attempted to move his African-American students toward standard American English usage by developing an approach called "Bridge" (Sheils, 1976), described in Figure 5.4.

In this approach, standard language is taught transitionally and gradually (Sheils, 1976). Students begin the year using their cultural language, black English, exclusively—all reading, writing, and oral communication reflect black English conventions. Midway through the instructional period, the students use black English part of the time and standard language part of the time. By the end of the instructional period, all writing, formal communication, and reading are in standard American English,

Teacher Tool Box

Language Learning Programs

The SDOL Program model mentioned on page 184 preserves cultural language and emphasizes standard English learning. Successful implementation of this program—if not any language learning program—requires the following stages (Taylor, 1988; p. 21):

1. *Developing positive attitudes toward one's own language.* Students learn about the history and components of their own dialects and cultural languages.

2. *Developing an awareness of language varieties.* Students seek examples of language variation in popular media.

3. *Recognizing, labeling, and contrasting dialects.* Students examine dialectal phonology and syntactics.

4. *Comprehending meanings.* Students examine dialectal semantics.

5. *Recognizing situational communication requirements.* Students match language usage to appropriate settings.

6. *Producing in structured situations.* Students practice with models.

7. *Producing in controlled situations.* Students practice without models.

8. *Matching the language to the situation.* Students role play realistic language use.

Figure 5.4
Bridging Language

Bridging Language		
BLACK VERNACULAR	TRANSITION FORM	STANDARD ENGLISH
...young dudes gonna be having they wheels Got to have them...You know how brothers be with they wheels. They definitely be keeping them looking clean, clean, clean.	...If you find teenagers, you find old cars...Most teenagers can't afford new or late model cars. But they can...buy an old car...Their love they cars. They spend most of their time taking care of them.	Young guys...love their cars. They must have a car, no matter how old it is. James Russell...had a...'59 Chevrolet. He spent a great deal of time keeping his car clean. He was always washing and waxing it.

Source: Adapted from three kinds of English: "Go for what you know about the story," *Newsweek,* December 20,1976. Used by permission.

but black English is still used for less formal communication or for emphasis or effect. The implementation of this approach yielded "extremely promising" results, but not without controversy. Critics in the African-American community in particular questioned the long-term wisdom of an approach that at least appears to be less rigorous than immersion approaches (Sheils, 1976).

Some educators are trying mastery approaches like the one designed by the San Diego Oral Language Program (SDOL) and used in Texas and California (Taylor, 1988). Indigenous language is performed, and the new tool is taught via mastery of language elements in sequential order.

Again and again in this chapter, you will read that knowing your students is crucial to addressing diversity effectively. (Actually, the refrain "Know your students" is repeated throughout this text!) Linguistic diversity is no exception. Keep in mind that not all minority students, students from other regions of the United States, or immigrants will use cultural language and not all Euro-caucasian students will be users of standard language or intolerant of nonstandard language users. Know your students and respect their linguistic backgrounds accordingly.

LEARNING STYLE

Another element of diversity in your classroom may be learning style. There is some controversy about whether cognitive style is influenced culturally, but let's first consider what we know about this element.

♦ What Do We Know About Diversity in Learning Styles?

learning styles biological and socialized differences or preferences for how students learn

Learning styles appear to be biological and, perhaps, socialized differences that influence classroom learning in particular and lifelong learning in general. They reflect qualitative differences or preferences; they do not reflect how smart students are or how well the students are developed cognitively. There are many types of learning styles (Butler, 1989).

♦ *Psychological/affective styles:* Students' inner strengths, sense of individuality, and personality traits (e.g., social and emotional traits) also influence how they learn. How the student feels about him/herself and how self-esteem is developed are linked to learning. You might want to look into taking the Myers-Briggs Type Indicator to find out about your **psychological/affective style** (Houston, 1997; Avitabile, 1998; Wilson, 1998).

psychological/affective style ways that students' personality traits influence learning preferences

physiological style students' preferred ways of learning through the use of their senses or environmental stimuli

♦ *Physiological styles:* There are consistent ways to facilitate learning through the use of the senses or environmental stimuli. Hemispheric specializations (i.e., right or left brain), auditory, visual, kinesthetic, olfactory preferences, or preferences for environmental conditions, e.g., light, noise, are examples of physiological styles. You can check your own **physiological style** using the self-assessment in Table 5.2.

Table 5.2 Modality Preferences Inventory

Directions: Think about how each statement below applies to you. Then, rate the statement using U = usually applies (3 points); S = sometimes applies (2 points); or N = never or seldom applies (1 point).

AUDITORY

1. While solving problems, I talk to myself or to a friend or I hum a tune.
2. During lectures in class, I can pay attention without looking at the instructor.
3. I remember material from class by repeating it orally to myself.
4. When learning something new, I like to listen to verbal explanations, records, or audio tapes.
5. I prefer to use mnemonics (or memory devices) to help me remember things from class.
6. I enjoy reading most when there is dialogue in the text.

VISUAL

1. While solving problems, I take an orderly methodical approach.
2. During lectures in class, I sit near the instructor and watch intently.
3. I remember class material by picturing it in my mind.
4. When learning something new, I prefer to see it demonstrated first.
5. I find highlighting to be most helpful when I study.
6. I enjoy reading when there is a great deal of descriptive imagery.

TACTILE/HAPTIC

1. While solving problems, I prefer to move around or pace.
2. During lectures in class, I take notes in my notebook.
3. I remember material from class that allows me hands on experiences.
4. When learning something new, I like to try it out for myself.
5. I prefer classes with project assignments.
6. I enjoy reading stories with action scenes.

Assessment:

For each category, use the number of points per response and calculate a subtotal number of points. The category of your highest subtotal is your modality strength, i.e., Visual. (It's possible to be multi-modal; you may have more than one modality strength, e.g., Auditory and Tactile/Haptic!)

◆ *Cognitive styles:* There are consistent ways of responding and using stimuli in the environment; how things are perceived and made sense of; the most comfortable, expedient, and pleasurable way to process information. For example, students may utilize field-dependent or independent, impulsive or reflective **cognitive styles.**

The more students grow, the more sophisticated they become, but each has preferred styles or ways of learning. Students' preferred styles of learning influence their achievement, and teachers' learning styles

cognitive style students' most comfortable, consistent, and expedient ways of perceiving and making sense of information in the environment influence their instructional choices. Students learn best when there is congruence between their preferred learning styles and the teacher's preferred teaching style. Students' styles should, therefore, influence teachers' instructional choices.

YOU MAKE THE CALL

Take a look at the figure. This is an example of an embedded figure task. Quickly, can you see the face in this figure?

Source: From Block, J. R., & Yuker, H. (1992). *Can you believe your eyes?* Bristol, PA: Brunner/Mazel, p. 49. Reprinted by permission of Taylor & Francis.

Field Independence and Dependence

Consider cognitive style alone. Some students will be **field-independent learners**, and some will be **field-dependent learners**. Field-independent learners perceive items as more or less separate from the surrounding field; they are interested in concepts for their own sakes. They have self-defined goals and function successfully in self-structured situations and impersonal learning environments. Other students may be field-dependent processors. Their mode of learning is strongly influenced by the prevailing context or setting; they are more aware of their surroundings as they learn. These learners value practical information.

Now, look back at the embedded figures task above. If you found it quickly, you may be a field-independent learner. Your teaching may also reflect your learning preferences. As a teacher, you may be more comfortable giving lectures and emphasizing cognition. You may prefer offering corrective feedback, using negative feedback as warranted, and you may use grades and personal goal charts motivationally. But, if it took you longer than a few seconds to find the embedded figure, or if you didn't find it at all, you may be a field-dependent learner and, as such, a field-dependent teacher.

As a field-dependent teacher, you may prefer interaction and conversation with your students. You may rely less on corrective feedback and little on negative evaluations. You also are likely to try to establish a warm and personal environment and prefer to motivate through verbal praise, external rewards, and the use of outlines and metacognitive structures.

On the other hand, if you are a field-independent teacher using field-independent strategies, your field-independent students will benefit most. If you are a field-dependent teacher using field-dependent strate-

field-independent learners
cognitive style variation emphasizing the perception and analysis of distinct pieces of information

field-dependent learners
cognitive style variation emphasizing the perception and analysis of distinct pieces of information as integrated wholes

Action Research

Learning Style Preferences

Being sensitive to the diversity of your students and aware of the research on student differences can assist you to develop teaching-learning activities tailored to your students' unique strengths and limitations. One example of this ability to adapt to the observed uniqueness of students was that presented by Jacquelyn, an eighth grade English teacher.

Early in her teaching career, Jacquelyn began to sense that some of her classes had what she called "distinct personalities." According to Jacquelyn, she began to realize that her students approached learning activities with a uniqueness of style. She was aware of some of the research on learning styles, and she wanted to assess if her classes, in fact, had distinct learning style preferences. Jacquelyn developed a simple set of descriptions of various learning styles and had her students identify what they felt best characterized or described their approach to learning. After surveying her three sections of eighth grade English, she discovered that a majority of students were classified as either visual or tactile learners. That is, the majority of her students reported learning more easily when the material was presented in some visual mode, for example through graphs, charts, or pictures, or when they were able to touch and manipulate the material, as might be the case when working with models. As a result, Jacquelyn developed a number of visual prompts to accompany her lectures, and she became especially interested in developing lessons with hands-on activities to use when teaching a class of tactile learners.

Being sensitive to the diversity and uniqueness of her own class, while at the same time being familiar with learning style and learning preference research, helped this one teacher to increase her effectiveness by adapting her HOW of teaching, to the WHO of her class.

gies, your field-dependent students will benefit most. Remember: Students learn best when there is congruence between their preferred learning styles and the teacher's preferred teaching style. Unfortunately and all too often, teachers ignore learning style variations and teach all students the same way. Despite the fact that many students are field dependent, most teachers utilize field-independent strategies (Dunn & Dunn, 1987). Why do teachers seemingly ignore learning style diversity?

That's not an easy question to answer. You probably feel a little overwhelmed by all of the elements of diversity addressed in this chapter so far. There are all of the cultural elements, the linguistic variations, and now, there are many variations of learning style. Practicing teachers often feel overwhelmed in trying to accommodate cognitive, physiological, and psychological and affective styles. As a result, several questions arise.

◆ Questions About Learning Styles and Teaching

If it's so difficult, should teachers even try to match instruction to students' learning styles? Some teachers and researchers say "no." They feel that to do so provides a crutch to learners and enables them to create excuses for not learning (Guild, 1994). Other teachers and researchers say "yes, we should try to match styles" (Dunne, 1987; Gardner, 1995; Shaughnessy, 1998). By so doing, we capitalize on the diverse strengths students bring to the classroom.

YOU MAKE THE CALL

Take a pencil or pen, and write your name on a piece of paper. When you've finished, take your pen, and switch it to your "nondominant" hand, and write your name again. Think about how you feel writing with your other hand. Do you feel frustrated? Awkward? Embarrassed? Did it take you longer to write your name with your nondominant hand? What might this exercise suggest about how "mismatched learners" feel in school?

Here is another question asked frequently: "Is it feasible to expect teachers to teach to each individual style?" Some teachers and researchers respond "no" again, suggesting that teachers who try to teach to individual styles will burn out or will reinforce resistance to learning. Teachers and researchers who think it is a good idea to teach to individual styles, however, say that effective teachers attempt to accommodate different learners all the time: they have a repertoire of instructional strategies related to learning style.

There is one additional, controversial question to consider: Is there a link between cognitive style and culture? One side of the debate denies just such a link. Opponents to the link theory suggest that it imposes unnecessary labels on students; it may be perceived as "racist" as well. Proponents of the theory, however, state it is neither. Jordan-Irvine (1990) suggests that majority teachers of minority students must be bilingual, bicultural, and bicognitive; and Hale-Benson (1986) encourages teachers to acknowledge the cultural-learning style link and utilize the variations to enhance instruction. In just one example, Pewewardy (1998) concluded that teachers' ignorance of Native American children's culture and learning styles was a great barrier to the children's learning. Review the cultural learning style preferences in Table 5.1. Was any of the information new to you? Some of it may have been. Do all minority learners prefer the styles listed? No—all minority learners probably do not.

Keep in mind, *some* learners—*not all*—from non-Western cultures, low socioeconomic status families, and/or who are racial or ethnic minorities or are female *may* have a tendency to be field-dependent and relational learners. Contrast this with the earlier finding that the majority of classroom teaching reflects a field-independent style, and you may have quite a segment of students who are left to feel awkward, frustrated, embarrassed, and slow about their difficulties in school.

Teacher Tool Box

Teaching to Learning Style Differences

It is not difficult to see how teachers might feel bewildered by diversity in general and learning style diversity in particular. Yet there is evidence that its influence on achievement is strong. To accommodate for differences, keep these strategies in mind:

◆ Introduce new material in learners' strongest modalities,

◆ Reinforce learning via the second strongest modality and again with the tertiary,

◆ Encourage older students to find preferable ways to represent material on their own (Kroom, 1985).

GENDER ROLE

Let's pretend that a colleague of yours tells you about a conversation with the parent of one of his students. The father of the student, a girl, informs you that his daughter will not be attending school regularly from now on so that she can work in the family business. After all, he suggests, she'll marry soon, and her education will be of little consequence after that. Your friend protests to the father, insisting that the daughter should be allowed to complete her education. The father is adamant: his daughter's place is at home. What do you think about this situation? Who is right—the father or the teacher? Should the girl work for her family or go to school?

◆ What's the Debate Surrounding Gender Differences?

The debate wages on over gender as an element of classroom diversity. Not too long ago, we openly debated whether to educate females outside of the home at all—as in the argument between your colleague and the father. Worldwide, 85 million more boys are educated than girls (Briscoe, 1994). For the most part, we realize that females and males alike should be educated, but we still are unsure if they are indeed different and, as such, in need of differing educational experiences.

> ### YOU MAKE THE CALL
>
> Close your eyes for a minute. Think about a scientist working alone in a lab and making a crucial discovery to help the world. Keep the image of that scientist in your mind for a few more minutes, we'll come back to it!

◆ Similarities and Differences in Girls and Boys

Prior to being able to categorize their own genders as preschoolers, we see little gender typed or stereotypical behavior in young children. These relative similarities suggest that boys and girls should be able to learn and achieve similarly as well. Therefore, we should be able to expect girls to perform in school as boys do and vice versa—but we don't. Largely, the reason for academic variations across gender is socialization, or how we've treated boys and girls, first at home, and then at school.

Newer theories like **gender schema theory** suggest that genetic predispositions such as hormonal levels, may account for some behaviors, personality traits, and interests as they are differentially displayed in males and females early on. Genetic influences, however, are thought to account for only a limited amount of such variation.

Gender schema theory points to socialization or differential treatment as the major reason for gender differences in attitude, behavior,

gender schema theory the explanation that most differences in thinking and behavior between females and males are due to socialization and achievement (Bem, 1981). Such environmental experiences as child-rearing, media exposure, and schooling are thought to account for the majority of gender-typed behaviors. Schools, in particular, have molded female students' academic choices and achievement in gender-specific ways through socialization. Even teachers themselves have been socialized to view males and females differently and to have differing expectations for them. Remember the scientist you envisioned a few moments ago? Well, if you conjured up the image of a male scientist, then the results of years of both direct and indirect gender associations is evident. We have been "programmed" by our own childrearing, media exposure, school experiences, and other societal interactions to see males as greater achievers than females.

Let's be a little cautious, however, with our charges of **gender typing.** We need to remember that gender typing is a two-way street. Boys can be affected by gender typing as well. The male image of the scientist shows that you have been socialized, but what about the effects on our students? Our expectations for males and females are affected greatly, but we know that the way children behave and view themselves is also influenced and starts quite early.

gender typing the oversimplification of gender-based characteristics

◆ Gender Typing Across the Ages

Early gender typing experiences result in distinguishable play labels and styles in young children (e.g., rough and tumble play for boys), clothing choices, toy preferences, even career choices (Alexander & Hines, 1994; Stroeher, 1994). Boys often are rewarded—directly or vicariously—for aggressive behaviors, while girls are rewarded for "ladylike" behaviors. Both parents and teachers can hold stereotypical expectations for young children (Leung, 1992). At home, sons are encouraged to test their freedom, while girls are kept closer to home.

By elementary school, children become sensitive to gender role expectations. The external manifestations witnessed in the younger child (e.g., clothing, toys) are joined by internalized gender typing (e.g., personality traits, school subject choices). Schoolage children themselves view male students as the more "prominent" members of the class (Safir et al., 1992). Athough some girls may attempt to cross gender-typed lines, for example in sports, few males do. If we think that gender typing potentially narrows opportunities for girls, it can be limiting for boys as well.

Early adolescents experience gender typing intensely. Gender role identity heightens from sixth grade on. Fewer females are allowed to traverse even the borders they crossed in middle childhood. In school, selected and differential academic achievement and subject area preferences (e.g., avoidance of science and math by girls) provide key evidence (Sadker & Sadker, 1994). In earlier grades, almost one third of young girls reported that they were good in math, but by middle school that figure has dropped to only 18% (Sadker & Sadker, 1994).

Consider the research on Hispanic adolescents in particular. The high school completion rate for Latinos is much less than it is for white

Recommendations for eliminating gender bias are broad and sound easy, but they are not. They urge teachers to become aware of the gender bias and to become knowledgeable about its pervasive effects. ◆

or African American students, and while it is slightly higher for Hispanic girls than for males, Latinas suffer more from **gender bias** in our society. They face greater difficulties in obtaining higher wage jobs and advanced levels of education (Romo, 1998).

gender bias favoring one gender over the other

Teachers of young children and especially teachers of young adolescents interact with male students more often than with female students. Boys regularly receive more praise, more negative feedback, more neutral procedural feedback—more teacher-student communications of all types—than girls do (French, 1984; Irvine, 1985; Merrett & Wheldall, 1992). Particularly disturbing is the drop in self-esteem in female students during adolescence (Sadker & Sadker, 1994; Orenstein, 1994).

◆ General Recommendations for Eliminating Gender Typing

Recommendations for eliminating debilitating gender typing and bias in classrooms are broad and sound easy, but they are not. At the very least, they urge teachers to become aware of the possibility of gender bias entering into their teaching and to be knowledgeable about its pervasive effects (Edge et al., 1997). Current recommendations warrant careful consideration:

◆ Avoid stereotypical language (e.g., "Okay, guys, let's get to work");

◆ Provide equal opportunities for males and females (e.g., science club membership for boys and girls); and

◆ Reduce or oust gender-typed activities in classrooms (e.g., "Girls will serve the snack, boys will move the chairs").

But, teachers—and society—have vested interests in enacting the recommendations. As Biklen and Pollard (1993) state: "Teachers and counselors should provide all children with opportunities for engaging in behaviors like curiosity, cooperation, assertiveness, and helpfulness. This way appropriate school behavior, not gender behavior, will be demonstrated" (p. 177).

✦ Newer Controversies About Educating Girls and Boys

Gaining a little steam across the country as a remedy for gender typing and bias in school is the controversial return to segregated classes and schools. The belief is that girls can learn more and be more assertive in all-girl classrooms and that, in some cases, boys can learn more in all-boy classrooms. The constitutionality of such recommendations is questionable, but school districts and parents are exploring this option for girls with greater frequency (Sadker & Sadker, 1994). A Maine high school saw a decrease in the math achievement gap when girls entered into same-gender algebra classes (Durost, 1996). Achievement scores for girls and boys improved when a Virginia middle school offered gender-based math and science classes (Perry, 1996). The Illinois Math and Science Academy tested single-sex physics classes for gifted girls and found that girls responded more positively to the classes. One of the few worries was that boys would see the girl-only classes as less rigorous than their classes (Sadker & Sadker, 1994).

Ethnicity and culture interact with gender bias in classrooms as well. Teachers have a tendency to respond less favorably to male student behavior, and especially to the behavior of African-American males (Simpson & Erickson, 1983). For this reason and because African-American male academic achievement declines steadily after third grade (Kunjufu, 1985), some communities are exploring male-segregated classrooms. Special classrooms in Dade County, Florida, Washington, D.C., Camden, New Jersey, Baltimore, Maryland, and Milwaukee, Wisconsin, are trying or have tried to educate black male students separately (Tifft, 1990; Holland, 1989). Such efforts are controversial and, although the intentions have been praised, they have been criticized by African Americans and Anglo Americans alike (Lawton, 1990; Morgan, 1991). The earlier general recommendations sounded easy, but there are no simple solutions.

Teacher Tool Box

Teacher Response to Gender Typing

Sadker and Sadker (1994) see school-based gender typing and bias as a continuing problem. It results in females in lower-paying jobs, earning less than less-qualified males. Teacher change, more than anything, is crucial to any change in schools. So, they recommend that

- Teachers encourage girls to be assertive,

- Teachers monitor textbooks used in class to ensure coverage of women,

- Teachers be aware of "seating arrangement inequities" because the children who sit up front get the most attention, and

- Teachers should praise and encourage girls for their academic achievement and not for their appearance or handwriting (Sadker & Sadker, 1994).

SOCIOECONOMIC STATUS

Think for a minute about a school that you know. Visualize the students walking from class to class, visualize the school building, and visualize the community in which the school is found. There are probably plenty of examples of the varied social and economic conditions students encounter in your visualizations. But what is socioeconomic status, and what, if any, effect does it have on academic achievement?

◆ Defining Socioeconomic Status and Dispelling Myths

Socioeconomic status (SES) is the term used to distinguish between people's relative position in the society in terms of family income, political power, educational background, and occupational prestige. It is often described via stratified groupings. Those families with an income in excess of $100,000, who enjoy broad political power, who possess college and professional degrees, and who head corporations and large family businesses are categorized at the top of the SES hierarchy or *upper SES*. Families earning between $25,000–40,000, who hold power in state and local politics, who have at least high school educations, and who hold white collar or skilled labor jobs are part of the *middle SES* in the United States; *upper middle SES* families earn between $40,000–100,000 (Macionis, 1991).

Some families are considered part of the vast *working SES*. Working SES families have incomes of $12,000–40,000, limited local power, high school degrees, and hold blue collar jobs. *Lower SES* families' incomes are below what is called "the poverty line" or below $12,000, and low SES families enjoy no political voice. The heads of households are often minimally educated and are minimally employed in low wage, unskilled jobs (Macionis, 1991). Despite the setting of your school, in all likelihood you will meet socioeconomic diversity.

socioeconomic status (SES) students' relative position in society relative to their family income, political power, educational background, and occupational prestige

◆ Dispelling Myths Surrounding Low SES Families

As with the other elements of diversity, many myths surround SES, particularly in terms of low SES families. One often surprising realization is that poverty is not limited to inner cities (Reed & Sautter, 1990). Fewer than 9 percent of low SES people live in cities, while the largest number live in rural areas; more than 50 percent of the populations of some rural communities are poor. Even more surprising is the fact that more than a quarter of low SES families live in suburban communities. Even the affluent suburban county of Westchester, New York, has thousands of homeless people living within its borders (Reed & Sautter, 1990).

Another myth is that poverty is confined to racial minorities. The truth is that, although the rate of poverty is higher for minorities (i.e., given minority population statistics, there are disproportionate numbers of minority families living below the poverty line), the majority of poor children in the United States are Caucasian; two-thirds of the poor are white (Reed & Sautter, 1990). Many people also mistakenly believe that families are impoverished because the household heads are unemployed or welfare recipients. In fact, most poor families have employed members, and although households headed by single females have a greater tendency to live below the poverty line, at least half of all poor children come to school from two-parent households (Reed & Sautter, 1990).

We need to consider the issue of values relative to socioeconomic status. Many people think that poor families have no values or, at least, do not value education. By contrast, many people also think that high SES families *do* value education. Either case might be true, of course, but by the same token, we cannot rule out the fact that many poor families value education and some high SES families do not. Often, because low SES family culture differs from high SES family culture, we interpret this difference as illustrating a lack of caring in low SES families (Finders & Lewis, 1994).

YOU MAKE THE CALL

CONSIDERING SES

Ask yourself critically: What are two ways parents can show that they value education?

- They come to school.
- They see that homework is done.

Ask also: Why might low SES parents not come to school?

- Low wage jobs have less flexible hours.
- They feel intimidated or alienated by school culture and personnel.
- Transportation is inaccessible.
- They have day care constraints.

Now, ask yourself: Why might a low SES parent not monitor a child's homework closely?

- They themselves were poorly educated, and they cannot do the work.
- They are at work during "homework time."
- Low income housing for families often leaves little space for a consistent "homework place."

---

affluenza a perceived decrease in support of teachers and schooling by middle and high socioeconomic parents

In fact, recently teachers have reported increased incidences of "**affluenza**," described as the reduction of middle and high SES parents' support of teachers and schools (McCormick, 1990). Affluent parents, busy with careers and travel, seem to visit school less frequently, monitor homework less frequently, and do not encourage the work ethic in their privileged children (McCormick, 1990). The bottom line here is that values are culturally diverse and are not indigenous to a particular SES group, although it is true that upper SES families (i.e., upper middle and high SES) often are more attuned to school culture.

♦ What Is the Relationship Between SES and School Achievement?

The research shows that children from upper SES families earn higher achievement test scores, better grades, and stay in school longer than lower SES students (Reed & Sautter, 1990; Knapp & Shields, 1990). We know that there are positive correlations between low SES and lower self-esteem, ability or readiness, and school-oriented resources; and negative correlations between low SES and learned helplessness, achievement test scores, the dropout rate, discipline problems (Rice, 1993; Dodge, Pettit, & Bates, 1994). We increasingly see low SES adolescents as members of resistance cultures (Rice, 1993; Reed & Sautter, 1990). We also see many students who are academically able to continue their schooling fail to do so because of the low income status of their families (Jordan & Plank, 1998). Coryman (1998) examined the discrepancies between lower and upper SES families' abilities to pay increasing school fees for textbooks, sports, etc.

YOU MAKE THE CALL

Did your elementary or secondary school offer field trips, or did it require student projects for a grade? Did your parents have to pay a fee for you to attend some field trips? Or did they have to purchase materials for you to complete your projects? What happened to the students whose parents could not afford the field trip fees? What happened to the students whose parents could not afford the project materials? Could the parents' lack of funds for field trips and project materials affect their children's achievement in school? Should schools require such things?

◆ How Do We Address SES in School?

Let's consider a hard reality. As teachers, we cannot remedy all of society's ills. The conditions in the United States that contribute to such disparate levels of socioeconomic status and send so many poor children to school ill-prepared are often beyond our control inside our classrooms. Coordinated and concerted societal efforts will be needed (Reed & Sautter, 1990; Lewis, 1997). More schools are attempting to address the manifestations of poverty (e.g., inadequate clothing, hunger, the need for after-school care) if not for humanitarian reasons, than because Maslow's hierarchy of needs (see Chapter 8) implies that hungry children, poorly dressed children, abused children, and homeless children cannot learn as we have planned for them. Seidman et al. (cf. Huston et al., 1994) point to the significance of addressing developmental needs of poor children by schools, especially from preadolescence on. Such efforts may help "children's self esteem, social adjustment, and long-term academic performance" (p. 80). Some recommendations suggest addressing the literacy level of impoverished parents—a factor that can impact student achievement (McCormick, 1995; Zady et al., 1998). Inconsistent parenting, inadequate health care, and biased teacher expectations must be addressed (McLoyd, 1998).

However, the recommendations offered in the effective teaching literature, in general, can address socioeconomic diversity. We can hold all students accountable for work, offer a variety of instructional methods, and ensure a classroom environment conducive to learning. Utilizing what children bring to school—poor or affluent—and emphasizing the

Teacher Tool Box

Reshaping Curriculum

Means and Knapp (1991) and others recommend that we reshape our curricula to accommodate the needs of educationally disadvantaged children. Teachers can serve poor children best if we

- Focus on complex, meaningful problems,

- Embed basic skills instruction in the context of more global tasks,

- Make connections with students' out-of-school experience and culture.

Along with curricular reform, newer instructional strategies are recommended also. Teachers are encouraged to

- Model powerful thinking strategies,

- Encourage multiple approaches to academic tasks,

- Provide scaffolding to enable students to accomplish complex tasks,

- Make dialogue the central medium for teaching and learning (Means & Knapp, 1991; pp. 286–287).

process of learning are effective. Reliance on content areas deemed relevant by the students themselves (e.g., examinations of community problems, societal issues, human differences, real-life experiences) and encouraging students to make associations between concepts and ideas and principles are useful instructional approaches (Haberman, 1991). Students can benefit when they are helped to become aware of their own learning processes and metacognitive approaches to meaningful learning (e.g., orienting, critiquing, reflecting) (Haberman, 1991, 1995). Challenging curricula, effective teaching, and high yet attainable standards are needed (Lewis, 1997). It's funny—these recommendations are good not just for students from impoverished families, but for all students.

◆ Recommendations for Teaching Poor Children

Many poor children are low ability students, meaning that they lack the necessary prerequisite skills or background experiences to be successful in school. The effective teaching research states that when students have little prior knowledge, the instructional method chosen by the teacher is crucial (Coolican in McNergney, 1988). Some researchers have recommended that we utilize direct instructional approaches, emphasizing basic skills remediation for poor children and employing more than one teaching cycle per lesson (Ziomek, 1982). Direct instructional approaches often offer little challenge and are repetitive (Means & Knapp, 1991). Recently, however, we have realized that poor children may benefit from the incorporation of higher order thinking skills in school (Means & Knapp, 1991). Specifically, cognitive psychologists recommend teaching students "comprehension, composition, and mathematical reasoning" (Means & Knapp, 1991; p. 283).

EMBRACING DIVERSITY

Many teachers are overwhelmed by the notion of having to recognize and incorporate issues of diversity in our classrooms. Some of us celebrate diversity, others are a little reticent about addressing it; while still others resist addressing diversity altogether.

One important recommendation for teachers of diverse children calls for them to examine their own concerns, beliefs, expectations, and biases about diversity. Stacey, Singer, and Ritchie (1989), for instance, explored teenagers' views of poverty—teens attributed poverty to family inadequacies—and teachers should continue to do the same. Let's consider what may be keeping teachers from embracing diversity in school. York (1992) suggested that sometimes teachers are reluctant because they lack adequate knowledge, materials, and time to embrace or even address diversity. Some teachers feel that they are too tired, too overwhelmed, and too fearful of change or of being the lone teacher to advocate change. They may not be up to the challenge or may not want to rock the boat. Still others have other priorities, or they don't care about diversity, don't want to commit to it, don't value the commitment, and may hate change. Some teachers resist addressing diversity in their classrooms because they are prejudiced (York, 1992).

YOU MAKE THE CALL

RELUCTANCE TO FACE DIVERSITY

Take a look at the list of "excuses" described above. Think carefully about which ones may reflect any reluctance you might have about facing diversity. It's natural to be reluctant, but it's necessary to confront our feelings. Then, it's necessary to start thinking about how the excuses can be eliminated.

It is possible that reluctance to embrace diversity may reflect biases, or tendencies to favor one group over another; it may reflect **prejudices** or preconceived opinions about student diversity. Teachers' biases and prejudice could manifest in their using **stereotypes**, or oversimplified characteristics, to describe student variations. It could manifest in **discrimination** also, where preferential treatment is given to students belonging to particular groups.

prejudices preconceived opinions about differences between people

stereotypes oversimplified characteristics used to describe students generally

discrimination preferential treatment given to one group over another

We should acknowledge that we may possess these faults. We know, for instance, that teachers have lower academic expectations for teen mothers and children from mother-only families, and for households with working mothers (Cooper & Moore, 1994; Tetenbaum, Lighter, & Travis, 1981). We know that teachers treat students differentially with respect to gender, race, and socioeconomic status (Simpson & Erickson, 1983; Madden et al., 1992; Dodge et al., 1994). In classrooms, we know also that students are sensitive to speech differences (Light et al., 1978), prefer students who look like them (Kistner et al., 1993; Ramsey, 1991) and internalize stereotypes early (Elrich, 1994). Awareness of beliefs, expectations, and biases is important to effectively addressing the academic—if not social—needs of children in our classrooms as well.

One last word: Regardless of the amount of diversity in our classrooms, **cooperative learning** also called group assisted learning, can be utilized. It represents the closest thing to "generic teaching strategies" for addressing diversity. Cooperative learning has been covered elsewhere in this text, but it can serve several instructional and humanitarian purposes in the classroom. Facilitating small group work can foster group connectedness, responsibility, communication, interaction skills, and group processing skills (Johnson, 1990). Additionally, cooperative

cooperative learning students representing various cultural groups work together in class to facilitate academic as well as social skills; also called "group assisted learning"

learning activities are motivating (Nichols & Miller, 1994), can increase performance (Eldredge, 1990), and can promote the traversing of student worlds (Johnson & Johnson, 1981). Be cautioned: Some family cultures do not view cooperative learning as positively as the growing body of educational research does (Dunn & Griggs, 1990; Hickson, Land, & Aikman, 1994). Be sensitive to the interactions between culture and instructional methodologies.

Reflections from the Field

1 After 31 years of classroom teaching, I am still in awe and somewhat amazed about how important it is to understand the unique values, culture, and approach to learning that each child brings to my class. Assuming common learning values and styles is a BIG mistake!

—Alice R. (high school mathematics teacher), Roanoke, VA

2 One of the things I found very helpful was at the beginning of the year assign each child the project of interviewing family members to identify unique cultural activities, artifacts or values. The children generally focused on things like holidays, special foods, and dress. We would establish each month as a special culture month, and I would group the kids together to work on the decoration for the classroom for that month. I have also invited members of the family in to share foods or practices that reflect their culture. The children really like this and we end up celebrating cultural diversity throughout the year . . . not just on national holidays.

—Robert D. (fourth grade social studies teacher), San Diego, CA

3 I work with preschoolers and find that they are most often very genuine and open in their ignorance and interest about other cultures. I am a woman of Irish descent, my teaching partner is an African-American woman. As part of our curriculum, we try to get the children to recognize their uniqueness (making body templates—cut outs of hands, etc.). As part of that, we will team up and have the children identify our physical differences. They really like to touch and contrast my very red curly hair, with my partner's. The children have also noted our nose and lip differences and even our skin texture. They are curious, and they seem to become more comfortable with these physical differences when we give them permission to look-touch-and-ask.

—Kathleen O. (preschool teacher), Canton, OH

4 I teach high school psychology (twelfth grade). I often employ gender and culturally biased exercises and tests (e.g., Chitlin test—an alternative, cultural biased IQ test) as a way to discuss stereotypes, prejudice and real cultural differences. I find providing some degree of shock helps the students question their own bias.

—Thomas D. (social studies/psychology teacher, high school), Chicago, IL

5 I provide my students with a learning styles inventory at the beginning of the year. I explain to them about learning styles, and I invite them to take the test so that we can decide on the best ways for them to approach my class as well as to give me some direction regarding the best possible ways to approach my instruction. The test I use costs about $5 to have computer scored. The kids (and their parents) really get into discussing the results and what they mean in terms of approaching homework. If nothing else, it opens your eyes to the variety of learning styles. Further, it helped me to understand that often I teach to my style . . . which is not always that of the children in my class.

—*Laura C. (middle school language arts teacher), West Chester, PA*

THEORY TO PRACTICE

A Look at Escalante as Decision Maker

Take a look back at the varied movie scene that opens this chapter: The camera pans the campus outside of the high school. We see students walking to class, standing around, conversing with friends, standing in groups, standing alone. We see students with dark complexions, light complexions, tall students, short students, well-dressed students, not-so-well dressed students, smiling students, and students who are expressionless. The scene moves next to the hallways and the main office, where we see the same mixtures of people. Next, we see Mr. Escalante in his first classroom, where he looks out over a sea of students walking and standing, dark and light, well-dressed and not . . .

How do we assess those scenes from the standpoint of diversity? Ask yourselves: How do Mr. Escalante's students appear to differ from each other? How will he find out about their differences? In that sweeping look, in his review of their records, and in the weeks to come as he gets to know his students, Mr. Escalante will begin to make determinations about the nature and extent of diversity among the students in his classroom. He will gain first-hand experience about their family cultures by talking to the students and by visiting their homes and communities. He will ascertain learning styles and language diversity, and he will find out who comes from an impoverished or an affluent family, who has the necessary background experiences, and who does not. Mr. Escalante will also be able to see the effects of gender typing and gender-biased socialization on both his male and female students.

You—as Teacher, as Decision Maker

Case Illustration 1:
One encounter with diversity, Kara Holland's social studies class

Now, consider the following scene, only this time, you look for possible diversity.

Kara Holland's social studies classes are in a suburban school that draws most of its students from the surrounding middle-class communities. Some of her students have plans to attend college, while others plan to start jobs as soon as possible. Although the curriculum in her school is fairly traditional, at least a quarter of her students recently have come from a middle school emphasizing independent learning.

As you attempt to analyze this scene, think about these questions: What do you possibly know about the students in Ms. Holland's classes? Are your views of the diversity in her class influenced by biases, expectations, prejudices, and attitudes you might be bringing to this exercise? Given the elements of diversity possible in Ms. Holland's class, which instructional methods are viable?

Case Illustration 2:
A community, a school . . . a class in transition

Now, consider the following scene, again *looking for possible diversity* and attempting to anticipate the possible impact on the teacher and the teacher's approach to his classroom.

Jeffrey Taylor has been teaching seventh grade language arts for 23 years, all at the J. P. Morgan middle school. Over the last few years, the community in which J. P. Morgan is located has gone through some transitions. A number of the older families have moved and many of the new families moving in are of Asian heritage. Last year, Mr. Taylor had 8 students with Asian surnames, and this year he has 17.

As you attempt to analyze this scene, think about these questions: What do you possibly know about the students in Mr. Taylor's classes? Are your views of the diversity in his class influenced by biases, expectations, prejudices, and attitudes you may be bringing to this exercise? Given the elements of diversity possible in Mr. Taylor's class, what recommendations might you give him in reference to the context of his classroom, the mode of his teaching, and the content of his class?

SUMMARY

Increasing Diversity

In Chapter 5, we examined student diversity. The preceding chapters have addressed optimal student development and relative uniformity within student populations. However, we must all realize that student diversity—the ways in which our students differ from each other as well as the ways in which they differ from their teachers—is increasing. But at the same time that we acknowledge that diversity is increasing, we must accept the fact that diversity or difference is just that—different! In this chapter, we take a look at several of the many areas of diversity that may be present in contemporary classrooms, and we consider the recommendations for teaching diverse students. Each of these areas is rife with ongoing controversy; researchers and practitioners continue to examine ways to incorporate diversity successfully within the context of classroom teaching.

Cultural Diversity

The first area addressed is cultural diversity. Cultural diversity includes the ways in which individuals, families, and larger social groups think, feel, behave, and live. Rather than shun differences in individuals and families, we are encouraged to embrace cultural pluralism and incorporate it into our instructional decision making. Culture is a broad and encompassing concept and may influence the other areas of diversity addressed in the chapter, including linguistic diversity.

Race and Ethnicity

Race is another element of microcultural diversity and should be examined like all others in this chapter. Ignoring race means that we may be ignoring an important aspect of our students' cultural makeups. The differences in achievement between racial groups in schools are well-documented. We remain uncertain about why this is the case. There is no lack of possible explanations. The fact is, we are just not sure why the gaps persist. We do know, however, that teacher expectations can be a contributing factor. Teachers' differing expectations for students may be influenced by students' race, and teachers' attitudes may manifest in biased student attitudes as well. Effective teachers of racially and ethnically diverse students know their students through interaction and exploration. Teachers also examine their own attitudes and beliefs about racial diversity and racial differences. They hold challenging expectations for all students and have a deep commitment to the increased achievement of all students.

Linguistic Diversity

Language is an element of culture. Demographers project that many students in the public schools will come from families where American English is not the primary language. Many myths surround the inclusion of language-diverse students in the classroom; effective teachers acknowledge their own biases, and accept language diversity, while seeking ways to move all students into American English usage. However, there is some debate about the best ways to do just that.

Learning Style

There has been debate about the need to address learning-style differences in students as well. Students may vary in several ways according to their learning preferences. Learning style is a broad category and students may differ in their cognitive processing preferences, their physiological styles, and their psychological/affective styles. We know that "as we learn so do we teach"; therefore, it is a good idea for teachers to have a sense of their own learning styles before we attempt to address variances in our students.

Gender Role

The debate surrounding gender differences is ongoing. Males and females are different, of course, but in their early lives they share many more similarities. Gender typing begins when children are young and can become gender bias in the school years and beyond. Many recommendations attempt to ameliorate the effects of biased socialization on both girls and boys, but newer controversies have arisen as we try to address this area of diversity in the classroom.

Socioeconomic Status

Socioeconomic status distinguishes between people's relative standing in society in terms of family income, political power, educational background, and occupational prestige. Myths abound about the characteristics of poor and affluent families. Socioeconomic status does correlate positively with school achievement for many reasons. Although teachers cannot remedy all of society's ills, we can attempt to teach both the children of affluent families as well as those from impoverished families effectively. Several research-based recommendations are offered.

Embracing Diversity

Many teachers are overwhelmed at having to incorporate issues of diversity into their instruction. One significant recommendation calls for teachers to examine and acknowledge their own concerns, beliefs, expectations, and biases about diversity. Then, in making our choices we should be sensitive to the interactions between culture—broadly defined—and instructional methodologies.

◆ Field Experience Questions

As with previous chapters, it may be valuable for you to see these concepts in action, by systematically observing what goes on in classrooms you visit. Below are a series of field experience questions related to topics covered in this chapter. Consider each, as you make your classroom observations.

1. Observe teacher interaction with differing individuals in a classroom. (You may have to ask the teacher privately and IN ADVANCE to help with the identification.) Look to see how many times a student in each of the following groups asks for help and then receives positive or neutral assistance, receives a reprimand, or is ignored:

   ◆ Females and males;

   ◆ African American, white, Hispanic, Asian;

   ◆ High SES and low SES;

   ◆ standard and nonstandard American English users;

   ◆ field-dependent and field-independent learners.

   Note the percentages of interaction and make comparisons. OR,

2. Identify the apparent preferred teaching style of the teacher using the descriptions presented in class or in your readings.

   ◆ Does the teacher try to vary teaching style?

   ◆ How does the teacher's style appear to affect student learning in general?

   ◆ How does the teacher's style appear to affect certain students in the class?

◆ Key Terms

affluenza
amalgamation theory
antibias education model
assimilation theory
biases
bicultural education model
cognitive style
cooperative learning
cultural pluralism
culture
dialectal language

discrimination
diversity
field-dependent learners
field-independent learners
gender bias
gender schema theory
gender typing
human relations approach
immersion approach
learning styles
linguistic diversity

multicultural education
physiological style
prejudices
psychological/affective style
single group study approach
socioeconomic status (SES)
standard language
stereotypes
transformative multicultural
   education model
transitional approach

◆ Additional Resources

Baker, G. (1983). *Planning and organizing for multicultural instruction.* Reading, MA: Addison-Wesley.

Hyde, S. H., & Linn, M. C. (Eds.). (1986). *The psychology of gender: Advances through meta-analysis.* Baltimore: Johns Hopkins University Press.

Knapp, M. S., Turnbull, B. J., & Shields, P. M. (1990). New directions for educating children of poverty. *Educational Leadership, 48*(1), 4–9.

Linn, M. C. & Hyde, J. S. (1989). Gender, mathematics, and science. *Educational Researcher, 18,*17–27.

Noll, J. W. (1991). *Taking sides: Clashing views on controversial educational issues* (5th ed.) (pp. 44–63) Guildford, CT: Duskin.

Pine, G. J., & Hilliard, A.G., III (1990). Rx for racism: Imperatives for America's schools. *Phi Delta Kappan, 71,* 593–600.

Tettegah, S. (1996). The racial consciousness attitudes of white prospective teachers and their perceptions of the teachability of students from a different racial/ethnic backgrounds: Findings from a California study. *Journal of Negro Education, 65*(2), 151–163.

Learning Theories: Behaviorism

T he teacher stands before his class with an inquiring look, a raised baton, a bucket of ice cubes, and a ship's captain's uniform. He distributes sheet music for the "Main Theme from *Titanic*." The sounds of excerpts of the work fill the practice room. He points to a nearby student with an oboe poised at the ready and asks, "Who has the melody?" She looks puzzled and cannot answer. He waits a moment, then moves on to a student holding a flute in her lap. He asks again, "Who has the melody?" The flutist looks at the music for a second and then responds, "The string section." The teacher smiles broadly and replies, "Good!" A third student, a percussionist, has little trouble answering the question and receives a smile and a compliment as well.

The music teacher's smiles and praise were certainly sincere personal gestures, but they were also tools of an effective teacher-designed behavior to increase the likelihood of both participation and thoughtful answers in his classroom. The learning about melody was evident. But why? Do learning and performance need to result in a payoff? Do learners need incentives? If so, what kinds of incentives are necessary? Do learners need goals to work towards? Should teachers help students control and monitor their behavior? Should teachers consider what their students are thinking about in learning?

The music teacher clearly realized the need to have a clear understanding of "What" he was about to teach. Further, as discussed in previous sections, an effective teacher has to consider the unique cognitive, social-emotional, cultural, and individual characteristics of the "Who" they are about to teach. With both the "What" and "Who" of teaching identified, you, we, and the music teacher can begin to consider the "How" of our teaching. Identifying this "How" is a way for us to understand the theories that explain the learning process.

Remember that in Chapter 1 you learned that theories are reasoned explanations for various phenomena in education. As you work through this chapter and the next, you will come to understand more about the phenomena of human learning. You will come to understand various reasoned explanations of human learning and their applications in classroom settings. These theories are often prescriptive, meaning that they can offer instructional suggestions, regardless of developmental level, subject area, or the social context of the class. An understanding of learning theories is crucial to teachers, especially to new teachers.

◆ Chapter Objectives

When you have mastered the material in this chapter, you will be able to

1 Define learning and distinguish it from maturation;

2 Describe the behaviorist approach to learning and differentiate it from other approaches;

3 Describe the role of contiguity and repetition in the classical conditioning response;

4 Define key concepts in the classical conditioning paradigm (e.g., unconditioned stimulus, unconditioned response, conditioned stimulus, conditioned response);

5 Define key concepts associated with Skinner's operant conditioning (e.g., positive reinforcement, extinction, punishment, shaping) and explain how operant conditioning differs from classical conditioning;

6 Define the key concepts associated with the work of Bandura and other social learning theorists: modeling, imitation, and vicarious learning;

7 Describe and give examples of classroom applications of behaviorist and neobehaviorist principles, including classroom use of contiguity, reinforcement, alternatives to punishment, and modeling.

CHAPTER 6 CONTENT MAP

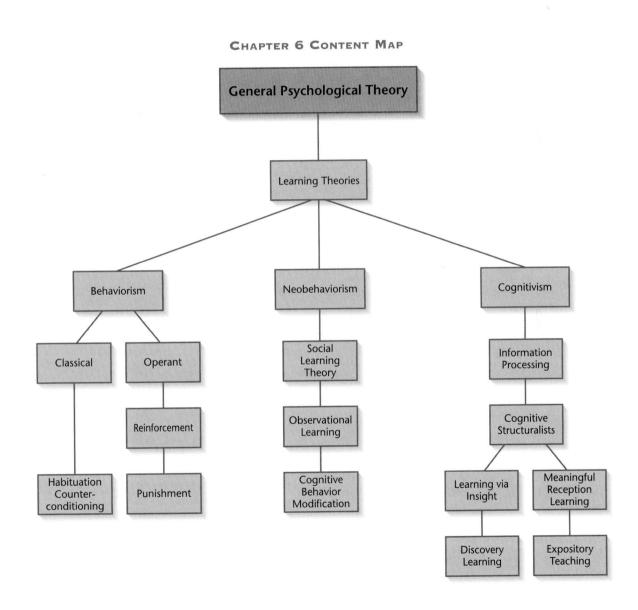

WHAT IS LEARNING?
AN OVERVIEW OF LEARNING THEORIES

What is learning? This sounds like such a simple question until you really start to think about it. Consider the following examples. Which are instances of **learning**? Which are not?

learning permanent change in behavior or capacity acquired through experience

◆ An infant babbles "Da-da-da-da-da";

◆ The toddler sings, "Old MacDonald had a farm";

◆ The second grader jumps when a door slams unexpectedly;

◆ The middle schooler screams when a neighbor's dog approaches.

The toddler singing and the middle schooler screaming are examples of learning. The infant babbling and the second grader jumping are not. Why?

What's the difference between the examples of learning and "not learning"? The difference is . . . experience. In other words, the toddler's behavior is the result of her experience. She was not biologically programmed to sing "Old MacDonald." Sure, learning is acquiring knowledge; it's an enduring change in living beings not dictated by genetic predisposition; it is also a relative yet permanent change in behavior resulting from practice. But, for the most part, learning is change in behavior or capacity acquired *through experience*, and learning theories attempt to explain how we are changed by our experiences. Learning theories are subdivisions of general psychological theory and as such offer differing explanations of types or perspectives on how we are changed by our experiences.

◆ Basic Premises of Learning Theories

Despite the differences in theoretical perspectives, there are overall premises of learning theories that are *true across perspectives*:

◆ *We can learn things that are beneficial and not so beneficial to us.* Sometimes, our behavior changes in ways that are not helpful to us. We learn things that do not help us to advance either as individuals or as a species. An example might be phobias.

◆ *We are not always aware of what we've learned.* Learning is not always deliberate, and we may not be conscious of what we've learned. Sometimes, we learn things without realizing it. We are unaware of what we have learned, or we learn something that we did not set out to learn.

◆ *The results of learning are not always easy to see.* Most contemporary theorists agree that not all learning yields readily observable change. Bandura (1977, 1978) noted that learning can take place even though no overt behavioral change is witnessed in learners.

◆ *There are different types and levels of learning.* In the last thirty years, psychologists have determined that learning varies from simple and mechanistic (e.g., instincts or reflexes) to complex and organized (e.g., solving a quadratic equation).

These assumptions appear to be agreed upon by all of the major theorists attempting to explain the learning process. The more specific details of "how," "when," and "how best" to learn are not so commonly agreed upon. There are many different sets of beliefs about the learning process, which we will begin to explore. But first it may be useful to consider your own set of beliefs about how people learn.

◆ A Personal View of Learning

Take a few minutes to become aware of what beliefs you're bringing to this chapter. Review each of the following. (Adapted in part from Seaberg, 1974, pp. 7–8.) Do you believe that

1. Learners need grades, gold stars, and other incentives as motivation to learn and to accomplish school requirements?

2. Teachers are powerful models for learning new behaviors?

3. Teachers need to determine what students are thinking about while solving math problems?

4. Students should be graded according to uniform standards of achievement, which the teacher sets for the class?

5. Culture influences learning?

6. Curriculum should be organized along subject matter lines that are carefully sequenced?

7. The teacher should help students to monitor and control their own learning behavior?

Your beliefs and assumptions about the learning process are the seeds of your preformed theories about how students learn. It is good to acknowledge these beliefs now, but keep in mind that theories are reasoned explanations for phenomena and not absolute fact. Thus, we should be open to review all theories of learning as they serve to explain human behavior.

◆ An Overview of Classic Theories

Take a look at the content map on page 205, and you'll notice that learning theories represent some of the subdivisions of general psychological theory and that there are varied explanations for change via experience.

A Brief Overview of Cognitivism

The **cognitivist** explanation suggests that learning is a change in internal processes that cannot be observed directly. Review your responses to the previous questions. If you support the notions found in questions 3 and 6, you may have a cognitivist orientation to learning. The cognitivist regards changes in thinking or emotions or in a person's ability to respond to a particular situation as the key to learning. (Some cognitivists consider changes in overt behavior as simply symptomatic or

cognitivism theory in which learning is equated with changes in the organization and use of internal processes reflective of the "real" changes, which occur internally.) The cognitivist perspective has been championed by such researchers and theorists as Jean Piaget, Robert Gagne, Jerome Bruner, Lev Vygotsky, and David Ausubel. Chapter 7 will examine the cognitivist explanation of learning in more detail.

A Brief Overview of Neobehaviorism

A second perspective on the process of learning, which as you will see is positioned somewhere in between the behaviorist and the cognitivist explanations of how people learn, is *neobehaviorist theory.* (Some people have suggested that the neobehaviorist explanation could have just as easily been called the "neocognitivist" perspective.)

neobehaviorism theory which believes that changes in behavior are observable and influenced by internal processes

Neobehaviorism offers an explanation of learning that emphasizes both changes in observable behavior *and* in internal processes. In attempting to explain change, the neobehaviorist looks at obvious evidence and the "less-than-obvious" motivations behind it. If you found yourself supporting the positions presented in questions 2 and 6, then you may adhere to a neobehaviorist orientation. This theoretical perspective has been offered by noted researchers and theorists like Albert Bandura and Daniel Meichenbaum and derives from both lab study and observation of human behavior. We will return to a more in-depth presentation of neobehaviorism near the end of this chapter.

A Brief Overview of Behaviorism

Look at the concept map again. Another theoretical perspective—or alternative explanation for experiential changes in human behavior—is behaviorism. "Behaviorism" is a termed coined by John B. Watson (1914), who took the position that as scientists, psychologists should focus only on overt, measurable behaviors. Watson and others favoring a behaviorist perspective would answer in the affirmative to questions 1, 4, and 7. Review your own thoughts on those questions; perhaps you subscribe to behaviorist notions about learning.

behaviorism theory which equates learning with changes in observable behaviors

The behaviorist explanation suggests that learning is a change in the way people act overtly—observable behaviors and observable behavior change. (Some "old school" behaviorists have believed so strongly in the latter part of the explanation that they have ruled out changes in thinking or emotions as being learned since we cannot see changes in thinking or emotions always.) The behaviorist perspective has been championed by noted researchers and theorists such as Ivan Pavlov, John Watson, E. L. Thorndike, and B. F. Skinner. Many of their theories and the theories of other behaviorists began

Teacher Tool Box

Preferred Theories?

Acknowledging our "pet" theories about how humans learn is important. But after acknowledgement comes "knowledge." We should consider that our students' behavior can be changed—and will be changed—in a variety of ways. We should be open to exploring explanations different from our "preferred" theory. When we ask ourselves, "Why are my students behaving this way?", we should keep the following in mind:

- Don't underestimate the power of experience;
- Don't underestimate the extent of behavioral change;
- Consider engaging differing types of learning.

in experimental laboratories and as observations of animal behavior, which were generalized later to explain human behavioral change. The current chapter will describe two behaviorist perspectives: classical conditioning and operant conditioning.

YOU MAKE THE CALL

UNDERSTANDING CLASSROOM EXPERIENCE

Think back to the scene that opened this chapter:

Hadn't the first student learned anything?

Will the second student continue to learn?

Will the teacher's responses increase or decrease the likelihood of future learning?

Whether we are examining behaviorism, cognitivism, or neobehaviorism, *all* of these theories are crucial to teachers in classrooms. They help us attempt to explain the student behavior we see in class as well as what might be going on in the minds of the students emitting the behaviors. (For a review of the differing perspectives, see Table 6.1.)

As you work your way through this chapter and the next, keep in mind the basic premises we examined at the beginning of this chapter. They become evident across theoretical perspectives. Now let's consider the first theoretical perspective: behaviorism.

Table 6.1   Perspectives on Learning

	Behaviorism	*Neobehaviorism*	*Cognitivism*
ASSUMPTION	"Learning is overt action."	"Learning is overt action and internal processes."	"Learning is internal processes."
PROPONENTS	Watson Thorndike Skinner	Bandura Meichenbaum	Piaget Bruner Ausubel
RESEARCH	Lab study with animals	Lab study with animals and human study	Human study
PROCESSES	Classical conditioning and operant conditioning	Social learning and modeling	Information processing, cognitive structuralism

HOW DO BEHAVIORISTS EXPLAIN HOW WE LEARN?

B. F. Skinner opens his book *About Behaviorism* with the statement: "Behaviorism is not the science of human behavior; it is the philosophy of that science" (p. 3). An intriguing quote no doubt! But what does it mean? What does it mean to teachers?

Remember that the behaviorist explanation of how we change through experience focuses on overt and observable behavior change. At the core of this view of learning is the idea that whenever two events occur together over and over again, they will become associated, so, at another time, when only one of the events occurs, the association will persist. This notion of learning via associations sounds simplistic, but is really quite profound, so much so that some psychologists feel that it can explain almost every aspect of learning. Think about it—events that occur together often enough may become indelibly linked. Why do you think a language arts teacher might lead a class in chanting, "I before E except after C," over and over again? Clearly, the teacher wants that grammatical rule indelibly linked in the students' minds, so that when they come across new words, they'll automatically remember the rule.

principle of contiguity
theory that if two events are presented together repeatedly, they will become so associated, that when only one event is present, the missing event will be remembered also

Yet for all of the **principle of contiguity**'s benefits and service, we can't forget our basic premises about learning theories. *Learning via association* (or contiguous learning) does not yield deliberate or adaptive behavior, which means that through this founding principle we sometimes learn things that we did not intend or that are not good for us. Some psychologists feel that stereotypes are learned contiguously. For example, if we consistently see minorities depicted as criminals in the media, those images may become connected unforgettably. Again, if we consistently see women depicted as sex objects, those images become joined as well. In either case, we all could agree reasonably that such images are not productive and may not be learned intentionally. Still, contiguous learning provides a powerful, general explanation of learning and is highly useful in classrooms. In the popular 1988 movie *Stand and Deliver*, when Mr. Escalante ordered his class to line up and field calculus questions from him one at a time—in other words, when he engaged them in a drill and practice—he was relying on the principle of contiguity to establish a memorable association between the questions and answers.

With the significance of contiguous learning as a foundation, let's consider two behaviorist explanations of how people learn: classical conditioning and operant conditioning.

A LOOK AT CLASSICAL CONDITIONING

The teacher in the opening scene transforms his students' boredom into positive attitudes. Through his use of humor, they start to view learning new music as enjoyable and exciting. This change may be due in part to classical conditioning. **Classical conditioning** is sometimes referred to as stimulus-substitution learning, in that it represents a condition where, through contiguity and repetition in presentation of stimuli, a learner generalizes an existing stimulus-response connection to some new stimuli. The focus is on a pattern of learning where the catalyst for behavior change is what precedes a behavior (Bigge & Shermis, 1992; Ney, 1981; Jones 1975; Mikulas, 1972).

◆ Association of Stimuli

Perhaps the most famous representation of classical conditioning was the Russian physiologist, Ivan Pavlov. Pavlov had been investigating the salivation response in animals when—by accident—he and his colleagues conditioned a dog to salivate to the sound of a bell. In Pavlov's study, dog food (or meat paste as was the case in the actual study) automatically elicited a physiological response in dogs; that is, salivation. Since the "meat-salivation" connection seemed to be "pre-wired" or natural, Pavlov termed it "unconditional," as a way of identifying it as not having been learned voluntarily. As an unlearned, natural elicitor of a response, the meat in this experiment was identified as an **unconditioned stimulus (US)**. Further, the salivation was an automatic reaction to the presentation of meat and thus was termed the **unconditioned response (UR).** Other unconditioned stimuli and unconditioned responses could be found in reflex actions such as showing a "startle" reaction to an unexpected loud noise, or blinking to a puff of air aimed near the eye, etc.

The uniqueness of Pavlov's work was not in its identification of the "meat-salivation" connection. Rather, Pavlov demonstrated that if he paired a stimulus, which to that point did not elicit a salivation response automatically, with a stimulus that did have this characteristic, then through repetition and contiguity the two stimuli would become associated and share the characteristic of eliciting salivation. It was not hard for Pavlov to teach his dog—we'll call him "Boris"—to associate the sound of a bell with the presentation of meat through repetitive pairings of these two signals. They were paired often enough to become associated, so much so that later, when the bell was presented alone, Boris salivated to its sound. In this situation, once the bell acquired the characteristic of eliciting salivation, it became

classical conditioning type of behaviorist learning in which associations are established between automatic emotional or physiological responses and a new stimuli; also called "s-r pattern learning"

unconditioned stimulus (US) stimulus which automatically evokes an emotional or physiological response

unconditioned response (UR) an automatic emotional or physiological response to an unconditioned stimulus

The uniqueness of Pavlov's work was not in the identification of the meat-salivation connection. Instead, it was the demonstration that dissimilar stimuli can become associated. ◆

conditioned stimulus a stimulus which evoked a different emotional or physiological response after conditioning

conditioned response an emotional or physiological response to a conditioned stimulus after learning

a learned or **conditioned stimulus**, and the response to that learned stimuli was also learned and was termed a **conditioned response.**

Another, more readily available example is presented in your own response to a "surprise" toy such as a Jack in the Box. Do you remember the childhood toy consisting of a music box with a crank and a clown attached to a spring inside? The crank makes the song play and the clown jumps out at the end of the song. The clown jumping out of the box at the end of the song has surprised you so often that now you cringe when you hear the song, even if the clown is not present!

With the Jack in the Box episode in mind, let's review some key terminology:

1. *Unconditioned stimulus (US):* A stimulus that automatically produces a physiological or emotional response (e.g., the sudden appearance of the clown).

2. *Unconditioned response (UR):* a naturally occurring physiological or emotional response (e.g., your startle response).

3. *Neutral stimulus (NS):* a stimulus that—prior to conditioning—evoked no physiological or emotional effect or even a different effect (e.g., the little song emitted). (Prior to its pairing with the clown release, the song may have evoked no response in you or maybe even a pleasurable response.)

4. *Conditioned Stimulus (CS):* a stimulus that evokes a physiological or emotional response *after* conditioning or pairing (e.g., the little song).

5. *Conditioned response (CR):* a learned response to a previously neutral stimulus (i.e., your cringing when you hear just the song).

It should be noted that while the UR (e.g., salivation to meat) and the CR (salivation to the bell) may appear to be the same, they are not exactly the same response. Often, the CR differs in intensity or presentation. It may even be a subtle adaptation of the initial UR.

Two psychology professors demonstrated classical conditioning to their classes by popping balloons in class after counting "one, two, three" aloud (Kohn & Kalat, 1992). They showed their students that the CR can be different from the UR, because in their in-class experiment, although the UR was flinching at the sound of the balloons, the CR inevitably became the students' muscle tightening to keep from flinching.

✦ Classical Conditioning in the Classroom

Now, let's move this familiar classical conditioning paradigm from the laboratory to the schoolhouse. Imagine that this is the first day of school and little Jamillah is standing at the door to her classroom. As she stands looking into her brightly lit and colorfully decorated classroom, she is startled by a loud, booming voice shouting "Everybody QUIET!" Startled by the noise and on the brink of tears, Jamillah sees the sound coming from Mr. Henry, her teacher. It happens again and again. While reactions typically are not conditioned so rapidly, it is pos-

Table 6.2 **Example of a Classical Conditioning Paradigm**
Conditioning an Emotional Reaction

Before Conditioning	*Conditioning*	*After Conditioning*
US = loud sudden noise	Present neutral stimuli (Mr. Henry)	CS = Mr. Henry
UR = startle, fear, withdrawal	+	
	Unconditioned stimuli (Loud sudden noise)	
NS = Mr. Henry (Neutral signal)		CR = fear, withdrawal
	Unconditioned response (startle, fear, withdrawal) Repeat	
	Repeat	

sible that the "fear" and "startle" and "tendency to withdraw" (UR) responses, which may be elicited naturally in situations of loud, sudden noise (UR), will now be associated with Mr. Henry (CS) to the degree that Jamillah begins to feel anxious, on edge, and withdrawn (CR) in his presence. This example of classical conditioning is summarized in Table 6.2.

Classical conditioning can provide a powerful explanation for the changes in human behavior. Take a minute to think about what might happen to Jamillah as a result of her classically conditioned fear of this one teacher.

◆ Stimulus Generalization

One demonstration of the possibility of classically conditioning an individual's fear response was dramatically presented in the early 1920s by the work of J. B. Watson. It was a demonstration that resulted in more information than was initially expected!

With his colleague Rosalie Rayner, Watson embarked on what has come to be known as the Little Albert study (Jones, 1975, 1924b). As the story goes, Watson and Rayner invited a young mother and her toddler son, Albert, into their lab. They utilized the time-honored classical conditioning paradigm of stimulus substitution. In this case, a white lab rat was paired with an unconditioned stimulus, a loud noise. Through associations of the rat and noise, Little Albert learned to fear the planned CS, the rat. So far, pretty predictable stuff as far as classical conditioning is concerned. What set this study apart was the discovery that not only did Albert fear the direct CS, but he began to fear multiple conditioned stimuli or things that resembled the direct CS. He learned to fear a white hamster, a white toy bunny, a white fur coat, and—in what was probably the most insidious finding of all—a Santa Claus mask! Watson

stimulus generalization
responding emotionally or physiologically not only to the conditioned stimulus, but also to stimuli that resemble the conditioned stimulus

and Rayner discovered that sometimes what is a learned response to one particular stimulus can spread to similar stimuli; they termed the process, **stimulus generalization.** Our behavior changes because of the CS, but also because of things like the CS; we may respond to similar, multiple stimuli in the same way as to the initial CS.

Let's consider Jamillah again. If she learned to associate fear with Mr. Henry, that fear could generalize to other teachers, or even to other classroom settings or to the entire school, since these signals were also paired with the startle noise made by Mr. Henry!

Both Albert and Jamillah seemed to learn generalized, irrational fears—why? What determines the extent of the generalization? Experience—or its lack—determines extent!

We suspect that the degree or amount of generalization is influenced by the amount of experience students have. Let's say you have very little experience cooking, but are preparing a special dinner for friends due to arrive at any moment. Suddenly, one of your featured dishes catches fire! You will probably be mortified—and it's possible that you may vow to never cook for friends again! You also may vow to stay out of the kitchen altogether. Now, let's examine this scene again: Suppose, instead of being a novice cook, you are a great restaurant chef, and one of your featured dishes goes up in flames as well. As a chef, you won't be happy to see your creation charred, but you'll get over it and will start to cook again. The fact that chefs have more experiences with cooking mishaps than people who are new to cooking results in differing degrees of generalization.

Little Albert's fear of so many things that were similar to the white lab rat (or direct CS) may have been the result of his having so little experience with these events. (Remember that Albert was a young child.) Jamillah's fear of Mr. Henry and other teachers may have been influenced by the fact that this was her first encounter with school. Students with limited experience are more apt to have massive stimulus generalization than students with many experiences.

Connections

Find current information about the use of behaviorist principles in effective teaching for yourself via the Internet. Go into <http://Yahoo.com> and enter its *Quick Search directory;* start a search of *classroom management* entries. Evaluate the tips offered with respect to the behaviorist and neobehaviorist learning theories studied in this chapter (e.g., use of reinforcers, punishment, models).

◆ Stimulus Discrimination

Let's suppose for now that, interestingly, Jamillah is not fearful of entering the school building or any of her other classes. She is not anxious about stopping to talk to other teachers or interacting with them at assemblies or community functions. Her classically conditioned response seems to be limited to one stimulus, Mr. Henry. What's going on with Jamillah now? It would appear that Jamillah is showing signs of *stimulus discrimination.* Her response to similar stimuli is different even in similar situations.

◆ Extinction

Sometimes, as in the examples we have used above, students learn things via classical conditioning that are not intended or beneficial to them. We need to consider how to *extinguish* or "undo" such classically conditioned bonds. Many strategies for **extinction** are familiar, but some have unanticipated results and problems, and we are warned about their use. In fact, although popular, the first three of the following strategies are ineffective.

extinction (in classical conditioning) strategies used to undo classically conditioned associations

First, when a student has learned something that is not beneficial—let's say, an irrational fear—we may try to break the bond between the CS and CR by removing the student from the situation. We feel that we can help the student forget the fear. Jamillah's well-meaning parents might insist she stay at home or be placed in another class or may even send her to a new school. However, this strategy is ineffective because classically conditioned bonds—for example, irrational fears—are *not* forgotten.

Second, sometimes when children have learned something that we did not want them to—for example, a fear of the water—we inappropriately use ridicule, teasing, and scolding to undo the fear bond. We'll say things like "Don't be a chicken! Don't be a wimp!" This strategy is ineffective also because ridicule, teasing, and scolding may enhance—not extinguish—a bond, especially a fear bond.

Third, often we try to *talk* students out of classically conditioned bonds that are not adaptive. We attempt to appeal to their logic and rationality. This is another ineffective strategy because classically conditioned bonds are not always rational or logical. In the case of an irrational fear, for example, the emotional response usually outweighs the rational solution offered.

The previous "strategies" are used frequently but are not recommended to extinguish classically conditioned bonds, since they are not only ineffective but may be counterproductive! In the 1920s, researcher Mary Cover Jones examined several ways to unlearn classically conditioned bonds (Jones, 1924a, 1924b); these techniques are still applicable today. The following two extinction strategies do work—*provisionally*, meaning that they should be used knowledgeably and with empathy and caution.

Habituation

Sometimes, we try to undo bonds by presenting the student with the object of their fear over and over again. We attempt to achieve extinction via repeated presentations of the direct CS. Repeated presentations of the CS may cause it to lose its power to elicit the conditioned response. This strategy often *is* effective but should be used with sensitivity. Plunging a child who is terrified of the dark into a darkened room repeatedly is neither humane nor an effective use of **habituation**. The teacher's repeated presentation of sample items from the AP Calculus test, however, may be a more effective application.

habituation strategy used to extinguish classical conditioning by repeated presentations of the conditioned stimulus until the conditioned response is lessened

Counterconditioning

Sometimes, we can undo a classically conditioned bond by attempting to pair the CS and CR with a different and incompatible stimulus and response. Thus, we may have Jamillah witness Mr. Henry's tirade at the same time she is enjoying her favorite ice cream. The ice cream elicits a positive feeling, which replaces the fear associated with Mr. Henry.

We can "interfere" with the bond until it is extinguished. However, there is again a caution. This strategy is effective also, but warrants careful deliberation. If the diversionary stimulus is less powerful than the conditioned stimulus, the strategy falls flat. In fact, since the stimuli become associated, it is quite likely that the fear value of Mr. Henry may actually spread to the ice cream! A friend of one of the authors of this text tells this story, which illustrates the dangers of counterconditioning: Years ago, cod liver oil manufacturers tried to pair cod liver oil—something children hated—with orange flavoring—something children liked. The result was that the children ended up hating both the cod liver oil *and* anything orange! Ostensibly, the children's enjoyment of orange flavoring could not overpower their hatred of the thick, smelly oil. But the smelly oil certainly could overpower the liking for orange!

A more common experience of **counterconditioning** occurs when a student learns to enjoy a part of music class, for example new music learning, which he had previously learned to hate, simply because he enjoyed the style and humor of the teacher. In our opening scene, the teacher's use of tongue-in-cheek humor (i.e., displaying a bucket of ice cubes) to introduce the arduous task of new music learning would have been an effective use of counterconditioning. The teacher's dressing up like a ship's captain made the instruction more enjoyable to his students, thus changing their initial associations.

There are many practical applications of the two effective strategies for extinction cited above. In terms of counterconditioning, kindergartners' racial views were "modified" through the pairing of the color black with slides of positive words (Parish & Fleetwood, 1975), and, similarly, young girls were conditioned to show more positive attitudes about females through the pairing of pictures of females and positive words (Parish, Bryant, & Prawat, 1977).

In a clinical application, Joseph Wolpe helped patients unlearn irrational fears through a technique called "systematic desensitization" (1958, 1982). Dr. Wolpe's strategy utilizes both habituation and counterconditioning to extinguish classically conditioned bonds. From habituation, the clinician repeatedly presents the CS, but along a hierarchy of stimuli that are related but somewhat

counterconditioning strategy used to extinguish classical conditioning by pairing the conditioned stimulus with a new stimulus that will interfere with the association between the conditioned stimulus and conditioned response

Teacher Tool Box

Preventing—or at least anticipating—harmful associations with classroom learning is an important task for teachers. Remember, learning can be intentional *and* unintentional, productive *and* nonproductive. Using your critical thinking skills, consider the following issues:

- Alerting young or new students to fire drill procedures;

- Discouraging a highly competitive "do or die" testing atmosphere in class;

- Linking curricular content meaningfully to students' everyday lives;

- Utilizing noncompetitive games and cooperative learning activities in instruction; and

- Keeping the classroom climate relaxed and supportive.

dissimilar to the direct CS. The presentation of the CS continues until it eventually loses its eliciting power. From counterconditioning, the clinician also helps the patient find an incompatible response to "interfere" with the bond between the direct CS and CR.

For example, through the desensitization technique, a patient with an irrational fear of snakes will be presented with the direct CS along a hierarchy. First, perhaps, the word "snake" written on paper will be presented; then, perhaps, pictures of snakes will be presented; and so on until the patient is presented with a live snake itself. Concurrently, whenever the patient exhibits conditioned responses (in this case, fearful reactions), he will be trained to evoke an incompatible response; he may be trained in relaxation or deep breathing techniques, techniques that will interfere with the direct CR. Desensitization and counterconditioning techniques have been used to extinguish school phobia, test anxiety, and other academic anxieties in children (cf. Prout & Harvey, 1978).

YOU MAKE THE CALL

USING DESENSITIZATION

Suppose Jamillah generalizes her fear of Mr. Henry to everything connected with school. How could systematic desensitization—habituation and counterconditioning—be used to eliminate her fear? How could a classroom teacher "desensitize" students to test taking so that their performance would not be inhibited by their test anxiety?

Finally, how could the processes of habituation or counterconditioning be used to help a student prepare for presenting a public speech, for example, as graduating valedictorian?

Effective Use of Classical Conditioning

Is there a single rule of thumb for utilizing classical conditioning in the classroom? There is probably no single rule, but there is something to keep in mind. The name of the game in classical conditioning is *association*. As teachers, we can establish helpful associations, and we can help students avoid the pitfalls of detrimental associations if we carefully consider possible associations in advance. Planning for the positive associations and preventing the detrimental associations are ways teachers can use classical conditioning in their classrooms.

FOCUSING ON OPERANT CONDITIONING

Not all learning is the S-R, *stimulus-response*, pattern learning found in classical conditioning. Some learning can involve the association of a response followed by a stimulus or R-S pattern learning. For example, sometimes it is the *result* or *consequence* of a behavior that makes that behavior more likely to be repeated and thus more likely to be learned.

Consider the puppy that attempts to sit at the master's command because sitting leads to a doggie treat!

What's important to behavior change in R-S pattern learning is whatever *follows* the behavior. Noted early behaviorist E. L. Thorndike (Skinner, 1968, 1953) extended Pavlov's work to show the influence of environmental manipulations. He trained animals—cats and pigeons—to respond in desired ways, based on stimulus contingencies. For example, a cat placed in a laboratory box would be trained to escape the box and reach food outside by pressing a bar—if the cat pressed the bar, the bar-pressing behavior (R) would be followed by escape and food (S). Through experiments like this, Thorndike delineated several laws of behaviorist learning (Bigge & Shermis, 1992). Let's focus on two key laws:

law of exercise Thorndike's rule that repetitions strengthen learned associations

1. **Law of Exercise** Thorndike theorized that repetitions strengthen paired learning. (Again, we can see the continuing influence of the principle of contiguity.)

law of effect Thorndike's rule that any act that produces a satisfying effect will be repeated

2. **Law of Effect** Thorndike also theorized that any act that produces a satisfying effect in a given situation will tend to be repeated in that situation.

◆ Skinner and Operant Conditioning

One of the champions of the theory of operant conditioning was B. F. Skinner. In using the term **operant conditioning**, Skinner wanted to focus on the type of learning that occurs when voluntary behaviors are controlled by the manipulation of consequences or follow-up stimuli (Kazdin, 1994; Bigge & Shermis, 1992; Nye, 1981; Mikulas, 1972; Skinner, 1978, 1968, 1953).

operant conditioning type of behaviorist learning in which voluntary behaviors are controlled by the manipulation of follow-up stimuli; also called "r-s pattern learning"

Unlike many theorists, Skinner (1968) considered the problems of educating children in his interpretations of operant conditioning. He strongly encouraged teachers to make use of the principles of operant conditioning in their classrooms (Epstein, 1982). In fact, Skinner suggested that teachers could be more effective if they acted as "behavioral engineers." The teacher as behavioral engineer observes the students' behaviors and the *consequating*, or follow-up, stimuli and then uses the information to bring about increases or decreases in behavioral strength (i.e., frequency, duration, or intensity of behavior). In other words, the teacher as behavioral engineer gets desirable behaviors to increase in behavioral strength and gets undesirable behaviors to decrease in behavioral strength by controlling the consequating stimuli in the classroom (Brantley & Webster, 1993; Smith & Misra, 1992).

Unlike many theorists, Skinner considered the problems of educating children. He strongly encouraged teachers to make use of the principles of operant conditioning. ◆

Take a few minutes to interview a classmate or roommate: Ask what this person likes to eat most. What things does he like to drink? What does this person like to do? Jot down the responses and keep them. Now, you have a list of potential consequences or "contingencies" that could be used to manipulate and change your friend's behavior in ways that you desire. Sounds empowering, doesn't it? Sounds potentially dangerous, doesn't it? Well, it's not.

◆ Reinforcement

Skinner and other operant theorists believed that the primary mechanism for changing behavior was **contingent reinforcement**. That is, by expanding upon Thorndike's Law of Effect, Skinner contended that a behavior that was followed by a desired event would be strengthened or reinforced. And if one were to make the reception of that pleasurable consequence contingent on the performance of a particular behavior, that behavior could be manipulated. Thus, for Skinner, a reinforcer or a reinforcement would be anything that strengthened the response.

contingent reinforcement
the use of follow-up stimuli to strengthen a desired behavior

Let's pretend that you have a student, Suzy, who is a good student but is reluctant to participate in drills and practices or in class discussions. You want her to participate more; in other words, you want to strengthen her participation behavior. To increase her participation behavior you would have to

1. catch her at participating and

2. follow her participating with some desired event.

While that may appear easy enough, there are a number of nuances or subtleties that you need to consider when using operant conditioning. To illustrate, consider the following example.

Mr. Galarago is a third grade teacher. Mr. Galarago states that he is at his "wits end" with one of his students, Roberto. Apparently, Roberto has been making belching sounds in class. Mr. Galarago has spoken with Roberto, reprimands him in class when he does it, has even gone over to his desk and somewhat loudly and angrily chastised him after a belch. But according to Mr. Galarago, Roberto's noise making is happening more often. From what we now know about reinforcement, it would appear that Roberto's noise making is being reinforced, since it is increasing in frequency. A reinforcement is *anything* that increases the frequency of the behavior that has led to it. In reviewing Roberto's situation, it would appear that each time he belches, Mr. Galarago pays attention to him. It could be suggested, therefore, that Mr. Galarago's attention to Roberto is the reinforcement, even when that attention is loud and chastising. What defines a reinforcer is that way it operates rather than what it appears to be. If it increases the behavior that preceded it, it is a reinforcer!

◆ Types of Reinforcement

Let's assume that you are seeking to increase Suzy's participation in your classroom. You have two kinds of reinforcement at your disposal, positive and negative.

Before we continue, it is important that you shake off all your old notions or associations that "positive" means good and "negative" means bad. "Good" and "bad" are not at issue here. In fact, in thinking

positive reinforcers desired, follow-up stimuli added to strengthen a behavior

negative reinforcers inhibiting, follow-up stimuli withdrawn to strengthen a behavior

about **positive** and **negative reinforcers** it may be helpful to associate positive reinforcement with the symbol (+), as in adding, and negative reinforcement with the symbol (–), as in subtracting. Take a look at Table 6.3. The terms positive and negative refer to the way a stimulus works to become a reinforcer. If the stimulus is added in the aftermath of a desired behavior and the intention is to get the behavior to increase in strength, then that reinforcer is positive. If the behavior is followed by the removal of an inhibiting stimulus, then the reinforcer is negative.

Positive Reinforcement

As noted above, a positive reinforcer adds desirable consequating stimuli to a behavioral event in the hope that the event will increase in strength. In Suzy's case, you follow up her infrequent attempt to participate with "Good try, Suzy!" or you walk over and smile right at her. You are adding something Suzy likes to her participation behavior to get her to participate more. Consider the way the music teacher employed a smile and a "Good!" as a way of positively reinforcing the students' effort and achievement.

Negative Reinforcement

Responses that are followed by the escape from or removal of an undesirable situation are likely to be repeated and constitute negative reinforcement. Let's say that our fictitious music teacher is attempting to encourage a student to play a difficult passage correctly. He stands over

A teacher uses positive reinforcement to increase the likelihood that a behavior will be repeated. A pleasant stimulus (gold stars, praising comment, privilege, etc.) follows the desired classroom behavior or performance. ◆

Table 6.3   **Reinforcement and Punishment**

Positive Reinforcement	*Presentation Punishment*
Adding (+) a desired stimulus	Adding an aversive stimulus
"Good answer, Suzy!,"	"Davy, be QUIET!"
"Suzy, you get the 'star' today!"	"Davy, write, 'I must not call out in class' 100 times and have your parents sign it."
Negative Reinforcement	*Removal Punishment*
Withdrawing an inhibiting or aversive stimulus	Withdrawing a desired stimulus
"Davy, I know you are unhappy standing in the corner. You have calmed down and so we would like you to come back to your seat and rejoin the class."	"Suzy, because you didn't do your seat-work when you were supposed to, you will lose your recess privileges today."
"Let's hear from Suzy, this time."	Move Davy's seat away from his friend.

the student commanding, "Again! Again!" When the student plays the passage correctly, the music teacher moves away from the student's desk and toward the front of the classroom. If the special attention the student was receiving was "uncomfortable" for that student, then the removal of that special attention following the correct response will reinforce the student's responding in class. Thus the next time the teacher hovers over his seat, the student may play correctly again.

Positive or Negative?

It is important to remember that one is not better than the other nor is one a reward and the other a punishment. Both positive and negative reinforcement increase behavior and are received as desirable by the person behaving. For the individual doing the reinforcement, in either case—positive or negative reinforcement—the goal is the same: Get a desirable behavior to increase in strength!

YOU MAKE THE CALL

Think critically for a minute: Who's reinforcing whom? Imagine the following scenario. A newborn baby cries and the mother runs to the nursery and picks the infant up. As the mother picks the child up, the baby stops crying. Let's assume that the baby begins to cry more frequently and the mother begins to run and pick up the infant more rapidly.

What behaviors are being reinforced? What behavior is followed by positive reinforcement? What behavior is followed by negative reinforcement?

◆ Identifying Student Reinforcers

Knowing the *kinds* of reinforcement is not all there is to knowing how to use reinforcement effectively to change behavior. You also need to know *what* is reinforcing to your students. (Again, "knowing your students" is important!) There are levels of reinforcers: primary and secondary.

Primary reinforcers are things like air, food, shelter, warmth, human touch—things tied to the physiological survival of the human species. But here's a free tip given with "tongue-in-cheek": School districts frown on teachers' manipulation of primary reinforcers to get students to learn appropriately. It's not advisable to tell Suzy that if she participates, you'll let her breathe! So, we are left with a vast host of *secondary reinforcers* instead: verbal praise, tokens, privileges, certificates, stickers, stamps, snacks, peer recognition, release from homework or tests, and so on. Secondary reinforcers are stimuli that have acquired their reinforcing value by being associated with a primary reinforcer. Thus a smile and a "Good job!" may have been paired with a hug or a comforting touch.

You must know something about your students, however, to choose a secondary reinforcer wisely. All reinforcers are not appropriate with all students. There's an old story about administrators at a middle school with a high rate of absenteeism and lateness, offering a dollar to each student who came to school on time. The first few days of the "Come to school, get a buck$" program were wildly successful, but then attendance dropped off drastically. Why, why, why?—the staff was stumped. Then, they found out that some children were being bullied out of their dollars on the way home from school, while others had to turn their dollars over immediately to impoverished families. As a potential secondary reinforcer, money was *not* effective.

Sometimes, the only way to make wise choices for reinforcers is to ask the students themselves just as you did with your classmate or roommate. You have a list of things this person likes to eat, likes to drink, and likes to do—a host of reinforcers! A teacher might use a variety of reinforcers, including praise (e.g., "I knew you could do it"), smiles, and pats on the shoulder, and even candy and toys! (Please note: Before patting a child on the shoulder, make sure you understand the possible cultural and special needs implications. In some cultures touching is not accepted; for tactile defensive special needs children, touching is not advised either.)

◆ Delivering a Reinforcement

In addition to knowing what is reinforcing, we must understand the way to deliver a reinforcer in order for it to be effective. We have already suggested one rule about the delivery of the reinforcer: *It must follow the behavior we are attempting to strengthen!* Consider what could happen if a teacher asks a student a question and the student politely smiles, and provides the correct answer. The teacher continues with the lesson asking other students a variety of additional questions. The first student feels somewhat cheated and ignored and starts to frown and mumble under his breath. In the time that has elapsed the teacher remembers that he should employ more verbal praise as positive reinforcement. He turns to the first student and says, "That was a good job, Anthony!" Yikes! What did he do? What behavior was just reinforced? For reinforcement to produce the desired result, it must be introduced in close temporal sequence to the behavior that we are attempting to strengthen. Beyond this fundamental point, we must also consider the frequency or schedule with which we will deliver a reinforcement following the desired behavior.

Schedules

In considering the use of reinforcement, we also need to consider a schedule for utilizing the reinforcers. In general, we can administer reinforcers continuously (i.e., "all the time, every time") or intermittently (i.e., "sometimes"). The question is—what is the difference?

Let's say a teacher offers verbal praise (e.g., a quick "Good!" or a smile or a pat on the shoulder) continuously—until students are comfortable participating in math class. After their participation is established, she praises less frequently, reserving reinforcers for larger accomplishments. In other words, there is a need for both types of schedules: continuous reinforcement schedules help establish the behavior change initially and intermittent schedules help maintain the change. We can break the **schedules of reinforcement** down a little further:

schedules of reinforcement variations in the frequency in the presentation of reinforcers

1. *Fixed ratio schedules* (FR) are predictable; reinforcement is dispensed following a constant number of desired behaviors. An example of an FR might be putting coins in a soda machine and getting a soda every time.

2. *Fixed interval schedules* (FI) are predictable; reinforcement is dispensed following a constant amount of time. An example of a FI might be getting a snack at school every day at 10:45.

3. *Variable ratio schedules* (VR) are unpredictable; reinforcement is dispensed following a varying number of desired behaviors. An example of a VR is winning the lottery. You never know when it will happen!

4. *Variable interval schedules* (VI) are unpredictable; reinforcement is dispensed following a varying amount of time. Periodic breaks during a long period of seatwork would be an example of a VI.

If all this information about primary and secondary reinforcers, and schedules of reinforcement is a little confusing, visit a local zoo! No kidding! Some psychology instructors in Georgia help their students to learn about operant conditioning principles by having them shadow zookeepers who utilize the principles in animal care (Lukas et al., 1998).

◆ Operant Conditioning in the Classroom

Now that we have established the nature of reinforcement, the kinds of reinforcers, and the levels of reinforcers, we are now ready to examine several reinforcement strategies to use in our classrooms to change behavior: **cueing** and prompting, shaping and fading, the Premack Principle, and behavioral contracts.

cueing strategy in which a reinforceable behavior is set up by a stimulus or signal; may be accompanied by a verbal reminder called a "prompt"

Cues and Prompts

As a way of introducing the concepts of cues and prompts, consider the following scene from the movie *Stand and Deliver.* In this scene, Mr. Escalante makes a scooping motion with his hands to symbolize digging in the sandy beach. The students are encouraged to explain what a negative number is, so the teacher can then reinforce their response.

Mr. Escalante utilized a *cue*—a signaling stimulus that sets up a reinforceable or desirable behavior. He was setting the student up to give a response that the he could reinforce. Many teachers, when faced with a restless class, will use a signal like flicking the lights or raising a hand to get their attention and so set them up for positive reinforcement when they settle down. If the teacher had followed the signalling stimulus with a verbal reminder ("What does this signal mean?" "What am I waiting for you to do?"), the teacher would have used a *prompt* also. A prompt follows a cue to make sure the person reacts appropriately to the cue.

In the movie, the teacher leans in close to the truculent student, waiting for a response. He whispers, "Come on, you can do it. It's easy," thus prompting the student toward attempting the solution.

Shaping and Fading

Consider the situation with Willie. Willie is a first grader who has a great deal of difficulty staying seated at his desk. His teacher has placed a three-minute egg timer on Willie's desk. Each time Willie remains in his seat through the entire three minutes, he is given a gold star. As Willie demonstrates his ability to sit for the three minutes, a new, longer period is implemented. Now Willie will have to stay seated for seven minutes in order to receive his gold star. If the teacher keeps lengthening the amount of time Willie has to remain seated in order to gain the reinforcement of the gold star, that teacher is **shaping** Willie's "sitting at the desk" behavior, moving it successively from three minutes to the entire 30-minute period by providing reinforcement following successive approximation of the final desired behavior (i.e., 30 minutes in his seat).

shaping reinforcement strategy in which remote approximations of a target behavior are rewarded

The teacher in this situation was attempting to shape the student's behaviors. Shaping means that the teacher reinforces small—even remote—approximations of target behavior until progress toward a targeted behavior is established. In the case of Suzy, we might reinforce eye contact at first or mouthing an answer to help her get into the habit of participating. Once she is participating appropriately and regularly, we may want to *fade* the reinforcers. Fading, like shaping, is accomplished in small steps, through successive approximations, moving from reinforcing every correct response to perhaps reinforcing every other correct response. Fading continues until the lowest rate and form of reinforcement that maintains the response is achieved. Once Suzy becomes an active participant in class, we may choose to reinforce her participation on an intermittent schedule rather than the continuous schedule previously used, and we may change the secondary reinforcers, moving from demonstrative verbal praise ("Good answer, Suzy!") to a less effusive smile and eye contact.

The Premack Principle

A useful strategy, especially when working with classroom management is described by David Premack (1965), who noted that a behavior that is performed spontaneously at a high rate can be used as a reward for increasing the frequencies of behaviors performed spontaneously at lower rates. Consider the student who loves working at the art center. Suppose the teacher informs him that he can move to the art center as soon as his seatwork is completed but not until then. The teacher is employing the **Premack Principle.** The Premack Principle uses an "if-then" statement where a preferred activity is used as a reinforcer for a less-preferred one. It is popularly called "Grandma's Rule" because a lot of grandmas (and grandpas, too!) use it to get grandchildren to do what they want. You probably remember hearing, "Honey, if you'll get my reading glasses, I'll give you a cookie." It was effective for grandma and can be effective for teachers. Preservice teachers are often skeptical, but the Premack Principle can be used in balanced amounts over a protracted period effectively. For example, first you can offer five minutes of extra recess for every minute of attentiveness in class; then, offer four minutes of recess for every two minutes of attentiveness; then, three minutes of recess for three minutes of attentiveness; and, so on. (Don't be surprised—it does work!)

Geiger (1996) found that middle school and junior high school students' on-task classroom behavior could be strengthened if contingent upon the seemingly unlikely reinforcer of playground time! McNamee-McGrory and Cipani (1995) observed a decrease in preschoolers' "clinging" behavior and an increase in their classroom independence when a Premack contingency was used. (They noted that the reinforcement strategy was more effective than "pleading" with the child to comply.)

One of the authors of this text encountered a teacher who very creatively employed the Premack Principle to reduce the disruptive behaviors of one of her students. Apparently this eighth grade student enjoyed making humorous comments throughout the class and often would tell jokes, which became very distractive to those around him. The teacher suggested to the student that after the seatwork had been completed and assuming that the student was nondisruptive for the

Premack Principle
reinforcement strategy in which an if-then contingency is established between a preferred reinforcer and a less-preferred activity; also called "grandparents' rule"

entire 45 minutes of the lesson, he could get up in front of class and tell his "joke of the day." This made his joke telling contingent on his nondisruptive, task-focused behavior. The strategy increased his acceptable behavior, and the other students began to remind him not to be disruptive so that they could enjoy the "joke of the day," at the end of the period.

Behavioral Contracting

In Miss Lewis' class, the students were greeted with a piece of paper, which each member of the class was required to sign, pledging to complete all homework assignments. While the students protested the fact that she wanted them to do homework on weekends and holidays as well, Miss Lewis simply reminded them, "If you complete all homework, you'll receive extra credit!"

Miss Lewis was establishing a *behavioral contract* with her students. Behavioral contracts roll the three strategies we have discussed into one. They are written "if-then" statements in which a teacher and student collaboratively decide on a target behavior and a planned, desired reinforcer (Carter, 1994). The contract usually also includes a time frame for working towards the goal and a description of the methods for evaluation of the student's progress.

Research has shown a variety of successful applications of behavioral contracting in classrooms and with diverse students. Hishinuma (1996) used behavioral contracts to increase motivation in gifted students, while Bender and Mathes (1995) used contracting as part of a management hierarchy for students with attention deficit/hyperactivity disorder.

Token economies can be examples of the Premack Principle in action and/or behavioral contracting. When teachers decide to award a number of tokens (e.g., marbles, special school currency) to students for desired behavior, they are promoting the Premack Principle. But, the tokens alone are not reinforcing; it is the fact that they may be "cashed in" for more popular secondary reinforcers like prizes or privileges. On-task behavior is encouraged to persist as students "save up" tokens. Plans for this system may become a part of a behavioral contract. In one example of a token economy, Adair and Schneider (1993) employed a point system to reinforce study habits and appropriate classroom behaviors to help learning challenged, secondary students.

YOU MAKE THE CALL

OPERANT CONDITIONING IN ACTION

Take another look at our opening scene. What type of reinforcer did the teacher use? Was it a primary or secondary reinforcer? What is the likely effect on the second and third students' behavior? What was the teacher's response to the first student when she was unable to respond desirably? What is the likely effect of that antecedent?

All of these reinforcement strategies can lead to increased behavioral strength of desired behaviors. But what if a student is behaving inappropriately? What if you want to decrease the likelihood a behavior will be displayed in your classroom again? Can you use any of the above strategies? Technically, no—they are all designed to increase behavioral strength. So—technically—what can you use?

Punishment

Another mechanism often employed in operant conditioning is **punishment.** Athough most people would argue that punishment will reduce a behavior, this is not technically accurate. Behavior that results in some painful or undesirable consequence (a punishment) will most likely be suppressed by the learner, but the learner's behavior has not been changed and the behavior potential remains intact and may re-emerge. The presence of a punishment can lessen the frequency, duration, and intensity of an inappropriate behavior.

The use of punishment as a means of changing an individual's behavior or eliminating an undesirable behavior is somewhat complicated and in most cases ineffective unless it is used in combination with the reinforcement of an appropriate, incompatible behavior. Like reinforcement, there are two kinds of punishers: presentation and removal.

Presentation punishment is probably the most familiar kind; it involves following an undesirable behavior with an aversive stimulus. Consider the case of David: David is an annoying talker all through class, and you want him to stop. The next time he talks in an off-task manner, you yell at him, "Shut up!" The loathsome yell is designed to decrease the likelihood that David will talk out of turn again. The effects of such an application of a punishment has many potential consequences, most of which are highly undesirable. Yet yelling, sarcasm, and verbal attack are all too familiar in schools. We'll consider theoretical opposition to regular use of presentation punishment later.

Unless your childhood experiences included the infamous "grounding," you are probably less familiar with **removal punishment** as an approach to decreasing the frequency of undesirable behaviors. Removal punishment is the process in which we follow unacceptable behaviors with the removal of a desired stimulus. Something the student values is taken away after an undesirable behavior is displayed. In the case of David, when he talks inappropriately, you move his seat to another part of the classroom—away from his friends (the valued stimulus), or you withhold school privileges.

Just as there were primary and secondary reinforcers, there are universal and individual punishers. Universal punishers include those stimuli that involve physical or emotional pain. Even though the use of these punishers appears to prove effective in the short run, they are *not* advocated. In fact, as a rule punishment is the least desirable mechanism one could use to change behavior. Presentation punishment can elicit aggression, creates anxiety, leads to escape/avoidance behavior (e.g., students who cannot escape punishment physically by leaving

punishment follow-up stimuli used in operant conditioning to decrease the strength of the performance of undesired behaviors

presentation punishment aversive, follow-up stimuli added to decrease the strength of an unwanted behavior

removal punishment desired, follow-up stimuli withdrawn to decrease the strength of an unwanted behavior

The teacher as behavioral engineer observes students' behaviors and the follow-up stimuli and uses the information to get desired behaviors to increase and undesired behaviors to decrease. ◆

"Hey, wait a minute! You're cleaning erasers as a punishment? I'm cleaning erasers as a reward!"

© Tony Saltzman, 1991.

class, may tune it out psychologically via daydreaming), leads to imitative behavior, and can result in students who become so accustomed to punishment that it yields no effects (Skinner, 1953; Parke, 1972; Kazdin, 1994). Skinner and others would oppose the use of presentation punishment. It is as the African saying implies: "You can't call a dog to come with a whip in your hand."

Suppose a teacher yells at a young woman who is talking during a quiz. This would be an example of presentation punishment. While the punishment DID NOT teach her what to do, it did temporarily suppress her talking and yielded conformity. If punishment does not remove unacceptable behaviors, what can we do?

◆ Modifying Undesirable Behavior

There are a number of strategies that allow a teacher to modify a student's unacceptable behavior within the classroom. These techniques include extinction, response costs, time out, utilizing extinction with reinforcement, and satiation (or negative practice.)

Extinction

Let's say a short-tempered student stamps her foot loudly on the classroom floor, but the teacher doesn't even turn around to acknowledge the outburst. A student acting out or performing in some unacceptable manner in an attempt to gain a pay off (e.g., a teacher's reaction) may come to surrender that behavior if it is not reinforced. This is basis for the process of **extinction**.

Although many people are skeptical about this technique, extinction can be an effective technique for reducing previously reinforced,

extinction (in operant conditioning) strategy in which voluntary, undesired behavior is followed by no stimulus, or is ignored undesirable behavior. In this situation, the teacher appeared to ignore the misbehavior, therefore denying the student any possible reinforcing consequences that may strengthen it. (Often, this operant conditioning strategy is used in conjunction with another, as we will see soon.) It is obvious that such ignoring should not be employed in conditions where harm to the student or to others could result. Also, it needs to be stated that one should not attempt to extinguish behavior by ignoring it unless it is certain that the response can be consistently ignored. Should the student increase the inappropriate behavior (e.g., slamming the door) and the teacher then attends to the student, the teacher may reinforce the misbehavior, rather than extinguish it.

Response Costs

If students experience situations in which their behavior seems to be costing them in some way, most individuals will attempt to stop acting in that way. Removing a unit of some pre-established reinforcement each time an undesirable behavior is displayed is employing a method called **response cost**. The teacher who takes away five minutes of recess time for every infraction of class rules is implementing a response cost strategy. It can be an effective alternative to presentation punishment (Reynolds & Kelly, 1997).

> **response costs** strategy in which units of reinforcement are removed for each display of undesired behavior; used as an alternative to presentation punishment

In the movie *Stand and Deliver*, Mr. Escalante notes that the class has not been working hard enough on calculus and they must forfeit their vacation days to make up for lost time. Such a loss of "free" time follows the students' off-task behavior. As such, off-task behaviors should be reduced.

Response cost procedures are only effective if a reinforcement program has been instituted. You have to have something of value to remove! Some behaviorists believe it is most effective when used with individual students, but many teachers use it effectively to alter the behavior of a small group or the whole class. You may remember a teacher who put a mark on the blackboard when your class was noisy, which told you and your classmates that five minutes of recess time had been lost.

Time Out

One of the most familiar and probably most misused operant strategies to stop undesirable classroom behaviors is **time out**. Time out is a process whereby a student exhibiting an undesirable behavior may be removed from the reinforcing situation (Carter, 1994; Costenbader & Reading-Brown, 1995). Time out is effective particularly in classrooms where other students' laughter, attention, comments, and looks can reinforce unacceptable behaviors in some students. But, unbeknownst to some who would use time out, there are guidelines for its use and caveats to consider.

> **time out** strategy in which a student who is acting inappropriately is removed to a non-reinforcing setting; used as an alternative to presentation punishment

1. *Students must understand what's going on.* For example, "You need to go to the time out area to settle down." Students should *not* be sent in anger, and they should *not* feel that they are being rejected or

One of the most familiar and most misused operant discipline strategies is time out. Time out is effective, but there are guidelines for its use and caveats. ◆

banished or that you can't stand the sight of them! Betz (1994) recommends explaining the infractions to the student at eye-level and walking the child to the time out area.

2. *Teachers must be aware, too.* Time out won't work if the student is using it to avoid an unpleasant situation. For instance, the child who causes a disruption on the brink of test time may be using the time out to avoid the test!

3. *The time out area should be humane and safe.* This guideline may sound like common sense, but you'd be surprised to learn that some schools allow children to be placed in cardboard boxes or in soundproof, dark, poorly ventilated rooms in the name of time out.

4. *The time out area should be nonreinforcing.* Time out areas filled with toys or where communications—or antics!—with other students are still possible are *not* nonreinforcing.

5. *Time out should not be used for extended periods.* Betz (1994) warns, "Don't forget a child in time out!" Students placed in time out for hours—or days—are not being changed, they're being punished ineffectively. Protracted time out results in resentment, not desired behavior change. If there is a rule of thumb, time out for young children should not exceed four to five minutes or, perhaps, a minute per year of age and not to exceed fifteen minutes at any age.

6. *Time out cannot be used to exclude a child from education.* As an extension of point 4, teachers must recognize a child's right to be part of a classroom and to be provided with a free public education. The use of time out cannot be so frequent, nor for such lengths of time as to restrict the child's access to education. In cases where the child is simply unable to function appropriately within the classroom, special due process procedures will be needed to remove the child or to place the child in an appropriate educational setting.

Combining Extinction and Reinforcement

Imagine the situation in which a middle school teacher ignores the faint murmurs coming from a student in the back of the class. As the talker stops the murmuring, the teacher is quick to praise him for his quiet listening. The teacher in this scene used an effective combination approach, *differential reinforcement of other behavior (DRO) or reinforcement of competing or incompatible stimuli.*

This method combines **extinction with reinforcement;** extinction (the teacher ignored the misbehavior) and positive reinforcement (the teacher rewarded the desirable behavior) (Carter, 1994). Some people call this the "catch them being good" method. As the reinforcement of the desired response leads to an increased frequency of that response, the misbehavior will automatically diminish, not only because it is being extinguished but also because the incompatible response of "silent listening" has increased, thus making it more difficult to murmur!

Geiger (1997) found that extinction, coupled with cueing, was very effective for decreasing inappropriate classroom behaviors, such as talking or whispering and getting out of seats. This worked for more than 700 students in 35 classrooms! In an even more fascinating application of this method, Dr. Harold Strang of the University of Virginia designed a teaching apparatus called "Mr. Big Ear," used to curb school noise (Strang, 1975). Mr. Big Ear looks like a giant, mechanized "happy face." His smile (the reinforcer) consists of single light bulbs, which light up successively if the noise level remains low (the desired behavior). When the noise rises above the target number of decibels (an undesired event), the progression of the lights on Mr. Big Ear's face stops (removal punishment); earned lights in Mr. Big Ear's smile are not lost, as that would be punishing. In his limited empirical applications, Mr. Big Ear has been a surprising success, with students not only desiring to light all of the light bulbs but successfully accomplishing that task through modulation of their own noise levels. Interestingly, Strang (1975) noted that the students eventually internalized Mr. Big Ear's presence in the classroom!

extinction with reinforcement strategy pairing extinction (or ignoring undesired behavior) with positive reinforcement of desired behavior; also called "reinforcement of competing stimuli"; used as an alternative to presentation punishment

Satiation and Negative Practice

The unsuspecting teacher ducks as the paper airplane sails past her nose, as she stands in the front of the class. The teacher approaches the student "pilot" and states, "Since you like to make airplanes, here is a ream of paper to make planes for all the students in the school." After about the twenty-fifth airplane, the student feels as if his fingers will fall off!

The teacher in this scene is using a strategy that does not often have a classroom application. **Satiation** or **negative practice** attempts to decrease the likelihood that an unacceptable behavior will be displayed again through the overload of that enjoyable behavior. Intriguingly, in this approach we heap on "too much of a good thing" to get misbehavior to stop.

The process is actually quite understandable when you consider that each action, when repeated in rapid succession brings with it a certain

satiation or negative practice strategy emphasizing the introduction of the overloading of enjoyable (to the student), yet inappropriate behavior (to the teacher) until the behavior loses its attractiveness; used as an alternative to presentation punishment

amount of discomfort and fatigue. Because of the principle of association, discomfort and fatigue will be paired with the previously enjoyed action, to the point that the action, like the discomfort and fatigue, will be avoided.

Sometimes, well-meaning teachers misuse satiation. A student is caught writing notes at school so the teacher gives the student a ream of paper and commands, "Since you like to write notes, write your note 1,000,000 times!!" Technically, this may be a strategy for stopping note writing in the short run, but we need to remember that this is still a behaviorist strategy where *associations* are important. Think about the association established with the process of writing, if used as a means of satiation!

Some Cautions and Considerations

There are tremendous advantages to operant conditioning. For one thing, it works. Operant conditioning is successful, especially for special populations like learning-challenged children (Remington, 1996). It is useful when working towards larger, more valued goals. Students awarded in small increments learn to persist toward the more significant and desired accomplishment. Operant conditioning can result in self-management—if used properly (Chance, 1993). Skinner would suggest that it is crucial to vary the kinds and schedules of reinforcement. If a behavior is established with a continuous schedule of a highly desired reinforcer and then maintained via a thinned, scheduled, and faded presentation of reinforcers, eventually the behavior will persist on its own. Extrinsically reinforced behavior is now reinforced intrinsically.

But, by the same token (no pun intended!), many theorists and practitioners have great concerns about operant conditioning: It can be expensive. If there is a heavy reliance on extrinsic rewards—stickers, candy, movie passes, toys, etc.—a reinforcement program can be costly to teachers, many of whom end up paying for the secondary reinforcers themselves. An extensive operant strategy can be difficult to manage. Different contracts with different students utilizing differing reinforcers can seem unwieldy, especially to new teachers. The effects may be temporary (Ferguson & Houghton, 1992). It also can result in a reduction of intrinsic motivation in students (Kohn, 1994), a point that will be more fully discussed in Chapter 8.

Another issue for you to think about critically before using operant conditioning in your classroom stems from what you studied in Chapter 5: student diversity. It is safe to assume that the selection and use of effective rewards and appropriate deterrents may be influenced by your students' cultural groups

Teacher Tool Box

Operant Conditioning?

What do you think about operant conditioning? Does it appear useful for classroom teaching? Operant conditioning is not as simple as it seemed at the beginning of this unit. There are guidelines for its effective use (Bacon, 1989):

♦ Decide how frequently to reinforce students (there are developmental differences);

♦ Decide what percentage of available reinforcers are necessary to reap rewards (100% of the reinforcers may not be realistic);

♦ Decide how often and how many reinforcers you will give throughout a day;

♦ Determine when students will be able to receive rewards.

(e.g., race, ethnicity, gender, SES). While there are suggestions that Native American students' self-esteem might be enhanced by the teachers' use of positive reinforcement (Stachowski, 1998), that both black and white students prefer intermittent reinforcement (Casteel, 1997), that boys worry more about their teachers' use of punishment than do girls (Jules & Kutnick, 1997), and that low socioeconomic parents may employ harsher forms of discipline at home (Dodge, 1996), we actually know relatively little about the relationship between diversity and the effective use of behavioral principles (Iwamasa & Smith, 1996). It is an area where greater research to inform teacher decision making is needed.

A LOOK AT NEOBEHAVIORISM

We have seen that the behavioral approach to learning emphasizes the S-R and R-S patterns of learning. However, behaviorism goes beyond these presentations. While the classical behaviorism of John Watson exalted the need to focus only on overt behavior as the focus for investigation, expansion of the behavioral model in the last three decades has begun to investigate behaviors that are not directly observable but can be inferred.

The S-O-R behavioral approach investigates, not only the influences of the Stimuli (S) and the Response (R) but also the internal processes of the Organism (O) as they impact learning. This extension of behavioral perspective has been termed a neobehaviorist model.

◆ How Do Neobehaviorists Explain Learning?

The neobehaviorists acknowledge that the overt behaviors in S-R pattern and R-S pattern learning theories are evident in learning, but they also believe that sometimes there is an intervening variable; sometimes, there is something within the organism—in our cases, human beings—that may influence learning. Further, they believe that these personal, subjective experiences or cognitive information processes are needed to fully explain how human learning occurs in social situations.

◆ Social Learning Theory

According to the neobehaviorists, complex human social functions, such as the use of language or the demonstration of socially and culturally appropriate behaviors, do not seem explainable without some reference to the organism's (O) covert mental activities of affective experiences. Understanding how humans come to employ appropriate social behaviors has been the special focus of social learning theory. Proponents of social learning theory maintain that while the specific behaviors that result from social learning vary from culture to culture, the acquisition of these behaviors appears to be consistently determined by the processes of identification and imitation (Bandura, 1978; Khan &

Cangemi, 1979). These processes have been targets of investigation and are presented through our discussion of observational learning and cognitive behavior modification.

Observational Learning

observational learning a social learning strategy which emphasizes learning by watching others; also called "modeling"

The kind of social learning theory that focuses on imitation and modeling is **observational learning.** One of the primary researchers in social learning theory and observational learning is Albert Bandura (1977, 1986). Bandura's work is highly significant and instructive for the classroom teacher, both in the areas of instruction and motivation (see Chapter 8).

Bandura examined how children learn through a process of observation. According to Bandura, much of what humans learn occurs through a process of observing and imitating others (modeling). He concluded that students learn to imitate by being reinforced for specific acts of imitation. Classical associations and operants are important to learning, but Bandura also feels that one must also consider the intervening conditions of the organism, "unseen" or internal conditions. His work is often referred to when society questions whether children learn via television viewing.

In his classic study, Bandura (1977) showed a group of children a film of "an adult committing novel, aggressive acts" against a Bobo doll. The adults were viewed punching the large stand up doll, pushing it down, or even throwing the doll. At the conclusion of the viewing, the children were instructed to make a list of all novel, aggressive acts shown. They were divided, then, into two groups: Group A was offered a prize for the number of acts they had learned, Group B was not.

Action Research

Model Educational Television

M r. Warner, a seventh grade social studies teacher, was interested in studying which educational television programs provided the best models for geography learning. Prior to taking a unit test, he required 60 of his seventh grade students to keep logs for three weeks in which they recorded their reactions to educational programs about geography, which they watched at home and at school. Mr. Warner then looked for patterns in his students' viewing by observing and asking them to complete questionnaires about which shows sustained their attention, three facts retained from each show, their ability to actually identify geographical content after viewing, and their motivation to study for the upcoming unit test. He found that certain programs served as better models, exemplifying Bandura's characteristics, than others. As a result of this project, Mr. Warner is now selecting the instructional aids he will use in class and will recommend for home viewing more carefully.

Group A came up with a lengthy list of acts, but Group B did not. What was different about Group A? Was it smarter? Did it have a better view of the film? Was it more imaginative?

Bandura surmised that Group A probably was not smarter, more imaginative, nor sitting in better seats. However, it had been offered an incentive. While initially producing only a limited list of aggressive acts, Group B was able to generate a more extensive list of novel aggressive acts viewed in the film once offered an incentive, even though that incentive was offered later within the experiment. Two significant conclusions should be highlighted:

1. Children—and people, in general—*do* learn from observing others.

2. The potential for learning is always there, but observable evidence may fool us. Both Group A and Group B had the potential for learning from the film and did learn, but initially only Group A was willing to show what it had learned. Therefore, internal factors (e.g., incentives in Bandura's classic study) intervened to influence the learning.

YOU MAKE THE CALL

OBSERVATIONAL LEARNING

Let's return to the scene that opened the chapter. Think critically about it for a minute. Did the teacher get the students' attention? How? What could he do to get them to hold on to the learning longer? Should he assume that all students have the prerequisite skills and knowledge recognize the melody? Does he offer them any incentives for learning? In addition to the intended focus of his teaching, what else might the students learn by simply "observing" this teacher's behavior?

Factors involved in observational learning. In observational learning, there are four interrelated factors significant to the learning process: attention, retention, production process or motoric reproduction, and motivation (Bandura, 1977). Let's examine each.

For students (observers) to learn from a teacher (model), the teacher must get the students' *attention*. Proximity (or nearness) to the teacher may help attract students. Students sitting in the front row may stand better chances at attending to the lesson. Other characteristics may influence attention (e.g., use of aggression, appearance of warmth, gender, age). Did you know that *Mr. Rogers' Neighborhood* seems to be more successful at teaching children prosocial behaviors (e.g., cooperation, sharing, caring, helpfulness) than other children's TV shows? Of course, as adults we may be bored with the show, but children identify with Mr. Rogers' personal characteristics and mannerisms and are more willing to learn prosocial behaviors from him (Tower et al., 1979).

Despite proximity and identification with personal characteristics of the teacher, students may not learn via imitation unless there also is *retention*. Retention processes ensure that the student can retain or hold onto whatever is to be learned. It facilitates learning if we get students to rehearse or practice learning—even learning via imitation. Madison Avenue in New York—the site of many major advertising firms—aids our observational learning about their products by getting us to rehearse or practice product information. The jingles used in commercials and the popular logos of print ads enable us to hold onto product information. It's a good bet that you learned and can hum on command several popular vehicles of retention.

Now, let's say you are a physical education instructor who wants to teach basketball to your students. You roll out the VCR, sit your students up close, and show them tape after tape of Michael Jordan driving to the basket. You have your students' attention, and you have offered them an opportunity to rehearse the images of Jordan in their minds. At the conclusion of the videos, you hand each student a basketball and shout, "Go for it!" Do you really expect that you have now "created" a class full of Michael Jordans and that all of your students can successfully imitate "The Great One"? Probably not.

For some students, observational learning may depend on their *production processes* or *motoric reproduction*. Despite the establishment of attention and retention, unless the students also have the ability to actually perform the task to be learned, they may not be able to show what—if anything—they've learned. However, different from the actual physical ability to perform an observed task, it may be just as important for students to be able to represent internally—visualize or imagine—what they'd look like accomplishing the task.

Now, suppose that your students have attended to your teaching, have opportunities to practice the lesson, and have the ability to actually perform the task. Still, they may not show you what they've learned. (Remember Bandura's Group B?) Sometimes, a remaining, intervening variable can influence observational learning. That variable is *motivation* or *incentive*. Often, there has to be "something in it" for the students or observers. A direct reinforcement can motivate. (Remember secondary reinforcers?) It is also possible to influence observational learning through vicarious reinforcement—or punishment. When a student observes another student rewarded *or* punished, the first student is reinforced or punished also—but indirectly. That indirect benefit or hindrance is vicarious reinforcement or vicarious punishment. Again, Madison Avenue loves to motivate you to learn about their products via vicarious learning. Any time you turn on the TV, you will observe a person being rewarded for using the sponsor's product or see a person being "punished" for using the Brand X commodity. Many ads—like the ones with the Energizer Bunny—inspire you to buy the featured battery through the use of vicarious reinforcement ("the bunny keeps going and going!") *and* vicarious punishment ("the Brand X battery fizzles out").

Thus, to be effective models, teachers (or even peers must juggle several characteristics. They must grab the students' attention, they must provide for the retention of the learning, they must ensure that the student has the capability to learn observationally, and they must provide some kind of incentive for learning.

Observational learning is a powerful learning concept. Christensen et al. (1996) found that observational learning enabled learning-challenged preschoolers to learn basic first aid lessons, while Wilson (1995) advocated its use by teachers to enhance young children's learning about nature. Weiss and colleagues (1998) found observational learning techniques useful in helping children who were fearful in a physical education swimming class, and videotaped models were effective in teaching instrumental music (Linklater, 1997; Lanners, 1999).

Observational learning figures prominently also in the research about the influence of TV on children's behavior. For instance, recent researchers have concluded that, immediately after watching the "Power Rangers" on television, children harass and karate kick and shove playmates (Boyatzis in Franey, 1994). The potential power of observational learning and the subtle or not so subtle effects on children that may result from their observing television, movies, and real adult models (including teachers) are things that need to be considered, reviewed, and researched. And, as teachers who are daily models for the children in our classrooms, we all need to consider the behaviors we may be exhibiting.

◆ Cognitive Behavior Modification

A second type of social learning that we need to examine is **cognitive behavior modification (CBM)** (Swaggart, 1998; Berger, 1995; Meichenbaum, 1977; Meichenbaum & Burland, 1979). Cognitive behavior modification, as a strategy, wears "two hats": it can be a neobehaviorist strategy, emphasizing social learning; and it can be a metacognitive strategy, emphasizing self-regulation. (Its self-regulatory or metacognitive role will be described in Chapter 12, Learner-Centered Instruction: Metacognition and Constructivism.)

cognitive behavior modification (CBM) a social learning strategy utilizing both modeling and self-instructional verbalization

Suppose you are an English teacher attempting to teach your students to conjugate verbs. You may enhance their learning by utilizing cognitive behavior modification or CBM. Cognitive behavior modification involves the manipulation of thoughts as a means of affecting overt behavior change. (Sounds like diabolical mind control, doesn't it?) It's not—and you've probably used it again and again. (Think about the primary school dance, "The Hoky Poky.") Cognitive behavior modification techniques attempt to assist learners in their capacity for controlling their own behaviors through goal setting (learning the "Hoky Poky"), planning, self-instruction ("you put the right foot in!"), self-monitoring and self-reinforcement. More specifically, CBM consists of two basic parts: (1) direct instruction or demonstration of a task to be learned and (2) teaching a set of verbalized self-instructions to carry out the task.

In CBM, teachers go beyond telling students what to do. They model the process and teach verbalized instructions for task completion. As in observational learning, both the overt stimuli and responses as well as internalized characteristics are significant influences. In utilizing this theory in a classroom, a teacher might demonstrate a task (e.g., a

Teacher Tool Box

Social Learning and CBM

Social learning theory can be helpful in several ways, especially in classroom learning. Keep in mind that teachers are powerful models for

- teaching new behaviors,

- refining already learned behaviors,

- strengthening or weakening behaviors in students via direct or vicarious reinforcement and punishment,

- focusing attention via the demonstration of strategic skills, and

- fostering good and bad feelings in students in social situations.

Increase the value and efficiency of observational learning and CBM by

- gaining the students' attention, to facilitate retention and provide opportunity for production,

- talking through your own problem-solving strategies,

- combining modeling with verbalized self-instruction as a way to maximizing the impact of these instructional techniques.

science lab) while at the same time verbalizing the steps for completion of the task (e.g., "First, we pick up our 5 ml flask"). The teacher, then, invites the students to follow along with repetition of the steps and instructions; the students attempt the physical steps of the lab, but must also chime in aloud with the verbalized self-instructions. Subsequently, the students can perform the task without the teacher's demonstration, but by continuing the self-instructions softly. Eventually, they can perform the task and internalize the instructions.

Your English students may learn to conjugate verbs after watching and listening to you conjugate verbs on the blackboard. Next, you would encourage them to conjugate the verbs at their seats while verbalizing aloud the conjugations. Eventually, they can continue the task silently. Voilà—your students are learning via CBM!

Kubany and Sloggett (1991) found that CBM has worked well teaching self-control procedures to students; Douglas, Parry, Marton, and Garson (1976) showed its use with aggression-prone students. Lest we think CBM is only utilized for management problems, Meichenbaum (1975) concluded that it is effective in training students to be more creative, and Loera and Meichenbaum (1993) proposed using CBM to teach metacognitive skills to deaf students.

We've now reviewed learning theories generally and behaviorist and neobehaviorist explanations of learning specifically. In the next chapter, we will examine cognitivists' perspectives on how we are changed by our environment and experiences. However, prior to moving on to another theory, let us first see the theory in action, behaviorism as a basis from which teachers can make decisions!

Reflections from the Field

1 I never thought I would use extrinsic motivators, like candy, stickers, etc. but to be honest for some children these types of reinforcers really do work!

—*Helen B. (second grade teacher), Philadelphia, PA*

2 I have found that I can often gain a child's attention, or return him or her to task, by praising another child, sitting close to the one off task, for being such a "good worker." It is almost as if the child who is off task models the good behavior and even feels some vicarious reinforcement from my praising of his/her neighbor.

—*Timothy K. (fourth grade language arts teacher), Wilmington, DE*

3 I have been teaching for 6 years and I am a big believer in the use of praise as a reinforcer. The last year, however, I began to ask the students for what they felt should be rewards for working especially hard. I anticipated they would want "things"! To my surprise, they really began to list privileges, like collecting homework, running the milk money to the office, clapping erasers (do you believe it?), etc. So now I have developed a whole token economy where each child has a list of things they can do to earn points (I try to tailor it for each child's needs and abilities) and then each Friday they can cash them in to "purchase" a privilege. They seem to love it!

—*Andrea K. (fifth grade self-contained classroom), Louisville, KY*

4 I have learned a very valuable lesson that I would like to share. We all learned about extinction. However, what you need to know is that if a child is seeking attention and you have been giving it to them AND then you decide to ignore (extinguish) . . . trust me, the behavior will get worse before it gets better. Further, if you begin to then pay attention, you not only reinforce the acting out . . . but increase persistence. So before you use ignoring as extinction make sure you can do it!

—*Alfonso D. (seventh grade social studies), Slidell, LA*

5 One of the benefits of using cooperative learning groups is that I've noticed placing a child who has previously been a distraction, an attention seeker, into a group of children that are bright, achieving, and focused—they seem to shape the disrupter's behavior and he/she begins to model the prosocial, pro-achieving behavior of the other group members. It is important, however, to be sure that the pro-achieving children are strong and independent so that they do not model the disrupter's style!

—*Joanne K. (second grade self-contained class), Baltimore, MD*

THEORY TO PRACTICE

A Look at the Music Teacher as Behaviorist and Decision Maker

As we begin to bring the information presented within the chapter together, it would be helpful to review the classroom scene with which we opened the chapter:

The teacher stands before his class with an inquiring look, a raised baton, a bucket of ice cubes, and a ship's captain's uniform. He distributes sheet music for the "Main Theme from *Titanic*" and the sounds of excerpts of the work fill the practice room. He points to a nearby student with an oboe poised at the ready and asks, "Who has the melody?" She looks puzzled and cannot answer. He waits a moment, then moves on to a student holding a flute in her lap. He asks again, "Who has the melody?" The flutist looks at the music for a second and then responds, "The string section." The teacher smiles broadly and replies, "Good!" A third student, a percussionist, has little trouble answering the question and receives a smile and a compliment as well.

The teacher certainly provided an interesting approach to music instruction! Assuming behavioral theory to be his informational base for his decision making, how do we now understand his teaching method? Was it effective? Could he have done something that would have increased his effectiveness?

Faced with students whose previous experience with learning new music had apparently "taught" them to anticipate boredom, the teacher begins a process of counterconditioning. The visual presentation as a "captain," and the "interesting" addition of ice cubes, certainly made this class . . . well, different. The students' responses demonstrated that these stimuli were clearly arousing, interesting, and motivating. The music teacher was presenting stimuli that elevated interest and paired those stimuli with another less than interesting one (analyzing new music). He was beginning a process of *association*, of *classical conditioning*, of *counterconditioning*, which would hopefully "generalize" (*stimulus generalization*) beyond this one lesson and result in his students' increased interest in the work.

He also demonstrated the process of *extinction* when he "ignored" the student's calls of "Catastrophe ahead!" and other inappropriate responses. As he moved through the class, he looked and sounded (*modeled*) enthusiasm—interest and excitement. And when a student responded correctly, he followed the response with a *secondary, positive reinforcer* ("Good!").

An interesting expansion of the application of behavioral theory occurs when the music teacher "reinforces" the soft-spoken student in the back of the class by not only stating "good" following her correct response, but by asking, "Is it true that intelligent people make better clarinetists?" Given what we know about adolescent development, their obvious interest in how others see them, the teacher hopes to associate (condition) "musical achievement" with "intelligence"!

You, as Teacher, Behaviorist, Decision Maker

Below you will find examples of classroom experiences that you, as teacher, may encounter. Using the concepts discussed in this chapter as the data base or guides for your own decision making, what decisions would you make? How would you respond?

Illustration 1:
H. W. Mann Elementary
The School
You are teaching at the H. W. Mann Elementary School, an elementary school located in a large urban setting, with a predominately Latino student population.

Your Class
You are teaching third grade. You are responsible for all subject matter with the exception of physical education. You have 35 children in your class, which makes it very difficult for you always to attend (immediately) to every student's request.

Your Student
One of your students has you both concerned and exasperated. Jose is a bright, energetic child who currently sits in the back of your classroom. You have placed him there because he has been extremely disruptive in class. He moves in his seat, makes noises to "entertain" the other students and often calls out answers (which by the way are most often correct). You have consistently corrected him for these behaviors by (1) calling his name out in class; (2) stopping what you were doing and going over to his desk; and (3) even keeping him in with you at recess. But none of this seems to help. In fact his behavior keeps getting more disruptive. Since placing Jose in the back of the class you have noticed that his disruptive behavior has seemed to have gotten worse! He is not only calling out more frequently . . . but with a lot more volume!

Guides for Reflection
In reviewing the situation with Jose, how would you explain the reasons for his disruptive behavior? How

would you explain his recent increase in disruptive behavior? What would a behaviorist suggest you were doing by your (1) calling his name out, (2) going over to his desk, or even (3) keeping him in at recess? What do you think you should do? Use the following concepts to guide your decision making:

> Extinction
> Reinforcement
> Shaping
> Schedules of Reinforcement.

Illustration 2:
Behaviorism Applied To Self Management

Identify a behavior (e.g., exercising more, smoking less, studying more, etc.) that you would like to develop. Set a specific goal for that behavior and then using the following concepts to guide your decision making, establish a plan for achieving this goal.

> Positive Reinforcement
> Premack Principle
> Shaping
> Schedules of Reinforcement.

SUMMARY

What Is Learning?

Learning is a change in behavior due to experience. Learning theories attempt to explain how we are changed via environmental interaction. Distinctions between three theoretical perspectives (behaviorism, neobehaviorism, and cognitivism) were examined along with several premises that are true across the perspectives.

How Do Behaviorists Explain How We Learn?

Behaviorists take the position that learning yields overt, measurable change. At the core of the behaviorist perspective is the concept of learning via association. Association learning explains the efficacy of both classical and operant conditioning.

A Look at Classical Conditioning

Association learning is a key factor in classical conditioning and so is the substitution of contiguous stimuli. Not only can we learn to respond differently to a once-neutral stimulus, but, due to experience, we may respond similarly or differentially to multiple stimuli. Classical conditioning can enable us to explain student behavior and can provide strategies for changing harmful associations in the classroom as well.

Operant Conditioning

Skinner and other operant learning theorists believed that through the use of contingent reinforcement teachers could change any behaviors they desired in the classroom. Skinner's "teacher as behavioral engineer" is knowledgeable about different types, levels, and schedules of reinforcement, strategies for the effective use of reinforcement in the classroom, as well as strategies that attempt to avoid overuse of presentation punishment. Although there are tremendous advantages to using operant conditioning in the classroom, some theorists and practitioners have concerns.

Neobehaviorist Learning Theory

A second theoretical perspective is the neobehaviorist orientation, which emphasizes the overt and observable change of the behaviorist, but considers the changes in internal processes championed by the cognitivists. Learning in social situations—as in the case of observational learning or modeling—is an important part of the neobehaviorist perspective. Albert Bandura explored several factors that may influence social learning. Donald Meichenbaum's strategy, cognitive behavior modification (CBM), attempts to change behavior via the use of demonstration and goal setting, self-monitoring, and self-reinforcement.

The two theoretical perspectives described—behaviorism and neobehaviorism—offer teachers a host of strategies to attempt to change student behavior. They provide teachers with a basis for instructional decision making.

◆ Field Experience Questions

In addition to action research, you can begin to gather data about teaching and the use of behavioral principles by way of classroom observations. The following questions could guide your observations. Be sure to take detailed field notes of what you observe, asking teachers and students interview questions, and recording the frequency and nature of certain types of behaviors. Try to answer these questions based on classroom observations.

1. Based on your observations, what forms of reinforcement did this teacher employ? (Primary, Secondary? Positive? Negative?)

2. What percentage of praise is given to individuals and to the entire class?

3. What percentage of verbal rebukes or punitive remarks is given to individuals and to the entire class?

4. Is there a behavioral consequence system used by the teacher? What is it? Is it used consistently and fairly?

5. Are extrinsic reinforcers used? Are intrinsic reinforcers used? Which reinforcement schedule does the teacher use?

6. Did you notice the teacher "inadvertently" or "accidentally" reinforcing undesirable student behavior?

7. Did the teacher employ extinction procedures? Time out?

8. Were cues and fading procedures employed?

9. Was cognitive behavioral modification employed as part of the instructional process or classroom management procedures?

◆ Key Terms

behaviorism
classical conditioning
cognitive behavior modification (CBM)
cognitivist
conditioned response
conditioned stimulus
contingent reinforcement
counterconditioning
cueing
extinction (in classical conditioning)
extinction (in operant conditioning)

extinction with reinforcement
habituation
law of effect
law of exercise
learning
negative reinforcers
neobehaviorism
observational learning or modeling
operant conditioning
positive reinforcers
Premack Principle

presentation punishment
principle of contiguity
punishment
removal punishment
response costs
satiation or negative practice
schedules of reinforcement
shaping
stimulus generalization
time out
unconditioned response
unconditioned stimulus

◆ Additional Resources

Bannerman, D. J., Sheldon, J. B., Sherman, J. A. (1991). Teaching adults with severe and profound retardation to exit their homes upon hearing the fire alarm. *Journal of Applied Behavior Analysis, 24(3),* 571–577.

Barth, R. (1979). Home-based reinforcement of school behavior: A review and analysis. *Review of Educational Research, 49(3),* 436–458.

Chance, P. (1993). Sticking up for rewards. *Phi Delta Kappan, 74,* 787–790.

Kosakowski, B. J. (1998). A behavioral approach to student tardiness. *NASSP Bulletin 82,* 113–116.

McCurdy, B. L., Cundari, L., Lentz, F. E. (1990). Enhancing instructional efficiency: An examination of time delay and the opportunity to observe instruction. *Education and Treatment of Children, 13(3),* 226–238.

McDaniel, T. R. (1993). Practicing positive reinforcement. In K. M. Cauley, F. Linder, and J. H. McMillan, *Educational Psychology 93/94* (pp.74–77) (8th ed.). Guilford, CT: Dushkin Group.

Pica, L., Jr., Margolis, H. (1993). What to do when behavior modification is not working. *Preventing School Failure, 37(3),* 29–33.

Cognitive Learning Theories

A s class begins, the teacher directs the students' attention to the problem written on the board. She proceeds to have them read it aloud. In sing-song unison, the class recites: "Jamal's dog, Rex, weighs a total of 35 kilograms while soaking wet after a bath. After being dried, Rex loses 2,500 grams. How much does Rex weigh now?" Engaging several students, the key pieces of the problem are discovered. Punctuated by humorous asides, several attempts are made until the problem is solved.

S urely, you have sat in a similar class, where a teacher directs you to review a problem on the chalk board and then proceeds to invite the entire class to recite and begin to solve. Perhaps you have also experienced the teacher who focused you on various pieces of the problem in an attempt to facilitate your problem solving. He or she may have also employed humor at various time in the problem solving process. Why?

What happened in this case or in your own class experience? What was the impact of this teaching technique? Was it merely that the students enjoyed the process? Was it simply that a solution was derived? Or were the students, themselves, somehow significantly changed by the relatively simple learning activity?

There are a number of theorists, called cognitivists, who would suggest that not only was a problem solved, but the students' internal cognitive structures were changed as a result of this and similar learning activities. Cognitive learning theorists, like Jean Piaget, Jerome Bruner, and David Ausubel put less emphasis on overt behavioral change in learning and greater emphasis on changes we cannot always readily see. While they may acknowledge overt behavioral change, they also view it as symptomatic of "more significant" changes internally.

Learning, according to cognitive theorists, involves the acquisition or reorganization of cognitive structures. It is through these structures that we as human beings process and store and, hopefully, make later use of information.

In this chapter we will review the cognitive perspective on learning. We will discuss cognitive theory and research, which presents the learner as an active, purposeful, and deliberate participant in the learning process. Further, we will review what is known about the way individuals receive, record (store), and retrieve information. Finally, we will review the implications of what is known about cognitive science for instructional design—or, the choices that we make in our classrooms (Tennyson et al., 1992). As noted by others, knowing how our students process, store, and retrieve information can inform our decision making about the teaching of subject matter to our students (Tennyson, 1990; Aubrey, 1992).

◆ Chapter Objectives

After completing this chapter, the reader should be able to

1 Explain the cognitive perspective on learning and how it differs from other theoretical perspectives.

2 Discuss the origins of the contemporary cognitive perspective, including Gestalt psychology and the role of perception.

3 Describe the information-processing approach to learning and distinguish the features of the multistore model.

4 Discuss the importance of attention, rehearsal, chunking, and elaboration to memory.

5 Describe Gagne's "instructional phases" model as it relates to information processing.

6 Examine dual coding theory and, in particular, schema theory.

7 Link schema theory to cognitive structuralism (or connectionism) and examine the role of insightful learning and meaningful reception learning.

8 Describe Ausubel's expository teaching model and give examples of research-derived structuring strategies.

9 Describe several factors known to affect rote learning and meaning verbal learning.

CHAPTER 7 CONTENT MAP

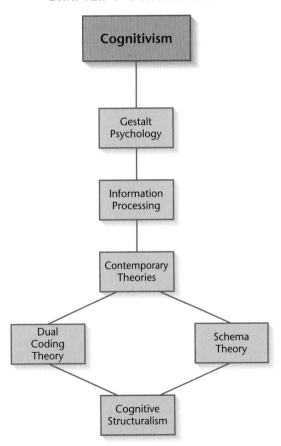

FOUNDATIONS OF COGNITIVE LEARNING THEORY

While much of the research that supports cognitive learning theories is relatively new and contemporary, the theory itself has longstanding roots. Before we begin our discussion of the origins of the cognitive learning theory, however, exercise your critical thinking skills in the "You Make the Call."

YOU MAKE THE CALL

ARE WE SIMPLY DATA RECORDERS?

As we attempt to process our various experiences in life and make sense out of them, we need to question the degree to which our personal experiences directly reflect the reality of that experience. Review the following figures. Does your experience "make sense"? Is what you received and recorded an accurate reflection of what is really there?

Figure 7.1
Visual Illusions

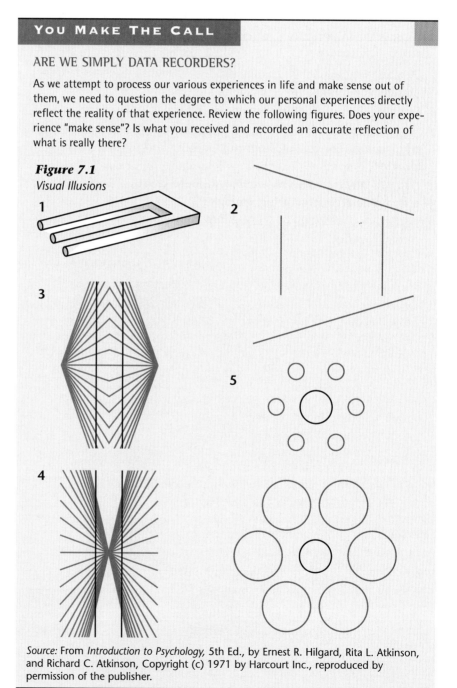

Source: From *Introduction to Psychology,* 5th Ed., by Ernest R. Hilgard, Rita L. Atkinson, and Richard C. Atkinson, Copyright (c) 1971 by Harcourt Inc., reproduced by permission of the publisher.

Obviously, the figures presented are visual illusions. What you receive is clearly not an accurate reflection of what is really there. For example, the middle circles presented in item 5 ARE the same size, as are the two vertical lines presented in item 2. Why do you think we are vulnerable to such illusions?

It is the way we "perceive" the input (i.e., give it meaning) that leads to the distortion of that information. Further, it is the process that we use for receiving, storing, and retrieving data that makes us vulnerable to such perceptual illusions. Thus, understanding those processes is important, if we are to assist our students to receive, store, and retrieve—accurately!

The first group of researchers interested in this process and the impact that this process may have on learning were German psychologists called **Gestaltists**.

Gestalt Psychology

Many **Gestalt psychologists** emigrated from Germany to other parts of the world before World War II and continued to study both the process and products of perceptual organization (Koffka, 1963). The term, "gestalt," means "form" or "configuration" (Benjafield, 1992 p. 15). Scientists like Max Wertheimer, Wolfgang Kohler, Kurt Koffka, and Karl Duncker brought with them ideas that perceivers (or learners) are not passive, but rather active (Benjafield, 1992; Farnham-Diggory, 1992). They believed that we do not simply record data, rather that we actively gather and restructure data in order to make sense of it. The ways we restructure these data, however, can be quite subjective (Benjafield, 1992) and can be influenced by our previous experiences (learning) and even our current states (e.g., needs, attitude, context , etc.). Consider the following:

Gestalt psychology type of perceptual psychology in which our perceptions are believed to be active and subjective, and influential to learning

---

YOU MAKE THE CALL

WHAT IS IT?

Take a look at Figure 7.2.

What do you see?

Some people see a dog sniffing the ground, just beyond a shady tree. Did you see all that? Why do you think you did—or why not? What about your previous learning or experiences may have influenced how you saw that figure?

Figure 7.2 *Spots?*

Source: From Block, J. R., & Yuker, H. (1992). *Can you believe your eyes? Over 250 Illusions and Other Visual Oddities*, p. 43. Reprinted by permission of Francis & Taylor.

Some people are unable to see the dog because they focus disproportionately on the individual "splotches" in the picture. They have hope that the splotches will come together into a recognizable pattern. Other people do see the pattern of the dog in Figure7.2 because they are able to perceive the picture in its entirety—as interrelated, rather than isolated, splotches. Or, perhaps they were able to see it because they have had a great deal of experience with visual illusions; or, perhaps because they have a dog at home who sniffs the ground near shady trees.

The way we organize our experiences is not totally random or subjective. The Gestalt psychologists discovered there are a number of organizing principles that we all seem to employ. These principles, or laws of perceptual organization, predict how we perceive in the ways that we do. Consider these laws (and reflect back to the visual illusions shown previously):

figure-ground discrimination the tendency to perceive images in the foreground first, while other images fade into the backdrop

* The Law of **Figure-Ground Discrimination.** Sometimes we discern a particular figure in the foreground of an image while everything else fades into the backdrop (Farnham-Diggory, 1992). The dog seems to loom at some of us, and the other splotches seem to move to the background.

closure the tendency to fill in gaps in our perceptions

* The Law of **Closure.** Perceptually, we have the tendency to fill in gaps (Farnham-Diggory, 1992). In other words, we may see these figures—[ ] [ ] [ ]—as squares or boxes, when they are brackets with spaces at the top and bottom.

law of proximity theory that the placement of images near each other influences our perception of them

* The **Law of Proximity.** When things we are perceiving are close together, we have a tendency to discern them as "belonging" together (Farnham-Diggory, 1992). For instance, we see these figures—oo oo oo oo oo—as five pairs of circles first, rather than as 10 separate circles because of proximity.

good form law theory that our perceptions are influenced by our past experiences; also called Pragnanz Law

* The Law of **Good Form or Pragnanz.** Based on our experiences with perceptual organization, we anticipate certain patterns or figures. Perhaps past experiences with dogs or visual illusions facilitated our seeing the dog in the previous illusion.

law of similarity theory that our perceptions are influenced by stimuli with comparable characteristics

* The **Law of Similarity.** We also tend to "pick up" on figures with like characteristics (Farnham-Diggory, 1992). We perceptually link the large circles with other large circles, and the smaller circles with other small circles, as in this pattern—O o O o O o O o.

At any rate, concepts like figure-ground discrimination, closure, proximity, similarity, and the good form law influence our perception. These same principles influence our learning. Consider the impact on learning when out of all the things that a teacher is saying, she turns and writes one word on the board. Such a simple action can take that word, that concept, and make it emerge as a figure, against the ground of all her other words. Further, consider the child who has difficulty knowing how to group letters on a page to make a word (closure) or the student who highlights everything in the text, since he is unable to discern what is important (i.e., figure-ground discrimination). Clearly, these Gestalt principles are useful as guides for teachers as they organize their material and learning activities. Again, refer to You Make the Call as a way of more fully appreciating this Gestalt-classroom connection.

YOU MAKE THE CALL

GESTALT–CLASSROOM CONNECTION?

Review the previous five Gestalt laws of perceptual organization. Below you will find "typical" classroom activities. Can you match an activity with one or more of the Gestalt principles?

◆ Why might teachers change tone of voice to emphasize important points?

◆ Why might color chalk be used with some of the words written on the board?

◆ Why do teachers insist that students keep their columns straight when performing multiple number additions?

◆ Why might a teacher have her class chant "'I' before 'e' except after 'c'" over and over and then abruptly stop them and ask "How do you spell 'receive'?"

◆ Why is it useful to relate new material to something the student has already experienced?

Work on perception originating with the Gestalt psychologists has, within the last twenty years, been expanded to include a computer-based metaphor for understanding how we gather, represent, hold, and get information we learn and use. This model is called the **information processing model** (IPM).

> **information processing model** theory emphasizing the influence of selective perception on memory, and subsequently, on learning

◆ The Information Processing Model

The influential IPM theorist, W. R. Garner, described "information" as "something we get when some person or machine tells us something we didn't know before" (cf. Benjafield, 1992, p. 22). Like the Gestaltists, IPM theorists believe in the significance of perception to learning. In fact, the IPM theorists believe that we are bombarded with things to perceive, and, for that reason, we are selective in what we actually try to understand. The information processing model suggests that humans develop increasingly varied, sophisticated, and integrated cognitive structures. Bombarding stimuli are filtered through these structures; what we perceive is filtered and processed selectively.

The terminology of the information processing model appears to be a very contemporary one, emphasizing the significance of the "encoding" or "input" of information, the "storage" of information, and the "retrieval" or "access" of information. The language and the metaphor often used is one of the mind as computer. IPM theorist, U. Neisser, maintained that the correlation between cognition and computers is a powerful one (Benjafield, 1992). And while those IPM theorists interested in artificial intelligence try to design and program computers to receive, store, and retrieve information in order to solve problems like humans (Schunk, 1991), most IPM theorist see the computer as only a metaphor for human mental activity.

◆ The Multistore Model

There are several models that depict the processing of information via our cognition. Broadbent described an "analysis of stage models," and Gibson took an ecological view of information processing, but the model used most often is the one appearing in Figure 7.3, the Atkinson and Shiffrin model (Barsalou, 1992; Benjafield, 1992; Mayer, 1998).

This model, the Atkinson and Shiffrin information processing model, hinges on a **multistore** or three-port processing system. As human beings we are bombarded with much more environmental stimuli than we can ever deal with, so the first port makes an attempt to delimit what we can and will process. This first port is the sensory register.

multistore model information processing system consisting of the sensory register, the short term memory, and the long term memory

Sensory Register

sensory register the first port or site in the information processing model featuring the converting of information gathered via our senses

As the name suggests, the **sensory register** contains receptors that briefly hold on to only that information that enters through our senses. That may not sound like much, but when you think about all the possible sources of stimuli we might encounter in a single moment, we must acknowledge how helpful the sensory register is! The sensory register, according to gestaltist principles lets in only those things which we can see, hear, taste, smell, and/or touch; all else fades away.

Figure 7.3
Human Information Processing Model

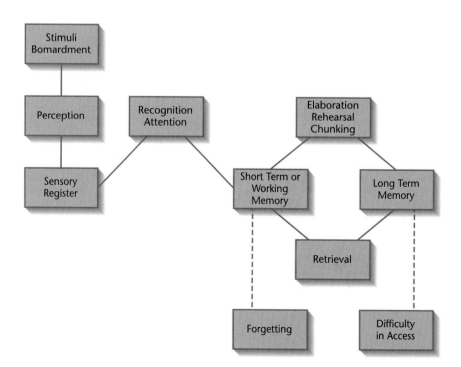

As young students learn to read, one of the most important steps is the recognition of phonemes (i.e., sound units). It is necessary for new readers to recognize that words are made up of discrete phonemes, which can be combined into words (Mayer, 1998). Arguably, this recognition or attention to sound units begins in the sensory register. Things that we attend to sensorially, that we recognize via feature analysis or anticipated associations, are held briefly before being passed on to the second port, the short term memory.

Short Term Memory

The **short term memory** (STM) is as its name suggests, a temporary storage facility. Information entering the short term memory, also called the working memory, is held just long enough for use. The STM allows us to use information without its becoming a part of our permanent storage. Storage capacity is limited and increases with age but varies developmentally; our STM is very brief when we are young, extends somewhat as we get older, but then drops off again as we age further.

STM storage is limited and can hold only a limited number of pieces of information at a time. Only five to nine pieces of information can be held in the STM at a time. If, for example, we asked you to listen to a series of random numbers such as 8-3-9-6-2 and then after a few seconds repeat them back, most people would have little difficulty as long as the length of the sequence was less than seven. However, as we approach a string of nine separate, random numbers, some of us might have difficulty repeating the entire string since we are most likely reaching our STM maximum storage capacity.

Short term memory is not only limited in its capacity but in the duration with which it can actively retain information. To keep information activated in short term memory requires that a person repeat the information in his or her mind (i.e., **maintenance rehearsal**) (Craik & Lockart, 1972). Thus in our little digit span experiment, you may actually "hear" yourself repeating the random sequence of numbers over and over in your mind until you are finally permitted to state them aloud.

Another process that is sometimes used to expand the capacity of short term memory is the process of **chunking**. Chunking is a process by which we group individual bits of information into some type of large, more meaningful unit. Again, if we consider our little digit span experiment we may find that individuals who have difficulty retaining more than five or seven bits of information within their short term memory may find it relatively easy to repeat a social security number such as 189-56-7620. If this is true, it is probably due to the use of chunking. A person would group the nine bits of information into three bundles, or chunks, with each chunk having less than five bits of data. Listen to the way a person repeats a social security number or a phone number. Typically, it is in a rhythm that implies chunking!

Often, more recent memories seem hazier than longer memories, which seem clearer. If we don't use short term memories or don't use

short term memory site in the information processing system in which a limited amount of information is held until use; also called the working memory

maintenance rehearsal keeping information active in short term memory by repeating the informantion

chunking information processing strategy which groups bits of information into more meaningful and processable units

them right away, they decay or are forgotten. If some other potentially memorable event occurs, existing short term memories may be displaced or interfered with (Barsalou, 1992). Unless we actively transfer our short term memories to long term storage, their storage and recall will be short lived. In an interesting study of memory decay, Cooper et al. (1996) found that students do indeed forget quite a bit over summer vacation. Although the researchers reported no gender or race differences, they did find that students tend to forget more as they get older.

YOU MAKE THE CALL

WHY DO WE REMEMBER SOME THINGS?

As we begin to discuss the information processing model and the factors that affect our ability to receive, store, and retrieve information, you may want to review your own experience with memory and retrieval. Consider the following:

What did you wear yesterday?

What did you wear last Thursday?

What did you wear to your last Thanksgiving Day dinner?

Which memory was clearer? Even if Thanksgiving was some time ago, you may discover that you may have more difficulty remembering what you wore yesterday or last Thursday than remembering what you wore last Thanksgiving. To understand why, we need to understand how material is moved from short term memory to long term memory.

Long Term Memory

long term memory a permanent storage facility with unlimited capacity

The **long term memory**, or third port, is a permanent storage facility. As best as we can currently determine, it has unlimited capacity and memories remain indefinitely. How do we move information from our short term storage to this more permanent form of storage? Two processes appear to be invaluable in facilitating our efforts to enter information into long term storage. They are **rehearsal** (practice) and elaboration (Byrnes, 1996).

rehearsal information processing strategy in which practice or repetiton of information enhances recall

Crawford and Baine (1992) examined methods of rehearsal and the benefits of employing distributed practice (i.e., practice with breaks) versus massed (i.e., extended practice periods). These authors found that breaking material down into smaller parts and practicing them a little at a time (i.e., distributed practice), instead of trying to commit everything all at once to memory (i.e., massed), was a more effective way to encode information for long term memory entry and retrieval. There is a scene in the movie *Stand and Deliver* when Mr. Escalante is teaching an ESL (or English-as-a-Second Language) course at night. He states a phrase or two of American English and his students repeat the phrase. He dictates a little more, they repeat. By reducing the lesson to phrases and encouraging them to practice, Mr. Escalante is incorporating IPM ideas into his instruction.

YOU MAKE THE CALL

INCREASING MEANINGFULNESS

Think critically: Suppose you were shown eight words—tulip, hippo, fork, bottle, trunk, toe, doorknob, and leaf—and told to remember them in fifteen seconds or less. What would you do? What would be an efficient and effective way to complete the task?

Repetition is certainly one strategy, but with a fifteen-second deadline, there really isn't enough time for effective distributed practice. Another process that facilitates entry and storage into long term memory is elaboration. **Elaboration** is a process by which we try to tie something we already have stored in long term memory to this new material. In this way, we add and extend the meaning of the new material by connecting it with existing memories. In the words of Ritchie and Karge (1996), it is a "thoughtful pause" (p. 28). For example, if you happen to be familiar and skilled with computers, then the computer as a metaphor for remembering the information processing model will facilitate your storage and assist in your retrieval of that new information.

> **elaboration** information processing strategy emphasizing links between information stored in long term memory and new information

There are two basic categories of elaborations: macrolevel and microlevel elaborations. Macrolevel elaborations help students comprehend entire lessons. They assist students in the identification of schema that can be associated with new information. Some macrolevel elaborations rely on generality: they present a consolidated description of a similar topic and, therefore, provide an "anchor" to the new information to be learned. Some macrolevel elaborations are described as being "general-to-detailed" (Ritchie & Karge, 1996). These elaborations start with a few simple, concrete ideas and then follow them up with increasingly specific details (Ritchie & Karge, 1996).

Microlevel elaborations help students store and recall specific pieces of information from within a lesson. Some microlevel transformations are facilitative when students are largely unfamiliar with the new content in a lesson. Students may then establish associations with a new term by pairing it with an acoustically similar one or through the use of selective highlighting. Still other microlevel elaborations build on pre-established inferences within the material. This may occur through the use of precise contextual cues, imagery, or references to prerequisite material (Ritchie & Karge, 1996).

Sometimes we refer to microlevel elaborations as paired associates. When learners chunk lists of terms like the one in the previous You Make the Call into pairs and then attempt to associate a hippo with a tulip and a fork in a bottle, perhaps, through the use of imagery, they

---

Connections

There has been a great deal of growth in the contemporary literature of cognitive psychology. You can search for some of the more recent information on your own on the Internet. Using the <http://www.AltaVista.digital.com> search engine, use both the *LookSmart* and *AltaVista* directories to find information, by grade level, on study strategies. Sift through what you find and evaluate the sources relative to what you learned in this chapter.

stand to remember the words better. Estes & Chovan (1992) used paired associates imagery with kindergarten students and found that their memories were better as a result. Teacher questioning as an elaboration technique was investigated (Cassidy & DeLoache, 1995); students were directed to connect or apply new information to something they already understood. In another study, reader-generated elaborations were examined (Spires, 1992). Both were found to be effective memory strategies.

episodic long term memory our memories for times or places

There are different kinds of long term memory: episodic, semantic, and procedural. **Episodic memories** are the memories we have for times and places (like Thanksgiving Day dinner). Information encoded in our episodic memory is in the form of images. Again, you probably can actually "see" the seating arrangement at that Thanksgiving Day dinner!

semantic long term memory our memories for facts and concepts

Semantic memories are our memories for general facts and concepts. Most of what we learned in school (instructional content) is stored in our semantic memory. That doesn't mean that you still can't remember (see?) your locker or senior prom (i.e., episodic memory), but that content of our schooling years is most likely stored in semantic memory. The last type of long term memory is called **procedural memory**, which helps us recall particular skills or steps for accomplishing a task (like tying your shoes).

procedural long term memory our recall of specific skills or steps used in task completion

While it may be comforting to break down long term memory into nice, clean categories or types, the reality is that in operation there is probably much overlapping and working back and forth. For instance, what kind of memory contributed to your learning about the Revolutionary War—episodic or semantic? What kind of memory contributed to your learning to calculate arithmetic means—semantic or procedural? There is quite a bit of overlap in the types of long term memory we use, and perhaps a teacher who employs techniques which incorporate content with imagery and action may facilitate storage by eliciting each of the memories discussed.

YOU MAKE THE CALL

EARLIEST SCHOOL MEMORY

What is your earliest school memory? Was it a memory of a time or place or event? Or was it a memory of an early skill you learned? What kind of long term memory is it? Now, why do you think you've remembered this for so long? Did something special happen to you? Did the teacher do something special? Have you had any reason to recall this memory repeatedly through the years? What would information processing theorists suggest caused you to retrieve this memory?

Information Processing— Implications for the Classroom Teacher

phases of learning Gagne's translation of the information processing model for classroom teaching

Gagne (1985) translated the information processing model into an instructional one with his **"phases of learning."** As detailed in Table 7.1, Gagne (1985) parallels information processing stages such as attending with instructional events like . . . gaining student attention! Berlyne

Table 7.1 Gagne's Internal Processes and Corresponding Instructional Events with Action Examples (Phases of Learning)

Internal Process	Instructional Event	Action Example
Reception Expectancy	1. Gaining attention 2. Informing learners of the objective	Use abrupt stimulus change. Tell learners what they will be able to do after learning.
Retrieval to working memory	3. Stimulating recall of prior learning	Ask for recall of previously learned knowledge or skills.
Selective perception	4. Presenting the stimulus	Display the content with distinctive features.
Semantic encoding	5. Providing "learning guidance"	Suggest a meaningful organization.
Responding Reinforcement Retrieval & reinforcement	6. Eliciting performance 7. Providing feedback 8. Assessing performance	Require additional learner performance, with feedback.
Retrieval and generalization	9. Enhancing retention and transfer	Provide varied practice and spaced reviews.

Source: Table from *The Conditions of Learning and Theory of Instruction* by Robert M. Gagne, copyright © 1985 by Holt, Reinhart & Winston. Reproduced by permission of the publisher.

(cf., Benjafield, 1992) observed that we attend to information if it is possesses the collative (or comparative) variables of uncertainty, surprisingness, and complexity. Imagine the impact if on the day a teacher planned to teach his tenth grade American history class about the Revolutionary War, he waited in the hall until the students had settled and ran in, dressed in colonial garb yelling, "The red coats are coming!" After the initial startle response and expected comments and catcalls, the students would most certainly wonder what all this was about. Although this is a radical and perhaps extreme way to gain attention, it does demonstrate the instructional value of gaining student attention in a way that has them not only focused but wondering! Additional things to consider when attempting to gain student attention as your first step in your instructional process can be found in the Teacher Tool Box.

As we continue to review Gagne's model, we see that he drew parallels between the short term memory store and pre-instructional review, long term memory store, and instructional strategies like practice and reinforcement (which mirror rehearsal

Teacher Tool Box

Gaining Student Attention

Teachers can facilitate this important phase of learning for students by remembering these characteristics of attention:

◆ Cognitively, we attend to things for which we are physically oriented (e.g., things that appeal to our senses like demonstrations, visual aids, etc.);

◆ We attend to things that are provocative (i.e., things that engage our cognitive disequilibrium like "Mystery of Life Questions," or "Why are driveways places where we park and parkways places where we drive?");

◆ We attend to things that are oriented emphatically (e.g., things that have been emphasized via changes in voice or via cues and reminders); and

◆ We attend to emotionally oriented stimuli (e.g., things that appeal to our emotions like hearing our names used or inquiries about our attitudes or humor).

and elaboration in an IPM context). He suggested that these pre-instructional and instructional practices enhance the likelihood of transfer of information back from the long term memory into the working short term memory where it can be used.

Our own experiences will tell us that it is not always easy to retrieve information that we have stored in our long term memory. Gagne's suggestion of specific pre-instructional and instructional practices that would enhance this process of storage AND retrieval is useful for teachers to know. But, in addition to Gagne, a number of contemporary cognitive theories have addressed this issue of retention, retrieval, and transfer of information. They are the next focus for our discussion.

CONTEMPORARY COGNITIVE THEORIES

Your students' knowledge *about* something, or facts, is their *declarative knowledge*, while their knowledge of how to *do* something, or skills, is their *procedural knowledge* (Arends, 1988; Farnham-Diggory, 1992; Byrnes, 1996). Fourth graders may know their home addresses ("declarative ") and how to get from their homes to school on foot ("procedural"). Students may know also that dinosaurs lived during the Jurassic Period of life on earth ("declarative") and how to find sources for further research of facts ("procedural"). Teachers are in the business of facilitating both declarative and procedural knowledge in students, but they also hope to promote the transfer of knowledge across contexts and conditions.

When students can apply facts or skills to situations beyond the context in which the initial learning took place—or *transfer of learning*—these facts or skills are more useful. Knowing dinosaur facts is good, knowing how to research them is better; but knowing how to research any topic and commit facts of any type to long term memory (and be able to access them when needed!) is best.

◆ Dual Coding Theory

dual coding theory cognitive theory that memory is facilitated when two processes are engaged, e.g., visual learning and verbal learning

Some theorists explain the efficient processing of long term memories via the dual coding theory. **Dual coding theory** suggests that we remember better when two processes are engaged: visual learning and verbal learning. If we see a demonstration and are taught to verbalize the steps for completion, we remember the task instructions—and are more likely to complete it successfully!—than if we just hear or just watch. For example, a teacher instructing a young child in writing a cursive "t" may provide verbal instruction as well as visual presentation. She may begin with pencil on the student's paper, saying; "let's make a line starting here on the base of our writing line and going up to touch the top of the page guide line and then sliding back down and touching the base line and then swooping up to mid-way. All the time that she is providing these verbal guides, she would also be demonstrating the process on the student's paper.

The research supports the interest in dual coding. Baumann et al. (1993) used a dual coding technique described as "think aloud" to encourage comprehension in students and Matsumi (1994) saw improvements in student learning of Japanese via visual and verbal coding. Elementary students improved their reading and writing posttest scores when taught to use a Vygotskian (see Chapter 2) strategy promoting the use of inner speech (Liva et al., 1994). Robinson et al. (1999) caution, however, that the two modes used should be distinctive and different from each other (e.g., processing text and processing a graphic organizer).

◆ Cognitive Behavior Modification

Cognitive behavior modification (described in Chapter 6) is a dual coding learning strategy and is certainly an effective one. The guided demonstration and self-instruction of CBM offers an effective means of verbal and visual coding. Information is rehearsed and elaborated to make access easier.

cognitive behavior modification a verbal and visual coding strategy combining guided demonstration with self instruction

◆ Schema Theory

Contemporary learning theory embraces **schema theory** in an attempt to explain how information is best encoded in the long term memory (Hyde & Bizar, 1989). The theory emphasizes the nature and purpose of schemata as the fundamental elements of cognitive processing (Douchy & Bouwens, 1990). They are prior knowledge linkages, and they influence the amount and proficiency of our learning (Bigenho, 1992; Leinhardt, 1992).

schema theory cognitive theory which features the nature and purpose of schemata as fundamental elements in information processing

Even though there are slightly different descriptions of schema theory in the cognitive literature, most would agree that it attempts to explain the store of long term memory information in networks of facts and concepts that provide a framework for making sense of new information. In other words, we recall what has been linked successfully to what we already know.

While this theory would suggest that our **prior knowledge** can facilitate or enhance transfer of a learning task, it is also true that prior knowledge can inhibit or interfere with our acquisition of new information (Leinhardt, 1992; Alexander, Kulikowich, & Schulze, 1994). Many people have expressed difficulty learning to use a new software package because their prior familiarity with the preceding versions seemed to interfere. Sometimes students will lament that the reason they are having difficulty with a subject is that they have not "seen it in the real world." In the former case, existing prior knowledge may have been inhibiting, yet in the second case, the lack of prior knowledge seemed to inhibit transfer of learning.

prior knowledge past experiences or previously-learned material

◆ Cognitive Structuralism

One "school" of cognitivists, the **cognitive structuralists**, believe that the awareness of interrelationships between stimuli or the use of

cognitive structuralism cognitive theory that emphasizes an awareness of interrelationships between stimuli of the appropriate use of schemata

appropriate schemata are significant to cognitive learning and to teaching and classroom learning (Leinhardt, 1992). Schemata serve several functions in learning: categorizing, remembering, comprehending, and problem solving (Byrnes, 1996). Remember reading Piaget's use of "schemata" and "schema" in Chapter 3?

First, schemata or prior knowledge links categorize our experiences more efficiently for processing. This categorization of information facilitates the processes of remembrance (recall), and comprehension (understanding), all of which make problem solving more productive (Byrnes, 1996). Alba and Hasher (cf. Benjafield, 1992) suggest that schema facilitate the selection of information based on our interests. Further, once selected, the schema enable the selected material to be organized abstractly and assist the individual in the processes of interpreting and integrating the new material, based on what he or she know already.

Implications for the Classroom Teacher

These are all worthwhile processes for teaching, for they facilitate student learning (Weaver, 1994; Doch, 1988; Leal, 1993; Burgess, 1994). Further, Smilkstein (1993) concluded that schemata-based learning encourages the growth of new brain structures—structures that develop further with practice in making linkages and networks.

As noted by Leinhardt (1992), the question for teachers is "What do I do about schema theory in my classroom?" Clearly, the cognitive structuralists' (or "connectionists") responses suggest that to promote more effective learning the teacher needs to link new information to familiar information selectively in as learner-satisfying a format as possible (Hinson, 1988; Sanchez & Lopez, 1993; Ellis et al., 1994). Some cognitivists stress that students need to learn to extrapolate meaning from limited information, while other theorists have emphasized that students need to learn to use the information in the environment more efficiently and effectively (Miklus, 1974). Cognitivists like Jerome Bruner and David Ausubel described ways of utilizing schema theory in classroom learning, and although they both might be categorized as cognitive structuralists, their perspectives on the structuring of prior knowledge linkages differed. Each is discussed in the next section.

◆ Bruner and Learning via Insight

Jerome Bruner, a noted Harvard psychologist, was interested in the effect of internal processes on perception and learning. He concluded that we are bombarded by more stimuli than we can perceive reasonably and maintains that we perceive the world selectively and subjectively. In other words, we perceive what we are interested in, what we are motivated to perceive (1978).

Bruner presented a developmental model suggesting that our motivations to perceive, and thus the focus for our perception, change developmentally (1978). When we are very young, we are motivated to perceive things that we can manipulate physically via our overt hands-on

Action Research

An Insightful Learning "Mini-Experiment"

Ms. Alicia B is a middle school science teacher. She has taught for fifteen years and has become increasingly concerned that the students, while learning concepts, don't seem to be able to recall information meaningfully. She recently learned about a program in which school-aged students explored the environment via a scientific inquiry method and a study using concept mapping and other structuring strategies. She wondered which strategy would facilitate her students' learning and might create a little fun in the classroom besides. She is trying a "mini-experiment."

She has decided to teach her morning and afternoon classes differently: the morning classes would utilize the scientific inquiry method exclusively and the remaining classes would be taught to integrate concept mapping into their study of the environment. With the insightful learning groups, Ms. B used a series of guided questions and structured lab exercises. These lab exercises required that the student employ naturalistic observations of their neighborhood stream and pond area. Ms. B knew that the "upper portion" of the stream appeared viable, alive, whereas the lower portion and the pond areas were beginning to become stagnant as a result of pesticide runoff. Ms. B structured the students' labs so that they would measure the clarity and odor of the water, as well as making a timed sampling of evidence of aquatic life, at ten different sections of the stream and pond, moving from the top portion to the bottom. At each station, she had the students make "predictions" (hypotheses) about what they thought they would find, and the predictions and the observations were compared and discussed in class.

Ms. B supplemented the afternoon classes' inquiry with structuring strategies. First, she utilized advance organizers at the start of each subunit and integrated mediators throughout the lesson. She also challenged students to derive their own mnemonics and instructed them on how to construct concept maps. She then guided them in the application of the steps when constructing maps relative to the topics in the unit.

Following the completion of the unit, she compared the student groups in terms of (1) unit test scores, (2) interest in joining the schools "green team," an environmental group, and (3) the parents survey assessing student enthusiasm. She found that, in terms of the grades on the unit test score, the latter group scored a little better. However, the group that employed the "inquiry" approach alone produced more volunteers to the green team and parents scored higher on the "student enthusiasm survey." It would appear that at least for this unit, the insightful learning increased the students affective involvement.

One interesting side point was that one of the parents of a child in the morning group noted that his daughter was frustrated with this unit (i.e., didn't like science now) because she didn't know what she was trying to learn. For this student, the insightful learning exercise may have been inefficient.

Ms. B was very enthusiastic about the results and intends to use the information gained to guide her instructional decision making.

experiences. Our motivation to perceive and learn is "enactive." When we reach school age, we are motivated to perceive things that are tied less to the physical manipulation, but still are tied to the physical environment. We are motivated to perceive and learn from pictures and visual aids or images and memories from familiar experiences. Our motivation, then, is "iconic." In adolescence as in adulthood, our motivation to perceive is "symbolic," meaning that we learn what is presented neither enactively nor iconically. We can understand and utilize abstract concepts without having to handle them or having them represented concretely (Bruner, 1978). Does Bruner's developmental sequence

Insightful experiences intrigue us and pique our interests. We seek answers to questions, we solve problems, we make connections between clues because we want to. ◆

seem familiar? It should—it parallels Piaget's developmental sequence for cognitive reasoning (see Chapter 3)!

Bruner concluded that at any age we learn best when we are motivated to perceive and that we are motivated to perceive by insightful experiences. Insightful experiences evoke our powers of induction—we're intrigued, our interest is piqued. We seek answers to questions, we solve problems, we make connections between clues because we want to answer, solve, and make those connections. This idea—**learning via insight**—was embraced much earlier by gestaltist, Wolfgang Kohler in 1925. Kohler also concluded that problem solving occurs when we discover new relationships (Farnham-Diggory, 1992). Consider the mind-bender presented in the next You Make the Call.

learning via insight theory highlighting the influence of our motivations on our selected perceptions and learning

---

YOU MAKE THE CALL

Keesha, Marcus, Neil, and Rolanda are best friends. They've given each other special nicknames: Mouse, Jay, Red, and Bean. Use the clues to find the nickname of each person.

1. Bean is two years older than Neil and one year younger than Mouse.

2. Keesha is shorter than Bean and is taller than Jay, who had her hair braided last weekend.

Can you solve this puzzle?

By itself, this problem is an insightful learning task. The learner is allowed to discover an effective structure for organizing the clues and retrieving a solution. That's certainly one way to approach the puzzle, and many students will find this delightful. Many teachers attempt to pique their students' interests and desire to solve problems. For example when she directed her class's attention to the problem on the board and let them try to solve it, piece by piece, she was encouraging their learning through insight. The fun of the recitation in unison and the humorous yet familiar nature of the problem sparked their organization of previously encoded and stored methods for solving it.

If you attempted to solve the problem presented above, you were using your inductive reasoning skills to try to link the clues in order to find that solution. (Incidentally, the solution appears at the end of this chapter!) Student-centered strategies that capitalize on insightful learning are explored in greater detail in Chapter 12.

However, the other school of cognitive structuralists—the **meaningful reception learning** theorists—maintain that we do not "discover" organizing structures, we "receive" them. Therefore, they anticipate that a more efficient approach to the puzzle would have included the suggestion of a grid, like the one in Table 7.2 to facilitate the organization of clues.

By exposing possible structures for organizing learning, the learning itself can be facilitated. Learning via insight theorists like Bruner and meaningful reception learning theorists like David Ausubel agree in many ways, except when it comes to the "who" of the organization of structures. Bruner wants the student to do it; Ausubel would like the teacher to help.

> **meaningful reception learning** theory highlighting the receipt, not the discovery, of selectively organized information

✦ Ausubel and Meaningful Reception Learning

David Ausubel and theorists from the meaningful reception learning school believe in the significance of the organization of stimuli for efficient recall (Ausubel, 1968). Like Bruner, the meaningful reception learning (or MRL) theorists agree that the linkage of new information to familiar information selectively in as learner-satisfying a format as possible is key to cognitive learning. But unlike Bruner, the MRL theorists suggest that discovery learning alone is an inefficient way to learn. Whereas Bruner stressed subjectivity in the link between perception and learning, Ausubel and the meaningful reception learning theorists stress "selective linkages" (Ivie, 1998).

Table 7.2 Grid for the Organization of Clues

	Keesha	Marcus	Neil	Rolanda
Mouse				
Jay				
Red				
Bean				

Implications for the Classroom Teacher— the Expository Teaching Model

expository teaching teaching model which emphasizes the provision of organizing structures to facilitate learning

The MRL theorists translated their ideas about the significance of the provision of organizing structures into a teaching model called "**expository teaching**" (Ausubel, 1968). This method requires the teacher to provide the students with possible ways of organizing the information for more efficient encoding, storage, and retrieval. If teachers do not expose students to the underlying and selective interrelationships in cognitive learning, the students may draw inappropriate conclusions.

YOU MAKE THE CALL

ACCURACY WITHOUT ASSISTANCE

Take a look at the following excerpt and make your judgments carefully:

"Also important is two-part or binary form, which is symbolized AB. In a binary form the second part may take on the character of an answer to the first. The AB form was very important during the seventeenth and eighteenth centuries. . . . Because there is no sense of large-scale repetition and return, the binary form is not so immediately apparent . . . as is the ternary." (Politoske, 1974, p. 35)

Now, what do you think this excerpt is about? What kind of textbook was it taken from? History? Literature? Music? Math?

If you thought the above excerpt was taken from a music text, you'd be correct! The point is that we all bring our own subjective experiences—our own schemata or prior knowledge— to the process of learning. These experiences influence how we learn. Unless teachers expose the intended schemata or intended underlying structure, students may fill in the gaps inappropriately; therefore, information about music theory may be interpreted inaccurately.

◆ Organizing Strategies

Expository teaching stresses the *importance of teacher-directed organization*. There are several strategies that can mediate concept development in students (Dixon-Krauss, 1996). You are probably familiar with many of the structuring strategies advocated by MRL theorists, and you've probably had teachers who recommended them to you to facilitate your learning in class. One such structuring strategy is the advance organizer.

Advance Organizers

advance organizers cognitive strategy made up of deliberately prepared, slightly abstract passages presented orally or in writing in advance of the main material

David Ausubel is well-known for his research in the area of **advance organizers** (Ausubel, 1968; Hinson, 1988; Pagliocca, 1988; Ritchie & Karge, 1996) . He found that by providing students with deliberately prepared, slightly abstract passages in advance of the main material to be learned, student learning of subsequent material was facilitated.

Advance organizers provide "mental scaffolding." Think for a minute what a scaffold does. When you see a window washer or construction worker standing on scaffolding attached to a building, what purpose does the structure provide? Exactly, it provides a place for workers to anchor things. That's what advanced organizers do for verbal learning. They provide an anchor for subsequent, relevant ideas—a familiar structure for anchoring newer information.

Advance organizers share these characteristics: They are always brief, are written, are presented in advance of the body of material, and are presented at a slightly higher level of abstraction than the students' present level of cognition (Hinson, 1988). In other words, there may be some information or concepts within the advance organizer that are not readily familiar to students. That's okay for an advance organizer because, as we learned when we examined Piaget's view of cognitive reasoning, we know that disequilibrium can be motivating. We are motivated to seek subsequent relevant information to complete the structure.

You may realize already that you have encountered several advance organizers in this text. The brief narrative scenes that begin each chapter are advance organizers. You may be puzzled when you first read about their relationship to the subsequent content, but that's okay. Hopefully, the linkages become clearer as you move toward equilibrium or understanding of chapter content. Most advance organizers are expository advance organizers, presented as prose, as are the advance organizers in this text, but some are comparative advance organizers presented graphically or in tables (Ritchie & Karge, 1996). Look at the two organizers, designed by members of the University of Georgia's Anthropology Curriculum Project and cited in Pagliocca (1988), about Africa in Table 7.3a and Table 7.3b; one is an expository organizer, and the other is comparative.

Expository organizers facilitate introductions of completely new material, while comparative organizers enable clearer linkages between new information and familiar information (Pagliocca, 1988; Ritchie &

Table 7.3a Expository Organizer

Acculturation takes place when the people of one culture acquire the traits of another culture as a result of contact over a long period of time. The British governed Kenya for about 80 years. During this period, the direction of cultural change was largely one way.

Table 7.3b Comparative Organizer

Cultural Universal	*African Trait*	*European Trait*
Social Organization	Tribe and smaller kin groups	National government
Family	Extended; husband has more than one wife	Nuclear; husband has only one wife
Work	For self or in exchange for work	Day laborers for wages

Source: Adapted from Clauson & Rice, 1972; cited in Bryce Joyce & Marsha Weil, *Models of Teaching,* Third Edition, copyright © 1980 by Allyn & Bacon. Adapted by permission.

Karge, 1996). By starting each chapter with an advance organizer, initial encoding and storage as well as subsequent retrieval and storage are facilitated (Ausubel & Fitzgerald, 1962; Ausubel & Youssef, 1963; Mayer, 1979; Meese, 1992; Downing, 1994; Thompson, 1998; Story, 1998)—and without greatly increasing the amount of time spent on learning new material (Hatch & Dwyer, 1999). In a meta-analysis of 135 studies of advance organizer use, Luiten, Ames, and Ackerson (1980) concluded that advance organizers do offer such benefits.

Mediators

mediators cognitive structuring strategy of verbal phrases designed to link new and familiar concepts

Another structuring strategy advocated by expository teaching is the **mediator.** Mediators, at first glance, may resemble advance organizers in that they are often brief written passages. Unlike advance organizers, however, mediators do not have to be written and often are presented orally by teachers. They do not have to be presented at a higher level of abstraction either, nor do they have to be used in advance of the primary information. In fact, mediators are designed by teachers to expose intended links between new and familiar concepts (Gage & Berliner, 1984; Hinson, 1988).

Mediators are brief written or verbal passages linking concepts to be learned with concepts learned already (Hinson, 1988). This sounds so simplistic that we are tempted to think it is unimportant, but it is crucial. Suppose you were presented with this list of terms to remember: *city, crime, car, cave, dark, comics.* By itself, it might seem like a list of random terms and therefore difficult to encode and store meaningfully. But, if your teacher had exposed the mediating phrase that links the terms early on—"Batman, the Caped Crusader"—you may have a better chance of encoding and storing the terms for easier access. Without deliberate exposure to the linkages, almost any verbal learning can seem like an attempt to memorize random word patterns.

Mediators can be used at any point in the lesson, as in this set of mediators, which could be used in an English class. This set of mediating phrases establishes the teacher's intended link between Shakespeare's character, Ophelia and "rejection": "Hamlet's rejection of Ophelia led to her unstable condition; seemingly unwarranted rejection left Ophelia delirious; the inability to cope with rejection resulted in Ophelia's suicide." (Hinson, 1988, p. 197). Teachers facilitate cognitive learning by showing where possible links and connections occur.

Vygotsky advocated the use of mediators, especially with young children, but possibly with learners at any age (Bodrova & Leong, 1996). Developmentally, mediators can vary from being rather simple to being quite complex. They can range from external and overt to internal and covert. For instance, a young learner's mediators probably will be quite obvious: "When Linda is learning how to read, the teacher says, 'Look at the first letter. What sound does it make?' Linda thinks to herself, 'Look at the first letter.' . . . Tony is learning to add numbers. He uses his fingers to help him calculate" (Bodrova & Leong, 1996, p. 69). The overt mediator offered by the teacher sparked the use of an internal mediator in Linda and facilitated her reading; Tony's use of his fingers overtly mediated his ability to do the arithmetic problem. Adults' mediators are internal, automatic, and often, they are not aware they are using them! When adults think, "What do I have to do next?" they are enlisting mediators to facilitate task completion. However, sometimes adults must rely on overt mediators as well. For instance, when switching from one software package to another, the adult computer user may have to rely on multiple templates to keep track of the varied tool bars and functions.

Mnemonic Devices

Another structuring strategy is the mnemonic device. **Mnemonics** are memory gadgets; they provide a familiar structure for processing information so that it can be recalled easily (Hinson, 1988). Mnemonic devices help students recall through the use of elaboration and chunking (Carney et al., 1988; Byrnes, 1996). New information is associated with familiar terms or phrases through evocative images or is broken down into more manageable units for processing. Mnemonics are probably the most "learner-satisfying" of the structuring strategies. Mnemonics have been successful in increasing memory in a range of settings: alphabet learning (Raschke et al., 1999), reading for intermediate students (Solvberg et al., 1995), geography classes (Wright, 1995; Bednarz, 1995), math classes (Lombardi, 1995), foreign languages (Kasper, 1993; Lu et al., 1999), music history (Brigham & Brigham, 1998), and with learning disabled students (Heaton & O'Shea, 1995).

mnemonics cognitive structuring memory devices which facilitate recall via elaboration and chunking

Many mnemonics take the form of *acronyms*. Each letter of a term is associated with new concepts, or concept information is associated with phrases designed to link the terms. Many of us remember one, primarily because they're a little quirky and fun to evoke. A very popular one is the device for remembering the lines of the treble clef in music, EGBDF. Were you ever taught the phrase, "Every good boy does fine" or "Every good boy deserves fudge" or some similar phrase to help you store the names of the lines? Or were you ever told to think of the word "HOMES" as a way of processing the names of the Great Lakes for easier access? (Incidentally, they are Huron, Ontario, Michigan, Erie, and Superior.) Acronym mnemonics, for example, have facilitated the learning of proofreading by young children (Buchanan et al., 1996) and to aid learning disabled students' academic work and social skills (Heaton & O'Shea, 1995). Table 7.4 provides additional examples of mnemonics used for a variety of subject areas.

There are other kinds of mnemonic devices, including pegword mnemonics, keyword mnemonics, loci mnemonics, and face-name mnemonics. *Pegword mnemonics* evoke visual images to make associations. Icon-driven computer programs utilize pegword mnemonics when they get you to remember the "SAVE" function by representing it with the image of a computer disk or the way to open a new file with the image of an open file folder.

Table 7.4   Sample Mnemonics

Subject	Concept(s)	Mnemonic
Directions	North, East, South, West	Never Eat Shredded Wheat.
First Aid	Treating an injury: Rest, ice, compression, elevation	RICE
	Soluble vitamins: A, D, E, K	All Dogs Eat Kibbles.
	Foods to curb diarrhea: Bananas, rice, apples, toast	BRAT
Music	Lines of the treble clef: EGBDF	Every Good Boy Does Fine.
	Spaces of the treble clef	FACE
Mathematics	Order of operations: parentheses, exponents, multiply, divide, add, subtract	Please Excuse My Dear Aunt Sally.
Social Studies	Great Lakes: Huron, Ontario, Michigan, Erie, Superior	HOMES
	Countries of North Africa: Morocco, Algeria, Tunisia, Libya, Egypt	My Apples Tasted Like Eggs.
Science	Planets: Mercury, Venus, Earth, Mars, Jupiter, Saturn, Uranus, Neptune, Pluto	My Very Excited Mother Just Served Us Nine Pizzas.
	Colors of the spectrum: red, orange, yellow, green, blue, violet	ROY G. BiV
	Zoological classifications: species, genus, family, order, class, phylum	Some Good Families Order Class Photos.

Keyword mnemonics are "sound-alike" mnemonics (Byrnes, 1996; Ritchie & Karge, 1996). You encode new information by associating it with a rhyming term. Therefore, if you want to encode the name of the great physician and inventor Charles Drew, you might associate it with the color "blue"—a sound alike. Think back to the childhood counting song about the ants in which children sang, "The ants go marching one by one and the little one stopped to suck his thumb." Not only is the image of marching ants helpful, but rhyming of the number "one" with the word "thumb" is a keyword mnemonic and is helpful, too. Content learning in areas including foreign language learning and social studies have been facilitated by keyword mnemonic strategies (Baehre & Gentile, 1991; Kasper, 1993).

Loci mnemonics enable us to efficiently and effectively encode information for subsequent retrieval by linking them with places (Byrnes, 1996). For instance, given a number of things to remember in some type of sequencing—say, presidents—the teacher makes students' processing easier by linking the presidents' names to rooms in a house, perhaps.

Thus, the learner can visualize George Washington standing near the entryway, and subsequent presidents standing at appropriate spots one might see while walking through the house. Perhaps as the student visually proceeds through the house he encounters Eisenhower in the playroom with army figures, or Reagan watching TV, and ending at the back door with Clinton, who is pictured cooking burgers and so on.

Carney et al. (1988) used the little-known *face-name mnemonics* to help students learn about famous paintings and artists. First, students are taught keywords associated with the artists' names. Then, distinguishing features of the artists' faces are identified, and last, the features and keywords are linked.

YOU MAKE THE CALL

ORGANIZING FOR LEARNING

If you were asked to think about many of the concepts introduced in this chapter so far, how might you go about it? If you had to represent your understanding of the interrelationships between those terms in a diagram, what would you draw? Try it! Arrange the following chapter terms based on your understanding of how they relate to each other: cognitive structuralism, guided class demonstrations, David Ausubel, discovery learning, advance organizers, student questions, mnemonics, mediators, Jerome Bruner, expository teaching, class discussions.

Hierarchical Retrieval Systems

Cognitivists also offer **hierarchical retrieval systems.** If advance organizers and mediators emphasize linking new and familiar information and if mnemonic devices emphasize learner-satisfying formats, then hierarchical retrieval systems (or HRS) probably stress selective organization over the other elements of cognitive structuralism. HRSs present material hierarchically, from the most general representations of concepts to specific and detailed representations (Hinson, 1988; Byrnes, 1996; Ritchie & Karge, 1996). Often, they are represented graphically using a visual "scaffold" or diagram emphasizing interrelationships and levels of concept understanding. One of the early Gestaltists, Karl Duncker, introduced "decision trees"—hierarchical depictions of a concept—precursors to modern day hierarchical retrieval systems (Farnham-Diggory, 1992).

Many of us have been encouraged to represent concepts we are learning via tree diagrams and the like. We might represent our understanding of a concept by representing it as shown in Figure 7.4 or our understanding of a particular English unit as in Figure 7.5. The former is a conceptual HRS, while the latter is an associative one (Hinson, 1988).

Hierarchical retrieval systems expose the student's understanding of the key concepts and subconcepts and their interconnectedness. The information is linked and organized to facilitate encoding, storage, and eventual recall.

hierarchical retrieval systems strategy utilizing a graphic structure which depicts information from the broadest representation of the concept to the most detailed representation

Figure 7.4
Conceptual Hierarchy

Example of a Hierarchical Structure

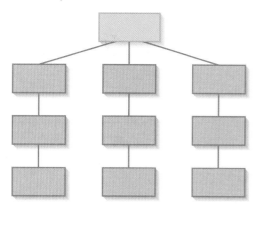

Figure 7.5
Associative Hierarchy

Example of an Associative Hierarchy for an English Unit

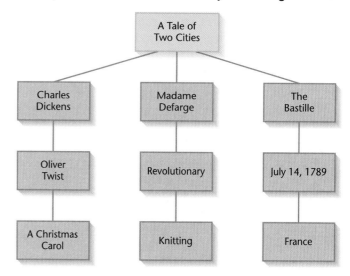

Again, learning is enhanced by these structures (Bower et al., 1969; McCarthy-Tucker, 1992; Gallini et al., 1993). In one study, test scores of basic skills of remedial students in a South Carolina high school increased after the students were taught to organize content via hierarchical schemes.

Concept Mapping

concept maps cognitive strategy utilizing graphic and hierarchical structures and linking phrases added to expose student understanding of interrelationships

Recently, there is much interest in concept mapping. **Concept maps** provide a little more information than the typical hierarchical retrieval systems. They offer the teacher and the student added insight into the student's understanding of the interconnectedness of concepts and subconcepts (Novak, 1993; Perrone, 1994; Boyle & Yeager, 1997). In addition to the hierarchical diagram there are words and phrases—mediators—which serve to clarify not only the top-down organization of concepts, but also the relationships between them. Concept maps offer a greater level of structural understanding than is possible in standard HRS formats. Students can check their own understanding and teachers can check student comprehension as well. Examine the concept map about concept maps by Novak (1993) in Figure 7.6.

Now, using your critical thinking skills, consider the diagram you devised of terms related to this chapter. Unless your diagram was arranged hierarchically and included mediators, it probably was not a concept map.

Figure 7.6
Concept Map about Concept Maps

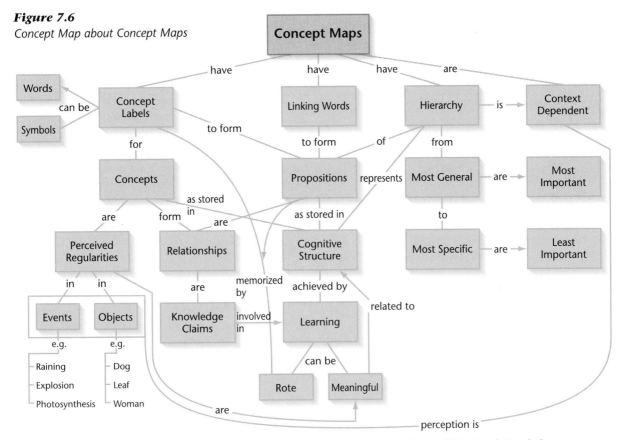

Source: Used with permission of NSTA Publications from "Clarify with Concept Maps, Figure 1" by Joseph Norak, from *The Science Teacher,* October 1991, published by The National Science Teachers Association, Arlington, Virginia.

Concept maps have been helpful in facilitating higher-order thinking (Daley et al., 1999), especially in science classes (Okebukola, 1992b). They have been used to enhance information processing in biology (Okebukola, 1992a), physics (Roth & Roychoudhury, 1993; Roth, 1994), and chemistry (Pendley et al., 1994). They are used in cooperative learning groups (Okebukola, 1992a) and for assessment (Rafferty & Fleschner, 1993). Concept maps also have been used to facilitate student teachers' understanding of multicultural education (Troutman et al., 1999).

Structured Overviews and Outlines

Structured overviews and outlines are also examples of hierarchical organizing structures. In fact, structured overviews combine features of advance organizers, concept maps (or mediators + HRS), and cognitive behavior modification. They are pre-instructional strategies that facilitate the processing via dual coding of a representation of the hierarchical arrangement of key vocabulary (Pagliocca, 1988). In other words, through visual and verbal coding, the teacher can use key terms in a

structured overviews
pre-instructional, dual coding strategies featuring the hierarchical arrangement of key terms

Teacher Tool Box

Using Concept Maps

Teachers can encourage the use of concept maps in their classrooms by having students

- Hierarchically organize concepts at all levels,

- Use directional arrows to indicate linkages and overlapping connections,

- Use mediators or linking phrases between concept levels.

unit to introduce new concepts. Structured overviews clarify the teacher's instructional intentions or objectives and provide students with a framework to anchor new learning (Pagliocca, 1988).

In utilizing a structured overview, first the teacher lists key terms and represents them hierarchically in a concept map. Then, at the beginning of the new unit, the teacher draws the concept map on the board (or using an overhead projector) while students watch. As the teacher draws, however, she verbalizes for students the steps and reasoning. Later, additional terms and mediators may be added as new learning evolves (Pagliocca, 1988).

Additional Techniques Used to Organize Learning Material

In addition to previously mentioned systems for organization of conceptual material, a number of techniques have been suggested by cognitive researchers. These are use of outlining, analogies, selective underlining, selective note taking, and reviews. Each of these techniques is briefly discussed.

Many of us are familiar with the process of **outlining**. In fact, most textbooks today are organized in such a way that teachers need only refer students to the unit headings, chapter headings, major concepts or topics, major subheadings, and bold or "bulleted" items, for effective examples of outlines. This text provides an outline at the beginning of each chapter. Some cognitive researchers advocate the use of teacher-directed **analogies**, which point out similarities between otherwise unlike concepts (Ritchie & Karge, 1996). In many cases, analogies, such as encouraging students to think of "the mind" as a "computer," are helpful (Theile et al., 1995; Dagher, 1995). Other scientists propose the teaching of **selective underlining** techniques, but the evidence is mixed: Underlining is a beneficial strategy for some students (Idstein & Jenkins, 1972; O'Shea & O'Shea, 1994; Harris, 1990), but not for others (Idstein & Jenkins, 1972; Peterson, 1992). Ritchie and Karge (1996) recommend the use of visual aids like directional arrows, boldface type, and varying colors throughout note taking. Harris (1990) found that underlining was effective for short term learning only. It was often more effective when coupled with another information-processing strategy (e.g., keyword mnemonics, annotations) (O'Shea & O'Shea, 1994; Harris, 1990).

Selective note taking, often coupled with distributed practice and/or highlighting, is an effective cognitive strategy (Bretzing, et al., 1987; Loulou, 1995; Georgiady & Romano, 1994). Bretzing, Kulhavy, and Caterino (1987) found that it was a successful strategy for junior high school students, regardless of student ability level.

outlines cognitive structuring strategy which facilitates learning via the organization of information into hierarchically arranged, highlighted headings and subheadings

analogies cognitive strategy used to highlight similarities between otherwise dissimilar concepts

selective underlining cognitive structuring strategy in which the key points in material are underlined

selective note taking cognitive structuring strategy utilizing selective chunking and facilitated by the use of arrows, boldface type, and colors

Reviews, as a post instructional strategy, can be effective also. Once students have learned the material, it is necessary to assist them in maintaining the information and keeping it ready for retrieval. Reviews, in which previous learning is (a) recapitulated and (b) extended to new areas, provide such assistance (Pagliocca, 1988).

In addition to identifying strategies to assist in learning complex material, cognitive learning theorists have also identified strategies to facilitate rote learning.

reviews post-instructional cognitive strategies which feature the recounting and summarizing of information and its link to new material

FACTORS AFFECTING ROTE AND MEANINGFUL VERBAL LEARNING

Rote learning, the kind of learning that emphasizes memorization of disconnected material (e.g., lists of numbers or words), can be facilitated if teachers take into consideration the factors that influence it. There are several factors that affect rote learning by students: practice, transfer, interference, organization, serial position, state-dependence, and level of processing effects (Good & Brophy, 1995); some are helpful, others are inhibiting, many have been addressed elsewhere in this chapter.

rote learning a type of learning which emphasizes the memorization of disconnected material, e.g., lists

Practice, especially distributed practice, improves retention and retrieval (Mumford et al., 1994; Shany, 1995). It is useful for long lists, quick turnaround in learning, and completely unfamiliar material. The language arts teacher who encourages his students to recite the assigned poem a few times each day is facilitating practice effects.

practice effects learning improves when repetition or rehearsal is used

Transfer, as an influential factor, cannot be taken for granted. It is described as the effects of prior learning on the learning of new material. Positive transfer makes new learning easier; specific transfer facilitates tasks that share elements; general transfer expedites the learning of tasks without shared elements. The biology teacher who took her class to the beach last week may have facilitated their learning about mollusks this week. Fuchs et al. (1995) found that students taught peer-assisted learning strategies showed exceptional mathematics growth.

transfer effects prior learning influences the processing of new material

Sometimes our learning of rote material is hurt by past or future experiences. This is called **interference**. There are different kinds of interference: proactive interference occurs when previously learned material hinders new learning; and, retroactive interference occurs when subsequent learning disrupts the retention of already learned material. For example, if a person had learned to type on an electric typewriter which required him to make a carriage return at the end of every line, he may have difficulty on a word processor, where such a carriage return is unnecessary. He may find that, rather than allowing the word processor to wrap, he keeps inserting a return at the end of each line. This would be an example of proactive interference, where the previously learned way is interfering with the new learning.

interference effects rote learning is hindered by our past or future experiences

An example of retroactive interference occurs when a person, having moved to a new apartment finally comes to remember her new telephone number. If that memory of the new phone number blocks her ability to retrieve the old number, it could be said to be retroactively interfering with the old number. Howe (1995) observed that young children, in particular, were more likely to be affected by interference effects.

organization effects learning is enhanced when material is organized structurally, e.g., hierarchically

Organization is a well-established facilitator of cognitive learning. Structuring material hierarchically as reviewed in this chapter—e.g., HRS, concept maps, outlines—is more helpful than using serial order arrangements. The teacher who assigns a mapping exercise for the concept "animalia" is more facilitative of student learning than the teacher who emphasizes serial lists of zoological classifications.

serial position effects recall may be hindered or helped due to the position or placement of words in lists

Related to organization effects are **serial position effects**, in which rote learning is hindered or helped by the placement or position of words in a list—beginning, middle, or end. Memory is better for words appearing at the beginning of a list (primacy effects) and words at the end of a list (recency effects), rather than for words in the middle. The teacher who presents the key terms first or last utilizes this research to facilitate student learning. However, Marmie (1997) found declining serial position effects with practice.

state-dependent or context effects learning is facilitated when material is presented in a context similar to the one in which the information was presented; also called "context effects"

Rote learning is influenced also by **state-dependent factors or context effects** (Brennan, 1992; Talbert et al., 1993). When the context for the encoding of material is similar to the context in which the information must be retrieved, recall is made easier. In other words, the teacher who teaches the rules for croquet to the class as they sit in a sunny field probably will be disappointed by the performance on a paper-and-pencil test of those rules in the closed classroom.

level of processing effect learning will be facilitated if processing occurs at multiple levels, e.g., sensorily and semantically

The deeper the processing, the greater the likelihood the lesson will be remembered. So states the principle of the **level of processing effect**. Information that is processed at more than one level—sensorily and semantically—persists and is more easily accessed (Hamann & Squire, 1996). By offering students advance organizers, mediators, demonstrations, concept maps, and reviews, the teacher encourages processing at a variety of levels.

The learning of information that is verbal and disconnected, yet not in lists—that is not considered rote learning—is influenced by several factors as well. Cognitive scientists conclude that abstraction, levels, schema, text organization, and mathemagenic effects either hinder or enhance **meaningful verbal learning** (Good & Brophy, 1995).

meaningful verbal learning information presented in verbal, disconnected forms, yet not in lists
abstraction effect learners remember the crux or main theme, while details are lost

levels effect learners believe that some information is more important to process than other information

When processing verbal learning, learners often remember the crux or main theme of the learning, while details are lost. This is the **abstraction effect.** For some learning, teachers are comfortable with this effect; they will instruct students to "Read for the main points." But for other learning—learning in which details are crucial—this effect poses a problem. **Levels effects** occur when learners believe that some portions of the material are more important than others. The teacher who distributes sheets of learning objectives with each unit is encouraging this type of selective preparation. Vershaffel and Corte (1997) reported that teachers could change students' dispositions towards mathematical modeling through greater emphasis on word problems.

The degree and type of organization built into the material correspondingly influence the degree and type of information that learners input, store, and recall. These are called **text organization effects.** If the morning class is assigned a poorly presented essay to read, while the afternoon class is given a well written passage, chances are the afternoon class will learn more effectively.

The teacher who is aware of the influence of **mathemagenic effects** will have little difficulty predicting which of his students will be effective learners. Mathemagenic effects consider what learners do to facilitate their own learning. The teacher who observes Maria engaged in selective note taking, Siobhan reading intently but relying on her "photographic memory," and Chris sleeping on his book, will be able to predict reasonably that Maria will learn best. As a matter of fact, we will examine what students can do for themselves to facilitate verbal learning in the next chapter.

We have reviewed the origins of cognitive learning theory, and examined the fundamentals of those theorists who stress the organization of cognitive structures to enhance learning. We can conclude from the research of cognitive science that teachers can facilitate both rote and verbal learning by encouraging the activation of appropriate schemas, helping students to draw inferences, using well-organized material, and assisting students to break material into manageable, processable chunks.

Up to this point, the recommendations stress what teachers can do to make learning meaningful—the responsibility for meaningful learning is the teacher's. But there are newer ideas about the students' role in meaningful learning. In the next chapter, we will examine the student's role in meaningful learning by reviewing the theories and research in metacognition and look at the recent movement towards social constructivism.

Postscript

Incidentally, the answer to the mind-bender is as follows: In the nicknames puzzle, if you concluded that Keesha is Mouse, Marcus is Bean, Neil is Red, and Rolanda is Jay, then you were correct!

text organization effects the degree and type of learning processed is influenced by the degree and type of organization built into the material

mathemagenic effects learning will be facilitated by the use of organizing, structuring strategies

Teacher Tool Box

Promoting Memory

Scruggs and Mastropieri (1992, pp. 33–36) list nine ways that teachers can assist students with the "forgotten art of memory":

1. Promote attention,
2. Promote external memory,
3. Increase meaningfulness,
4. Use pictures or imagery,
5. Minimize interfering information,
6. Encourage active participation,
7. Promote active learning,
8. Increase practice and review,
9. Use mnemonic techniques.

Reflections from the Field

1 I have been teaching American history for close to twenty years. I have found that the students seem to be "less interested." Over the last two years I have begun a "ritual" in which each Monday I enter class dressed as one of the significant figures we will be talking about, or I may simply use a phrase or a gesture that will become more significant as we discuss the topic for that week. I have found that this simple activity has led to students' increased attention (at least on Mondays), and they even try to "guess" who I am. This guessing has led to them actually discussing class material OUTSIDE OF CLASS!

—*Mr. Len J. (social studies teacher), Wilkes Barre, PA*

2 As a health/physical education teacher, I have been concerned that students do not simply "memorize" the material, but try to apply it. I have found that having them make concept maps that we review each week seems to help them organize the material. I have found this has been particularly useful when talking about food groups and physiological systems. And they seem to enjoy constructing them!

—*Ms. Jill S. (middle school health teacher), Boca Raton, FL*

3 I teach senior high mathematics—primarily trig and algebra II. I have found that it helps if before each unit I can present a "real life situation or problem" that would require the use of the principles we will be covering. Presenting the problem before the unit provides both an advance organizer for the students and a point for elaboration as I move through the unit.

—*Mrs. Carol N. (high school mathematics teacher), Aston, PA*

4 Whenever I have a series of terms that I want the children to remember, I provide extra credit for any students who can develop a mnemonic device to be used by the class. I have been doing this now for about four years and have gathered quite a collection. I have found that allowing the students to "discover" or "create" their own mnemonics seems to work much better than if I supply it for them.

—*Mr. Antonio D. (elementary language arts teacher), Needham Heights, MA*

THEORY TO PRACTICE

Revisiting the Classroom—
Is This Teacher a Cognitivist?

Take a look at the opening scene again:

> As class begins, the teacher directs the students' attention to the problem written on the board. She proceeds to have them read it aloud. In sing-song unison, the class recites, "Jamal's dog, Rex, weighs a total of 35 kilograms while soaking wet after a bath. After being dried, Rex loses 2,500 grams. How much does Rex weigh now?" Engaging several students, the key pieces of the problem are discovered. Punctuated by humorous asides, several attempts are made until the problem is solved.

How do we analyze this scene in a cognitive learning context? First, the teacher utilizes dual coding theory by encouraging students to read the problem from the board not only visually but orally as well. She is almost certainly using insightful learning by posing a problem such as this to the class and, through humorous and encouraging comments, guiding them through the problem solving. You also might say that the nature of the problem—Jamal and his dog Rex—and the injection of humor into the task by both teacher and students provided elaboration to the learning.

You, as Teacher, as Decision Maker, as Cognitivist

Illustration 1:
Lisa's Biology Course

Now, consider the following scene, only it's your turn to make the call. As you attempt to analyze this scene, think about these questions: What can you as the teacher do to help? Can you offer opportunities for dual coding as well as opportunities for structuralist or connectionist strategies? Is insightful learning war-ranted? Which meaningful reception learning or expository teaching strategies might be effective? How can you account for—and ameliorate—any hindering effects?

> Lisa is taking a biology course in which her worst problem is remembering the functions of the various systems of the body and the terms within those systems. No matter how hard she tries—she repeats them to herself frequently—she can't remember them.
> (Adapted from Kaplan, P. S. (1990). *Educational Psychology for Tomorrow's Teacher.* New York: West Publishing Company, 101)

Illustration 2:
Mr. Z's Geometry Class

Again, consider the following scene and make the call. As you analyze this scene, think about these questions: What can you as the teacher do to help? Can you offer opportunities for dual coding as well as opportunities for structuralist or connectionist strategies? Is insightful learning warranted? Which meaningful reception learning or expository teaching strategies might be effective? How can you account for—and ameliorate—any hindering effects?

> No matter how many ways he has tried, Mr. Z finds that his tenth grade students have a great deal of difficulty remembering the axioms in geometry. He has tried to make games out of the axioms, he has even used flash cards—but the students struggle with remembering these axioms. His concern is that the students become so anxious about remembering the axioms that he can't get them to enjoy the process of geometry and the value it brings to their lives. He would love your assistance.

SUMMARY

Foundations of Cognitive Learning Theories

Cognitive learning theories boast the most contemporary of the theoretical perspectives, yet even they have longstanding roots in Gestalt psychology. The modern-day information-processing model theorists further developed the Gestaltists' notions that perception is key to learning by adding the influence of perception on memory and memory's role in learning. The multistore system for the processing of information has evolved.

Contemporary Cognitive Theories

Contemporary cognitive psychology acknowledges the role of dual coding in learning, as in cognitive behavior modification, and the efficacy of establishing links with prior knowledge, schema theory, in learning.

One school of cognitivists, the cognitive structuralists, believes that long-term learning is facilitated when learners can link new learning to old, can organize information selectively, and when information is presented in as learner-satisfying a format as possible. From these ideas stem several implications and models for classroom teaching, including discovery learning and expository teaching.

Jerome Bruner believes that we are motivated to perceive and therefore must be motivated to learn effectively. Left to process information on their own, learners will organize the information for encoding, storage, and retrieval in the most personally efficient, expedient, and comfortable way possible.

Theorists like David Ausubel, however, emphasize selective organization over learner-satisfying formats in learning. They believe that we learn more efficiently and effectively when we are exposed to or receive a structure for the organization of information rather than generate our own. The more direct role of teachers in the expository teaching model is described, and several structuring strategies are offered in the chapter.

Factors Affecting Rote and Meaningful Verbal Learning

Memorization of seemingly disconnected materials—known as rote learning—can be influenced by several factors including practice, transfer, interference, organization, serial position, state-dependence, and level of processing effects. Meaningful verbal learning can be affected also. Cognitive scientists maintain that effects such as abstraction, level, schema, text organization, and mathemagenics can either hinder or enhance learning.

◆ Field Experience Questions

As an alternative to engaging in action research, observation and discussion with those in the field can prove insightful. Your task is to observe and interview several practicing teachers. Try to answer the following based on your observations and discussions.

1. Was there evidence of the teacher's use of attention getters? Rehearsal techniques?

2. Did the teacher employ advance organizers? Concept maps? Mediators? Hierarchical retrieval systems?

3. Any evidence of insightful learning? Meaningful reception learning or expository teaching? What is the teacher's opinion of these?

4. In the teacher's experience, which activities are most effective in helping students to remember?

5. Does the teacher teach the students how to organize material?

◆ Key Terms

abstraction effect	interference effects	practice effects
advance organizers	law of proximity	prior knowledge
analogies	law of similarity	procedural long term memory
chunking	learning via insight	rehearsal
closure	level of processing effect	reviews
cognitive behavior modification	levels effect	rote learning
cognitive structuralism	long term memory	schema theory
concept maps	maintenance rehearsal	selective note taking
dual coding theory	mathemagenic effects	selective underlining
elaboration	meaningful reception learning	semantic long term memory
episodic long term memory	meaningful verbal learning	sensory register
expository teaching	mediators	serial position effects
figure-ground discrimination	mnemonics	short term memory
Gestalt psychology	multistore model	state-dependent or context effects
good form or Pragnanz	organization effects	structured overviews
hierarchical retrieval systems	outlines	text organization effects
information processing model	phases of learning	transfer effects

◆ Additional Resources

DiVesta, F. (1987). The cognitive movement and education. In J. Glover & R. Ronning (Eds.), *Historical foundations of educational psychology* (pp. 203–236). New York: Plenum.

Leinhardt, G. (1992). What research on learning tells us about teaching. *Educational Leadership*, April, 20–25.

Pearsall, N. R., Skipper, J. E., Mintzes, J. J. (1997). Knowledge restructuring in the life sciences: A longitudinal study of conceptual change in biology. *Science Education, 81,* 193–215.

Shuell, T. (1986). Cognitive conceptions of learning. *Review of Educational Research, 56,* 411–436.

Wilcox, R. T. (1987). Rediscovering discovery learning. *The Clearing House, 61,* 53–56.

Motivation in the Classroom

E ntering the room, the teacher is "greeted" with 30 students, some standing, some sitting (some two on a lap), and all appearing unruly. Rolled up balls of paper, along with various comments, are being "tossed" around the classroom. Announcing that "this is Introduction to Computers," the teacher is greeted with the response "Oh good now we can find those porno pictures on the Internet?"

Presented with a class clearly determined to do anything BUT learn the curriculum as planned, this teacher finds himself being "saved" by the unauthorized pulling of the fire bell.

Twenty-five or 30 high school students, throwing papers around the room, making disparaging comments about the teacher's appearance, and announcing, quite mockingly, their lack of need to understand computer science—all this could certainly intimidate both the novice and seasoned teacher. But the classroom need not be as blatantly hostile as this one to make a teacher feel intimidated and frustrated. Consider the teacher facing 20 fourth graders who, at varying points throughout the lesson, demonstrate most of their interest and concern with the children next to them or with the fact that lunch is next period or that someone "is teasing me." They are not much concerned with the learning objectives and the task at hand.

Under these conditions of distraction and competing interests, it is understandable why a teacher may question the intent and motivation of the student. As one middle school teacher noted of her class, "These kids are not only unmotivated, they are unmotivate-able!"

The truth of the matter, fortunately, is that her children, as with the students in the classroom depicted in the introductory scene, ARE motivated. Arthur Combs noted, "People are always motivated; in fact, they are never unmotivated. They may not be motivated to do what we would prefer they do, but it can never truly be said that they are unmotivated" (Combs, 1962, p. 85). Thus, the issue is not one of motivating students; rather it is motivating the—to attend selectively to the tasks presented and engage in learning so that they can move toward the learning objectives and goals.

Faced with students who are often motivated to do things that are not part of a teacher's plan, teachers need to understand the nature of motivation, its connection to learning and performing, and the various factors that may contribute to the motivation of a student at any one time. This chapter begins with the question "What is motivation?" and proceeds through a discussion of the current theories and research that provide answers.

◆ Chapter Objectives

When you complete this chapter, you should be able to do the following:

1 Define motivation;

2 Describe the connection of motivation to learning and performing in the classroom;

3 Give examples of intrinsic and extrinsic motivation;

4 Explain what is meant by the value/expectancy theory;

5 Describe the practical implications of Abraham Maslow's need hierarchy for the motivation of classroom learning;

6 Describe the effect of arousal and anxiety on achievement motivation;

7 Discuss the possible impact of success and failure on continued motivation and how these experiences relate to a student's belief about ability;

8 Describe the characteristics of mastery-oriented, failure-avoiding, and failure-accepting students;

9 Develop a list of five specific conditions you would hope to establish for your classroom in order to maximize student achievement motivation.

CHAPTER 8 CONTENT MAP

WHAT IS MOTIVATION?

"Why?" is probably the most widely asked question in the English language. Why did he do that? Why didn't she come? Why would anyone want to be like that? Why didn't that student complete the assignment? Why does he always pay attention in class? These are all questions that attempt to understand the "motive" that drives people to act or not act in certain ways. They are all questions which attempt to understand and explain human motivation.

YOU MAKE THE CALL

Take a moment and reconsider our opening scene.

Were the students motivated? By what? Was the teacher motivated? Why?

How about the students who silently stood by? What motivated that behavior?

Was anyone depicted who showed the absence of motivation?

---

motivation an internal state that energizes, directs, and maintains behavior

So, what is motivation? Simply stated, *motivation is the force that energizes and directs a behavior towards a goal* (Baron,1992; Schunk, 1990).

Typically, the concept of motivation is applied when a person is energized to satisfy some need or desire. The person will engage in, or be attracted toward, activities that are perceived as having the potential to meet this need or desire. The students presented in the opening scene clearly are acting in ways designed to meet various needs: Social? Sexual? Artistic? Rebellious? Safety? Could you think of other needs that may be inferred from their actions?

Since activities that appear to satisfy "unmet" needs will appear attractive and interesting, the teacher who observes an "unmotivated" student may really be observing someone for whom "life in the classroom" is not meeting needs. When the classroom activities allow for the satisfaction of the student's needs, even this "unmotivated" student will actively engage in the learning experience.

THE MOTIVATION-LEARNING CONNECTION

Motivation is a crucial element to the learning process. The research clearly shows a positive correlation between motivation and achievement (Ringness, 1965; Ugurogulu & Walberg, 1979; Wang, Haertel, & Walberg, 1993). Therefore, knowledge of the factors that facilitate motivation to learn and achieve is critical for a teacher to be truly effective or for a student to achieve!

The concept of motivation has been surrounded by numerous myths and misgivings, such as "failure is a good motivator!"

(Wlodkowski, 1984). The effective teacher must be able to discern fact from fancy when deciding on a process to motivate. Perhaps one of the most counterproductive "myths" is that **anxiety** and fear are useful ways to simulate a student's motivation to learn.

anxiety a state of arousal, marked by tension and uneasiness

◆ Arousal: Necessary for Learning?

Although extreme anxiety and fear appear less than productive motivators for learning, a level of general **arousal** seems essential. Arousal is both a psychological and a physiological state. Psychologically, arousal refers to alertness or attentiveness. We know that the introduction of novel stimulation, for example, a movement or change in the teacher's voice level, or the assignment of a task can all elevate the level of arousal. Simply consider your own state of alertness and how it was affected when a teacher moved from the desk and started walking down the aisle past your desk. Or consider the experience of stepping into a classroom and having the teacher state, "Everybody clear your desk for a little pop quiz!"

arousal a physical and psychological state of readiness in which one feels alert and attentive

Arousal is an important variable in the motivation-learning equation. Even though many commercial products attempt to sell us on the idea of "passive learning" and the ease of learning as we sleep, it is clear that we gather and process information much better when we are alert than when we are asleep. However, this arousal-motivation-learning connection is not a simple linear one in which more is better. Arousal needs to be at an optimal level, since too little or too much can be detrimental to performance (Morris, 1988).

◆ Fear and Anxiety:
Arousal as Detriment to Learning

One manifestation of increasing arousal is anxiety, a feeling characterized by varying degrees of fear and worry. Anxiety is most often presented as a self-protection mechanism that surfaces in response to threatening situations. Thus, if while jogging down the street, you find yourself confronted by a large, teeth baring, growling dog, you may find your level of alertness, your level of arousal increases. Typically, increased levels of physiological and psychological arousal, which accompany anxiety, are intended to prepare for coping with the possible threat. The change in physical and psychological arousal prepares us either to flee (flight response) from the source of the threat or fight off the danger. This fight-flight response can take many forms besides the obvious manifestation of actually running from the danger or physically attacking the threat. Often, fight can take a verbal form or even be a facial gesture, as when a person

Alert and attentive ◆

makes a sarcastic comment back to someone who has just made a threat. Flight can also occur internally, as when a person escapes from a threatening situation by daydreaming, or fantasizing.

The classroom is not void of threats and the resulting anxiety and fight-flight response. Consider the student with a mild speech impediment who is asked to stand and read aloud before the class or the student who anticipates being mocked by his peers for being too "stupid" to know the answer and who thus resists the teacher when told to go to the board to do "problem number 5." These students may be experiencing the classroom, the teacher, or the task as threatening. Thus, they experience a high and nonproductive level of arousal. With such a high level of anxiety, the student may engage in flight behaviors, as when our "reader" acts as if he simply does not hear the teacher or really doesn't know the place to start. Flight behavior is also evident in the resistant expression and behavior of our math student. In either case, the level of arousal for each of these students is not motivating effective learning behavior.

As Naveh-Benjamin, McKeachie, and Lin (1987) noted, anxiety can interfere with attention, learning, and testing. The idea that anxiety may interfere with a student's ability to demonstrate what they have learned is not new. The detrimental effects of anxiety are clearly demonstrated in the research on test anxiety (Hembree, 1988).

Anxiety can also interfere with learning in that anxious students are more easily distracted by irrelevant or incidental aspects of the task at hand, having trouble focusing on significant details (Hill & Wigfield, 1984). Gaudry and Speilberger (1971) studied the behavior of anxious students who perceive the classroom experience to be threatening perhaps because of history and expectation of failure or because they anticipate negative consequences if they attempt to achieve (e.g., humiliation, punishment, etc.). These researchers reported that highly anxious children engage in behaviors that are self-disparaging and unadventurous. Further, these researchers noted that highly anxious children often indulge in daydreaming (Gaudry & Speilberger, 1971). These behaviors appear to be ways of protecting ourselves from a perceived threat, but each interferes with our productivity and achievement. In addition, it has been proposed that highly anxious students divide their attention

YOU MAKE THE CALL

Most of us have experienced the interference of anxiety with our test taking ability. Consider a time when you found yourself experiencing anxiety during a test. It could have been a major exam, a standardized test, like the college board, or even something like a driver's test. How did (do) you experience anxiety? How does your body react? What are your thoughts? How did (do) these physical and psychological changes impact your performance?

between the new material and their preoccupation with their anxiety (Tobias, 1985). Rather than processing the information they are hearing or reading, they are more attentive to the heart palpitation, tension in the chest, or the fear of how poorly they will perform (Hill & Wigfield, 1984; Paulman & Kennelly, 1984).

The relationship between anxiety and academic performance is complex. Although high levels of anxiety may improve performance on simple, well-practiced tasks, it seems to interfere with performance on new or difficult assignments (Covington & Omelich, 1987). In general, anxiety that is too high can block learning and performance and teachers with highly anxious students may need to concentrate on building relationships that allow the students to feel not threatened in that environment.

Teacher Tool Box
Reducing Student Anxiety

Taking steps to reduce debilitating anxiety in our students, while difficult, is certainly not impossible. Consider each of the following:

- Promote a safe environment, free from physical or psychological "attack":
  - Don't embarrass;
  - Use competition carefully;
  - Don't make public display out of failures;

- Help students set realistic, acceptable goals;

- Consider changing instruction and evaluation procedures:
  - Reduce time pressure on students completing assignments by teaching student time management strategies;
  - Vary level of assignment difficulty, matching more carefully student skill level to task;
  - Provide clear instructions for assignments.

UNDERSTANDING MOTIVATION

To be effective, a teacher must go beyond the materials and processes typically used to stimulate and understand the underlying elements involved in the motivation to learn.

◆ Extrinsic and Intrinsic Motivation

Researchers and theorists in the area of human motivation generally identify two generic classes or types of motivation: extrinsic and intrinsic (e.g., Deci, 1975; Deci & Ryan, 1985; Lepper & Green, 1978; Malone & Lepper, 1987).

Extrinsic Motivation

Extrinsic motivation is operative when an individual is motivated by an outcome that is external or somehow related to the activity in which she is engaged. It is the motivation to engage in an activity as a means to an end (Pintrich & Schunk, 1996). The piece worker on the production line of the widget factory may attempt to increase her production if a special bonus or money incentive is provided. In this situation it is not the process of making widgets that is motivating but the fact that additional money can be made. In most cases, the individual engaged in some activity because of extrinsic motivation often will be very goal oriented and goal directed.

extrinsic motivation
motivation that is based on external factors such as rewards and punishment

Teacher Tool Box
Strategies for Reducing the Negative Impact of Extrinsic Motivation

- Use extrinsic rewards when students demonstrate they are unable to experience interest or joy in just doing the activity;

- Limit the use of extrinsic rewards to tasks that hold low value for most people, for example, performing a repetitive drill;

- Use extrinsic rewards so that they add to the students' sense of control and self-determination. That is, allow the student to know the "payoff" for particular choices, prior to engaging in that choice.

- Attempt to use extrinsic rewards that are most "natural" to the setting. That is, if praise and smiles are normally present in that environment, whereas, candy or gifts are not, use praise and smiles;

- When using "tangible" rewards, such as stickers, candy, or toys, pair the tangible with a word of praise, pointing to the student's success as a result of his effort.

- Encourage the student to employ self-praise, again pointing to the value of her effort in producing this success. Specifically, have the student repeat after you, "I really worked hard, and it paid off!"

The use of extrinsic motivators in the form of awards, grades, privileges, or praise is clearly widespread and will continue to be so not only within our schools but in our society; but the sole use of reinforcers as motivators is not without its criticism (Harter & Jackson, 1992; Kohn, 1992). Heavy emphasis or reliance on extrinsic motivation and reinforcement has been criticized along the following grounds.

- *Practical/logistical problems.* Other than the use of teacher praise, which is readily available and easy to deliver, the use of reinforcers may often result in a disruption of the flow of the class, added expense or simply inconvenience for the teacher.
- *Devaluation of learning.* Research (e.g., Calder & Staw, 1975; Kohn, 1993) has found that in situations that are intrinsically interesting, the utilization of extrinsic rewards results in decreased motivation and interest. It is suggested (e.g., Cohen, 1985) that the utilization of extrinsic motivation actually detracts from learning for learning's sake.
- *Restricts learning.* As Crooks (1988) noted in classrooms where emphasis is on passing a test or getting good grades, students may restrict their interest and their learning to areas to be tested. Many have experienced the student who asks the teacher, "Do we have to know this?" or "Is this going to be on the test?" Clearly, in situations like this learning is restricted to that which will earn a payoff.

Intrinsic Motivation

intrinsic motivation finding value and motivation within the activity itself, regardless of the outcome

Intrinsic motivation exists when an individual works simply because of an inner desire to accomplish a task successfully, whether it has some external payoff or value, or not. This is engaging in an activity simply for its own sake (Pintrich & Schunk, 1996; Reeve, 1996). Consider our widget producer. In the process of performing the job, the worker starts to enjoy the process of assembling the widgets. Further, let's assume that this worker begins to compete with himself, attempting to set personal records for the number of widgets he can produce in an hour, even though he receives no additional monetary incentive. Under these conditions, the worker is operating from intrinsic motivation. He is finding satisfaction within himself by simply doing the action of making widgets.

People involved in a task because of intrinsic motivation appear to be engaged and even consumed, since they are motivated by the activity itself and not some goal that is achieved at the end or as a result of the activity. Deci and Ryan (1985) have suggested that this state wherein a person attends so closely to the activity she is engaged in, even to the point of tuning out the rest of the environment, as being in the "flow" (p. 28). Research indicates that students who are intrinsically motivated achieve higher than those who are only extrinsically motivated (Gottfried, 1985).

◆ The Classroom: A Setting of Intrinsic and Extrinsic Motivation

It is clear that in any one classroom on any one day, numerous children can be seen engaging in learning for its own sake (i.e., intrinsic motivation). However, that same cursory glance at a "typical" class or school may lead one to conclude that emphasis is placed on extrinsic motivational factors (Lepper & Hoddell, 1989). Student of the month posters, honor cards, smiley faces, grades, special forms of recognition are all examples of the payoffs teachers employ to motivate (extrinsically) their students. Even the right to engage in extracurricular activities, such as playing sports or attending proms, are sometimes contingent on a level of academic performance.

Students do bring a desire and interest to the classroom to learn and grow. Sometimes the direction and timing of those desires, however, may not always be in line with the needs of the teacher, the pace of the class, or the objectives of the curriculum. Further, for some the use of extrinsic payoffs may fail to stimulate the students' motivation to achieve. Under these conditions, the teacher is left with the questions of "why" and "what to do?" To answer these questions effectively and to make appropriate decisions to facilitate each student's achievement, the teacher needs a fuller understanding of the research and theory behind both intrinsic and extrinsic motivation.

◆ Value and Expectancy

Feather (1982) provides a second and perhaps more useful way to conceptualize motivation, in contrast to simply identifying motivation as intrinsic or extrinsic, in what he termed the **value/expectancy theory**. This theory postulates that the effort people are willing to expend on a task is a product of: (a) the degree to which they value the rewards they anticipate from successfully completing a task and (b) the degree to which they expect to be able to perform the task successfully if they apply themselves. It is important to note that this model suggests that motivation is a PRODUCT, not a SUM, of value and expectancy. That is, if either of the two components is missing, there will be no motivation

value/expectancy theory of motivation which emphasizes the need for both a belief that the action will lead to goal attainment (expectancy), and that the goal has value (value) to engage in that activity. Without valuing the activity the goal, there will be no motivation, even when one believes he/she could successfully complete the task. For example, you know that you CAN successfully dig a hole, but without the need to plant a tree, get some exercise, find a treasure, or some other such need, your motivation to do so will be low or nonexistent. Similarly, if the value is high, but a person, a student, truly does not believe that he can perform the task successfully, there will be no motivation to engage in the task.

The issues of "value" and "expectancy" are so essential to student motivation that we will use them to organize our remaining discussion.

VALUE: AN ESSENTIAL MOTIVATIONAL INGREDIENT

One of the basic assumptions in motivation theory is that people behave in an attempt to reduce their felt or experienced needs. Thus, one is motivated to engage in an activity when it is perceived as having value for reducing need.

YOU MAKE THE CALL

Take a moment and reconsider a classroom where students state, "This is boring," "I don't need this — when will I ever use it?"; "Can we have class outside?"; or "Could we get in a circle and discuss our feelings?" What needs are being met or expressed by each of these comments?

◆ Need/Drive Theory

One of the earliest theorists to investigate human motivation and the concepts of need and drive was Henry Murray. Murray (1938) described the concept of need as a force, a tension that leads an organism to move in the direction of the goal. In this formulation, the goal state is an event capable of releasing the felt tension.

It is assumed that when needs are activated, an individual is compelled to act in ways that reduce or satisfy that need. This desire to act has been called a **drive**. The stronger the need, the stronger the drive, and the more the individual will engage in goal-directed activity. A very sad, yet poignant demonstration of the need/drive/activity connection is provided by the all too familiar news reporting of the crimes committed by addicts in support of their habit.

drive the desire to act when needs are activated

Primary and Secondary Needs

While there are many specific needs that could be motivating, needs are generally grouped into two classes: primary and secondary. *Primary needs* are essential for survival. Thus, the need for food, water, and oxygen are all primary needs. *Secondary needs*, while not essential or fundamental to physical survival, clearly are needed for psychological well being and happiness. These secondary needs include the need for companionship, prestige, status, affirmation.

From a need/drive theory, a student's lack of motivation could be explained in any of three possible ways. Each of these possible explanations for the low motivation has its own directive for changing the situation. First, it may be possible that the student simply does not engage in the activity because of low felt need. That is, the student at this time is quite satisfied and finds no "push" to engage in this activity. Secondly, the student may be reacting to a stronger, competing need. This may be the case with the boy and girl in our opening scene. Somehow expressing and receiving affection and physical contact appear stronger than learning about Math-1A! A third explanation for a student's low motivation may be that the student, while possessing the need and drive to achieve, simply lacks the skills to do so. Under this scenario, the student may not only experience a need to engage in the activity but also a felt sense of frustration with not being able to participate. Perhaps this explains our students' desire to "sit in a circle and discuss feelings" rather than engage in a math lesson.

With the exception of the last possibility, which involves skill training, motivating the student requires the teacher to understand and identify the student's need state as well as to know how to reduce competing needs while increasing the need to achieve. The discussion to follow will assist you to develop the skills and understanding necessary to do just that!

◆ Maslow's Hierarchy: Categorizing Needs and Motives

Abraham Maslow (1954, 1968, 1970), a key participant of the humanistic movement, agreed that humans were motivated to satisfy needs. However, he also felt that previous psychological theories underestimated human potential and failed to consider the reality of higher needs, motives, and capacities. As with many other "need" theorists, Maslow believed that unsatisfied human need creates tension, which serves as a force to direct behavior toward goals that the individual perceives as tension reducing. Somewhat unique to Maslow's presentation of needs, however, is his belief that humans have two classes of needs: deficiency and growth needs, and the specific needs within these classes are arranged in a hierarchy (Figure 8.1).

Deficiency Needs

Deficiency needs are needs that disrupt psychological and/or biological balance, causing a response to the discomfort. Deficiency needs include such physical requirements as food, water, sleep, and pain reduction.

deficiency needs Maslow's lower four needs, which take precedence and must be satisfied before moving to growth needs

Figure 8.1
Maslow's Need Hierarchy

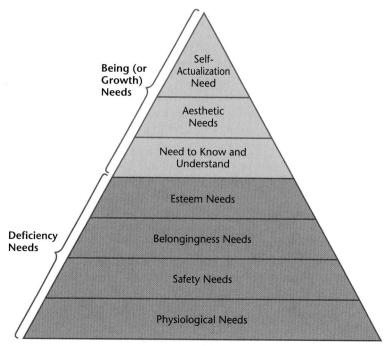

Source: From *Motivation and Personality*, by Maslow, © 1971. Reprinted by permission of Prentice-Hall, Inc., Upper Saddle River, NJ.

Also included in this group are needs for security, belongingness, and self-esteem.

When activated, deficiency needs energize an individual to remove or satisfy the deficiency. For example, when a person is dehydrated, he is motivated to increase his fluid intake. Deficiency needs appear to have an automatic cap or completion point. For instance, once an adequate amount of fluid has been ingested, an individual is no longer motivated to acquire more. Deficiency needs could be viewed as having an off-on characteristic, where once satisfied they cease to be motivating, until once again a need arises. Contrast this to the second category of needs, growth needs.

Growth Needs

growth needs in Maslow's hierarchy these are the highest three needs, which appear to be insatiable and thus growth oriented

Growth needs are those that apparently have an unlimited capacity for satisfaction. As a class, they are needs that motivate us to develop the fullness of our unique capabilities. Growth needs, according to Maslow, include our quest for understanding, appreciation of beauty, and our own personal development. These needs are never truly "met" in the same way that the deficiency needs could be "met" or "fulfilled." Rather, growth needs continue to expand and take on new directions each time the individual experiences them. This would explain why a person having begun to learn about music or electronics, for instance, may truly desire to learn more. It is a reflection of the adage "the more you know, the more you want to know!"

Needs in Hierarchical Order

In addition to placing human needs into two groups, deficiency and growth needs, Maslow also suggested that within each group needs are arranged in a hierarchy of precedence (Figure 8.1). Implied in this **hierarchy** is the proposition that a lower, survival-based, deficiency need takes precedence over the higher-level growth needs. Thus, the higher needs are more predominant and directive of our actions only when the lower needs have been satisfied.

From this perspective, it is understandable why free breakfast or lunch programs are so essential to the proper motivation of students who lack resources to meet those needs outside of school. One must be free of the pain of hunger before one can truly appreciate the beauty of the Mona Lisa or be interested in quadratic equations!

As Figure 8.1 demonstrates, the physiological needs (food, water, sleep, pain reduction) are the one that most demand satisfaction. As with the other need levels of the hierarchy, once this level is satisfied, the next level emerges. Safety needs include good health and security from harm and danger. Safety needs also arise in anticipation that physiological needs will need to be satisfied again. Thus, an individual is motivated to save for a rainy day or to ration water or food when confronted with limited supplies.

It could be argued that when a student asks the teacher, "Is this important?" or "Will this be on the test?" the primacy of the safety need is interfering with the need to know. Under these conditions, the role of the teacher may be to facilitate learning through providing for the safety (physical and psychological) of the student. By being specific in telling students their learning objectives, along with telling them what they will need to do, the teacher can satisfy or at least reduce this safety need and open the way to activate higher-order needs, such as the need to know and understand. Additional ways to provide for the safety of the student will be discussed later within this chapter.

Next in the hierarchy of needs are what have been termed **belongingness needs**. These are the needs to feel connected with others. Needs for friends, family, and interpersonal connectedness are all reflections of this level of motivation, as is the need to give and receive love. As we continue up the hierarchy, the next needs to emerge are those involving the need for esteem, or the desire to have respect, confidence, and a sense of personal worth and value.

The needs to know and to understand include the need to satisfy curiosity, to seek knowledge, and to gain understanding. The final needs in a person's path toward self-actualization are the aesthetic needs. These are the needs to experience order, truth, beauty, symmetry, closure, and the sense of completion of an act.

Maslow's position was that as these more fundamental needs are met, an individual will be directed toward the ultimate growth need, **self-actualization**. This refers to the drive to develop one's potential in order to become what one is capable of becoming. The paths toward self-actualization can be many and varied, ranging from career or vocational

hierarchy of needs Maslow's model of seven levels of human needs that are arranged in order of precedence

belongingness needs the need to feel connected with others

self-actualization fulfilling one's potential

choices, life-style choices, and even leisure activity choices. As one author noted, self-actualization is "not so much a matter of what a person does, as how he feels about what he's doing" (Kolesnik, 1975, p. 42).

◆ Implications and Directions for Teachers

There have been numerous criticisms of Maslow's need hierarchy. Some have questioned the precision of the categories; others debate the rigid precedence of lower needs over higher needs, at least as suggested by the hierarchy. But perhaps one of the most commonly recurring criticisms of this presentation is that it is a bit oversimplified, in that no behavior can be described exclusively in terms of a single need. Just consider the process of selecting a partner or a mate for a life-long commitment. This selection process is certainly motivated by multiple needs and would be multi-leveled in terms of Maslow's hierarchy. In fact, the process of selecting a mate may engage all the levels of needs identified in Maslow's hierarchy. Similarly, the way a student behaves in a classroom may reflect a single need or, more than likely, several levels of needs.

Even with the possible limitations of the theory, one element seems to hold some intuitive value for teachers. This is the concept of prepotency of lower-level needs. Without arguing for the absolute domination of lower-level needs, one can consider the potential for distraction of lower needs when attempting to facilitate a child's curiosity and desire to learn. A child who is distracted by headache, fatigue, or hunger will have a great deal of difficulty attending, or even wanting to attend, to a history lesson. Under these conditions, the source of the physiological need must be addressed. Further, this interference of lower needs is NOT restricted to physiological conditions alone. Consider the child whose need for safety or belonging has been activated by his parents' recent divorce and his subsequent displacement from his house. Clearly, this child may not be motivated to attend to the filmstrip on the "life cycle of the fern"! Certainly, the child who feels threatened and unsafe will achieve less than those whose learning environment (either at home or in school) is safe and stable (Blumenfeld, 1992).

Teacher Tool Box
Addressing Needs and Drives

- It is important to understand the concept that students operate with multiple levels of needs and that some of these needs may interfere with the motivation to learn and achieve.

- Time to address the "physical" needs of children (e.g., bathroom needs, the need to stretch or move, the need to relax, as well as the need to eat and drink) should be built into the classroom regimen, especially for younger children, whose ability to delay such gratification may be more difficult. For the middle school child, who is going through so many physiological changes and growth spurts, snack times may prove useful.

- "Buddy systems" whereby new students are paired with buddies to show them around the school and to assist them to fit in with their peers are good ways to satisfy belongingness needs.

- Be sensitive to procedures that may "threaten" the students' sense of security or safety (physical and psychological) within the classroom. Research supports the notion of a nurturing, safe, and orderly learning environment as essential to learning and achievement (Brophy & Good, 1986; Rosenshine, 1980; Soar & Soar, 1978).

- Employ strategies (e.g., cooperative learning) that provide for the belongingness needs of your students.

- Model your respect and the valuing of all students within the classroom.

◆ Achievement Need:
A Motivation of Special Interest to Teachers

Achievement need is the term most often applied to the drive to excel in learning (Atkinson, 1980, 1983). Thus, students who persistently attempt to do well in school and succeed with high grades have high achievement needs and high achievement motivation. Those with high achievement motivation are generally perceived as being more intrinsically motivated, ambitious, competitive, and independent in decision making than people with low achievement needs. People with high achievement motivation generally do not require immediate gratification or rewards but can work for delayed, future rewards (Kukla, 1972). Students with high need for achievement tend to be motivated by challenging assignments, opportunities for second attempts, and corrective feedback, whereas students with a high need to avoid failure seek small, clearly defined assignments with clear, achievable payoffs. Studies (e.g., Klienke, 1978) have shown that students with high achievement motivation generally earn better grades in high school and college, and are more likely to attribute their success to their own ability and their failures to a lack of effort, a point that will be further discussed later within this chapter.

These characteristics of students with high achievement motivation certainly point to the desirability of having students within your classroom who exhibit a high achievement need.

EXPECTANCY: A SECOND ESSENTIAL INGREDIENT TO MOTIVATION

But value is only one of the components in this equation of motivation. The second component is expectancy, the degree to which a person expects to be able to perform the desired task successfully. Albert Bandura (1982), for example, suggested that an individual's beliefs (expectations) about his/her ability to reach a goal will determine how much effort is expended and how long it will persist. This belief about what one can and cannot do in a particular situation Bandura termed: Self-efficacy.

Teacher Tool Box

Affecting Achievement Motivation

1. *Assign Do-able Tasks:* Alschuler, Tabor, and McIntyre (1971) suggest that students initially focus on "do-able" assignments along with assignments that engage the student through personal involvement. The experience of success can then promote higher achievement motivation.

2. *Provide Moderately Difficult Tasks:* Providing "do-able" tasks does not mean providing easy tasks or easy goals. Easy goals are not the answer, since they provide very little satisfaction or sense of mastery, whereas difficult goals may provide little hope of accomplishment.

Atkinson felt that students' motivation to learn was influenced by their perception of the difficulty of the task. Achievement-oriented students prefer tasks that they consider to be moderately difficult (Maehr & Sjogren, 1978). Therefore, it is important to help students develop more realistic goals and predictions around moderately difficult tasks.

3. *Provide Specific Help:* According to David McClelland and his associates (McClelland, 1973, 1985), giving students concrete ideas about how to reach their goals increases their motivation to achieve, whereas abstract advice (e.g., "just keep trying"), or clichéd directives ("you'll get it, practice makes perfect!") are not very useful.

4. *Reduce the Fear of Failure:* Research (e.g., Stipek, 1984a, b; Weisz, 1979) suggests that students appear to develop a stronger need to avoid failure, as they progress along in their education.

Whereas younger children often plunge in and attempt tasks, older students often devote more energy to developing strategies to reduce failure than they do to those strategies that increase achievement.

Self-perception of competence also generally decreases during the elementary grades. Initially, overly optimistic perceptions of ability drop. This drop appears to correlate with the increased use of objective performance measures (Eshel & Klein, 1981). It would appear that another drop in self-perceptions occur after students enter junior high as do attitudes toward school (Eccles, 1987).

Thus, for those with high fear of failure and shifting self-perceptions of competence, the teacher needs to minimize failure by providing support and praise for legitimate effort as well as for outcome.

◆ Self-Efficacy:
Personal Expectations as Motivation

This belief in one's ability to reach a goal, whether accurate or not, affects choices of activities. If a student believes he can do the activity, he will try it, if not, he will avoid it! Thus, the unmotivated student may, in fact, be quite motivated, but the motivation is to avoid a task that he feels he cannot complete successfully!

self-efficacy beliefs about one's personal competence within a particular situation

According to Bandura (1977), high **self-efficacy** is a function of a person's believing (a) that she can successfully perform the behavior required to produce the goal, and (b) that the behavior will lead to the desired outcome. Thus, students who have low self-efficacy may be demonstrating either (a) their belief that they cannot perform the task (such as study, present a speech, memorize an assignment) or (b) that they can perform the needed action, but that other factors will prevent that action from leading to the desired outcome. Thus, a student who knows that he can study and memorize the material for the spelling test may still not perform because he believes that even when he studies, the teacher will find a way to give him a bad test grade. A very poignant demonstration of this self-efficacy theory is found in the movie *Stand and Deliver* (see Class Illustration).

CLASS ILLUSTRATION
Stand and Deliver

The movie *Stand and Deliver* is a powerful presentation of the potential impact of self-efficacy. Throughout the movie, the teacher, Jaime Escalante, "fights" with the students' beliefs in their inability to perform at the advanced placement level. Through his efforts, the students slowly come to believe that they can pass the A.P. exam. The second component in Bandura's theory suggests that not only must one believe one can perform the activity, but that one needs to believe the activity will lead to the desired outcome. Having successfully passed the A.P. examination, the students in Mr. Escalante's class receive word that all of their passing scores are being discounted because ETS had suspicion of cheating, even though no cheating had occurred. The students (and Mr. Escalante) are not only devastated, but the students demonstrate no willingness to try again. They know they can do the work, but what's the use if they're never rewarded?

Self-efficacy is an important theoretical and practical concept for educators. As one researcher noted, "A sense of efficacy for performing well in school may lead students to expend effort and persist at tasks, which promotes learning. As students perceive their learning progress, their initial sense of efficacy is substantiated which sustains motivation" (Schunk, 1990, p. 33). Feelings of efficacy motivate students to tackle a task. Further, this sense of efficacy can foster the ability to concentrate on the task at hand, whereas feelings of inefficacy can lead to preoccupation with feelings of incompetence (Bandura, 1986, 1993; Schunk, 1990, 1995). Therefore, fostering a student's feeling of efficacy is a valuable tool in a teacher's tool box and may assist students to set reasonable, achievable goals.

◆ Motivation, Self-Efficacy, and Goal Setting

Locke and Latham (1990) have demonstrated the value of goal setting for increasing motivation and self-efficacy in learners. They suggest that goals should not only give the students a standard against which to measure their progress but should also encourage them to develop new strategies when old ones prove unsuccessful. Goals that are focused on the challenge and mastery of a task have been described as learning goals (Pintrich & Garcia, 1991). These goals often lead students to become more task-oriented (Stipek, 1996) and motivated to seek understanding rather than simply to avoid failure (Nicholls, 1984). Further, Bruning, Schraw, and Ronning (1995) found that students who adopt learning goals persist when encountering difficulty, and they attribute success to internal, alterable (i.e., unstable) causes. They also focus on personal mastery rather than on competition or avoiding failure. However, for goals to work they need to be (1) specific; (2) close at hand, and (3) moderately difficult (Jagacinski, 1997). Furthermore, increased motivation appears to result more readily when the goals are developed by, and thus owned by, the student (Pintrich & Schunk, 1996; Ridley, McCombs, & Taylor, 1994).

> ### Teacher Tool Box
> **Fostering Self-Efficacy**
>
> ◆ Help students set appropriate learning goals toward which they can make genuine progress. Research indicates that getting students to set goals and make a commitment to try to reach those goals increases their performance (Bandura & Schunk, 1981; Tollefson et al., 1984).
>
> ◆ Goals need to be specific, with clear standards of achievement attached to them.
>
> ◆ Goals are best if they are moderately challenging.
>
> ◆ Goals should be attainable with a reasonable amount of time and effort. Break down long-term goals into smaller, more readily attainable subgoals.
>
> ◆ Help students experience success that is attributable to past and present effort. Focus on seeing how hard they worked to get here, rather than telling them "if you work hard, you will get there!"
>
> ◆ Model goal setting, effort, persistence.

In addition to the work of Albert Bandura, the importance of developing and maintaining a student's expectancy of personal competence and predictive success has been supported by a number of theories and areas of motivational research. Two of these areas of research will be presented in some detail. First, we will look at attribution theory and later in the chapter we will discuss the effect of teacher expectancy on student self-perception and expectancy.

◆ Attribution Theory

Attribution theory (Weiner, 1979, 1980, 1984) attempts to discover how people perceive the cause of their behavior and then looks at the way their beliefs may affect their later behavior (Fiske & Taylor, 1984). **Attribution theory** suggests that the element(s) or target(s) to which a person attributes his successes and failures, influences his expectations for future success and therefore affects motivations. Consider the dialogue between two seventh graders.

attribution theories theories which point to a person's explanation of the factors impacting performance as influencing their motivation and behavior

Penny on seeing her friend Joan at lunch asks, "Hi, Joan! How did you do on Mrs. Baywell's math test?"

"Yeah, right! You know that old bag hates me. How do you think I did—I failed!" "How did you do?" asks Joan.

"I failed too! But to be honest I didn't even crack a book last night. I thought I could just wing it. Boy, was I wrong!"

While Joan and Penny share a common experience (i.e., failing the math test), they attribute their failure to different causes. Joan clearly attributes her failure to the teacher's dislike for her, whereas Penny clearly sees her own lack of preparation as the source of the bad grade.

Attribution theory (Weiner, 1979, 1980, 1984) attempts to systematically describe people's explanations for success and failure in classroom situations. It holds that understanding student attributions is the key to understanding student motivation.

The theory suggests that people attribute success and failure to four factors: *ability, effort, luck* (good or bad), and *task difficulty*. According to Weiner (1972), a student will first assess the task that they are asked to perform and then make what he termed a **causal attribution**. That is, the student will estimate if the outcome is most likely to be affected by his ability, effort, or luck, or by degree of difficulty of the task. The student's level of motivation will be the result of the causal attribution derived. Thus, if a student, such as Penny in our previous illustration, feels the outcome is a function of her effort, then she will be more motivated to "try" than would be the case if she firmly believe the outcome is strictly a matter of luck! Figure 8.2 provides a look at an attributional approach to understanding achievement motivation.

causal attribution the way an individual estimates if the outcome is most likely to be affected by his/her ability, effort, luck, or degree of difficulty of the task

Figure 8.2

The Attributional Approach to Explaining Achievement Motivation

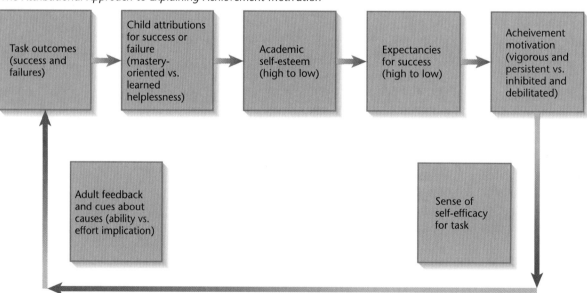

Source: From L. E. Berk, *Child Development,* 5th Edition, Copyright © 2000 by Allyn & Bacon. Adapted with permission.

The four factors used to explain one's success and failure (ability, effort, luck, and task difficulty) can be conceptualized along three other dimensions: locus of control (Rotter, 1966), stability, and control. Characterizing the attributes along these three dimensions will help clarify how they influence a person's expectations for future success and therefore current motivation.

Locus of Control

The **locus of control** describes a person's belief as to the location of the cause for his success or failure. Much of the conceptualization and research in this area stems from the social learning theory of Julian Rotter (1966), who presented locus of control as having two dimensions: external locus of control and internal locus.

An "external" person perceives the causes for events as located outside himself, thus external to the person. An external person believes that he has little control over the outcome and fails to perceive a cause-and-effect relationship between his actions and the consequences. Thus, Joan, who feels that she always fails the test because "the teacher hates her" is clearly placing the source for her success or failure onto the teacher. In contrast to such an external locus of control, the student who feels that she didn't do very well on the quiz because she really didn't study is placing the cause of the failure within herself and as such is demonstrating an internal locus of control.

Certainly, there will be less motivation to work hard when the locus of control is external. If a student does not perceive any value or causal connection between her effort and the outcome, why should she try? Similarly, if a student perceives success as a matter of luck or the good will of the teacher (external locus of control), it will be difficult to motivate the student to assume personal responsibility for her learning. Thankfully, locus of control is not felt to be a fixed, unchangeable orientation. Rather, locus of control is a learned perception that can be altered. It will not, however, happen as a result of simply being successful or failing on one task. However, the more a student believes that he can control outcomes—success and failure—the more internal a sense of control will develop. As might be evident, teachers concerned about the motivation of their students will do well to set up their classrooms in such as way as to allow their students to experience choice and control. This point will be elaborated upon later in this chapter.

locus of control where a person places the source of their experience; is success and failure a result of factors outside of the individual's responsibility (external) or within the individual (internal)?

Stability

Stability refers to a person's perception that the cause of her performance will or will not change over time. A person with a stable attribution orientation may point to her basic intelligence or genetic makeup as an explanation for the outcome. Someone who attributes the outcome of her efforts to genetic make-up is likely to believe that the outcome will remain the same over time and perhaps even across situations. A person employing an unstable attribution will tend to see the outcome as fluctuating or varying across settings or tasks. This would be the case when a student who usually believes himself capable of success blames another student for bothering him during the test and thus upsetting his test performance.

This stability/instability dimension is believed to underlie a student's expectation for future success or failure (Weiner et al., 1983). Students who attribute success to stable factors will expect to succeed at the same task the next time. Conversely, those who attribute their success or failure to an unstable factor (such as unusual help from the teacher or luck) will not feel as sure of future success. The same pattern holds for the experience of failure. Failure ascribed to a stable cause, such as low ability, will generally lead to decreased expectations of future success and lowered motivation. Whereas failure ascribed to a temporary condition (e.g., head cold, temporary emotional upset, having a bad day) likely would not affect expectations for later success.

Control

The final dimension to consider is that of control. This factor describes the extent to which the student feels she has control over the learning situation as opposed to the source or locus of that control. This dimension (controllable versus uncontrollable) characterizes students' perceptions of whether the conditions leading to their success or failure are either under their control (e.g., effort) or not under their control (e.g., luck). If you believe that the active factor is controllable, you are more apt to attempt the task.

CLASS ILLUSTRATION

Imagine the case of Sister Alice's fourth grade math class. As we observe the class, we note that one student is at the board, struggling to complete a problem. Sister Alice continues to press the student to try harder, to remember what he has learned, and to see the task as "easy," as simple. The student, out of a sense of frustration, announces that he can't do it. It's too hard. He is not as smart as everyone else in the class. The student almost pleads for Sister to help him. "Show me how to do it!"

This classroom presentation clearly demonstrates one student's attributional profile in relationship to that particular problem. The student clearly believes that his own low ability (being the dumbest in the class) makes this problem (task difficulty) beyond his reach. Since both ability and task difficulty are stable, uncontrollable conditions, the student loses all motivation to continue trying at the task and surrenders.

The relationship of these dimensions and attributes is summarized in Table 8.1.

Attribution and High or Low Achievers

As demonstrated in our class illustration, one's attribution of success and failure is critical to one's motivation and later performance (Bar-Tal,

Table 8.1 Relationship of Dimensions of Locus, Stability, and Controllability to Attributions

Example		*Locus of Control*	*Stability*	*Controllability*
Ability	"I was born with an ear for music."	I	S	UC
Effort	"I really studied for this exam."	I	US	C
Luck	"I just flipped a coin for all those true and false questions."	E	US	UC
Task	"Nobody could pass her tests, they are impossible."	E	S	UC

1979; Weiner, 1972, 1979). Research, for example, has demonstrated that low achievers tend to blame themselves for failure, emphasizing their low ability. They make external, unstable attributions for success (such as luck). Low achievers don't believe that their efforts are responsible for success or that their lack of effort is responsible for failure (MacMillan, et al., 1986). Without a sense of connection between their actions and the outcome of success or failure, low achievers will have little motivation to try.

High achievers, on the other hand, are found to attribute success to internal and stable causes. They believe they are smart (i.e., high ability) and that when they work (i.e., high effort), they succeed. If they fail, they may make external attributions, such as suggesting the test was unfair, or internal attributions, such as not studying hard enough.

Weiner (1984, 1986) summarized the salient characteristics of students high in achievement motivation:

a. They prefer situations in which performance outcomes can be ascribed to their own actions;

b. They have learned to attribute outcome to effort, and

c. They notice and react to cues indicating the importance of effort expenditure.

These are desired responses and typically result in increased effort, achievement, pride, and sense of control (Ames, 1990). High achievers expect success in the future and will strive to attain it (Fennerma, 1987).

To increase the achievement motivation of their students, teachers need not only to provide tasks of appropriate difficulty, but also to focus on helping students to perceive the relationship between effort and success. Without this, students can develop a condition of **learned helplessness** (Seligman, 1975), the feeling that no amount of effort can lead to success. With this perspective, a student is left with feelings of shame and self-doubt, and with little motivation to succeed.

learned helplessness an expectation of failure due to a previous experience with the belief that there is nothing that one can do to succeed

Changing Attribution: A Personal Causation Model

A number of attribution-changing programs have been developed and investigated. Wittrock (1986) noted that the major objective of most of these programs is to move students in the direction of effort attributions. That is, these programs attempt to lead students to understand that their successes and failures should be attributed to their personal efforts, as opposed to other, uncontrollable attributes. One approach discussed by deCharms (1972) focuses upon the development of a **personal causation** perspective. When a person believes the reasonable use of his/her knowledge or habits will lead to the desired outcomes, she can develop a sense that she is the *origin* of these changes. DeCharms (1972) developed a program that attempted to teach students to shift their locus of control from an external orientation, in which they see themselves as helpless pawns who have no responsibility for their own learning and achievement, to an internal orientation, in which they perceive themselves as *origins* and assume greater responsibility for the outcomes of their behavior. He believed that in order to enhance motivation, one needs to believe that he is an active agent who can interact with the environment. In support of his theory, deCharms (1976) demonstrated that when teachers were trained to use motivation-enhancing exercises designed to increase, among other things, the students' "origin" orientation, even low-income students exhibited improved achievement test scores, reduced absences and tardiness, and increased willingness to take moderate academic risks.

> **personal causation** a person's belief regarding the degree to which his/her knowledge or habits will lead to the desired outcomes

In his personal causation theory, deCharms (1984) suggests there is an optimal level of structure in the classroom to be motivational. According to deCharms (1984), over-structured and under-structured classrooms are likely to inhibit origin enhancement. It appears, therefore, that the classroom structure which provides choices and control for students will increase student motivation (Kounin, 1970).

◆ Achievement Motivation: Beliefs About Ability and Self-Worth

As evident in the previous discussion, there is a connection between a student's belief about her ability and her resulting achievement. Research has also discovered a linkage between students' beliefs about their ability, their **achievement motivation,** and their sense of self-worth (Covington, 1984).

> **achievement motivation** a drive to succeed, desire to excel

Self-worth theory assumes that achievement behavior is in some way an attempt to maintain feelings of competence and self-worth (Covington, 1984; Covington & Beery, 1976). Self-worth theory stresses that although people have drives to achieve and succeed, they also have a powerful need to remain competent and to avoid anything that might imply low ability or incompetence. Thus, if success is in doubt, one's priority is to act in a way that minimizes the possibility of failure and its reflections on one's ability. Covington (1984) posited that often an able student who does not put in the effort necessary to achieve may be demonstrating a pattern aimed at protecting his own sense of worth or personal value. Thus, for many students what appears to be a lack of motivation is, in fact, a high degree of motivation. However, the motivation driving their behavior is aimed at protecting their sense of self-worth by avoiding achievement activity. It is not a motive to demonstrate competence and mastery through achievement. Clearly, when confronted with such a student, the task of the teacher is not to draw attention to achievement or failure but to find ways to reduce the perceived "threat to one's self-worth," which this achievement task obviously holds for that student.

◆ Motivational Sets Reflecting Self-Worth Orientations

Research (Covington, 1984; Covington & Omelich, 1987) reports patterns or styles of approaching achievement tasks, patterns that reflect the individual's way of responding to the need to feel worthwhile. The three kinds of motivational sets identified by Covington were mastery oriented, failure avoiding, and failure accepting (see Table 8.2).

Mastery-oriented students value achievement and see ability as improvable. These students focus on goals in order to increase their skills and abilities. Mastery-oriented students generally attribute success to their own efforts and thus become persistent, successful learners (McClelland, 1985).

mastery-oriented students
studentswho focus on mastering the material presented within the class because they value achievement

Failure, while not desirable, is not perceived as threatening for those with a mastery orientation. Mastery orientation tends to insulate the individual from fear of failure, since failure is not a reflection of self-worth, merely evidence that they have to work harder. Thus, for high achievers, failure often leads to sustained, successful learning (McClelland, 1985). These mastery-oriented learners experience failures as opportunities to adjust their goals, or develop new approaches to achieving the old goals. Quite often, they simply resolve to work harder in the future (Graham & Weiner, 1996).

Failure-avoiding students lack a strong sense of their own competence and self-worth separate from their performance. When they can demonstrate success on a task, they feel that they have worth. When they fail, they feel worthless. Therefore, in order to feel competent they must protect their self-images from failure.

failure-avoiding students
students who are motivated more by a desire to avoid failing rather than attempting to succeed and as such do not take risks, or attempt to avoid responsibilities

Students with a failure-avoiding orientation most often play it safe. They stick to tasks they have mastered, risk responding only when it is clear that they will be successful, and generally stay with what they know. When presented with new or novel situations, these students employ failure-avoiding strategies. They expend energy looking for ways to appear smart, or they make excuses and rationalizations for failure.

In addition to procrastinating and finding excuses, two of the most common failure-avoiding strategies are (1) to set very low, almost no-lose goals, or (2) to establish unrealistically high goals. While the first is obvious, in that it attempts to ensure success, the latter protects the student's self-worth. Even though failure is almost a guaranteed outcome, there is comfort in knowing that this task was so difficult that no one really could have done it. With this frame of reference, the student does not feel that his competence or self-worth can be questioned.

The problem with such failure-avoiding strategies is that while they may prove effective for the short run, eventually they erode a student's will to learn. The student shifts from simply avoiding failure to accepting failure (Covington, 1984).

failure-accepting students
students who believe that they are unlikely to be successful since their failure reflects their low ability

Failure-accepting students are those who have given up. Convinced that their lack of achievement reflects their lack of ability, they see little hope for success. At this level, students feel that they can no longer avoid failure, and they take up a helpless, hopeless, position. For example, Butkowsky and Willows (1980) found that poor readers (fifth grade boys) had lower expectations for success, gave up more quickly in the face of difficulty, tended to attribute failures to internal and stable causes, and attributed success to more external causes. Further, these low perceptions of competence and control translated into helplessness in achievement settings and reduced motivation and effort (Boggiano & Barrett, 1985).

The teacher who can increase a student's effort attribution, help the student distance personal worth from achievement, and reduce the competitive nature of the task completion, will increase the achievement motivation of that student.

Action Research

Mrs. Nelson: Study of Locus of Control

As discussed in Chapter 1, acting as decision makers, teachers frequently conduct their own action research. Mrs. Nelson, a high school English teacher, became intrigued with the concept of locus of control after studying it in her graduate course. She wondered to what extent her students' locus of control orientation affected their academic performance in her class. She obtained permission to use some of the questions from a published locus of control survey and developed a survey appropriate for her class of adolescents. She then administered the newly created survey to her students.

While her students' locus of control orientations varied, she did find a relationship between external locus of control and poor academic performance in her English class. Mrs. Nelson is now making special efforts with students identified as having an external locus of control orientation. She is demonstrating to them the link between effort expended and the concrete results of that effort.

Table 8.2   Self-Worth—Expectancy and Motivational

Orientation	View of Success	View of Failure	Motivation and Behavior
Mastery	Result of effort	Evidence of a need for more work	Select tasks that are challenging and increase effort with failure
Failure-avoidant	Evidence of personal worth	Evidence of personal worthlessness	Play it safe; develop protective strategies, for example, excuses & rationalizations
Failure-accepting	Not possible	Inevitable; reflective of lack of ability	Hopeless, helpless and therefore non-motivated. Surrender!

THE CLASSROOM—IMPACTING STUDENT MOTIVATION

Much of the previous discussion focused on student elements that were involved in achievement motivation such as need, attribution, and self-worth. However, implied throughout the previous discussion is the role that structure and organization of the classroom play in the motivation of the student. The next section will discuss the specific role the teacher and classroom climate play in creating and maintaining a student's achievement motivation.

◆ Teacher Expectations: A Motivational Element

Few educators would question the potentially serious impact that **teacher expectancy** can have on a student's behavior and achievement in the classroom (Dusek & Joseph, 1983). A student's levels of aspiration (i.e., expectations of future successes or failures) can be influenced not only by his or her own history of success or failure but also by the teacher's behavior. Good and Brophy (1977) suggested that a teacher expecting specific behavior and achievement from a student will behave differently toward that student. For example, the teacher may wait less time for students who are assumed to be low achievers to answer, or she may criticize these low expectancy students more often. This treatment by the teacher tells each student what behavior and achievement the teacher expects from him and affects his self-concept, achievement motivation, and level of aspiration. Weinstein (1998, p. 83) suggests that the "expression of low expectations by differential treatment can

teacher expectancy beliefs a teacher holds regarding a student's behavior performance

Teacher Tool Box

Managing Expectancy and Self-Worth

◆ Increase effort attribution:
- Praise students for efforts as personal characteristics rather than for the effort itself (E. Gagne, 1985). For example, it is more beneficial to state: "You are a hard-working student" as opposed to "You worked hard on that project, this time." This encourages students to view their effort as stable.
- Manipulate the classroom environment to emphasize the importance of student effort, to match task difficulty to student abilities, and to downplay the influence of luck on student achievement (Wheller, 1988).
- When encouraging students, emphasize past effort and its relationship to positive achievement, rather than simply encouraging the student to work harder. Andrews and Debus (1978) report research that demonstrates that students can be taught to make effort attributions and that such training increases achievement.

◆ Develop supportive environment:
- Use noncompetitive learning structures (mastery learning, for example) where everyone is expected to achieve, with standards of performance high and constant but with a flexible amount of time to achieve these standards (Covington & Omelich, 1979a).
- Create structure to increase "origin" perceptions. Allow the student to be an active agent in interacting with the environment in such a way that his knowledge or habits will lead to the desired outcomes (deCharms, 1984).
- Build success into a program and increase the possibility that effort will lead to success (Weiner, 1984, 1986).

◆ Increase student competency:
- Teach students how to set goals and develop problem-solving strategies to assist in reaching those goals (Bandura & Schunk, 1981; Tollefson et al., 1984).
- Assist students to identify self-worth as more than the possession of ability or the success at a task (Covington, 1984).
- For low achievers, minimize competition and emphasize individualistic goal setting (Stipek, 1988).

inadvertently lead children to confirm predictions about their abilities by exerting less effort & ultimately performing more poorly." Some researchers (e.g., Cooper & Tom, 1984; Cooper, 1979) suggest that the real impact of teachers' expectations is in sustaining motivation. Thus, a teacher who expects a student to be disinterested may either not notice the student's interest or may respond inappropriately when the student shows enthusiasm, thus stifling the student's motivation.

Research has demonstrated that teachers often treat those students they perceive as lower achieving in ways that may prove counter-motivational. Good (1987), for example, found that teachers often seat lower-achieving students farther away from them, pay less attention to the slower student, call on slower students less often, wait less time for them to answer, fail to provide follow-up questions, criticize more frequently, praise less often, and give less frequent and less detailed feedback. All of these teacher behaviors reduce a student's interest in or desire to engage in achievement activities.

◆ Classroom Climate: A Motivational Element

Classrooms are certainly unique settings. They are places with unique social and psychological characteristics, which may facilitate or impede a student's motivation. The classroom can be a safe, orderly place where students believe they can learn. Under these conditions, learning will be facilitated (Brophy & Good, 1986; Rosenshine, 1980; Soar & Soar, 1978). The classroom can also appear threatening to students, as a place for performance and personal evaluation.

At its most fundamental level, the classroom is a social environment where much interaction and interpersonal dynamics occur, as those involved move toward common goals. This interpersonal dimension, or the way students relate to one another as they attempt to complete their learning tasks, can influence their motivation to learn. David and Roger Johnson (1985) termed this interpersonal dimension of the learning task the goal structure.

Goal Structures: A Key to the Classroom Environment

In a series of investigations, Johnson and Johnson (1987) introduced the concept of **goal structures** as a key ingredient in the classroom climate and a pivotal element in a student's motivation. These authors suggest that it is through the interaction with others (e.g., teacher and peers) that students come to value learning for its own sake, as well as to enjoy the process of learning itself (Johnson & Johnson, 1985). Furthermore, they suggested that different goal structures will establish different learning atmospheres and relationships in the classroom, thus impacting student motivation in different ways (Johnson & Johnson, 1987).

These authors proposed three different forms of goal structures:

◆ **Cooperative,** in which students work together to achieve a goal. In this situation, students believe that the goal is attainable only if others reach the goal as well. This is the basis for "pulling together" as a team.
◆ **Competitive,** in which students work against each other while pursuing an instructional goal. Students believe that they can reach their goal (for example, to be the classroom spelling bee champ) if and only if others do not reach that goal.
◆ **Individualistic,** in which student's activities are unrelated to each other as they work toward a goal. The student believes, "I can do my thing and achieve my goal. You may or may not reach your goal, but it won't affect me."

Certainly, a classroom structured around any one of these goals, for example, competition, will look and feel different from a classroom that has another goal structure, such as a cooperative one. Not only will the classroom climate be different, but so too will the impact on student motivation.

Competitive Goal Structures and Classroom Climates

Competition can certainly be exciting and energizing, but this energizing effect is often limited to those who win. Those who find themselves consistently on the losing end can quickly become defeated and employ avoidance strategies rather than engaging in the competition.

goal structures the way students relate to one another when working toward an academic goal

cooperative learning students work together to achieve a goal, believing that the goal is attainable only if others reach the goal as well

competitive goal structures students work against each other while pursuing an instructional goal, believing that they can only reach their goal if and only if others do not reach that goal

Spelling Bee: Competitive goal structures ◆

Cooperative learning: Students working together ◆

Consider the impact on the child who hears that we are about to have another spelling bee, knowing full well she is always the first one to sit down. Her enthusiasm for the activity will most likely be minimal. Indiscriminate use of classroom competition does not appear advisable, and the consequences of winning or losing must be carefully considered. Otherwise, competition can produce detrimental anxiety.

Research on the impact of competition suggests it works best with those who have the ability to succeed (Michaels, 1977). Competition appears to be an effective source of motivation when the competitors have a chance to succeed and when they are fairly evenly matched. In situations where there may be a variety of competencies, competition still may prove useful. It would appear, however, that the usefulness of competition is limited to simple or mechanical tasks as opposed to more complex problem solving (Clifford, Cleary, & Walster, 1972). This suggests that competition can be useful for drill activities, once *everyone* has acquired the knowledge and skill required to compete.

The implication of this research for the classroom teacher appears to be that teachers can enliven the climate of the classroom with playful competition, but at the same time, teachers need to de-emphasize the value of winning or losing as the desired outcome. Too much emphasis on outcome may increase anxiety to a detrimental level for many pupils (Johnson, Johnson, & Holubec, 1993; Johnson, Johnson, & Smith, 1991).

Connections

Using any Internet search engine, do a generalized search on one of the following terms and share your findings with your classmates. Is this concept still hot? What is the latest research on this issue? Did you find anything that conflicted with what was suggested in this chapter? Yahoo! is one search engine with an education category. It can be found at: <www.yahoo.com/education>. Search on the following terms:

Self-fulfilling prophecy

Attribution theory

Competitive versus cooperative goal structures

Extrinsic versus intrinsic motivators

Locus of control

Cooperative Learning—Increasing Achievement

Morton Deutch (1979) compared students in a competitive environment to those in cooperative classrooms and found that the competitive group tended to produce

1. Higher levels of anxiety;

2. Students who think less of themselves and their work;

3. Students with less favorable attitudes toward their classmates; and

4. Students with lowered feeling of responsibility toward others.

Deutch (1979) concluded that the more cooperative the group tasks students can be involved in, the more positive will be the general classroom atmosphere.

Cooperative learning (Johnson & Johnson, 1987; Slavin, 1990, 1995) environments focus on the interdependence among the classroom members rather than on competition between them. Typically, cooperative learning employs mixed-ability student groups who are given a set of instructional procedures that direct them to work collaboratively to master skills and increase achievement.

A number of benefits have been reported to be associated with cooperative learning climates, including increased student achievement, improved acceptance of the academically challenged student, increased student self-esteem, and higher levels of intrinsic motivation, especially among less able students (Sharan, 1980; Slavin, 1991).

In discussing the elements to a cooperative classroom, Slavin (1990) noted the following key characteristics. A cooperative classroom is characterized by (1) group goals, (2) individual accountability, and (3) equal opportunities for success. What follows are the steps to be implemented to creating a cooperative classroom environment (Slavin, 1990, 1991).

Step 1: Instruction Phase. The teacher should present the material and review as he typically would do. However, rather than assigning independent practice following the review of the material, the teacher in a cooperative learning atmosphere might employ teamwork to reinforce the learning.

Step 2: Team Study. The teacher needs to prepare works sheets to provide practice in applying the concepts and material presented in the lesson.

Teacher Tool Box

Developing a Motivational Climate

◆ Reduce the negative effects of teacher expectations:
  • Monitor your verbal and nonverbal communications to students. Check to see if your tone, body language, body distance, and choice of words vary dramatically from student to student.
  • Make special note of children whom you find yourself discussing with colleagues. Do you discriminatly interact with the child in your classroom?

◆ Employ varied materials to ensure challenge, involvement, and personal relevance for all students:
  • Monitor your use of examples to ensure that they provide adequate gender representation and a wide range of ethnic groups.
  • Provide materials and tasks that challenge, while at the same time provide opportunity for success for all achievement levels.

◆ Monitor your attending and facilitating behaviors, especially for students who are low achieving:
  • Call on low-achieving students as volunteers as much as high-achieving students.
  • Invite low-achieving students to roles of "power" and "prestige" (e.g., running errands, distributing or collecting papers, etc.)
  • Provide low-achieving students prompts or cues to guide correct response.
  • Allow low achievers ample time to respond.

◆ Employ competitive goal structures constructively:
  • Use competitive goal structures sparingly and with materials all students have mastered.
  • Establish the excitement and energy of competition, without the anxiety, by creatively arranging the activity so that all students are competing against their own previous performances.

◆ Emphasize cooperative goal structures for the classroom.

Two work sheets should be employed per team, along with two answer sheets. The members are encouraged to solve the problems individually and check answers on the answer sheet. Any questions a member may have are directed first to the other team members, before asking the teacher. If any one member fails to get the correct answer, the team is responsible to explain and assist that person. Teams are finished only when everyone gets 100 percent on the work sheets. The teacher should circulate among the teams, encouraging and praising their effort and promoting their interdependence and cooperation. It is important to realize that simply putting students together is not sufficient to make a team. Students need help and encouragement to work toward group goals while maintaining individual responsibility (Slavin, 1991). According to Slavin (1990), teams can be changed after five or six weeks.

Step 3: Quiz. After all team work is complete with 100% accuracy from all members, students will be given quizzes, which are now taken individually.

Step 4: Team Scoring. Team scores are based on the IMPROVEMENT of individual team members. Team members are awarded points, based on their quiz scores as compared to their base scores. Gains in quiz scores will be translated into team improvement scores using a teacher-made formula, such as perfect quiz score or improvement of 10 or more points would give 30 team points; improvement of 5–9 points would give 20 points; 4 points improvement to 4 points below base would give 10 improvement points; and 5 or more below would give no points. Team scores are determined by averaging the improvement points. Recognition is given for team performance.

Step 5: Evaluation and Grading. In situations where an individual's base score is used, the student's grade should not only reflect the individual quiz score but also the team improvement score.

The importance of teacher expectancy and behavior, goal structures, and classroom climate cannot be overemphasized. The teacher tool box on page 309 provides a number of recommendations for maximizing the motivational composition of the classroom climate.

Reflections from the Field

Motivating in the Real World of the Classroom

1 I use rewards, such as bonus points. For example, I give my students a bonus point if they come in, get unpacked, open a book quietly, and read until class starts. After they accumulate a set number of points, I let them exchange points for a privilege to go down to lunch a minute early (they can get in line first!) or even go out to recess early (when I am on duty). They love this!

—*Kim M. (emotional support teacher, grades 3, 4, 5), Philadelphia, PA*

2 I have a child who is in my fourth grade class. He has a long history of abuse, and he came to me very unorganized, very messy, impulsive, and angry. I had a negative feeling for him at first, but quickly realized that positive expectations would prove much more effective so . . . He and I set goals for him, together. These were goals we knew he could achieve if he tried. For example, our first goal was to simply keep his desk and floor area picked up by checking every 30 minutes. Once that was met, we set the goal of keeping the top of his desk clear so that he could work on it . . . rather than on his lap. He likes the fact that he has "some say" in setting the goals. If he fails, he is not punished or chastised, we simply problem solve and set new goals. He is responding beautifully, and he clearly feels good about his new "power" and "responsibility."

—Melissa S. (fourth grade teacher), Chadds Ford, PA

3 I used to rely on extrinsic motivators, like homework passes, extra free time, etc. I find that most of my seventh graders do much better and appear much more motivated when I simply convey an attitude of achievement expectation and help them establish their own goals and strategies. At the beginning of each week, the students set some specific academic and behavioral goals for themselves — me too! We keep these in a journal along with three specific things we are going to do to help them achieve those goals. I review the goals and plans, making suggestions regarding their strategies or pushing them toward higher goals. On Fridays, we take time to evaluate our own progress and make plans for the next week. This has taken a little time to set in place, but now that the students have been doing it for a month, it is getting easier and faster. It is working wonderfully— they all feel like they are achieving and mastering their own fate! Very motivating!!

—Howard Z. (seventh grade language arts), Lawrence, KS

4 I teach in a very poor district. Our school has limited resources, and most of the families are just above poverty level. While I generally do not like the use of extrinsic motivators, I have found that my children (first graders), love to receive little treats (krispie treats, cookies, homemade fudge) or even little "toys" (fancy erasers, glow pencils, crayons). These are things that they don't experience often at home, so they seem to have special value. I have all the children on a contract system, each with their own goal (some academic and some behavioral—like raising your hand before calling out!). They earn points for each day they are successful. To be truthful, I am pretty liberal in defining success. At the end of the week, they can choose from a menu of items—each with different point values. This allows each child to be able to get something at our "We did it!" store.

—Sister Elisa A. (first grade), Brooklyn, NY

5 For years, I have tried to motivate seventh grade science students, not always successfully. For the past two years, I have employed a cooperative learning structure in my class, with students working in groups of four. They work together on various labs and projects, and receive a group and individual grades for their involvement. Probably breaking away from a strict cooperative approach, I have encouraged each group (there are five) to come up with their own nicknames and even mascots (e.g., panthers, smurfs, etc.). As they complete their lab work, I announce which team has been successful, simply referring to them by their nickname. I also have picture cutouts of their mascots, and each week we place a mascot in the "future Nobel prize winner" bulletin board. I try to find ways to be sure every group eventually gets there! This little twist seems to have helped form tighter work groups, and they all work hard to help each other finish the lab successfully as a way of competing with the other groups.

—Richard D. (seventh grade science), Boca Raton, FL

THEORY TO PRACTICE

Mr. Hallahan's Introductory Class: Decisions to Maximize Motivation

Mr. Hallahan is a sixth grade science teacher for students in an urban school district. This is his tenth year of teaching, and it is the beginning of a new school year. His first period class is pretty large, over 26 students. They all appear energetic—though not necessarily focusing on science. Two of the boys are teasing one of the girls in the back of the class; four girls are showing pictures to one another; a number of students appear to be negotiating where they are going to sit; and a couple appear somewhat lost, simply looking around the room.

Clearly, the energy is high, and these students are motivated, but are they motivated to learn and achieve in science class? From his past experience, Mr. Hallahan understands that not all of his students see the value of science, and some, especially those who have a history of academic problems, may fail to see the relevance of school in general. With this in mind, Mr. Hallahan may do well to use the various theories and research on motivation and achievement as a base upon which to make his instructional decisions.

From Maslow's hierarchy, perhaps Mr. Hallahan will need to understand the importance of belonging needs for his students so that he can integrate those needs as part of the learning environment. Perhaps he would do well to appreciate the concepts of failure-avoiding and failure-accepting styles as he reviews the students' comments and actions. But perhaps most importantly he needs to appreciate the implications of value/ expectancy theory, for students who may fail to see the value of education (given their social or economic backgrounds) or the expectancy of success (because of their own personal history of academic failure).

As a teacher who is able to call upon his knowledge of these theories and research, Mr. Hallahan will most like employ the following strategies to facilitate his students' motivation to learn:

1. A safe, structured classroom environment, where goals are clear, concrete, and attainable,

2. High, yet realistic expectations for academic achievement;

3. Success as a function of effort; achievable goals, emphasis on and support for effort;

4. Consideration of Maslow's hierarchy and the apparent need for belongingness operating within this classroom; use of cooperative goal structures and attempts to mold the class into a "learning team" or a "community of learners";

5. Concrete and personal examples of the learning concepts;

6. Tasks that are personally worthwhile; connection of learning tasks to the felt needs of the student (for example, the need to be respected);

7. Building students' confidence and expectations; starting at a level where they will achieve and encouraging self-comparison rather than competition;

8. Attempts to "arouse" the students' curiosity by employing stimulating presentations;

9. Opportunities for both high achievers and low achievers to participate;

10. A teacher who demonstrates motivation to learn and achieve, and modeling a belief that with effort improvement is possible.

You—as Teacher, and Decision Maker— Using Motivational Theory for Instructional Decision Making

As with the other case presentations, you will find two illustrations of classroom situations. The following illustrations describe a number of the salient characteristics of the school, the classroom, and the students. In reviewing these illustrations, you are to apply your knowledge of motivational theory and research in order to identify

1. Those factors that may interfere with the students' motivation to achieve in the learning environment;

2. Those factors needed to increase student motivation; and

3. Four specific decisions or steps you would make as the teacher of that class to maximize student motivation.

Case Illustration 1:
P.S. 142

The School
Public School 142 is in a poor, urban location. The neighborhood is marked by many abandoned houses, a high level of drug trafficking, and repetitive gang activity, drive-by shootings, and domestic violence.

Your Class
Your class is a self-contained fourth grade. There are 22 children, 9 boys and 13 girls. The racial composition of your class reflects the community at large, 9 are African American, 3 Latino, 1 Asian, and 9 Caucasian.

All of your students qualify for public assistance and federally provided lunch programs. The children all live within two blocks of the school and generally walk to and from home.

Guides for Reflection

In reviewing the description, consider how each of the following may provide insight and direction for a teacher concerned about motivating this class.

◆ Maslow's theory,
◆ Value/expectancy theories,
◆ Learned helplessness,
◆ Locus of control

Case Illustration 2:
J. L. Learner Preparatory School

The School

J. L. Learner Prep is a middle school, grades 5–8, located in an upper-class community. Most of the people living in this suburban setting commute and work in the city, some 25 miles from this community. The school reflects the high achieving values of the community and attempts to prepare its students to move on to the best private high schools in the country and eventually to the best universities.

Achievement is valued and recognized, with public announcements of individual student successes, prizes, and honors.

Your Class

You are teaching seventh grade social studies. Throughout the first two months of school, you note that your students are extremely energized, active, and competitive with one another. This competition appears to extend to the point where they outdo each other in class by giving answers, criticizing each other, and almost taking pride in beating out each other in test or project grades.

Student

One student, Brad, has you concerned. He appears to lack motivation. He doesn't volunteer answers in class, rarely participates in the sometimes "heated" discussions, and is always ready to give an excuse for why he was unable to complete his homework or perform the assignment. Brad appears well liked by his peers, and they seem to enjoy his antics in class. For example, when you call on Brad, he always makes a face and provides some silly comment to make the class laugh.

Guides for Reflection: In reviewing the description, consider how each of the following may provide insight and direction for a teacher concerned about motivating that class.

◆ Maslow's theory,
◆ Self-worth,
◆ Competitive goal structures,
◆ Mastery, failure-avoiding, failure accepting.

SUMMARY

What Is Motivation?

Simply stated, *motivation is the force that energizes, sustains, and directs behavior toward a goal* (Baron, 1992; Schunk, 1990). The issue is not one of motivating the student, rather it is motivating the student to attend selectively to the academic tasks presented and to engage in learning activities to move toward desired objectives and goals.

The Motivation-Learning Connection

Motivation is a crucial element in the learning process. Research clearly shows a positive correlation between motivation and achievement. This arousal-motivation-learning connection is not a simple linear one in which more is better. Not only does too little arousal impede performance, but if the task is especially complex, increased arousal may hamper performance.

When arousal takes the form of anxiety, it can interfere with attention, learning, and testing. Anxiety interferes with learning in that anxious students are more easily distracted by irrelevant or incidental aspects of the task at hand, having trouble focusing on significant details. Anxiety may even block students' ability to demonstrate what they have learned. They tend to freeze at a test or go blank and forget. Therefore, the goal is to develop the optimal level of arousal and anxiety, which will vary across students and even across moments for each student.

Understanding Motivation

Researchers and theorists in the area of human motivation generally identify two generic classes or types of motivation, extrinsic and intrinsic. Extrinsic motivation is operative when an individual is motivated by an outcome that is external or somehow related to the activity in which she is engaged. Intrinsic motivation exists when an individual works because of an inner desire to seek out and accomplish a task simply in pursuit of personal interest, regardless of other payoffs (Reeve, 1996).

A second way to conceptualize motivation is through the lens of the value/expectancy theory

(Feather, 1982). When presented with a student who states that he wants to do well, but who does very little work, a teacher needs to decide if the lack of motivation reflects the limited value of the activity or goal and/or the low level with which this child expects that he may successfully attain it.

Value: An Essential Motivational Ingredient

It is assumed that when needs are activated, an individual is compelled to act in ways that reduce or satisfy that need. This desire to act has been called a drive. The stronger the need, the stronger the drive, and the more the individual will engage in the goal-directed activity.

In addition to placing human needs into two groups, deficiency and growth needs, Maslow also suggested that within each group, needs are arranged in a hierarchy of precedence. Implied in this hierarchy is the proposition that a lower-level, survival-based, deficiency need takes precedence over the higher-level growth needs. Thus, the higher needs can become more predominant and directive of our actions, only after the lower needs have been satisfied.

Achievement need is the term most often applied to the drive to excel in learning tasks. The tendency to approach an achievement goal is a product of three factors:

1. the need for achievement or the motive for success,
2. the probability of success; and
3. the incentive value of success.

Expectancy: A Second Motivational Ingredient

Albert Bandura (1982) suggested that an individual's beliefs (expectations) about his or her ability to reach a goal will determine how much effort is expended and how long it will persist. Attribution theory attempts to discover how people perceive the cause of their behavior and then looks at the way their beliefs might affect their later behavior (Fiske & Taylor, 1984). The theory suggests that people attribute success and failure to four factors: *ability, effort, luck* (good or bad), and *task difficulty*. Low achievers don't believe that their efforts are responsible for success or that their lack of effort is responsible for failure (MacMillan, et al., 1986). Without a sense of connection between their actions and success or failure, low achievers will have little motivation to try. High achievers, on the other hand, attribute success to internal and stable causes. They believe they are smart and when they work, they succeed. If they fail, they may make external attributions such as suggesting the test was unfair, or internal attribution such as not studying hard enough.

The Classroom: Impacting Student Motivation

A student's levels of aspiration (i.e., expectations of future successes or failures) can be influenced not only by his or her own history of success or failure but also by the teacher's behavior. The impact of a teacher's expectations on student performance has been a focus of much debate. However, even with the various limitations of this particular research it appears that teacher expectations can impact student motivation and thus affect student achievement. Another factor that impacts student motivation is the way students relate to one another as they attempt to complete their learning tasks. David and Roger Johnson (1985) termed this interpersonal dimension of the learning task the goal structure. Goal structures can be cooperative, in which students work together to achieve a goal; competitive, in which students work against each other while pursuing an instructional goal; or individualistic, in which students' activities are unrelated to each other as they work toward a goal. Each specific goal structure can differentially impact student behavior and student achievement.

✦ Field Experience Questions

Applying Motivational Theory to Teacher Decision Making

If you are not yet teaching, another way to conduct action research is through classroom observation. Below are a series of field experience questions, related to the concepts presented in this chapter. Use the questions to guide your field observations.

1. How would you assess the general level of anxiety of the students in that classroom? What steps does the teacher take to "optimize" student anxiety (that is reduce it if it is too high or increase arousal, when it is too low)?

2. Based on your observations which forms of motivation appear to be dominant? Intrinsic? Extrinsic?

3. Observe the students in the class. Which of Maslow's needs are being manifested? How does the teacher attempt to satisfy the lower-level needs

to make them less likely to distract from the impact of the growth needs?

4. How has this teacher attempted to enhance the students' self-efficacy? Were the goals moderately challenging? Were the students helped to experience success, a success that was attributable to their effort?

5. Did you find evidence of any students having external locus of control? Internal locus?

6. What did the teacher say or do that might suggest his or her expectations regarding the self-efficacy or achievement potential of the students? Did the students perceive these teacher expectations?

7. How would you describe the classroom climate? Goal structures (cooperative, competitive, individualistic)?

✦ Key Terms

achievement motivation
anxiety
arousal
attribution theories
belongingness needs
causal attribution
competitive goal structures
cooperative learning
deficiency needs

drive
extrinsic motivation
failure-accepting students
failure-avoiding students
goal structures
growth needs
hierarchy of needs
intrinsic motivation
learned helplessness

locus of control
mastery-oriented students
motivation
personal causation
self-actualization
self-efficacy
teacher expectancy
value/expectancy theory

✦ Additional Resources

Ames, C. (1992). Classrooms: Goals, structures and student motivation. *Journal of Educational Psychology, 84,* 261–271.

deCharms, R. (1976). *Enhancing motivation: Change in the classroom.* New York: Irvington.

Johnson, D., Johnson, R., & Holubec, E. J. (1994). The new circles of learning: Cooperation in the classroom and school. Alexander, VA: Association for Supervision and Curriculum Development.

Raffini, J. P. (1996). *150 ways to increase intrinsic motivation in the classroom.* Boston: Allyn & Bacon.

Slavin, R. (1995). *Cooperative learning: Theory, research and practice* (2nd ed.). Boston: Allyn & Bacon.

Thorkildsen, T.A., & Nicholls, J. G. (1998). Fifth graders' achievement orientations and beliefs: Individual and classroom differences. *Journal of Educational Psychology, 90,* 179–201.

Tomlinson, T. M. (Ed.). (1993*). Motivating students to learn: Overcoming barriers to high achievement.* Berkeley, CA: McCutchan.

Classroom Ecology and Management

T he walls were bare and the room poorly lighted. The only visual stimulation was that created "graffiti style" by the students. Desks were scattered throughout the room with no discernible pattern. Students either walked about the room or stood against the wall because the classroom did not have enough desks. Crumpled papers lay on the floor, and the teacher had some difficulty finding chalk to write his name on the chalkboard.

An observer of this classroom and the interactions occurring within it will soon come to realize that the teacher in this middle school classroom is truly the "outsider" and that within the class there are a number of tightly knit groups. It is this physical, social environment that the teacher is called to craft into a learning community—an efficient, productive classroom!

If you can imagine the classroom depicted in the above scenario, you will certainly appreciate the importance of both the physical and social environment to the work of a teacher. The development of a positive learning environment is essential to effective teaching (Evertson & Emmer, 1982). With planning and organization of the learning environment, the effective teacher can prevent, or at least significantly reduce inappropriate behavior by students and also stimulate behaviors and attitudes that support learning. But where do you start? What are the factors, the variables that are going to facilitate or hinder the students' learning?

◆ Chapter Objectives

The current chapter discusses the factors and elements that make the classroom one that facilitates learning. When you have mastered the material in this chapter, you will be able to:

1 Describe what is meant by the phrase the "ecology of the classroom";

2 Explain how the physical setting of the classroom affects student attitudes and behaviors;

3 Describe how factors such as visibility, accessibility, and freedom from distraction should guide a teacher's decision regarding the physical arrangement of the classroom;

4 Explain what is meant by the "action zone" and identify strategies to expand this zone;

5 Discuss the benefits and limitations of the cluster, circle, stack, and straight line configurations for teacher-directed or cooperative learning activities.

6 Define what is meant by the terms "entitavity," "task goals," "social-emotional goals," "norm" and "group cohesiveness";

7 Describe the steps a teacher can take to facilitate the development of group cohesiveness within the classroom;

8 Describe the stages of group evolution and discuss the steps that a teacher can take to facilitate group development of the class at each stage.

CHAPTER 9 CONTENT MAP

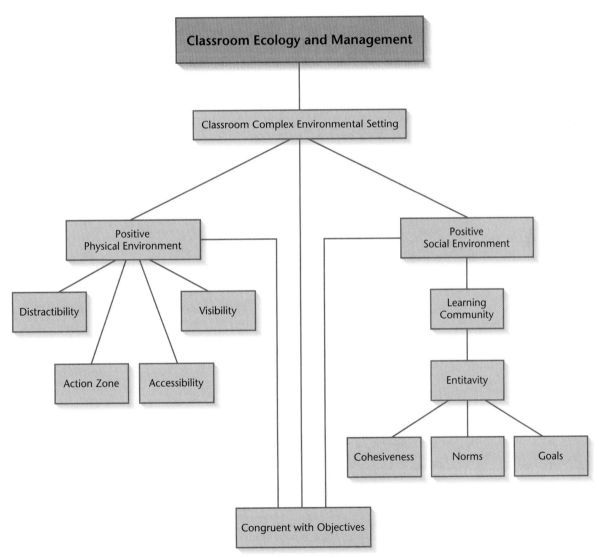

THE CLASSROOM: A COMPLEX ENVIRONMENT

Classrooms are complex environments. In fact, there may not be any other setting where the manager, or in this case the teacher, is required to juggle so many separate activities and demands simultaneously. Doyle (1979, 1986) described the classroom as multidimensional, simultaneous, immediate, and unpredictable. Classrooms are *multidimensional* in that on any one day, within any one classroom, we can find a variety of individuals, all with their own personal goals, approaches, and abilities, called upon to interact with each other in specific learning activities. Further, these learning activities, which in themselves may be quite varied, can be and most often are occurring simultaneously, each requiring immediate teacher attention and feedback. It is no wonder that the outcome is so often unpredictable! For example, in observing a "typical" class, we may find a small group of students engaged in a cooperative learning task; in another section of the room, students may be completing individually assigned work sheets; while in another area, the teacher may be providing additional instruction to a couple of students—many activities, all occurring simultaneously, all requiring some level of teacher attention and immediate reaction. Consider the teacher who introduces a new concept only to be required to attend to the student who apparently has a bathroom need or the two students in the back who seem to be more interested in passing notes, or to the child who is still unclear about the previous point. Starting, responding, reviewing, and managing this multidimensional and simultaneous environment require the teacher fully to understand the nature of this complex human ecology and to be skilled in environmental planning and management.

◆ The Classroom—A Setting of Human Ecology

Perhaps the term "ecology" is somewhat surprising. While the term has often been applied to advocacy of protection of our natural resources from pollution it is also applicable to instances describing interactions, relationships, and interdependency of people to people and people to their environment. With this latter meaning in mind, it becomes obvious that the classroom is a setting of human ecology. Classrooms are complex environments in which people interact, interdependently with one another, and with the unique characteristics of the specific physical and social environment. The environment and those within it (teacher, students, aides, etc.) are constantly interacting and affecting one another. The specific characteristics of this environment, along with the learning activities and the needs and characteristics of the participants, all contribute to the total classroom experience. Further, it is through balancing the various needs exhibited within that environment, along with the resources provided, that effective teaching-learning can occur and the teacher as ecologist will function.

So what are these interactive, interdependent elements that constitute a classroom and affect the efficiency of the teacher-learning process? As noted below, the classroom is composed of physical, social, and personal elements, which interact to affect the learning process and the educational experience.

Physical Components of the Classroom Environment

The **physical environment** includes the school building, the classroom, the furnishings, etc. Each of these physical factors contributes to the ultimate nature of the classroom and of the educational experience.

physical environment the physical conditions and materials characterizing a classroom

> ### YOU MAKE THE CALL
>
> ### THE IMPACT OF THE PHYSICAL ENVIRONMENT
>
> Consider the depiction of the classroom which opened this chapter. Now place this classroom in a school environment where the building is surrounded by high fences topped with barbwire and the inside has lockers which are destroyed, walls with holes in them, and tiles falling from the ceiling.
>
> Contrast that school classroom scene with your own middle school or junior high. Would the physical environment of either school impact your desire and enthusiasm about going to school differently? Would your expectations and behavior in school be influenced by these differing physical environments? How do you feel your actual academic achievement may have been different if you went to the school which was described?

The Classroom as a Social Environment

The classroom is more than brick and mortar, more than a physical space; it is a setting composed of individuals who interact around a number of common purposes. As such, the classroom develops into a unique **social environment.**

When effective, the classroom more than just a social setting—it is a group—a community of learners with common goals and **social structures** that help them to achieve those goals.

social environment the social climate and atmosphere characterizing a classroom

social structure includes the establishment of common goals and the articulation of specific roles to be played (e.g., teacher-student; leader-follower; note taker-reporter, etc.), and the establishment of the social norms

The classroom: A place of interaction and interdependence ◆

THE CLASSROOM AS SOCIAL ENVIRONMENT

It may be helpful to take a moment to reflect on your own school experiences. Attempt to identify a particular class or grade level where you felt that you belonged. Was there a class where the students were inclusive of all the members of the class? Did you have a class in which you felt that the teacher, while playing a different role for the class, was still truly a member of the class? If you have experienced such a learning environment, or at least could envision such a setting, contrast it to a classroom in which there are very tightly organized cliques or subgroups who do not allow new members. Imagine that a number of these cliques are openly hostile or at least competitive with one another and make fun of anyone who is not a member. Further, imagine that this class is taught by a teacher who is unapproachable and who truly cannot relate to the students' needs or interests.

In which of the classrooms would you feel safe to try new things or to risk active participation? In which classroom would you feel free to call on your fellow students or your teacher for assistance? In which class would you want to continue or maintain relationships once the class was over?

An environment in which you feel safe and accepted, one in which you are willing to risk new things and ask for assistance, will certainly result in higher levels of achievement than one that does not. Wouldn't you agree?

The Personal Nature of a Classroom

Finally, the classroom is more than desks, chairs, chalkboards, and equipment—or a group called "second grade" or "home room 210." The classroom is viable and organic in that it is "peopled" with students and teachers. Each individual brings to this experience a unique history, special expectations, talents, concerns, and challenges. These unique personal characteristics—which each child, and adult, brings to this setting—contributes to the personal environment within which one will function. The special, diverse ways in which each individual approaches the task of learning, along with the preferred conditions under which this learning should occur, makes each classroom a highly individualized experience.

ME AND THE LIBRARY JUST DON'T GET ALONG

Alicia was a bright, energetic college freshman. She had never taken school too seriously but always managed to get by with Bs and some Cs. Now, as a college freshman, Alicia made a personal commitment to get serious about education and to use her time wisely and productively.

With this new attitude and sense of purpose, she started the semester by going to the college library every time she had a free moment between classes. Her goal was to review her notes, read for the next class, or begin projects and assignments as early as possible.

While staying true to her decision to go to the library, Alicia soon found that she was spending a lot of time without being very productive. It appeared that she had trouble sitting in the large reading room, with its bright lights, its very quiet atmosphere, its large, uncomfortable wooden chairs, and its prohibition about bringing food or drink into the room.

Alicia found that almost as soon as she sat down she would begin to fidget, or tap her fingers, or hum to herself. Further, after a few minutes she would get up to get some water or simply walk about looking for some friends with whom to chat.

While Alicia may have begun to feel that there was something wrong with her and that she was perhaps too immature to be in college, the truth, which was later discovered, was that Alicia's learning style conflicted with this physical-social environment. Alicia was actually better able to concentrate and do her school work in the Student Pie Shop. It appears that this setting with its low-intensity lighting, its background music and chatter, the informal seating which provided the opportunity to move about, interact with friends and snack while studying, proved much more conducive to her learning. Which physical environment appears conducive to your own learning?

When our own preferred style of learning is in conflict with the particular physical or social environment of our classroom, or in Alicia's case her place of study, it can prove quite detrimental to our overall academic achievement.

CREATING A POSITIVE PHYSICAL ENVIRONMENT

The subtle impact of the environment on a person's work performance has been studied by psychologists for a number of years. For example, Tinker (1939) found that workers were more efficient when lighting was evenly distributed throughout the work area.

Even though the physical arrangement of your classroom will not guarantee minimal classroom disruptions or maximum learning, it can significantly impact the psychological climate of the classroom and the facility of the teaching-learning process. This is true, regardless of whether the classroom is new . . . or quite old. It is true whether or not the classroom houses the latest in technology or is limited to a chalkboard. Although research does not provide conclusive evidence that the physical features of a classroom affect actual achievement, it does suggest that the physical features, including the classroom's spatial arrangement, affect student attitudes and behaviors (Weinstein, 1979).

The effect of the physical setting can be twofold. First, the physical arrangement can influence the teacher's behavior, which in turn influences the students' (Arlin, 1979). For example, a classroom arranged in a tiered, amphitheater style, with special lab equipment set up in the left front section of the class may restrict the teacher's movement to the front, right of the classroom. Under these conditions, a major proportion of the interaction between the teacher and students may be focused on the students seated in the front, right portion of the classroom. Thus, these students may be more engaged, more attentive, and more participative than those seated in the back, left quadrant. Another example of the impact of physical arrangement on student participation was presented by Rosenfield, Lambert, & Black (1985). These researchers found that students seated in circles brainstormed during writing assignments better than when seated in rows or clusters (Rosenfield, Lambert, & Black, 1985). These authors suggest that the circular arrangement made it easier to see one another, thus encouraging interaction. Further, the circular arrangement also facilitated the teacher's ability to monitor the brainstorming process and the level of student involvement.

A second impact of the physical arrangement is that it can affect the type of task structures that can be employed (Doyle, 1986). For example, the teacher described above, who is teaching within that tiered, fixed-seat amphitheater may find it difficult to employ small group cooperative learning activities or to engage the students in general student-to-student discussions or debates.

Therefore, teachers need to give time and energy to answering the questions "What do I want my students to do in my classroom?" and "What learning activities would I like to employ?" prior to considering the ways of arranging or designing their classroom.

YOU MAKE THE CALL

KNOWING WHAT I HOPE TO ACCOMPLISH

In designing your physical environment, it is important to first identify what you hope to accomplish within that space. Further, it is essential to identify how you want the students to behave within that environment. It may prove useful to answer each of the following:

♦ Do you want your students to do more listening or more talking?

♦ Do you want the students to interact only with you, or one another?

♦ Do you want to promote independent work or cooperative, interdependent work?

The arrangement of your classroom—space allocation, furniture placement, decoration—can play an essential role in creating/answering these questions.

♦ Fundamental Considerations

While there are a number of subtle aspects of the classroom's physical environment that will obviously impact the learning climate and experience, two areas—the material components of the classroom and class size—are fundamental considerations when designing a positive learning environment.

Material Aspects of the Classroom

The material aspects of a classroom include its shape and size, the predominant color or colors, and the presence or absence of specific furnishings. These are the essential raw materials with which the teacher has to work. Prior to any considerations about the creative utilization or arrangement of these components, a number of preliminary, yet essential, details need to be considered, the first of which may be called a space audit. The teacher needs to take a "tour" of the classroom. If windows or lights are in ill repair, they need to be repaired. Is there storage space? If not, what will be needed, and where could it be placed? Is there a lock on the closet? Is one needed? And even more fundamentally, are there enough desks?

Although one might assume that a classroom would at a minimum be equipped with lights, storage, and desks, one need only speak to a veteran teacher to realize that sometimes the most assumed elements are the most neglected. One clear illustration of just such a situation is found in the movie *Stand and Deliver*.

YOU MAKE THE CALL

STAND AGAINST THE WALL

Mr. Escalante entered his classroom that first day of class and found himself greeted by eight students standing against the wall. When he invited the students to take a seat, it was quickly pointed out to him that there were no seats available!

With not enough desks in the classroom to accommodate all the students, any learning activities planned would have to be modified. Can you imagine the impact on the learning environment, the student attitudes, the student behaviors, and the teacher's activities that result from having eight to ten students standing around the room? What would your initial reaction be to this space-management issue?

Class Size

This illustration highlights another concern when creating a positive physical environment. That is class size. The number of persons occupying a space will affect the educational climate and the behavior of everyone present. For example, research on group behaviors has long supported the notion that under conditions of crowding people tend to react more negatively to each other (e.g., Griffit & Veitch, 1971). Further, the size of the class can affect the teacher's ability to manage the class.

Although all teachers hope to have small classes, they typically do not have ultimate decision-making power over the number of students assigned to them. However, even when the actual numbers of students assigned to a class are quite large, some creativity in classroom arrangement and resource management may gain the benefits of a smaller class size (i.e., the opportunity to monitor individuals, provide immediate feedback, and adjust teaching style to maximize participation). One example would include incorporating other "teachers," such as parent volunteers, student interns, aides, and even peer-tutors into the environment and dividing the class into smaller units. This would allow the teacher more time to spend supervising individual and group work. In circumstances where such added pairs of hands are not available, a teacher may be able to achieve the benefits of small group instruction by employing a variety of classroom strategies. For example, the creation of learning centers or the arrangement of classes into cooperative learning groups can free the teacher to provide small-group instruction or individual assistance as needed.

While the arrangement and management of the classroom's physical environment is open to each teacher's own unique creativity, there are a number of factors that should be taken into consideration when approaching the task of creating a positive classroom environment.

◆ Creating a Positive Environment: Some Guiding Principles

As a teacher begins arranging the classroom, all plans should be guided by the desire to ensure that each student has ease of **visibility, accessibility**, and **freedom from distraction** (Evertson, 1987).

Visibility

visibility a classroom arrangement in which students can clearly and easily see all learning materials and activities and the teacher can see each student

accessibility degree to which students and teachers have access to learning materials and one another

freedom from distraction an environment which is stimulating with factors which may compete with the teacher for student attention

It is important to maintain clear sight lines between the student and the teacher or between the student and the learning activity being presented. Further, in situations where children have additional adult support provided, as may be the case with hearing-impaired children who are supported by aides who can sign for them, the organization and arrangement of the classroom need to allow the language-support person to see all learning activities and have a direct sight line to the student.

These may seem like obvious considerations, but often it is the obvious that is overlooked or taken for granted. It is not unusual to have a student's visibility impeded by the structure of the actual classroom or by poor placement of specific learning aides (e.g., posters, projectors, etc.). For example, each of the authors has taught in an older college building in which the only place to mount a permanent screen for use of overheads and projectors was in the front and extreme right of the classroom. The positioning was such that anything projected on to the screen was not easily seen by those in the seats close to the front, left-hand portion of the classroom. Certainly, the decision to place the screens in that location was motivated by engineering concerns and not educational needs. Under these conditions, the teacher needs to adjust the seating arrangement to allow each student to see projected materials.

The placement of materials is certainly key to visibility but so is the actual presentation. Often, teachers and, notoriously, college professors write too small or too illegibly to make their visuals of much use. When writing on the board or preparing overheads or posters, it is important to write clearly and in a size that is easily readable from the back of the room and from any angle. A good idea is for the teacher to take up various positions throughout the classroom to see if the visual presentations can be seen and read, with little strain, from every position in the classroom.

In addition to ensuring that students have clear and easy visibility of all learning materials and activities, teachers need to arrange materials, equipment, desks, in such a way as to allow them to be able to make eye contact with each of the students.

Accessibility

Students need easy access to all learning materials. The classroom should be arranged in such a way that students can move easily to and from their desks, to learning materials and the chalkboards, to storage areas, and even in and out of their classroom. For classrooms with children with physical disabilities, who may employ orthopedic supports such as crutches, walkers, or wheelchairs, special attention needs to be given to providing sufficient aisle space or row configuration.

When placing materials that will have frequent use, such as the pencil sharpener, bookcase, or storage units, the teacher should ensure that these high-traffic areas are free of furniture or students. In fact, any path that will be heavily traveled should be free from obstacles, materials, etc., and be wide enough to reduce the chances of students' bumping into one another, which is almost always an invitation to disruption. Further, it is often helpful to disperse these high-traffic areas throughout the classroom to avoid congestion and having a large number of students gathering into a single restricted area.

In addition to arranging the classroom in a way that allows easy access to learning materials, it may be important, especially for those working with younger children, to provide a spatial arrangement that allows the children to handle routine tasks and personal needs on their own. In these elementary classrooms, students may need to be provided spaces which are easily accessible and which they can use for keeping their personal belongings. Thus, the creation of cubbies, lockers, or spaces with coat hooks may need to be created and assigned to individual students. It is important to be sure that these spaces are within the students' reach. Further, student identification of their specific area needs to be facilitated. Perhaps the spaces can be color coded, or the students can place their own pictures or pictures of their pets over their lockers or special spaces. This personalization of the space should increase the independent use of the space and reduce the amount of instructional time that has to be devoted to such housekeeping and personal needs.

While the focus to this point has been on providing students with ease of access to learning materials, it is also important for the teacher to

Connections

As suggested throughout the chapter, the creation of a supportive classroom environment is essential to effective teaching and learning. Establishing cohesiveness and a sense of group identity (i.e., entativity) facilitates this supportive environment by providing the students with a feeling of safety and a sense of belonging.

Make a *connection* with teachers by entering a chat room at either <http://www.classroom.net> or <http://www.newmaine.com/progressive-educators>. Ask teachers in the chat room for suggestions on how they develop a sense of entitavity and cohesiveness within their classrooms. Share your findings with your classmates.

have easy access to all learning materials. Teachers should be sure to organize materials so that they can move easily, fluidly, and quickly from one set of materials to another. Further, since research (e.g., Wolfgang, 1995) suggests the importance of a teacher's maintaining some closeness or proximity to the students, the classroom should be arranged in a way to provide such access. As student seating arrangements are designed, the teacher should be sure to set the aisle spacing so that everyone can easily move between students without bumping against the desks or the material on the desks. For classrooms where space is at a premium, the teacher may need to become creative. In these situations, clustering desks can provide more room for movement, or when rows are desired, placing two rows together may provide increased aisle spacing.

Distractibility

Although we would like to believe that the teacher's very presence, materials, and presentation will be enough to captivate the students' attention, the reality is that students often find other things more compelling. It is important to provide a stimulating environment while at the same time identifying factors that may compete with the teacher for student attention.

Seats should be positioned in such a way that they focus the students' attention while minimizing distraction. Thus, when employing a teacher-focused arrangement, seats should be arranged neatly, with students facing the teacher. When employing small work groups, it is important to close the space within each group to facilitate communication while providing sufficient spaces between groups to reduce visual and auditory distraction.

Although each teacher needs to be sensitive to the presence of distractions within the classroom, this is especially important when working with children with attention deficit disorder. These children have difficulty directing and maintaining attention under even minimally stimulating circumstances and would be greatly disadvantaged if barraged by distracting stimuli, as might be the case if seated next to a cage of gerbils actively playing on cage toys.

Action Zone

action zone areas of the classroom marked by the highest degree of interaction

The last general guideline to consider is to arrange the room in such a way as to broaden the **action zone.** Adams and Biddle (1970) found that verbal interaction between teacher and students was concentrated in the center front of the classroom and in a line directly up the center front of the classroom (Figure 9.1). The concentration was so obvious that these authors termed this area of the room the action zone.

Although the original work identified the action zone the area in the front center of the classroom, other research has demonstrated that the action zone is any area in the seating arrangement where a teacher is most likely to direct his or her attention (Good, 1983; McGown,

Driscoll, & Roop, 1996). The location of the action zone is a function of the classroom arrangement and the placement of the teacher. Thus, for teachers who employ a straight row arrangement of the seating, the action zone is most typically those desks in the front (see Figure 9.1). Since earlier research (e.g., Daum, 1972; Delefes & Jackson, 1972) has demonstrated that students who are not in this action zone tend to participate less and achieve at lower levels than the students located in the action zone, it behooves each teacher to increase the action zone to be as inclusive as possible. This does not mean that you have to constantly change the seating arrangement of your classroom. Action zones can be broadened through seating arrangements and more simply through teacher movement.

Teacher movement can shift the action zones around the classroom, especially if teachers establish eye contact and direct communication with students who are both near and far (Weinstein & Mignano, 1993). But such movement also requires a classroom arrangement that ensures accessibility and visibility. Jaime Escalante, the teacher in *Stand and Deliver,* used mobility quite effectively to broaden the action zone. In one scene, for example, he walks down the aisle, visually sweeping from left to right, looking at his students as he asks a series of questions. "Have you ever been to the beach?" "Have you ever played in the sand?"* As he continues to move throughout the class, the students fix their attention on him, perhaps because of the unusual questions, as well as because of his movement and changing proximity. Changing location while interacting with different students throughout the class will continue to broaden and shift the action zone.

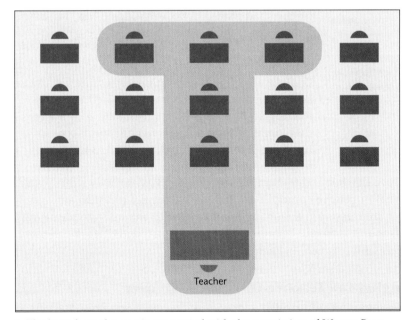

Figure 9.1

Action Zone with Traditional Teacher-Focused Arrangement

Source: Figure adapted from *Realities of teaching: Explorations with Video Tape* by Raymond S. Adams and Bruce J. Biddle, copyright © 1970 by Holt, Rinehart & Winston, reproduced with permission of the publisher.

* The lines from the movie are quoted with the permission of Warner Bros.

◆ Physical Environment: Congruency with Learning Activities

Certainly, a teacher needs to consider visibility, accessibility, and freedom from distraction when beginning to arrange and organize the classroom environment. It is also important to remember that the optimal desk arrangement ultimately depends on the type of instruction to be employed and the classroom dynamic desired.

The room arrangement not only channels the flow of information, it also communicates and elicits the kinds of behaviors a teacher may be seeking from students. Thomas Good and Jere Brophy (1990) presented an interesting illustration of the power of the physical environment on student behavior. The scenario involved a fourth grade class who were engaged in a creative-writing assignment. The students were presented with a gigantic box and asked to describe all the interesting things they could do with it. As reported by these authors, the students were excited and actively and eagerly responding. Following this initial exercise the teacher asked the students to write an original story about the fun things they could do with a frog that was bigger than they were. These authors reported that the students, who only moments before had been creatively brainstorming ideas, now sat silent, apparently unable to start their assignment. The reason for the apparent difficulty was, according to Good and Brophy (1990), due in part to the physical arrangement of the room. It appeared that the teacher had placed desks in groups of six, forming a rectangular table. This stimulated eye contact between students, which was good for "brainstorming." However, when the task was changed to drafting a private composition, this same seating arrangement and eye contact appeared to be distracting and perhaps even intimidating. It appears that while some arrangements are conducive to one type of learning activity, such as small group work like brainstorming, that same arrangement may prove detrimental to another learning activity, such as writing an individual or private composition. It is clear that the physical arrangement of the classroom should be congruent with the intended learning objectives and facilitate the intended instructional activities (Emmer et al., 1994; Gump & Good, 1976).

Arranging for Teacher-Directed Activities

With teacher-directed learning activities such as lectures, presentations, demonstrations, or teacher-led discussions, students need to be arranged

Teacher Tool Box

Creating an Effective Physical Environment

As with most things teachers do, planning is essential to the development of a facilitative physical environment. As you plan and begin to implement the arrangement of your own classroom, consider each of the following:

◆ *Tour your space.* Is it sufficiently equipped? Is it safe? Does it provide storage space? Is the furniture congruent with your style of teaching and the needs of the students? How large is it? Any restrictions (e.g., fixed cabinets, columns, etc.) on arranging within the space?

◆ *Experience the classroom.* Sit and stand at various locations within the classroom. What do you see? What is hard to see? How freely can you move from space to space? What draws your attention? Will it compete with the teacher?

◆ *Check congruency with learning activities.* What type of learning activities will you employ? Will you vary the types of learning formats? How does the space lend to flexibility of arrangement? Can you establish home base and special activities sections?

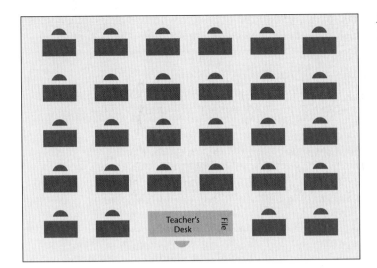

Figure 9.2
Teacher-Directed Activity

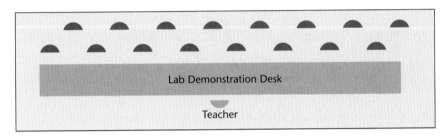

Figure 9.3
Stack Formation for Quick Demonstrations

in a way that facilitates clear visibility and interaction with the teacher. Arrangements such as that found in Figure 9.2 draw student attention to the teacher and support teacher direction of the learning activity.

In situations where the teacher is providing a quick demonstration or illustration, a **stack formation** (Figure 9.3) can be used, even with the back row standing. However, because it is not very comfortable and encourages physical contact, this formation can lead to disruptions if maintained too long.

Arranging for Student Participation

In situations where the teacher is seeking to increase student participation, a semicircular arrangement may prove more effective than a straight row arrangement (Rosenfield, Lambert, & Black, 1985). Or if the teacher feels that his/her learning objectives are best accomplished through small group activity, then a design such as that found in Figure 9.4 may be more effective. Arrangements such as that in Figure 9.5 will foster student cooperation, small group sharing, and positive student relationships.

Arranging for Flexibility

As illustrated by the experience of Good and Brophy (1990), it would appear that as a teacher's behavioral and instructional goals for students

stack formation seating arrangement in which students align themselves behind a row, sitting in an offset, with visibility gained by squaring the the back row so that students sit in the gap between students immediately in front

Figure 9.4 *Semi-Circular Arrangement for Increased Student Participation*

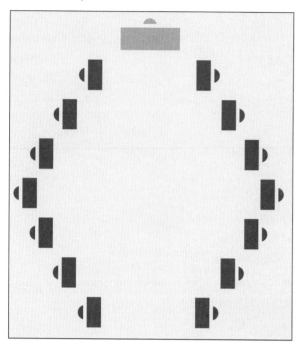

Figure 9.5
Facilitation Cooperative Activities

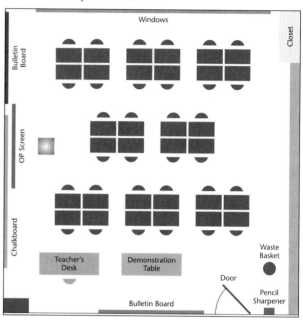

Source: Emmer, E. T., Everston, C. M., Clements, B. S., & Worsham, M. E., *Classroom management for secondary teachers,* 4th edition, © 1977 by Allyn & Bacon. Adapted by permission.

change, so too should the physical arrangement of the learning environment. The classroom should provide flexibility in seating to allow for that arrangement which facilities achievement of different goals. Having said that, one must remember that changing the seating patterns too frequently would not only occupy instructional time but also prove distracting to the students. Thus, in planning the organization of the classroom it may be helpful for the teacher to develop a couple of seating configurations, which the students can rapidly and easily create, and which they understand signals movement into a different type of learning activity. Musgrave (1975), for example, distinguished between **home-based formations**, which are semipermanent arrangements that are suitable for a wide number of learning activities and **special formations**, which provide needed variety when special lessons or lesson activities require it.

For those teachers fortunate enough to have a large space, the classroom could actually be arranged in sectors, with students asked to move to different sectors as the learning activities change. One such multipurpose arrangement was presented by M. Wang (1973) and illustrated in Figure 9.6.

home-based formation
classroom formations that are semi-permanent and suitable for a wide number of learning activities

special formation classroom formations which provide the needed variety and change when particular lessons or lesson activities require it

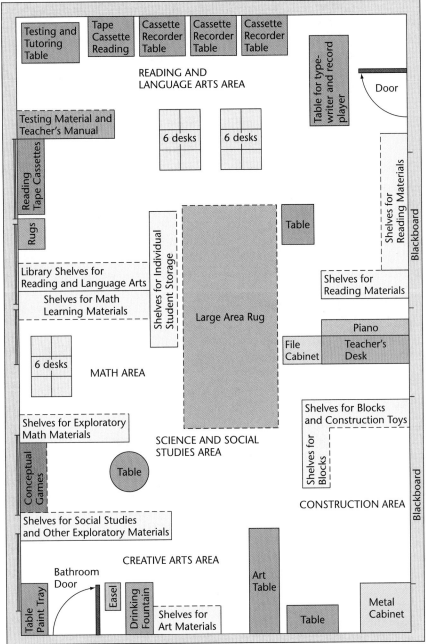

Figure 9.6
A Multipurpose Design for First Grade

Source: Adapted with permission from M. Wang (1973). Teacher's manual for the exploratory learning component of the LRDC Individualized instructional program for the early learning grades. Pittsburgh: University of Pittsburgh Learning Research Development.

CREATING A POSITIVE SOCIAL ENVIRONMENT

The classroom is not simply a matter of desks, chalkboards, textbooks, and wonderful decorations. The classroom is "peopled" and is a social, as well as a physical, environment. While the physical environment plays an important role in facilitating or hindering particular learning objectives, it is not the only factor influencing the outcome. For example, breaking the class down into small clusters of four students and sitting them close to one another in a face-to-face configuration, while increasing the possibility of small group exchange and cooperation, does not guarantee such a social dynamic.

The classroom is an active, viable, social-psychological experience. To be an effective teacher, one needs to understand the dynamics of this social-psychological experience as well as how to create a climate and a dynamic that facilitates the learning processes.

◆ Creating an Effective Learning Community

Even though we have made numerous references to the various examples of teaching principles and theory demonstrated in the movie *Stand and Deliver*, perhaps one of the most impressive and effective things the teacher in that movie achieved was taking a collection of diverse, energetic adolescents and molding them into an interdependent group of learners. As we follow the development of this class, we see that not only do the students take on a group identity as *Escalante's class*, but they also support each other as they move toward academic achievement and advanced placement status. Through a variety of actions and decisions on the part of this one teacher, not only was the physical environment of his class changed, but so too was the social-psychological environment.

A number of researchers (e.g., Glasser, 1990; Johnson & Johnson, 1984; Schmuck & Schmuck, 1992; Slavin, 1991) suggest that individual academic achievement goes hand in hand with high levels of group support and cooperation. In fact, some researchers (Cohen, 1986; Slavin 1984, 1990; Webb, 1982) suggest that cooperative learning in groups produces higher levels of academic achievement involving conceptual learning and problem solving across a variety of curriculum areas than do individualistic learning formats. However, cooperative learning or the establishment of group support and cooperation entails much more than merely physically grouping students together, it requires the melding of teacher and students into a singular learning group. Unless it possesses essential "group" elements, the classroom will remain simply a collection of individuals who happen to share a time and space. Consider, for example, the following two computer programming classes. In the first class, students are seated at individual computer stations and employ individualized programmed texts as the primary learning activity. The class was structured to allow the students to progress at their own rate, and the teacher moved throughout the class, providing individual support and instruction. The second class was significantly different in both design and operations. It was arranged to allow for group instruction in which the teacher would employ a large, projection screen of her computer on which she would demonstrate the specific commands to be used in the programming. The teacher in this second class would follow the large group presentation with small group assignments. Each group would be assigned a specific programming problem and would be given time to work together, sharing information and strategies to solve the problem. Following the small group activities, the students would gather in a large group to share information and strategies and to discuss the specific problems they encountered. Finally, the students were provided time to work individually at a computer.

It is clear that while both classes may provide instruction in computer programming, the second employed teacher-student, student-student, and individualized modes of instruction. Further, in this second class, interpersonal contacts were encouraged, and the possibility of molding this class into a group, a learning community, was far better than it was for the first class. The opportunity to *interact* and work *interdependently* will help to mold this second class into a group, into a community of learners.

Social psychologists and specialists in group dynamics have, for many years, studied the processes of group formation, development, and functioning. Many of the social psychological principles that have been observed and applied in industry, mental health, and government have been used to study the life in a classroom (e.g., Flanders, 1963, 1964; Getzels, 1969; Schmuck & Schmuck, 1992). Molding a class, which starts as an aggregate of individuals, into a group requires that the teacher help the class develop a perception of *entitavity* and group *cohesiveness*.

✦ Entitavity

Donald T. Campbell (1958) coined the term **entitavity** to describe the situation where a group of individuals begins to be perceived as a unique team or group. It is a condition in which a group takes on its own real existence, its own identity. This becoming of a unit, an entity, also occurs in classrooms that are forming as a group and who are developing as a community of learners.

Entitavity, or developing a sense of "We-ness," will be facilitated by any efforts that draw a distinction between the "We" and the "They." Thus, a teacher whose students select a class nickname and even develop a class logo will be facilitating the development of entitavity.

entitavity a group's perception of being a unique entity; 'we' versus 'they'

YOU MAKE THE CALL

MURRAY'S MARAUDERS!

Michael Murray, teacher of a fifth grade class, asked his students to come up with a class nickname. After some discussion and some silliness they decided on Murray's Marauders! The following day, a couple of the students showed Mr. Murray an idea they had for a logo, and a couple of the others asked if they made up a plaque in wood shop would he hang it up. Well, the word spread that Mr. Murray and his marauders were doing all kinds of things. While the curriculum being followed was the same as the other two fifth grade classes, the social dynamic was quite different. Students could be heard at lunch talking to other students and saying things such as: "Oh, yeah I'm a Murray's Marauder!" or "Aren't you a Murray's Marauder?"

Can you think of strategies your teacher employed to increase "entitavity"?

Teacher Tool Box

Developing Entitavity

In order to develop a sense of entitavity, a class has to create a uniqueness, a distinctiveness that demarcates "who they are" and "who belongs" as opposed to who they are not and who does not belong. The following can increase this sense of "we-ness" and thus contribute to the development of entitavity.

1. The development of a class nickname, logo, or slogan.

2. The embodiment of these nicknames, etc. on a classroom plaque, sign, button, badge, etc.

3. The distribution of class "membership" cards, which can also include on the back of each card the "rules" of the class.

4. The sharing of some special class experience, perhaps a field trip, special speaker, or the opportunity for a unique, personal experience in class.

5. The establishment of special routines, such as having pizza parties at the successful completion of a unit of study; or a special activity to celebrate members' birthdays, etc.

6. The creation of a class newspaper or newsletter.

As members of Mr. Murray's class began to identify with the class, in the midst of a number of classes within the school, they were quick to note those who were members from those who were not! And, in this process, they began to take on an existence as a group and give life to the entity called Murray's Marauders. Other ideas for facilitating the development of this entitavity within a classroom can be found in the teacher tool box.

◆ Cohesiveness

While entitavity is the result of developing a unique identity distinct from others, thus contrasting the "we" from the "they," **cohesiveness** points to the degree to which the members within the class see themselves as one. Cohesiveness exists when individual students not only recognize the existence of a unique class, but also feel that they are an integral part of it. With the development of cohesiveness, students see themselves as group members, rather than as isolated individuals or parts of some subgroup, or clique in the class. When students belong to a cohesive class, they will note that they are part of the class, involved in and contributing to the action. Students in a cohesive class feel accepted. This is an important point, since research has demonstrated that students who perceive themselves as

cohesiveness tightness, closeness found within a group

liked and accepted within the classroom actually learn more than those that don't (Lewis & St. John, 1974; Cohen, 1985; Slavin 1987,1990, 1991). Obvious indications of cohesiveness may appear when class members are seen hanging around together outside of class; or showing a willingness to work, study, and play together, and when they use inclusive language such as "we" instead of "I."

Cohesiveness is facilitated by all processes that (1) promote the interaction and **interdependence** of members (i.e., relationships) (2) establish common goals, and (3) create social structures.

interdependence a social environment which requires students interacting and working together

Fostering Cohesion Through Interaction and Interdependence

For a class to become a cohesive group, its members must interact in such a way that each person influences and is influenced by each other person. Thus, a group of screaming football fans at Saturday's game, while an aggregate in close physical proximity, are not a cohesive group, since they have limited interaction and certainly lack this interdependency.

Building cohesiveness through establishing common goals and promoting interdependence ◆

A key ingredient to the formation of a cohesive group, therefore, is that the members are encouraged and supported in the process of forming relationships. Teachers can promote relationships and group cohesiveness within the classroom by (1) minimizing individual or subgroup competitions, (2) avoiding playing favorites, and (3) encouraging the students to work cooperatively (Johnson & Johnson, 1975; Slavin et al., 1985). Additional techniques that can develop cohesiveness are promoting pro-social behaviors (e.g., sharing, assisting), maintaining high levels of trust, helping the student to identify with the class as a whole, promoting group norms that encourage the expression of individuality, trusting and trustworthy behavior, and concern and affection among group members.

Interacting Around Common Goals: A Process Fostering Cohesiveness

Each student enters a class with individual goals. Further, most classrooms are designed to promote individual achievement, rather than group achievement. However, while such individual, academic goals should be encouraged, teachers can introduce activities that are aimed at promoting group achievement and in so doing facilitate the development of classroom cohesiveness.

The teacher who can tap the common goals of students and structure activities and interaction around these goals will assist the establishment of cohesiveness in that class. This is not to suggest that individual academic goals should in any way be ignored. In fact, researchers have found that individual achievement can be assisted by helping the entire class perform group tasks (e.g., Schmuck, 1971). But it is not only around academic tasks that group goals and group achievement can be structured.

Schmuck and Schmuck (1988) suggest that classroom goals can be either **task goals**, or **social-emotional goals**. Task goals are involved with academic learning and achievement. Social-emotional goals are directed toward helping students satisfy needs such as the need for acceptance, the need to develop a positive self-image, etc. Further, each of these goals can be achieved at either the individual level or at a group level. Since higher individual achievement has been found to result when group goals are addressed, Schmuck and Schmuck (1988) proposed that the highest degree of group cohesiveness will be attained in classrooms that work toward all four types of goals (i.e., task-group; task-individual; social-emotional group; social-emotional individual).

The classroom structured to build cohesiveness will be designed to provide a variety of experiences to meet these four types of goals. Thus, time and energy will be given to create individual and group learning activities. These could include small group activities, structured time for individuals to work alone, large group discussions, and even time to allow informal sharing among students. In such a classroom, students will have ample opportunity to participate and contribute as well as to meet their own unique needs, blending efforts to complete their learning tasks, both group and individual, and social-emotional needs, also at both the group and individual levels.

task goals those goals involved with academic learning and achievement

social-emotional goals goals that are directed toward helping students satisfy needs such as the need for acceptance, the need to develop a positive self-image, etc.

norm rules of conduct within a group setting

YOU MAKE THE CALL

STRUCTURING FOR GOAL ACHIEVEMENT

For the teacher attempting to facilitate the development of group cohesiveness, the use of a variety of teaching activities is important. Such a teacher will provide activities geared to meet the students' academic (task) goals through individual and group formats. Similarly, student social-emotional needs will be met also through both individual and group activities. Below is a list of activities that may be found in a classroom. Which goals (task or social-emotional) are addressed by these activities? Which of the activities are group, and which are individual in focus?

- Cooperative projects,
- Class discussions,
- Seat work,
- Programmed instruction,
- Student participation in establishing classroom rules,
- Providing and receiving help,
- Sharing personal opinions and seeking feedback.

Norms that Foster Cohesiveness

A final element that contributes to the creation of group cohesiveness is the establishment of a rudimentary social structure. Although this includes the establishment of common goals and the articulation of specific roles to be played (e.g., teacher-student, leader-follower, note taker-reporter, etc.), it is the establishment of the social **norms** that will be the focus of this section.

Norms are simply the rules of behavior that one is expected to follow when operating within a particular social situation (e.g., the classroom). Norms influence interpersonal interaction and thus relationships, by helping individuals to know what is expected of them and what they can expect from the others in their group. For example, the behaviors that you would feel comfortable exhibiting or expect others to exhibit will certainly vary, depending on whether you are in church, at a concert, in a library, or at a sporting event. In each of these settings, there are very clear articulate rules, such as No Smoking (at a concert) or Please Be Quiet (in the library), indicating which behaviors are acceptable and which are not. These rules are the norms of that social setting.

Teacher Tool Box

Developing Class Cohesiveness

1. Structure class time to allow for student-to-student communications and interaction.

2. Encourage pro-social behaviors such as sharing, assisting, etc.

3. Reduce competition and subgroups by
   ◆ periodically changing academic work group compositions,
   ◆ employing a grading system that recognizes individual achievement and group progress,
   ◆ reducing evaluation procedures that pit one student against another.

4. Provide learning exercises that require students to share information and resources in order to be successful.

5. Recognize individual students' special talents and encourage them to share these talents with others in the class as would be the case with peer tutors.

6. Promote activities that encourage student sharing on a personal level to facilitate the development of personal relationships.

School norms can build teamwork and mutual support. ◆

Teacher Tool Box

Developing a Facilitative Social Environment

♦ Establish norms that encourage trusting and trustworthy behavior, foster cooperativeness, and promote the expression of affection and support.

♦ Articulate goals, both task and emotional, for the class and elicit personal goals, again both task and emotional, from the students.

♦ Structure time for personal sharing and relationship maintenance.

♦ Empower the students to monitor norm adherence. Perhaps form a classroom student council who can review classroom rules and sanctions and adjust as needed.

Within the classroom, norms serve several functions (Froyen, 1993; Putnam & Burke, 1992; Schmuck & Schmuck, 1992; Zimbardo, 1992). First, as noted above, norms orient group members to which social interactions are appropriate and which are not. Thus, in one classroom all communication may be directed through the teacher. Students are not allowed to talk to each other, only to the teacher. All questions, all answers, all information is to be channeled through the teacher. However, in another classroom the rules may be that there are times when the teacher talks and students listen, and times when student-student discussion occurs.

A second function of norms within the classroom is that they help to regulate the way social interactions are to occur. Thus, students can begin not only to know how they are to act, but what to expect from others. For example, in one classroom the norm may direct the students to ask before borrowing materials from other students, while at the same time supporting the notion of sharing. Or a classroom may specify that copying homework is unacceptable and students should respond with an assertive no when asked to share their homework. A third possible function of norms is to help create a group identity and facilitate group cohesiveness. When a new student entering the classroom hears from the others students, "We don't do that in here" or "This is how we do that," the new student is not only given evidence of the entitavity of the group (i.e., "We . . .") but also is given direction on how to behave as a member of that class (i.e., cohesiveness). Norms that facilitate cohesiveness will also promote academic achievement and positive relationships among class members.

MATCHING ENVIRONMENT TO LEARNING STYLE

The classroom that is too hot, cold, or dimly lit, or one that is marked by uncontrollable chaos or violence will not only prove to be a distraction to a student's attention, but may even elicit behaviors that are disruptive to instructional activities. It may appear obvious that extremes in temperature, lighting, or ventilation, or social conditions which are potentially dangerous to one's well-being will most certainly impact the students' ability to concentrate and perform. What may not be as obvious is that the physical and social characteristics of the classroom can also prove influential on student learning and performance, even when they are not present in their extreme forms. The research on student

learning styles suggests that there exists an important interaction between a student's learning style and the teacher's manner and style, the nature of the instructional activity, and the physical and social conditions of the learning environment. Dunn and Griggs (1988) have suggested that some students learn or perform better in a bright, noisy environment, whereas others do their best work in quiet places with subdued lighting. According to these authors, some students excel with highly structured teacher-directed instructional activities, whereas others do better in informal, unstructured, peer-driven environments.

What may be concluded from the research on learning style is that the ideal classroom should be arranged to provide students with learning condition options. Not only will the manner of presentation vary from teacher-directed activities to peer teaching or self-instruction, but the setting in which the instruction occurs will vary as well.

In the ideal classroom, children have the opportunity to learn through their preferred modality (i.e., visual, auditory, tactile, etc.) or through multiple modalities if this is preferred. Further, in the ideal classroom students can have the opportunity to work alone or with

learning style an individual's approach to learning and performance

Action Research

Why Won't They Participate?

K ristian, a tenth grade social studies teacher, consulted with one of the authors because he "was getting frustrated with his two advanced placement history classes." This was his first year teaching the advanced placement course, and he had developed objectives (see Chapter 11) that required class discussions and active involvement on the part of the students. His frustration stemmed from finding it difficult to motivate students to "open up and share their ideas and feelings" about the topics being taught.

He described his classroom as colorfully decorated, with posters and signs, which he changed regularly to reflect the specific topics or times being discussed. Further, since he employed a lecture format along with overhead visual aides, he arranged the seating so that the students were in straight rows, facing the front. Kristian was informed about the possible impact of this seating arrangement, especially when he attempted to move to a discussion.

Following a brief consultation, which focused on the importance of matching the physical arrangement to learning objectives, Kristian decided to attempt a "mini-experiment." While he would do nothing differently in his fifth period class, he would modify the seating in his fourth period. For his fourth period advanced placement class, he would assign the students to small discussion groups. He would have them sit in straight rows during the lecture portion of the class but then have them rearrange their seats into small circles for discussion. Following the discussion period, he would ask representatives of each group to present their group's major observations.

While he reported that the movement of the desks caused some minor loss of time and a bit of off-task "horsing around," overall he observed that the fourth period not only became more lively and participative but they even appeared to be "enjoying the class more." As a result Kristian applied the same approach to his fifth period and was now considering additional configurations, including a cluster arrangement.

small groups. They can function at formal settings, including tables and chairs, or perhaps in less formal locations with bean bags or carpet seating.

While not every classroom lends itself to such variations of learning conditions, it is possible with some creative planning to arrange a classroom to provide students with some physical and social options. These options would be provided in an attempt to maximize the congruency between the classroom environment and the students' learning style preferences. For example, students might be given permission to select their seats near a bright light or window or away from these light sources, as a function of their learning style. Or perhaps a student with a preference for background noise could select a seat in a location where such noise is maximized (e.g., near the corridor). Further, the creative teacher can establish learning centers or learning activities that elicit engagement of various modalities (e.g., visual, auditory, tactile, etc.) with the students free to select the version of the activity most aligned with their preferred learning modalities.

Those interested in learning more about the way one can configure the physical and social environment of the classroom to maximize the congruency of the environment with students' preferred learning styles are referred to the work and research of Rita Dunn and her associates (Dunn, 1987; Dunn, Beaudry, & Klavas, 1989; Dunn & Dunn, 1978, 1987; and Dunn, Dunn, & Price, 1984).

Reflections from the Field

Classroom Ecology

1 I often move seats in groups, in pairs, and individually, putting students in situations where they need to work cooperatively and at other times independently. Simply changing the seating seems to establish a completely different atmosphere.

—*Kim M. (emotional support class, grades 3,4,5), Philadelphia, PA*

2 A wonderful book for educators is called *Caring Spaces and Learning Places,* great ideas with plans, room arrangements, environmental concerns related to teaching.

—*George J. (reading specialist), Las Vegas, NV*

3 I have arbitrarily divided my class into three equal groups and arranged the classroom to support these different group activities. For about 30 minutes, one-third of the class "does" learning centers (each child at one previously explained hands-on center); one-third of the class works on seat work (math review, spelling sentences, journal entries, etc.); the other one-third works on "reading folders" (trading books and writing minireports on their level) (second grade various levels). I meet individually with the reading folder people each day. After 30 minutes the "white group" moves to learning centers; the "green group" moves to seat work; and the "orange group" works on reading folders. Each day, all the children work in this rotation. Luckily, I have the space in the classroom to organize areas for independent seating, learning centers, and reading folders.

—*Adele G. (second grade), Dallas, TX*

4 I have found that when I decorate (or even paint, since I am allowed) in lavenders and minty greens, the children seem much more energized. These seem to be uplifting colors. I have found that neon lights are a negative. They are not great for the eyes and tend to be depressing and tiresome under long hours of the day. For my older students, I have found traditional desks work best, the ones with movable straight chairs, whereas when I teach younger children (under fourth grade) it seems that a more relaxed learning environment with throw rugs, bean bag chairs, and pillows work best.

—*Joe B. (learning specialist—all grades), New Orleans, LA*

5 When I was in high school, each home room would get shirts with logos on them. We would use these any time we were involved in intramurals. Well, I have adopted that process to my fifth grade class, and over the past seven years I have had the students come up with a name for the class—like Logan's Legends etc., and we even try to "draw" a symbol or mascot. The shirts are relatively inexpensive to buy, and for those kids that can't afford it, we raffle some off. (I pick up the tab, about $5 each.) I let the students wear the shirts on field trips, or at assemblies, etc. It really has given them a sense of cohesiveness, and even though I can't prove it, it seems to help build cooperation among them.

—*Logan M. (sixth grade science teacher), Dover, DE*

THEORY TO PRACTICE

A look at Howard Katz making decisions as teacher and effective learning ecologist

It is a very warm August morning, when Mr. Katz, the seventh grade language arts teacher, takes one of his last days of summer vacation to visit his classroom. Over the course of the summer, work has been performed on the school, and most of the classrooms have been left in great disarray.

As he looks about the room, not only is he struck by its "lifelessness" (without the students), but by how bare and outright ugly it appears. The walls are bare and the room poorly lighted. The only visual stimulation to be seen was that created "graffiti style" by some of the students who must have entered during the summer. Desks were scattered throughout the room with no discernible pattern. Crumpled papers lay on the floor, and there was no chalk to be found. As he anticipated the opening days of school, he knew there was much to be done. The cleaning and putting in order would be handled by the workers. However, the creation of an effective teaching environment would be his responsibility. In addition to addressing the physical demands of the classroom, Mr. Katz was more than aware that he would be facing a group of adolescent students who he would need to mold into a learning community. The new class of seventh graders would come to his class having formed friendships, cliques, and expectations about the school encounter. In this social setting, he would be viewed as an "outsider." He knew that not all of the students would come to his class having previously been taught how to behave in this class. Mr. Katz liked an independent, somewhat loose classroom environment, but he was aware that many students would see this as an invitation to play, rather than an opportunity to be self-directed in their learning. Norms that govern play behavior would have to be corrected and new norms formulated. Identities as "me" would have to be shaped into an identity as "we."

Mr. Katz was very excited about the challenge and opportunity awaiting him. Turning this barren classroom into a stimulating environment was but a small part of that excitement. Having the opportunity to shape a group of individuals into an effective learning community was what really excited him as he viewed these last few days before the ringing of the school bell. In these days of preparation, Mr. Katz would have to engage in a number of activities.

He would have to ensure that the desks he needs would be available as well as the chalk, the overheads, and all the other components of an effective learning environment *(fundamental materials)*. Since his primary teaching strategy was to lecture and to employ large group discussions, he started to imagine how he could arrange the desks in a large semicircle, being sure that the students could easily see the chalkboard and one another *(physical arrangement congruent with goals and methods)*. Mr. Katz placed his own desk off to the corner of the front of the class so that he would have free access to the board as well as be able to move freely back and forth across the front of the room and thus to maintain eye contact with each of the students as he lectures. (Increasing his *action zone*).

In addition to cleaning the room and providing a number of posters as wall decoration *(creating an effective physical environment)*, Mr. Katz planned to make very clear the goals for the class and his expectations as to the students' level of performance, starting the very first day of class. He decided to employ a formal contract arrangement as a way of formalizing the rules, goals, and expectations of the class *(establishing goals and social structure)*.

But of all the things he wanted to accomplish, he felt that molding these individual students into a cohesive, interdependent community of learners *(group cohesiveness)* would be the most important. In addition to providing a group goal and explicit norms for classroom behavior, he also decided to employ a number of strategies aimed at increasing cohesiveness. He would use inclusive language ("we") when referencing class activities. He thought that he would ask each of his sections to establish a nickname (e.g., Katz' Kool Kats), and he thought he would try to start each class with a group chant, almost like a pregame pep activity. Finally, he realized that he would need to help the students see the freedom he was providing as part of their responsibility as mature students rather than as simply an opportunity to play. He thought he would attempt to instill in them the sense of their "maturity" by focusing on their new roles as seventh graders, no longer the children of elementary school *(re-normed)*.

If we were able to observe the first few days of Mr. Katz's class, we would most likely notice that all is not immediately ideal. At first, the students are confused by this new teacher, not sure what to expect *(forming)*. Soon, a number of the students attempt to test the authority of the teacher and even the rules of the class *(storming)*. But as the members begin to spend time in and out of class *(cohesiveness)*, they begin to adopt the norms established for the class and enforce the adherence of those norms, as evident by their chastising of one student for acting "immaturely," noting "hey—we're seventh graders!" *(norming)*. As we observe, we see Mr. Katz moving within the class, offering special attention to individual students while the others work independently *(performing)*. Hopefully, as they progress through the academic year, we will note that not only has the class developed strong emotional bonds to one another and to their teacher, but they also have been prepared to move on. If we could see this class to the end of the year, we would see them celebrating their achievement and formally recognizing their appreciation for their teacher and saying goodbyes (*adjourning*) and preparing for the beginning of the cycle once again.

You, as Teacher, as Decision Maker, as Classroom Ecologist

In the following case presentations, you will be given a description of a number of salient characteristics of a school, the classroom, and the students with whom you are to work. In reviewing the illustrations and the questions that follow, apply your knowledge of the impact that a physical and social environment has on student behavior and academic achievement.

Case Illustration 1:
M. L. King Middle School

The Classroom

The classroom under consideration is a sixth grade class in the M. L. King middle school. M. L. King is a brand new, high tech facility. The classrooms are arranged in an "open format," so that they have only three walls, a front, a back, and an outside—a solid glass wall. The inner wall has been removed, and the classroom is completely open to the center hallways.

The sixth grade class is located on the east side at the rear of the building. The room receives a lot of daylight, and the windows look over the athletic fields where all physical education classes are held.

The interior of the classroom is large (twice the size of typical classrooms), with half of the room having a tile floor and the other half carpeted. Rather than having fixed desk-chair furniture, the room is furnished with moveable student chairs and small tables. The lighting is on a number of electrical switches, and each can be turned up or down to maximize or reduce the lighting in any one area of the room.

The Class

This is a social studies class for students who have all been identified as gifted. In addition to mastering the material, a goal for this class is for the students to develop a sense of social awareness and concern and to engage in some form of social action.

The class members were all in the same class in the previous year. They have a class reputation of being bright, yet somewhat unruly. Their previous social studies teacher was very autocratic in his style of classroom management, and he employed a strict lecture, note-taking approach. In discussing the class with the chairperson of the department, you find that the class includes a child, Tina, who is a double amputee and

requires the use of an electric wheel chair. Further, you find that another child, Robert, has just recently been diagnosed as having a "mild" attention deficit.

Illustration 2:
Your Own Educational Psychology Class

As a second illustration of a classroom ecology, review the following questions and suggestions as applied to your own educational psychology class.

The Classroom

How would you describe the arrangement of the classroom? What are the significant physical characteristics of the room? How does the physical arrangement provide visibility, freedom from distraction, and accessibility? Is it congruent with the learning objectives?

How does the physical environment facilitate or inhibit the development of the students and teacher into a learning community?

The Class

What are the unique characteristics of the students and teachers that they bring to this learning environment? What goals and norms do they share? What stage of group formation would you feel this class is in?

1. What specific elements or characteristics of the physical environment appear to be a real plus for the teacher in this classroom?

2. What elements or characteristics of the physical environment appear to be a challenge for the teacher?

3. What specific elements or characteristics of the class and class members appear to be a real plus for the teacher?

4. What elements or characteristics of the class and class members appear to be a challenge for the teacher?

5. What special considerations would you give to the physical arrangement if it were your class?

6. What special consideration would you give to the social structuring of this class?

7. Identify specific types of learning activities anticipated, types of student participation desired, and climate expected (list specifics). Identify how you would arrange the physical space so that it was congruent with these goals and activities.

8. How would you arrange space for:
   (a) a large group,
   (b) a small group,
   (c) a demonstration,
   (d) private/quiet-work space?

9. Do you anticipate any seating which may be limited in visibility or accessibility, or at maximum risk for distractibility?

SUMMARY

The Classroom: A Complex Environmental Setting

Classrooms are *multidimensional* complex environments in which people interact interdependently with one another and with the unique characteristics of the specific physical and social environment. The classroom is composed of physical, social, and personal elements that interact to affect the learning process and the educational experience. The specific characteristics of this environment, along with the learning activities and the needs and characteristics of the participants all contribute to the total classroom experience. Further, it is through the balancing of the various needs exhibited within that environment, along with the resources provided, that effective teaching-learning can occur and the teacher as ecologist will function.

Creating a Positive Physical Environment

The physical arrangement of your classroom will not guarantee minimal classroom disruptions or maximum learning, but it can significantly impact the psychological climate of the classroom and the facility of the teaching-learning process. Further, the physical arrangement of a classroom can affect the type of task structures (e.g., cooperative) that can be employed.

When designing a positive learning environment, teachers need to ensure the availability of fundamental materials (e.g., desks, storage, etc.). Further, creating a positive learning environment requires that the teacher consider the impact of class size and consider arranging the class in ways that maximize student-teacher contact. A teacher beginning the process of arranging the classroom should be guided by the desire to ensure that each student has ease of visibility, accessibility, and freedom from distraction, that the action zone is maximized, and that the physical environment is congruent to the specific learning goals and activities desired.

Creating a Positive Social Environment

In addition to being a physical location, the classroom also provides an active, viable, social-psychological experience. An effective teacher needs to understand the dynamics of this social psychological experience, as well as know how to create a climate and dynamic that facilitate learning. Molding a class, which starts as an aggregate of individuals, into a group requires that the teacher help the class develop a perception of *entitavity* ("we-ness") and group *cohesiveness (tightness, closeness)*. These can be fostered through interaction, interdependence, and the development of common goals.

Matching Environment to Learning Style

Research on student learning styles suggests that there exists an important interaction between a student's learning style and the teacher's own manner and style, the nature of the instructional activity, and the physical and social conditions of the learning environment.

What may be concluded from the research on learning style is that the ideal classroom should be arranged to provide students with learning condition options. Not only will the manner of presentation vary from teacher-directed activities, to peer teaching or self-instruction, but the setting in which the instruction occurs will also vary. In the ideal classroom, children have the opportunity to learn through their preferred modality (i.e., visual, auditory, tactile, etc.) or through multiple modalities, if this is preferred. Further, in the ideal classroom, students have the opportunity to work alone or with small groups. They can function at formal settings, including tables and chairs or perhaps in less formal locations with bean bags or carpet seating.

While not every classroom lends itself to such variations of learning conditions, it is possible with some creative planning to arrange a classroom to provide students with some physical and social options. These options would be provided in an attempt to maximize the congruency between the classroom environment and the students' learning style preferences.

◆ Field Experience Questions

*Increasing Awareness
of the Classroom Environment*

If you are not yet teaching, another way of conducting action research is to collect a variety of different data about teachers and students through observation. The following field experience questions, related to the topics covered in this chapter, can be answered by making classroom observations (even of your college or university classes) or by interviewing teachers and recording their responses to the questions.

1. Observe a classroom (even your college classroom). Do you notice any fixed features of the physical environment that could impede learning or restrict the type of teaching-learning activities the teacher could employ?

2. How would you characterize the primary network of communication within this class. Is it centralized? Decentralized?

3. How would you characterize the social climate of the classroom? Is there evidence that the members of the class perceive themselves to be an entity (entitavity)? How cohesive does the class appear? Did the teacher employ inclusive language or group learning activities geared to increase group cohesiveness?

4. What were the learning objectives for the class you observed? Was the physical arrangement and social environment congruent and conducive for achieving these objectives?

5. Were there any students with special learning needs in the class? If so, how was the physical and social environment supportive of these special learning needs?

◆ Key Terms

accessibility
action zone
cohesiveness
entitavity
freedom from distraction
home-based formation

interdependence
learning style
norm
physical environment
social environment
social structure

social-emotional goals
special formation
stack formation
task goals
visibility

◆ Additional Resources

Borich, G. (1993). *Clearly outstanding: Making each day count in your classroom.* Boston: Allyn & Bacon.

Epanchin, B. C., Townsend, B., & Stoddard, K. (1994). *Constructive classroom management: Strategies for creating positive learning environments.* Pacific Grove, CA: Brooks/Cole.

Schmuck, R. A., & Schmuck, P. A. (1992). *Group processes in the classroom* (6th Ed.). Dubuque, IA: William C. Brown.

Weinstein, C.S. (1996). *Secondary classroom management: Lessons from research and practice.* New York: McGraw-Hill.

Weinstein, C. S., & Mignano, A. J. (1997). *Elementary classroom management: Lessons from research and practice* (2nd Ed.). New York: McGraw-Hill.

Wolfgang, C. H. (1995). *Solving Discipline Problems* (3rd Ed.), Needham Heights, MA: Allyn & Bacon.

Classroom Management

I t was very warm that first day of class. Twenty-four energetic, scrubbed cleaned second graders all sporting new school clothes, pencil cases, and a wide variety of superhero lunch boxes marched into Ms. Thompson's classroom.

No sooner had the bell rung announcing the beginning of this new school year than a student was crying, another complaining that the boy next to her was poking her, one was at the teacher's side, asking to go to the bathroom, and two were "experimenting" with the gerbil in the back of the class.

Into this mix came an announcement over the P.A. system asking the teachers to send the names of those students who ride the C-bus to school to the principal's office as soon as possible.

It was warm and getting warmer in Ms. Thompson's classroom that opening day of school, and on top of it all she realized she was short five desks!

Imagine that this is your first day as a teacher; this is your first class! While you may have prepared a wonderful lesson plan, one to engage these children and arouse their motivation for this new school year, your curriculum and lesson plan often take a back seat to the personal needs of your students (e.g., bathroom breaks, personal anxieties, and interpersonal annoyances) or the organizational demands of the school system (bus schedules, milk orders, fire drills).

The novice teacher confronted with such chaos, apparent disrespect, and open rebellion may truly appreciate the words of William Bagley, of the University of Illinois, who wrote in 1907:

> Absolute fearlessness is the first essential for the teacher on whom rests the responsibility for governing an Elementary or Secondary school. This fearlessness is not alone or chiefly the expression of physical courage, although this must not be lacking. It is rather an expression of moral courage . . . standing firm in one's convictions (cited in Curwin & Mendler, 1988, p. 1, used with permission of ASCD.).

However, transforming the children in our opening scene into a class of highly motivated, self-controlled, task-focused, and responsible learners will take more than moral courage. Such a situation requires that the teacher be skilled in classroom management, management that will not only bring order to chaos or control to what could become anarchy, but more importantly will facilitate student motivation (Brophy, 1988) and academic achievement (Evertson, 1987; Good, 1979).

If you are typical of many teachers in training, you may have a major concern about your ability to be an effective classroom manager. You are not alone in your concern. The issue of classroom management and student discipline has been found to be the most challenging task faced by novice teachers (Bulloch, 1987; Lashley, 1994; Sardo-Brown, 1993; Veenman, 1994). Further, this concern about classroom management and student discipline is not unique—nor limited —to the teacher in training or the first-year professional. Classroom management and discipline have been identified as major concerns of administrators (Boothe et al., 1993); teachers (Elam, 1989), and the general public (Elam, Rose, & Gallup,1994). Further, it has been identified as a significant reason for teachers' leaving the profession (Curwin, 1992). To gain a sense of how "hot" this issue is, review the Web site in *Connections* on page 354.

Effective classroom management is clearly an essential element, contributing not only to student motivation and achievement but also to teacher satisfaction. The current chapter will review the theory and research that point to the various elements of an effective classroom management plan. It will highlight the specific types of knowledge and skills required of the classroom manager.

◆ Chapter Objectives

After completing this chapter the reader should be able to

1 Define classroom management and differentiate it from punishment and discipline;

2 Describe three dimensions of an effective classroom management program: prevention, intervention, and remediation;

3 Identify the elements of effective planning that prevent management problems (Kounin's model);

4 Identify examples of essential management skills for effective intervention;

5 Explain how key aspects of classroom management and student socialization change across developmental stages;

6 List and explain characteristics of classroom rules that assist classroom management;

7 Describe response cost, soft and hard reprimands, and explain the effects of the use of punishment;

8 Describe Gordon's six-step "no-lose" method of solving student-teacher conflict

CHAPTER 10 CONTENT MAP

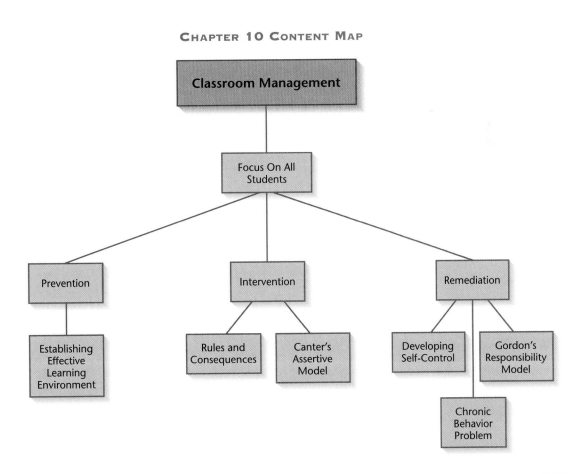

351

CLASSROOM OR STUDENT MANAGEMENT?

Listen to a group of educators as they discuss terms such as "classroom management," "discipline," and "codes of behavior," and you will discover that these terms elicit a number of different images and reactions. For some, "classroom management" is the predominant metaphor for establishing relations of authority (McLaughlin, 1994). The images or metaphors they may employ are those of "teacher as prison guard," "boss" (e.g., Lashley, 1994; Randolph & Evertson, 1994; Weinstein et al., 1994), or "overseer" (cf. Good & Brophy, 1994). The teacher with such an orientation focuses his/her management skills and energies on identifying **misbehavior** and punishing the "culprit" who has tested the teacher's authority.

This view of the teacher as controller or overseer of the student is not only limiting but may actually increase the difficulties of managing student behavior (cf. Good & Brophy, 1994). Such an orientation can turn the classroom into an arena for power struggle, **punishment**, and negativity.

misbehavior actions defined as inappropriate to the particular setting or in violation of the group norms

punishment a process of introducing an aversive condition or removing a desirable condition geared to weaken or repress a behavior

---

YOU MAKE THE CALL

IDENTIFYING OUR OWN IMAGES AND METAPHORS!

How one imagines a role can greatly impact how one enacts that role. In thinking about your role as classroom manager, what are the behaviors you envision employing? What is the relationship between the teacher, as classroom manager, and the students?

Do you see yourself in the role of "guard" or "mentor"; "controller" or "facilitator"? Do you image your role to be one of identifying, controlling, or eliminating the "trouble maker" or one of organizing and facilitating the learning activities and environment of your classroom?

◆ Classroom Management: More than Student Control

The terms "classroom management" and "discipline" are often used interchangeably (Bellon, Bellon, & Blank, 1992). However, too often the term "discipline" focuses attention only on misbehavior, ill deeds, and punishment. We feel the term "discipline" has two significant limitations. First, discipline highlights the individual (rather than the classroom), and secondly it connotes negative behavior only.

Classroom management is the term we will use to highlight *all of those positive behaviors and decisions a teacher makes to facilitate the learning process of their students*. It refers to all of those activities necessary to create and maintain an orderly learning environment.

Under such a broad definition, one could include activities such as planning and preparation of materials, organization, and decoration of

Teacher as classroom manager: Making decisions to facilitate learning ◆

the classroom (see Chapters 9 and 11), and certainly the establishment and enforcement of routines and rules.

◆ Goals of Classroom Management

The aim of such classroom management is to create and maintain a positive, productive learning environment. This point needs to be highlighted since, as previously stated, classroom management has been the predominant metaphor for establishing relations of authority (McLaughlin, 1994). The goal of classroom management is NOT absolute control. The goal is not to create an inert, docile, totally compliant classroom and student body. Rather, an effective classroom management plan not only reduces the incidents of misbehavior but maintains student interest, motivation, and involvement (Curwin & Mendler, 1988). Thus, the focus is on activities that create a positive, productive, and facilitative learning environment, with the teacher continually asking him/herself how management contributes to learning (Evertson & Randoph, 1995). The goals of an effective classroom management plan are

1. *To assist students to keep task focus.* Research demonstrates a significant relationship between the amount of content covered and student learning (e.g., Berliner, 1988; Rosenshine, 1979).

2. *To reduce distractions from learning.* This is as an extension of the goal to keep students task focused.

3. *To organize and facilitate the flow of learning activities.* Access to learning is assisted by the development of rules and routines that increase involvement and participation. Therefore, management goals must complement learning goals (Morine-Dershimer & Reeve, 1994).

Assisting a student to keep task focus ◆

4. *To help the students to manage themselves.* That is, to assist students to take responsibility for their own actions as they impact their work within the classroom (Curwin & Mendler, 1988; McCaslin & Good, 1992).

◆ The Need for "Schoolization"

Curwin & Mendler (1988) suggest that classroom management is more than simply correctional or even therapeutic, it teaches children how to behave in ways that facilitate learning. The effective classroom manager understands that behavior is not necessarily automatic for children. In fact, in many ways the behavior we request of children, as members of our classes, is not only nonautomatic but may be contrary to their natural inclinations. Consider the degree of folly involved in a teacher expecting healthy six-, seven-, and eight-year-old children, with all of their energy and enthusiasm, to automatically and naturally "sit at their desks," "be quiet," "wait to be recognized before speaking," etc. Similarly, is it reasonable to assume that the preadolescent, middle school child, experiencing the rush of hormones and the renewed interest in peers, would automatically and "naturally" attend only to the teacher and restrain from "passing notes," "speaking to neighbors" or "laughing at the noises coming from that child in the back," etc.?

In most cases, sitting at one's desk, remaining quiet, waiting to be recognized before speaking, and attending to the lesson rather than one's peers all facilitate learning, but they are not auto-

Connections

While the current chapter provides you with theory and research that should help guide your decisions and your critical thinking about classroom management, it is the experience of applying the theory and research that will prove most fruitful.

There are a number of teacher forums found on the Internet where teachers can exchange information, ideas, and even problems. Go to <http://www.pacificnet.net/~mandel/ ClassroomManagement.html> and review the topics presented within the forum. What is the current concern? Latest approach? Suggested programs?

matic, nor are their opposites (i.e., fidgeting in the seat, playing with peers, talking, etc.) evil or terrible acts. To attend to the business of the classroom and to maintain academic focus and attention, children have to forgo behaviors that are often desired, encouraged, and often appropriate in other contexts.

Like other lessons to be learned, schooling behaviors need to be taught, not simply demanded. Thus a major purpose of classroom management procedures is **schoolization**, that is, socializing the student to the behavioral "dos" and "don'ts" of the school environment.

schoolization the process of socializing the child to the role of student

◆ Classroom Management: Reflecting Student Developmental Needs

As a process of teaching appropriate "schooling behaviors," classroom management needs to consider the child's developmental level. This is certainly in line with the theme we have incorporated throughout the text. The classroom teacher needs to consider both the "Who" (that is the child with his or her own unique developmental tasks, interests, and limitations) and the "What," which in this case is facilitative classroom behaviors, when developing specific teaching-learning activities (i.e., the "How"). The goals and methods of classroom management must reflect the ever-changing needs of the learner. For example, Brophy and Evertson (1978) suggest that the tasks of classroom management change in the following manner.

The early grades. The major focus during the early school years is on socializing the child to the role of student, what we are calling "schoolization." Children at this level of development typically tend to follow adult authority. Thus, the emphasis is on teaching them what to do, more than on compliance with rules and regulations. With this emphasis on instruction and teaching, the primary techniques would be establishing and introducing routines within the classroom. The nature of routines will be discussed more fully in a later section of this chapter.

Upper elementary. By the time students reach later elementary school, they are most likely familiar with school routines and generally able to maintain an appropriate learning environment.

Middle school. A testing of the routines appears during the middle school years. Developmentally, a student's interest and control shift from adults to peers. The student may resist the teacher as authority. Classroom management will need to be developed that focuses on compliance, rather than instruction. Getting the student to behave through rules and consequences will take more of center stage in the classroom management plan.

Upper high school. With the exception of serious problems, which require special attention and remediation, most of the students are mature and socialized to the school environment (i.e., "schoolized"). Classroom management should take less energy and time, with the exception of setting the stage during the beginning of the year and perhaps refocusing students who may sway off course.

FOCUSING ON THE MANY AS WELL AS THE FEW

Classroom management procedures, as facilitators of the learning process, should be designed to be maximally beneficial for all the students within the classroom and not targeted just at the disruptive child. As previously suggested, too often the emphasis or focus of classroom management is on "controlling" or even "eliminating" the extremely disruptive and abrasive child. Such a focus can be both of limited utility for managing the disruptive child as well as work to the detriment of the others within the class.

Curwin and Mendler (1988) suggest a "80-15-5" view of the "typical classroom." These authors suggest that while the actual numbers will vary from classroom to classroom, there are fundamentally three groups of students in a typical classroom. According to Curwin and Mendler (1988), the majority of students (the 80 percent) have developed the appropriate school behaviors and rarely break rules. Classroom management procedures for these students need to be designed and implemented in ways that support them, acting as reminders of desired behavior, and refocusing them when they are in violation of the "rules of the classroom." A few students (15 percent) may break the rules with some regularity. These students need clear, consistent guidelines, expectations, and consequences. They need a classroom structure and set of procedures (intervention strategies) that will reduce the frequency and degree of their disruption, as well as "restrain" their disruptive behaviors and refocus them on the appropriate, facilitative schooling behaviors.

Action Research

Cooperative Learning Methods as a Classroom Management Tool

A s with previous chapters, and keeping in line with our own perspective of the teacher as a "research-practitioner," the following is an example of one teacher's approach to the research and practice of classroom management to assess the effect of a cooperative learning method (Sardo-Brown, 1994).

Dennis, an eighth grade teacher, wanted to know if using a cooperative learning method would improve classroom management. Dennis videotaped his eighth grade class before, during, and after his use of the cooperative learning method. In order to see if the classroom management improved, he analyzed the video for evidence of the number of times he had to remind students to stay on task during a class period.

Dennis found that during cooperative learning, students were reprimanded less for off-task behavior. Further, when after four weeks Dennis stopped using a cooperative learning method, he noted that the number of reprimands given returned to the higher level recorded prior to the intervention.

Finally, the last 5 percent are students who are chronic rule breakers and, according to Curwin and Mendler (1988), are out of control most of the time. These students need extraordinary assistance and attention.

With this "breakdown" as a backdrop, we suggest that teachers need to distribute their energies in their approach to classroom management in a way that parallels the 80-15-5 needs of their classrooms. Specifically, teachers need to place their energies and primary emphasis on developing organizational strategies and techniques that address the needs of the 80 percent and thus PREVENT possible problems from emerging. Secondly, it is clear that all students need assistance, at times, to remember and reapply appropriate schooling behaviors, and some of the teacher's classroom focus and energy needs to be devoted to INTER-VENING when children appear to sway from the desired behaviors. Finally, while certainly most dramatic, a small number of your students may need special attention and assistance in developing and applying school behavior. For these students, we need to employ strategies and techniques with a REMEDIAL focus. This three-layered plan of classroom management—prevention, intervention, and remediation—will be the focus of the remainder of this chapter.

PREVENTION

Early research (e.g., Kounin, 1971, 1977) concluded that the ways teachers handle misbehavior, once it occurs, are not the keys to future student behavior. Rather, it was what the teachers did to prevent management problems from occurring that was key. Waiting for a violation, a distraction, a problem is not when classroom management should be engaged. Rather, classroom management skills are essential to each of the decisions a teachers makes as she plans, organizes, and delivers her lessons. Teachers who see classroom management as a process of "establishing and maintaining effective learning environments tend to be more successful than teachers who place more emphasis on their roles as authority figures or disciplinarians" (Good & Brophy, 1994, p. 129).

Prevention measures occur prior to the class meeting. As noted in the previous chapter, the sociology and ecology of a classroom can go far in setting the stage for increased learning and reduced disruption. The physical layout of the room and the preparation of the materials are essential elements of a classroom management program. For example, the physical layout—including visibility, accessibility, and distractibility—can be an asset or liability to classroom management (Evertson, 1987). Just consider the situation encountered by Ms. Thompson, the teacher whose first day of class was depicted in the beginning this chapter. Her classroom had too few seats for the number of students present. Such a physical arrangement invites disruptions as students walk about, attempting to find a place to stand, or come into physical contact with one another due to the crowding. Thus, simply having ample room and appropriate seating can prove to be valuable preventive factors.

prevention arranging conditions as a pre-emptive strike against the occurrence of some problem

Classroom management starts even before meeting with students. ◆

In addition to actual physical arrangement, the operation and psychological climate of the classroom are also key management elements when creating and maintaining a learning environment that lowers classroom disruption.

◆ Establishing Effective Learning Environments

In one longitudinal study (Rutter et al., 1979) conducted in the schools in Great Britain, the authors identified a number of factors associated with positive student behavior. This research highlighted the importance of establishing an effective learning environment as a preventive classroom management strategy in that it found:

1. Very little class time (under 13 percent) spent in setting up equipment and materials was associated with better student behavior.

2. Starting class on time, pacing throughout the lesson, and not ending early was associated with better student behavior.

3. A high proportion of topic time per lesson (65–85%) spent in interaction with the whole class rather than with individuals was positively related to good student behavior.

Others (e.g., Brophy, 1988; Evertson & Harris, 1992; Jones & Jones, 1995) lend additional support to the intuitively appealing position that being organized and creating an effective learning environment is the best way to establish discipline in the classroom.

To establish an effective learning environment, geared to the prevention of disruptions, a teacher needs to (1) set the tone at the beginning of the year; (2) provide worthwhile classroom activities; (3) establish routines that facilitate progression, and (4) establish rules for classroom behaviors.

Set the Tone at the Beginning of the School Year

The initial interactions of any group of people (including students and teachers) set expectations for the interactions to follow. Research consistently demonstrates that the early tone and patterns set during the beginning of the school year are "critical" to the establishment of classroom behavioral patterns (Everston et al., 1994). Because of this "precedent-setting" nature of the first day (Evertson, 1987), it is essential that the teacher not only structure worthwhile activities but begin to articulate and model the expected classroom behavior. These expected behaviors will be communicated through the creation of classroom routines and rules.

Providing Worthwhile Classroom Activities

Rutters and colleagues (1979) suggest that classroom management problems can be prevented or at least significantly reduced by having students actively and continuously engaged in worthwhile activities. This is intuitively quite appealing. That is, classrooms with motivated students, enthusiastic teachers, and stimulating, meaningful activities have fewer problems. Table 10.1 provides a number of guidelines for creating such an engaging classroom.

Routines

In addition to preparing meaningful learning activities, the effective classroom manager should also develop and communicate a set of classroom **routines** and rules (Emmer, 1987; Emmer et al., 1989, 1994; Evertson & Emmer, 1982; Evertson et al., 1989).

routines sets of procedures organized around a particular time, concept, or activity

---

Table 10.1   Guidelines for Preventing Classroom Problems through Increasing Student Engagement

1. *Worthwhile lessons:* Make curriculum worthwhile and enjoyable.

2. *Student-focus:* Develop lessons that satisfy student needs to belong, to initiate, to have fun (Glasser, 1990).

3. *Humor:* Moskiowitz and Hayman (1976) found that effective managers smiled and joked more with their students.

4. *Preparation:* Teach a prepared lesson by (Kounin, 1971,1977)

   ◆ Beginning on time,

   ◆ Employing routines to begin and end class,

   ◆ Making transitions quick and orderly,

   ◆ Direct talking to the class not to the book or chalkboards.

Routines are sets of procedures organized around a particular time, concept, or activity. Routines are especially effective with time-consuming, non-instructional activities, such as roll taking or homework collection (Jones & Jones, 1995). Routines facilitate transitions from activity to activity. By facilitating such smooth transitions, they help to create effective classrooms that experience fewer disruptions (Kounin, 1971, 1977).

YOU MAKE THE CALL

WORKING WITH AND WITHOUT ROUTINES

Perhaps you have experienced classrooms that employed a set of routine procedures to facilitate administrative duties such as roll taking or homework collection. As you review the two scenarios below, begin to think of the conditions that may invite student misbehavior and how these may be reduced by effective routines.

Teacher A: Teacher A enjoys interacting and being personal with her fourth grade class. She starts each class by walking from desk to desk greeting her students and individually collecting their homework.

Teacher B: Teacher B begins each class with the following instructions: "Take a deep breath, let it out slowly and with your eyes closed remind yourselves to become focused, active learners, respectful of each other. Now slowly open your eyes and begin the day!" Following this exercise, she asks the students who are aisle captains for that week to please collect the homework. While the captains are collecting the work, she asks the class if there were any questions about the problems they did for homework.

Routines can be used for reviewing assignments, assigning homework, or even for responding to students who may come late to class. Again, using this last example as an illustration, it becomes clear that if the class is not aware of the routine to follow when coming late to class, the latecomer can be a major distraction from the learning activity and invite additional disruption. However, latecomers entering the classroom in which a lateness routine has been established may proceed immediately to the teacher's desk to deliver their late note, or perhaps place their books at their desks and return to the main office or perhaps just take their seats and see the teacher after class. Regardless of the specifics decided upon, the essential ingredient of a routine, such as one governing lateness, is that it involves a procedure that is well known, standardized across students, and invites minimal classroom interruption. Table 10.2 provides a general listing of the types of routines a teacher may wish to develop (Weinstein and Mignano, 1993).

Rules: Clear and Concrete

In addition to establishing meaningful, efficient routines, a teacher can prevent, or at least reduce, the potential for classroom problems by communicating a set of meaningful and relevant **rules** to the students.

rules a listing of appropriate and inappropriate behaviors within a classroom

Table 10.2	**Categories of Classroom Routines** **Adapted from Weinstein and Mignano (1993)**
1.	*Administrative activities:* These include developing procedures and routines for taking attendance, responding to lateness, etc.
2.	*Movement:* This includes procedures for going to the bathroom, pencil sharpener, locker, etc.
3.	*Housekeeping:* This includes cleaning up after an activity, storing folders, or materials, returning seats to desks, etc.
4.	*Lesson routines:* Examples of lesson routines would be procedures for collecting assignments, homework, etc.
5.	*Interactions:* These are routines or procedures for getting the teacher's attention (e.g., call out, come to the desk, raise hand, etc.) or providing peer support and assistance (e.g., "In small groups how do we give and receive help?" "Can we socialize while we do our activities?", etc.)

Source: Adapted with permission of McGraw-Hill Companies.

Research has demonstrated the value of creating an orderly environment, and the role played by clear, reasonable rules that are fairly and consistently enforced (Emmer et al., 1994; Evertson et al., 1994; Purkey & Smith, 1983). These "dos and don'ts" of classroom behaviors need to be communicated to the students during the first days of class and consistently monitored and enforced.

It is important that the rules be clear, concrete, and understood by all. This may seem like an obvious point, but the following illustration suggests that what might appear clear, concrete, and understood by all is not always the case. For example, asking children to be "nice," "act their age," etc., allows for multiple interpretations. Thus, when setting rules it is important to describe the behaviors one would exhibit or not exhibit when following the rule. Perhaps being "nice" means "not hitting another child," or "using the words 'please' and 'thank you' when borrowing materials," etc. Thus, classroom rules need to be clear, concrete, and unambiguous if they are to be effective. It is helpful for the rules to be presented and discussed with examples that demonstrate what is appropriate and what is not. Further, it may even be useful to "test" the students by requesting that they repeat, recite, or demonstrate the rules.

Research on classroom management (e.g., Emmer, 1987; Emmer et al., 1989, 1997; Evertson & Emmer, 1982; Evertson et al., 1989, 1997) suggests that effective managers have a workable system of rules, which they teach their students. Further, they had procedures for systematically and carefully monitoring student behavior in order to react swiftly to violations.

As to the type of rules to establish, it is important that the teacher remember that the goal is not to gain and exert power or to enforce blind obedience, but rather to establish and maintain an effective learning environment. According to Brophy and Putnam (1979), an optimal

Our Rules for Getting Along

1. Everyone has a right to be safe.
2. We will treat people with courtesy and respect.
3. We will include people who are left out.
4. Stopping violence is everyone's job.

Rules need to be clear and concrete. ◆

approach to classroom management is one that establishes the desired learning environment while imposing the least or fewest restrictions. Thus, the measuring stick applied to rule development should be "does it enhance and facilitate an effective learning environment?" Certain practices and rules may be inappropriate, since they simply do not result in effective learning. For example, demanding that the children keep absolutely quiet at all times, or sit perfectly still, or attend to tasks, regardless of the task's level of "worthwhileness," is not only undoable, but counterproductive to effective learning. It would appear that a short list of general rules such as no hurting, come to class with needed materials, listen when others are speaking, etc., is better than a long list of specific "do's" and "don'ts." Identifying the least and the fewest is not always an easy task.

It is important to assert both your authority and responsibility for the safety and effectiveness of your classroom and therefore your need for establishing rules. It is also important to involve the students in the development of these rules (Curwin & Mendler, 1988; Liconia, 1991; Glasser, 1990; Schap & Solomon, 1990). This not only facilitates their understanding and ownership but also cultivates their sense of power and self-esteem (Emmer, 1987). Working together, negotiating teacher and student needs, as rules are developed can serve as a base for establishing "power with" students, rather than simply "power over" them (Kreisberg, 1992).

◆ Maintaining Effective Learning Environments

The preparing of effective teaching activities, routines, and rules is essential to the creation of an effective learning environment. However, preparation alone is not enough. A teacher has to successfully implement the activities, routines, and rules if the classroom is to be managed effectively.

Jacob Kounin (1971, 1977) was one of the first researchers to identify the effect that a teacher's behavior had on student behavior. Kounin focused on highlighting teacher behaviors that led to increased student involvement in the lesson, while reducing classroom misbehavior. Thus, rather than focusing on teacher reactivity to disruption, Kounin focused on teacher behaviors that engaged students' "on-task" behaviors. In sum, he found that good preparation, which in turn produced good pacing and smooth transitions, and provision of appropriate individual work assignments were basic to successful classroom management.

From his research, Kounin was able to identify a number of variables, which further research (Brophy & Evertson, 1976; Anderson, Evertson, & Brophy, 1979; Good & Grouws, 1975) suggests characterizes teachers and classrooms with effective learning environments and reduced student problems. These factors include: "withitness," "momentum and smoothness," "group alerting," "student accountability," "overlapping," "satiation and challenge."

A "withit" teacher has eyes in the back of her head. ◆

Withitness

Kounin (1971,1977) found that effective classroom managers knew what was going on at all times and in all parts of their classroom. This characteristic of being fully aware has been termed **withitness.**

We are sure that you have experienced teachers who seemed to have eyes in the back of their heads. These teachers exhibited "withitness," knowing what was going on at all times.

Kounin found withitness to be associated with reduced incidence of classroom disruptions. A teacher with "withitness" was able to respond to prevent minor incidents from becoming serious issues. Teachers who were less aware often would make timing errors (i.e., waiting too long and thus allowing minor problems to become major), target errors (failing to identify all those involved or who did what), and even response errors (e.g., overreacting in situations which called for calm).

withitness having an awareness of everything that is happening within the classroom (Kounin's concept)

Momentum and Smoothness

A class or lesson that progresses without major disruption and flows from start through closing is one with momentum and smoothness. Teachers who demonstrate **momentum** and **smoothness** often employ classroom routines that promote efficiency in changing from one activity to another. Thus, a teacher exhibiting momentum and smoothness will employ a routine such as that previously described for having students relax and focus, moving next to having aisle captains collect the homework, while the teacher asks the students for questions or concerns with their homework. If there are no questions, the teacher is ready to move to recapping the previous lesson and processing the homework at the board.

momentum a characteristic of a class noting "movement" from one activity to another; a progression within the lesson

smoothness the degree to which a class or lesson progresses without major disruption and flows from start through finish

The teacher with momentum and smoothness moves from roll and review to new lessons and assignments without missing a beat. The lesson has been designed with logical sequencing and preparation of materials and proceeds smoothly from start through finish. In addition to a progression within the design and implementation of the lesson, teachers demonstrating momentum and smoothness avoid being distracted by questions or actions of one student or by giving out too many specific instructions that are repeated unnecessarily.

Group Alerting

Another characteristic of effective classroom managers was their ability to employ techniques to gain student attention and focus. These managers would gain student attention *prior to proceeding*. The techniques employed directed the entire group to what they needed to be doing, rather than attempting to focus one student at a time.

group alerting a classroom management technique which alerts the entire class to a transition about to occur

Some of the techniques used in **group alerting** included (1) looking around the group to gain attention; (2) using choral, as well as individual responses; and (3) keeping students in suspense and/or throwing out challenges.

In the movie *Stand and Deliver,* there is a scene in which the teacher, Jaime Escalante, is about to introduce the algebraic concept of multiplying negative and positive numbers. At first, he wanders around the class, aisle to aisle, asking students if they had ever gone to the beach. Did they ever dig in the sand? Clearly, his movement and the unusual nature of the questions have the students' wondering what he was doing. As a result, they stayed attentive. As they begin to respond affirmatively to his questions, he points out that the hole is like a negative and the mound of sand is like a positive. Next, he moves to a student and asks him what a negative 1 plus a positive 1 would equal. The student is at first resistant and requires a lot of individual attention. But with prodding and encouragement he finally responds, "Zero."

This activity at first involves small groups of the students (the ones sitting near where he was walking) and eventually focuses on the one student in the back. Now, prior to continuing his lesson, he attempts to refocus the entire class by providing a group alert. Having explained what a negative and positive number is, he goes to the chalkboard and writes $(-) * (-) = +$. Next he turns to the class and pointing to the board states: " A negative times a negative equals a positive." He then follows with the directive, "Say it." He continues to encourage and prod the class to "Say it," gaining full participation and having them respond with increased intensity and loudness. Having gotten their attention and involvement, he stops them to ask, "Why?" Now having gained their attention, their involvement, he is ready to move on.

While a number of excellent classroom management procedures are demonstrated in this scenario, it is clear that the teacher employs a mixture of individual "attention getters" with "group alerts" to effectively engage his students and thus manage his classroom.

Student Accountability

Another variable that characterized effective classroom managers and proactive learning environments was that the students were kept accountable and on their toes, involved in the lesson. Many of the techniques demonstrated in the previous illustration with Jaime Escalante, such as walking around the class, asking students directly for answers, etc. promote such student accountability.

A number of other creative techniques can be used to maintain student accountability. Hunter (1982), for example, reported on a process in which the teacher would circulate among the students and have them respond to grammar questions by holding up a specific color card to identify their answer. In Hunter's (1982) illustration, the teacher asks the students if the proper form would be "have run" or "has run." The teacher would ask the class: "Who thinks the answer is 'have run'? If you do, hold up the red card. If you think the answer is 'has run,' hold up the green card." Such a technique maximizes student involvement.

Student accountability can occur by simply having the students attend to another student who may be reciting her work, or responding to a problem on the board. The effective classroom manager will have those in their seats check the board work or perhaps hold props for their peer as she recites, or even employ feedback sheets to provide their peers with critiques of their presentations. All of these techniques are geared to keep as many students as possible involved in appropriate class activities. With such student involvement and accountability for the learning activity, disruptions or off-task behavior are reduced.

Overlapping

Overlapping is the ability of a teacher to attend simultaneously to two or more events in the classroom. For example, helping Ramon with his tissues, while being able to separate and redirect Harold and Annie, who are beginning to tug over the earth-moving toy in the sandbox, is essential for the preschool teacher. But overlapping is not limited to those working with the young children. The senior AP calculus teacher needs to be able to provide hints and directions for the students working at the board, while at the same time guiding those working at their seats and quietly refocusing the two in the back who would rather be sharing notes about the upcoming dance.

overlapping overseeing or supervising multiple tasks at the same time

The effective classroom manager will certainly be a juggler of multiple tasks. The key is not only the ability to recognize the multiple tasks that are required but to address these tasks in a way that does not disrupt the flow of the lesson. For example, if two students are talking to each other while the teacher is presenting a lesson, a teacher who can overlap will continue to lecture, rather than stop to correct the students. This teacher will continue to provide the lesson, while at the same time walking toward the two in conversation. Closing the distance between the teacher and the students can be an effective and unobtrusive tool for returning the students to the task. Further, such an intervention does not disrupt the lesson.

Satiation/Valence and Challenge Arousal

There is a good chance that you have experienced times when the activity in which you are engaged simply becomes "overdone." Whether it be working on a puzzle, balancing your check book, reading a book, or talking on the phone, you probably have gotten to the point where you simply need to stop and do something else. Well, just like ourselves, our students can get to a point where they have simply "had it" with a particular lesson or learning activity. Having their fill of this or that particular learning activity, students may become bored or frustrated, at least for the moment, and thus become at risk for engaging in off-task, disruptive activities. This experience of having "had it" is termed **satiation**.

satiation when an activity is repeated beyond the point of interest or motivation

valence the experienced level of value of a particular moment

During these times, an effective classroom manager will employ a variety of techniques to change the value (**valence**) of the moment in order to arouse the students with a challenge. For example, the teacher may employ a prop or prod the student with a challenge, or provide a dramatic pause and invite them to put on their "thinking caps," all as a means of delaying satiation and bringing enjoyment and challenge back to the lesson.

Consider the case of Mr. McCusker, a tenth grade social studies teacher. For the past three days, he had been discussing the origins of the American Revolution, showing a filmstrip and reviewing the many political, economic, and social forces active at the time. It became quite obvious that while the students were attending and making notes, they were losing their "enthusiasm" for the topic and their ability to empathize with those about to take such a significant political and personal step. He realized that the students were becoming satiated. Mr. McCusker then decided to vary his lesson plan. On the next day of class, he waited in the hall until the class bell had rung and the students had settled. Then he swung open the door, ran into the room dressed in revolutionary clothing yelling, "The Red Coats are coming! The Red Coats are coming!!" With his entrance, he not only introduced the content of that day's lesson but aroused feelings he would use to help the students appreciate the "shock," the anxiety, the fear of those hearing those same words over 200 years ago. What resulted was a new valence and an increased challenge arousal for his students.

Teacher Tool Box

General Considerations for Preventing Classroom Management Problems

A number of general conclusions can be gleaned from the research and should be placed within your tool box of considerations and techniques for effective classroom management.

- *Be prepared:* Develop engaging learning activities and facilitative routines and rules.
- *Be alert:* Know what is happening in your classroom at all times and let the students know that you know.
- *Be multitasking:* Learn to deal with more than one thing at a time.
- *Keep a group focus:* Alert and engage the entire class, avoid one-on-one absorption.
- *Be challenging:* Vary material and mode of delivery to avoid satiation.
- *Employ rapid response:* When necessary, intervene quickly and smoothly with minimal disruption to the lesson.

INTERVENTION

While a good management plan and a developed instructional program will minimize misbehavior, they will not totally prevent it. Remember, we are not suggesting that misbehavior is bad, evil, or in some way abnormal. What we are suggesting is that sometimes everyone can have a bad day and may engage in activities that are not instructionally related, or task focused.

Any disciplinary intervention employed at these times should be aimed at

1. stopping, suppressing, or redirecting the misbehavior; and

2. serving as an opportunity and method to foster the development of the appropriate classroom response.

Most "off-task" behaviors that you will experience from your students can be effectively managed by unobtrusive techniques that alert the students to your awareness of their misbehavior and perhaps redirect them to task. These unobtrusive reminders may include actions such moving closer to the student, making eye contact, or even some facial gesture (e.g., a frown). More serious or continued misbehavior will need more direct intervention. Under these conditions, the "what" and the "how" of the disciplinary intervention are important if it is to be effective not only in stopping the misbehavior, but also in assisting the student to develop and employ appropriate classroom behavior.

◆ Rules and Consequences

Earlier in this chapter we discussed the need to develop rules of behavior targeted to increasing the effectiveness of the learning environment. Further, we suggested that when these rules are developed collaboratively they may have a positive impact, with students taking increased ownership for the rules and thus becoming more willing to follow them. Even under the best of circumstances, students may on occasion violate a rule. At these times, an effective classroom manager will intervene with the appropriate application of consequences.

Consequences: Positive and Negative

Following the rules of a classroom or choosing to violate the rules of the classroom are decisions for which the student should experience some form of consequence. We have stated that following as well as violating the rules should have consequences, since we do not want you to simply interpret our suggestions for the use of consequences as a nice way of saying "punish!" Rather, the focus in this text is on positive behaviors and the use of positive consequences (reinforcement) for compliance.

Negative consequences (punishment) can be effective in discouraging or suppressing specific, unwanted behaviors, but they are not effective for teaching what is desired. As such the use of punishments should NOT be the core or mainstay of your classroom management-intervention system. Emphasizing positive behaviors that can be reinforced is much more effective than focusing on elimination of unwanted behaviors (Sulzer-Azaroff & Mayer, 1986).

Intervening entails stopping misbehavior and teaching what is desired. ◆

RIP (Rules-Ignore-Praise) a strategy for intervening with a student misbehavior that entails a reminder of the rule, ignoring the reaction, and praise adherence

RRP (Rules-Reward-Punishment) an alternative strategy for intervening with a student misbehavior which introduces punishment if the reminder of the rule or the reinforcement of adherence prove insufficient

Stopping Misbehavior

Charles (1992) suggested two approaches to responding to misbehavior: **Rules-Ignore-Praise (RIP)** and **Rules-Reinforce-Punish (RRP)** methods. Charles's (1992) technique of rules-ignore-praise (RIP), works in the following fashion: rules are established, misbehavior is ignored, students who follow the rules are praised. According to Charles (1992) such an approach appears to work for the younger students, who are still in the process of learning the rules, but perhaps less effective for those at the secondary levels. For older students, Charles (1992) suggests a modification of RIP to include the sequence rules-reward-punishment (RRP). As with the previous system, RRP starts with the establishment of rules and emphasizes positive reinforcement. Unlike RIP, this model does not ignore misbehavior, but rather employs a system of punishments.

Caveats When Using Punishment

In using punishment, it is important to remember that punishment controls undesirable behavior by making aversive consequences contingent on such behavior. The use of punishment as a classroom management tool is a stopgap at best and may be counterproductive, by causing anger, resentment, and power struggles. As noted previously, punishment does not change students' underlying desire nor provide guidance as to what is desired. If punishment is used to stop the misbehavior, the teacher needs to be alert to catch the student being good and following the rules so that such appropriate behavior can be reinforced. Thus, the child who has received a reprimand for calling out also needs to receive verbal praise as soon as he appropriately raises his hand, waits to be recognized, and then responds to the teacher's question.

Response Cost

One form of punishment that has been found to reduce off-task and socially inappropriate behavior is the process of **response cost** (Little & Kelly, 1989; Abramowitz & O'Leary, 1990; Stratton, 1989). Response cost is a technique aimed at reducing bothersome behavior by connecting misbehavior with loss of previously earned rewards. For example, people who violate certain driving rules by speeding or going through traffic lights may lose the privilege of driving for some length of time. Within the classroom, the teacher may establish a system in which each time a student breaks a rule, following an initial reminder, that student will receive a check mark next to his or her name. For each check mark received during the class period, a student could be "docked" a certain amount of time (e.g., one minute) of recess.

> **response cost** a behavioral strategy which employs the loss of a reinforcer as a punishment

Ideally, the costs employed should logically relate to the offenses. For example, the student who destroys materials will not get to use them for a time, or a student who breaks rules at recess will have to stay in; or one who fails to do her work during the time assigned will lose the privilege of free activity, using that time instead to make up the missed class work, etc.

◆ The Need to Stop and Train

In addition to stopping the misbehavior we want to use the incident as a teachable moment. The goal for such intervention is to increase effective, appropriate behaviors rather than simply to suppress misbehavior.

Thus, when providing a more direct intervention, it is important to remind the student of the rule that is being violated and the consequence assigned before applying the consequence. Consider the situation in which a student is playing with an electronic game even though the teacher has now directed the class that recess is over, and it is time to return to the lesson. As the teacher directs the class to open their math books and she begins to call on volunteers to go to the board, the teacher may start to walk toward the student with the game (**closing space**). As she continues to direct the class, she looks down to catch the distracted student's eyes but he fails to pick up on these less directive techniques. At that point, the teacher would do well to lean down and calmly and softly remind the student of the class rule regarding games during recess and games during work time. The teacher may note that recess is over and that it is time for math. Further, she should remind him that he is

> **closing space** reducing the physical space or distance between a teacher and a student who needs correction

---

Teacher Tool Box

Guidelines for Intervening

As you begin to consider your own plan for intervention with classroom disruptions, you need to consider each of the following:

◆ *Classroom rules:* Clear, concrete, understood?

◆ *Consequences*: Emphasize the positives of doing. Use negative consequences only as stopgap to allow the child to desist and return to on-task behavior.

◆ *Ignore* minor, not dangerous incidents.

◆ *Respond* quickly, consistently, yet calmly.

◆ *Develop and employ a response hierarchy,* ranging from unobtrusive techniques (e.g., close space, eye contact) to more formalized systems (e.g., response costs).

◆ *Allow students to keep self-esteem* (and image intact). Employ soft reprimands rather than loud public reprimands.

◆ *Employ a caring style* that does not provoke power struggles.

◆ *Catch the child at being good!* Remember to reinforce the child's appropriate behaviors.

◆ *Emphasize* cooperative goal structures for the classroom.

soft reprimand a reprimand presented in a tone which only the student being reprimanded hears

loud reprimand a reprimand which is noticed by others; a public reprimand

supposed to put away his game and take out his mathematics workbook and that if he does not do so (1) he will have his game placed in the teacher's desk until the end of class and (2) he will not be allowed to bring that type of game to class for one week. Such an intervention demonstrates the use of a hierarchy of responses terminating with a **soft reprimand** and direction rather than a **loud reprimand**.

Style/Manner

Since the goal of such intervention procedures is to both stop the misbehavior and encourage, reinforce, or teach the desired behavior, the teacher must approach the interaction with a style and manner that facilitates such learning. If this is a teaching situation, the teacher needs to be consistent when responding to misbehavior. Further, as noted previously, it is important to highlight or identify the misdeed and the nature of the rule violation that is resulting in this consequence.

There are a number of additional style or manner considerations for effective classroom management, especially when imposing a negative consequence for a rule violation. These suggestions have been adapted from the work of a number of researchers (e.g., Canter & Canter, 1992; Gordon, 1989; Glasser, 1990) and are outlined in Table 10.3.

Table 10.3   Style and Manner Guidelines for Delivering Negative Consequences

1. *Be close, use the power of proximity:* This appears to be more effective with younger children or those not exhibiting anger or hostility. In the latter case, it is preferable to allow for a comfort zone.

2. *Attempt to make eye contact:* Address the student at his/her physical level rather than speaking down or up to him/her, maintaining comfortable, non-threatening eye contact.

3. *Employ soft reprimands:* Present the consequence in a low or soft voice, which only the student can hear. Provide feedback in a way that helps to insure the student's dignity.

4. *Remain calm:* Provide consequences in a matter-of-fact style.

5. *Don't accept excuses:* Acknowledge the student's feeling, but simply repeat the rule and the consequence that was previously assigned.

6. *Avoid power struggles:* Ignore invitations to argue, defend, or engage in power struggles.

7. *Redirect the student:* Help the student refocus and engage in positive behaviors and employ reinforcement once the student demonstrates rule-appropriate behavior.

8. *Provide an escape mechanism:* For the students who are upset allow them to leave the room, or write down their concerns, take a moment to "gather" themselves, etc.

REMEDIATION

◆ Developing Self-Control

Some students present classroom behaviors that create chronic disruption and problems to learning. These students may continually break the same rules, blatantly forget to bring materials, or even refuse to participate in the classroom activities. Other students may present as much more openly hostile and defiant in class. In either case, there are some students, perhaps the 5 percent previously discussed, for whom the process of "schoolization" has not worked and the typical classroom rituals, rules, and procedures prove ineffective. These are children who need additional attention and assistance.

It is important for the classroom teacher to understand how to intervene with these chronic disrupters and, when necessary, how to work with others (e.g., counselors, school psychologists, parents) in helping these children adapt to the learning environment.

◆ Remediating Chronic Behavioral Problems

Chronic misbehaviors do not come with easy answers. Quite often, the child with such chronic misbehavior will require the assistance of mental health professionals such as the school counselor, school psychologist, or even an outside mental health specialist. For others, however, the teacher may be able to develop strategies that assist the student in gaining control of his behavior and learning to adhere to the classroom rules and procedures. Three specific approaches—applied behavior analysis, contingency contracting, and alternative response training—will be discussed in some detail.

Applied Behavior Analysis

Applied behavior analysis (e.g., Alberto & Troutman, 1990; Kahn, 1999) is a process of analyzing a problematic behavior and employing remedies based on behavioral learning principles. The process of applied behavior analysis requires that the behavior be identified, along with the conditions and events that precede and follow it. By identifying the (A)ntecedent conditions, the (B)ehavior, and the (C)onsequences, a teacher may be able to develop a clearer understanding of how to manipulate the environmental conditions that seem to be eliciting or supporting these behaviors.

applied behavior analysis a system for analyzing a behavior and the possible controlling antecedent and consequential factors

Consider the following example. Harry is a member of Mr. Callugo's fifth grade class. Harry has a long history of making noises and calling out in class, but more recently he has expanded his disruptive behaviors to include throwing books. Mr. Callugo reported that he has attempted a number of interventions such as hollering at Harry, going back to his desk to speak with Harry, asking him to go out in the hall, and even sending Harry down to the principal's office. However, according to Mr. Callugo nothing seems to work.

The school counselor, working with Mr. Callugo, went in to observe Harry in class. She attempted to study the A-B-C's (i.e., antecedent, behavior, consequence) of the book throwing in order to detect if anything happened before it or after it that may account for its frequency. What she found was that Mr. Callugo was a very energetic teacher. He had his class working at tables in small learning groups, all except Harry, who sat in the back of the room at a desk, doing worksheets. Mr. Callugo would move from table to table, attending to the various learning groups. At each table, he would become very involved, and the students appeared to enjoy interacting with him. In all his excitement, however, Mr. Callugo rarely went back to check on Harry. In fact, it appeared that the only time Mr. Callugo paid any attention to Harry was right after he had thrown a book.

It seemed to the counselor that the book throwing was Harry's technique for gaining attention and that Mr. Callugo's reprimanding, which at first glance may appear negative, was in fact giving Harry the attention he desired and acted as a positive reinforcement, thus increasing the book throwing rather than reducing it. From this applied behavioral analysis, the counselor and Mr. Callugo came up with a plan to use an RIP approach (rules-ignore-praise) to the problem (Charles, 1996).

While the rule of not throwing books (or anything for that matter) was something Mr. Callugo assumed the fifth graders would know, he decided to remind the class that throwing paper planes, pencils, books, etc., could be dangerous and therefore was not acceptable. Then Mr. Callugo instituted a plan in which he would ignore Harry right after he had thrown a book. However, because the counselor had pointed out that Harry would typically refocus on his work sheet and get back to work right after throwing a book, Mr. Callugo would not only ignore the book throwing but look for the first sign of appropriate behavior. He began to praise Harry as soon as he refocused on the work sheet. Mr. Callugo would walk near Harry's desk, checking and commenting on the other students' work. When he was close to Harry, he would provide a word of praise for Harry's ability to sit and do his seat work like the other students. Within two days after instituting this "rules-ignore-praise" plan, not only had the book throwing stopped, but Harry asked for and received permission to rejoin his learning group.

Sometimes systematically studying the events that precede a behavior or immediately follow it may provide insight into what needs to be changed to modify the undesirable classroom behavior.

Contingency Contracting

contingency contracting
influencing behavior through the manipulation of the consequences for that behavior

Contingency contracting is a process by which a student and a teacher actually sign a contract indicating which behaviors are desired and which consequences will result from performing and not performing them. Contracts could be developed around instructional issues so that specific amounts of work and levels of proficiency would be targeted. For example, Ms. Spellman developed a contract with Jonathan, a second grader who rarely completed or returned homework. The conditions of Jonathan's contract stated that "for each day Jonathan brings in his homework, which is both neat and complete, he will receive one (1) gold star. Stars will not be given for homework that is either incomplete or not neat. Further, after gaining 10 stars, Jonathan can serve as aisle captain and collect the homework for the next two days (an activity Jonathan liked).

Contracts can also be used to improve classroom behavior. Thus, a teacher may develop a contract specifying the need for a specific child to stay in her seat or raise her hand prior to asking or answering questions. In general, contracts are useful for reducing or eliminating lesson disruptions when the disruptions are serious and can be concretely defined.

In developing a contract you should specify (1) the terms or conditions under which appropriate behaviors will be displayed or the limits of misbehavior and (2) the consequence or contingencies tied to these behaviors. Figure 10.1 provides an example of one such contingency contract for a child who called out in class. Although the focus here is on teacher-student contracts, Blechman, Kotanchik, and Taylor (1981) reported that school-based contingency contracts written by families were helpful in developing students who were more consistent in classroom performance.

Figure 10.1
A Sample Contingency Contract

Student's Name:_____ Grade:_____ Date:_____

Teacher's Name:_____

I, _____(student), understand the expectations in our classroom are

that a student who wishes to respond to the teacher's question will:

    1. Raise his/or her hand directly in the air,

    2. Wait quietly until recognized by the teacher,

    3. And if another student is called upon, quietly lower his or her hand until

        the teacher asks for an additional response.

I agree to follow these rules for responding. Each time that I follow the three

steps listed above without being reminded, I will receive a check mark (✓). If I forget

the rules of the classroom and I call out an answer rather than following the 3 steps

listed above, I will not be given a check mark.

    When I have 10 check marks I will be allowed to ring the bell signaling the end

of recess for one week.

Student Signature:_____ Date:_____

Teacher Signature:_____ Date:_____

Teacher Tool Box

When Remediation Is Needed

When working with the student who is a chronic misbehaver, a number of behavioral approaches appear to be of value.

♦ Remember that attention, even negative teacher attention, can sometimes work as a positive, reinforcing consequence.

♦ Apply behavioral analysis to the situation to determine if teacher attention is reinforcing the undesired behavior.

♦ When attention is the controlling factor, consider employing the RIP approach (i.e., Rules-Ignore-Praise).

♦ Attempt to "attend" to the student when on task as a way of increasing on-task behaviors.

♦ Punishment may suppress the misbehavior, but it does not teach the child what to do. Attempt to "catch the child being good" and praise appropriate behaviors, especially following incidents of employing punishment.

♦ Some students need to be taught how to relax, how to assert (rather than aggress), how to reflect and problem solve rather than simply act out. For these students teach them how to
  • Stop and relax.
  • Ask themselves "What is my problem? What am I supposed to do?"
  • Use cognitive reminders such as "Slow down, I can do this," "Raise my hand," etc.
  • Request teacher assistance.

♦ Use behavioral contracts as a way of assisting the child to gain some self-control.
  • Develop the contract collaboratively with the student.
  • Be sure that the student understands what is expected and is able to perform the expected behaviors.
  • Have the student identify consequences that would be reinforcing and include these as the contingencies for completing the contract.
  • Remember the Premack principle, quite often the behavior that occurs with high frequency (e.g., getting out of the seat) can be creatively used (e.g., permission to take notes down to another teacher, or counselor) as the reinforcement for sitting still in the seat for a given length of time.

Alternative Response Training

Alternative response training is a self-control procedure that consists of teaching students responses that either interfere with or replace an undesired behavior, for example, teaching children with impulsive response styles to be sure to repeat the question out loud (or silently to themselves) prior to responding would be an example of alternative response training. Similarly, the old, tried and true method for reducing anger by counting to ten before saying anything is an alternative response training.

Quite often, students who chronically misbehave do so because they simply do not know how not to misbehave or what to do in the place of misbehavior. Under these conditions, the child needs to be taught alternative responses. A number of programs are available and appropriate for teachers to help students develop alternative responses to a variety of problematic behaviors such as impulsivity (Camp et al., 1977) and ineffective problem solving (Meichenbaum, 1977).

While behavioral management techniques, such as applied behavioral analyses and contingency contracts, appear effective in modifying much of the chronic misbehavior experienced within the classroom, some (e.g., Gordon, 1989; Curwin & Mendler, 1988; Glasser, 1990; Kohn, 1993) suggest that such modification is not enough. These authors argue that what is needed is the development of student responsibility and self-control.

♦ Developing Student Responsibility and Self-Control

Students who have failed often and who have frequently misbehaved may come to believe that doing anything other than misbehaving and failing is truly impossible or hopeless. They may believe that they can not change their situation or themselves (Curwin & Mendler, 1988). Managing these children can be a difficult and most likely unsatisfying experience unless the student is helped to gain some self-control and encouraged to take responsibility for her own choices and actions. Thus, rather than emphasizing rewards, punishment, or other forms of coercion for this type of student, some researchers (e.g., Gordon, 1989; Curwin & Mendler, 1988; Glasser, 1990; Kohn, 1993) suggest the teacher attempt to help the child develop self-control and personal responsibility. One model is presented by Thomas Gordon (1989).

◆ The Gordon Model: Discipline Through Self-Control

One of the proponents of a student responsibility model is Thomas Gordon (1989). Gordon's perspective is that good classroom management results, ultimately, in the students' developing their own inner sense of self-control. The techniques and approaches he suggests emphasize teaching rather than controlling or coercing. Brophy and Rohrkemper (1981) found that teachers rated as effective by both their principals and classroom observers behaved in ways generally consistent with the principles advocated by Gordon. That is, (1) they were willing to assume responsibility for solving problems; (2) they worked with problem students (rather than excluding); (3) they used long-term solution-oriented approaches (as opposed to controlling, punitive techniques); and (4) they focused on helping the student understand and cope with the problems underlying disruptive behavior.

This perspective implies that teachers who seek to foster self-control within their students must first give up their own need to employ controlling power over those students. In place of "power" and "control," the teacher needs confrontive skills, **helping skills**, and preventive skills.

The confrontive skills assist the teacher in meeting his own needs and thus are useful when the problem is primarily that of the teacher. Helping skills are useful for helping students meet their needs, when it is primarily the student who has the problem. Preventive skills, such as establishing routines, rules, etc., are employed prior to problem development and help establish a mutually satisfying environment.

Diagnose the Problem—Who Owns It?

Gordon (1989) suggests that misbehavior is actually an adult concept. What a teacher identifies as misbehavior is most often something the student experiences as useful and functional. It is only the adult who feels that this behavior produces undesirable consequences. This is not to suggest that children do not have their own problems, which may manifest in some form of disruptive behavior, but rather that often what has been identified and labeled as disruptive is only "bad" and "disruptive" to the teacher.

This is an important distinction, since quite often what a teacher labels as misbehavior are in reality normal and desirable types of responding when viewed from the perspective of the student. Thus, simply assuming that the student will automatically give up such behavior is ill-conceived. If a solution is to be effective, it must address

alternative response training a behavioral training strategy in which a person is taught to employ a substitute response for a behavior that has become problematic

helping skills interpersonal skills which convey a person's willingness to attend, listen, and assist another in their problem solving

teacher-owned problems problems in which the student's behavior causes a problem for the teacher

student-owned problems problems in which the student's behavior causes a problem for the student

the nature and the ownership of the problem. A teacher working with any child, but specifically one who is a chronic violator of classroom rules and procedures, needs to identify who owns the problem as the essential first step to successful intervention. Classroom problems can be placed into one of two categories: (1) **teacher-owned problems**, where the student's behavior causes a problem for the teacher; or (2) **student-owned problems**, where the behavior is causing a problem for the student.

Resolving Teacher-Owned Problems

For handling teacher-owned problems, Gordon (1989) suggests appropriate and effective confrontive skills. According to Gordon, teachers can meet their needs by appropriately confronting the misbehavior with a positive, nonadversarial approach. Gordon suggests the use of "I messages," "shifting gears," and "no-lose" conflict resolution strategies as part of an effective confrontive approach to teacher-owned problems.

Communicating through "I" messages. Since the ownership of the problem is with the teacher, Gordon (1989) suggests phrasing the problem from the perspective of "I" rather than a scolding "you." An **I message** communicates the specific behavior that is causing the teacher the problem along with how the teacher feels about the behavior and why that behavior is causing a problem. For example, a teacher who encounters three of his students in the back of the class talking and not attending might state: "When others are talking as they are now, I feel upset and concerned since it makes it difficult to complete the work selected for today's class." What do you feel might be the impact of such an "I statement," especially when contrasted to a more blaming, attacking "you message" such as, "You guys in the back stop acting like infants. Knock off the loud talking!"

The importance of the way a teacher communicates, as a factor influencing the nature and climate of the classroom, has been suggested by others as well as Gordon (e.g., Ginott 1971; Glasser, 1990).

Shifting gears. It is not unusual for a teacher's "I message" to elicit a defensive reaction from the student. Although this may not have been intended, the student may become defensive. When this occurs, Gordon suggests that the teacher **shift gears**, moving from asserting her own statement of concern to listening and understanding the position of the student. Such a shift will allow the student to feel less threatened, less coerced, and more considered. For example, in the situation previously highlighted, the teacher asserts: "When others are talking as they are now, I feel upset and concerned, since it makes it difficult to complete the work for today's class." Assume that one of the students responds somewhat emotionally: "This class is not always the most important thing in somebody's life! Some of us have REAL concerns." Recognizing that, at least for that student, other issues are interfering with his ability to follow class rules, the teacher might shift gears, away from asserting the rule of no talking. Shifting gears, the teacher needs to demonstrate sensitivity and understanding of the student-owned prob-

I message non-accusatory statements about how something is affecting a person

shifting gears a strategy to reduce student defensiveness by moving from asserting the teacher's own statement of concern to listening and understanding the position of the student

lem. Such a teacher might state: "It sounds like there might be a lot going on right now. Is there something I can do to help?" Or "You sound very upset. Would you like to go get a drink of water or simply take a moment to compose yourself?" In addition to active listening, the teacher redirects the student. Such a shifting of gears can defuse the student's defensiveness and perhaps invite a sharing of the student-owned problem. In those cases in which the student does not wish to share the problem, such a shifting may allow the time and support they need to refocus on the work at hand.

Using no-lose methods of conflict resolution. A third skill that Gordon advises is the use of **no-lose conflict resolution**, which attempts to defuse the situation and bring about a solution that is acceptable to all involved. This is contrasted to a win-lose dynamic, which typically pits one person (the teacher) against another (the student) in a struggle for which there will be only one winner.

no-lose conflict resolution a strategy for conflict resolution in which both parties' needs are met

No-lose methods require that the teacher minimize authoritative control over the student and approach the situation from a position of interdependence. Taking a no-lose approach to conflict resolution invites the parties to begin to operate from the perspective that the satisfaction of one person's needs is intricately connected to the satisfaction of the other person's needs. Table 10.4 identifies the steps involved in developing a no-lose approach to conflict resolution.

Table 10.4   No-Lose Conflict Resolution

Step 1: *Define the problem.* Identify in very clear and concrete terms what that each party is attempting to achieve. This is perhaps the most important and most difficult step. Often, when taking a closer look at a conflict one may find that the parties are arguing over incompatible strategies to two different needs, and if the needs and goals were highlighted, creative solutions, satisfactory to both, could be found. For example, a student may find it difficult to sit still for a great length of time. In fact, he may find sitting to actually impede learning. As a result he moves from his seat whenever he begins to feel frustrated. Similarly, a teacher recognizes that such out of the seat behavior is distracting to the other students in the class and results in some interference to their learning. Now, if the conflict was regarding "in" or "out" of seat behavior, then there could only be one person who would be satisfied. However, when looked at from the perspective of what goal each party is attempting to achieve—in the case of the student, to reduce frustration, for the teacher, to reduce distraction—a solution, such as allowing the student to "run" notes once a unit is complete, or moving the student's desk to the back so that he could stand or stretch without distracting others, may be found which would be mutually satisfying. So being clear on what the goal is for each of the parties involved is essential to the no-lose strategy.

Step 2: *Generate possible solutions.* It is important to develop as many solutions as possible. Using techniques such as brainstorming (Osborn, 1957; Corey, 1990; Parsons 1995) can often lead to creative solutions.

Step 3: *Assessing and selecting a solution.* After generating a list of possible solutions, all involved must evaluate the possible solutions, to identify which solutions provide the most benefit with the least cost to all involved (Corey, 1990; Parsons, 1995).

Step 4: *Implement the selected solution.*

Step 5: *Review and assess.* It is important to review and assess how well the solution worked and be willing to revisit the process.

Resolving Student-Owned Problems

active listening the ability to attend and reflect the essence of a message conveyed by another

When working with student-owned problems, Gordon (1989) suggests the use of helping skills such as **active listening**, acceptance, and valuing of the students. In addition to using skills that facilitate the student's sharing of his or her problem, it is also important for teachers to understand when and how to involve others with the student and his or her problem. We suggest that teachers working with a student-owned problem learn when and how to reach out as well as when and how to refer.

Reaching out. The focus is to create a condition where the student can freely express their problems and feel accepted and understood. Thus, instead of telling the student what to do or not do, the teacher simply demonstrates a willingness to listen and try to understand. The skills employed convey to students that they are respected and valued and that the teacher is able and willing to listen and support them in this time of need.

The specific skills needed for such helping are beyond the scope of this chapter. Readers interested in learning more about these helping skills are referred to a counseling primer such as *The Skills of Helping* (Parsons, 1995).

Referring when necessary. In addition to Gordon's suggestions for providing caring support to a student with a student-owned problem, a teacher may need to know when and how to find the student additional, professional assistance. It is important for teachers to understand the various student support services available within their school, school district, and community (e.g., counselors, psychologists, academic support, social workers, health care, etc.). It is also important to understand how to access these services. A visit to the school psychologist or counselor's office might be the first step in identifying and employing these services. For those interested in learning more about knowing when and how to make a referral, we recommend a counseling primer (e.g., Corey, 1990; Parsons, 1995; Parsons & Wicks, 1994).

Reflections from the Field

Facing the Challenges to Classroom Management

1 I have been teaching seriously emotionally disabled students for seven years. The best advice that I can give to a new teacher includes the following. There is never a reason to argue with a student. If there is a discussion that needs to take place, it is most helpful to wait until the student is ready. There will always be enough time to take care of a problem . . . don't rush it! When a student begins to argue, he/she needs to be told, "You're arguing, and you need to stop." Coupling statements can work wonders by allowing the teacher to remain emotionally distant, yet mentally prepared to handle difficulties.

—Ann F. (special educator), Decatur, IL

2 I just read a book *"Positive Classroom discipline"* by Fred Jones. It is a must. It has teaching strategies that encourage and reward positive behaviors from students. Limit-setting, communicating with body language, and responsibility training . . . great stuff.

—Vicki T. (seventh grade art teacher), Miami, FL

3 I like the concept of keeping expectations simple. No class rules, just procedures! For broken rules, there must be consequences. For disregarded procedures, there must be re-teaching. If these procedures are few in number and rather generic, then you can continue to reteach them, ask for each procedure to be demonstrated by individual and student groups, until they become almost a mantra. For example, (1) Eyes on me or on the board; (2) Ears—listening; (3) Hands to yourself or on your desk; (4) Mouths—quiet or one at a time or after being called on; (5) Bodies—still or in your own personal space.

—Maryanne M. (resource room teacher, middle school), Detroit, MI

4 Here's an idea for controlling the number of times kids call out for help, thus reducing the disruption. I have my students working at computer lab, and they are to use a colored card on top of the computer to alert my attention. White means it's fine, yellow they have a question but it is not urgent, and red means come quick (usually the computer has crashed). It is a nice way to keep everyone working without neglecting those who need help.

—Adam H. (computer science teacher, high school), Boston, MA

5 I'm a first year teacher with a fifth grade class. I use a system of behavior folders that go home every Friday to be signed by a parent. In the folders, I document on a chart any class rule that the student may have broken. I send a letter home to be signed by the parents letting them know what the class rules are and what the consequences will be if the children break the rules. This really does work for the majority of my class. I also use a group point chart, and each time I see a group following directions, I give that group points. Each Friday, I reward the group with the most points with a treat (maybe a free homework pass or stickers). I also send postcards home to parents when a student has really worked on improving his/her behavior. Communicating with parents seems to be the thing that works best!

—Juan C. (fifth grade social studies teacher), Camden, NJ

THEORY TO PRACTICE

Ms. Thompson, Decision Maker and Classroom Manager

We opened this chapter describing the first day in Ms. Thompson's classroom. In that scene, we are given an opportunity to watch as a new teacher enters her classroom for the first time. We can only assume that this teacher had given some thought to the prevention of classroom problems through the development of rituals and rules. However, regardless of the amount of thinking she had given to classroom management, prior to entering the classroom, much of this preparation may need to be adjusted, given the reality she experienced during those first few moments of that initial class. Without the appropriate number of chairs, with children showing emotional upset, and unexpected interruptions from the main office, Ms. Thomspon will need to be a flexible, adapative decision maker.

Entering her class, she was soon greeted by multiple demands and challenges. Some of her students were simply walking around, talking, teasing each other, investigating the gerbils and the materials in the back of the room, and some simply stood looking confused, without desks to go to. Ms. Thompson was confronted by the need for a classroom—not a student—to be managed! It would appear that many of these students had not learned appropriate school behaviors (*schoolization*), or, if they had, were choosing not to employ them. It would be this teacher's role to teach them. Continuing our observations of this new teacher, we find her rearranging the room so that students who were standing are now seated; students who appeared most upset or anxious moved to the front; and *routines* regarding homework, weekly quizzes, and board work are all discussed, posted, and initiated.

The transformation of this room of multiple, often conflicting, demands into a learning environment is dramatic, yet it is a transformation performed daily by every effective teacher. While the chaos often experienced in the beginning of any new school year, or even any new school day, can be challenging, effective teachers like Ms. Thompson will employ the principles discussed in this chapter to transform these classrooms into effective learning environments. As we continue our observation of Ms. Thompon, we see her as a teacher who provides enthusiastic, creative learning activities (*worthwhile activities*), in which she moves smoothly and continuously from one activity to another (*momentum, smoothness*). Further, she engages her students individually, and collectively, through choral responding as a way of maintaining *group attention*.

Throughout the next few days, we see Ms. Thompson not only discussing the need for rules but

assisting her students in identifying the rules that seem appropriate for this class. Through this process, the students not only learn to know the *rules* of the class but own them as well. They will come to class with their homework and the materials they need for their class work. And when the rules are violated, perhaps when a student comes late to class, not only will Ms. Thompson give evidence of knowing the rule and the rule violation but so will the violator and the other students. Similarly, when we see a student resisting a *routine* of engaging in independent quiet reading and engaging, rather, in note writing and talking to those around her, we also see students asking her to please be quiet and read. When this occurs, we can see that the rules and the routines were not simply imposed but were in fact embraced by the students. Continuing with our observations, we note that the students' requests for our independent reader to be quiet prove ineffective. Ms. Thompson then approaches the girl, asking her what is wrong, and then reminds her that if she cannot do what is expected now, then she would have to come later, losing her free time, to do her work (*response cost*). The reprimand is given in a tone of voice that only she could hear (*soft reprimand*), thus reducing the chance of embarrassing her or inviting her into a power struggle.

Throughout our observations of Ms. Thompson, it becomes clear that she is a teacher who was consistent, yet flexible. She exhibited "withitness," knowing when one student came late, even though her back was to the student and she was writing on the board. When disruptions occurred, she was able to identify who owned the problem and adjusted her interventions accordingly. For example, when one student put her head down on the desk, apparently upset, Ms. Thompson *shifted* focus from attempting to enforce the rules of the classroom, to calling for seat work, and directed the class to continue on their own (*overlapping*) while she went down to the girl's seat and asked her to come out in the hall, where Ms.Thompson provided caring and support (*helping skills*) for this student who was experiencing her own personal problems (*student-owned problem*).

All was not perfect in this class for every student. Ms. Thompson became aware that this little girl was having serious emotional and academic problems, and was in need of additional assistance. The student demonstrated extreme frustration at the work she was attempting, poor self-esteem, and a feeling of extreme sadness. She is certainly a student in need of *remediation*, and the teacher decided to call on the assistance of the school psychologist for additional support or *referral*.

You as Teacher, as Decision Maker, as Classroom Manager

Case Illustration 1:
Summer Preparation for One Second Grade Teacher

Below, you will find a description of how one second grade teacher prepared during the summer for the upcoming school year. As you read about her actions and her decisions, see if you can identify which principles, concepts, or theories, discussed in this chapter, are reflected in her own behaviors. Specifically, see if you can identify evidence or examples of

◆ Prevention planning

◆ Withitness,

◆ Focus on classroom management verses individual discipline,

◆ Hierarchy of response,

◆ Establishing an effective classroom through rules and routines,

◆ Diagnosing student and teacher problems,

◆ Schoolization and developmental appropriateness,

◆ Response costs.

It's August and Maura Kelly is busy thinking about the upcoming school year and her second grade class. Maura has been teaching second grade for the last ten years, and yet each summer she devotes a lot of energy to the preparation of her learning objectives, activities, and materials.

Maura's experience has taught her that the children, while eager to please, also come to her after a summer of running, yelling, playing, etc. Further, she is aware that while such activities are clearly very healthy summertime fun, they can prove quite disruptive to the learning process if they are carried over into the classroom. She is presently making up posters which dramatize the *rules* of the class. For example:

Rule: Raise your hand and be recognized by the teacher before answering in class (a brightly painted poster showing students eagerly raising their hands).

Rule: Take your seat when the bell rings (again the poster shows the clock pointing to 8:15 and all the children taking their seats).

Rule: Clean up all of your materials at the end of class and place your materials in your cubby.

Rule: Never fight, push, or scream on the playground or in class.

In addition to making up the posters showing each rule, Maura develops a couple of "role plays" that she wants to use. She intends to have the children act out what each rule looks like and how violating the rule may appear.

Next Maura makes a big poster that will remain on the bulletin board stating the *consequences* for the rule violation. The list is as follows:

Rule Is Broken	*Consequence*
First Time—no ☹	You will get a reminder, a warning.
Second time—no ☹ ☹	You will have to miss five minutes of recess.
Third time—no ☹ ☹ ☹	You will miss ten minutes of recess, and you and I will work out a plan to help you follow the rules.
Fourth time—no ☹ ☹ ☹ ☹	We will need to call your mom and dad and see if they can help us to help you follow the rules.

In addition to making up the rules for the class, Maura is also busy establishing the procedures she will be using to take roll, collect homework, pass out papers, and respond to children who need to go to the nurse or to the bathroom, or who may come late. There are a lot of routines that need to be considered.

As the first day of class approaches, Maura develops her lesson plans (including an assessment process) for the first few days of class. The primary focus for these initial lessons is on teaching the classroom management plan to the students. Clearly, if children are to become self-controlled and responsible, they need to understand what is expected and how to achieve it. Therefore, if the classroom management plan is to be effective, it will not be enough just to read and post the rules and consequences with an outline of the routines. She will need to (1) explain why these are needed, (2) demonstrate how each desired behavior looks, (3) discuss the consequences (both positive and negative) for those who follow or violate the rules, respectively, and (4) check the students' understanding. This year she decides to have the students take home the list of rules and share them with their parents. Further, as a homework activity, she wants the children, with their parents or guardians, to identify which rules will be easy to follow and which rules may be more difficult to learn. She intends to use the homework response as a way of identifying the children who may need additional assistance to develop appropriate schooling behaviors.

The only other thing that Maura considers as she prepares for that first day is whether she should have her hair cut shorter. As she states with a grin: "You know, so that I have an unobstructed view with the eyes in the back of my head."

Case Illustration 2:
You, Challenged and Confronted

Imagine that you are teaching high school in an urban setting. At the end of your first period class, two students approach you. They swagger up to you, presenting as "tough guys" and attempt to negotiate with you to get passing grades just by coming to class. As you resist, they threaten you, and one even taps you on the cheek in a symbolic slapping motion.

While these two would be the exception to any classroom, the reality is that they do represent one portion of the student population you may encounter. Along with a colleague, consider each of the following questions as you begin to plan your management strategies.

1. Is this an issue of prevention, intervention, or remediation?
2. Would RIP or RRP work in this situation?
3. Would you attempt to use response costs?
4. Would applied behavioral analysis be useful? Alternative response training?
5. How might you use no-lose conflict resolution or contingency management?
6. How would you use this situation to respond to your entire class on the next day?

SUMMARY

Classroom Management: More than Student Control/ Student Discipline

The terms "classroom management" and "discipline" are often used interchangeably. The term "discipline" has two significant limitations. First, "discipline" highlights the individual (rather than the classroom), and secondly it connotes negative behavior only. Classroom management is the term used to highlight *all of those positive behaviors and decisions a teacher makes to facilitate the learning process of the students.*

The aim of such classroom management is to create and maintain a positive, productive learning environment. The goals of an effective classroom management plan are

1. To assist students to keep task focus,
2. To reduce detractions to learning,
3. To organize and facilitate the flow of learning activities,
4. To help the students to be better able to manage themselves.

Classroom Management: Reflecting Student Development Needs

As a process of teaching appropriate "schooling behaviors," classroom management procedures need to take into consideration the child's developmental level.

The major focus during the *early school years* is on socializing the child to the role of student. A testing of the routines appears during the *middle school years.* Developmentally, a student's interest and control shift from adults to peers. As such, the student may resist the teacher as authority. Classroom management procedures will need to be developed that focus on compliance, rather than instruction. With the exception of serious problems, which will require special attention and remediation, most of the students by *high school* are mature and socialized to the school environment. Classroom management should take less energy and time.

Focusing on the Many as Well as the Few

Classroom management procedures, as facilitators to the leaning process, should be designed in ways to be maximally beneficial for all the students within your classroom and not targeted just for the disruptive child. The majority of them (80 percent) have developed the appropriate school behaviors and rarely break rules. Classroom management procedures for these students need to be designed and implemented in ways that support these students (preventive planning), acting as reminders of desired behavior and refocusing them when they are in violation of the rules of the classroom. A few students (15 percent) may break the rules with some regularity. These students need clear, consistent guidelines, expectations, and consequences. They are in need of a classroom structure and set of procedures (intervention strategies) that will reduce the frequency and degree of their disruption, as well as restrain their disruptive behaviors and refocus them on the appropriate, facilitative schooling behaviors. Finally, the last 5 percent are those students who are chronic rule breakers and in need of remediation.

Prevention

Teachers who see classroom management as a process of "establishing and maintaining effective learning environments tend to be more successful than teachers who place more emphasis on their roles as authority figures or disciplinarians" (Good & Brophy, 1994, p. 129).

To establish an effective learning environment, geared to the prevention of disruptions, a teacher needs to (1) provide worthwhile classroom activities, (2) establish routines that facilitate progression, and (3) establish rules for classroom behaviors. Further, teachers who appear to establish and maintain effective learning environments also demonstrate: "withitness," "momentum and smoothness," "group alerting," "student accountability," "overlapping," "satiation and challenge."

Intervention

Sometimes everyone can have a bad day and may engage in activities that are not instructionally related or task focused. Any disciplinary intervention employed at these times should be aimed at

1. stopping, suppressing, or redirecting the misbehavior; and

2. serving as an opportunity and method to foster the development of the appropriate classroom response.

Most "off-task" behaviors can be effectively managed by unobtrusive techniques that alert students to your awareness of their misbehavior and perhaps redirect them to task. These unobtrusive reminders include actions such moving closer to the student, making eye contact, or even some facial gesture (e.g., a frown). More serious or continued misbehavior will need more direct action, with the appropriate application of consequences.

Two approaches to responding to misbehavior are the Rule-Ignore-Praise (RIP) and Rule-Reinforce-Punish (RRP) methods. In addition to stopping misbehavior, we want to use the incident of misbehavior as a teachable moment. The goal for such intervention is to increase effective, appropriate behaviors rather than simply to suppress misbehavior. Thus, when providing a more direct intervention, it is important to remind the student of the rule that is being violated and the consequence assigned, before applying the consequence.

One model of intervention discussed is assertive discipline (Canter, 1992). The central focus of Canter's approach is on having teachers take responsibility for and in the classroom. Being an assertive teacher does not suggest or imply that one is uncaring or hostile. Rather, Canter (1992, 1988) sees assertive teachers as caring about themselves and their students so that they will not allow students to take advantage of them or behave in ways that harm themselves. This caring is demonstrated through the development of assertive discipline into their teaching styles, a style that includes each of the following:

- Recognizing and removing roadblocks to assertive discipline,
- Practicing an assertive response style,
- Making a discipline plan that contains good rules and effective consequences,
- Teaching the discipline plan to students,
- Teaching students how to behave responsibly.

Remediation

It is important for the classroom teacher to understand how to intervene with chronic disrupters and, when necessary, how to work with others (e.g., counselors, school psychologists, parents) in helping these children adapt to the learning environment. Three approaches: applied behavior analysis, contingency management, and alternative response training were discussed.

The process of applied behavior analysis requires that the behavior, along with the conditions/events that seem to precede and follow it, be identified. By identifying the (A)ntecedent conditions, the (B)ehavior and the (C)onsequences, a teacher may be able to develop a clearer understanding of how to manipulate the environmental conditions that seem to be eliciting or supporting these behaviors

Contingency contracting is a process by which a student and a teacher actually sign a contract indicating which behaviors are desired and which consequences will result from performing and not performing these behaviors. Often, however, students who chronically misbehave do so, because they simply do not know how not to misbehave or do not know what to do in the place of misbehavior. Under these conditions, the child needs to be taught alternative responses.

One model discussed, which seems to have value when working with those chronically misbehaving, is the Gordon Model: discipline through self-control. Gordon's perspective is that good classroom management results, ultimately, in the students' developing their own inner sense of self-control. The techniques and approaches he suggests emphasize "teaching" rather than controlling or coercing. Brophy and Rohrkemper (1981) found that teachers rated as effective by both their principals and classroom observers behaved in ways generally consistent with the principles advocated by Gordon. That is, they (1) were willing to assume responsibility for solving problems; (2) they worked with problem students (rather than excluding); (3) they used long-term solution-oriented approaches (instead of controlling, punitive techniques); and (4) they focused on helping the student understand and cope with the problems underlying their disruptive behaviors.

◆ Field Experience Questions

Developing your own classroom management plan!

In addition to performing your own research as a guide to practice, it is also useful to observe other teachers as they practice their profession and discuss with them the rationales for the decisions they make. This can be a very beneficial way of turning the theory of classroom management into a reality. It is also a useful strategy for stimulating the development of your own management plan.

Below you will find a series of field experience questions related to the topics covered in this chapter. You may find that the data you collect while observing a teacher in action will not only help you to answer these questions but may also provide greater insight and understanding of the concepts discussed within this chapter.

1. Was there evidence of prevention planning or was the approach one of reaction to disruption?

2. Based on your observations, was there a connection between class disruption and a loss of classroom momentum or smoothness?

3. What specific routines did you observe, and how did they help in making the class maintain momentum and smoothness, even through transitions.

4. In your observations, was there evidence of RIP or RRP plans of intervention? In your opinion, were they effective?

5. If you observed a teacher reprimand a student, was it "loud" or "soft"? What was the impact of the reprimand?

6. Did the classroom routines and rules appear to be developmentally appropriate for the students in that class?

7. Did the routines and rules reflect an orientation of teacher authority and control or one of student responsibility and self-control?

8. Were there any examples of alternative response training or contingency contracting?

9. Were there any examples of "I messages" or "shifting gears"? What was their effect?

◆ Key Terms

active listening	momentum	satiation
alternative response training	no-lose conflict resolution	schoolization
applied behavior analysis	overlapping	shifting gears
closing space	prevention	smoothness
contingency contracting	punishment	soft reprimand
group alerting	RIP (rules-ignore-praise)	student accountability
helping skills	RRP (rules-reward-punishment)	student-owned problems
I message	response cost	teacher-owned problems
loud reprimand	routines	valence
misbehavior	rules	withitness

◆ Additional Resources

Albert, L. (1996). *A teacher's guide to cooperative discipline* (rev. ed.). Circle Pines, MN: American Guidance Service (original work published 1989).

Blendinger, J., et al. (1993). *Win-win discipline.* Bloomington, IN: Phi Delta Kappa Educational Foundation.

Kohn, A. (1996). *Beyond discipline: From compliance to community.* Alexandria, VA: Association for Supervision and Curriculum Development.

Schell, L., & Burden, P. (1992). *Countdown to the first day of school: a 60 day get-ready checklist for first time teachers, teacher transfers, student teachers, teacher mentors, induction-program administrators, teacher educators* (NEA Checklist series). Washington, DC: National Educational Association.

Weinstein, C. S. (1996). Secondary classroom management: Lessons from research and practice. New York: McGraw-Hill.

Weinstein, C. S., & Mignano, A. J., Jr. (1997). *Elementary classroom management: Lessons from research and practice* (2nd Ed.). New York: McGraw-Hill.

Planning: Essential to Instruction

1 magine you are Sarah, a brand new teacher, entering your school for the first time. Certainly, you are nervous, but after all, you have prepared. You know your material. You have expertise in your field. You are ready to meet your class.

However, as you approach the front desk of the main office to introduce yourself and locate your classroom, you are told that the classes you were to teach in American government have been given to another teacher because of a last-minute retirement. Rather than teaching the class for which you are prepared, you are told that you will be teaching American history instead.

The secretary in the school office also informs you that you will be a "floater," meaning that you will not teach any of your classes in the same room, but move from classroom to classroom. As you enter your first class, a teaching colleague also mentions to you that there are not enough history books to go around.

A disaster—not quite! A set back—most certainly! This depiction of a teacher's first day is indeed unsettling and requires Sarah to regroup and rethink her plans. Being a creative, flexible, and effective planner will be critical to Sarah's success. As Sarah begins to regroup and prepare for her American history classes, she, like all effective teachers, has to consider many things. Certainly, as part of her planning, she needs to answer questions about "What" was she going to teach and "How" was she going to teach it. But to answer these questions fully, she needs to consider many things as she develops this plan, including the expectations of the school, the age and ability of her students, the students' prior background with history, the students' attitudes toward history, the materials that will be required, the adaptations that may have to be made for students with special needs—just to name a few. In Chapter 1, we learned that teaching is a decision-making process. In this chapter, we will learn that planning for instruction is a critical part of that decision-making process. We will consider the purposes or functions of planning. Next we will review terminology related to planning and how lesson planning fits into the broader educational system. We also will overview research done on teacher planning with respect to the models and types of planning used by teachers as well as the factors which affect teachers' planning decisions. In addition, we will review the three taxonomies of objectives and how to write an instructional objective. We will also consider Gagne's outcomes of instruction. Finally, we will describe the Hunter planning model as well as some alternatives to this model.

◆ Chapter Objectives

When you have mastered the material in this chapter you will be able to

1 Explain at least three purposes of instructional planning for the classroom teacher;

2 Distinguish between a goal and an objective;

3 List five major factors found to influence teacher planning;

4 Explain Mager's three-step model for writing behavioral objectives;

5 Differentiate among the nature of objectives found in the cognitive, affective, and psychomotor domains;

6 Specify what each level of Bloom's taxonomy requires the learner to do;

7 List the five different levels of affective objectives;

8 Describe what each level of the psychomotor taxonomy requires the learner to do;

9 Describe Gagne's five types of learning capabilities or outcomes;

10 Identify the seven steps of the Hunter planning model;

11 Give an example of how each step of the Hunter planning model could be used in a lesson;

12 Summarize the major differences between a direct instruction model of planning and a constructivist model;

13 Discuss the difference between a thematic unit and an integrated thematic unit.

CHAPTER 11 CONTENT MAP

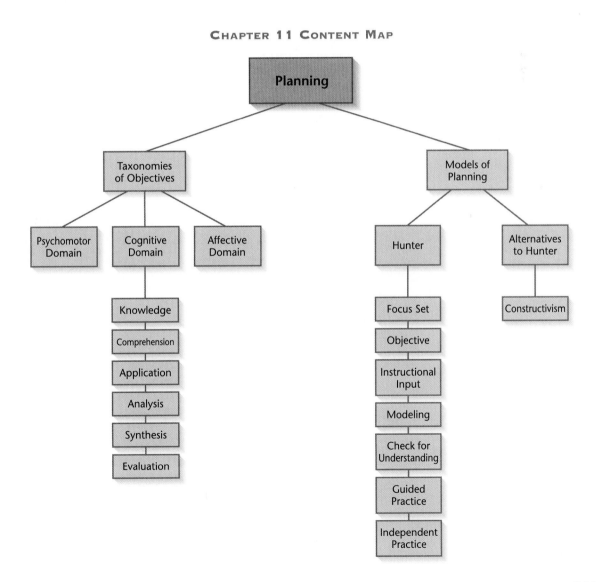

THE PURPOSES OF PLANNING

As in any other aspect of life, planning ahead enables us to be prepared. Imagine walking into a room of highly active, very energetic seventh graders without having a clue about how to spend the next forty-five to fifty minutes. Now add to this picture the fact that this is only one period out of the next 140 or more that you will spend, not only with this class, but with perhaps four or five additional classes, and the value of planning and preparation becomes quite obvious.

One of the key functions of planning for a teacher is organization. Have you ever taken a class in college that appeared disorganized? How did this make you feel as a student? Probably very frustrated and perhaps even confused. On the other hand, think about the well-organized lessons you have observed—lessons that are appropriate for the level of the students, that are logical in organization, and in which needed materials are readily available, lessons, in other words, in which learning takes place from start to finish with little "down time." Such lessons do not occur accidentally; they are a byproduct of adequate planning.

Another function served by planning is that it builds a teacher's confidence, particularly if you are a student teacher or a new teacher (Clark & Peterson, 1986). While all teachers experience some "performance anxiety," this anxiety can certainly be mitigated with sound planning. In other words, you'll feel less anxious if you have a firm grasp of the content that you are teaching, have planned a lesson

One of the key functions of planning is organization. ◆

appropriate for the level of the students, have planned so that all necessary materials are available, have planned and structured so that there is a flow to the lesson, and have more than enough planned for the time allotted. There is an additional benefit that results from the fact that you feel more confident. You are going to appear more confident to your students. This aura of confidence will lead them to respect you and anticipate that yours will be a valuable and effective class.

Still another purpose of planning is that it affords teachers the opportunity to solve a myriad of problems, often before these problems even emerge! We have already suggested how this might be true in the area of classroom management. But even beyond the question of management, planning can help a teacher to know how and when to condense content, how to motivate students, and how to assess student performance (Borko, Lalik, & Tomchin, 1987; Calderhead, 1984, 1993).

It should be obvious that without adequate course and lesson planning, effective teaching is impossible. Effective teachers not only plan before teaching but also after they teach as they reflect upon the quality of their teaching and how they can change their plans in the future.

YOU MAKE THE CALL

OFTEN, EVEN THE BEST LAID PLANS OF . . .

Imagine that a student teacher who is teaching her second lesson is following a step-by-step plan that isn't going well. Do you think the student teacher will be likely to drop her plan in an effort to improve instruction or continue with the original plan? Why? Now, suppose an experienced teacher faces this same scenario. Would you predict that this teacher will discard her plan to improve instruction or continue with the original plan? Why? Remember teaching is a decision-making process—planning simply provides a guide or a structure to operate within. Effective teachers are able to adapt and adjust as the "what" and the "who" interact with the "how" of their teaching.

CLASSROOM PLANNING: REFLECTING THE MISSION OF THE EDUCATIONAL SYSTEM

Perhaps you have been in a class where a student asks a teacher, "Why do we have to know this?" Perhaps you were that student—or may one day be that teacher. How will you respond to that student's questions? Relying on statements such as "because I said so" will simply not do. The question is important and deserves a reasonable explanation. Part of that explanation can be found in understanding the mission, goals, and objectives of the educational system in which the teacher is employed.

It is important to understand that teachers often make their plans for instruction in the context of the mission or purpose for which the community has invested in this educational system and for goals that a community has decided its members should achieve.

Thus, at the most fundamental level, a school's mission is to fulfill the educational needs that have been identified for its community members. Many districts and schools now display framed copies of their **mission statements** in their offices and hallways. These are, however, very important statements and not simply wall hangings. The unique needs of any one community may dictate that the types of educational programs to be delivered may be different from those of another community. With this in mind, it behooves you, as future teachers, to understand the mission of the schools to which you apply and to think critically about the implications the mission may have on the "what," the "who," and the "how" of your teaching.

mission statement statement defining the purpose of school and its unique characteristics

While the mission tends to be quite succinct and often written in somewhat global terms, a more expanded and concrete presentation of the goals of a school district can be found in a direct outgrowth of its mission, the academic and **unit goals.** These unit goals pertain to a particular unit of study and thus are more closely related to classroom teaching than mission goals.

unit goals objectives written for a unit of instruction that centers on one theme and usually lasts several weeks

goals broad or general educational outcome

You may be wondering how these **goals** are translated into practice. Typically, school districts have **curriculum guides**, which contain goal statements followed by student instructional objectives. **Objectives** state what students should be able to do; they may be specified for programs, units, or individual lessons. Objectives are much more specific than goals as explained in the following example.

curriculum guide specifies district instructional goals for various subject matters and grade levels

objective a specific instructional goal

Let's return to the initial scenario in this chapter. As Sarah begins to plan for her American history classes, she will need to identify the specific things she hopes to have her students do. For example, one goal for this class might be understanding how conflict, caused by economic, social, or political reasons, may be postponed but not necessarily prevented by compromise. A particular unit goal might include understanding the major causes of the Civil War. However, under the unit goal of understanding the major causes of the Civil War, you may find these specific instructional objectives:

1. Describe how Eli Whitney's invention of the cotton gin made it possible for the South to supply most of the world's cotton.

2. Explain the terms of the Missouri Compromise.

3. Discuss why Southerners came to believe that slavery was essential to their economic survival.

In theory, when presented with this new job expectation, Sarah would have to turn to the school district's curriculum guide before planning what topics to teach. In order to estimate how long she would spend on the Civil War, she also has to have a good idea about what other topics her district wants her to cover during the school year. As you can see, teachers nearly always must plan their daily lessons in a broader context. Further, the teacher who plans within this broader context will be able to respond to the student who asks "Why do we have to know this?" with an explanation of connectedness from topic to topic, from unit to unit; and from course to course, all reflecting an integrated plan for addressing the identified needs of members within their community. Be especially cognizant of this issue as you work with diverse student populations.

YOU MAKE THE CALL

THE VALUE OF KNOWING THE OBJECTIVE!

Think back to your own schooling. How often did your own teachers share specific instructional objectives with you? If teachers routinely share instructional objectives with students, what effect do you imagine this may have on the class?

FACTORS AFFECTING PLANNING

A host of factors affects the way in which teachers plan and how they make planning decisions. We will review factors that recent research has indicated influence the planning of both experienced and novice teachers.

◆ Experienced Teacher Planning

Research has shown that the plans of experienced teachers are affected by the school calendar, the physical facilities of the school, the content of textbooks, standardized tests, curriculum guides, and a variety of student characteristics (Brophy, 1982). Additional research has also demonstrated the influence of the principal's planning requirements, interruptions in the flow of activities within a given period, school schedule interruptions, students' interests and abilities, the availability of materials, and previous teaching experience (McCutcheon, 1980). Other work has shown that in-service programs, professional journals, and colleagues are also important influences on teacher planning (Sardo-Brown, 1990).

You may be wondering which of all of these influences are the most important. While that probably depends on where you teach and your years of teaching experience, one study has offered some intriguing answers (Sardo-Brown, 1988). In this

Teacher Tool Box
First Steps in Planning

◆ During student teaching, try to make sure you have access to all the necessary materials that frame your daily lesson plans. These may include such items as your co-operating teacher's unit plans, several different resources for textbooks, and the district curriculum guide objectives for your grade level and subject.

◆ In addition, make sure you consult your school calendar when making plans, as this alerts you to special events such as assemblies and early dismissals. Also have a calendar of marking term dates available, including dates by which grades must be handed in.

◆ Allow yourself plenty of time to order necessary materials. These often include audiovisual equipment as well as films, videotapes, records, and other library materials.

study of unit planning among middle school teachers, objectives listed in the district curriculum guide and in state competencies were found to influence planning "often" to "very often" (see Table 11.1) The only factors to influence the planning of this sample of teachers more often were students' previous learning and teachers' lesson goal beliefs.

♦ Novice Teacher Planning

Research indicates that some additional factors to these may strongly influence novice teacher planning (Bullough, 1987; Sardo-Brown, 1993). These factors that affect novice planning include the influence of cooperating teachers during student teaching, university supervisors, and

Table 11.1 Influences on Unit Planning of Twelve Middle School Teachers

Rank	Influence	Mean Rating
1	Student learning	1.17
2	Lesson goal beliefs	1.33
3	**District curriculum guides, objectives**	**1.66**
4	Orderly transition between activities	1.68
5	Student attention	1.75
6	**State competencies**	**1.81**
7	Previous teaching experiences	1.83
8	Avoidance of interruptions during class	1.91
9	**State objectives**	**2.08**
10	Teaching team requirements	2.17
11	**State curriculum guides**	**2.33**
12	Principal's requirements	2.54
13	Standardized tests	2.63
14	Parents	2.75
15	Department chairperson's requirements	2.90
16	Other teacher's suggestions	2.91
17	Professional journals	3.25
18	In-service training	3.33
19	Undergraduate training, textbooks	3.75
20	Teachers' manual	4.08

Note: 1 = very often influences; 2 = often influences; 3 = sometimes influences; 4 = rarely influences; 5 = never influences

Source: Adapted with permission from D. S. Brown, 1986, unpublished doctoral dissertation entitled "A Case Study of Twelve Middle School Teachers' Planning", University of Delaware, Newark, DE.

mentor teachers, as well as perceptions of one's subject matter. In addition, a variety of "newcomer stresses" were identified as profound influences on planning. These included learning and establishing beginning-of-the-year routines and procedures, attempts to fit in socially with teaching colleagues, and a variety of curricular decisions such as learning content, adjusting the pace of instruction, developing a grading system, and designing long-range plans. More recent studies also have suggested that factors related to the psychosocial development of the novice teacher may affect planning. These could include changes in social status or relationships such as a new marriage (Sardo-Brown, 1996a; Sorenson, 1993) or changes in developmental interests or needs, as might be the case as teachers enter Erikson's generativity stage (Sardo-Brown, 1996b). As you can see, planning is both a complicated process and a process complicated by many other issues!

INSTRUCTIONAL OBJECTIVES

One of the most widely emphasized topics in preservice teacher education courses concerns how to write instructional objectives. Think about it. If you are not sure what you want your students to be able to do, then how can you proceed to plan the rest of your lesson? If the instructional objectives are unclear, how can you plan to assess student performance? And how will you be able to answer the questions regarding what students have learned, which may be asked by your cooperating teacher, principal, or parents?

◆ Mager's Format for Writing Objectives

A very influential system for writing instructional objectives has been developed by Robert Mager (1975). Mager emphasizes that a well-written objective, sometimes called a behavioral objective, should describe what students are doing as they demonstrate their achievement and how you, the teacher, will know that they are doing this. Mager's concept of **behavioral objective** has three parts. These include the performance component or what the student will actually do, the conditions under which this performance will be assessed or how this behavior will be recognized and tested, and the criteria for acceptable performance. Table 11.2 illustrates how Mager's system works.

Mager's three-part system or behavioral objective stipulates that a well-written objective include performance, conditions, and criterion

Let's pause to consider the case of the novice high school teacher, Rachel. An objective for her class might read as follows:

> In class, without the use of a calculator, students will be able to calculate the percentage they will save on selected items in a school bookstore sale. It is expected that students will be able to compute accurate percentages 95 percent of the time.

◆ Gronlund's Approach for Writing Objectives

An alternative approach for writing objectives has been suggested by Norman Gronlund (1995). In contrast to Mager's system, **Gronlund's**

Gronlund's instructional objective format stipulates an objective; includes a general term such as to understand or know followed by specific learner outcomes

Table 11.2 Mager's Three-Part System

Part	Central Question	Example
Student behavior	Do what?	Mark statements with an F for fact or an O for opinion
Conditions of performance	Under what conditions?	Given an article from a newspaper
Performance criteria	How well?	75% of the statements correctly marked

Source: Adapted with permission from Prentice-Hall Publishers. Eggen & Kauchak's *Educational Psychology: Windows on Classrooms,* 3rd edition, p. 447, copyright 1993.

instructional objectives include a general term such as *understand* or *know,* followed by specific learner outcomes that operationally define what we mean when we say *understand* or *know.* For instance, specific learner outcomes for *understands concepts* may include the following: (1) lists definitions of concepts; (2) labels examples of concepts; (3) formulates examples of concepts; and (4) predicts coordinate examples of concepts.

You can see that Gronlund's approach does not involve specifying conditions or criteria. Gronlund (1995) argues that in the classroom these restrict the freedom of the teacher because they result in cumbersome lists. While Mager's work is historically significant, you will find that most curriculum materials employ a variation of Gronlund's format.

DOMAINS AND TAXONOMIES OF OBJECTIVES

As we plan our courses and lessons, we will need to consider not only the content we wish to convey but also the level of complexity that is to be involved. To illustrate, consider the number of times you have had a literature course through your elementary and high school education. Why so many? Is it because pieces of literature change over time? As you reflect on your experience with reading and studying literature as a fifth grader and contrast it with the literature course you had in tenth grade, you may discover that it wasn't the content that changed, but the level at which you approached the content. Perhaps in the fifth grade course you remember having to memorize the name of central characters and events in a story, whereas the tenth grade course may have focused on helping you to understand and appreciate the underlying themes in a story and the motives of the central characters. If this reflects your experience, then you have encountered the different levels of complexity with which something can be taught.

Connections

There are several teacher chatrooms available on the Internet for teachers new to the field. Try using the following Web site to access information on lesson plans and curriculum materials. <http://california.teachers.net/chatboard/topic167/3.02.99.02.19.58.html>

In order to differentiate levels of complexity of learning, a group of educators led by Benjamin Bloom (1956) developed a system, a **taxonomy**, to classify objectives. A taxonomy is a set of classifications based on one or more principles (Krathwohl, Bloom, & Masia, 1964). They began their work by classifying learning into three broad domains or categories including cognitive (thinking), affective (having to do with attitudes and emotions), and psychomotor (having to do with physical activities). Within each domain, they then categorized objectives according to complexity. In formulating a taxonomy, an analysis of the content of objectives was considered as well as how the objectives related to each other. In other words, the taxonomy was developed around a cumulative hierarchical structure. It is important to understand that as you consider a taxonomy of objectives, the higher objectives in a taxonomy are designed to further develop the activities of the lower objectives.

taxonomy a classification system; educational taxonomies have been developed for the cognitive, affective, and psychomotor domains

◆ Cognitive Domain

The **cognitive domain** of objectives is of the utmost concern to many educators. Objectives in this domain pertain to intellectual knowledge, skills, and abilities, which are classified on the basis of increasing complexity (Bloom, 1956). The six **levels of Bloom's taxonomy** occur in increasing complexity—knowledge, comprehension, application, analysis, synthesis, and evaluation (see Table 11.3). Often, the first two levels of the taxonomy (knowledge and comprehension) are referred to as lower-level

cognitive domain a part of Bloom's taxonomy of educational objectives

levels of Bloom's taxonomy a system for the classification of cognitive teaching objectives that includes six levels; knowledge, comprehension, application, analysis, synthesis, and evaluation

Action Research

Use of Bloom's Taxonomy in Written Lesson Plans

A fter attending a student teaching practicum, Roxanne, a student teacher about midway through her fifteen-week placement with a class of sixth graders wondered if she was planning appropriately. Specifically, as she reflected on her own teaching, she became concerned that she might not be planning enough activities that involved higher level thinking as described in Bloom's taxonomy.

With the help of her cooperating teacher, she undertook an informal analysis of her lesson plans from the last six weeks. Together, Roxanne and her cooperating teacher developed a checklist containing each level of Bloom's taxonomy. Each time a planned lesson objective required students to perform at one of the six levels of Bloom's taxonomy, they would record a tally in a box next to that level. Upon completion of their analysis, they discovered that most of Roxanne's planned objectives for the thirty-two lesson plans analyzed were developed for either the knowledge, comprehension, or application levels of Bloom. Only two lesson objectives required students to perform at the analysis level, while none were written for the synthesis or evaluation levels. As a result of this action research, Roxanne now systematically consults Bloom's taxonomy as she plans her lessons to make sure that at least once a week she plans objectives at the synthesis and evaluation levels.

Table 11.3 Taxonomy for the Cognitive Domain

1.0	**Knowledge.** This category of objective involves recall of specifics and universals; recall of methods and processes; or recall of any pattern, structure, or setting.
1.1	*Knowledge of specifics.* The recall of specific bits of information, such as terms or their definitions and the recall of specific facts (for example, dates, events, persons, or places) and given examples.
1.2	*Knowledge of ways and means of dealing with specifics.* The recall of ways to organize, study, judge, or criticize something. This subcategory includes knowledge of conventions (rules of punctuation or etiquette), trends and sequences (historical developments), classifications (types of literature), criteria (for assessing the nutritional value of foods), and methodology (the scientific method, methods of coping with emotional stress, bookkeeping procedures).
1.3	*Knowledge of the universals and abstractions in a field.* The recall of the schemes and patterns by which a subject field is organized, including principles or generalizations (laws of heredity, basic chemical principles, axioms of geometry) and theories or structures (the theory of evolution, the principles, behind the organization of Congress).
2.0	**Comprehension.** This lowest level of intellectual skill requires understanding material (knowledge of what is being "said" in verbal, pictorial, or symbolic form) without necessarily relating it to other information or gaining insight into its full implications.
2.1	*Translation.* Care and accuracy in paraphrasing, or rendering the content in one form of communication to another (paraphrasing a speech, translating material from one language to another, plotting points on a graph).
2.2	*Interpretation.* Explaining or summarizing a communication. Whereas translation involves a part-to-part correspondence, interpretation involves a reordering, rearrangement, or new approach to information (interpreting graphs, distinguishing accurate from unwarranted or contradicted conclusions, explaining a concept in one's own words).
2.3	*Extrapolation.* Extension of what is given to intermediate, past, or future situations; inference with regard to implications, consequences, and corollaries, in accordance with the conditions described in the original communication (estimating or predicting consequences of a described action).
3.0	**Application.** This category of objective includes using abstractions in general situations. The abstractions may be general ideas, rules, methods, principles, or theories to be applied in a particular situation (using trigonometric laws to solve a word problem, applying social-science generalizations to social problems).
4.0	**Analysis.** Breaking down a communication into its constituent parts to detect the relations between the parts or to clarify the organizing principles. Analysis may also be directed at the techniques or means used to communicate an effect (describing a style of writing).
4.1	*Analysis of elements.* Detection of elements that permit full comprehension or evaluation (the identification of unstated assumptions or motives, the distinction of facts from hypotheses or premises from conclusions).

(continued)

4.2	*Analysis of relationships.* Determining the relationships among elements or parts of a communication; detecting connections or interactions of parts in the whole (determining consistency of hypotheses with assumptions, distinguishing cause-effect relationships, detecting logical fallacies, comparing and contrasting to identify patterns of similarity or difference).
4.3	*Analysis of organizational principles.* Discovery of purpose, point of view, attitude, or general conception of a work; general form, pattern, structure, or organization of evidence or elements (analysis of a work of art for its organization, inference of an author's point of view, discovery of an author's concept of science, discovery of bias in a historical account).
5.0	**Synthesis.** The putting together of parts so as to form a whole. Arranging or combining elements to constitute a pattern or structure not clearly present before.
5.1	*Production of a unique communication.* Developing a communication to convey ideas, feelings, or experiences to others (telling a personal experience, writing a creative story or essay).
5.2	*Production of a plan or proposed set of operations.* Developing a plan or proposal to satisfy requirements of a given or self-set task (development of a plan to solve a problem, test a hypothesis, or teach a unit; the design of a building).
5.3	*Derivation of an abstract set of relations.* Developing a set of abstract relations to classify or to explain phenomena; deducing propositions or relations from a basic set of propositions or representations (formulation of a hypothesis or critical theory, discovery of mathematical principles).
6.0	**Evaluation.** Judging the value or worth of material and methods for given purposes. Making quantitative and qualitative judgments about the extent to which something satisfies criteria. Criteria may be determined by the student or given.
6.1	*Judgments based on internal evidence.* Judging accuracy from internal criteria such as logical accuracy and consistency (consistent style, logical development, precise wording).
6.2	*Judgments based on external evidence.* Evaluating material by criteria appropriate to its type (weighing different courses of action, evaluating health practices, comparing products with works of excellence).

Source: John W. Wakefield. *Educational Psychology: Learning to Be a Problem-Solver.* Copyright © 1996 by Houghton Mifflin Company. Adapted with permission.

objectives, while the remaining four levels are termed higher-level objectives because they require students to engage in more sophisticated types of thinking. However, it is not always the case that every level of the taxonomy directly builds on the level below it. For instance, evaluation does not depend on synthesis. For the most part, however, the higher levels of the taxonomy do depend on the lower levels. That is, synthesis and evaluation both depend on analysis, analysis depends on application, and application depends on comprehension.

Now let's consider how the novice teacher Rachel, who was refered to earlier, might write objectives at various levels of Bloom's taxonomy for her mathematics class. At the synthesis level, one objective may be as follows:

> Using local newspaper ads as a model and your own set of materials, create an ad for a store sale in which you advertise to customers how they will be able to save 40 percent on selected clothing items, 60 percent on selected houseware items, and 75 percent on selected sporting good items. The ad must contain a description of the regular retail price of each item as well as the sale price.

At the analysis level an objective might be stated as follows:

> Given statistics on the performance of two local high school baseball teams, diagram the percentage chance with regard to wins at home compared to wins away.

Remember that as you construct your lesson plans, you should be planning to address not only lower-level objectives, but also those represented in the higher levels of the taxonomy. In fact, the focus of the outcomes-based education movement is on the specification of what learning outcome or product we can expect to see students achieve as a result of a learning experience. Objectives at the synthesis and analysis levels, such as the two given above, afford the teacher and student a very direct, clearcut idea as to the nature of these outcomes or products.

affective domain objectives for student attitudes, values, and emotional growth; domain includes five basic categories: receiving, responding, valuing, organization, and characterization

◆ Affective Domain

A second domain of objectives, which is receiving increased attention with the advent of outcomes-based education, is the **affective domain.** Similar to the cognitive domain, it too is divided into a hierarchical taxonomy (Krathwohl, Bloom, & Masia, 1964). However, unlike Bloom's taxonomy, affective objectives focus on emotions and attitudes. The hierarchy describes the least commitment (pay attention) to the most commitment (adopt an idea or value and act consistently with that idea). Table 11.4 summarizes the five levels of the affective domain.

One affective objective that perhaps Rachel might set for her students is as follows: "Each student will comply with the rules regarding bringing necessary materials to math class."

You should be aware that action research strategies can be very helpful to you when assessing students with regard to the affective domain. Among the data-gathering procedures you may use to ascertain changes in student attitude are such things as student journals, interviews with students, transcripts of audiotapes containing student dialogue, as well as attitude surveys.

Teacher Tool Box
Using the Affective Domain

◆ As you prepare objectives from the cognitive domain, keep a separate column of objectives from the affective domain related to your subject area.

◆ As you work with students who seem to lack motivation, critically examine what you could do differently in your planning process to facilitate their achievement of affective objectives.

◆ As you plan student assignments, you will want to remember to encourage students to at least occasionally undertake assignments in which the affective domain is used, such as written or oral expression of their feelings, interviewing others, producing audiotapes, surveying others, or attending community events.

◆ Psychomotor Domain

psychomotor domain objectives involving physical ability

Overlooked until recently by most classroom teachers, with the exception of those who teach physical education, objectives in the **psychomotor**

Table 11.4   Taxonomy for the Affective Domain

1.0	**Receiving (Attending).** Exhibition of *awareness* or consciousness of an affect or value (e.g., awareness of aesthetic factors); *willingness to receive* a communication (listening to others speak); and *controlled or selected attention* given to affects or values (discrimination of mood in music; alertness toward human values recorded in literature).
2.0	**Responding.** Paying active attention or expressing interest through *acquiescence in responding* (obedience or compliance); *willingness to respond* (voluntary participation, acceptance of responsibility); or *satisfaction in response* (enjoyment of self-expression, conversation, or reading).
3.0	**Valuing.** Adoption of consistent behavior that reflects an independent assessment of worth or a characteristic attitude. These objectives include *acceptance of a value* to the point of being identified with it (continuing desire to speak effectively); pursuit of or *preference for a value* (active participation in making arrangements for an art show); and *commitment* or conviction (devotion to ideas of democracy).
4.0	**Organization.** Gradual development toward a system of values in which interrelationships and predominance of particular values are determined. Includes *conceptualization of a value* held (identifies attributes of an admired object, forms judgments as to the responsibilities of society); and *organization of a value system* in which values are in a dynamic equilibrium (weighs alternative policies with the criterion of the public good).
5.0	**Characterization by a Value or Value Complex.** Development of a life outlook characterized by an internally consistent set of values. Includes *generalized set* or selective response at a very high level (readiness or predisposition to revise judgments in light of evidence); and *characterization* by a philosophy of life or view of the universe (development of a code of behavior based on ethical principles consistent with democratic ideals).

Source: John W. Wakefield. *Educational Psychology: Learning to Be a Problem-Solver.* Copyright © 1996 by Houghton Mifflin Company. Adapted with permission.

domain also have been classified into a taxonomy (Harrow, 1972). The levels of the taxonomy are described in Table 11.5. One of the advantages of this taxonomy is that it depicts how certain activities are often related. For example, skilled movements are often dependent upon physical abilities.

Besides those who teach physical education, objectives in this domain should be of interest to many educators, including those who teach special education, driver's education, music, art, and vocational education. Other subjects such as computer science and science courses, which involve the manipulation of fine motor skills, also involve psychomotor objectives.

In terms of how to assess student skills in the psychomotor domain, you should again be aware that a variety of action research methods are at your disposal. These include the use of checklists, the analysis of videotapes of student performance, and anecdotal records of student performance.

Subjects such as computer science also involve psychomotor objectives. ◆

Table 11.5. Taxonomy for the Psychomotor Domain

1.0	**Basic-Fundamental Movements.** At this level of objective, the learner develops basic *locomotor* movements (walking, running, jumping, hopping, rolling, climbing), *nonlocomotor* movements (pushing, pulling, swaying, swinging, stooping), and *manipulative* movements (handling, gripping, grasping, manipulating). A typical child enters school with these movements mastered, but objectives may be established for early childhood or special education children.
2.0	**Perceptual Abilities.** Early childhood educators are interested in the refinement of a child's perceptual abilities, as are teachers of older students. This level of objective includes *auditory* perception (following instructions), *visual* perception (dodging a moving ball), *kinesthetic* perception (adjusting body in a handstand), *tactile* perceptions (determining texture, identifying coins through touch), and *coordinated* perceptions (jumping rope, punting, catching).
3.0	**Physical Abilities.** The goal of "physical fitness" generally comprehends this category of objective, which includes *endurance* or strenuous effort (distance running, swimming), *strength* or muscular exertion (weightlifting, wrestling), *flexibility* or axial movements (toe touching, sit-ups, twisting exercises, ballet exercises), and *agility* or quick, precise movements (shuttle run, typing, dodge ball).
4.0	**Skilled Movements.** A *physical skill* is defined as a "degree of efficiency in performance of a specific, reasonably complex movement behavior" (Harrow, 1972, p. 75). A skill's complexity distinguishes it from basic-fundamental movements. Activities in this classification include skills of sports, dance, recreation, and manipulation in three categories. *Simple adaptive skills* refer to adaptations of basic-fundamental movements (sawing as an adaptation of push-pull, waltzing as an adaptation of walking, piano playing, archery skills, typing and clerical skills, handicrafts, industrial skills). *Compound adaptive skills* require skill in the simultaneous manipulation of a tool or implement in addition to skill in use of the body (racket games). *Complex adaptive skills* require mastering the mechanics of total body involvement (aerial gymnastics stunts, complex dives). Each of the three categories of skilled movements is further subdivided into four levels of proficiency (beginner, intermediate, advanced, highly skilled).
5.0	**Nondiscursive Communication.** This level of movement involves communication through bodily movements from facial expressions to dance compositions. Its two subcategories are *expressive movement* (posture and carriage, gestures, facial expressions) and *interpretive movement* (art forms of aesthetic and creative movement). Objectives are not typically written for expressive movements, but expressive movements are modified, exaggerated, and utilized in movement interpretations by highly skilled athletes, fine arts students, and even children (the ability to design one's own series of movements in free response activities).

Source: John W. Wakefield. *Educational Psychology: Learning to Be a Problem-Solver.* Copyright © 1996 by Houghton Mifflin Company. Adapted with permission.

GAGNE'S OUTCOMES OF INSTRUCTION

A more cognitively oriented approach to conceptualizing student learning capabilities is found in the work of Robert Gagne (see Chapter 7 of this text for an earlier discussion of Gagne's work). While Gagne proposed that learning begins with the students' exposure to certain environmental events, which he termed the events of instruction, he also believed that these events of instruction interact with the cognitive states the student brings to the classroom, as well as with the cognitive processes the student uses to interpret the environmental stimuli (Gagne & Driscoll, 1988). The interaction of these external and internal conditions of learning produces what Gagne described as the **outcomes of learning.** According to Gagne, these outcomes of learning or learning capabilities include the following:

1. Verbal information,

2. Intellectual skills,

3. Cognitive strategies,

4. Attitudes,

5. Motor skills.

> **Gagne's outcomes of learning** includes verbal information, intellectual skills, cognitive strategies, attitude, and motor skills

Gagne contends that when teachers plan for instruction they should be making critical decisions about these outcomes of learning.

◆ Verbal Information

Verbal information is the learned capability that enables children to communicate about objects, events, or certain relationships. For example, the novice teacher Sarah may decide that an important learning outcome for her students is that they should be capable of talking about historical events. So a child's declaration "George Washington was our first president" enables her to communicate verbal information. Likewise, a series of questions asked by a child such as "What is that?", a teacher's attempt to teach new vocabulary before the start of a unit, as well as a teacher's quizzing students on important labels, such as phone numbers, are all illustrations of verbal information. Thus, verbal information addresses the "what" of learning and provides a vehicle for thought (Gagne & Driscoll, 1988).

◆ Intellectual Skills

Intellectual skills, instead of addressing the "what" of learning, focus on the "how." Gagne organized intellectual skills into the following hierarchy from the lowest level of complexity to the highest level:

1. Discrimination,

2. Concrete concept,

3. Defined concept,

4. Rule,

5. Higher-order rule.

Gagne did not mean to imply that intellectual skills are necessarily more complex than verbal information. They are merely different in nature. By *discrimination* he referred to the ability to distinguish between two or more stimuli. Young children for instance learn to discriminate between adults who are parents and adults who are not parents. As children enter school they learn to discriminate between the letter *T* and the letter *F*. As children progress into junior and senior high school, the discriminations they are required to make become finer and finer. For instance, the novice teacher Sarah may plan the following outcome of learning for her secondary students: *Students will be capable of making historically significant discriminations when given a series of dates* (some that are historically significant to the American Revolution and some that are not).

According to Gagne, after the child has developed the capability to discriminate, she is then ready to learn about *concrete concepts* or objects, events, and relations that can be observed or experienced. Sarah, for example, may plan the following student learning outcome: *Students will be capable of identifying the critical features present in a city*. Another instance of a concrete concept is when young children learn about the critical features that make an animal a horse but not a dog. Spatial relations between objects are also included in concrete concepts such as the concepts "higher" and "lower," "above" and "below."

Defined concepts, in contrast, are abstractions that cannot be observed in the environment but must instead be defined. For example, Sarah may want her students to understand and define the concept "liberty." Obviously, students cannot point to "liberty" in the environment. However, she can use liberty in a discussion of historical events and the Constitution.

Concrete concepts can acquire the properties of defined concepts. It is important to note that a student who first learns the concept "horse" by identifying concrete instances in her environment can go on to learn the same concept in abstract terms; for instance, "a horse is a large, herbivorous mammal."

Gagne proposed that *rules* exist next in order of complexity. Rules explain the way that phenomena work and allow students to use symbols. For instance, students may recognize that certain nonverbal teacher signals mean that they need to be quiet because the students have acquired rules (see the discussion in Chapter 10 for additional examples relative to classroom management). Students may also learn grammatical rules, such as rules for how to put a heading on a letter or rules for spelling. The novice teacher Rachel may plan a learning outcome as follows: *Students will learn the rule for finding the area of a rectangle*.

Once students have learned rules, Gagne contended that they are ready to learn *higher-order rules,* which are formed by combining two or more rules in order to solve problems. For instance, Rachel may plan the following learning outcome for her students: *The students must use the rules of multiplication, subtraction, and simple division to solve long-division problems.* Sarah, the novice social studies teacher, may ask her students to apply the economic principle of "supply and demand" in an analysis of fluctuating gasoline prices.

◆ Cognitive Strategies

In addition to verbal information and intellectual skills, Gagne believed that a set of skills termed *cognitive strategies* were very important for teachers to consider as they undertook the planning process. Cognitive strategies refer to the capability to internally organize skills that regulate the use of concepts and rules (Gagne, 1985). In essence, these cognitive strategies serve a metacognitive function, for they enable students to organize and monitor the cognitive processes they use to represent the environment (see the discussion of metacognition in Chapter 12). For example, Sarah's students may develop a cognitive strategy similar to the PQ4R technique to study for the semester final in American history. Or Rachel's students may develop a series of personal mnemonic devices to memorize the order of operations in math. See Chapter 12 for a discussion of the teacher's role in training students to utilize metacognitive strategies.

◆ Attitudes

Similar to Bloom's notion of the affective domain, Gagne described an *attitude* as an acquired internal state that influences a student's choice of personal action (Gagne, 1985). The things toward which students acquire attitudes are termed *attitude targets*. Students may acquire an attitude toward teachers, an attitude target, which may influence student behavior in the presence of teachers. Certainly students' attitudes toward various subject areas vary tremendously. It is no wonder then that both Sarah and Rachel would be concerned with their students' attitudes toward social studies and mathematics, respectively.

◆ Motor Skills

Finally, Gagne proposed that *motor skills* were another critical skill for teachers to consider as they made planning decisions. Obviously parallel to Bloom's psychomotor domain, motor skills are physical capabilities to do such things as ride a bike, write with a pencil, or use a computer keyboard. But this set of skills is not confined to the area of physical education. For instance, Sarah may be concerned with her students' ability to collect historical artifacts from a field site. Even in cases where the skill in question may involve a prototypical physical movement such as learning to play kickball, there are still cognitive and affective components to that skill. Students have a cognitive representation or schema (see the discussion in Chapter 7) for how kickball is played as well as an individual predisposition for kickball in terms of whether they like to play it or not. Thus, motor capabilities rarely develop in the absence of the previously reviewed categories proposed by Gagne.

Although learning to play soccer involves motor skills, there are still cognitive and affective components to that skill. ◆

▌EFFECTIVE PLANNING AND TEACHING

The connection between the planning practices of teachers and the actual delivery of their lessons is critical. In this section, we will review two popular ways of conceptualizing this connection. First, we will

YOU MAKE THE CALL

APPLYING GAGNE

For how young an age can teachers plan to teach their students cognitive strategies? How were you taught to use cognitive strategies in school?

How do you envision that the defined concepts you are learning about in educational psychology will affect decision making during your student teaching semester?

How did your own teachers gather information about your attitudes toward the subjects you were learning?

explore how the Hunter model of planning can be incorporated into teaching. Second, we will consider how to implement alternative planning models of a constructivist nature.

Hunter model of planning a seven step model incorporating focus set, objectives, input, modeling, monitoring, and guided and independent practice

◆ The Hunter Model of Planning

One widely advocated model of instructional planning, based on the notion of formulating very specific instructional objectives from the above domains, is called the Madeline **Hunter model of planning** (Hunter, 1982). The Hunter steps, described in Table 11.6 are a model of planning

Table 11.6. Hunter's Seven Elements of Effective Lessons

Focus Set	An activity intended to *focus* on what the student will learn during today's lesson. It also provides *practice* of previous learning and develops readiness for learning.
Objective	Tells the students what they will learn (*stating the objective*), *shows the purpose* for the learning, and *indicates the relevance* of the learning.
Instructional Input	Shows *what* information is needed by the student in order to achieve the objective and *how* that information will be presented.
Modeling	Shows the learner what an *acceptable finished product or a process* looks or sounds like, rather than just telling about it. In other words, the students need to see the teacher do what the teacher expects students to do.
Check for Understanding—Monitor	This is a *validation of learning*. It is important that the teacher not assume that the students have learned what has been presented. The teacher should determine immediately following the presentation that the information just presented has been understood by the learners.
Guided Practice	This occurs when *relevant tasks* are practiced with the *teacher present* and available to help students the moment they need assistance.
Independent Practice	This practice involves *unassisted performance* by the students on relevant tasks, which will allow them to develop *fluency of the objective* without the teacher.

as well as a model of teaching; they are also known as an example of the direct model of instruction. That is, within the model there are the following four phases: (1) introduction and review; (2) presentation; (3) guided practice; and (4) independent practice.

The essential feature of the Hunter model of planning is that all of the steps must be related back to the objective. Although the Hunter model of planning is not the only way in which to put an effective lesson together, it does seem to be helpful to novice teachers (Sardo-Brown, 1993). First, it provides an organizational framework, which, if followed, ensures the teacher that she will not deviate from the lesson objective. It also ensures the students of a well-organized lesson that provides them with adequate opportunities to clarify misunderstood material and to practice their skills.

Let's consider how Rachel, the novice mathematics teacher, could use the Hunter model to plan the lesson on percentages which we discussed previously within this chapter.

Focus Set. To catch students' attention, Rachel could pass out the sales section from a local newspaper, which consists of price markdowns reported as percentages off. This focuses the students' attention on the topic of percentages and sets the students up for the lesson objective.

Objective. The objective of Rachel's lesson might be as follows: Given ten problems from the math book involving retail sales, each student will be able to calculate the percentage discount received by the customer.

Instructional Input. This refers to the actual content that Rachel teaches the students. This could include reading material and sample problems presented in the textbook as well as material presented in class.

Modeling. Rachel might illustrate several different problems on the board or on an overhead projector by showing students how they can use a step-by-step process to calculate percentages.

Check for Understanding. After Rachel takes students through the step-by-step process, she could monitor for understanding in a variety of ways. She might ask students to calculate the answer to one or two additional percentage problems. As students did this, Rachel could circulate throughout the classroom to check their answers. Or Rachel might ask students oral questions about percentages by calling on a random number of students. This way, she will get an idea as to whether students are really grasping percentages. Still a third strategy Rachel might employ to check for understanding is to ask the entire class to individually work a problem involving percentages and then to ask for students to hold their thumbs up if they got it right or put their thumbs down if they did not. Once again, this method allows the teacher to quickly assess if any reteaching is necessary.

Teacher Tool Box
Some Additional Tips for Using the Hunter Model

- Some additional ideas for establishing focus include having students write down the most important thing they learned from yesterday's lesson, having students write down their answer to a question you have written on the board, or having students write or share what they already know about a topic. It is essential that all of these strategies be directly linked to your lesson objective.

- As you write your lesson objectives, it may be helpful to also force yourself to write out the reason these objectives are important to the students so that you remember to share this rationale with them. In some cases, this will require you to really think about why your lesson objectives matter and how students might use what you are teaching in their lives.

- When modeling the steps of what you are teaching for students, remember to do so in a developmentally appropriate way. That is, make sure that for preoperational and concrete operational students especially, you use many visual aids, hands-on props, and familiar examples.

Guided Practice. Once Rachel checked for understanding and assuming students did in fact understand the material, she would next assign them practice problems to begin in class. As students worked on these problems, she could make herself available by scanning their work and offering assistance and feedback. This step is essential so that students don't begin their homework outside of school, only to find that they are clueless as to what to do.

Independent Practice. Rachel would assign students problems (which perhaps they had begun to do in guided practice) for homework. It is critical that this homework assignment require students to fulfill the objective(s) specified above.

Numerous school districts, you should be aware, conduct extensive in-service training on the use of the Hunter model and may even evaluate their teachers' performance based on their use of the steps listed above. A few caveats to this approach are in order. First, Madeline Hunter herself never intended for this model to be used to evaluate teacher performance. Second, there are no research data available to show that teachers who use the Hunter model compared to those who do not have higher achieving students. Third, it is not always appropriate to expect a teacher to use all of the steps listed above in any one lesson. These steps, in fact, may be used over several days' time.

◆ Alternatives to the Hunter Model

You should be aware that while the model of teaching described above is very effective for teaching basic skills, there are alternative approaches to consider, especially if your objective concerns the teaching of critical thinking skills. It is argued that expert teachers should also be able to construct lessons that help students learn content in a meaningful way (Marshall, 1992). The illustration in Table 11.7 shows how a teacher could implement such a lesson in a math class.

There are several differences between the approach described in Table 11.7 and the Hunter model. First, it is assumed that students actively construct their own understanding of knowledge rather than having it directly delivered to them by the teacher. Second, the social nature of learning is acknowledged by having the students interact often with the teacher as well as each other. Third, the lesson should focus on not only the importance of getting the right answer, but also on students' understanding of the process behind the right answer.

constructivist model the philosophical position that a child builds his or her own knowledge

This **constructivist model** of learning, which is presented in Chapter 12, has several implications for how teachers plan their lessons. These include the following: (1) teachers should plan instructional activities in the form of problems for students to solve; (2) as teachers plan, they should recognize that substantive learning takes place over long periods of time and often entails periods of confusion; and (3) teachers should plan lessons that allow students to interact socially as they learn.

Returning to the case of Sarah, who was asked to teach an American history class in the initial scene in this chapter, we could consider another illustration of constructivist lesson planning. Perrone (1994) has described a constructivist mode of planning in which the focus is on the process of learning and the thinking behind the products. So Sarah,

Table 11.7. Excerpts from a Constructivist Lesson

As a homework assignment, Keisha Coleman had given her third graders a worksheet with a number line on it that appeared as follows:

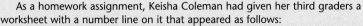
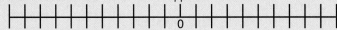

She had told the students to put the numbers on the number line. Below the line were 12 different problems, some of which involved adding and subtracting negative numbers. Keisha and her students spent a half hour discussing the problem:

$$10 + 10 = ? \text{ How do you know?}$$

In introducing the problem Keisha emphasized that students were supposed to give an answer and then explain why their answer was correct. Keisha then asked someone to volunteer the answer.

"Zero," Marta answered.

Keisha wrote $-10 + 10 = 0$ on the board saying, "negative 10 plus 10 equals zero," as she wrote. "Now, can you explain why you know that, Marta?"

Marta nodded.

"What did you say? I would like for the rest of you to listen very carefully because I want you to be able to tell us, or Marta, if you agree with what she says."

"You have to count 10 numbers to the right," Marta went on.

Keisha then asked Marta to repeat what she had said, and Keisha wrote her exact words on the board. She then continued, "All right. Marta says that negative 10 plus 10 equals zero, so you have to count 10 numbers to the right. What do you people think about that? . . . Harold?"

"I think it's easy, but I don't understand how she explained it."

"Does anyone else have a comment on that? . . . Tessa?"

"I think it's zero' cause negative 10 plus 10 equals zero."

"Okay. Right now I'm asking about what Marta said," Keisha intervened.

"There's not . . . I don't agree," Tessa continued.

"What do you disagree with?"

"You have to count numbers to the right. If you count to the right you couldn't get zero. You'd have to count to the left," Tessa argued.

"Could you explain a little bit more about what you mean by that? I'm not sure if I follow you. And the rest of you need to listen very carefully so you can see if you agree or disagree," Keisha probed. "Tessa?"

"Because if you went that way (pointing to the right) then it would have to be a higher number."

To this point in the dialogue, the interaction has been mostly teacher-student-teacher-student. Keisha then made an effort to turn the dialogue to student-student.

(continued)

Table 11.7. Excerpts from a Constructivist Lesson *(Continued)*

"Tessa says if you're counting right, then the number is . . . I don't understand. I don't know what she's talking about. Negative 10 plus 10 is zero," Chang argued.

"Do you want to ask her?" Keisha gestured.

"What do you mean by counting to the right?" Chang turned to Tessa.

"If you count from 10 up, you can't get to zero. If you count from 10 left, you can get to zero," Tessa returned.

"Well, negative 10 is a negative number, . . . smaller than zero," Chang went on.

"I know," Tessa nodded.

"Then why do you say you can't get to zero when you're adding to negative 10, which is smaller than zero."

"OHH! I get it! This is positive," Tessa blurted out.

"Excuse me?" Keisha queried.

"You have to count right," Tessa motioned.

"You're saying in order to get to zero, you have to count to the right? From where, Tessa?"

"Negative 10."

Source: Reprinted with permission from Ablex Publishing, (from) *Redefining student learning: Roots of educational change.* Author: P. Peterson, Ch. 6, "Revising their thinking; Keisha Coleman and her third grade mathematics class," pp. 157–176. Copyright 1992.

as a teacher of American History might propose that her students be able to

- Generate and solve problems,
- Handle multiple points of view,
- Be critical readers and active writers, and
- Use primary historical sources from which they can formulate hypotheses.

Perrone (1994) would next suggest that Sarah try to identify themes and issues in American history that would aid students in arriving at important understandings. For Sarah's class such themes might include "slavery," "fairness," or "democracy and revolution." Perrone would recommend that Sarah create a map of the theme that would help to elucidate how the topic could stimulate her students' thinking and understanding of critical issues and relationships between and among these issues. An illustration of one such topic map based on the theme "Immigrants in America" is provided in Figure 11.1 Using this topic map as a guide, Perrone (1994) would then advocate that Sarah and her students co-plan projects, materials, and activities, which will help facilitate student learning.

It should be pointed out that planning and teaching with themes and integrated content are very popular features of lesson and unit

Figure 11.1
Planning with a Topic Map

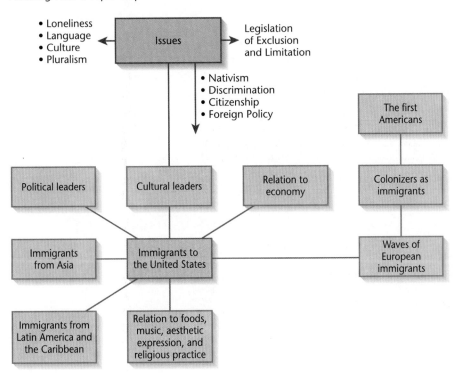

Source: Vito Perrone. "How to Engage Students in Learning." *Educational Leadership 51,* 5, Figure 1, p. 12. Used by permission of the Association for Supervision and Curriculum Development. Copyright © 1997 by ASCD. All rights reserved.

planning from kindergarten (Roskos & Neuman, 1995) through high school (Clarke & Agne, 1997). When conventional units are organized around a theme of study, such as railroads, they are called **thematic units.** When a thematic unit integrates disciplines together, it is called an **interdisciplinary thematic unit.** For instance, in planning an inter-disciplinary unit on the study of railroads, Sarah could integrate not only content from American history but from other disciplines as well, such as science, mathematics, and language arts (Kellough & Kellough, 1996). Imagine reading short stories or novels about life on the railroads in English class, studying the engineering aspect of railroads in science class, and formulating the speed at which railroad cars travel in math class at the same time as learning about the role railroads played in key historical events in history class. Many educators argue that such an experience is much more authentic and meaningful to students, because in the real world life is not divided up into history, English, science, and math classes. Rather, to understand phenomena in the real world, one has to understand how the disciplines integrate together.

thematic units units organized around a theme of study

interdisciplinary thematic units (ITU) units based on themes interwoven across content areas

To understand phenomena in the real world, one has to understand how the disciplines integrate together. ◆

Reflections from the Field

1 In teaching middle school kids, I have found that student mood and variations in mood are the most important factors that affect how I make daily plans. One day the kids will come in all jazzed up and the next day they may be very low.

—*Sally (middle school social studies teacher), Andover, KS*

2 I've found that my experience working as a supervisor in business is a major factor that affects my planning. That is, just as I used team leaders to lead small groups of people who worked under me, I found it helpful to use team leaders in cooperative learning groups. I rotate these assignments, just as I did in business so everyone gets a turn.

—*Jeff (senior high social studies teacher), Derby, KS*

3 When I do the focus step, I make sure it involves something students can relate to from their personal lives. For example, when teaching about the conflict in the myth "Echo and Narcissus," I first had students write about a conflict they had experienced in a journal for the first few minutes of class.

—Jill (middle school language arts teacher), Panama city, FL

4 One of the big factors that affected my plans as a first-year teacher was my allergy to chalk. I had to plan an alternative teaching style which involved using the overhead projector and rearranging seats so everyone could see.

—Richelle (senior high math teacher), Wichita KS

5 I've found that the students just love synthesis-level activities. At first, they may complain that they are hard, but then they get into the activity. The key is that you lay out everything they are to do and how they will be graded ahead of time. I had one of my high school sections work in small groups to create an economic development for a third world nation. They really felt they had learned a lot by the end.

—Steve (senior high English teacher), Warminster, PA

THEORY TO PRACTICE

A Look at Teacher as Decision Maker, as Planner

Throughout the chapter we have made reference to the actions of Sarah, a social studies teacher and to Rachel, a mathematics teacher. Remember that both teachers' instructional plans did not occur by happenstance. That is, both teachers developed an instructional plan to guide their teaching. They had to consider what resources were available and be sensitive to diverse student characteristics, the school schedule and calendar, and the larger K-12 curriculum. As teachers such as Sarah and Rachel plan, they do many hours of work that is rarely seen by anyone else. They specify behavioral objectives or specific expectations as to what students should be able to do for each lesson they teach. Increasingly, in many subjects, these behavioral objectives are not only cognitive in nature but also draw from the affective and psychomotor domains. Effective teachers, in addition, need to consider the wide gamut of objectives represented in each of the taxonomies described in this chapter. That is, in order to maximize student learning, teachers must plan both lower-level and higher-level objectives for their students as well as

carefully consider Gagne's outcomes of learning. New teachers especially profit from using some sort of organizational framework to guide their planning. One that has helped thousands of teachers, the Hunter model, is a framework you may find helpful to consult. On balance, though, and depending upon the level of your lesson objectives, the constructivist approach may also be of value to both you and your students.

You, as Teacher, as Decision Maker, as Planner

In the following case presentations you will be provided with a number of salient characteristics of the school, classroom, and the students. In reviewing these illustrations, try to apply your knowledge of instructional planning in order to

1. Determine if all of the major factors related to the classroom situation and students were adequately taken into account as lesson plans were developed;

2. Identify if behavioral objectives were clearly shared with the students;

3. Decide if both lower- and higher-level objectives were used;

4. Decide which of Gagne's outcomes were focused on;

5. Specify how employing either the steps of the Hunter model or the constructivist model could facilitate student learning.

Case Illustration 1:
Groveton Middle School

Your School

Groveton Middle School is located in a working class neighborhood in which the local steel mill has recently closed. The majority of the student population comes from middle class households. However, a growing number of students are from families who recently emigrated from Cambodia and Laos. Many of these students are in the school's English-as-a-Second-Language program.

Your Class

Your class is one of five sections of American government you teach at the seventh grade level. There are twenty-three students in your class. Seventeen are white, and five are Laotian.

Your Students

You begin your class by explaining to students the importance of understanding how their government works. You write the lesson objective on the board for them as follows: "To be able to identify the three branches of government and explain the role of each branch." After a brief presentation of the facts, you ask students to read a brief article about the current budget crisis and to answer a set of questions to identify the role of each branch of government in resolving the problem. A few minutes later, you notice that while several students have finished with the assignment, the majority are still reading the article. You begin to worry about what you will do with those who have finished early.

In reviewing the above features, consider how each of the following may provide insight and direc-tion for a teacher concerned about using research on instructional planning to help her students learn:

Mager's three-part system,

Bloom's taxonomy,

Gagne's outcomes,

The Hunter model, and

The constructivist model.

Case Illustration 2:
The Northend Elementary School

Your School

The Northend Elementary School is situated in a grow-ing, economically affluent area outside of a major south-ern city. Parental involvement in the nearly all-white school is high, and teachers routinely experiment with new teaching methods they learn at a nearby university.

Your Class

You are teaching a group of twenty-eight third graders, two of whom are African American, and one who is from India. The remainder of the class is white. Three students who have been labeled as having a learning disability have recently joined your class and receive periodic help from a special education teacher who cir-culates into your room.

Your Students

You announce that the objective for the week in science is for students to be able to identify the properties of light and shadows. During the first lesson, you bring in a light and a basket of objects with interesting shapes. You then ask the children questions about what kinds of things have shadows and whether the objects in the basket have shadows. As the students become more interested, you ask them to make predictions about what the shadows of selected objects will look like. For several days, the class experiments with shining a light on selected objects to test if their predictions are true. While you are pleased with the enthusiastic response the children have to your lessons, you are disappointed when they do poorly on an end-of-week quiz in which they respond to questions about the properties of light and shadow.

SUMMARY

The Purposes of Planning

Without adequate course and lesson planning, effective teaching is impossible. Planning helps a teacher to become organized, builds teacher's confidence, enables a teacher to be more effective as a classroom manager, and reduces the opportunity for off-task disruptions. In addition, planning can help a teacher to know how and when to condense content, how to motivate students, and how to assess student performance.

Classroom Planning: Reflecting the Mission of the Educational System

Educational planning—whether it is lesson planning, unit planning, or overall curriculum—is done in the context of the community's mission for its educational system and in the context of the goals that the community has decided its members should achieve.

The mission of a school system or district is a statement that depicts its reason for existence along with its unique characteristics. The mission tends to be quite succinct and often written in somewhat global terms. A more expanded and concrete presentation of the goals of a school district can be found in its academic unit goals, which are a direct outgrowth of its mission. Unit goals pertain to a particular unit of study and thus are more closely related to classroom teaching than mission goals.

Factors Affecting Planning

Research has shown that the plans of experienced teachers are affected by the school calendar, physical facilities of the school, the content of textbooks, standardized tests, curriculum guides, and a variety of student characteristics. In addition to these factors, the principal's planning requirements, interruptions in the flow of activities within a given period, school schedule interruptions, students' interests and abilities, the availability of materials, and previous teaching experience can affect teacher planning.

Research indicates that additional factors may strongly exert an influence on novice teacher planning. Identified as profound influences on planning were such factors as the influence of cooperating teachers, university supervisors, and mentor teachers during student teaching, as well as perceptions of one's subject matter, and a variety of "newcomer stresses."

Instructional Objectives

Robert Mager (1975) has developed an influential system for writing instructional objectives. Mager emphasizes that a well-written objective, sometimes called a behavioral objective, should describe what students are doing as they demonstrate their achievement and how you, the teacher, will know that they are doing this. According to Mager a

good behavioral objective has three parts. These include the performance component or what the student will actually do, the conditions under which this performance will be assessed or how this behavior will be recognized and tested, and the criteria for acceptable performance.

In contrast to Mager's system, Gronlund's instructional objectives include a general term such as understand or know, followed by specific learner outcomes that operationally define what we mean when we say understand or know.

Domains and Taxonomies of Objectives

In order to differentiate different levels of complexity of learning, a group of educators led by Benjamin Bloom (1956) developed a system, a taxonomy, to classify objectives. Learning was classified into three broad domains or categories including cognitive (thinking), affective (having to do with attitudes and emotions), and psychomotor (having to do with physical activities). Within each domain, objectives were categorized according to complexity.

Gagne's Outcomes of Instruction

Gagne proposed that learning begins with the students' exposure to certain environmental events that he termed the events of instruction. He also believed that these events of instruction interact with the cognitive states the student brings to the classroom, as well as the cognitive processes the student uses to interpret environmental stimuli.

The interaction of these external and internal conditions of learning produce what Gagne described as the outcomes of learning. These outcomes of learning or learning capabilities include verbal information, intellectual skills, cognitive strategies, attitudes, and motor skills.

Effective Planning and Teaching

Madeline Hunter presented a model of planning and teaching that includes the following four phases: (1) introduction and review; (2) presentation; (3) guided practice; and (4) independent practice. The essential feature of the Hunter model of planning is that all of the steps must be related back to the objective.

Those taking a constructivist view of learning have developed an alternative approach to the somewhat directive model offered by Hunter. This constructivist view of learning has several implications for how teachers plan their lessons including: (1) teachers should plan instructional activities in the form of problems for students to solve; (2) as teachers plan they should recognize that substantive learning takes place over long periods of time and often entails periods of confusion; and (3) teachers should plan lessons which allow students to interact socially as they learn.

◆ Field Experience Questions

1. *Mission of the educational system and teacher plans.* When you do your observation look for some of the items referred to in this chapter, including the school's mission statement and curriculum guide for the grade and subject you are observing. You may also want to ask the teacher to look at her lesson plan book.

2. *Factors affecting plans.* As you observe, try to list all of the factors that this teacher most likely had to consider as she planned the lesson you are watching. With regard to the students, especially, record what factors the teacher perhaps did not take into account as she planned the lesson.

3. *Writing objectives.* Record the objective(s) for the lesson, either by writing down the objective the teacher shares with the students or inferring what it is. Based on the information in this chapter, evaluate the following: (1) What were the conditions of the objective? (2) Did students know what behavior they were expected to perform? and (3) What were the criteria for student performance?

4. *Bloom's taxonomy.* For at least one period of your observation, record the number of lower-level (knowledge and comprehension) and higher-level (application, analysis, synthesis, and evaluation) questions asked by the teacher or implied in class activities or assignments.

   (a) First, report how often lower- and higher-level questions or activities were used;

   (b) Second, give one example of both a lower- and higher-level question or activity used in the class;

   (c) Third, if higher-order questions or activities were not observed, how would you suggest that the classroom teacher implement these?

5. *Gagne's outcomes.* Over the course of your observation be looking for teacher attention to as many of Gagne's learning outcomes as you can identify from class activities or assignments.

   (a) First, report what outcomes were stressed most (verbal information, intellectual skills, cognitive strategies, attitudes, or motor skills);

   (b) Second, give examples of the following capabilities: verbal information, intellectual skills, and cognitive strategies;

   (c) Third, if any of the above were not focused on, suggest ways in which they could have been for the students you observed.

◆ Key Terms

affective domain
cognitive domain
constructivist model
curriculum guide
Gagne's outcomes of learning
goals
Gronlund's instructional objectives

Hunter model
interdisciplinary thematic
  unit (ITU)
levels of Bloom's taxonomy
Mager's three-part system of
  behavioral objectives
mission statement

objective
psychomotor domain
taxonomy
thematic units
unit goals

◆ Additional Resources

Anderson, L. W., & Sosniak, L. A. (1994). *Bloom's taxonomy: A forty-year retrospective.* Chicago: National Society for the Study of Education.

Bloom, B. (Ed.). (1984). *Taxonomy of objectives: Book 1. Cognitive domain.* White Plains, NY: Longman.

Bullough, R. V. (1987). Planning and the first year of teaching. *Journal of Education for Teaching, 12,* 231–250.

Good, T., & Brophy, J. (1994). *Looking in classrooms* (6th ed.). New York: HarperCollins.

Reiser, R. A., & Mory, E. H. (1991). An examination of the systematic planning techniques of two experienced teachers. *Educational Technology Research and Development, 39(3),* 71–82.

Zahorik, J. (1975). Teachers' planning models. *Educational Leadership, 33,* 134–139.

Learner–Centered Instruction: Metacognition and Constructivism

There is an air of concern in the room. The teacher sits down to pore over his students' recent tests. He thinks to himself, "If I can find their errors, I can figure out just what they need to learn next."

Frankly, the focus of this chapter, metacognition and constructivism, is only implied in this scene. This teacher isn't interested in just seeing his students' tests or test scores; he is also interested in seeing their errors! A constructivist teacher is as interested in students' errors as in their correct test responses, because their errors offer insight into their thinking. The concern over how students resolve problems, process information, and think is a key focus of constructivism.

Chapter 7 examined the foundations of cognitive learning theories and highlighted a number of strategies a teacher could use to making learning meaningful. The theories and strategies targeted in Chapter 7 were primarily *teacher-centered or teacher-directed;* the current chapter will focus on more *learner-oriented theories* and more *learner-centered* strategies for instruction. The current chapter will also highlight students' ability to think and the students' role in the process of making learning meaningful as well as the teacher's role in promoting such cognitive activity.

Concern over the ability of students to think is all too familiar among teachers, as illustrated by the following exchange:

History Teacher: I'm so frustrated with my class today. For homework, I asked them to compare the major campaign strategies of the two candidates. That seems straightforward enough. . . . You should see what they turned in. It's awful! Sometimes they just don't *think.*

American Literature Teacher: It's almost as though they need to be taught how to think.

History Teacher: I always assume that by this age kids know how to think. So when I ask them to compare two ideas in an essay question, I expect them to automatically outline similarities and differences—how the two ideas are alike and how they differ.

American Literature Teacher: But they simply tell one way they're different and think they're answering the question. They never fully explore the idea by comparing and contrasting many characteristics.

History Teacher: You know, we probably need to teach them strategies for thinking. . . . We need to actually demonstrate good thinking. They need the tools to work with so they can approach any question, any situation, and think it through. (Fogarty & McTighe, 1993; p. 161)

◆ Chapter Objectives

Students' thinking about their own thinking and student assembly of new information are the targets of this chapter. Upon the completion of this chapter, you will be able to:

1 Define metacognition and recognize its significance for cognitive learning theory;

2 Describe the research findings about metacognition and development;

3 Analyze the research findings distinguishing novice and expert problemsolvers and readers;

4 Describe several strategies for encouraging metacognition in your students;

5 Explain the major tenets of the constructivist movement in cognitive psychology and its philosophical implications;

6 Link the current constructivist movement to the work of Jean Piaget;

7 Evaluate the research findings concerning constructivism in student thinking; and,

8 Offer general recommendations as well as specific examples of constructivism in classroom teaching.

CHAPTER 12 CONTENT MAP

421

WHAT IS METACOGNITION?

◆ Definitions

metacognition thinking about one's own thinking; examining one's own information processing

Metacognition is thoughtfulness. It is thinking about your own thinking and about how you process information effectively. As Hyde and Bizar (1989) state, "Metacognition (literally, *over* or *overseeing* cognition) refers to our ability to understand and manipulate our own cognitive processes. It involves thinking about our thinking and purposely making changes in how we think" (p. 51).

In other, almost tongue-twisting words, it's "what you know about what you know"! (Benjafield, 1992; p. 8). Although it is probably impossible for any conscious human *not* to think, it is clear that too many students, in fact, too many people in general, fail to think about their thinking! We do not think about how we think or what we know about what we know, which means we cannot control our information processing or use our cognitive capacities to their full advantage. We may be failing, then, to engage in the "self-planning, -monitoring, -regulating, -questioning, -reflecting, -reviewing" that is necessary to critical thinking and learning (Hyde & Bizar, 1989).

A key to grasping the concept of metacognition is the word *purposeful*. We may find ourselves engaged in some of the above processes randomly or accidentally, but research in cognitive psychology emphasizes that in metacognition, the engaging of these processes is intentional and deliberate. Metacognition is controlled; it is purposeful thoughtfulness. But don't be fooled; how we engage our cognititive processes is not always clear and unambiguous. In fact, when we think about our own thinking, we are far from having an absolute picture of how we think. There is always uncertainty about how our minds work, but the active search for increased understanding is adaptive. Awareness and action, as depicted in Table 12.1, are important to the enhancement of critical thinking (Sternberg, 1998; Byrnes, 1996; Willen & Phillips, 1995; Garcia & Pintrich, 1992).

You should know that there is debate in the theoretical literature about whether the source of our metacognitive activities is *explicit* or *implicit*. Some theorists suggest that when we solve a problem, explicit features of the problem spark our metacognitive strategy choice, while other theorists maintain that it is an internal, "rapid feeling of knowing" or our first impressions that guide our metacognitive actions and attempts to solve the problem (Reder, 1996).

Nonetheless, the awareness, reflection, control, and cognitive action that participate in metacognition enable us to think more effectively (Sternberg, 1998; Byrnes, 1996; Hyde & Bizar, 1989; Willen & Phillips, 1995; Ganz & Ganz, 1990; Benjafield, 1992). But we have to develop metacognitive capability as we grow and mature.

◆ Metacognition and Development

Metacognition relies on a fair amount of abstract thinking; the skills engaged are often highly representational and internalized. We may sus-

Table 12.1 A Strategy for Helping Learners Acquire Critical Thinking Skills

A Metacognitive Approach in Teaching Critical Thinking Skills

1. Explanation by the Teacher

   Introduce the skill.

   Show examples and non-examples.

   Use exercises to practice the skill.

2. Modeling by the Teacher

   "Think aloud" the modeling process by the teacher/expert.

   ◆ identification of problem

   ◆ initiation of strategies

   Learner interpretation of the modeling process.

   Teacher provides cues and prompts if there is a lack of understanding.

3. Modeling by the Learner

   "Think aloud" the modeling process by learners in different situations.

   Comparison of their modeling processes.

   Silent modeling whereby learners are on their own.

Source: From "Teaching Critical Thinking: A Metacognitive Approach," by William W. Wilen and John Arul Phillips, March 1995 *Social Education, 59* (3), 135–138. © National Council for the Social Studies. Reprinted by permission.

pect there will be little evidence of metacognitive activity in preschool-age and early school-age students.

Our suspicions are verified in the research. Hennessey (1993) reports that when she studied science students in grades 1–6, she found developmental differences in their metacognitive capabilities. Specifically, she observed that the students became better able to engage in metacognitive activity over time; second graders were less likely to engage in metacognition than third graders, who were less likely to engage metacognition as fully as fourth graders.

On the other hand, Fang and Cox (1999) and Schwanenflugel and colleagues (1994) were surprised to see evidence of metacognitive awareness in preschoolers and in students as young as eight years old, respectively—they had speculated a much later start for such abstract thinking. Schwanenflugel and colleagues (1994) suggested that the period between eight and ten years of age is important for the increasing "awareness of a number of distinct mental processes" (p. 1561). They found, however, that even if children as young as eight years can start to think metacognitively, they often do not. In fact, eleven- and twelve-year-old students failed to engage in needed self-monitoring (Schwanenflugel et al., 1994).

Thus, the good news is that, in theory, most of our students should be able to think about their own thinking and the significant processes that influence their learning. The downside of the research is that "should" and "do" are not the same: students who should be able to engage metacognition frequently do not. We need to consider, then, how teachers can encourage metacognitive activity in students.

A growing body of research strongly supports a role for teachers in the metacognition of students, despite the fact that what is at issue is *students'* thinking about *their* thinking. Teachers can teach students cognitive strategies to facilitate their metacognition. But before we examine a few of those strategies, let's consider their foundations in the comparisons between novice and expert information processors in cognitive psychology.

◆ Comparing Novices and Experts

In the last two decades, cognitive psychologists have observed several distinctions between learners in the ways they approach and process information. Expert learners read, study, and engage in problem solving in ways that are distinct from those employed by the novice learner. Byrnes (1996), citing numerous research summaries, notes that experts are more efficient in their use of their working memories and illustrate better self-monitoring skills.

Expert learners have more knowledge in subject areas than novice learners and "practice their knowledge" by seeking complex linkages and interrelationships between concepts. They are *Gestaltist* in their cognition, meaning they seek to see things as integrated wholes, rather than as isolated parts. Thus, in reading about Piaget's presentation of the pre-operational stage, the expert learner may attempt to connect the child's new ability to internally represent experiences with the increased frequency and intensity of nightmares among these children. A second distinction between novice and expert learners can be found in the way they approach problem solving. Unlike novice learners, who jump right in when they attempt to solve problems, expert learners first try to understand the problem, look for the boundaries of the problem, and attempt to build a viable mental picture of all the problem entails. The orientation process of expert learners enables them to process information more quickly and efficiently (Byrnes, 1996).

self-questioning metacognitive strategy in which students generate and answer questions designed to facilitate information processing; also called "self-interrogation"

A key finding in the research in metacognition is that expert learners are "purposeful, attention-directing, **self-questioning**" in their studying, while novice learners hold few ideas about what is necessary cognitively to be successful (Ganz & Ganz, 1990). While experts tailor their study, reading, or problem-solving strategies to the particular task at hand, novices often engage in rigid strategies that may be inappropriate. Experts even design new strategies for processing information when old strategies prove inadequate; novice, less mature learners do not. Experts also utilize their skills in prediction and are able to extract crucial ideas from texts early on to make the most efficient use of their study time; they are selective in their processing. Novices, on the other hand, attempt to process everything; they woefully lack selectivity (Ganz & Ganz, 1990). This last point is often evident to the teacher who observes those students who underline everything in their texts, who try to take down every word the teacher says verbatim, and who attempt to read every word in the text and in their notes just before the big exam!

Thus, the research offers several features of expert learners that distinguish them from less apt learners. In summary, expert learners activate orienting schemas, draw inferences, use well organized existing **schemas**, and break down information into manageable chunks.

schemas cognitive structures which allow us to represent actions, people, places, events, etc.

TEACHERS' ROLES IN TRAINING METACOGNITION

While it appears obvious that the approach of the expert learner is much more efficient and effective, the question is what do we, as teachers, make of these features? Do teachers just sit back and observe their manifestations in classrooms? Can we use this information to guide our instructional choices? Can we facilitate metacognition, or *self-regulated learning*, for our classrooms?

Metacognitive strategies or self-regulated learning can be taught (Boekaerts, 1997). Teachers can play a significant role in the establishment of structure and networks in meaningful learning in students. In fact, there are strong recommendations that teachers should carefully train students in purposeful, strategic studying, reading, and problem-solving (Gourgey, 1998; Willen & Phillips, 1995; Lucangeli et al., 1995; Feden, 1994; Ganz & Ganz, 1990; Hydes & Bizar, 1989). Remember the history teacher's remark: "We probably need to take some time to teach them strategies for thinking" (Fogarty & McTighe, 1993; p. 161).

If the appropriate strategies are employed, teachers can make learners better users of their metacognitive skills (Dixon-Krauss, 1996). Teachers, through careful student training, can invite students to be purposefully thoughtful (Fogarty & McTighe, 1993). Precise training in engaging metacognitive strategies has, in fact, improved the level of knowledge and performance in fifth graders (Lucangeli et al., 1995). Interestingly, however, Zohar (1999) found that many teachers do not employ their own metacognitive skills, which makes it difficult for them to teach the skills to their students!

But what kinds of things, then, do teachers teach to encourage students to know what they know? In addition to supplying study guides, opportunities for collaborative discussion (emphasized in the latter sections of this chapter), and written summaries to students, there are a number of specific metacognitive learning strategies that a teacher can teach to students.

◆ Metacognitive Learning Strategies

A teacher interested in facilitating her students' use of metacognitive learning strategies would do well to teach them strategies such as self-questioning, KWL, PQ4R, and IDEAL. Fascinatingly, cross-cultural studies have shown that similar strategies are used in different parts of the world: Japanese, Australian, and American students were taught to use very similar metacognitive problem-solving strategies (Jones & Davenport, 1996; Purdie & Hattie, 1996).

Self-Questioning

To facilitate metacognition, teachers can present divergent questions (or questions with a range of possible answers) for students to answer, or they can encourage the students to generate their own questions (Cardiello, 1998). We will focus on the latter strategy.

A teacher can assist students in their use of self-questioning or self-interrogation (Ganz & Ganz, 1990). Ganz & Ganz (1990) suggest that self-questioning encourages the students' monitoring of their own cognition, along with the assessment of their feelings about the efficacy of their thinking. It also assists students in the employment of self-correction and the development of newer understanding (Ganz & Ganz, 1990).

cognitive behavior modification metacognitive strategy in which the teacher demonstrates a task and guides students through the use of self-instruction and practice

In attempting to teach students the process of self-questioning, a teacher would do well to use many of the **cognitive behavior modification** techniques discussed in Chapter 6. Specifically, the teacher should demonstrate the procedure, then encourage students to execute the strategy along with the teacher, and finally, provide opportunities for students to enact the strategy alone.

Wilen and Phillips (1995) enumerate three steps for helping learners, as described in Table 12.1. Step 1 requires the teacher to (a) identify the skills to be taught, (b) outline the steps necessary to complete the skill, and (c) explain to students both the significance of the skill and the circumstances of its use, often through illustrative examples. Step 2 requires that the teacher model the cognitive processes necessary to use the skill. Finally, the third step directs the teacher to

Teachers can help students with self-questioning or self-interrogation. In turn, students are assisted by self-correction and the development of newer understanding. ◆

guide the student in the exercise of the skill (Wilen & Phillips, 1995). Ideally, teachers will become less involved in the exercise of the skill over time, as the students have greater opportunities to practice (Hyde & Bizar, 1989).

When applying this model to teaching self-questioning skills we would expect that a teacher would first identify self-questioning as the specific metacognitive skill that she wishes to teach and then describe to her students the significance of that skill for effective study. The teacher might then model self-questioning prompts for the student. To facilitate student self-monitoring the teacher might include the following prompts (Ganz & Ganz, 1990; p. 181):

"Should I slow down here?"

"Can I skip the clarifying explanation?"

"Can I picture this situation or information in my mind?"

Or, these prompts (Hyde & Bizar, 1989; p. 99):

"Have I ever encountered any similar problems?"

"What information is irrelevant?"

"Should I take notes on this part?"

"Do I understand what is going on?"

"Am I on the right track?"

The teacher then guides the student to use these prompts in appropriate situations.

Different skills require somewhat different prompts that should be taught to students. For example, **prediction**, a skill that calls on students to "pause to hypothesize" about the content (Dixon-Krauss, 1996), can be practiced through the use of the following self-questioning prompts (Hyde & Bizar, 1989; p. 99):

prediction skill requiring students to hypothesize about content to be learned

"What do they really want here?"

"What are the different assumptions I could make?"

Or the following (Ganz & Ganz, 1990; p. 181):

"What do I think will happen next?"

"Was that piece of information related to what I read on the last page or paragraph?"

Further, in situations in which comprehension and review are desired, teachers might model the following prompts (Ganz & Ganz, 1990; p. 181):

"Did this make sense?"

"Can I say this in my own words?"

"Can I make a judgement now?"

"Will this make sense later?"

In general, effective teachers facilitate development of metacognitive skills by teaching students specific strategies and allowing them time to practice the strategies (Feden, 1994).

KWL Strategy

KWL metacognitive strategy focusing on what students know, what they want to know, and what they did learn

KWL is a strategy enabling students to know what they *know*, what they *want* to learn, and what they did *learn* (Dixon-Krauss, 1996). This metacognitive strategy starts with student discussion of what they know and a listing of the information. Then, students are encouraged to make predictions about what they want to learn. Having read the content information, students are guided to recall the information they learned. Figure 12.1 depicts a KWL chart designed by third graders studying the life of Johnny Appleseed.

PQ4R Method

PQ4R metacognitive strategy encouraging students to predict, question, read, reflect, recite, and review material to be learned on their own

The **PQ4R** is a popular metacognitive strategy with steps similar to KWL, albeit in greater detail. PQ4R is an acronym for: *Preview, Question, Read, Reflect, Recite,* and *Review.* This PQ4R strategy assists students to process a lot of information in a relatively short amount of time. It helps the student to orient cognitively to the task at hand prior to actual reading. The following teacher tool box provides suggestions for assisting students in the utilization of the PQ4R method.

Figure 12.1
KWL Chart of Johnny Appleseed

K What you KNOW	W What you WANT to learn	L What you LEARNED
He took a lot of journeys.	Is he still alive?	His mother and brother died when he was two.
He was nice.	How old was he when he died?	He made friends with the Indians.
He liked apple trees.	Why did he wear a pan on his head?	He was born September 26, 1774.
He died 156 years ago.		He was 70 years old when he died.
He loved the forest animals.		He carried his pan on his head so his hands would be free.
His real name was John Chapman.		There are many legends about Johnny Appleseed.
Everywhere he went he planted apple trees.		

Source: From *Vygotsky in the Classroom* by Lisbeth Dixon-Krauss. Copyright 1996 by Longman Publishers USA. Reprinted with permission of Addison-Wesley Educational Publishers, Inc.

IDEAL

Another approach to metacognition is to *Identify, Define, Explore, Act,* and *Look.* **IDEAL** is the acronym for these strategies, which are important for effective and efficient thinking and problem solving (cf. Byrnes, 1996). Each of these specific metacognitive skills can be taught to students by a teacher who is concerned with facilitating effective thinking and problem solving.

Effective problem solving should begin with *identification* or the careful anticipation of potential difficulties. Novice learners rarely anticipate problems, while expert learners do. However, identifying the existence of problems is not enough. It is also necessary to attempt to ascertain just what makes this problem so difficult, to ask "What's wrong here?" Thus, after identification, *problem definition* is a significant step (Byrnes, 1996). Through this step, the efficient learner examines goals and looks for obstacles to those goals.

The third strategy in problem solving is *exploration.* Following the identification and definition of the obstacles to understanding, the student explores solution options. Expert learners are more reflective and open-minded to possible solutions, while novice learners are more rigid and narrow. Both expert and novice learners act on their solution options, but only expert learners think purposefully before acting (Byrnes, 1996).

The last strategy in IDEAL, after trying a solution option, is for the student to look and note which actions lead to successful resolution and which do not. This is a critical step. Comparison research indicates that only expert learners monitor the outcomes of their choices, while novices are inattentive (Byrnes, 1996).

Teacher Tool Box

PQ4R Method

As teachers, we can facilitate metacognition in our students by modeling the PQ4R method through the following steps:

P	PREVIEW	Skim the material. Read the titles. Note the length. Use headings as guides.
Q	QUESTION	Construct questions about the material. Ask yourself, "What do I need to know?" Use headings.
R	READ	Read, using questions as guides. Pay attention to introductory paragraphs. Reread difficult passages. Look up unfamiliar terms.
R	REFLECT	Think about what has been read. Relate ideas to what you already know.
R	RECITE	Close book and answer questions. Relate information to headings. Recall main points.
R	REVIEW	Organize information. Restudy difficult material. Remember linkages. (Thomas & Robinson, 1972.)

IDEAL a metacognitive strategy featuring student processing skills, i.e., identification, definition, exploration, action, and looking, to facilitate thinking and problem-solving

YOU MAKE THE CALL

FACILITATING METACOGNITION

Examine these questions: How will you promote self-questioning? How will you encourage prediction? Do you know how you might encourage your students to monitor their own learning? What is the role of teachers in metacognition?

◆ Instructional Methods that Promote Metacognition

Reciprocal teaching, developed by Anne Marie Palincsar (cf. Hyde & Bizar, 1989), is an instructional method that can promote metacognition. It not only supports metacognition, but adds an important

One commonly used metacognitive method is journal writing. It helps students to reflect on classroom learning and to modify their cognitive structures. ◆

affective component—peer interaction—to purposeful thoughtfulness as well. It brings to mind the old shampoo commercial in which sudsy models tell the television audience that they were so happy with their shampoo that they told two friends about it, who then told two other friends, and so on and so on. In reciprocal teaching, a teacher will first model a metacognitive strategy like PQ4R for the students and practice it with them. In time, however, the teacher turns the process over to the students, who in turn instruct other students in the class to execute the metacognitive strategy. Collaboration between students is viewed as an added benefit of reciprocal teaching, and, as with any of the strategies, the role of the teacher and the time involved lessen as the students become more familiar and more comfortable with the process (Hyde & Bizar, 1989). One teacher-peer modeling technique similar to reciprocal teaching was used to improve the learning of underachieving gifted students (Manning et al., 1996).

Other types of instructional tools qualify as metacognitive systems as well. One method commonly used is **journal writing.** Which induces students to reflect and modify cognitive structures by encouraging student questions and comments on their classroom learning (Hettich, 1993; Cole, 1993). Similarly, the growing interest in the use of portfolios has increased teacher introspection and **self-regulation** of learning (Deming & Valeri-Gold, 1994; Gordon, 1994).

journal writing metacognitive strategy in which students reflect on and identify cognitive strategies in written records

self-regulation metacognitive strategy in which students monitor their own processing of information

The Value of Increasing Student Metacognition

What are the benefits for increased metacognition in students? What kind of classroom promotes thinking about thinking? Consider Fogarty and McTighe's (1993) description of a classroom emphasizing metacognitive awareness:

> [S]tudents meet in small groups at the beginning of math class to review their homework problems. They discuss only the ones with differing answers,

trying to reconcile the differences. Only when agreement is reached do they turn in their papers. In this scenario, group members trace their problem-solving steps in an effort to find the best answer. Students may reason that they need to multiply at one point in the problem because they know the answer has to be a larger number. (Fogarty & McTighe, 1993; p. 165).

What's important here is the students' awareness of their own thinking as well as the thinking of others. The awareness and cognitive control developed facilitates problem solving. We noted in Chapter 6—and it bears repeating now—that Meichenbaum (1975) has done interesting work in using metacognitive skills to enhance student creativity as well.

Now, let's not forget that we will be teaching in classrooms with students who differ from each other in additional ways. Recent research in metacognition has started to examine the relationship between individual differences in students and cognitive learning. This research has demonstrated that lower-ability students especially gain from metacognitive instruction (Spence et al., 1995; Cardelle-Elawar, 1995). Further, training in metacognitive strategies has been reported to enhance the thinking and social skills of learning-disabled students (Powell & Makin, 1994; Rosenthal-Malek, 1997). But, what about cultural differences (refer to Chapter 5)? Will differences in gender or learning styles or race/ethnicity or language influence the use of metacognitive strategy? They certainly can. Several studies in recent years have reported possible links between such individual differences and student use of metacognitive problem solving strategies (Hartman et al., 1996; Carr & Jessup, 1997; Lee et al., 1995; Turner, 1993). Yet further study is needed in this area, especially as we try to understand why and how differences in cultural groups influence cognitive learning. The effective teacher, nonetheless, tries to take into consideration the need for varied approaches that may be required in a diverse classroom.

CONSTRUCTIVISM: THE "NEW" MOVEMENT

Benjafield (1992) writes, "Cognitive psychology is not in a finished state" (p. 8). We continue to learn about how the brain processes information. Over the course of the last two decades, we have begun to shift attention from information processing (see Chapter 7) and metacognition to a new theoretical focal point—**constuctivisim.**

◆ Rationale and Philosophical Implications

In the traditional classroom, there is an emphasis on the transmission of knowledge, and meaning is conveyed, largely, via the spoken and written word of teachers (Wadsworth, 1996). The teacher decides which topics, concepts, and skills are to be taught, and then teaches them directly and intact (Yager and Lutz, 1994). But traditional orientations to teaching are getting a new look. Contemporary research in neuro-

constructivism cognitive theory emphasizing learner interest in and accountability for their own learning which manifests in student self-questioning and discovery

psychology suggests different roles for both teachers and students for effective learning (Lord, 1999; Smilkstein, 1991). These new roles have been embraced by the constructivist movement in education.

Constructivism is a theory of how learning occurs (Henson, 1996). Its philosophical roots suggest that if learning is viewed as important to the lives of learners, they will be intrigued by learning enough to seek their own understandings and insights. Learners will seek meaning via the questioning of their own knowledge and via new discoveries (Henson, 1996). Thus, from this perspective and in the words of Bransford et al. (cf. Saunders, 1992; p. 136), "Wisdom cannot be told."

The constructivist perspective emphasizes that learning occurs only when learners actively engage their cognitive structures in schema-building experiences (Yager & Lutz, 1994; Fosnot, 1996). Saunders (1992), for example, stated: "Learners respond to sensory experiences by building or constructing in their minds, schemas or cognitive structures which constitute the meaning and understanding of their world" (p. 136). Thus, pre-existing schemas, or what the learner brings to the learning episode, figure prominently in constructivist learning (Saunders, 1992; Byrnes, 1996; Yager & Lutz, 1994).

From the constructivist perspective, learners try to make sense of the world by relying on their pre-existing schemas. Learning is aided by social interaction with peers and teachers and via real world experiences. Some—if not all—of the assumptions of constructivism may sound familiar to you, and with good reason. There are theoretical parallels to be drawn between the recent constructivist movement and the work of previously studied cognitive psychologists Jean Piaget, Lev Vygotsky, and Jerome Bruner, although Piaget's work is most often described as the impetus for the current orientation (Kamii, 1981; Valsinger, 1996; Wadsworth, 1996; Byrnes, 1996).

◆ Modern-Day Piaget

The constructivists believe that cognitive structures enable learners to use past experiences. Sounds a lot like the Piagetian notion of assimilative triggers to schema development. Further, the constructivist belief that the cognitive structures can be modified for newer explanations reminds us of Piaget's "**accommodation**" (Saunders, 1992). Indeed, Piaget's **interactionist** ideas about the individual building of knowledge in a context of environmental stimulation are at the heart of the current movement. The child is primarily responsible for construction, although social interaction can provide a framework for internal change.

As you remember from the earlier chapter on cognitive development, when confronted with new experiences, we seek first to assimilate the experience into an existing schema. But when the newly encountered proves too discrepant, we modify our existing schemas or add new ones altogether—we accommodate—thereby internalizing the encounter. The Piaget school stresses, however, the importance of confronting the discrepancy *ourselves* (Byrnes, 1996). Cognitive constructivists such as Piaget view social interaction as beneficial, but emphasize

accommodation Piagetian term for changing or modifying cognitive schemes to encourage understanding of new information

interactionist theoretical perspective which reflects the influence of nature and nurture on development and learning

that the initial spark that moves the learner towards adaptation comes from within. Consider the following 1940s dialogue between Piaget and a young student named Claude:

> *Piaget:* What is Switzerland?
>
> *Claude:* It's a country.
>
> *Piaget:* And Geneva?
>
> *Claude:* A town.
>
> *Piaget:* Where is Geneva?
>
> *Claude:* In Switzerland. (Claude draws two circles side by side; the circle for Geneva is smaller.) I'm drawing the circle for Geneva smaller because Geneva is smaller. Switzerland is very big.
>
> *Piaget:* Quite right, but where is Geneva?
>
> *Claude:* In Switzerland.
>
> *Piaget:* Are you Swiss?
>
> *Claude:* Yes.
>
> *Piaget:* And are you Genevese?
>
> *Claude:* Oh no! I'm Swiss now (cf. Kamii, 1981; p. 12).

From Claude's drawing as well as from his comments we can discern that the child's understanding of the relationship between "countries" and "towns" is quite different from what we might imagine and do not reflect what he may have been told.

Thus, the issue of balancing the impact of nature and nurture in learning finds an interesting resolution in constructivism (Wadsworth, 1996). Students are motivated to learn because of **disequilibrium** or **cognitive conflict.** Cognitive conflict, according to Wadsworth (1996), occurs when a learner's predictions for learning—based on their pre-existing schemas—are not confirmed. From the Piagetian perspective, we are made "mentally uncomfortable" by cognitive conflict, and we seek the comfort found in understanding newly encountered experiences. But the movement from current conceptualization to new cognitive conflict to newer, constructed meaning occurs within the individual.

disequilibrium or cognitive conflict learners' predictions based on their pre-existing, unconfirmed schemata that motivate them to seek answers

---

YOU MAKE THE CALL

A CONTRUCTIVIST VIEW

Think about these questions for minute: How do you respond to each of the following? How would a contructivist?

◆ Who should control students' learning?

◆ Is it left to the individual student alone?

◆ Can others help students arrive at meaning and understanding?

◆ Constructivist Perspectives

There are differing schools of thought on how we acquire schema. Each has distinctive implications for the role of teachers. The *nativists* (e.g., Immanuel Kant and Noam Chomsky) reject the value of "outside inter-

Teacher Tool Box

To further understand these distinction, let's examine the following analogy by Byrnes (1996):

Imagine that a student's knowledge is like a brick wall. Each brick is a piece of information that is interconnected to other pieces of information. Empiricists think that a child's mind is merely a receptacle for a teacher who builds the wall inside the child's head. As they teach something, they metaphorically lay another brick in just the right spot. In contrast, nativists think the that the wall is already built when children are born. All teachers do is help students turn inward and see what they already know. Or, they can wait for the wall to build up by itself much as we stand back and watch a child grow taller. . . . Constructivists think that teachers do provide the bricks, but they merely toss them to students who try to lay the bricks themselves. Sometimes students do not understand a brick, so they drop it or lay it in the wrong place. Sometimes they have not built the wall up high enough to be able to lay a certain kind of brick (e.g., a really abstract idea) (pp.13–14).

vention." The nativists believe that construction is the sole responsibility of the individual: we are innately predisposed to understand complex concepts in the world. Our understanding of concepts such as time, space, and grammar are inborn (Byrnes, 1996). The nativists emphasize that the initial spark which moves the learner towards adaptation comes from within—and not from without. From such a biological orientation, there is little role for teachers or organized instruction.

On the other hand, the *empiricists* believe that teachers—and others—are central to construction. The empiricists (e.g., John Locke and E. L. Thorndyke) believe that there is no "pure" discovery but *only* discovery mediated by others (Byrnes, 1996). The empiricists view the human mind as a "blank slate" waiting for the stroke of the pen of experience. The empiricists see social interaction with teachers, parents, and peers as providing a key stimulus for internalized exploration (Byrnes, 1996). They believe that active participation of multiple learners is crucial to construction (Dixon-Krauss, 1996).

While these two positions present quite different orientations, reconciliation in the guise of a multiple model can be found: both the cognitive or nativist and the social or empiricist views contribute to the development of the learner (Fosnot, 1993). Hence, the *constructivists* represent a third position. They agree with the nativists' view that people impose their own schema on the world, but they do not agree that understanding of complex concepts is inborn. Additionally, they agree with the empiricist view that our experiences with others are important to our learning, but they disagree with the empiricists' belief that social integration is solely responsible for learning and that such understanding occurs immediately because of interaction (Byrnes, 1996). The constructivist model, therefore, blends the best of the previous two schools.

The constructivist position, therefore, offers suggestions to teachers about learner-centered instruction. We will investigate, then, the role of teachers in the multiple model of constructivism.

◆ Characterizing Constructivist Teaching and Classrooms

Constructivist philosophy can alter—and perhaps should alter—the culture of the classroom (Windschitl, 1999). The research suggests that three factors—autonomy, interaction, and exploration—are most frequently identified as characterstics of constructivist teaching and classrooms.

Action Research

Metacognitive Techniques in Mr. Goodwin's Science Class

M r. J. L. Goodwin was a high school science teacher for more than 21 years prior to attending a workshop on metacognition. At the workshop, he discussed his frustration with what he felt was the students' difficulty in not only applying logical problem-solving approaches to his course material but also in their inability to learn from their mistakes. He was encouraged to use some of the metacognitive techniques discussed at the workshop.

Using two of his general science classes, he decided to modify his method of homework review for one and continue his typical approach with the other. In this "experimental" class, he allowed the students to meet in small groups at the beginning of the period in order to discuss their homework assignments. They were told to share their answers, and when there was disagreement, they were to discuss how they came to their conclusion. Mr. Goodwin allowed the students to modify their answers following their discussion with their peers.

A second adjustment that he made was to have the students in this class maintain a journal in which they described how they approached their homework assignments and how they modified their approach following the discussion with their peers. In his second class he simply collected the homework and explained the correct approach and answer. This was his typical approach to correcting homework.

He hypothesized that by helping the members of the "experimental class" identify and share their own approach to problem solving they would not only become more aware of their thinking but would begin to develop more effective problem-solving approaches. After one marking period Mr. Goodwin noted that his "experimental class" were not only more active and participative within the class but were advancing through the material at a faster rate than the second class. Further, on a standardized district test, the average grade for experimental class was nine points higher than that of the second class. Mr. Goodwin decided to implement this procedure with his other classes in order to see if the same results could be obtained.

Student autonomy is an important element in the classroom (Yager & Lutz, 1994; Wadsworth, 1996; Li, 1993). Constructivist teachers are able to relinquish control of student learning. They trust their students to be responsible for their own learning. They allow students' interests to drive the lessons and let the students make intellectual choices for themselves.

One of the fascinating aspects of constructivism is that, to be successful in its implementation, all must be fully engaged (Li, 1993). Teachers *and* students need to reflect on their own thinking, seek interactions with others, and explore the world from differing viewpoints. Constructivist teaching, therefore, encourages *social interaction* between students and between teachers and students (Yager & Lutz, 1994; Saunders, 1992; Wadsworth, 1996; Mason, 1994; Henson, 1996). Fosnot (1996) writes that "dialogue within a community engenders further thinking" (p. 29). In the classroom, social interaction provides opportunities for cognitive conflict and cooperation. When children work together, they are exposed to differing points of view. Students are encouraged to articulate their differing constructions to each other and to the teacher. These discussions in turn stimulate higher order thinking. Yet, in the constructivist classroom the teacher limits intraclass competition to further collaboration.

student autonomy entrusting students with their learning and allowing their interests to guide lessons

But, wait! Perhaps a little mystery might help pique your interest in constructivist teaching. Consider the case of the Walking Sweater.

THE CASE OF THE WALKING SWEATER

Lena Jones had already concluded for the tenth time that today was not the day to be a store manager, when the head store detective ushered in a very red-faced young man.

"This kid just walked out with this," the detective said, and he threw a crumpled sweater onto Lena's desk. "I got him down the street. He was at least a hundred yards away. And he's admitted it. Open and shut."

"Very well." Lena sighed and looked at the young man. "We'll take your name and address. You realize that the police will be involved too, don't you?" She began to get angry. "Don't you realize that shoplifters are so easy to catch?"

The young man reddened even more, and fought to keep back the tear that was beginning to roll down his cheek.

"No!" he almost shouted. "I was like . . . trying it on in the dressing room, and got it on all inside out back to front. I mean, here it was on wrong, and the tags were inside and all, and I thought nobody would see it was from the store so I just, I mean, I just . . . walked out! I didn't plan it! Nobody saw it either . . . until this guy stopped me."

Lena looked at the detective. "Who tipped you off?" she asked.

"That's part of the problem," the detective answered. "The security light went on when he went out the door so I just followed him. But the problem is that there are two different clerks claiming the store reward. They both say they saw him leave, and each of them says she turned on the alarm light. . . . Borelli's one," he said. "She claims she saw the kid coming toward her and when she saw the label of the sweater, she figured out what he was doing and hit the light as soon as he got to the door."

Lena pondered a moment. "And the other story?"

"That's Singh," the detective replied. "She's a part-timer. Her story is that she saw him stop at the door for a minute and check the street. That's when she saw the sweater label, and she too figured it was a lift and hit the light. Both her [*sic*] and Borelli work right beside the exit door," he offered, "so really, both their stories check."

"In all but one respect," Lena said. "It looks like we've not only got a lifter here, we may have a liar, too!"

What made Lena suspicious? And which clerk does she suspect is lying?

Source: Adapted from Ken Weber's *Five Minute Mysteries* (1989), pp. 151–152.

---

cognitive exploration direct, hands-on investigation which facilitates higher order thinking skills

Did you attempt to solve the mystery? (The answer appears at the end of this chapter.) If you did, you were using your inductive reasoning skills to try to link the clues in order to find the solution. Opportunities for **cognitive exploration** and higher-order thinking skills are promoted by constructivist teachers (Yager & Lutz, 1994; Wadsworth, 1996; Hwang-bo & Yawkey, 1994; Saunders, 1992). Constructivist theory suggests that direct, active, hands-on exploration facilitates higher order thinking (Smilkenstein, 1991). The teacher is the mediator of these types of experiences. The emphasis of the constructivist teacher, then, is not on what to teach, but on how to teach (Yager & Lutz, 1994). Thus, content is viewed as a vehicle for the development of higher-order cognitive processes (Henson, 1996). As depicted in the scene described in the beginning of the chapter, the constructivist teacher is intrigued by his students' errors. In wanting to examine their test errors, he is attempting to reconstruct their thinking to facilitate both his students' and his own future learning. In a technique derived from Piaget's clinical interview technique, the constructivist teacher might pose questions to students such as "How did you arrive at this answer?" or "How did you approach this problem?" to explore even their incorrect answers (Wadsworth, 1996).

Teachers in the constructivist classroom are skilled at asking thoughtful, divergent questions and allowing enough wait time for students to be reflective. Teachers provoke cognitive conflict through skilled questioning, also known as critical exploration. Guiding students in the use of questioning, like that depicted in Figure 12.2, can assist critical exploration. Henson (1996) summarizes contrasts between the pre-constructivist and constructivist teaching in Table 12.2.

Constructivist-style Questioning		
WHAT?	**WHERE/WHEN?**	**WHICH?**
What is it?	Where/when is it?	Which is it?
What did it do?	Where/when did it do it?	Which did it do?
What can it do?	Where/when can it do it?	Which can it do?
What would it do?	Where/when would it do it?	Which would it do?
What will it do?	Where/when will it do it?	Which will it do?
What might it do?	Where/when might it do it?	Which might it do?
WHO?	**WHY?**	**HOW?**
Who is it?	Why is it?	How is it?
Who did it?	Why did it do it?	How did it do?
Who can do it?	Why can it do it?	How can it do?
Who would do it?	Why would it do it?	How would it do?
Who will do it?	Why will it do it?	How will it do?
Who might do it?	Why might it do it?	How might it do?

Figure 12.2
Constructivist-Style Questioning
Source: Adapted from Resources for Teachers, Inc.

Table 12.2 The Roles of Constructivist and Preconstructivist Teachers

Preconstructivist Teaching Roles	Constructivist Teaching Roles
The teacher:	The teacher:
Provides information	Invites students to discover information
Preidentifies important information	Invites students to identify additional content that interests them
Helps students remember information by giving clear explanations and examples	Helps students discover information
Continuously strives for clarity	Arranges for discontinuity
Keeps students quiet and on task	Encourages students to create learning; allows a reasonable amount of noise
Strives to convey all information designated for the particular grade level	Strives to help students reach a deeper understanding of fewer topics
Uses threats and other punishments to motivate	Uses students' personal interests to motivate
Uses intraclass competition to motivate	Uses interclass competition to motivate

Source: From *Methods and Strategies for Teaching in Secondary and Middle Schools* by Henson (1996). Reprinted by permission of Addison Wesley.

To generate disequilibrium, the constructivist teacher surprises his students with the unknown and the unpredictable. Students' constructions benefit from multiple experiences rather than one-shot opportunities. Discovery learning-type activities and hands-on investigative labs are the rule.

◆ Discovery Learning Model

discovery learning teaching model which highlights the learners' interests, self-motivation, and self-regulation

Jerome Bruner—studied in Chapter 7—is noted for translating the learning through insight or constructivist perspective into a particular teaching model, **discovery learning** or guided discovery. He wrote: "The most urgent need of all is to give our pupils the experience of what it is to use a theoretical model, with some sense of what is involved in being aware that one is trying out a theory. . . .We shall, of course, try to encourage students to discover on their own . . . we want to give them opportunity to develop a decent competence at it and a proper confidence in their ability to operate independently" (Bruner, 1978, p. 96).

The discovery learning model does all the things a cognitive structuralist model should do: New information is linked to familiar information via selective organization in a learner-satisfying format. However, discovery learning puts a greater emphasis on the motivational or "learner satisfying" aspects of encoding, storage, and retrieval

(Bruner, 1978) than is perhaps true of other cognitive structuralist models.

Discovery learning or guided discovery encourages students to make guesses based on incomplete information and stimulates them to find their own systematic means to solve problems. In discovery learning, teachers serve only as guides. But the teacher's role is not to be taken lightly—discovery learning is not "blind trial and error" learning (Ausubel, 1968, p. 536). In fact, teachers "set up" the eventual discoveries by offering basic information and some details without giving students too much information. In discovery learning, students do all the work. Students determine the best ways to organize new and familiar information for efficient future transfer. Bruner maintained that problems and puzzles stimulate students to discover the underlying structure of the subject matter themselves. Left to "fill in the gaps" in their learning, they will determine ways to organize the information for encoding, storage, and eventual recall in the most personally efficient and comfortable way.

Several studies support the significance of insight and discovery to learning. Primary school students explored the environment via a scientific inquiry/discovery learning method (Klein, 1991). Junior high school students increased their learning in science using discovery learning approaches (e.g., an inquiry approach) as well (Scruggs et al., 1993; Lord, 1998), and guided discovery enabled seventh graders to ask thoughtful questions, become less dependent on the teacher and textbook, and perceive math as useful, regardless of ability (Higgins, 1993). Teachers at Pound Junior High School in Lincoln, Nebraska, encouraged their students to learn about forces, speed, energy, acceleration, and Newton's laws through rocket building (Winemiller et al., 1991). Mokros and Russell (1995) observed students' productive and nonproductive constructions as they tried to understand the concept of "averages"; hands-on encounters with a data set facilitated their understanding. Discovery techniques have also facilitated student reading and participation in discussions, science constructions, and understanding of culture (Carter & Holden, 1997; Garnett et al., 1995; Wadsworth, 1997; Gregg et al., 1996). It also has been helpful in the training of blind students (Boone & Boone, 1997).

Many of you may have learned via the discovery method. Perhaps you participated in "The Famous Egg Drop," developed by Cal Tech students, in which students learn science principles by having to creatively devise a way to package an egg so that it can survive a drop from the top of a building (Hyde & Bizar, 1989). Or perhaps you had creative teachers who helped structure your learning environment in ways that maximized your own discovery. If you have, your experience may support the position taken by Cardellichio (1995) and Frid and Malone

Connections

You might want to find some information about discovery learning on your own through your internet sources. Ask questions about discovery learning of the educational experts which can be found at the <http://FamilyEducation.com> site. Compare and contrast constructivist theory and the practice of teaching for insight.

Teacher Tool Box

Guided Discovery—Developed Insight

Teachers can provide insightful experiences to students in a variety of ways. Teachers can promote discovery learning through the use of

- Warmups or short practice exercises at the beginning of class,

- Student questioning or "Ask me about . . ." sessions,

- Examples and non-examples where students establish links,

- Class discussions that are open and free-wheeling,

- Set induction or discovery via analogies,

- Problem-solving exercises in math, science, moral dilemmas,

- Socratic questioning where students link exemplars,

- Guided lab exercises which leave students to hypothesize,

- Guided class demonstrations where teachers withhold clues,

- Individualized assignments of planned, independent projects.

Wilcox, 1987; pp. 53–56.

(1994) that to provide students with only factual knowledge undermines meaningful learning.

Limitations of the Discovery Learning Model. Teachers familiar with Bruner's model can attest that it is a good model for testing students' application of prior learning. It is a wonderful teaching method for self-motivated students with sufficient background knowledge. However, inherent in each of these advantages are disadvantages also.

Yes, discovery learning is a wonderful method for self-motivated students—but not all students will come to your classroom with the level of motivation required for successful discovery learning activities. The deliberate uncertainty of the activities is frustrating—too frustrating for some students. Also, sometimes, if left to their own devices, students will fill in the gaps purposefully provided in discovery learning with activities that are purposeful to the student but are not appropriate for the lesson. Others may draw wrong conclusions or will go off on tangents that the teacher neither intended nor anticipated.

Think back. How well did you do with the Five-Minute Mystery? Too long, too frustrating to continue? Did you check to see if you came up with the correct solution? What happens if you were wrong? Garnett et al. (1995) found that chemistry students do indeed harbor many misconceptions, or *misconstructions*, about chemistry at the beginning of the semester. If left on their own, these misconceptions may persist and compound. There are also concerns about the evaluation of discovery learning and about their effectiveness with low-ability students (Heywood et al., 1992).

One additional limitation has been identified for constructivist-type teaching in general. In an interesting study by Brown and Rose (1995), teachers were reported to be fairly knowledgeable about constructivism, its major theorists, and recommended teaching activities. Yet the teachers reported engaging in little actual constructivist teaching in their classrooms. Why? One reason was that the teachers were so preoccupied with the other demands on their time and expertise—e.g., handling inclusive classrooms, meeting mandated curricular standards—that they just could not integrate constructivist activities into their teaching. Although worthwhile, these strategies can be time-consuming and complicated (Bevevino et al., 1999).

As a result of these possible limitations, some cognitive theorists view the constructivist perspective and teaching methods like discovery

Many teachers use the discovery method via the Famous Egg Drop experiment. Students learn science principles by having to creatively devise a way to package an egg so that it can be dropped without breaking. ◆

learning as good for motivating students but inefficient ways to learn. They prefer more teacher-directed approaches like those of the expository teaching method—described in Chapter 7. However, Heywood et al. (1992) compared discovery and expository teaching and found, despite few differences in test results, classrooms where students engaged in discovery methods had environments that were more conducive and supportive of learning.

Postscript

In the "Mystery of the Walking Sweater," if the sweater was inside out and backwards, the label would not have been prominent from the rear, therefore, the clerk who said she saw the tag as the accused was standing in the door was lying. (Adapted from Weber, 1989; p. 195.)

Reflections from the Field

1 The use of journal writing as allowed by students to take the material discussed in class and find through their own reflection a way to elaborate upon the concepts and to make them meaningful to their own experience and as such facilitate their long-term storage.

—Lew K. (eleventh grade American literature teacher), Newark, DE

2 Probably one of the hardest things for me to have learned—and yet one of the most rewarding—is to "relinquish control" of the student learning. But providing my students with intellectual choices has really led not only to increased student involvement but to a more personal level of knowing for my students.

—Kevin McK. (eighth grade social studies teacher), Albany, NY

3 I have taught my tenth grade social studies students the PQ4R method, and it has significantly improved their test grades. They are thrilled knowing "how their brain works"!

—Jonathan F. (tenth grade social studies teacher), New Orleans, LA

4 I have used the "snowball method" in my earth science course with the students identifying the types of topic-related questions they want answered (usually two questions), and then I have them pair up with a partner to compare questions and discuss the reason for their selection. I ask them to come to an agreement about the two questions they want answered, and then I combine this group with another pairing to come to agreement. It really helps them not only take ownership of the material to be presented but it has increased their eagerness to answer the questions.

—Emilho L. (sixth grade science teacher), Lawrence, KN

5 I have found that teaching my lower ability students about how they process material and help them to develop strategies for effective problem solving, like IDEAL, has really helped them not only improve achievement but increase their feelings of power and self-esteem. They really love to discuss their perspectives on the problems I present.

—Cheryl M. (fifth grade social studies teacher), Boca Raton, FL

THEORY TO PRACTICE

A Look at the Teacher as Decision Maker

As we observe a teacher in a learner-centered classroom, we soon come to appreciate the degree to which he obviously values metacognition and a constructivist approach. In addition to assisting his students to employ *mnemonics*, the effective teacher continually challenges the students to think about their approach, say, to the calculus problems he presents. Further, as he instructs his students on problem-solving strategies, he models the approach and then practices it with them as they employ these strategies (*reciprocal teaching*).

We have already seen a teacher demonstrate his own interest in constructivism. As he pores over his students' tests to examine their errors, he gives evidence of his interest to understand how they problem-solved, even if that knowledge came through an investigation of their errors. But there may be other examples of his employment of a constructivist approach to his classroom. Consider the skill with which the teacher might *use thoughtful questions* to provoke cognitive conflict. The silence that follows such questioning sometimes is evidence of the *creative cognitive tension* this question stimulated. The result is that each student is positioned for *critical exploration* of an answer that will help them out of this cognitive tension.

You, as Teacher, as Decision Maker

Illustration 1:

As you revisit the exchange between the history teacher and the american literature teacher, consider each of the following questions:

1. How do you analyze this scene in a metacognitive context?

2. What options can we offer these teachers?

3. How could the teachers guide the students in self-questioning—for prediction, monitoring, and reviewing?

4. How could reciprocal teaching be used to guide their students in the development of a strategic reading or problem-solving strategy like the PQ4R or IDEAL?

History Teacher: I'm so frustrated with my class today. For homework, I asked them to compare the major campaign strategies of the two candidates. That seems straightforward enough. . . . You should see what they turned in. It's awful! Sometimes they just don't *think*.

American Literature Teacher: It's almost as though they need to be taught how to think.

History Teacher: I always assume that by this age, kids know how to think. So when I ask them to compare two ideas in an essay question, I expect them to automatically outline similarities and differences—how the two ideas are alike and how they differ.

American Literature Teacher: But they simply tell one way they're different and think they're answering the question. They never fully explore the idea by comparing and contrasting many characteristics.

History Teacher: You know we probably need to teach them strategies for thinking . . . We need to actually demonstrate good thinking. They need the tools to work with so they can approach any question, any situation, and think it through.

(Fogarty & McTighe, 1993, p. 161)

Illustration 2:

As you reflect on the following scene, think about what you know about the constructivist approach to teaching and learning. What suggestions can you make to aid this teacher and his students?

Mr. Green would like to encourage divergent thinking in his sophomore social studies class. He decides to say something outlandish and wait for the students to react, disagree, and, he hopes, come up with some original and appropriate solutions to a problem. To his horror, not one student in the class responds, and some even take down his ridiculous statement in their notes (Kaplan, 1990; p. 141). How might you explain the students' lack of response? Why might Mr. Green want to facilitate their divergent thinking? Which other strategies could he use to encourage them to construct solutions to the problem on their own?

SUMMARY

Metacognition

The awareness, reflection, control, and cognitive activity of metacognition enable more efficient and effective thinking. Young children may show little metacognitive activity, but it develops over time with experience. Much of the present research has examined differences between novice and expert learners in the areas of reading, studying, and problem solving. Experts often are found to be purposeful in their efforts and rely on attention-directing and self-questioning strategies. The research notes that teachers can facilitate metacognition in students by teaching self-questioning and self-monitoring skills and other metacognitive strategies, such as the PQ4R and IDEAL.

Constructivism: The "New" Movement

Constructivism centers around how learning occurs. Philosophically, it stresses learning deemed important in the lives of learners. The constructivist movement relies heavily on the early theories of Jean Piaget, who believed that individuals build knowledge in a context of environmental stimulation. Learning primarily rests with the child, although social interaction can provide a framework for changes in cognitive structures. In classrooms, the provision of direct, active, hands-on exploration links constructivist theory with teaching practice. Frequently, classroom applications of constructivist theory emphasize student autonomy, teacher-student interaction, cognitive exploration.

Discovery Learning

Discovery learning is a constructivist teaching method. It encourages students to make guesses based on incomplete information and stimulates them to find their own solutions to problems. In discovery learning, teachers serve as guides, while students do all of the work. Several studies support the significance of this approach. There are several research-based discovery learning teaching strategies, but, as a teaching methodology, discovery learning is not without limitations.

◆ Field Experience Questions

Observe classroom teaching in action and record your perceptions of whether the teacher

1. Uses competition or cooperation as the main motivating force,

2. Offers tangible rewards and punishments to motivate students or relies on their personal interests to motivate them,

3. Provides pre-prioritized information to students or invites the students to discover and prioritize information themselves,

4. Emphasizes clarity in instruction or arranges for cognitive conflict and critical exploration,

5. Insists that students work quietly and stay on task or promotes student creativity and allows for a reasonable amount of conversation and movement,

6. Allows students to process new information on their own or offers training in metacognitive skill development.

Observe in a kindergarten or first grade, a fifth or sixth grade classroom, and an eleventh or twelfth grade classroom to examine any developmental differences.

◆ Key Terms

accommodation	disequilibrium or cognitive conflict	PQ4R
student autonomy	IDEAL	prediction
cognitive exploration	interactionist	schemas
cognitive behavior modification	journal writing	self-questioning
constructivism	KWL	self-regulation
discovery learning	metacognition	

◆ Additional Resources

Alexander, J. M., Carr, M., Schwanenflugel, P. J. (1995). Development of metacognition in gifted children: Directions for future research. *Developmental Review, 15,* 1–37.

Atwater, M. M. (1996). Social constructivism: Infusion into the multicultural science education research agenda. *Journal of Research in Science Teaching, 33,* 821–837.

Clough, M. P., Clark, R. (1994). Cookbooks and constructivism: A better approach to laboratory activities. *The Science Teacher, 61(2),* 34–37.

Czarnecki, E., Rosko, D., Fine, E. (1998). How to CALL UP notetaking skills. *Teaching Exceptional Children, 30(6),* 14–19.

Irvin, J. L., Rose, E. O. (1995). Starting early with study skills: A week-by-week guide for elementary students. ERIC Document Service No.: ED379066.

Macmillan, A. (1990). Constructivism in a kindergarten mathematics class. *Mathematics Education Research Journal, 2(2),* 12–27.

Pirie, S., Kieren, T. (1992). Creating constructivist environments and constructing creative mathematics. *Educational Studies in Mathematics, 23,* 505–528.

Valli, L. (1994). Professional development schools: An opportunity to reconceptualize schools and teacher education as empowering learning communities. ERIC Document Service No.: ED381484.

Yell, M. M., Scheurman, G. (1998). Resources for constructivist teaching. *Social Education, 62(1),* 54–55.

Classroom Assessment

he teacher instructs her students to line up against the classroom wall for "History Baseball." After several words of encouragement, she fires the first quiz item to the first student in line. "In 1972," she begins, "Barbara Jordan became the first black woman to serve in the United States Congress from which state?" The first student responds incorrectly and is sent to the end of the line. "You've forgotten already?" the teacher cries. She turns to the next student and again asks the question. When this student responds correctly, the teacher looks pleased, shakes the student's hand, and says, "I knew you could do it!" The student advances to "first base."

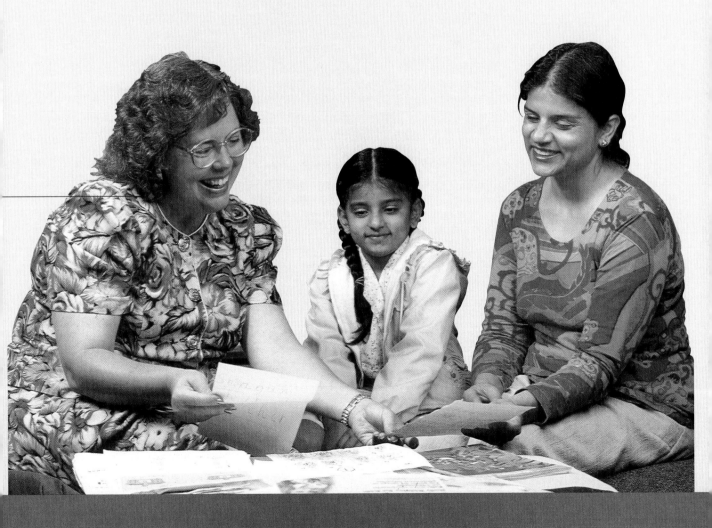

While it may look like a game, with the snakelike line and students moving about the room, it is actually much more than a game; it is an essential element within an effective teaching plan. The rapid-fire questioning, along with the adjustment of the students' placement within the line and along the "base path" as a result of the accuracy of their answers, is an assessment procedure used by this teacher. Assessment procedures within the classroom serve many purposes and come in many types, forms, and styles. Classroom assessment should be an integral part of instruction; it should be planned; it should be woven within the lesson; it should reflect the content and nature of the instruction; and it should be discussed clearly with students.

Too often for most students and for many teachers, the term *assessment* elicits visceral anxiety, even full-blown dread. Each of us has experienced the fear, apprehension, and general anxiety produced by the instructions: "Everybody, take out a piece of paper and clear your desks." The general moan that often engulfs the classroom, along with the panic-stricken looks on many of the students' faces, are sad commentaries on the use and abuse of assessment procedures within the classroom. These reactions are not innate to the assessment process or intrinsically tied to the evaluative process. Assessment is not alien or repugnant to our nature. The toddler eagerly "tests" her ability to support his/her body and take those initial steps; the preschooler tests her social prowess by racing, joking, and making new friends; and the adolescent seeks evaluation on her dancing and dating skills. If assessment is not by nature aversive, then we must ask what has gone wrong in the classroom that has fostered this aversion?

As will be discussed within this chapter, assessment is not simply restricted to the end of a lesson or a semester, nor to the grading and classification of students. Assessment should be a pervasive process which contributes to the quality of the learning experience. Classroom assessment procedures should be an integral part of instruction; they should be planned; they should be woven within the lesson; they should reflect the content and nature of the instruction; and they should be discussed clearly with students. Stiggins (1997), for example, calls for teachers to be "assessment literates," meaning that they should understand solid assessment principles (p. 7). The effective teacher can construct and use assessment effectively to inform their decision making (Carmichael & Caldwell, 1988). Assessment enables us to ask—and hopefully, answer—instruction-related questions such as: "Are my students ready to go on to the next concept?", "Should I review those last concepts?", "Should I use additional materials?", or "Did I teach that unit as effectively as possible?"

◆ Chapter Objectives

Clearly, being assessment-literate is essential to effective teaching. The material presented within this chapter will serve as a basis for the development of your own assessment literacy. By the end of this chapter, you will be able to

1 Define the term *assessment* and distinguish it from related terms;

2 Articulate the reasons for classroom assessment;

3 Describe different kinds of assessment;

4 Explain the major issues and concerns surrounding the use of teacher-made tests and standardized tests;

5 Discuss authentic assessment and distinguish between new developments in classroom assessment; and

6 Describe the significance of effective communication in assessment.

CHAPTER 13 CONTENT MAP

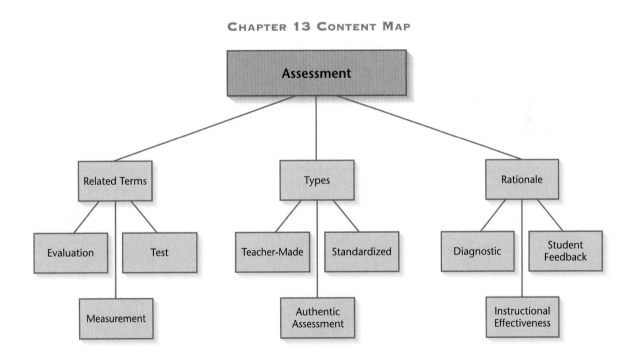

WHAT IS CLASSROOM ASSESSMENT?

Before we start on the long road toward assessment literacy, which will and should be a much longer road than this chapter can convey, we need to come to terms with key terms!

♦ Defining Assessment

In an early scene from the 1988 movie *Stand and Deliver*, the teacher Jaime Escalante states, as he distributes sheets of paper to his students, "Today is Monday; tomorrow is Wednesday; and Friday is payday-the weekly test." Typically, that's how many of us view **assessment.** We see it as synonymous with regular testing—the daily quiz, the weekly test, the final exam! Even more specifically, we see assessment as synonymous with paper and pencil testing, and although paper and pencil weekly tests may be one aspect of assessment, they are only a part.

assessment general term used for all forms of information gathering

Assessment is a general term. It refers to all types of teacher information gathering. Whenever teachers collect data about their students, analyze and synthesize it, interpret it and use it in their classroom decision making, they are performing assessments! Assessment procedures are "more than scoring and grading paper and pencil tests" (Airasian, 1997; p. 3), they are broad processes, common to instruction at all levels in all subject areas, and many teachers indeed do have a working knowledge about assessment (Adams & Hsu, 1998). Let's examine the terms related to *assessment*, including those that are often used interchangeably with it, but should remain distinct.

♦ Distinguishing Related Terms

Terms such as *evaluation, measurement*, and *test* are often used as substitutes for the word *assessment.* Teachers may use these words almost interchangeably, but they do have characteristics that make them distinguishable within the general concept of assessment. While it may not

The term "assessment" refers to all types of information gathering. Teachers collect, analyze, and interpret data about their students and use it in their decision making. ♦

be necessary to finely discriminate in the use of the terms *assessment* and *evaluation*, the terms *measurement* and *tests* are more specific and distinct concepts.

Evaluation

A related term is **evaluation**, which is the process by which teachers make specific judgments about students. During the evaluation process, teachers ask themselves: "How are my students doing? Did I teach them what they need to know?" Evaluation allows both information gathering about student performance and about the efficacy of instructional choices. A teacher attempting to develop a profile of a student's areas of achievement and areas of deficiency is engaging in an evaluation.

evaluation process by which teachers make specific judgments about student knowledge, performance, or attributes

Measurement

A more specific term is **measurement.** When teachers score a quiz or test, they are involved in measurement. Measurement allows teachers to quantify or assign numbers to student performance or particular student characteristics. The process of measurement permits teachers to answer the question, "How much?" as in "How much progress have my students made?" or "How much remediation is needed?" Thus, identifying that a particular child has increased the equivalence of two grade levels in reading would be the result of measuring the child's level of reading achievement.

measurement allows teachers to quantify or assign numbers to student performance or attributes

Tests

Often, however, we think about **tests** when we hear the term assessment. Tests are formal, systematic procedures or instruments for measuring a sample of student knowledge and skills. They are collections of tasks that are administered to our students, often in the form of paper-and-pencil procedures. We should remember, however, that tests are but one of many assessment procedures available for teachers to use and not all assessment procedures rely on paper-and-pencil formats. Consider the scene depicted at the beginning of the chapter. The teacher employed a system of oral questioning as her assessment tool. In addition to pencil and paper procedures and oral questioning, assessment procedures can include procedures such as observations, interviews, projects, and portfolios.

tests formal, systematic procedures for measuring student knowledge

---

YOU MAKE THE CALL

CRITICAL THINKING ABOUT ASSESSMENT

As a prospective teacher, take a few minutes to think about how you see yourself using the above assessment terms in the context of your teaching. Which *processes* do you think you will be engaged in most? Do you think you will be making a lot of decisions about your students' progress? Or do you see yourself regularly administering instruments that sample student knowledge or skills? Or, will you be more likely to calculate numerical scores to represent certain characteristics of your students?

If you are having a little difficulty deciding which of the previous *processes* you might engage in most, your confusion is understandable. As teachers, you will engage in all of them, frequently. Assessment literates ask themselves, "How good are my students and my instruction?" They construct effective instruments which facilitate their data gathering, and they look for quantifiable indicators of progress. But why go to all this trouble? What is the rationale behind sound assessment?

WHY PLAN FOR ASSESSMENT?

Let's face it, effective assessment takes quite a bit of time and effort! Assessment needs to be planned and purposeful, and it should provide the information teachers (and students) need to be effective. So why would teachers, with all of the other demands on their time and energy invest in assessment planning?

One answer to the question "why" might simply be that school effectiveness has become a question of local, state, regional, and national interest. Assessment plans and strategies are often the focal point of the bureaucratic concerns of national, regional, state, and local education officials who require data gathering. Broad-based curricular choices, fiscal determinations, and hiring patterns are the kinds of bureaucratic concerns that require such data. To promote educational accountability—or to expose the lack of it—teachers, students, school administrators, and programs are often assessed to provide needed information to the public at large, including legislators, administrators, and parents.

The value and necessity of effective assessment, however, extend well beyond these bureaucratic interests. Assessment is key to effective teaching! Assessment facilitates student diagnosis, instructional effectiveness, and student feedback.

◆ Diagnosis

Sound assessment enables teachers to identify both problems and strengths of students (Kindsvatter et al., 1996; Carmichael & Caldwell, 1988). A well developed assessment program can assist teachers in identifying students who may benefit from special programming. Through such assessment, students needing additional tutoring, special learning support, or additional services can be identified and directed to such services. Similarly, by gauging students' strengths as well as their areas of weakness, a good assessment plan helps teachers provide programs of enrichment or additional stimulation to those students showing special skills and talents.

◆ Instructional Effectiveness

Sound assessment can provide indicators of instructional effectiveness to teachers (Kindsvatter et al., 1996; Carmichael & Caldwell, 1988). In addition to the planning that occurs prior to teaching, teachers need to reflect on what they have done within the classroom in order to make decisions about the next steps to take. Well developed assessment plans will provide teachers with the data needed to make decisions regarding the effectiveness of their instructional efforts. Assessment allows teachers to see what worked and where re-teaching might be warranted. These data can help teachers answer questions such as "How well did my lesson go?" "Did I reach my instructional objectives?" "Do I need to re-teach the material?" "Is additional reinforcement needed?" "Were the techniques I used effective?" Sometimes, even after lecturing and providing examples and opportunities for problem solving, concepts simply do not make sense to students, and they will say so! In addition to testing and instructional questions, student feedback can help teachers realize that they may have to re-teach a concept and employ an alternative teaching strategy, such as a field trip, to make this process more concrete for these students.

◆ Student Feedback

One value of sound assessment, which is often misunderstood, especially by students, is that good assessment can provide each student with valuable information and feedback (Kindsvatter et al., 1996; Carmichael & Caldwell, 1988). For too many students and teachers, assessment procedures are used solely as ways of labeling, grading, excluding, or even punishing those who fail to meet the standard. This is not a natural consequence of assessment. It is a misuse of assessment procedures. Each of us has experienced the benefits to be accrued from the information we can receive through assessment of our performance. Whether it is the toddler who "tests" her ability to complete a puzzle, making adjustments and rotating pieces as she assesses the need; or the teen who wants instruction on how to play a particular riff on the guitar or how to shoot a sky hook, assessment provides feedback, which is valuable for the person being assessed as well as for those doing the assessment.

The data collection of teachers, when communicated to students, can help them gauge their own progress in class. If communicated sensitively, assessment information can serve as an incentive to motivate students (Carmichael & Caldwell, 1988).

Regardless of whether assessment is implemented for diagnostic, instructional, or student feedback reasons, the bottom line is that assessment is important to classroom teaching because it improves student learning and teacher effectiveness (Carmichael & Caldwell, 1988).

WHAT ARE THE DIFFERENT KINDS OF TRADITIONAL ASSESSMENT?

Teachers are assessing students in a variety of ways all day long! Many times, teachers gather information during the course of instruction through use of questions, conversations with students, and observation

informal methods of assessment the gathering of data about student knowledge during the course of instruction

formal methods of assessment data gathering procedures devised in advance, not scheduled during instruction, and including exams, and tests, quizzes

of their performance in classroom activities. While these are **informal methods of assessment**, somewhat spontaneous, they are no less important to a teacher's decision making than the more formal types of assessment to be discussed in the remainder of this chapter.

Formal assessments are generally devised in advance and typically involve a disruption in the teaching process to implement. Formal assessment includes classroom examinations, tests, and quizzes, as well as the more standardized measures such as achievement tests, ready readiness tests, etc. Since both forms of assessment, formal and informal, have value, the effective teacher will employ both. The degree to which any one form is employed depends largely on the purpose or role such assessment is to play.

◆ Formative, Summative, and Diagnostic Assessments

As noted previously, assessment procedures serve a variety of functions in the classroom. For example, Bloom, Hastings, and Madaus (1981) suggested that assessment can serve formative, summative, and diagnostic purposes within the classroom.

Formative Assessment

formative assessment information about student knowledge and performance provided by interim data gathering by teachers during teaching and learning

When teachers gather data while teaching and learning are still going on, they are employing **formative assessment**. Formative assessment is the type of assessment that provides interim information to both teachers and students. As noted previously, teachers need feedback about what works, just as students need data about their progress, even before the end of instruction. Formative assessment allows changes to be made, which can ensure ongoing improvement. Since formative assessments are employed as part of the teaching-learning sequence, they are typically informal in nature. Oral questioning to probe student comprehension and being sensitive to students' body language as evidence of their understanding are informal means of formative assessment. However, the use of quizzes, seat work, challenge bees, etc., while more formal, can also be formative in nature.

Some teachers begin each class with a quiz, and when they do, they are integrating formative assessment within instruction. Quite possibly, the daily quizzes are used to keep the students informed about their performance regularly, and throughout the course they may be used to keep the teachers informed about their teaching efficacy.

Summative Assessment

summative assessment information about student knowledge and performance provided by teachers at the end of instruction

Teachers also find useful the kind of data that inform them about student performance at the end of instruction. This type of assessment, **summative assessment**, allows teachers to see how well they taught and how well students learned overall. Summative assessment may occur at the end of a unit, term, or year, and is often used for grade assignment and promotion decisions.

Mr. Escalante stated, "Friday is payday—the weekly test." By contrasting the weekly test with the daily quiz, he may have been letting his students know that the Friday test would be designed to show their accumulation of knowledge and skills for the week or unit. It served more of a summative purpose. Because of the comprehensive nature of summative tests, they require preparation and forethought and are thus based on formal assessments.

Diagnostic Assessment

Teachers seeking to identify the prerequisite skills and knowledge needed to achieve a particular instructional objective or to identify the causes for a particular student's difficulty are employing assessment for diagnostic reasons. **Diagnostic assessments** can be both formal and informal in nature. A standardized test or a teacher-designed test to assess a student's performance would be one example of a diagnostic assessment. For example, if your college had a foreign language requirement, you may have needed to take a placement test, which assessed your current level of proficiency, so that you could be properly placed within the curriculum.

diagnostic assessment information about student knowledge and performance sought by teachers for identification of student prerequisite skills

◆ Criterion- and Norm-Referenced Assessment

In addition to the role assessment plays, a teacher will need to consider how the data acquired are to be interpreted and used. For example, following the administration of a formal, summative examination, the teacher notes that one student received a 90. While our initial reaction might be that the student did well, such a reaction depends upon our particular frame of reference and the standards against which we would interpret this score. According to Oosterhof (1996), a score needs a reference in order to be interpreted.

The two types of references most often employed within the classroom are termed "criterion reference" and "norm-reference."

Criterion-Referenced Assessment

Teachers often need assessment that makes comparisons of a student's performance within a specific, well-defined content domain. When teachers choose the kind of assessment that yields information about the student relative to a pre-established standard or criterion, they are utilizing criterion-referenced assessment. **Criterion-referenced assessments** gauge the degree of mastery in students. They can yield clear information about individual learners' skills and what knowledge they possess. Criterion measures are interpreted in light of the specific skill the child can or cannot demonstrate. Examples of criterion-referenced testing include having students solve a specific algebraic equation, play a particular piece on an instrument, locate a particular book in the library, or make exact change. This type of assessment, emphasizing mastery, provides teachers with the means to monitor student progress toward of curricular objectives. However, sometimes teachers measure

criterion-referenced assessment information gathered about student knowledge and performance relative to a pre-established standard

students against each other with this as a goal, norm-referenced assessment may be employed.

Norm-Referenced Assessment

When we gather information about individual performance in relation to the performance of other individuals, we engage in **norm-referenced assessment**, which allows for comparisons between students along similar indicators of the quality of performance. Thus, knowing that the student can perform more sit-ups than 90 percent of the others in his class or demonstrate word knowledge at a level above 45 percent of those his age would be an example of norm-referenced assessment. Similarly, tests like the Advanced Placement calculus and English exams are norm-referenced assessment vehicles. Students' achievement in calculus or English are not compared to a specific set of skills but to the achievement of a representative group of students.

norm-referenced assessment
information gathered about individual student knowledge and performance measured in relation to other individuals

✦ Assessment Origin

Whether assessments occur during instruction or at the end (i.e., formative or summative), whether they compare students to each other or to a criterion (i.e., norm- or criterion-referenced), there may be issues about where and how the assessment originated and who controls it. In many situations—as we sincerely hope!—the assessment originates and is controlled by the teacher (i.e., teacher-made assessment). At other times, the nature of the assessment is such that even though it is administered in classrooms, its origin and control do not rest with the classroom teacher (i.e., standardized assessment).

Teacher-Made Assessment

Teacher-made assessment is the kind for which teachers have primary authority. The teacher decides which students will be assessed, when they will be assessed, what they will be assessed about, how the assessment will be carried out, and what the scoring procedures will be. The teacher controls the interpretation and use of the results of the assessment. Teachers' daily quizzes—both written and oral—as well as weekly tests may evolve from the teachers' authority to assess students as the teachers deem appropriate and effective. We will discuss this type of assessment in a little more detail in the next section.

Standardized Assessment

Sometimes, however, although data collection occurs in schools and in classrooms, the teacher does not have a say in the planning of either the content or the data collection procedures. Despite the classroom teacher's lack of authority in this type of assessment, all assessment procedures are carried out in all classrooms uniformly. This type of assessment, which often utilizes tests and yields specific measurement information, is called **standardized assessment.** It is usually an empirically derived form of assessment, which relies on unambiguous instructions

standardized assessment
empirically derived procedures carried out uniformly and yielding statistically reliable and valid data

for administration, measures individual performance on norm-referenced skills, and yields statistically reliable and valid data. We will address standardized assessment, briefly, in a later section.

For either kind of assessment, tests are common data-gathering vehicles. We want to examine the tests that teachers make themselves and the kinds that are not developed by the average teacher and how both sorts facilitate assessment.

HOW DO TEACHER-MADE TESTS FACILITATE ASSESSMENT?

Teacher-made tests can be particularly effective if the teacher varies from a prepared or published curriculum. As vehicles of classroom assessment, they focus more on the instructional objectives of the teacher-developer. In developing your own test to assess your students, you begin with clear and unambiguous instructional objectives.

◆ The Need for Instructional Objectives

As noted in Chapter 11, detailed, systematic planning is an integral part of effective instruction, and such planning should include instructional objectives. These objectives can facilitate instruction and communication with students, but they also can guide the development of assessment procedures, e.g., formative or summative testing, as well.

Instructional objectives can be general and implicit (e.g., "The student will understand the sociopolitical elements that preceded Malcolm X's assassination"). Objectives that hope for increases in things like "understanding," "appreciation," or "realization" are worthwhile, but they do not describe specific tasks or skills to be accomplished. Although valid as instructional guides, general objectives do not translate easily into traditional test items. Therefore, some instructional objectives should be more precise and behavioral. For instance, if the teacher writes, "By the end of the unit, students will be able to list at least five sociopolitical elements preceding Malcolm X's assassination," the instructional intentions are a little clearer and a lot easier to translate into test items.

As you learned in Chapter 11, instructional objectives can reflect a variety of skill domains. Frequently, teachers rely on Benjamin Bloom's taxonomy of cognitive skills to identify targeted skills at a variety of cognitive levels, although there are also taxonomies of affective as well as psychomotor skill development (Table 13.1).

Objectives written for a variety of skill levels can be translated into test items that tap a variety of skill levels. Sound assessment should not tap disproportionately either lower-level or higher-level skills. Both should be tapped according to the instructional objectives. Thus, when planning assessment content, the teacher needs to establish a table of specification as a way of ensuring that the test measures all that it purports to assess.

instructional objectives clear, unambiguous statements of teachers' instructional intentions for students

Table 13.1 Bloom's Taxonomy of Cognitive Skills

1. KNOWLEDGE
   Definition: remembering facts, terms, definitions, concepts
   B: writes the meaning of; lists the sequence of; states in writing
   I: knows the meaning of; remembers the meaning of; recognizes how . . . is used
   Typical item stems: What? list, name, define, describe

2. COMPREHENSION
   Definition: understanding the meaning of material
   B: translates in writing
   I: comprehends the Spanish word for . . .
   Typical item stems: explain, interpret, summarize, give examples, predict, translate

3. APPLICATION
   Definition: selecting a concept or skill and using it to solve a problem.
   B: solves examples of . . .
   I: applies knowledge of . . .
   Typical item stems: compute, solve, apply, modify, construct

4. ANALYSIS
   Definition: breaking material down into its parts and explaining the hierarchical relations
   B: circles examples of . . . ; infers relationships
   I: distinguishes between; clarifies structure of . . .
   Typical item stems: How does . . . apply? Why does . . . work? How does . . . relate to . . . ?

5. SYNTHESIS
   Definition: producing something original after having broken the material down into its component parts.
   B: propose a hypothesis; composes a novel solution to . . .
   I: develops ideas; derives abstract relations
   Typical item stems: How do the data support . . . ? How would you design an experiment that investigates . . . ? What predictions can you make based upon the data?

6. EVALUATION
   Definition: making a judgment based upon a pre-established set of criteria
   B: makes written judgments; orally compares an argument
   I: makes judgments; compares arguments
   Typical item stems: What judgments can you make about . . . ? Compare and contrast . . . criteria for . . . ?

Note: B represents behavioral objective stems and I represents implicit objective stems.
Source: Adapted from Mackey & Appleman, 1988; p. 151.

◆ Tables of Specification

table of specification two-dimensional chart matching the targeted instructional objectives to the content areas to be addressed by the test

Once the relevant instructional objectives have been developed, they need to be matched with content areas to be addressed by a test. This two-dimensional chart is a **table of specification**. Stiggins (1997) writes: "Building a test without a plan is like building a house without a blueprint" (p. 124). The table of specification is a plan; it is a test blueprint, which enables teachers to get a preliminary look at their test's coverage of appropriate content and levels of skill development. The table can clarify instructional goals for both teachers and students. Without a testing plan, test development may take much longer for the teacher, and the completed test may not yield the information expected.

The table of specification usually graphically depicts the list of instructional objectives to be covered on the prospective test and allows for subsequent classification of test items by objective and domain (see Table 13.2).

As you can see, test blueprints typically appear as matrices and may be as detailed and as organized as the teacher desires. The table may specify which topics are to be tested, the nature of the questions to be asked, how many questions per topic, and the domain levels. The table can be developed in collaboration with students in some cases.

◆ Item Type

The teacher engaged in developing her own classroom tests has two main options for item writing, although many types of traditional items are possible. The teacher as test developer can write selected response items or supply items where the students generate their own responses.

Selected Response Items

Selected response items, usually called objective items, are those items that ask a series of questions accompanied by a predetermined set of possible answers. They are often presented in a pencil and paper format. There are several formats for writing selected response items: multiple-choice items, true/false or dichotomous items, and matching items. Let's briefly review each type.

selected response items
objective items which ask a question followed by a pre-determined set of possible responses

---

Table 13.2 Sample Table of Specification for Tenth Grade World History

Objectives	Content Areas	Number of Items	Percentage Coverage
Recognizes vocabulary and key terms	The Roman Empire: Pax Romana, senate, patrician, plebians	4 or 5 items	20%
Identifies specific facts related to . . .	Establishment of Roman Empire; importance of Senate; Roman leaders	7 or 8 items	40%
Identifies principles, concepts, and generalizations from content	Relationships between leaders and the fall of Rome; struggle between Christians, Hebrews, and Romans	7 or 8 items	40%
TOTAL		20 items	100%

Source: From H. Carmichael and M. Caldwell in Robert McNergney (Ed.), *"Evaluation" in Guide to Classroom Teaching.* Copyright © 1988 by Allyn & Bacon. Reprinted by permission.

Multiple-choice items consist of a statement or stem, which is followed by three to five viable response options. The student reads the stem and makes an informed choice—we hope!—from the possible responses displayed. Many of us are familiar with multiple-choice items, having been assessed with them on standardized tests of achievement or aptitude. Although they typically tap lower-level skills, they can be crafted carefully to assess higher-order performance as well. When developed well, multiple-choice tests offer a number of basic advantages. They provide a more adequate sampling of content and can be quickly and objectively scored (Oosterhof, 1996). To develop a good multiple choice test, one should consider each of the following guidelines.

1. Be sure there is only one correct or best answer.
2. Word response options as briefly as possible and be sure they are grammatically parallel.
3. Vary the number of response options presented as appropriate to create the item you want.
   (Stiggins, 1997; pp. 135–136)

True/False items are sometimes called dichotomous items because the teacher allows the students just two response possibilities. Given the appropriate stem, dichotomous items may be completed with one of two likely responses, including "true/false," "yes/no," and "correct/incorrect" (Airasian, 1997). Like multiple-choice items, dichotomous items require careful crafting to assess higher-order skills, and they are susceptible to student guessing. Stiggins (1997) offers but one emphatic rule for writing dichotomous items: "Make the item *entirely* true or false *as stated*" (p. 136). Dichotomous item stems that are too complex confuse learners and provide inadequate information. A common variation of a dichotomous test involves asking students to rewrite false items as correct statements. Such a procedure moves true and false tests into the realm of short answer or brief response items and may allow the teacher to gain a fuller understanding of how well the students understand the concepts tested.

Matching items are really just a special case of the multiple-choice format and as such follow the same general guidelines. Unlike multiple-choice, matching items are often formatted as two columns: one column contains the stems or *premises* and the second column consists of the possible responses. They are concise tools, yielding quick data, and are easier to write than traditional multiple- choice items. When constructing matching items, teachers are encouraged to

1. State the matching challenge up front;
2. Keep the list of things to be matched short;
3. Include more response options than are needed; and permit responses to be used more than once.
   (Stiggins, 1997, p. 137)

Some objective test items are **supply items**, meaning they require that students generate answers not already supplied as a set of options by the teacher. Short-answer, fill-in, and completion items are often considered supply items. Short-answer items regularly present direct questions to students and require concise, correct responses. Fill-in or completion items present test items as incomplete sentences; the teacher observes the students' ability to supply an appropriate response relative to the context of the partial stem.

The guidelines for writing short-answer or completion items include the following:

1. Ask a question of the respondent and provide space for an answer;

2. Try to stick to one blank per item;

3. Don't let the length of the line to be filled in be a clue as to the length or nature of the correct response.
   (Stiggins, 1997; p. 137)

Supply Response Items

Another type of supply item is the essay. It is perceived by some as an "untapped" source of information. Because pre-established response options are not presented to the test taker, the development and scoring of both short answer and completion items relies a little more on the teacher's professional judgment than selected response items might, and essay items rely most on professional judgment. *Essay items* offer students the chance to produce their own responses, since they are responsible for the scope and organization of the response. This format can showcase the development of higher-order skills but it can be time consuming for both test takers and scorers, and may necessitate abridged coverage of content and skills.

At any rate, essay items require careful planning. Teachers are reminded to

1. Identify the knowledge to be incorporated;

2. Specify the kind(s) of reasoning or problem solving to be carried out by the respondent;

3. Point the direction to an appropriate response without giving away the store.
   (Stiggins, 1997; pp. 164–165)

◆ Issues and Concerns About Teacher-Made Tests

There are many issues and concerns surrounding classroom assessment. Two of them—the use of item analysis to improve objective tests, and the appropriate assigning of grades—will be addressed below..

Test Item Analysis

Teachers should check on the efficacy of the tests they construct. **Test item analysis** is a procedure that enables teachers to do so and provides

supply items objective test items which require students to generate responses, not respond to options supplied by the teacher

test item analysis procedure by which teachers can evaluate the effectiveness of their tests

information about the functioning of the test itself. Especially in terms of selected response tests, item analysis can expose ambiguous items, miskeyed items, items that are too easy or too difficult, and ones that do not distinguish sufficiently between levels of student performance. Teachers who analyze tests systematically can enhance the technical quality of the test and can uncover student strengths and weaknesses not readily apparent. Unfortunately, many teachers do not evaluate the efficacy of the tests they construct, therefore limiting their usefulness.

Item analysis can be conducted using complex item-response theory or using a number of simple steps. Using a simplified approach requires that the teacher tabulate the responses that have been made for each item on the test. **Item difficulty** can be determined by examining the proportion of students who answered each item correctly. Thus if 20 out of the 25 students in the class got a particular test item correct, the item difficulty would be 0.80 (20/25). High values on item difficulty indicate that the test question is relatively easy. A second procedure is a **discrimination index** for test items. The discrimination index allows us to determine if a particular test item discriminates between those students who scored high on the test from those who did not. It can be computed by simply splitting the group into the top 50 percent and the bottom 50 percent on total test scores. Now, the discrimination index is computed by subtracting the number of students who got a particular test item correct in the lower group from the number who got it correct in the upper group and dividing the difference by the number in one of the groups. For example let us assume that there are 20 students in the class. We would rank the test scores from highest to lowest and then split the class in half. The top 10 would be considered the high performers, and the bottom ten the low performers. Next we would look at a particular test question. Thus, if for item one, 10 of the high scoring group got it correct and only 2 of the low scoring group got it correct we would subtract the 2 from the 10 (8) and divide that number by the number of students in any one group (10). Thus for item one our index of discrimination would be 0.8 or ((10 − 2)/10). It is desirable to have items that are positively discriminating, that is, where more people in the higher group get the item correct.

item difficulty procedure for examining the proportion of students who answered test questions correctly

discrimination index statistical procedure for examining whether a test item distinguishes between high-scoring and low-scoring students

Assigning Grades

Assigning grades to classroom assessment efforts is not as easy as it may seem. Even veteran teachers may think that they assign grades fairly, consistently, and with clarity, and yet, they may not. Canady and Hotchkiss (1989) enumerate many of the pitfalls teachers face in assigning grades. For instance, teachers often *vary grading scales* as is the case when an "80" on one test is assigned a "B," but an "80" on another test is assigned a "C+." Such variation in grading scales can undermine students' self-concept and lessen the value of the information obtained. Further, Canady and Hotchkiss (1989) suggest that teachers often rely too heavily on test score averages, or mean scores, even when it is not appropriate to do so and as a group often are reluctant to admit to and ameliorate measurement error. These authors also suggest that as teachers, we have a tendency to assign zeros haphazardly, meaning that we assign them to students despite their devastating effects on students' scores (Canady & Hotchkiss, 1989). In addition to these pitfalls, we could add that tests are often used to "ambush" students as may be the case with the pop quiz. Sometimes, teachers construct tests which inadequately reflect the actual content taught or the learning objectives articulated.

Thus, the effective teacher knows that planned test items should reflect instructional objectives and should represent a mixture of formats. Many of the pitfalls found in assigning grades can be reduced, if not completely avoided, by (1) determining the specific number and nature of assignments upon which the grade will be based, (2) identifying the weight given to each of these assignments, and (3) setting performance standards for each grade (Oosterhof, 1996).

> **Teacher Tool Box**
>
> Examine critically these general guidelines for writing effective selected or supply items in your classroom:
>
> 1. Write test items clearly, concisely, and without ambiguity;
>
> 2. Generate item stems that ask students questions;
>
> 3. Do not offer embedded grammatical clues to the correct responses;
>
> 4. Check all parts of your test for accuracy: item stems, response options, and scoring key.

HOW DO STANDARDIZED TESTS FACILITATE ASSESSMENT?

If you have seen the movie *Stand and Deliver* you know that half of the movie centers on standardized testing. There is a scene in the film where the viewer hears instructions for the administration of the AP calculus test being read aloud, juxtaposed with scenes of the students taking the multiple-choice test. For those who may not have seen the movie, a quick reflection on your own standardized testing experiences can make you appreciate that these standardized procedures often evoke both excitement and anxiety. Standardized testing, which has "enjoyed" a tempestuous relationship with society, has a dual effect on people: it is at once exciting and anxiety-provoking.

◆ Distinguishing Standardized Tests

Standardized tests, while often more dramatic, are no better as assessment tools than teacher-made tests. Standardized tests are better suited to large scale data collection and when uniform comparisons across students are crucial (Table 13.3).

Standardized tests, according to Airasian (1997), are "intended to be administered, scored, and interpreted in the same way for all test takers, regardless of where or when they are assessed" (p. 13). These tests can be administered individually or to groups, and although they can serve in diagnostic and instructional planning and provide students with feedback, such tests often serve the bureaucratic needs of educational leaders. Standardized tests are used to inform admissions and selection

Table 13.3 Comparison of Teacher-Made Tests and Commercially-Published Standardized Tests

	Teacher-Made	*Commercial*
Content and/or objectives	Specific to instruction; controlled by teacher; narrow range	Topics commonly taught in many schools; broad range
Item construction	Written/selected by teacher	Professional item writers
Item types	Various items used	Typically selected response items
Item Selection	Controlled by teacher	Many items written and screened and tried out with students before final selection
Scoring	By teacher	Typically, by optical scan machine
Interpreting scores	Norm- or criterion-referenced depending on teacher's preference	Norm-referenced relying on grade equivalent scores

Source: From Airasian, *Classroom Assessment*, Second Edition. Copyright © 1994 by The McGraw-Hill Companies. Reproduced with permission.

Standardized tests are often norm-referenced. They were designed to make comparisons between students along specified measurements. ◆

procedures, to sort and identify the special needs of students, and to provide accountability information about the efficacy of schooling at all levels. Many standardized tests, therefore, are norm-referenced by design; they were created to make comparisons between students along specified measurements. Most standardized tests measure aptitude or achievement. Examples include large-scale admissions vehicles like the

Scholastic Aptitude Test (SAT) and commercially published achievement test batteries like the California Achievement Tests.

In general, most teachers have little say in the construction or the selection of the standardized tests utilized in their school districts or schools. Although these tests can provide useful information to classroom teachers, many teachers are uneasy about them. Teachers often feel that standardized tests are not important to their daily instructional choices, and they express concerns about appearing—or being "encouraged" —to "teach to the standardized test" (Airasian, 1997).

BASIC CONSIDERATIONS AND CONCEPTS IN ASSESSMENT

The classroom teacher needs to be both a constructor of "good" assessment procedures as well as an informed consumer of those "standardized" procedures and tools in the marketplace. The current chapter provides only an introduction to many issues and concepts of assessment. Teacher education students are encouraged strongly to seek course work and additional sources of information to ensure assessment literacy. Nonetheless, there are a number of fundamental concepts that are key to assessment procedures in general and to standardized testing in particular. Teachers need to have a basic understanding of these, and they are briefly discussed below.

◆ Validity

Perhaps the single most important concept in assessment and therefore a necessary consideration for test makers, is the issue of **validity.** Validity addresses the issue of whether our test measures what we want to measure and what we say we are measuring. If tests measure what they were purported to measure, if they inform the decision maker as intended, they may possess validity. Both teacher-made tests and standardized tests should have validity, or the data yielded may not be useful.

validity psychometric concept concerning whether a test measures what it was intended to measure

Validity is not readily "seen" in a test; it is an abstraction. Rather than seeing validity directly, teachers often look for evidence that a test is valid, which is demonstrated by construct-related evidence, content-related evidence, and criterion-related evidence.

Construct validity refers to the fact that the students' performance on this particular measure provides a legitimate indication of the capability that is purported to be measured. Thus, a test of "intelligence" has construct validity IF it truly measures intelligence. **Content validity** refers to the fact that the specific questions or tasks that compose the test actually reflect that which is to be assessed. Thus, a test described as assessing a student's understanding of the solar system should not be designed to test reading abilities, problem-solving abilities, or creative responding. Each item within the test should be assessing elements of the solar system. Finally, a test might have validity if it can demonstrate

construct validity psychometric concept measuring whether a student's test score is a legitimate indicator of the skill or concept or attribute purported

content validity psychometric concept measuring whether specific test questions or tasks reflect the actual skill, knowledge, or attribute tested

criterion-related evidence psychometric concept which indicated how well a student's test performance correlates with the student's performance on relevant measures

criterion-related evidence. **Criterion-related evidence** indicates how well a student's performance on a test correlates to that student's performance on some other relevant criterion measure. For example, a test that is used to predict success in college would demonstrate criterion-related evidence of validity, if those students predicted to succeed, in fact, do succeed, and those identified as having low probability of success, perform less well.

◆ Reliability

A second characteristic of useful tests is that they are reliable. **Reliability**, as a psychometric concept, refers to the consistency or the stability of the responding. When concerned over a test's reliability, the teacher is not asking what the test measures, but how accurately and consistently it measures. If test performance remains consistent across testing times and settings, the test is reliable, and we can have faith in its results. For example, imagine that you just purchased a new bathroom scale. You step on the scale and find that you are eleven pounds over your desired weight. Committed to losing that weight, you go to have lunch and give up dessert. Later that day, you return to the scale and find that you are now eight pounds UNDER your desired weight. Not sure what is going on, you step off the scale and then try one more time. This time the scale reads that you just gained ten pounds. The inconsistency of data provided by the scale suggests not only that it is an unreliable measure, but that you probably should find the receipt as soon as possible. Typically, classroom teachers do not calculate the reliability of the tests that they construct, but many standardized tests do and are obligated to disseminate such information to consumers. In attempting to measure the reliability of a test, a test constructor might employ one of the following techniques. Sometimes, a retest, in which students are given the same test or measure, is employed. In this situation, the examiner is attempting to evaluate the degree to which student performance remains nearly the same on the repeated measures.

reliability psychometric concept concerning the statistical consistency or stability of responding

A second approach to assessing reliability employs a parallel or alternate test form. Under this condition, the examiner administers a second "equivalent" form of the test. The degree to which student performance across tests is similar (i.e., correlated) is the measure of reliability. Reliability can also be assessed when only one test is administered. A number of statistical techniques can be used to test the internal consistency and/or split half reliability of a single test. When using split half reliability, tests are divided to check reliability of their parts. One method attempts to assess reliability by comparing a student's performance on any one item to performance on another item. Another approach attempts to compare a student's performance on

Teacher Tool Box

Teachers should consider these questions when developing their own tests or reviewing commercially published standardized tools:

1. Does the test offer salient information to me?

2. Will the test format allow my students to indicate appropriate levels of performance?

3. Are the instructions and items clearly worded?

4. Does the test reflect actual teaching?

5. Is it possible that the biases of the test developer might influence scoring?

(Airasian, 1997, pp. 18–19)

one half of the test as compared to performance on the second, equivalent half of that test.

◆ Interpreting Results

Upon the receipt of students' test scores, teachers may be required to describe student performance to parents or other interested audiences. Under those circumstances, teachers may employ various data and statistics to effectively and efficiently describe the students' performance. A student's performance may be described using **raw scores,** which is the number of correct responses obtained on the test; it is the simplest concept to explain. **Percentages**—also easy to explain—are useful ways to describe a student's performance. Percentages present the number of correctly answered items relative to the total number of items; they can be calculated by dividing the total number of items into the student's raw score. Thus, a student may be described as successfully answering 80 percent of the problems presented.

Another way in which student performance is described is though the use of **percentile ranks,** which are crucial to the efficacy of norm-referenced testing. They address the need to know what percentage of the comparison group of students was outscored by the test taker. Thus, the student who answered 20 questions correctly (raw score) may have been successful on 50 percent of the items (percentages), assuming the test had 40 items. This same student may have performed better than 80 percent of his comparison group on that test and thus would be in the 80th percentile. **Stanines** are derivatives of percentile rankings, which simplify between-student comparisons by dividing the rankings into nine parts.

Quite often, teachers find themselves discussing **grade equivalents** with interested parties. Grade equivalents compare raw scores to typical grade-level scoring of a comparison group. For example, Joy's teacher may be able to tell her parents that, although Joy is in second grade, her reading achievement score is equivalent to that of a fifth grader.

raw scores the number of correct responses obtained on a test

percentages number of correct responses relative to the total number of items; can be calculated by dividing the total number of test items into the student's raw score

percentile rank score describing the number of students in the normal sample who scored at or below an individual student's score

stanines score which describes between-student comparisons based on rankings divided into nine parts

grade equivalents comparison of raw scores with typical grade-level scoring

◆ Ethics in Assessment

Assessment is social interaction; it is an enterprise that relies on effective communication between teachers and students and any other interested party. As social interaction, assessment depends upon trust, respect, and cooperation; otherwise, worthless data can result.

In the late 1960s, the National Education Association and the American Psychological Association published ethical guidelines for assessment situations. For the most part, their guidelines were designed for standardized achievement tests and psychological tests, but many are applicable to classroom assessment as well. To summarize them: the right to privacy and confidentiality should be

Some educators oppose the use of standardized tests for young children. It is suggested that testing should better reflect the test takers as well. ◆

afforded in assessment unless waived by the student. Testing material should be secured, so that the integrity of the results is maintained. Assessment results should be communicated to students and parents in as clear and unambiguous a manner as possible.

Worthwhile assessment should not be viewed as an obligatory toothache. If planned and executed knowledgeably and systematically—and let's not forget, sensitively—it can serve educational accountability and effective classroom decision making, and can make students *want* to learn.

✦ Special Concerns and Considerations with Standardized Tests

In addition to being sensitive to issues of validity and reliability and being able to interpret data, teachers need to be aware of additional concerns and considerations surrounding the construction and use of standardized test.

Undoubtedly, standardized tests have a powerful and useful place in society. Many students nationally take the AP tests to gain college credit in advance. Yet we hold mixed views about standardized tests. Historically, the development of standardized testing began not long after World War I. In this era, the United States was admitting an ever-increasing number of immigrants, primarily from postwar Europe, and educational and political leaders became concerned about a perceived loss of homogeneity in society. The growing cultural diversity of public schools in the 1920s and 1930s could be remedied, it was thought, if schools and school assessment became more "assembly line-like" (Stiggins, 1997). Stressing product uniformity in schools, standardized tests evolved as the *major means for sorting students*. In general, the concerns some teachers have about standardized tests today stem from their uneasiness with this possible sorting function and the possibility that such measures will stifle individual differences and diversity.

The sorting, or norm-referenced, nature of standardized testing has been criticized for *making adversaries of students and teachers*. Krumholtz and Yeh (1996) write that a "contentious relationship between students and their teachers" (p. 324) stems from the sorting attributed to standardized assessment; students cannot feel comfortable with the arbiters of rankings. Sorting, they maintain also, allows poor teachers to get off the hook, because some teachers see students' problems, not as the result of ineffective teaching choices, but due to the students' inability to "measure up."

Sheppard (1994) decries the use of standardized tests for young children in particular, observing that in the last ten years, their use has been "*excessive.*" It has resulted in curricular distortions and, to borrow David Elkind's term, "hurried children." Sheppard (1994) proposes that no such testing be administered to young children unless it will benefit the child's development. Further she suggests that all testing be language appropriate, that comparison groups be truly representative of the potential test takers, and that diagnostic tests be curriculum-free and more like aptitude tests.

Worthen and Spandel (1991) see the problem as a *"lack of appropriate use."* The overuse of standardized testing through the years has undermined the valuable role that it can play in children's lives, for even the best standardized test provides but a partial picture of the developing child.

Additionally, there is concern about *teacher preparation* of *tests and students' preparation* for *tests*. It is okay to inform students in advance that they will be taking a standardized test, but it is not okay to spend time teaching the specific items of the tests. It is acceptable for teachers to provide students with an explanation of or chance to practice the mechanics of test taking (e.g., effective "bubble filling"), but it is unacceptable for teachers to use actual or even parallel standardized test items during instruction or as a part of their own tests. Diverse students should never be excluded from standardized test administrations, but all students should be ensured adequate time, space, and materials for effective completion of the test.

In the last ten years or so, psychometricians, legislators, and educators have started examining alternatives to the traditional paper and pencil standardized test. Assessment reform efforts at the national, state, and local levels may soon increase the frequency of newer assessment vehicles like performance assessments and portfolios. In the next section, we examine some of these alternatives.

NEW DEVELOPMENTS: AUTHENTIC ASSESSMENT

Although traditional assessments such as the ones we have already described in this chapter are still widely used, these assessments have recently been criticized. Some authors, for instance, contend that objective formats, in particular, fail to measure the learner's ability to apply understanding of knowledge to the real world (Herman et al., 1992). As we examine more constructivist teaching methodologies—like those described in Chapter 12—we also should consider more "constructivist" forms of assessment (Brophy & Allman, 1998).

In answer to this criticism, a new movement termed **authentic assessment** has been proposed (Worthen, 1993). As the term implies, this movement proposes assessments that directly measure student performance through real-life tasks or products (Herman et al., 1992). These *alternative assessments*, as they are sometimes called, could include the following tasks or products:

authentic assessment measures of student performance which use real life tasks or products; also called "alternative assessment"

◆ Creating an original piece of artwork,

◆ Writing an editorial,

◆ Designing a week's worth of nutritionally balanced meals,

◆ Delivering a political speech.

Often teachers who use authentic or alternative assessments are interested not only in the products of learning as specified above, but also in the processes that students use to prepare such products. Thus, a portfolio of writing samples may be used to chart the development of students' writing skills over time as they relate to the production of a final editorial. Or, in some cases, teachers may videotape students practicing their delivery of a speech on successive occasions to document their growth in the development of a final version.

Such authentic or alternative assessment strategies are supposed to have the following advantages when compared to traditional assessments. First, they use real-world applications in which students are asked to be active participants in performing, creating, or producing something (Herman et al., 1992). Second, they are more likely than traditional assessments to call upon higher-level thinking or problem-solving skills (Baxter, Elder, & Glasser, 1995). A third advantage is that they ensure that students are actively involved in constructing understandings. You'll recall our discussion in Chapter 12 about constructivist views of learning. Clearly, authentic or alternative assessments are philosophically congruent with the notion that students should be actively involved in constructing knowledge that is contextualized within authentic tasks (Camp, 1992). Alternative assessments also ensure a closer link between assessment and instruction (McTighe, 1997).

While there are few systematic investigations of teachers' implementation of authentic assessment in the literature, the following is noteworthy. Kamen (1996) studied the use of authentic assessment in an elementary science context. The teacher he studied used science logs, performance assessments, creative drama, scrapbooks, and interviews. In this setting, the factors that contributed to successful implementation included administrative support, close contact with parents, teacher ownership, and the teacher's flexibility to try a variety of assessment strategies. Kamen found that the teacher's perception of assessment shifted toward an integrated model wherein assessment and instruction occurred simultaneously.

In the following sections, we will examine two of the most popular forms of authentic assessment more closely, performance assessment and portfolio assessment.

◆ Performance Assessment

performance assessment
form of authentic assessment in which student performance is evaluated against criteria that are as realistic as possible

Performance assessments have been described as authentic assessments that involve "the process of gathering data by systematic observation for making decisions about an individual" (Berk, 1986, p. 6). Performance assessments, through the direct measurement of performance in a natural setting, attempt to increase the validity of assessment by evaluating student performance against criteria that are as realistic as possible (Grady 1994).

Gronlund (1993) has identified the following four steps in generating classroom performance assessment. First, teachers should clearly describe the skill or process they require of the students. Table 13.4 provides a sample of how this could be done with regard to learning outcomes in the area of speech. Second, teachers need to discern whether the focus of assessment will be on products or processes (see Table 13.5). Third, teachers need to determine the appropriate degree of realism to incorporate in their assignment. Often, because of factors such as time and expense, some sort of simulation may be the most practical way to have students demonstrate their understanding. Finally, teachers must develop their evaluation procedures. The key concern here is that the performance assessment is reliable. To achieve reliability, the following criteria are suggested (Herman et al., 1992): (1) one or more dimensions that serve as a basis for judging student performance; (2) a description of each dimension; (3) a scale of values on which each dimension is rated, and (4) definitions of each value on the scale.

The following evaluation methods are those typically used in performance assessment. First, some teachers prefer to use systematic observations in which they specify the criteria for student performance and then take notes based on the criteria. In a scientific problem-solving task, teachers may expect to see some of the following criteria: (1) a stated problem or question; (2) an identified set of independent,

Table 13.4 Performance Outcomes in Speech

Oral Presentation
1. Stands naturally
2. Maintains eye contact
3. Uses gestures effectively
4. Uses clear language
5. Has adequate volume
6. Speaks at an appropriate rate
7. Topics are well organized
8.   Maintains interest of the group

Source: Educational Psychology, 3rd Edition, Windows on Classrooms by Eggen/Kauchack, © 1993. Reprinted by permission of Prentice-Hall, Inc., Upper Saddle River, NJ.

Table 13.5 Processes and Products as Components of Performance

Content Area	*Product*	*Process*
Math	Correct answer	Problem-solving steps leading to the correct solution
Music	Performance of a work on an instrument	Correct fingering and breathing that produces the performance
English composition	Essay, term paper, or composition	Preparation of drafts and thought processes that produce the product
Word processing	Letter or copy of final draft	Proper stroking and techniques for presenting the paper
Science	Explanation for the outcomes of a demonstration	Thought processes involved in preparing the explanation

Source: Educational Psychology, 3rd Edition, Windows on Classrooms by Eggen/Kauchack, © 1993. Reprinted by permission of Prentice-Hall, Inc., Upper Saddle River, NJ.

dependent, or controlled variables; (3) a methodology plan for how data will be gathered; and (4) an evaluation of the problem or question based on the gathered data. The teacher's notes would then make specific reference to these specific criteria.

Another way in which many teachers conduct performance evaluations is by using a checklist. In this method, teachers check off whether or not students have met a written description of dimensions that must be present for acceptable performance. Checklists are most appropriate when meeting a criterion that can be determined with a yes-or-no answer (see Table 13.6 for example).

In cases where yes-or-no criteria do not make sense, many teachers find it helpful to turn to a third form of evaluation called a rating scale. Rating scales are written descriptions of dimensions and scales of values on which each dimension is rated. They permit more precise gathering of information than does a checklist. For each dimension specified, the scale of values must be clearly articulated and described so that trained observers can achieve acceptable levels of reliability when judging student performance. Table 13.7 illustrates a sample rating scale.

Essay questions, in so far as they entail the use of a systematic scoring guides, are a fourth possible means of performance assessment. For restricted response items (essays that require a response ranging from a phrase to a paragraph), analytic scoring is suggested (Herman, Ashbacher, & Winters, 1992). This technique entails identifying different dimensions of a response and awarding points based on a rating scale for each dimension. For extended response items (essays that require more than a short paragraph), holistic scoring is recommended, in which essays are sorted into one of five categories of quality.

The reliability of scoring essays can be greatly enhanced with the use of a **rubric** or scoring guide. A scoring rubric consists of a set of rules the teacher employs for assessing the quality of a student's work, in this case essay responses. Typically, scoring rubrics are designed to

rubric set of rules teachers employ to guide their scoring of student assessment

Table 13.6 Checklist for Evaluating a Writing Assignment

DIRECTIONS: Place a check in the blank for each step performed.

_____	1.	It has a title.
_____	2.	It is at least three pages long.
_____	3.	It specifies a setting.
_____	4.	It contains at least three characters.
_____	5.	It has dialogue.
_____	6.	It contains a moral dilemma.
_____	7.	It uses correct grammar.
_____	8.	It uses correct spelling.
_____	9.	It contains at least one illustration.
_____	10.	It has a surprise ending.

Table 13.7 Rating Scale for Evaluating Experimental Technique

DIRECTIONS: Rate each of the following items by circling 4 for an *excellent* performance, 3 for *good*, 2 for *fair*, 1 for *poor*, and 0 for *nonexistent*.

4 3 2 1 0	States problem or question clearly and accurately.
4 3 2 1 0	States hypothesis that clearly answers the question.
4 3 2 1 0	Controls variables.
4 3 2 1 0	Uses appropriate data-gathering procedures.
4 3 2 1 0	Displays gathered data accurately and clearly.
4 3 2 1 0	Draws appropriate conclusions.

Source: Educational Psychology, 3rd Edition, Windows on Classrooms by Eggen/Kauchack, © 1993. Reprinted by permission of Prentice-Hall, Inc., Upper Saddle River, NJ.

assess one aspect of the performance or one learning target. If you are attempting to assess complex performances, you may need to use several different rubrics (Nitko, 1996).

Usually, the scale in a scoring rubric consists of numerals that reflect the various quality levels of performance. In Table 13.8, the number 4 denotes the highest quality, 3 the next highest, and so on. Note that each numerical rating is anchored by a written description of each level of quality. In Table 13.8 both general and specific scoring rubrics relative to the content standard being addressed are provided. The use of both types of rubrics assures you that when a teacher uses a specific rubric to actually assess a student's essay response it will be consistent with a general scoring framework (Nitko, 1996). Sarah, the novice teacher described in Chapter 11, would find such a scoring guide extremely helpful as she attempts to ascertain the quality of students' performance on written essays in her American history class.

> **YOU MAKE THE CALL**
>
> Design a performance assessment to evaluate if Rachel, the novice teacher whose practice is described in Chapter 11, is doing an effective job teaching her students mathematics.

◆ Portfolio Assessment

Portfolio assessment is still another form of authentic assessment popular among a growing number of teachers today. Portfolios are systematic collections of work compiled by students and teachers that are reviewed against preset criteria to judge a student or program (Herman et al., 1992). Portfolios may serve varied purposes in schools as are described in Table 13.9. These collections consist of the products of learning such as a videotape, piece of artwork, a journal entry, or an essay. Table 13.10 contains examples of portfolio items from different content areas.

portfolio assessment form of authentic assessment in which systematically compiled collections of student work are reviewed by teachers and compared to a preset criterion

Table 13.8 General and Specific Rubrics for a Declarative Knowledge Learning Target in History

Declarative knowledge content standard being assessed: Understands that war forces sensitive issues to the surface and causes people to confront inherent conflicts of values and beliefs.

General Rubric for Declarative Knowledge	Specific Rubric Adapted for this Content
4. Demonstrates a thorough understanding of the generalized concepts and facts specific to the task or situation. Provides new insights into some aspect of that information.	4. Demonstrates a thorough understanding of the generalization that war forces sensitive issues to surface and causes people to confront inherent conflicts of values. Provides new insights into people's behavior during wartime.
3. Displays a complete and accurate understanding of the generalizations, concepts, and facts specific to the task or situation.	3. Displays a complete and accurate understanding of the generalization that war forces sensitive issues to the surface and causes people to confront inherent conflicts of values.
2. Displays an incomplete understanding of the generalizations, concepts, and facts specific to the task or situation and has some notable misconceptions.	2. Displays an incomplete understanding of the generalization that war forces sensitive issues to surface and causes people to confront inherent conflicts of values and has some notable misconceptions about this generalization.
1. Demonstrates severe misconceptions about the generalizations, concepts, and facts specific to the task or situation.	1. Demonstrates severe misconceptions about the generalization that war forces sensitive issues to the surface and causes people to confront inherent conflicts of values.

Source: R. Marzano, D. Pickering, and J. McTighe. (1993) *Assessing Student Outcomes: Performance Assessment Using the Dimensions of Learning Model.* Alexandria, VA: Association for Supervision and Curriculum Development. Used by permission of McREL.

Portfolios are not as novel in other fields as they are in the class-room. Commercial artists, models, photographers, and journalists often use portfolios to showcase their achievement and skills. As such, a portfolio provides tangible evidence of accomplishments and skills that must be updated as the person grows and changes. For instance, writing samples collected over the course of a term can be used to document changes in student writing. Many classroom teachers have found that a portfolio of such writing samples is a far more effective means of communicating progress to parents than merely sharing letter grades from term to term (Tierney, Carter, & Desai, 1991).

One distinctive element of portfolio assessment compared to other means of evaluation is that portfolios involve students in the design, collection, and evaluation process. Students as well as teachers must answer the following two questions: "What content should go into a portfolio?" and "Based on what criteria will the students' work be evaluated?" In the following excerpt, one seventh grade language arts teacher shares her experience with regard to involving students in the selection of portfolio content:

> I introduced the idea that their portfolios might represent a broader picture—how students have changed and improved, what their particular interests are, and areas where they still have difficulties. This comment led my students to

Table 13.9 Examples of the Many Purposes that Portfolios May Serve in the Schools

General Purpose and Contents	Examples of Specific Purposes
Best Work Portfolios	
Evaluation portfolios: Contents focus on providing convincing evidence that specific types of accomplishments have been attained.	Evidence of subject-matter mastery and learning. Evidence of high levels of accomplishment in an area. Evidence of minimum competence in an area. Evidence of a school district's accomplishments.
Communication portfolios: Contents focus on providing examples of accomplishments that may be either typical or that may impress others.	A student's showcase for his or her parents. Pass on information about a student to the next teacher. A school district's showcase.
Growth and Learning-Progress Portfolios	
Monitoring progress portfolios: Contents focus on products and work that appear at intermediate stages in the course of a student's learning.	Teacher and/or students review progress. Student is able to look over the work and see the "long view" or the "whole picture."
Daily instruction: Contents focus on a student's recently completed correct and incorrect work, on data or recent findings, on a student's conceptual explanations of the work underway, etc.	Basis for discussions with a student of his or her work and ideas. Record of changes in thinking and conceptual explanations. Basis for diagnosing learning difficulties.
Self-reflection and self-guidance: Contents focus on work a student has completed at several points separated in time, records of a student's past and present conceptual thinking about the subject-matter, records of a student's past and present evaluations of his or her own work, etc.	Reflect on one's own progress in knowledge and skill. Reflect on one's own changes in conceptual thinking. With other students' portfolios to reflect on one's progress.

Source: Educational Assessment of Students by Anthony J. Nitko. © 1996. Reprinted by permission of Prentice-Hall, Inc., Upper Saddle River, NJ.

suggest the following items: an early and later piece of writing, a rewrite of something, examples of what they like and don't like, and reading logs that show how their thinking about books has changed. (Case, 1994, p. 46)

In the above classroom, criteria were also jointly established. These included the following: (1) how well students explained why certain pieces were selected; (2) the quality of the actual pieces of work; (3) clarity and completeness of the cover letter describing the contents and; (4) neatness and organization. The process of involving students in these decisions facilitates student reflection about what makes for quality in their own work.

Compared with traditional assessments, portfolios are said to provide several advantages (Tierney, Carter, & Desai, 1991). First, advocates of portfolios contend that they enable teachers to assess a wider range

Table 13.10   Portfolio Samples in Different Content Areas

Content Area	Example
Art	Two-dimensional art projects, including samples of drawing, cutting, and/or pasting
Elementary language arts	Reading logs, audiotape of student reading aloud, reading response journals, writing notebook samples
Science	Checklists of proficiency in lab skills, science concept maps, drawings of animals and plants studied
Social studies	Samples of current events scrapbook, student narrative self-assessments of unit test performance, videotapes of group reenactments of historical events
Elementary math	Samples of computation papers, peer critique checklists, and self-assessment narratives of math homework

of assignments than do traditional tests. Second, portfolios engage students in assessing their own work and establishing ongoing learning goals, whereas traditional assessments typically do not. Third, portfolios assess by allowing for individual differences between students, while traditional assessments assess students on the same dimensions. Fourth, portfolios address not only student achievement but also effort and improvement, whereas traditional assessments typically focus only on student achievement. Fifth, portfolios link assessment to learning and teaching. In contrast, traditional assessment separates these processes.

However, portfolio assessment is not problem-free. A recent survey of secondary teachers who implemented portfolio assessment indicated that teachers felt the most troublesome barrier to using portfolios was the amount of time required, followed by problems associated with scoring (Wolfe & Miller, 1997). It is recommended that teachers need to set standards relative to student learning goals ahead of time, evaluating portfolios either in terms of standards of excellence or on growth demonstrated within an individual portfolio (Valencia, 1990).

YOU MAKE THE CALL

Suppose your school district has announced that it wants to move away from the exclusive use of standardized tests to measure student achievement. Based on our discussion of performance assessment and portfolios, suggest three alternative ways that teachers can document student performance in the area of mathematics other than via standardized tests.

In addition to the traditional assessment methods teachers have in their repertoire and the performance and portfolio assessments described above, still another means of gathering data about students is called *action research*.

Action Research

A Questionnaire to Inform Instructional Decision Making

M rs. Porter teaches fifth graders and wants to know more about her students. She wants information in addition to what she has gathered already using traditional assessments and portfolios. Mrs. Porter decides to administer questionnaires to her class to gain a little insight into her students' learning style preferences, interests, and attitudes.

Mrs. Porter administered the questionnaires during the early days of school. She found that approximately 50 percent of the class enjoyed working with one partner, 30 percent preferred to work with a group, and 20 percent liked to work alone. She also found that 60 percent of her students preferred outdoor play to reading and watching television, while 90 percent reported that they liked computer work, 50 percent liked listening to books on tape, and 30 percent of the class preferred to use the library. (Some questions had response totals that surpassed 100 percent because the students could check more than one response option in a category.)

Mrs. Porter now feels that she can use these results to inform her instructional decision making. She can teach to her students' strengths and work to ameliorate their weaknesses, and she can utilize learn-alike groups and preferred environments. (For more information about learning style preferences, please refer to Chapter 5: Student Diversity.)

◆ Another Alternative Form of Assessment: Action Research

You'll recall our discussion of action research in Chapter 1, where we defined this as a classroom-based investigation conducted by the teacher in an effort to find an answer to a practical question. Action research methods can supplement data gathered about students in such alternative assessments as portfolios.

For example, if teachers are especially interested in how student attitudes or learning strategies in a particular subject change over time, they may find action research a valuable means to document such changes (Sardo-Brown, 1990). Formats including teacher-constructed questionnaires, open-ended questions, and student journals are useful ways to glean such data.

Questionnaires can be used to ascertain valuable data about students' learning style preferences, interests, and attitudes. The following items exemplify this:

A. On the next science unit, I prefer to
 1. work alone
 2. work with one partner
 3. work with a group of three or four

B. In my leisure time I most like to:
 1. read
 2. spend time playing outdoors
 3. watch television

C. For each activity listed below, circle the choice that best represents how you feel. SA means "strongly agree"; A means "agree"; D means "disagree"; and SD means "strongly disagree."

 1. I like to work on the computer.

 SA   A   D   SD

2. I enjoy going to the library.

   SA   A   D   SD

3. I like to listen to books on tape.

   SA   A   D   SD

In addition, many teachers find open-ended items to be another useful way of obtaining data about students. These incomplete sentences allow students to complete statements in any way they choose, thereby affording the teacher a glimpse at student feelings and attitudes. The following items serve as illustrations of open-ended items.

1. In today's lesson, the thing that surprised me the most was . . .

2. My favorite part of our last science unit was . . .

3. The thing I like least about this class is . . .

4. After learning about the metric system, I now will be able to . . .

Student journals are still another means of gaining information about students' feelings about classroom experiences. They can also be used to document students' use of learning strategies and how these may evolve over time. In this sense, it can be argued that student journals not only provide the teacher with valuable insights about students but also provide students with a means to metacognitively reflect upon their own study strategies.

Teacher Tool Box

1. Check to see what your school district's policies and procedures are with regard to the privacy of student journals. Increasingly, districts are requiring teachers to report written comments made by students in which the student either threatens to do harm to someone else or to him or herself. Another issue that of course you as the teacher are required to report pertains to indications of child abuse.

2. Try to focus student journal entries by giving students specific questions to write about, so that the entries contain meaningful information related back to your purpose for using student journals.

3. Give students specific feedback on their journal content. It is also of help to periodically write reflective questions in the journal so that students know you have carefully read its contents and so that students are stimulated to think more critically about their own writing.

4. Ask students to use journal entries to record their own use of learning strategies such as the PQ4R technique. Then, analyze entries in concert with your review of student academic performance to glean insights as to why students are performing as they do.

◆ An Additional Concern About Assessment: Old and New

One area where research could offer us even better information to facilitate our decision making concerns the relationship between diversity and educational testing, especially in terms of the newer assessments. You may have heard about questions of bias or differential results for diverse students on traditional measurements, yet some research indicates the same differential patterns of responding occur even when performance assessments are used (Murphy, 1995; Klein et al., 1997). There are findings on both sides of the issue. While Jovanovic and colleagues (1994) found that there were no individual differences—they focused on gender—on performance assessments administered to elementary students, Mawhinney (1999) and Garner and Engelhard (1999) suggest that there may be. At any rate, there are calls in the contemporary literature for greater consideration of the influence of diversity on the newer forms of assessment (Belcher et al., 1997; Gordon, 1995; Lensch, 1996).

Reflections from the Field

1 As an undergraduate student, I never quite understood why anyone would go through the process of making a table of specification just to develop a test. Well, now that I am in third year teaching, I really believe that making a test without a table of specification is like building a house without a blueprint.

—Tina D. (high school English teacher), Dubuque, IA

2 Our school recently purchase on op-scan machine for scoring multiple-choice exams. The machine also provides statistics on item difficulty and discrimination index. I never was one much for statistics, but this information has really helped me to develop better tests—even the students, who have had me before have commented on how "hard" yet "fair" my tests are.

—Howard L. (high school science (biology) teacher), Pittsburgh, PA

3 In my eighth grade health class—for my unit on nutrition—I decided to have the students plan with their family a full month of "balanced" meals. I used this as my assessment (authentic) for the unit. Not only did the children enjoy the project and seem to understand the concepts more fully, but I received notes from parents saying that the exercise helped them to reconsider their own dietary habits AND even saved them money at the market!!

—Sister Eva L. (health and science teacher), Philadelphia, PA

4 This past year I switched from using multiple-choice exams to assess my students' knowledge of "experimental" methodology to a more hands-on performance assessment. I have the students generate questions about anything to do with a possible cause and effect relationship in nature. They are then required to (1) develop this question into a hypothesis; (2) identify what the independent, dependent, and two control variables would be; (3) explain what data they would gather in at least two forms and how they would collect the data; (4) generate "pretend" data, and (5) finally, draw conclusions about their hypothesis based on the data they "collected." The students really get into the activity and seem to understand the concepts more readily with this "hands-on approach." An interesting side effect has been that a number of students actually attempt the experiments, and I have even had minor debates over the "validity."

—Maria S. (middle school science teacher), Wilmington, DE

5 Our English department has moved to portfolio assessment, in which we require our students from freshman through senior year to develop "best work samples" for each of their writing assignments through the course of the four years. Each teacher makes copies and keeps files (students do lose theirs over the summer). We have found it has been useful not only for the students but also for our department in reviewing our curriculum and the assignments we make. Students are also asked, during their senior year, to write an evaluation of their development. We have found this very useful.

—Robert K. (English/language arts teacher), South Bend, IN

THEORY TO PRACTICE

A Look at the Teacher as Decision Maker, as Assessor

The teacher instructs her students to line up against the classroom wall for "History Baseball." After several words of encouragement, she fires the first quiz item to the first student in line. "In 1972," she begins, "Barbara Jordan became the first Black woman to serve in the United States Congress from which state?" The first student responds incorrectly and is sent to the end of the line. "You've forgotten already?" the teacher cries. She turns to the next student and again asks the question. When this student responds correctly, "Texas," the teacher looks pleased, shakes the student's hand, and says, "I knew you could do it!" The student advances to "first base."

Think about the above scene again and the assessment depicted. Why might the teacher want to assess her students? What kinds of assessment are implied: informal or formal? formative or summative? teacher-made or standardized? What kind of test item did she employ?

This instructor is not seeking to diagnose special conditions or place any of her students in special programming, so we can rule out any diagnostic function for the baseball game. She may be interested in finding out what she needs to re-teach in preparation for an end-of-unit exam, or she may want the students themselves to see where they should focus their remaining study efforts. Therefore, both instructional and student feedback rationales may be at work. The baseball game is more of an informal means of assessment; the activity is woven within the instructional sequence. Since the game comes very near the end of the students' unit, it could serve either a late formative or early summative purpose. It did not appear that the questions the teacher fires at the students in the activity were uniform in administration, nor did they appear to have been developed based on a comparison group's performance; these are more than likely items developed by the teacher herself. They also were not selected response items—the teacher provided no predetermined response options—so, we can suggest that they were supply items. The teacher awaited viable responses generated completely by the students.

You, as Teacher as Decision Maker, as Assessor

Below you will find two case illustrations in which assessment issues are central to the teacher's decision making. Your task is to imagine that you are in that situation. Using the material discussed within this chapter, and decide how your would respond.

Case Illustration 1:
Ms. Lu's Sixth Grade

Now, it's your turn to analyze a scene. Read the following scene and reflect on the follow-up questions:

Ms. Lu is a sixth grade teacher who noticed during class that Fran is having trouble keeping up. Ms. Lu wondered whether she should move Fran to a slower group or to a remedial class. She decided that she needed more information before she could accurately judge Fran's ability.

◆ Which kinds of information should she seek?

◆ What should be Ms. Lu's first step?

◆ Whom should she share the information with?
   (Adapted from Carmichael and Caldwell, 1988.)

Case Illustration 2:
A Course in Educational Psychology

Below you will find the objectives outlined for a college course in educational psychology. The focus of this course is on both theory and application. It will investigate the major variables in the teaching-learning process. The goals for the course are

1. To help students identify their own beliefs about the teaching-learning process;

2. To help students understand variables such as instructional objectives, individual differences, learning principles, and methods of instruction and evaluation that influence the amount of learning in the classroom;

3. To help student teachers examine the effects of their decisions on their own student's learning;

4. To help students internalize and apply the material presented as guides to their own decision making as teachers.

For each of the goals listed, identify the form of assessment you would employ to measure goal attainment. It would be helpful to share your response with a colleague or classmate and discuss the advantages and disadvantages to the methods you selected.

SUMMARY

What Is Classroom Assessment?

The term *assessment* refers to all types of teacher information gathering. There are many terms that are related to assessment but which should remain distinctive in our minds, including *evaluation, measurement*, and *tests*.

Why Plan for Assessment?

Assessment facilitates instructional decision making as well as student learning in several ways. It enables teachers to diagnose student problems appropriately, and it yields information on specific indicators of teacher effectiveness. Assessment also can provide valuable feedback to students, thus enabling them to monitor their own progress.

What Are the Different Kinds of Traditional Assessment?

There are many ways in which teachers can formally gauge the progress of their students. This chapter examines briefly formative and summative kinds of assessment as well as criterion- and norm-referenced assessment. The contrasts between teacher-made and standardized assessments are introduced also.

How Do Teacher-Made Tests Facilitate Assessment?

Teacher-made assessment provides information to teachers who want to focus on *their* particular learning objectives rather than those of a national or published curriculum. The procedures for constructing a teacher-made assessment are articulated. Teacher-made assessment always begins with detailed systematic planning, including learning objectives. The objectives are incorporated into the "test blueprint" or table of specification. A variety of objective item formats are explored as are a number of issues and concerns surrounding the construction and use of teacher-made assessment.

How Do Standardized Tests Facilitate Assessment?

Although equal in effectiveness to teacher-made assessments, standardized tests are often used to serve larger, bureaucratic needs of educational leaders. They can inform admissions and selection procedures and can be used to sort and identify special student needs.

Basic Considerations and Concepts in Assessment

To use assessment effectively, teachers must be cognizant of terms such as *validity, reliability, raw scores, percentages, percentile ranks, stanines*, and *grade equivalents*. Several issues and concerns pertaining to the administration and use of assessment are weighed also.

New Developments: Authentic Assessment

There are new areas of assessment being explored in the research literature. The focus of the newer research is on authentic assessment. One type of authentic assessment that teachers are encouraged to use more and more is performance assessment. Another type is portfolio assessment. Teachers are also utilizing action research in their own classrooms to facilitate decision making.

An Additional Concern about Assessment: Old and New

The current research does not offer clear evidence of any relationship between individual differences and testing formats. Both traditional forms of assessment as well as the newer forms, such as performance assessments, may or may not be influenced by students' gender, socioeconomic status, race, or learning style variations. The effective teacher takes this information into consideration.

◆ Field Experience Questions

Airasian (1997) suggests the following activity. Select a chapter from a teacher's edition of a textbook. Read the chapter and examine the aids and resources provided for the teacher in planning, delivering, and assessing instruction. Compare the objectives of the chapter to the suggestions for instruction provided by the textbook author.

1. Will the suggested instructional experiences help pupils attain the objectives?

2. Is there a match between objectives and instructional experiences?

3. Examine the end-of-chapter test. Is it a good test in terms of the chapter's objectives and the instructional suggestions?

4. Does the type of item used match the objectives?

5. What is the proportion of higher- and lower-level items in the test? (pp. 150–151).

◆ Key Terms

assessment
authentic assessment
construct validity
content validity
criterion-related assessment
diagnostic assessment
discrimination index
evaluation
formal methods of assessment
formative assessment
grade equivalents

informal methods of assessment
instructional objectives
item difficulty
measurement
norm-referenced assessment
percentages
percentile ranks
performance assessment
portfolio assessment
raw scores
reliability

rubric
selected response items
standardized assessment
stanines
summative assessment
supply items
table of specification
test item analysis
tests
validity

◆ Additional Resources

Kane, M. B., & Khattri, N. (1995). Assessment Reform: A Work in Progress. *Phi Delta Kappan, 77(1)*, pp. 30–32.

Oosterhof, A. (1996). *Developing and using classroom assessments*. Englewood Cliffs, NJ: Merrill.

Tittle, C. K., Hecht, D., & Moore, P. (1995). Assessment theory and research for classrooms: From taxonomies to constructing meaning in context. In K. Cauley, F. Linder, & J. H. McMillan (eds.) *Educational Psychology 95/96* (pp. 202–208) (10th ed.). Guilford, CT: Dushkin Publishing Group/Brown and Benchmark Publishers.

Stiggins, R. J. (1991). *A practical guide for developing sound grading practices*. Portland, OR: Northwest Regional Educational Laboratory.

Stiggins, R. (1995). Assessment literacy for the 21st century. *Phi Delta Kappan, 77(3)*, 238–245.

abstraction effect learners remember the crux or main theme, while details are lost

acceleration educating gifted students by placing them in grade levels ahead of their peers in one or more academic subjects

accessibility degree to which students and teachers have access to learning materials and one another

accommodation Piagetian term for changing or modifying cognitive schemes to encourage understanding of new information

achievement motivation a drive to succeed, desire to excel

action research research which stems from a practical problem and is planned and implemented by the person most likely to be affected by the findings; it involves systematic observation, data collection, and incorporation of results into planning and practice

action zone areas of the classroom marked by the highest degree of interaction

active listening the ability to attend and reflect the essence of a message conveyed by another

adolescent egocentrism assumption that everyone else shares one's thoughts, feelings, and concerns

advance organizers cognitive strategies made up of deliberately prepared, slightly abstract passages presented orally or in writing in advance of the main material

adventitiously deaf those who acquire deafness sometime after birth

affective domain objectives for student attitudes, values, and emotional growth; includes five basic categories: receiving, responding, valuing, organization, and characterization

affluenza a perceived decrease in support of teachers and schooling by middle and high socioeconomic parents

AIDS acquired immunodeficiency syndrome, which interferes with the body's immune system leading to chronic and fatal infections

alternative response training a behavioral training strategy in which a person is taught to employ a substitute response for a behavior that has become problematic

amalgamation theory elements of individual culture are blended to become a new, synthesized culture

American Sign Language (ASL) a manual language, used by people who are deaf, to communicate a true language with its own grammar

analogical reasoning heuristic in which one limits the search for solutions to situations that are similar to the one on hand

analogies cognitive strategy used to highlight similarities between otherwise dissimilar concepts

animism Piaget's term for a child's tendency to attribute life to inert objects

anorexia nervosa an eating disorder in which individuals (primarily females) starve themselves to maintain a slim figure; the illness causes a distortion in one's perceptions of body image

antibias education model teaching model stressing the inequalities of society and problem-solving strategies; also called "antibias curriculum" and "bicultural education models"

anxiety a state of arousal, marked by tension and uneasiness

applied behavior analysis a system for analyzing a behavior and the possible controlling antecedent and consequential factors

arousal a physical and psychological state of readiness in which one feels alert and attentive

assessment general term used for all forms of information gathering

assimilation theory all student must conform to the rules of the Anglo American group culture regardless of family culture or to the rules of the groups to which they belong

assimilation Piaget's term for the process of making sense of experiences and perceptions by fitting them into previously established cognitive structures (schemata)

asthma characterized by difficulty breathing from narrowing of small airways in the lungs

attention deficit disorder (ADD) medical condition characterized by attention problems and impulsivity; may exist with or without hyperactivity

attention deficit hyperactivity disorder (ADHD) current term for disruptive behavior disorders marked by over activity, excessive difficulty sustaining attention, or impulsiveness

attribution theories theories which point to a person's explanation of the factors impacting performance as influencing their motivation and behavior

authentic assessment measures of student performance which use real life tasks or products; also called "alternative assessment"

autism a disorder characterized by extreme withdrawal, self-stimulation, cognitive deficits, language disorders, and onset before the age of thirty months

autonomous morality or morality of cooperation stages of development wherein children realize that people make rules and people can change them

autonomy versus shame and doubt independence autonomy versus shame and doubt marks stage 2 of Erikson's theory of psychosocial development

behaviorism theory that equates learning with changes in observable behaviors

belongingness needs the need to feel connected with others

biases the tendency to favor one group over another

Braille a system in which raised dots are used to allow blind people to "read" with their fingertips; consists of a quadrangular cell containing from one to six dots whose arrangement denotes different letters and symbols

brain tumor symptoms include blurred or double vision, dizziness, difficulty walking, and nausea

bulimia eating disorder characterized by overeating, then getting rid of the food by self-inducing vomiting or laxatives

cancer characterized by disorderly and uncontrolled growth of cells in the body

causal attribution the way an individual estimates if the outcome is most likely to be affected by his/her ability, effort, luck, or degree of difficulty of the task

centration the tendency to focus on one perceptual aspect of an event to the exclusion of others

cerebral palsy condition involving a range of motor or coordination difficulties due to brain damage

child abuse the deliberate physical, sexual or emotional injury of a helpless child

chunking information processing strategy which groups bits of information into more meaningful and processable units

classical conditioning type of behaviorist learning in which associations are established between automatic emotional or physiological responses and a new stimuli; also called "s-r pattern learning"

classification grouping objects into categories

cleft lip condition in which there is a rift or split in the upper part of the oral cavity or the upper lip

closing space reducing the physical space or distance between a teacher and a student who needs correction

closure the tendency to fill in gaps in our perceptions

cognitive behavior modification (CBM) a social learning strategy utilizing both modeling and self-instructional verbalization

cognitive disequilibrium a discrepancy between what is perceived and what is understood

cognitive domain a part of Bloom's taxonomy of educational objectives

cognitive exploration direct, hands-on investigation which facilitates higher order thinking skills

cognitive structuralism cognitive theory that emphasizes an awareness of interrelationships between stimuli of the appropriate use of schemata

cognitive style students' most comfortable, consistent, and expedient ways of perceiving and making sense of information in the environment

cognitivism theory in which learning is equated with changes in the organization and use of internal processes

cohesiveness tightness, closeness found within a group

communicative disorder an impairment in the ability to use speech or language to communicate

competitive goal structures students work against each other while pursuing an instructional goal, believing that they can only reach their goal if and only if others do not reach that goal

concept maps cognitive strategy utilizing graphic and hierarchical structures and linking phrases added to expose student understanding of interrelationships

concrete operational stage the third of Piaget's four major stages, characterized by children's ability to think logically, but only about concrete problems and objects

conditioned response an emotional or physiological response to a conditioned stimulus after learning

conditioned stimulus a stimulus which evoked a different emotional or physiological response after conditioning

conduct disorder a disorder characterized by overt, aggressive, disruptive behavior or covert antisocial acts such as stealing, lying, and fire setting; may include both overt and covert acts

congenitally deaf refers to those who were born deaf

conservation a Piagetian term for the realization that certain properties of an object (i.e., weight and length) remain the same regardless of changes in its other properties (i.e., shape and position)

construct validity psychometric concept measuring whether a student's test score is a legitimate indicator of the skill or concept or attribute purported

constructivism a growing movement in education that places primary importance on direct experience and students' active construction of mental structures, and that de-emphasizes lecturing and "telling" as instructional tools

constructivist classroom view that emphasizes the active role of the learner in building understanding and making sense of information

constructivist model the philosophical position that a child builds his or her own knowledge

content validity psychometric concept measuring whether specific test questions or tasks reflect the actual skill, knowledge, or attribute tested

contingency contracting influencing behavior through the manipulation of the consequences for that behavior

contingent reinforcement the use of follow-up stimuli to strengthen a desired behavior

conventional morality rules of conduct of older children (9-young adulthood) based on the conventions of society; is level II of Kohlberg's theory of moral reasoning

cooperative learning students work together to achieve a goal, believing that the goal is attainable only if others reach the goal as well

correlation coefficient a number, ranging between -1.00 and +1.00 which indicates the size and direction of a relationship between variables

correlational research research which identifies apparent relationships between variables or factors

counterconditioning strategy used to extinguish classical conditioning by pairing the conditioned stimulus with a new stimulus that will interfere with the association between the conditioned stimulus and conditioned response

criterion-referenced assessment information gathered about student knowledge and performance relative to a pre-established standard

criterion-related evidence psychometric concept which indicated how well a student's test performance correlates with the student's performance on relevant measures

cueing strategy in which a reinforceable behavior is set up by a stimulus or signal; may be accompanied by a verbal reminder called a "prompt"

cultural pluralism education attempts to address both shared national culture and/or individual/family culture

culture socialized influences that govern how we think, feel, behave, and live

curriculum guide specifies district instructional goals for various subject matters and grade levels

deaf hearing that is impaired enough so that other channels or senses, usually sight, are used to communicate

decision making the constant found within a teacher's day; selecting from options at any one moment with the intent of facilitating student learning

deductive reasoning drawing conclusions by applying rules or principles; logically moving from a general rule or principle to a specific solution

deficiency needs Maslow's lower four needs, which take precedence and must be satisfied before moving to growth needs

dependent variable the variable in an experiment which changes as a result of the independent variable; the effect, in a study of cause and effect

descriptive research research which employs systematic observation and recording of data without manipulation of the observed phenomenon

Descriptive Video Service provides audio narrative of key visual elements; available for several public television programs; for use of people with visual impairment

development orderly, adaptive changes we go through from conception to death

diabetes mellitus impairs body's ability to use glucose to obtain energy

diagnostic evaluation information about student knowledge and performance sought by teachers for identification of student prerequisite skills

dialectal language language of a particular cultural or family group

discovery learning teaching model which highlights the learners' interests, self-motivation, and self-regulation

discrimination index statistical procedure for examining whether a test item distinguishes between high-scoring and low-scoring students

discrimination   preferential treatment given to one group over another

disequilibrium or cognitive conflict   learners' predictions based on their pre-existing, unconfirmed schemata that motivate them to seek answers

diversity   ways in which students differ from each other and differ from their teacher

Down syndrome   a condition resulting from a chromosomal abnormality; characterized by mental retardation and such physical signs as slanted-appearing eyes, flattened features, shortness, tendency toward obesity; the three major types of Down syndrome are trisomy 21, mosaicism, and translocation

drive   the desire to act when needs are activated

dual coding theory   cognitive theory that memory is facilitated when two processes are engaged, e.g., visual learning and verbal learning

dyslexia   learning disability characterized by difficulty in reading, spelling, confusion between right and left, and the tendency to reverse letters in writing and speech

egocentric speech   speech characteristic of the preoperational child

egocentrism   the tendency of young children to assume that everyone views the world in the same way they do and that they are, quite literally, the center of everything

elaboration   information processing strategy emphasizing links between information stored in long-term memory and new information

emotional or behavioral disorder   a handicapping condition in which people have difficulty controlling their feelings and behavior

enrichment   an educational program that provides richer and more varied content through strategies that supplement or go beyond normal grade level work

entitavity   a group's perception of being a unique entity; "we" versus "they"

epilepsy   disorder marked by seizures and caused by abnormal electrical discharges in the brain

episodic long term memory   our memories for times or places

equilibration   achieving a proper balance between assimilation and accommodation

evaluation   process by which teachers make specific judgments about student knowledge, performance, or attributes

experimental research   research method in which variables are manipulated in order to observe and record effects

expository teaching   teaching model that emphasizes the provision of organizing structures to facilitate learning

external morality or moral realism   stage of development wherein children see rules as absolute

externalizing dimension   dimension of emotional/behavior disorder characterized by aggressive, acting-out behavior

extinction (in classical conditioning)   strategies used to undo classically conditioned associations

extinction (in operant conditioning)   strategy in which voluntary, undesired behavior is followed by no stimulus, or is ignored

extinction with reinforcement   strategy pairing extinction (or ignoring undesired behavior) with positive reinforcement of desired behavior; also called "reinforcement of competing stimuli"; used as an alternative to presentation punishment

extrinsic motivation   motivation that is based on external factors such as rewards and punishment

failure-accepting students   students who believe that they are unlikely to be successful since their failure reflects their low ability

failure-avoiding students   students who are motivated more by a desire to avoid failing rather than attempting to succeed and as such do not take risks, or attempt to avoid responsibilities

field-dependent learners   cognitive style variation emphasizing the perception and analysis of distinct pieces of information as integrated wholes

field-independent learners   cognitive style variation emphasizing the perception and analysis of distinct pieces of information

figure-ground discrimination   the tendency to perceive images in the foreground first, while other images fade into the backdrop

formal methods of assessment   data gathering procedures devised in advance, not scheduled during instruction, and including exams, and tests, quizzes

formal operational stage   Piaget's final stage of cognitive development, characterized by children's increasing ability to employ logical thought processes

formative assessment   information about student knowledge and performance provided by interim data gathering by teachers during teaching and learning

freedom from distraction   an environment that is stimulating with factors that may compete with the teacher for student attention

full inclusion   the belief that all students with disabilities should be educated in regular classrooms in their neighborhood schools

Gagne's outcomes of learning includes verbal information, intellectual skills, cognitive strategies, attitude, and motor skills

Gardner's multiple intelligences theory specifying eight different intelligences that presume a broadened definition of intelligence

gender bias favoring one gender over the other

gender schema theory the explanation that most differences in thinking and behavior between females and males are due to socialization

gender typing the oversimplification of gender-based characteristics

generativity versus stagnation characterized by either a sense of productivity or self-absorption; stage 7 of Erikson's psychosocial theory

Gestalt psychology type of perceptual psychology in which our perceptions are believed to be active and subjective, and influential to learning

gifted a category in special education that defines individuals who give evidence of high-performance capability in certain areas

Gilligan's ethics of caring refers to part of Gilligan's stage theory describing female moral development

goal structures the way students relate to one another when working toward an academic goal

goals broad or general educational outcome

good form law theory that our perceptions are influenced by our past experiences; also called Pragnanz Law

grade equivalents comparison of raw scores with typical grade-level scoring

Gronlund's instructional objective format stipulates an objective; includes a general term such as to understand or know followed by specific learner outcomes

group alerting a classroom management technique that alerts the entire class to a transition about to occur

growth needs in Maslow's hierarchy these are the highest three needs, which appear to be insatiable and thus growth oriented

Guilford's structure of intellect stipulates that intelligence depends on what we are thinking (i.e. contents), our mental operations (or process of thinking); and the products or end results of these operations

habituation strategy used to extinguish classical conditioning by repeated presentations of the conditioned stimulus until the conditioned response is lessened

hard of hearing a term describing those individuals with sufficient hearing potential (with hearing aids) to process linguistic information through audition

hearing impairment having a hearing loss significant enough to require special education or training; term includes both deaf and hard-of-hearing persons

helping skills interpersonal skills that convey a person's willingness to attend, listen, and assist another in their problem solving

hierarchical retrieval systems strategy utilizing a graphic structure that depicts information from the broadest representation of the concept to the most detailed representation

hierarchy of needs Maslow's model of seven levels of human needs that are arranged in order of precedence

home-based formation classroom formations that are semi-permanent and suitable for a wide number of learning activities

human relations approach teaching model in which the development of positive self concept and student interests are emphasized

Hunter model of planning a seven step model of planning incorporating focus set, objectives, input, modeling, monitoring, and guided and independent practice

hypoglycemia low blood sugar

hypothetical reasoning the ability to formulate many alternative hypotheses in dealing with a problem and to check data against each of the hypotheses to make an appropriate decision

hypoxia damage to the brain which stems from a lose of oxygen

IDEA individuals with disabilities education act extending rights of disabled beyond PL 94-142

IDEAL a metacognitive strategy featuring student processing skills, i.e., identification, definition, exploration, action, and looking, to facilitate thinking and problem-solving

identity achievement when the adolescent has a strong sense of commitment to life choices after careful consideration of options

identity diffusion when the adolescent has not made any firm commitments to any ideology, occupation, or interpersonal relationship and is not currently thinking about such commitments

identity foreclosure when the adolescent selects a convenient set of beliefs and goals without carefully considering the alternatives an example would be accepting one's parents' choice of lifestyle and career without considering other options

identity moratorium when the adolescent considers alternative choices, experiences different roles, but has made no final decision regarding his or her identity

identity versus confusion a sense of well being, a feeling of knowing where one is going, and an inner assuredness of anticipated recognition from those who count

I message non-accusatory statements about how something is affecting a person

immersion approach teaching model for addressing language diversity by placing students in classrooms where all instruction and verbal socialization are in the language to be learned

independent variable the variable in an experiment which is manipulated and being tested for its impact on other variables

individualized transition plan (ITP) a plan designed to prepare the mentally retarded student to function and work in the community

industry versus inferiority an eagerness to produce; typifies stage 4 of Erikson's theory of psychosocial development

informal methods of assessment the gathering of data about student knowledge during the course of instruction

information processing model theory emphasizing the influence of selective perception on memory, and subsequently, on learning

initiative versus guilt the quality of undertaking, planning, and attacking a new task; characterizes stage 3 of Erikson's theory of psychosocial development

instructional decisions decisions a teacher makes which are intended to induce learning

instructional expert the role a teacher assumes when he/she employs behaviors targeted to inducing learning

instructional objectives clear, unambiguous statements of teachers' instructional intentions for students

integrity versus despair a sense of understanding how one fits into one's culture and the acceptance that one's place is unique and unalterable; stage 8 in Erikson's theory of psychosocial development

interactionist theoretical perspective which reflects the influence of nature and nurture on development and learning

interdependence a social environment which requires students interacting and working together

interdisciplinary thematic units (ITU) units based on themes interwoven across content areas

interference effects rote learning is hindered by our past or future experiences

internalizing dimension dimension of emotional/behavior disorder characterized by immaturity, anxiety, and depression

intimacy versus isolation the state of having a close psychological relationship with another person; stage 6 of Erikson's theory of psychosocial development

intrinsic motivation finding value and motivation within the activity itself, regardless of the outcome

item difficulty procedure for examining the proportion of students who answered test questions correctly

journal writing metacognitive strategy in which students reflect on and identify cognitive strategies in written records

KWL metacognitive strategy focusing on what students know, what they want to know, and what they did learn

language disorder a lag in the ability to understand and express ideas that puts linguistic skill behind an individual's development in other areas, such as motor, cognitive, or social development

law of effect Thorndike's rule that any act that produces a satisfying effect will be repeated

law of exercise Thorndike's rule that repetitions strengthen learned associations

law of proximity theory that the placement of images near each other influences our perception of them

law of similarity theory that our perceptions are influenced by stimuli with comparable characteristics

learned helplessness an expectation of failure due to a previous experience with the belief that there is nothing that one can do to succeed

learning disability problem with acquisition and use of language; may show up as difficulty with reading, writing, reasoning, and math

learning styles biological and socialized differences or preferences for how students learn

learning via insight theory highlighting the influence of our motivations on our selected perceptions and learning

learning permanent change in behavior or capacity acquired through experience

least restrictive environment (LRE) placing children with disabilities in as normal a setting as possible

leukemia most frequent form of cancer in children

level of processing effect learning will be facilitated if processing occurs at multiple levels, e.g., sensorily and semantically

levels effect learners believe that some information is more important to process than other information

levels of Bloom's taxonomy a system for the classification of cognitive teaching objectives that includes six levels; knowledge, comprehension, application, analysis, synthesis, and evaluation

Lickona model model of character education encompassing self-esteem cooperative learning, moral reflecting, and participatory decision making

linguistic diversity ways in which students may differ relative to their language usage

locus of control where a person places the source of their experience; is success and failure a result of factors outside of the individual's responsibility (external) or within the individual (internal)

long term memory a permanent storage facility with unlimited capacity

loud reprimand a reprimand which is noticed by others; a public reprimand

lymphoma cancers which involve the lymph nodes

Mager's three-part behavioral objective stipulates that a well-written objective includes performance, conditions, and criterion

maintenance rehearsal keeping information active in short term memory by repeating the information

manager a role assumed by teacher in which he/she employs behaviors that help bring order and structure to the classroom environment as a way of fostering the learning process

manual approach approach in which finger spelling is used to aid the deaf, or representing letters of the alphabet by finger positions

Marcia's identity statuses theory descriptive of four ways in which adolescents resolve the issue of identity

mastery-oriented students students who focus on mastering the material presented within the class because they value achievement

mathemagenic effects learning will be facilitated by the use of organizing, structuring strategies

meaningful reception learning theory highlighting the receipt, not the discovery, of selectively organized information

meaningful verbal learning information presented in verbal, disconnected forms, yet not in lists

measurement allows teachers to quantify or assign numbers to student performance or attributes

mediators cognitive structuring strategy of verbal phrases designed to link new and familiar concepts

metacognition thinking about one's own thinking; examining one's own information processing

metalinguistic awareness knowledge about language and the ability to think about one's own knowledge of language

mild retardation a classification used to specify an individual whose IQ test score is between 55 and 69

misbehavior actions defined as inappropriate to the particular setting or in violation of the group norms

mission statement statement defining the purpose of school and its unique characteristics

mnemonics cognitive structuring memory devices that facilitate recall via elaboration and chunking

momentum a characteristic of a class noting "movement" from one activity to another; a progression within the lesson

moral reasoning the thinking processes involved in judgments about questions of right and wrong

moral reflection a process in Lickona's model that focuses on consideration of the cognitive aspects of moral development

morphology the study within psycholinguistics of word formation; of how adding or deleting parts of words changes their meaning

motivation an internal state that energizes, directs, and maintains behavior

multicultural education education in which a range of cultural perspectives are presented to students

multistore model information processing system consisting of the sensory register, the short term memory, and the long term memory

myelinization physiological changes in neurons that contribute to rapid cognitive growth

negative correlation a relationship between two variables in which change in one variable is marked by change in the opposite direction for the other variable; as one increases, the other decreases

negative reinforcers inhibiting, follow-up stimuli withdrawn to strengthen a behavior

neobehaviorism theory that believes that changes in behavior are observable and influenced by internal processes

neo-Piagetian updated research on Piagetian stages as applicable to transition from concrete to formal operations

neuroblastoma second most common cancer in children; found in adrenal glands

no-lose conflict resolution a strategy for conflict resolution in which both parties' needs are met

norm rules of conduct within a group setting

norm-referenced assessment information gathered about individual student knowledge and performance measured in relation to other individuals

note taking cognitive structuring strategy utilizing selective chunking and facilitated by the use of arrows, boldface type, and colors

object permanence Piaget's term for children's understanding that objects continue to exist apart from the children's perception of them

objective a specific instructional goal

observational learning a social learning strategy which emphasizes learning by watching others; also called "modeling"

operant conditioning type of behaviorist learning in which voluntary behaviors are controlled by the manipulation of follow-up stimuli; also called "r-s pattern learning"

Optacon a device used to enable persons who are blind to "read"; consists of a camera that converts print into an image of letters, which are then produced by way of vibration onto the finger

oral approach approach for aiding the deaf which includes hearing aids and speech reading

organization effects learning is enhanced when material is organized structurally, e.g., hierarchically

osteogenic sarcoma form of childhood cancer located in the bone

outlines cognitive structuring strategy which facilitates learning via the organization of information into hierarchically-arranged, highlighted headings and subheadings

overlapping overseeing or supervising multiple tasks at the same time

participatory decision-making a process in Lickona's model that holds students accountable for decisions that influence the quality of classroom life

pedagogical content knowledge knowledge about the effective ways to present information to learners along with an awareness of what makes topics difficult or easy to learn for students of different ages and background

percentages number of correct responses relative to the total number of items; can be calculated by dividing the total number of test items into the student's raw score

percentile rank score describing the number of students in the normal sample who scored at or below an individual student's score

personal causation a person's belief regarding the degree to which his/her knowledge or habits will lead to the desired outcomes

phases of learning Gagne's translation of the information processing model for classroom teaching

phonics approach approach to reading instruction that urges students to sound out words they read

phonological awareness one's awareness of phonemes as related to reading comprehension

phonology the study of the sound system of a language and the structure of those sounds

physical environment the physical conditions and materials characterizing a classroom

physiological style students' preferred ways of learning through the use of their senses or environmental stimuli

PL 94-142 the education for all handicapped children act, which contains a mandatory provision stating that to receive funds under the act, every school system in the nation must make provision for a free, appropriate public education for every child between the ages of three and eighteen (now extended to ages three to twenty-one) regardless of how, or how seriously, he or she may be disabled

portfolio assessment form of authentic assessment in which systematically compiled collections of student work are reviewed by teachers and compared to a preset criterion

positive correlation a relationship between two variables in which change in one variable is marked by change in the other variable in the same direction; as one increases, the other increases

positive reinforcers desired, follow-up stimuli added to strengthen a behavior

postconventional morality rules of conduct of adults who recognize the societal need for mutual agreement and the application of consistent principles in making judgments; this is level III of Kohlberg's theory of moral reasoning

PQ4R metacognitive strategy encouraging students to predict, question, read, reflect, recite, and review material to be learned on their own

practice effects learning improves when repetition or rehearsal is used

practitioner-researcher role of teachers in that they must use research and theory as a foundation or structure to guide their decisions, but those decisions must be professional judgments based upon knowledge, experience, and constructive reflection about their own situations and the effectiveness of their theory

pragmatics the study within psycholinguistics of how one uses language in social situations; emphasizes functional use of language rather than its mechanics

preconventional morality rules of conduct of children (birth-9 years) who do not yet understand the conventions of society, this is level I of Kohlberg's theory of moral reasoning

prediction skill requiring students to hypothesize about content to be learned

prejudices preconceived opinions about differences between people

Premack Principle reinforcement strategy in which an if-then contingency is established between a preferred reinforcer and a less-preferred activity; also called "grandparents' rule"

preoperational stage the second stage in Piaget's theory of cognitive development, in which the lack of logical operations forces children to make decisions based on their perceptions

presentation punishment aversive, follow-up stimuli added to decrease the strength of an unwanted behavior

prevention arranging conditions as a pre-emptive strike against the occurrence of some problem

principle of contiguity theory that if two events are presented together repeatedly, they will become so associated, that when only one event is present, the missing event will also be remembered

prior knowledge past experiences or previously learned material

private speech children's self-talk, which guides their thinking and action; eventually these verbalizations are internalized as silent inner speech

procedural long-term memory our recall of specific skills or steps used in task completion

psychodrama technique in which students act out potentially troublesome situation and discuss ways to resolve them

psycholinguistics the combined study of psychology and linguistics; refers most often to Chomsky's work on language development

psychological/affective style ways that students' personality traits influence learning preferences

psychomotor domain objectives involving physical ability

psychosocial development describing the relation of the individual's emotional needs to the social environment

punishment a process of introducing an aversive condition or removing a desirable condition geared to weaken or repress a behavior

raw scores the number of correct responses obtained on a test

reflective teacher teachers who are thoughtful and inventive, who review situations, analyzing what they did and why along with the impact of that decision in order to improve the future

Regular Education Initiative (REI) an attempt to restructure special education so that the regular classroom would serve as the primary setting for special education services a regular education initiative also attempts to include all special needs students (i.e., economically disadvantaged and non-English-speaking) in one basic program rather than establish separate programs for each type of need

rehearsal information processing strategy in which practice or repetiton of information enhances recall

reliability psychometric concept concerning the statistical consistency or stability of responding

removal punishment desired, follow-up stimuli withdrawn to decrease the strength of an unwanted behavior

response costs strategy in which units of reinforcement are removed for each display of undesired behavior; used as an alternative to presentation punishment

reviews post-instructional cognitive strategies which feature the recounting and summarizing of information and its link to new material

revolving door model model which proposes to include more students, up to 15 percent, in gifted programs

RIP (Rules-Ignore-Praise) a strategy for intervening with a student misbehavior that entails a reminder of the rule, ignoring the reaction, and praise adherence

rote learning a type of learning which emphasizes the memorization of disconnected material, e.g., lists

routines sets of procedures organized around a particular time, concept, or activity

RRP (Rules-Reward-Punishment) an alternative strategy for intervening with a student misbehavior which introduces punishment if the reminder of the rule or the reinforcement of adherence prove insufficient

rubric set of rules teachers employ to guide their scoring of student assessment

rules a listing of appropriate and inappropriate behaviors within a classroom

satiation or negative practice strategy emphasizing the introduction of the overloading of enjoyable (to the student), yet inappropriate behavior (to the teacher) until the behavior loses its attractiveness; used as an alternative to presentation punishment

scaffolding support for learning and problem solving; the support could be clues, questions, prompts, breaking a problem down into steps, and anything else that helps a learner become more successful

schedules of reinforcement variations in the frequency in the presentation of reinforcers

schema theory cognitive theory which features the nature and purpose of schemata as fundamental elements in information processing

schemas cognitive structures that allow us to represent actions, people, places, events, etc.

schizophrenia characterized by psychotic behavior manifested by loss of contact with reality, bizarre thought processes, and inappropriate actions

schoolization the process of socializing the child to the role of student

selected response items objective items that ask a question followed by a pre-determined set of possible responses

selective underlining cognitive structuring strategy in which the key points in material are underlined

self-actualization fulfilling one's potential

self-concept the way in which an individual perceives or thinks about him or herself

self-efficacy beliefs about one's personal competence within a particular situation

self-esteem the value each of us places on our own characteristics, abilities, and behaviors

self-questioning metacognitive strategy in which students generate and answer questions designed to facilitate information processing; also called "self-interrogation"

self-regulation metacognitive strategy in which students monitor their own processing of information

semantic long term memory our memories for facts and concepts

semantics the study of the meanings attached to words

sensorimotor stage Piaget's first stage of intellectual development, in which the child moves from the reflexive activities of reaching, grasping, and sucking to more highly organized forms of activity

sensory register the first port or site in the information processing model featuring the converting of information gathered via our senses

serial position effects recall may be hindered or helped due to the position or placement of words in lists

seriation arranging objects in sequential order according to one aspect, such as size, weight, or volume

severe retardation a classification used to specify an individual whose IQ test score is between approximately 25 and 40

shaping reinforcement strategy in which remote approximations of a target behavior are rewarded

shifting gears a strategy to reduce student defensiveness by moving from asserting the teacher's own statement of concern, to listening and understanding the position of the student

short term memory site in the information processing system in which a limited amount of information is held until use; also called the working memory

significance (statistically) an indication that the results are not likely a chance occurrence

single group study approach teaching model emphasizing self exploration of cultural elements and sources

smoothness the degree to which a class or lesson progresses without major disruption and flows from start through finish

social environment the social climate and atmosphere characterizing a classroom

social learning theory a theory of learning that places heavy emphasis on parent modeling and the child's imitation of adult behavior; used to explain the acquisition of language and complex behaviors

social structure includes the establishment of common goals and the articulation of specific roles to be played (e.g., teacher-student; leader-follower; note taker-reporter, etc.), and the establishment of the social norms

social-emotional goals goals that are directed toward helping students satisfy needs such as the need for acceptance, the need to develop a positive self-image, etc.

socialized speech speech characterized by marked decline in egocentrism

socioeconomic status students' relative position in society relative to their family income, political power, educational background, and occupational prestige

soft reprimand a reprimand presented in a tone which only the student being reprimanded hears

special formation classroom formations that provide the needed variety and change when particular lessons or lesson activities require it

speech disorder oral communication that involves abnormal use of the vocal apparatus, is unintelligible, or so inferior that it draws attention to itself and causes anxiety, feelings of inadequacy, or inappropriate behavior in the speaker

spina bifida congenital defect resulting from failure of bony spinal column to completely close

stack formation   seating arrangement in which students align themselves behind a row, sitting in an offset, with visibility gained by squaring the the back row so that students sit in the gap between students immediately in front

standard language   language of the marketplace within a shared national culture

standardized assessment   empirically derived procedures carried out uniformly and yielding statistically reliable and valid data

Stanford-Binet test   an individually administered standardized test of intelligence composed of verbal and performance subtests; correlates well with school success and teachers' evaluation of intelligence

stanines   score that describes between-student comparisons based on rankings divided into nine parts

state-dependent or context effects   learning is facilitated when material is presented in a context similar to the one in which the information was presented; also called "context effects"

stereotypes   oversimplified characteristics used to describe students generally

Sternberg's triarchic theory of intelligence   three-part theory of intelligence including componential, experiential, and contextual types of intelligence

stimulus generalization   responding emotionally or physiologically not only to the conditioned stimulus, but also to stimuli that resemble the conditioned stimulus

structured overviews   pre-instructional, dual coding strategies featuring the hierarchical arrangement of key terms

student autonomy   entrusting students with their learning and allowing their interests to guide lessons

student-owned problems   problems in which the student's behavior causes a problem for the student

stuttering   speech characterized by abnormal hesitations, prolongations, and repetitions; may be accompanied by grimaces, gestures, or other bodily movements indicative of a struggle to speak, anxiety, blocking of speech, or avoidance of speech

summative assessment   information about student knowledge and performance provided by teachers at the end of instruction

supply items   objective test items that require students to generate responses, not respond to options supplied by the teacher

symbolic function   emerges during preoperations; the ability to represent objects and events

syntax   the set of rules that one uses (often unconsciously) to put words together in sentences

table of specification   two-dimensional chart matching the targeted instructional objectives to the content areas to be addressed by the test

task goals   those goals involved with academic learning and achievement

taxonomy   a classification system; educational taxonomies have been developed for the cognitive, affective, and psychomotor domains

teacher expectancy   beliefs a teacher holds regarding a student's behavior performance

teacher-as-counselor   one of the roles a teacher may embrace; assisting students with their personal concerns and problems through availability, approachability, listening, and problem solving

teacher-owned problems   problems in which the student's behavior causes a problem for the teacher

telegraphic speech   children's speech using only essential words, as in a telegram

test item analysis   procedure by which teachers can evaluate the effectiveness of their tests

tests   formal, systematic procedures for measuring student knowledge

text organization effects   the degree and type of learning processed is influenced by the degree and type of organization built into the material

thematic units   units organized around a theme of study

time out   strategy in which a student who is acting inappropriately is removed to a non-reinforcing setting; used as an alternative to presentation punishment

transductive reasoning   feature of preoperations in which the child neither reasons deductively or inductively

transfer effects   prior learning influences the processing of new material

transformative multicultural education model   teaching model which focuses on the value of diversity

transition programs for secondary students   accommodations to help secondary students with learning disabilities make the transfer to adulthood and the world of work; these students often require additional support and assistance to make this transfer

transitional approach   teaching model for addressing language diversity by allowing students to learn and socialize initially in the students' cultural or familial language and moving students gradually to standard language usage

trust versus mistrust   stage of Erikson's psychosocial theory pertaining to first year of life

unconditioned response (UR)   an automatic emotional or physiological response to an unconditioned stimulus

unconditioned stimulus (US)   stimulus which automatically evokes an emotional or physiological response

unit goals   objectives written for a unit of instruction that centers on one theme and usually lasts several weeks

valence   the experienced level of value of a particular moment

validity   psychometric concept concerning whether a test measures what it was intended to measure

value-expectancy   theory of motivation which emphasizes the need for both a belief that the action will lead to goal attainment (expectancy), and that the goal has value (value)

VersaBraille   a device used to record Braille onto tape cassettes that are played back on a reading board; the VersaBraille II Plus is a laptop computer on which a person can type Braille that can be converted into print copies

visibility   a classroom arrangement in which students can clearly and easily see all learning materials and activities and the teacher can see each student

visual impairment   a difficulty in clearly distinguishing forms or discriminating details by sight at a specified distance, resulting in the need for special methods and materials

Wechsler test   an individually administered intelligence test with 13 subtests, of which 6 are verbal and 7 are performance oriented

whole language approach   a philosophical approach to teaching and learning that stresses learning through authentic, real-life tasks; emphasizes using language to learn, integrating learning across skills and subjects, and respecting the language abilities of student and teacher

withitness   having an awareness of everything that is happening within the classroom (Kounin's concept)

word decoding   ability to identify the sounds associated with the word's letters and blend them together to identify what the word is

zone of proximal development   Vygotsky's description for the difference between an individual's current level of development and his or her potential level of development

REFERENCES

CHAPTER 1

Anderson, L. W., & Burns, R. B. (1989). *Research in the classrooms: The study of teachers, teaching and instruction.* New York: Pergamon.

Bennett, W. (1993). *The index of leading cultural indicators.* Washington, DC: Heritage Foundation.

Berliner, C. D. (1986). In pursuit of the expert pedagogue. *Educational Researcher, 15(7),* 5–13.

Berliner, D. (1987). Knowledge is power. In D. Berliner & B. Rosenshine (Eds.), *Talks to teachers.* New York: Random House.

Berliner, C. D. (1987). Ways of thinking about students and classrooms by more and less experienced teachers. In J. Calderhead (Ed.), *Exploring teachers' thinking.* London: Cassell Educational Limited.

Berliner, C. D. (1988). The development of expertise in pedagogy. Charles W. Hunt Memorial Lecture presented at the Annual Meeting of the American Association of Colleges for Teacher Education, New Orleans.

Borko, H., & Shavelson, R. J. (1990). Teachers' decision making. In B. Jones & L. Idols (Eds.), *Dimensions of thinking and cognitive instruction.* Hillsdale, NJ: Erlbaum.

Brandt, R. (1988). *Content of the curriculum:* ASCD Yearbook. Alexandria, VA: ASCD.

Breuer, J. T. (1993). *Schools for thought.* Cambridge, MA: MIT Press.

Brophy, J., & Good, T. (1986). Teacher effects. In M. Wittrock (Ed.), *Handbook of research on teaching,* 3d ed., (pp. 328–375). New York: Macmillan.

Carter, K., Sabers, D., Cushing, K., Pinnegar, S., & Berliner, D. (1987). Processing and using information about students: A study of expert, novice and postulant teachers. *Teaching and Teacher Education, 3(2),* 147–157.

Carter, K., Cushing, K., Sabers, D., Stein, P., Berliner, D. (1988, May-June). Expert-novice differences in perceiving and processing visual classroom information. *Journal of Teacher Education,* 25–32.

Casanova, V. (1989). Research and practice—we can integrate them. *N.E.A. Today, 7(6),* 44–49.

Cochran-Smith, M. (1988). A new assignment for student teachers. *Harvard Education Letter, 4(4),* 3.

Cochran-Smith, M. (1991). Reinventing student teaching. *Journal of Teacher Education, 42(2),* 104–118.

Cochran-Smith, M., & Lytle, S. L. (1990). Research on teaching and teacher research: The issues that divide. *Education Researchers, 19(2),* 2–10.

Cruickshank, D. (1987). *Reflective teaching: The preparation of students of teaching.* Reston, VA: Association of Teacher Education.

Doyle, R. (1989). The resistance of conventional wisdom to research evidence: The case of retention in grade. *Phi Delta Kappan, 71,* 215–220.

Eisner, E. W. (1982). An artistic approach to supervision. In T. J. Sergiovanni (Ed.), *Supervision of teaching* (ASCD 1982 Yearbook). Alexandria, VA: Association for Supervision and Curriculum Development.

Feiman-Nemser, S., & Floden, R. (1986). The cultures of teaching. In M. Wittrock (Ed.), *Handbook of research on teaching* (3d ed.). New York: Macmillan.

Flinders, D. (1989, May). Does the "art of teaching" have a future? *Educational Leadership,* 16–22.

Gage, N. (1985). *Hard gains in the soft sciences: The case of pedagogy.* Bloomington, IN: Phi Delta Kappa.

Glaser, R. (1988). Cognitive science and education. *International Social Science Journal, 40(1),* 21–44.

Good, T. L. & Brophy, J. E. (1990). *Educational Psychology: A realistic approach.* New York: Longman.

Hovda, R., & Kyle, D. (1984). Action research: A professional development possibility. *Middle School Journal, 15(3),* 21–23.

Huling-Austin, L. (1994). *Becoming a teacher: What research tells us* (booklet). West Lafayette, IN: Kappa Delta Pi.

Jetton, T., & Alexander, P. (1997). Instruction importance: What teachers value and what students learn. *Reading Research Quarterly, 32,* 290–308.

Kerlinger, F. (1973). *Foundations of behavioral research.* New York: Holt, Rinehart and Winston.

Leinhardt, G., & Greeno, J. G. (1986). The cognitive skill of teaching. *Educational Leadership, 49(1),* 20–25.

Livingston, C., & Borko, H. (1989, July-August). Expert-novice differences in teaching: A cognitive analysis and implications for teacher education. *Journal of Teacher Education,* 36–42.

Moore, K. D. (1992). *Classroom Teaching Skills* (2d ed.). New York: McGraw Hill.

National Commission on Excellence in Education (1983). *A Nation at Risk: The Imperative for Educational Reform.* Washington, DC: U.S. Department of Education.

Parsons, R. D., & Brown, K. (in press). Action Research: Increasing the utility of theory and practice. New York: Addison-Wesley-Longman.

Peterson, P. L., & Comeaux, M. A. (1987). Teachers' schemata for classroom events: The mental scaffolding of teachers' thinking during classroom instruction. *Teaching and Teacher Education, 3,* 319–331.

Pintrich, P., & Schunk, D. (1996). *Motivation in education: Theory, research, and application.* Upper Saddle River, NJ: Prentice Hall

Purkey, W., & Novack, J. (1984). *Inviting school success* (2d ed.). Belmont, CA: Wadsworth.

Rubin, L. (1985). *Artistry in teaching.* New York: Random House.

Sardo-Brown, D. (1990). Middle level teachers' perceptions of action research. *Middle School Journal, 22(3),* 30–32.

Sardo-Brown, D. (1994). Descriptions of six classroom teachers' action research. *People and Education, 1(4),* 458–467.

Schon, D. (1983). *The reflective practitioner: How professionals think in action.* San Francisco, Jossey-Bass.

Shulman, L. (1986). Those who understand: Knowledge growth in teaching. *Educational Researcher, 15(2),* 4–14.

Slavin, R. (1987). Ability grouping and student achievement in elementary schools: A best-evidence synthesis. *Review of Educational Research, 57,* 293–336.

Spaulding, C. L. (1992). *Motivation in the classroom.* New York: McGraw-Hill.

Whittrock, M. C., & Farley, F. (1989). Toward a blueprint for educational psychology. In M. C. Wittrock & F. Farley (Eds.). *The future of educational psychology* (pp. 193–199). Hillsdale, NJ: Erlbaum.

CHAPTER 2

Adams, M. J. (1990). *Beginning to read: Thinking and learning about print.* Cambridge, MA: MIT Press.

Anglin, J. M. Vocabulary development: A morphological analysis. *Monographs of the Society for Research in Child Development, 58* (10 Serial No. 238).

Arlin, P. K. (1975). Cognitive development in adulthood: A fifth stage? *Developmental Psychology, 11,* 602–606.

Arlin, P. K. (1977). Piagetian operations in problem solving. *Developmental Psychology, 13,* 297–298.

Arlin, P. K. (1980). *The Arlin test of formal reasoning.* New York: Slosson Publishing.

Bandura, A. (1977). *Social learning theory.* Englewood Cliffs, NJ: Prentice Hall.

Bandura, A. (1986). *Social foundations of thought and action: A social-cognitive theory.* Englewood Cliffs, NJ: Prentice Hall.

Bee, H. (1992). *The developing child* (6th ed.). New York: HarperCollins.

Berger, K. S. (1986). *The developing person through childhood and adolescence* (2d ed.). New York: Worth.

Berk, L. E., & Garving, R. A. (1984). Development of private speech among low-income Appalachian children. *Developmental Psychology, 20,* 271–286.

Bivins, J. A., & Berk, L. E. (1990). A longitudinal study of elementary school children's private speech. *Merrill-Palmer Quarterly, 6,* 443–463.

Bradley, L. & Bryant, P. E. (1991). Phonological skills before and after learning how to read. In S. A. Brady and D. P. Shankweiler (Eds.), *Phonological processes in literacy* (pp. 118–137). Hillsdale, NJ: Erlbaum.

Bronfenbrenner, U. (1989). Ecological systems theory. In R. Vasta (ed.), *Annals of child development, vol. 6* (pp. 187–251). Greenwich, CT: JAI.

Brooks, J. G. (1990). Teacher and students: Constructivists forging new connections. *Educational Leadership, 47(5),* 68–71.

Brown, R. (1973). *A first language: The early stages.* Cambridge, MA: Harvard University Press.

Case, R. (1984). The process of stage transition: A neo-Piagetian view. In R. J. Sternberg (Ed.), *Mechanisms of cognitive development* (pp. 56–84). New York: W. H. Freeman.

Case, R. (1985). *Intellectual development: A systematic reinterpretation.* New York: Academic Press.

Chall, J.S. (1991). American reading instruction: Science, art and ideology. In W. Ellis (Ed.), *All language and the creation of literacy* (pp. 20–26). Baltimore: Orton Dyslexia Society.

Chomsky, N. (1957). *Syntactic structures.* The Hague: Morton.

Cowan, P. A. (1978). *Piaget, with feeling: Cognitive, social, and emotional dimensions.* New York: Holt, Rinehart and Winston.

Cronbach, L. J. (1990). *Essentials of psychological testing* (5th ed.). New York: Harper & Row.

Dorval, R., & Eckerman, C. O. (1984). Developmental trends in the quality of conversation achieved by small groups of acquainted peers. *Monographs of the Society for Research in Child Development, 49* (2, Serial No. 206).

Dudley-Marling, C. (1995). Whole language: It's a matter of principles. *Reading and Writing Quarterly: Overcoming Learning Difficulties, 11(1),* 109–117.

Elkind, D. (1981). Obituary Jean Piaget (1906–1980). *American Psychologist, 36,* 911–913.

Foorman, B. R., Francis, D. J., Fletcher, J. M., et al. (1998). The role of instruction in learning to read: Preventing reading failure in at-risk children. *Journal of Educational Psychology, 90,* 37–55.

Gardner, H. (1982). *Development psychology* (2d ed.). Boston: Little, Brown.

Goodman, Y. M., & Goodman, K. S. (1990). Vygotsky in a whole-language perspective. In L. Moll (Ed.), *Vygotsky and education: Instructional implications and applications of a sociohistorical psychology* (pp. 223–250). New York: Cambridge University Press.

Greenfield, P. M. (1984). Theory of the teacher in learning activities. In B. Rogoff & J. Lave (Eds.), *Everyday cognition: Its development in social context* (pp. 117–138). Cambridge, MA: Harvard University Press.

Hawkins, J., Pea, R. D., Glick, J., & Scribner, S. (1984). "Minds that laugh don't like mushrooms": Evidence for deductive reasoning by preschoolers. *Developmental Psychology, 20,* 584–594.

Hinson, S. (1988). Television viewing and pretend play in Black preschoolers. Unpublished doctoral dissertation. University of Virginia: Charlottesville, Virginia.

Inhelder, B., & Piaget, J. (1958). *The growth of logical thinking from childhood to adolescence.* New York: Basic Books.

Karpov, Y. V., & Bransford, J. D. (1995). Vygotsky and the doctrine of empirical and theoretical learning. *Educational Psychologist, 30,* 61–66.

Keating, D. (1979). Adolescent thinking. In J. Adelson (ed.), *Handbook of adolescent psychology* (pp. 211–246), New York: Wiley.

Keil, F. (1979). *Semantic and conceptual development.* Cambridge, MA: Harvard University Press.

Kozulin, A., & Presseisen, B. Z. (1995). Mediated learning experience and psychological tools: Vygotsky's and Feuerstein's perspectives in a study of student learning. *Educational Psychologist, 30,* 67–75.

Leinhardt, G. (1992). What research on teaching tells us about teaching. *Educational Leadership, 49(7),* 20–25.

Lemire, R. J., Loeser, J. D., Leech, R. W., et al. (1975). *Normal and abnormal development of the human nervous system.* New York: Harper & Row.

Lenneberg, E. (1967). *Biological foundations of language.* New York: Wiley.

Lonigan, C. J., Burger, S. R., Anthony, J. L., et al. (1998). Development of phonological sensitivity in 2- to 5-year old children. *Journal of Educational Psychology, 90,* 294–311.

Lowe, M. (1975). Trends in the development of representational play in infants from one to three years—An observational study. *Journal of Child Psychology, 16,* 33–48.

Mastrilli, T. (1995). *The use of verbal and visual relational comparisons in biology classrooms.* Unpublished doctoral dissertation, University of Pittsburgh: Pittsburgh, PA.

Mather, N. (1991). Whole language reading instruction for students with learning disabilities: Caught in the crossfire. *Learning Disabilities Research and Practice, 7,* 87–95.

Melzoff, A. N. (1988). Infant imitation and memory: Nine-month-olds in immediate and deferred tests. *Child Development, 59,* 217–255.

Nelson, K. (1981). Individual differences in language development: Implications for development and language. *Developmental Psychology, 17,* 170–187.

Niaz, M. (1991). Correlates of formal operational reasoning: A Neo-Piagetian analysis. *Journal of Research in Science Teaching, 28*(1), 19–40.

Pascal-Leone, J. (1987). Organismic processes for Neo–Piagetian theories: A dialectical causal account of cognitive development. *International Journal of Psychology, 22,* 531–570.

Piaget, J. (1969). *Science of education and the psychology of the child.* New York: Viking.

Piaget, J. (1968). *Six psychological studies.* New York: Vintage.

Piaget, J. (1964). Development and learning. In R. Ripple and V. Rockcastle (Eds.), *Piaget rediscovered* (pp. 78–119). Washington, DC: U.S. Office of Education, National Science Foundation.

Piaget, J. (1952). *The origins of intelligence in children* (M. Cook trans.). New York: International Press.

Piaget, J., & Inhelder, B. (1963). *The child's conception of space.* London: Routledge and Paul.

Reuter-Lorenz, P., & Gazzaniga, M. (1991). *Localization of function: A perspective from cognitive neuropsychology.* New York: Oxford University Press.

Reutzel, D. R., & Cooter, R. B., Jr. (1999). *Balanced reading strategies and practices.* Upper Saddle River, NJ: Merrill/Prentice Hall.

Robbins, P. A. (1990). Implementing whole language: Bridging children and books. *Educational Leadership, 47(6),* 53.

Rogoff, B., & Chavajay, P. (1995). What's become of the research on the cultural basis of cognitive development? *American Psychologist, 50,* 859–877.

Rubin, K., Fein, G., & Vandenberg, B. (1983). Play. In P. H. Mussen (Ed.), *Handbook of child psychology: Vol. 4, Socialization, personality, and social development.* New York: Wiley.

Santrock, J. (1992). *Children.* Dubuque, IA: Brown/Benchmark.

Sardo-Brown, D. (1990). Middle level teachers' perceptions of action research. *Middle School Journal, 22(2),* 30–32.

Schab, F. (1980). Cheating in high school: Differences between the sexes (revisited). *Adolescence, 15,* 299–324.

Selman, R. I., Newberger, C. M., & Jacquette, D. (1977, April). *Observing interpersonal reasoning in a clinic/educational setting: Toward the integration of developmental and clinical child psychology.* Paper presented at the meeting of the Society for Research in Child Development, New Orleans.

Shayer, M. (1978). The distribution of Piagetian stages of thinking in British middle and secondary school children 11- 14- to 16 year-olds and sex differentials. *British Journal of Educational Psychology, 48,* 62–70.

Siegler, R. S. (1985). Encoding and the development of problem solving. In S. F. Chipman, J. W. Segal, and R. Glaser (Eds.), *Thinking and learning skills* (Vol. 2). Hillsdale, NJ: Erlbaum.

Siegler, R. S. (1983). Information processing approaches to development. In W. Kessen (Ed.), *Handbook of child psychology: History, theory, and methods* (Vol. 1, pp. 129–212). New York: Wiley.

Skeen, P., Brown, M. H., & Osborn, D. K. (1982). Young children's perception of "real" and "pretend" on television. *Perceptual and Motor Skills, 54,* 883–887.

Spector, J. E. (1992). Predicting progress in beginning reading: Dynamic assessment of phonemic awareness. *Journal of Educational Psychology, 84(3),* 353–363.

Vygotsky, L. (1978). *Mind in society.* Cambridge, MA: Harvard University Press.

Vygotsky, L. (1993). *The collected works of L. S. Vygotsky,* Vol. 2 (J. Knox & C. Stevens, trans.). New York: Plenum.

Wadsworth, B. (1989). *Piaget's theory of cognitive and affective development* (4th ed.). New York: London.

CHAPTER 3

Aitken, J. (1963). *Section eleven: A longitudinal study of teacher learning and development.* Paper presented at the Annual Meeting of the American Educational Research Association, Atlanta, Georgia.

Berk, L. (1994). *Child Development* (3d ed.). Needham Heights, MA: Allyn & Bacon.

Bolger, N., Downey, G., Walker, E., & Steininger, P. (1989). The onset of suicidal ideation in childhood and adolescence. *Journal of Youth and Adolescence, 18,* 175–190.

Books-Gunn, J., & Furstenberg, F. F., Jr. (1989). Adolescent sexual behavior. *American Psychologist, 44,* 2249–2257.

Burton, R. V. (1963). The generality of honesty reconsidered. *Psychological Review, 70,* 481–499.

Calvert, P. (1986). *Responses to guidelines for developmentally appropriate practice for young children and Montessori.* Paper presented at the Annual Meeting of the National Association for the Education of Young Children. Washington, DC.

Castle, K. & Rogers, K. (1993/1994). Rule-creating in a constructivist classroom community, *Childhood Education, 3,* 77–80.

Childress, A., Brewerton, T., Hodges, E. L., & Jarrell, M. (1993). The kid's eating disorders survey (KEDS): A study of middle school students. *Journal of the American Academy of Child and Adolescent Psychiatry, 32(4),* 843–850.

Compas, B. E. (1987). Coping with stress during childhood and adolescence. *Psychological Bulletin, 101,* 393–403.

DeRidder, L. M. (1993). Teenage pregnancy: Etiology and educational interventions. *Educational Psychology Review, 5,* 87–107.

Erikson, E. (1950). *Childhood and society.* New York: Norton.

Frey, K., & Ruble, D. (1987). What children say about classroom performance: Sex and grade difference in perceived competence. *Child Development, 58,* 1068–1080.

George, P. (1987). *Long-term teacher-student relationship: A middle school case study.* Columbus, OH: National Middle School Association.

Gilligan, C. (1977). In a different voice: Women's conception of self and of morality. *Harvard Educational Review, 47,* 481–517.

Gilligan, C. (1982). *In a different voice.* Cambridge, MA: Harvard University Press.

Guttmacher (Alan) Institute. (1994). *Issues in brief, 14(2).* Washington, DC: Alan Guttmacher Institute.

Halmi, K. A. (1987). Anorexia nervosa and bulimia. In V. B. Van Haselt & M. Hersen (Eds.), *Handbook of adolescent psychology.* New York: Pergamon Press.

Harris, R. T. (1991). Anorexia nervosa and bulimia nervosa in female adolescents. *Nutrition Today, 26(2),* 30–34.

Harter, S., & Connell, J. (1984). A comparison of alternative models of the relationships between academic achievement and children's perceptions of competence, control, and motivational orientation. In J. Nicholls (Ed.), *Development of achievement-related cognitions and behavior* (pp. 34–59). Greenwich, CT: JAI Press.

House, D. (1997). The relationship between self-beliefs, academic background, and achievement of Asian-American students. *Child Study Journal, 27(2),* 95–110.

Kelly, J. B., & Wallestein, J. S. (1977). Brief interventions with children in divorcing families. *American Journal of Orthopsychiatry, 47,* 23–29.

Kohlberg, L. (1963). The development of children's orientation toward moral order: Sequence in the development of human thought. *Vita Humana, 6,* 670–677.

Kohlberg, L. (1984). *Essays on moral development: Vol. 2. The psychology of moral development.* New York: Harper.

Kohn, A. (1987). Shattered innocence. *Psychology Today, 9,* 54–58.

Kupersmidt, J. B., Coie, J. D., & Dodge, K. A. (1990). The role of poor peer relationships in the development of disorder. In S. R. Asher & J. D. Coie (Eds.), *Peer rejection in childhood* (pp. 274–305). New York: Cambridge University Press.

Lantierzi, L. (1995). Waging peace in our schools: Beginning with the children. *Phi Delta Kappan, 76(5),* 368–388.

Lester, D. (1995). Why are some nations experiencing an increase in youth suicide rates? *Homeostasis in health and disease, 36(4),* 222–233.

Lickona, T. (1983). *Raising good children.* New York: Bantam.

Marcia, J. (1966). Development and validation of ego identity status. *Journal of Personality and Social Psychology, 3,* 551–558.

Marcia, J. (1980). Identity formation in adolescence. In J. Adelson (ed.), *Handbook of Adolescent Psychology* (pp. 116–117). New York: Wiley.

Marsh, H. (1989). Age and sex effects in multiple dimensions of self-concept: Preadolescence to early adulthood. *Journal of Educational Psychology, 81,* 417–430.

Marsh, H. (1992). Content specificity of relations between academic achievement and academic self-concept. *Journal of Educational Psychology, 84(1),* 34–52.

Marsh, H., & Yeung, A. S. (1997). Causal effects of academic self-concept on academic achievement: Structural equations models of longitudinal data. *Journal of Educational Psychology, 89(1),* 41–54.

Marsh, H., & Shavelson, R. (1985). Self-concept: Its multifaceted hierarchical structure. *Educational Psychologist, 20,* 107–123.

McLean, R. (1997). Selected attitudinal factors related to students' success in high school. *Alberta Journal of Educational Research, 43(2/3),* 165–168.

Natale, J. (1995). The hot new work in sex ed. *American School Board Journal, 182(6),* 18–25.

Philadelphia Inquirer. (1997, Nov. 19). Personal briefing: The cheat sheet. *Features Magazine,* p. D03.

Phillips, D. (1990, April). *Parents' beliefs and beyond: Contributions to children's academic self-perceptions.* Paper presented at the Annual Meeting of the American Educational Research Association, Boston.

Piaget, J. (1965). *The moral judgment of the child.* New York: Free Press (original work published, 1932).

Pintrich, P., & Schunk, D. (1996). *Motivation in education: Theory, research, and applications.* Upper Saddle River, NJ: Prentice Hall.

Sardo-Brown, D. (1996). A glimpse into the life of one second-career novice teacher using the lens of instructional planning. *Journal of Research in Education, 5(1),* 20–22.

Seifert, K. L., & Hoffnung, R. J. (1991). *Child and adolescent development.* Boston: Houghton Mifflin.

Serovich, J. M. & Greene, K. (1995). Predictors of adolescent sexual risk-taking behaviors which put them at risk for contracting HIV. *Journal of Youth and Adolescence, 26(4),* 429–441.

Sonenstein, F. L., Pleck, J. H., & Ku, L. C. (1991). Levels of sexual activity among adolescent males in the United States. *Family Planning Perspectives, 23,* 162–167.

Sorenson, N. (1993, April). *Stories of teaching and reflections on practice: Year two.* Paper presented at the Annual Meeting of the American Educational Research Association, Atlanta, GA.

Stipek, D. (1993). *Motivation to learn* (2d ed.). Needham Heights, MA: Allyn & Bacon.

Walberg, H. (1984). Improving the productivity in America's schools. *Educational Leadership, 41(8),* 19–27.

Wingert, P. (1998, May). The battle over falling birthrates. *Newsweek, 131(19),* 40.

CHAPTER 4

AAMR Ad Hoc Committee on Terminology and Classification. (1992). *Mental retardation: Definition, classification, and systems of support* (9th ed.). Washington, DC: American Association on Mental Retardation.

Allen, T. E. (1986). Patterns of achievement among hearing-impaired students: 1974 and 1983. In A. N. Schildroth & M. A. Karchmer (Eds.), *Deaf Children in America* (pp. 161–206). San Diego, CA: College Hill Press.

American Speech-Language-Hearing Association. (1982). Definitions: Communicative disorders and variations, *ASHA, 24,* 949–950.

Andrews, G., Craig, A., Feyer, A., et al. (1983). Stuttering: A review of research findings and theories circa 1982. *Journal of Speech and Hearing Disorders, 48,* 226–246.

Barkley, R. (1990). *Attention deficits hyperactivity disorders: A handbook for diagnosis and treatment.* New York: Guilford Press.

Bates, P., Renzaglia, A., & Wehman, P. (1981). Characteristics of an appropriate education for severely and profoundly handicapped students. *Education and Training of the Mentally Retarded, 16,* 142–149.

Batshaw, M. L., & Perret, Y. M. (1986). *Children with handicaps: A medical primer* (2d ed.). Baltimore: Paul A. Brookes.

Begley, S. (1991, May 3). Why teens kill. *Newsweek,* 32–35.

Bower, E. M. (1981). *Early identification of emotionally handicapped children in school* (3d ed.). Springfield, IL: Charles Thomas.

Brandenburg, N. A., Friedman, R. M., & Silver, S. E. (1990). The epidemiology of childhood psychiatric disorders: Prevalence findings from recent studies. *Journal of the American Academy of Child and Adolescent Psychiatry, 29,* 76–83.

Brill, R. G., MacNeil, B., & Newman, L. R. (1986). Framework for appropriate programs for deaf children. *American Annals of the Deaf, 31(2),* 65–77.

Brooks, P. H., & McCauley, C. (1984). Cognitive research in mental retardation. *American Journal of Mental Deficiency, 88,* 479–486.

Callahan, C. M. (1991). An update on gifted females. *Journal for the Education of the Gifted, 14,* 284–311.

Cattell, R. (1971). *Abilities: Their structure, growth, and action.* New York: Houghton Mifflin.

Chall, J. S. (1991). American reading instruction: Science, art, and ideology. In W. Ellis (Ed.) *All language and the creation of literacy* (pp. 20–26). Baltimore: Orton Dyslexia Society.

Charlson, E., Strong, M., & Gold, R. (1992). How successful deaf teenagers experience and cope with isolation. *American Annals of the Deaf, 137(3),* 261–270.

Coleman, J. M., & Fultz, B. A. (1985). Special class placement, level of intelligence, and the self-concepts of gifted children: A social comparison perspective. *Remedial and Special Education, 6(1),* 7–12.

Collins, M. E., & Barraga, N. C. (1980). Development of efficiency in visual functioning: An evaluation process. *Journal of Visual Impairment and Blindness, 74,* 93–96.

Council of State Directors of Programs for the Gifted, (1991). *The 1990 state of the states gifted and talented education report.* Author Unknown.

Daniele, R. P. (1988). Asthma. In J. B. Wyngaarden & L. H. Smith, Jr. (Eds.), *Cecil textbook of medicine, part VII: Respiratory diseases* (p. 403). Philadelphia. W. B. Saunders.

Detterman, K., & Sternberg, R. (Eds.) (1982). *How and how much can intelligence be increased?* Norwood, NJ: Ablex.

Drabman, R. S., & Patterson, J. N. (1981). Disruptive behavior and the social standing of exceptional children. *Exceptional Education Quarterly, 1(4),* 45–55.

Fletcher, J. M. (1992). The validity of distinguishing children with language and learning disabilities according to discrepancies with IQ: Introduction to the series. *Journal of Learning Disabilities, 25(9),* 546–548.

Freeman, J. M., Jacobs, H., Vinning, E., & Rabin, C. E. (1984). Epilepsy and the inner city schools: A school-based program that makes a difference. *Epilepsia, 25,* 438–442.

Griffin, J. R. (1992). Prevalence of dyslexia. *Journal of Optometric Vision Development, 23(4),* 17–22.

Gailbraith, J. (1985). The eight great gripes of gifted kids: Responding to special needs. *Roeper Review, 7,* 15–18.

Gallager, J. J. (1985). *Teaching the gifted child* (3d ed.). Boston: Allyn & Bacon.

Gardner, H. (1983). *Frames of mind.* New York: Basic.

Gardner, H. (1987). Developing the spectrum of human intelligences. *Harvard Educational Review, 57,* 187–193.

Groenveld, M., & Jan, J. E. (1992). Intelligence profiles of low vision and blind children. *Journal of Visual Impairment and Blindness, 86 (1),* 68–71.

Goodlad, J. (1984). *A place called school.* New York: McGraw-Hill.

Guilford, J. (1967). *The nature of human intelligence.* New York: McGraw-Hill.

Guilford, J. (1988). Some changes in the structure-of-intellect model. *Educational and Psychological Measurement, 48,* 1–4.

Hallahan, D. P., & Kauffman, J. M. (1994). *Exceptional Children: An Introduction to Special Education* (6th ed.). Needham Heights, MA: Allyn & Bacon.

Hallahan, D. P., & Kauffman, J. M. (1997). *Exceptional Learners: Introduction to Special Education* (7th ed.). Boston: Allyn & Bacon.

Hardman, M. L., Drew, C. J., & Egan, M. W. (1996). *Human Exceptionality: Society, School, and Family* (5th ed.). Boston: Allyn & Bacon.

Hoare, P. (1984). The development of psychiatric disorder among schoolchildren with epilepsy. *Developmental Medicine and Child Neurology, 26,* 3–13.

Holbrook, M. C., & Koenig, A. J. (1992). Teaching Braille reading to students with low vision. *Journal of Visual Impairment & Blindness, 86(1),* 44–48.

Hynd, G. (1992). Neurological aspects of dyslexia: Comments on the balance model. *Journal of Learning Disabilities, 25,* 110–113.

Ingersall, B. (1988). *Your hyperactive child.* New York: Doubleday.

Janos, P. M., & Robinson, N. M. (1985). Psychosocial development in intellectually gifted children. In F. D. Horowitz & M. O'Brien (Eds.), *The gifted and talented: Developmental perspectives* (pp. 149–155). Washington, DC: American Psychological Association.

Katsiyannis, A. (1992). Policy issues in school attendance of children with AIDS: A national survey. *Journal of Special Education, 26,* 219–226.

Kauffman, J. M. (1993). *Characteristics of emotional and behavioral disorders of children and youth* (5th ed.). Columbus, OH: Merlin/Macmillan.

Kaplan, R., & Saccuzzo, D. (1993). *Psychological testing* (3d ed.). Pacific Grove, CA: Brooks/Cole.

Keogh, B. K., & MacMillan, D. L. (1996). Exceptionality. In D. Berliner & R. Calfee (Eds.), *Handbook of educational psychology* (pp. 311–330). New York: Macmillan.

Kirk, S., Gallagher, J. J., & Anastasiow, N. J. (1993). *Educating exceptional children* (7th ed.). Boston: Houghton Mifflin.

Klein, R. G., & Last, C. G. (1989). *Anxiety disorders in children.* Newbury Park, CA: Sage.

Lammers, J. W. (1991). *I don't feel good: A guide to childhood complaints and diseases.* Santa Cruz, CA: Network Publications.

Lane, H. (1987, July 17). Listen to the needs of deaf children. *New York Times,* p. B–32.

Lane, H. (1992). *The mask of benevolence: disabling the deaf community.* New York: Alfred A. Knopf.

Laski, F. J. (1991). Achieving integration during the second revolution. In L. H. Meyer, C. A. Peck, L. Brown (Eds.), *Critical Issues in the lives of people with severe disabilities* (pp. 409–421). Baltimore: Paul H. Brookes.

Leonard, L. (1986). Early language development and language disorders. In G. H. Shames & E. H. Wiig (Eds.), *Human communication disorders* (2d ed.) (pp. 291–300). Columbus, OH: Merrill/Macmillan.

Lewis, R. B., & Doorlay, D. H. (1990). *Teaching special students in the mainstream* (3d ed.). New York: Merrill/Macmillan.

Lovaas, O. I. (1987). Behavioral treatment and normal educational and intellectual functioning in young autistic children. *Journal of Consulting and Clinical Psychology, 55,* 3–9.

Love, R. J. (1992). *Childhood motor speech disability*. New York: Macmillan.

Mauer, M. (1991, May 20). All children should learn Braille: Here's why. Scripps Howard News Service.

National Joint Committee on Learning Disabilities. (1989, September 18). *Letter from NJCLD to member organizations*. Topic: Modifications to the NJCLD definition of learning disabilities.

Newcomb, M. D., & Bentler, P. M. (1989). Substance use and abuse among children and teenagers. *American Psychologist, 44*, 242–248.

Olefsky, J. M. (1988). Diabetes mellitus. In J. B. Wyngaarden & L. H. Smith, Jr. (Eds.), *Cecil textbook of medicine, part XVI: Endocrine and reproductive diseases* (pp. 1360–1380). Philadelphia: W. B. Saunders.

Patterson, D. (1987). The causes of Down syndrome. *Scientific American, 257(2)*, 52–57, 60.

Rapp, D. W., & Rapp, A. J. (1992). A survey of the current status of visually impaired students in secondary mathematics. *Journal of Visual Impairment & Blindness, 86(2)*, 115–117.

Renzulli, J. (ed.). (1986). *Systems and models for developing programs for the gifted and talented*. Mansfield Center, CT: Creative Learning Press.

Renzulli, J. S., & Reis, S. M. (1991). The schoolwide enrichment model: A comprehensive plan for the development of creative productivity. In N. Colangelo & G. A. Davis (Eds.), *Handbook of gifted education* (pp. 111–141). Boston: Allyn & Bacon.

Rudigier, A. F., Crocker, A. C., & Cohen, H. J. (1990). The dilemmas of childhood: HIV infection. *Children Today, 19*, 26–29.

Sailor, W. (1991). Special education in the restructured school. *Remedial and Special Education, 12*(6), 8–22.

Sardo-Brown, D., & Hinson, S. (1995). Classroom teachers' perceptions of the implementation and effects of full inclusion. *ERS Spectrum, 13*(2), 18–24.

Schultz, E. E., Jr. (1983). Depth of processing by mentally retarded and MA-matched nonretarded individuals. *American Journal of Mental Deficiency, 88*, 307–313.

Shaywitz, B. (1987). Hyperactivity/Attention-deficit disorder. *Learning disabilities: A report to the U.S. Congress*. Washington, DC: Interagency Committee on Learning Disabilities.

Shaywitz, S., & Shaywitz, B. (1991). Introduction to the special series on attention deficit disorder. *Journal of Learning Disabilities, 24*, 68–71.

Siegel, L. S. (1989). IQ is irrelevant to the definition of learning disabilities. *Journal of Learning Disabilities, 22(8)*, 468–478, 486.

Smith, D. D. & Luckasson, R. (1995). *Introduction to special education* (2d ed.). Boston: Allyn & Bacon.

Spearman, C. (1927). *The abilities of man: Their nature and measurement*. New York: Macmillan.

Stainback, S., & Stainback, W. (1992). Schools as inclusive communities. In W. Stainback & S. Stainback (Eds.), *Controversial issues confronting special education: Divergent perspectives* (pp. 29–43). Boston: Allyn & Bacon.

Sternberg, R. (1988). *The triarchic mind*. New York: Viking.

Sternberg, R. (1990). *Metaphors of mind: Conceptions of the nature of intelligence*. New York: Cambridge University Press.

Sternberg, R. J., & Davidson, J. E. (Eds.) (1986). *Conceptions of giftedness*. New York: Cambridge University Press.

Stinson, M. S., & Whitmore, K. (1992). Students' views of their social relationships. In T. N. Kluwin, D. F. Moores, & M. G. Gaustad (Eds.), *Toward effective public school programs for deaf students: Context, process, & outcomes* (pp. 149–174). New York: Teachers College Press.

Swallow, R. M., & Conner, A. (1982). Aural reading. In S. S. Mangold (Ed.), *A teacher's guide to the special educational needs of blind and visually impaired children*. New York: American Foundation for the Blind.

Terman, L. M., & Oden, M. H. (1959). *Genetic studies of genius, Vol. V: The gifted group at midlife*. Palo Alto, CA: Stanford University Press.

U.S. Office of Education (1977). Education of handicapped children. Assistance to the states: Procedures for evaluating specific learning disabilities. *Federal Register, Part III*. Washington, DC: U.S. Department of Health, Education, and Welfare, December 29.

Walker, H. M., McConnell, S., Holmes, D., Todis, B., Walker, J., & Golden, N. (1983). *The Accepts Program*. Austin, TX: Pro-Ed.

Warren, D. H. (1984). *Blindness and early childhood development* (2d ed.). New York: American Foundation for the Blind.

Weiss, G., & Hechtman, L. T. (1993). *Hyperactive children grow up: ADHD in children, adolescents, and adults* (2d ed.). New York: Guilford Press.

Westbrook, L. E., Silver, E. J., Coupey, S. M., & Shinnar, S. (1991). Social characteristics of adolescents with ideopathic epilepsy: A comparison to chronically ill and nonchronically ill peers. *Journal of Epilepsy, 4*, 87–94.

Whitmore, J. R., & Maker, C. J. (1985). *Intellectual giftedness in disabled persons*. Rockville, MD: Aspen.

Wolf, S., & Allen, T. E. (1984). A five-year follow-up of reading comprehension achievement of hearing-impaired students in special education programs. *Journal of Special Education, 18*, 161–176.

Wolf, S., & Schildroth, A. N. (1986). Deaf children and speech intelligibility: A national study. In A. N. Schildroth & M. A. Karchmer (Eds.), *Deaf children in America* (pp. 139–159). San Diego: College-Hill Press.

Zabin, L.S., & Clark, S.D., Jr. (1981, September/October). Why they delay: A study of teenage family planning clinic patients. *Family Planning Perspectives*.

Zelnik, M., & Shah, F. K. (1983, March/April). First intercourse among young Americans. *Family Planning Perspectives*, 64–70.

Zigmond, N., Jenkins, J., Fuchs, D., Deno, S., & Fuchs, L. S. (1995). When students fail to achieve satisfactorily: A reply to Leskey and Waldron. *Phi Delta Kappan, 77*, 303–306.

CHAPTER 5

Alexander, G. M., & Hines, N. (1994). Gender labels and play styles: Their relative contribution to children's selection of playmates. *Child Development, 65*, 869–879.

Appleton, C. (1983). *Cultural pluralism in education: Theoretical Foundations*. New York: Longman.

Avitabile, J. (1998). Interaction of presentation mode and learning styles in computer science. ERIC Document Service No.: ED 419492.

Banks, J., & Banks, C. (1989). *Multicultural education: Issues and perspectives*. Boston: Allyn & Bacon.

Bem, S. (1981). Gender schema theory: A cognitive account of sex typing. *Psychological Review, 88*, 354–364.

Biklen, S. K. & Pollard, D. (Eds.). (1993). *Gender and Education*. Chicago: University of Chicago Press.

Boutte, G. S., & McCormick, C. B. (1992). Authentic multicultural activities: Avoiding pseudomulticulturalism. *Childhood Education, 68,* 140–144.

Briscoe, D. (1994, January 31). Report describes education gender gap. Philadelphia Inquirer, p. A2.

Brown, G., & McGraw-Zoubi, R. (1995). Successful teaching in culturally diverse classrooms. *The Delta Kappan Gamma Bulletin, 61(2),* 7–12.

Canney, G. F., Kennedy, T. J., Schroeder, M., & Miles, S. (1999). Instructional strategies for K-12 Limited English Proficiency (LEP) students in the regular classroom. *Reading Teacher, 52,* 540–545.

Carter, R. T., & Goodwin, A. L. (1994). Racial identity and education. In L. Darling-Hammond (Ed.). *Review of Research in Education*. Washington, DC: American Educational Research Association.

Cochran-Smith, M. (1995). Color blindness and basket making are not the answers: Confronting the dilemmas of race, culture, and language diversity in teacher education. *American Educational Research Journal, 32,* 493–522.

Coeyman, M. (1998, September 8). Parents pay up. *Christian Science Monitor*, p. 7.

Coolican, J. (1988). Individual differences. In R. McNergney (Ed.), *Guide to Classroom Teaching* (pp. 211–230). Needham Heights, MA: Allyn & Bacon.

Cooper, H., & Moore, C. J. (1994). Teenage motherhood, mother-only households, and teacher expectations. *Journal of Experimental Education, 63(3),* pp. 231–248.

Crosby, M. S., & Owens, E. M. (1991). An assessment of principal attitudes toward ability grouping in the public schools in South Carolina. ERIC Document Service No.: ED364634.

Davidson, A. L., & Phelan, P. (1993). Cultural diversity and its implications for schooling: A continuing American dialogue. In P. Phelan & A. L. Davidson (Eds.). *Renegotiating cultural diversity in American schools*. New York: Teachers College Press, pp. 1–26.

Dodge, K. A., Pettit, G. S., & Bates, J. E. (1994). Socialization mediators of the relation between socioeconomic status and child conduct problems. *Child Development, 65,* 649–665.

Dunn, R., & Griggs, S. (1990). Research on learning style characteristics of selected racial and ethnic groups. *Journal of Reading, Writing, and Learning Disabilities, 6(3),* 261–280.

Dunn, K., & Dunn, R. (1987). Dispelling outmoded beliefs about student learning. *Educational Leadership, 44,* 55–62.

Durost, R. A. (1996). Single sex math classes: What and for whom? One school's experiences. *NASSP Bulletin, 80,* 27–31.

Eldredge, J. L. (1990). Increasing the performance of poor readers in the third grade with a group-assisted strategy. *Journal of Educational Research, 84(2),* 69–77.

Elrich, M. (1994). The stereotype within. *Educational Leadership, 51(8),* 12–15.

Finders, M., & Lewis, C. (1994). Why some parents don't come to school. *Educational Leadership, 51(8),* 50–57.

Fordham, S. (1988). Racelessness as a factor in black students. *Harvard Educational Review, 58,* 54–84.

French, J. (1984). Gender imbalances in the primary classroom: An interactional account. *Educational Researcher, 26(2),* 127–136.

Garcia, E. (1994). *Understanding and meeting the challenge of student cultural diversity*. Boston: Houghton Mifflin Company.

Gardner, H. (1995). A meta-analytic validation of the Dunn and Dunn model of learning style preferences. *Journal of Educational Research, 88,* 353–362.

Good, T., & Brophy, J. E. (1974). Changing teacher and student behavior: An empirical investigation. *Journal of Educational Psychology, 66(3),* 390–405.

Hayes, J., & Allinson, C. (1993). Matching learning style and instructional strategy: An application of the person-environment interaction paradigm. *Perceptual and Motor Skills, 76,* 63–79.

Graybill, S. W. (1997). Questions of race and culture: How they relate to the classroom for African American Students. *Clearinghouse, 70(6),* 311–318.

Grottkay, B. J., & Nickolai-Mays, S. (1989). An empirical analysis of a multicultural education paradigm for pre-service teachers. *Educational Research Quarterly, 13(4),* 27–33.

Guild, P. (1994). The culture/learning style connection. *Educational Leadership, 51(8),* 16–21.

Haberman, M. (1995). Selecting "Star" teachers for children and youth in urban poverty. *Phi Delta Kappan, 76,* 777–781.

Haberman, N. (1991). The pedagogy of poverty versus good teaching. *Phi Delta Kappan, 73(4),* 290–294.

Hale-Benson, J. E. (1986). *Black children: Their roots, culture, and learning styles*. Baltimore: The Johns Hopkins University Press.

Herbert, J., & Pitt, E. (1988). Teaching in context. In R. McNergney (Ed.), Guide to Classroom Teaching (pp. 1–22). Needham Heights, MA: Allyn & Bacon.

Hernandez, A. E. (1995). Enhancing the academic success of Hispanic females. *Comptemporary Education, 67(1),* 18–20.

Hickson, J., Land, A., & Aikman, G. (1994). Learning style differences in middle school pupils from four ethnic backgrounds. *School Psychology International, 15(4),* 349–359.

Hlvana, D. (1994). A multicultural perspective in developing and delivering training. *Performance and Instruction, 33,* 25–27.

Holland, S. H. (1989). Viewpoint: Fighting the epidemic of failure. *Teacher Magazine*, Sept/October, 88–89.

Houston, L. (1997). Knowing learning styles can improve self confidence of developmental writers. *Teaching English in the Two Year College, 24,* 212–215.

Huston, A. C., McLoyd, V. C., & Garcia Coll, C. (1994). Children and poverty: Issues in contemporary research. *Child Development, 65,* 275–282.

Irvine, J. J. (1983). Teacher communication patterns as related to race and sex of the student. *Journal of Educational Research 78(6),* 338–345.

Irvine, J. J., & Foster, M. (1996). Growing up African American in Catholic schools. ERIC Document Service No.: 396051.

Irvine, J. J. (1990). *Black students and school failure*. New York: Greenwood Press.

Janzen, R. (1994). Melting pot or mosaic? *Educational Leadership, 51(8),* 9–11.

Johnson, D. W., & Johnson, R. T. (1981). Effects of cooperative and individualistic learning experiences on interethnic interaction. *Journal of Educational Psychology, 73(3),* 444–449.

Jordan, W. J., & Plank, S. B. (1998). Sources of talent loss among high-achieving poor students. Report No. 23. ERIC Document Service No.: ED424342.

Kistner, J., Metzler, A., Gatlin, D., & Risi, S. (1993). Classroom racial proportions and children's peer relations: Race and gender effects. *Journal of Educational Psychology, 85*, 446–452.

Knapp, M. S., & Shields, P. M. (1990). Reconceiving academic instruction for the children of poverty. *Kappan, 71(10)*, 753–758.

Kochman, T. (1981). *Black and white: Styles in conflict.* Chicago: University of Chicago Press.

Krashen, S. (1997). Why bilingual education? ERIC Document Service No.: ED403313.

Kunjufu, J. (1985). *Countering the conspiracy to destroy black.* Chicago: African American Images.

Ladson-Billings, G. (1994). What we can learn from multicultural education research. *Educational Leadership, 51(8)*, 22–26.

Ladson-Billings, G. (1994). *The dreamkeepers: Successful teachers of African American children.* San Francisco: Jossey-Bass Publishers.

Lawton, N. (1990, October 10). 2 schools aimed for black males set in Milwaukee. *Education Week, 10(6)*, 1–12.

Leung, J. L. (1992). Music, physical education, and reading: Aspiring parents' and teachers' expectation for young children. *Educational Research Quarterly, 15(1)*, 47–57.

Lewis, H. (Ed.) (1988, August). Multicultural perspective for effective teaching (Available from Horacio Lewis, State Supervisor, Human Relations/Title IV Projects, Delaware State Department of Public Instruction).

Lewis, A. C. (1997). The price of poverty. *Phi Delta Kappan, 78*, 423–424.

Light, R. L., Richard, D. P., & Bell, P. (1978). Development of children's attitudes toward speakers of standard and non-standard English. *Child Study Journal, 8(4)*, 253-266.

Lipman, P. (1997). Restructuring in context: A case study of teacher participation and the dynamics of ideology, race, and power. *American Educational Research Journal, 34(1)*, 3–38.

Lockhart, J. (1991). "We real cool": Dialect in the middle school classroom. *English Journal, 80*, 53–57.

Luster, T., & McAdoo, H. P. (1994). Factors related to the achievement and adjustment of young African American children. *Child Development, 65*, 1080–1094.

Macionis, J. (1994). *Sociology* (4th ed.). Englewood Cliffs, NJ: Prentice Hall, Inc.

McCabe, J. (1996). Afro-American and Latino teenagers in New York City: Race and language development. *Community Review, 14*, 13–26.

McCormick, J. (1990). Where are the parents? Newsweek Special Edition Education: A Consumer's Handbook, *116(28)*, 54–58.

McCormick, S. (1995). *Instructing Students Who Have Literacy Problems.* Columbus, OH: Merrill/Prentice Hall.

McFadden, A. C., Marsh, G. E. II, Price, B. J., & Hwang, Y. (1992). A study of race and gender bias in the punishment of school children. *Education and Treatment of Children, 15(2)*, 140–146.

McLoyd, V. (1998). Socioeconomic disadvantage and child development. *American Psychologist, 53*, 185–204.

Means, B., & Knapp, M. S. (1991). Cognitive approaches to teaching advanced skills to educationally disadvantaged students. *Kappan, 73(4)*, 282–289.

Meier, T., & Brown, C. R. (1994). The color of inclusion. *Journal of Emotional and Behavioral Problems, 3(3)*, 15–18.

Merrett, F., & Wheldall, K. (1992). Teachers' use of praise and reprimands to boys and girls. *Educational Review, 44(1)*, 73–79.

Morales-Jones, C. (1998). Understanding Hispanic culture: From tolerance to acceptance. *The Delta Kappa Gamma Bulletin, 64(4)*, 5–12.

Morgan, J. (1991). All-Black male classrooms run into resistance. *Black Issues in Higher Education, 7(23)*, 121–122.

Narahara, M. (1998). Gender bias in children's picture books: A look at teacher's choice of literature. ERIC Document Service No.: ED419247.

Nichols, J. D., & Miller, R. B. (1994). Cooperative learning and student motivation. *Contemporary Educational Psychology, 19*, 167–178.

Nietlo, S. (1996). *Affirming diversity.* White Plains, NY: Longman Publishers.

O'Connor, S. (1988). Affective climate. In R. McNergney (Ed.), Guide to classroom teaching (pp. 247–262). Needham Heights, MA: Allyn & Bacon.

Ogbu, J. (1991). Minority coping responses and school experience. *The Journal of Psychohistory, 18*, 433–456.

Olson, P. (1992, May). Referring language minority students to special education. *NCBE Forum, 15(4)*, 1–5.

Pewewardy, C. (1998). Fluff and feathers: Treatment of American Indians in the literature and the classroom. *Equity and Excellence, 31(1)*, 69–76.

Phelan, P., Davidson, A. L., & Yu, H. C. (1993). Students' multiple worlds: Navigating the borders of family, peer, and school cultures. In P. Phelan & A. L. Davidson (Eds.). *Renegotiating cultural diversity in American schools.* New York: Teachers College Press pp. 52–88.

Phillips, C. B. (1998). Preparing teachers to use their voices for change. National Institute for Early Childhood Professional Development. *Young Children, 53(3)*, 55–60.

Pietras, T., & Lamb, P. (1978). Attitudes of selected elementary teachers toward non-standard black dialects. *Journal of Educational Research, 71(5)*, 292–297.

Pyle, A. (1996, February). Research favors native-language education. *The News Journal*, p. A8.

Ramsey, P. G. (1991). The salience of race in young children growing up in an all-white community. *Journal of Educational Psychology, 83(1)*, 28–34.

Reed, S., & Sautter, C. S. (1990). Children of poverty: The status of 12 million young Americans. *Phi Delta Kappan, 71(10)*, K1–K12.

Rice, P. F. (1993). *The adolescent: Development, relationships, and culture.* Boston: Allyn & Bacon.

Robinson-Awana, P., Kehle, T. J., & Jenson, W. R. (1986). But what about smart girls? Adolescent self-esteem and sex role perceptions as a function of academic achievement. *Journal of Educational Psychology, 78(3)*, 179–183.

Rodriguez, R. (1991). Non-English speaking preschoolers stymied by English instruction. *Black Issues in Higher Education, 7*, p. 5.

Romo, H. (1998). Latina high school leaving: Some practical solutions. ERIC Digest. ERIC Document Service No.: ED423096.

Sadker, N., & Sadker, D. (1994). *Failing at Fairness: How America's Schools Cheat Girls.* New York: Charles Scribner's Sons.

Safir, M.P., Hertz-Lazarowitz, R., BenTsvi-Mayer, S., & Kupermintz, H. (1992). Prominence of girls and boys in the classroom: Schoolchildren's perceptions. *Sex Roles 27*, 439–453.

Shaughnessy, M. F. (1998). An interview with Rita Dunn about learning styles. *Clearing House, 71(3),* 141–145.

Sheils, N. (1976, December 20). *Newsweek,* 72–73.

Sherman, J., & Thompson, M. (1994). Reflections on diversity: Implementing anti-bias curriculum in the primary grades. ERIC Document Service No.: ED380335.

Simpson, A. W., & Erickson, M. T. (1983) Teachers' verbal and nonverbal communication patterns as a function of teacher race, student gender, and student race. *American Educational Research Journal, 20(2),* 183–198.

Singham, M. (1998). The canary in the mine: The achievement gap between black and white students. *Phi Delta Kappan, 80(1),* 9–15.

Soto, L. D. (1991). Understanding bilingual/bicultural young children. *Young Children, 46,* 30–36.

Stacey, B. G., Singer, M. S., & Ritchie, G. (1989). The perception of poverty and wealth among teenage university students. *Adolescence, 24(93),* 193–207.

Steele, C. M. (1992). Race and the schooling of black Americans. *Atlantic, 269(4),* 68–78.

Steinberg, J. A., & Hall, V. C. (1981). Effects of social behavior on interracial acceptance. *Journal of Educational Psychology, 73(1),* 51–56.

Steinberg, L., Dornbusch, S. M., Brown, B. B. (1992). Ethnic differences in adolescent achievement. *American Psychologist, 47,* 723–729.

Stroeher, S.K. (1994). Sixteen kindergartners' gender-related views of careers. *The Elementary School Journal, 95(1),* 95–103.

Taylor, O. L. (1988). *Cross cultural communication.* Washington, DC: Mid-Atlantic Center for Race Equity.

Tetenbaum, T., Lighter, J., & Travis, M. (1981). Educators' attitudes toward working mothers. *Journal of Educational Psychology, 73(3),* 369–375.

Thomson, B. J. (1993). Words can hurt you: Beginning a program of anti-bias education. ERIC Document Service No.: ED387204.

Tifft, S. (1990, May 21). Fighting the failure syndrome. *Time,* 83–84.

Valli, L. (1995). The dilemma of race: Learning to be color blind and color conscious. *Journal of Teacher Education, 46(2),* 120–129.

Vasquez, J. A. (1990). Teaching to the distinctive traits of minority students. *The Clearing House, 63(7),* 299–304.

White, J. J. (1998). Helping students deal with cultural differences. *Social Studies, 89(3),* 107–111.

Wiley, T. G. (1997). Myths about language diversity and literacy in the United States. ERIC Document Service No.: ED407881.

Wilson, V. A. (1998). Learning how they learn: A review of the literature on learning styles. ERIC Document Service No.: ED427017.

York, S. (1992). *Developing roots and wings* (Trainers Guide). St. Paul, MN: Red Lace Press.

Zady, M. F., Portes, P. R., DelCastillo, K., & Dunham, R. M. (1998). When low SES parents cannot assist their children. ERIC Document Service No.: ED424317.

CHAPTER 6

Adair, J. G., & Schneider, J. L. (1993). Banking on learning: An incentive system for adolescents in the resource room. *Teaching Exceptional Children, 25(2),* 30–34.

Bacon, E. H. (1993). Guidelines for implementing a classroom reward system. In K. M. Cauley, F. Linder, and J. H. McMillan. *Educational Psychology 93/94* (8th ed.), Guilford, CT: Dushkin Group, 78–82.

Bandura, A. (1977). *Social Learning Theory.* Englewood Cliffs, NJ: Prentice Hall, Inc.

Bandura, A. (1978). The self system in reciprocal determinism. *American Psychologist, 33(4),* 344–358.

Bandura, A. (1986). *Social foundations of thought and action: A social cognitive theory.* Englewood Cliffs, NJ: Prentice Hall, Inc.

Bender, W. N., & Mathes, M. Y. (1995). Students with ADHD in the inclusive classroom: A hierarchical approach to strategy selection. *Intervention in the Schools, 30(4),* 226–234.

Berger, J. (1995). Self-instruction: Lessons from Charlotte. *LD Forum, 20(4),* 20–22.

Betz, C. (1994). Beyond time-out: Tips from a teacher. *Young Children, 49(3),* 10–14.

Bigge, M. L., & Shermis, S. S. (1992). *Learning Theories for Teachers* (5th ed.). New York: HarperCollins Publishers.

Brantley, D. C., & Webster, R. E. (1993). Use of an independent group contingency management system in a regular classroom setting. *Psychology in the Schools, 30(1),* 60–66.

Carter, S. (1994). Interventions. *Organizing systems to support competent social behavior in children and youth.* ERIC Document Services No.: ED380971.

Casteel, C. A. (1997). Attitudes of African American and Caucasian eighth grade students about praises, rewards, and punishments. *Elementary School Guidance and Counseling, 31(2),* 262–272.

Chance, P. (1993). Sticking up for rewards. *Phi Delta Kappan,* 787–790.

Chance, P. (1992). The rewards of learning. *Phi Delta Kappan,* 200–207.

Christensen, A. M., et al. (1996). Teaching pairs of preschoolers with disabilities to seek adult assistance in response to simulated injuries: Acquisition and promotion of observational learning. *Education and Treatment of Children, 19(1),* 3–18.

Dodge, K. A. (1996). The legacy of Hobbs and Gray: Research on the development and prevention of conduct problems. *Peabody Journal of Education, 71(4),* 86–98.

Douglas, V., Parry, P., Martin, P., & Garson, C. (1976). Assessment of a cognitive training program for hyperactive children. *Journal of Abnormal Child Psychology, 4,* 389–410.

Epstein, R. (Ed.). (1982). *Skinner for the Classroom: Selected Papers.* Champaign, IL: Research Press.

Ferguson, E., & Houghton, S. (1992). *Educational Studies, 18(1),* 83–93.

Geiger, B. (1997). Discipline in K through 8th Grade Classrooms. ERIC Document Service No.: ED413094.

Halsey, M. (1993). Positive rewards. *School Arts, 92,* 37.

Geiger, B. (1996). A time to learn, a time to play: Premack's Principle applied in the classroom. ERIC Document Service No.: ED4055373.

Hishinuma, E. S. (1996). Motivating the gifted underachiever: Implementing reward menus and behavioral contracts with an integrated approach. *Gifted Children Today, 19(4),* 43–48.

Iwamasa, G. Y., & Smith, S. K. (1996). Ethnic diversity in behavioral psychology: A review of the literature. *Behavior Modification, 20(1),* 45–59.

Jones, M. C. (1924). A laboratory study of fear: The case of Peter. *Pedagogical Seminary, 31,* 308–315.

Jones, M. C. (1924a). The elimination of children's fears. *Journal of Experimental Psychology, 7,* 382–390.

Jones, M. C. (1975). A 1924 pioneer looks at behavior therapy. *Journal of Behavioral Therapy and Experimental Psychology, 6,* 181–187.

Jules, V., & Kutnick, P. (1997). Student perceptions of a good teacher: The gender perspective. *The British Journal of Educational Psychology, 67,* 497–511.

Kazdin, A. E. (1994). *Behavior Modification in Applied Settings* (5th ed.). Pacific Grove, CA: Brooks/Cole Publishing Company.

Khan, K. H., & Cangemi, J. P. (1979). Social learning theory: The role of imitation and modeling in learning socially desirable behavior. *Education, 100(1),* 41–46.

Kohn, A. (1993). Rewards versus learning: A response to Paul Chance. *Phi Delta Kappan,* 783–787.

Kohn, A., & Kalat, J. W. (1992). Preparing for an important event: Demonstrating the modern view of classical conditioning. *Teaching of Psychology, 19(2),* 100–102.

Kubany, E. S., & Sloggett, B. B. (1991). Attentional factors in observational learning: Effects on acquisition of behavior management skills. *Behavior Therapy, 22,* 435–448.

Lanners, T. (1999). Teaching by example. *Clavier, 38,* 8–11.

Linklater, F. (1997). Effects of audio- and videotape models on performance achievement of beginning clarinetists. *Journal of Research in Music Education, 45(3),* 402–414.

Loera, P. A., & Meichenbaum, D. (1993) The "potential" contributions of cognitive behavior modification to literacy training for deaf students. *American Annals of the Deaf, 138(2),* 87–95.

Lukas, K. E., Marr, M., & Maple, T. (1998). Teaching operant conditioning at the zoo. *Teaching of Psychology, 25,* 112–116.

Mahoney, M. J. (1974). *Cognitive Behavior Modification.* Cambridge, MA.: Ballinger Publishing Company.

McNamee-McGrory, V., & Cipani, E. (1995). Reduction of inappropriate "clinging" behaviors in a preschooler through social skills training and utilization of the "Premack" Principle. ERIC Document Service No.: ED401001.

Meichenbaum, D. (1975). Enhancing creativity by modifying what subjects say to themselves. *American Educational Research Journal, 12(2),* 129–145.

Meichenbaum, D., & Burland, S. (1979). Cognitive behavior modification with children. *School Psychology Digest, 8,* 426–433.

Mikulas, W. L. (1972). *Behavior Modification: An Overview.* New York: Harper & Row.

Mosk, M. D., & Bucher, B. (1984). Prompting and stimulus shaping procedures for teaching visual-motor skills to retarded children. *Journal of Applied Behavior Analysis, 17(1),* 23–34.

Nye, R. D. (1981). *Three Psychologies: Perspectives from Freud, Skinner, and Rogers.* Monterey, CA: Brooks/Cole Publishing Company.

Parish, T. S., & Fleetwood, R. S. (1975). Amount of conditioning and subsequent change in racial attitudes of children. *Perceptual and Motor Skills, 40,* 78–86.

Parish, T. S., Bryant, W., & Prawat, R. S. (1977). Reversing the effects of sexism in elementary school girls through the use of classical conditioning procedures. *Journal of Instructional Psychology, 4,* 11–16.

Parke, R. D. (1981). Some effects of punishment on children's behavior—Revisited. In E. M. Hetherington, and R. D. Parke (Eds.) *Contemporary Readings in Child Psychology* (pp. 176–188). New York: McGraw-Hill.

Prout, H. T., & Harvey, J. R. (1978). Applications of desensitization procedures for school-related problems: A review. *Psychology in the Schools, 15(4),* 533–541.

Remington, B. (1996). Assessing the occurrence of learning in children with profound intellectual disability: A conditioning approach. *International Journal of Disability, Development, and Education, 43(2),* 101–118.

Reynolds, L. K., & Kelley, M. L. (1997). The efficacy of a response cost-based treatment package for managing aggressive behavior in preschoolers. *Behavior Modification, 21(2),* 216–230.

Ross, P. A., & Braden, J. P. (1991). The effects of token reinforcement versus cognitive behavior modification on learning disabled students' math skills. *Psychology in the Schools, 28,* 247–256.

Skinner, B. F. (1953). *Science and Human Behavior.* New York: The Free Press.

Skinner, B. F. (1968). *The Technology of Teaching.* New York: Appleton-Century-Crofts.

Skinner, B. F. (1974). *About Behaviorism.* New York: Alfred A. Knopf.

Smith, M. A., & Misra, A. (1992). A comprehensive management system for students in regular classrooms. *Elementary School Journal, 92(3),* 353–372.

Stachowski, L .L. (1998). Student teachers' efforts to promote self esteem in Navajo pupils. *The Educational Forum, 62,* 341–346.

Strang, H. (1975). Clowning around to stop clowning around: A brief report on an automated approach to monitor, record, and control classroom noise. *Journal of Applied Behavior Analysis, 8(4),* 471–474.

Swaggert, B. L. (1998). Implementing a cognitive behavior management program. *Intervention in School and Clinic, 33(4),* 235–238.

Watson, J. (1914). *Behavior.* New York: Holt.

Webster, R. E. (1976). Time-out procedure in a public school setting. *Psychology in the Schools, 13(1),* 72–76.

Weiss, M. R., McCullagh, P., & Smith, A.L. (1998). Observational learning and the fearful child: Influence of peer models on swimming skill performance and psychological responses. *Research Quarterly for Exercise and Sport, 69(4),* 380–394.

Wilson, R. (1995). Teacher as guide—the Rachel Carson way: Environmental education. *Early Childhood Education Journal, 23(1),* 49–51.

Wolpe, J. (1958). *Psychotherapy by reciprocal inhibition.* Stanford, CA: Stanford University Press.

Wolpe, J. (1982). *The practice of behavior therapy* (3d ed.). New York: Pergamon Press.

CHAPTER 7

Alexander, P. A., Kulikowich, J. M., & Schulze, S. K. (1994). How subject-matter knowledge affects recall and interest. *American Educational Research Journal, 31(2),* 313–337.

Aubrey, C. (1992). Educational psychology: The challenge for the 1990s. *Educational Psychology-in-Practice, 7(4)*, 195–200.

Ausubel, D., & Fitzgerald, D. (1962). Organizer, general background, and antecedent learning variables in sequential verbal learning. *Journal of Educational Psychology, 53(6)*, 243–249.

Ausubel, D., & Youssef, M. (1963). Role of discriminability in meaningful parallel learning. *Journal of Educational Psychology, 54(6)*, 331–336.

Ausubel, D. P. (1968). *Educational psychology: A cognitive view.* New York: Holt, Rinehart and Winston, Inc.

Baehre, M. R., & Gentile, J. R. (1991). Cumulative effects of the keyword mnemonic and distributed practice in learning social studies facts: A classroom evaluation. *Journal of Research in Education, 1(1)*, 70–78.

Barsalou, L. W. (1992). *Cognitive psychology: An overview for cognitive scientists.* Hillsdale, NJ: Lawrence Erlbaum Associates.

Baumann, J. F., et al. (1993). Monitoring reading comprehension by thinking aloud. National Reading Research Center, Athens, GA ERIC Document Service No.: ED360612.

Bednarz, S. W. (1995). Using mnemonics to learn place geography. *Journal of Geography, 94(1)*, 330–338.

Benjafield, J. G. (1992). *Cognition.* Englewood Cliffs, NJ: Prentice Hall, Inc.

Bigenho, F. W., Jr. (1992). Conceptual developments in schema theory. ERIC Document Service No.: ED351392.

Boyle, J. R., & Yeager, N. (1997). Blueprints for learning: Using cognitive frameworks for understanding. *Teaching Exceptional Children, 29(4)*, 26–31.

Brennan, R. L. (1992). The context of context effects. *Applied Measurement in Education, 5(3)*, 225–264.

Bretzing, B., Kulhavy, R. W., & Caterino, L. C. (1987). Notetaking by junior high students. *Journal of Educational Research, 80(6)*, 359–362.

Brigham, F. J. & Brigham, M. M. (1998). Using mnemonic keywords in general music classes: Music history meets cognitive psychology. *Journal of Research and Development in Education, 31(4)*, 205–213.

Bruner, J. S. (1966). *Toward a theory of instruction.* Cambridge, MA: The Belknap Press of Harvard University.

Buchan, L., Fish, T., & Prater, M. A. (1996). Teenage mutant ninja turtles counting pizza toppings: A creative writing strategy. *Teaching Exceptional Children, 28(2)*, 40–43.

Burgess, J. (1994). Ideational frameworks in integrated language learning. *System, 22(3)*, 309–318.

Byrnes, J. P. (1996). *Cognitive development and learning in instructional contexts.* Boston: Allyn & Bacon.

Carney, R. N., Levin, J. R., & Morrison, C. R. (1988). Mnemonic learning of artists and their paintings. *American Educational Research Journal, 25(1)*, 107–125.

Cassidy, D. J., & Deloache, J. S. (1995). The effect of questioning on young children's memory for an event. *Cognitive Development, 10(1)*, 109–130.

Cooper, H. M., Nye, B. A., & Charlton, K. (1996). The effects of summer vacation on achievement test scores: A narrative and meta-analytic review. *Review of Educational Research, 66*, 227–268.

Crawford, S. A. S., & Baine, D. (1992). Making learning memorable: Distributed practice and long-term reten-

tion by special needs students. *Canadian Journal of Special Education, 8(2)*, 118–128.

Daley, B. J., Shaw, C. R., & Balistrieri, T. (1999). Concept maps: A strategy to teach and evaluate critical thinking. *Journal of Nursing Education, 38(1)*, 42–47.

Dixon-Krauss, L. (1996). *Vygotsky in the classroom.* White Plains, NY: Longman Publishers, USA.

Dochy, F. J. R. C. (1988). The "prior knowledge state" of students and its facilitating effect on learning: Theories and research. Centre of Educational Technological Innovation. ERIC Document Service No.: ED387486.

Dochy, F. J. R. C., & Bouwens, M. R. J. (1990). Schema theories as a base for the structural representation of the knowledge state. Centre for Educational Technological Innovation. ERIC Document Service No.: ED387489.

Downing, A. (1994). An investigation of the advance organizer theory as an effective teaching model. ERIC Document Service No.: ED377150.

Ellis, E. S., et al. (1994). Research synthesis on effective teaching principles and the design of quality tools for educators. Executive summary. Technical report no. 6. National Center to Improve the Tools of Educators. ERIC Document Service No.: ED386854.

Estes, J. C., & Chovan, W. (1992). Efficacy of awareness of strategy and overt verbalization for recall by kindergarten students. *Perceptual and Motor Skills, 74(2)*, 499–508.

Farnham-Diggory, S. (1992). *Cognitive processes in education* (2d ed.). New York: HarperCollins, Publishers.

Farnham-Diggory, S. (1972). *Cognitive processes in education: A psychological preparation for teaching and curriculum development.* New York: Harper & Row, Publishers.

Fuchs, L. S., Fuchs, D., & Phillips, N. B. (1995). Acquisition and transfer effects of classwide peer-assisted learning strategies in mathematics for students with varying learning histories. *The School Psychology Review, 24(4)*, 604–620.

Gagne, R. (1985). The learning basis of teaching methods. Chapter II in *The conditions of learning and instruction* (4th ed.). Orlando, FL: Harcourt Brace.

Gallini, J. K., Spires, H. A., Terry, S., & Gleaton, J. (1993). The implications of macro- and micro-level cognitive strategies training on text learning. *Journal of Research and Development in Education, 26(3)*, 165–177.

Georgiady, N. P., & Romano, L. G. (1994). Focus on study habits in school: A guide for teachers and students to increase learning in the middle school. Michigan Association of Middle School Educators. ERIC Document Service No.: ED385346.

Good, T. L., & Brophy, J. (1995). *Contemporary Educational Psychology,* (5th ed.). White Plains, NY: Longman.

Hamann, S. B., & Squire, L. R. (1996). Level of processing effects in word completion priming: A neuropsychological study. *Journal of Experimental Psychology: Learning, Memory, and Cognition, 22*, 933–947.

Harris, J. (1990). Text annotation and underlining as metacognitive strategies to improve comprehension and retention of expository text. Paper presented at the annual meeting of the National Reading Conference (40th, Miami, FL, November 27–December 1, 1991). ERIC Document Service No.: ED335669.

Hatch, C. A., & Dwyer, F. M. (1999). The effect of varied advance organizers in complementing visualized prose instruction. *International Journal of Instructional Media, 26*, 311–328.

Heaton, S., & O'Shea, D. J. (1995). Using mnemonics to make mnemonics. *Teaching Exceptional Children, 28(1),* 34–36.

Hinson, S. (1988). Meaningfulness. In R. McNergney (Ed.), *Guide to classroom teaching.* Boston: Allyn & Bacon, 193–210.

Howe, M. L. (1995). Interference effects in young children's long term retention. *Developmental Psychology, 31,* 579–596.

Hyde, A. A. & Bizar, M. (1989). *Thinking in context: Teaching cognitive processes across the elementary school curriculum.* New York: Longman.

Idstein, P., & Jenkins, J. R. (1972). Underlining versus repetitive reading. *Journal of Educational Research, 65(7),* 321–323.

Ivie, S. D. (1998). Ausubel's learning theory: An approach to teaching higher order thinking skills. *The High School Journal, 82,* 35–42.

Kasper, L. F. (1993). The keyword method and foreign language vocabulary learning: A rationale for its use. *Foreign Language Annals, 26(2),* 244–251.

Koffka, K. (1963). *Principles of gestalt psychology.* New York: Harcourt, Brace & World, Inc.

Leal, D. J. (1993). A comparison of third grade children's listening comprehension of scientific information using an information book and an informational storybook. Paper presented at the annual meeting of the National Reading Conference (43d, Charleston, SC, December 1–4, 1993). ERIC Document Service No.: ED365954.

Leinhardt, G. (1992). What research on learning tells us about teaching. *Educational Leadership, 49(7),* 20–25.

Liva, A., Fijalkow, E., & Fijalkow, J. (1994). Learning to use inner speech for improving reading and writing of poor readers. Special issue: Learning and development: Contributions from Vygotsky. *European Journal of Psychology of Education, 9(4),* 321–330.

Lombardi, T. P. (1995). Teachers develop their own learning strategies. *Teaching Exceptional Children, 27(3),* 52–56.

Lu, M., Webb, J. M., & Krus, D. J. (1999). Using order analytic instructional hierarchies of mnemonics to facilitate learning Chinese and Japanese kanji characters. *The Journal of Experimental Education, 67,* 293–311.

Marmie, W. R. (1997). Serial position effects and the role of variability of practice in the performance of a spatial memory task. *Dissertation Abstracts International, Section B: Sciences and Engineering, 57,* 7751.

Matsumi, N. (1994). The difficult link: From research on memory to the practice of learning a foreign language. *Hiroshima Forum for Psychology, 16,* 35–37.

Mavrogenes, N., et al. (1989). A comparative study of three methods of promoting literacy in kindergarten and first grade, 1987–1988. Chicago Public Schools, Illinois. ERIC Document Service No.: ED339025.

Mayer, R. E. (1998). *The promise of educational psychology.* Upper Saddle River, NJ: Merrill/Prentice Hall, Inc.

Mayer, R. E. (1979). Can advance organizers influence meaningful learning? *Review of Educational Research, 49(2),* 371–383.

McCarthy-Tucker, S. (1992). Semantic webbing, semantic-pictorial webbing and standard basal teaching techniques: A comparison of three strategies to enhance learning and memory of a reading comprehension task in the fourth grade classroom. Paper presented at the annual meeting of the Western Psychological Association (72d, Portland, OR, April 30–May 3, 1992). ERIC Document Service No.: ED344200.

Medina, S. (1990). An application of Gagne's theory of instruction to the instruction of English as a second language. Paper presented at the annual meeting of the Teachers of English to Speakers of Other Languages (San Francisco, CA, March 1990). ERIC Document Service No.: ED352833.

Meese, R. L. (1992). Adapting textbooks for children with learning disabilities in mainstreamed classrooms. *Teaching Exceptional Children, 24(3),* 49–51.

Mikulas, W. L. (1974). Perception and learning. Chapter III in *Concepts in learning.* Philadelphia: W. B. Saunders Company.

Mumford, M. D., Costanza, D. P., & Baughann, W. A. (1994). Influences of abilities on performance during practice: Effects of massed and distributed practice. *Journal of Educational Psychology, 86,* 134–144.

Novak, J. D. (1993). How do we learn our lesson? *Science Teacher, 60(3),* 50–55.

Okebukola, P. A. (1992a). Concept mapping with cooperative learning. *American Biology Teacher, 54(4),* 218–221.

Okebukola, P. A. (1992b). Can good concept mappers be good problem solvers in science? *Research in Science and Technological Education, 10(2),* 153–170.

O'Shea, L. J. & O'Shea, D. J. (1994). A component analysis of metacognition in reading comprehension: The contributions of awareness and self regulation. *International Journal of Disability, Development, and Education, 41(1),* 15–34.

Pagliocca, P. (1988). Clarity of structure. In R. McNergney (Ed.), *Guide to classroom teaching.* Boston: Allyn & Bacon, 167–192.

Pendley, B. D., Bretz, R. L., & Novak, J. D. (1994). Concept maps as a tool to assess learning in chemistry. *Journal of Chemical Education, 71(1),* 9–15.

Perrone, V. (1994). How to engage students in learning. *Educational Leadership, 51(5),* 11–13.

Peterson, S. E. (1992). The cognitive functions of underlining as a study technique. *Reading Research and Instruction, 31(2),* 49–56.

Politoske, D. T. (1974). *Music.* Englewood Cliffs, NJ: Prentice Hall, Inc.

Rafferty, C. D., & Fleschner, L .K. (1993). Concept mapping: A viable alternative to objective and essay exams. *Reading Research and Instruction, 32(3),* 25–34.

Raschke, D. B., Alper, S. K., & Eggers, E. (1999). Recalling alphabet letter names: A mnemonic system to facilitate learning. *Preventing School Failure, 43(2),* 80–83.

Reinelt, R. (1994). The difficult link: From research on memory to the practice of learning a foreign language: Comment on Dr. Matsumi's paper. *Hiroshima Forum for Psychology, 16,* 33–34.

Ritchie, D., & Karge, B. D. (1996). Making information memorable: Enhanced knowledge retention and recall through the elaboration process. *Preventing School Failure, 41(1),* 28–33.

Robinson, D. H., Robinson, S. L., and Katayama, A. D. (1999). When words are represented in memory like pictures: Evidence for spatial encoding of study materials. *Contemporary Educational Psychology, 24(1),* 38–54.

Roth, W. (1994). Student views of collaborative concept mapping: An emancipatory research project. *Science Education, 78(1),* 1–34.

Roth, W., & Roychoudhury, A. (1993). The concept map as a tool for the collaborative construction of knowledge: A microanalysis of high school physics students. *Journal of Research in Science Teaching, 30(5),* 503–534.

Sanchez, A., & Lopez, L. E. (1993). Making connections: An in-depth concept teaching technique. Paper presented at a meeting of the Center for Critical Thinking (August 1–4, 1993). ERIC Document Service No.: ED375091.

Scruggs, T. E., & Mastropieri, M. A. (1992). Remembering the forgotten art of memory. *American Educator, 16(4)*, 31–37.

Scruggs, T. E., Mastropieri, M. A., Bakken, J. P., & Brigham, F. J. (1993). Improving reasoning and recall: The differential effects of elaborative interrogation and mnemonic elaboration. *Learning Disability Quarterly, 16(3)*, 233–240.

Shany, M. T. (1995). Assisted reading practice: Effects on performance for poor readers in grades 3–4. *Reading Research Quarterly, 30*, 382–395.

Simpson, P., & Wise, K. (1993). The mystery box and more. *Science Activities, 29(4)*, 22–26.

Smilkstein, R. (1993). Acquiring knowledge and using it. ERIC Document Service No.: ED382238.

Solvberg, A., & Valas, H. (1995). Effects of mnemonic imagery strategy on students' prose recall. *Scandinavian Journal of Educational Research, 39(2)*, 107–119.

Spires, H. A. (1992). Promoting text engagement through reader-generated elaborations. *Forum for Reading, 23(1–2)*, 22–32.

Story, C. M. (1998). What instructional designers need to know about advance organizers. *International Journal of Instructional Media, 25(3)*, 253–261.

Talbert, J. E., McLaughlin, M. W., & Rowan, B. (1993). Understanding context effects on secondary school teaching. *Teachers College Record, 95*, 45–68.

Tennyson, R. D., Elmore, R. L., & Snyder, L. (1992). Advancements in instructional design theory: Contextual module analysis and integrated instructional strategies. Special issue: Educational technology: Four decades of research and theory. *Educational Technology Research and Development, 40(2)* , 9–22.

Tennyson, R. D. (1990). Cognitive learning theory linked to instructional theory. *Journal of Structural Learning, 10(3)*, 249–258.

Thompson, D. N. (1998). Using advance organizers to facilitate reading comprehension among older adults. *Educational Gerontology, 24(7)*, 625–638.

Troutman, P. L., Jr., Prankratius, W. J., Gallavan, N. P. (1999). Preservice teachers construct a view on multicultural education: Using Banks' levels of integration of ethnic content to measure change. *Action in Teacher Education, 20*, 1–14.

Verschaffel, L., & Corte, E. (1997). Teaching realistic mathematical modeling in the elementary school: A teaching experiment with fifth graders. *Journal for Research in Mathematics Education, 28*, 577–601.

Weaver, C. (1994). Phonics in whole language classrooms. ERIC Digest. ERIC Document Service No.: ED372375.

Wright, D. R. (1995). Mnemonics: An aid to geographical learning. Teacher's notebook. *Journal of Geography, 94(1)*, 339–340.

CHAPTER 8

Alschuler, A., Tabor, D., & McIntyre, J. (1971). *Teaching achievement motivation*. Middletown, CT: Educational Ventures Inc.

Ames, C. (1990). *Motivation: What teachers need to know*. *Teachers College Record, 91*, 409–421.

Andrews, R. G., & Debus, R. L. (1978). Persistence and causal perceptions of failure: Modifying causal attributions. *Journal of Educational Psychology, 70*, 154–166.

Atkinson, J. (1964). *An introduction to motivation*. Princeton: Van Nostrand.

Atkinson, J. (1980). Motivational effects in so-called tests of ability and educational achievement. In L. Fyans (Ed.), *Achievement motivation: Recent trends in theory and research*. New York: Plenum Press.

Atkinson, J. (1983). *Personality, motivation and action*. New York: Praeger.

Bandura, A. (1977). Self-efficacy: Toward a unifying theory of behavioral change. *Psychological Review, 84*, 191–215.

Bandura A. (1982). Self-efficacy mechanisms in human agency. *American Psychologist, 37*, 122–147.

Bandura, A. (1986). *Social foundations of thought and action: A social cognitive theory*. Englewood Cliffs, NJ: Prentice Hall.

Bandura, A. (1993). Perceived self-efficacy in cognitive development and functioning. *Educational Psychologist, 28(2)*, 117–148.

Bandura, A., & Schunk, D. (1981). Cultivating competence, self-efficacy, and intrinsic interest through proximal self-motivation. *Journal of Personalilty and Social Psychology, 41*, 586–598.

Baron, R. (1992). *Psychology* (2d ed.). Needham Heights, MA: Allyn & Bacon.

Bar-Tal, D. (1979). Interactions of teachers and pupils. In I. H. Frieze, D. Bar-Tal & J. S. Carroll (Eds.), *New approaches to social problems: Applications of attribution theory*. San Francisco: Jossey-Bass.

Blumenfeld, P. (1992). Classroom learning and motivation: Clarifying and expanding goal theory. *Journal of Educational Psychology, 84(3)*, 272–281.

Boggiano, A. K., & Barrett, M. (1985). Performance and motivational deficits of helplessness: The role of motivational orientations. *Journal of Personality and Social Psychology, 49*, 1753–1761.

Brophy, J. (1981). Teacher praise: A functional analysis. *Review of Educational Research, 51*, 5–32.

Brophy, J. (1985). Interactions of male and female students with male and female teachers. In L. Wilkinson & C. Marrett (Eds.), *Gender influences in classroom interaction* (pp. 115–142). Orlando, FL: Academic Press.

Brophy, J., & Good, T. (1986). Teacher effects. In M. Wittrock (Ed.), *Third handbook of research on teaching* (pp. 328–375). New York: Macmillan.

Bruning, R., Schraw, G., & Ronning, R. (1995). Cognitive psychology and instruction (2d ed.). Upper Saddle River, NJ: Prentice Hall.

Butkowski, I. S., & Willows, D. M. (1980). Cognitive-motivational characteristics of children varying in reading ability: Evidence for learned helplessness in poor readers. *Journal of Educational Psychology, 72*, 408–422.

Calder, B., & Staw, B. (1975). Self-perception of intrinsic and extrinsic motivation. *Journal of Personality and Social Psychology, 31*, 599–605.

Clifford, M. M., Cleary, T. A., & Walster, G. W. (1972). Effects of emphasizing competition in classroom testing procedures. *Journal of Educational Research, 65*, 234–238.

Cohen, M. (1985). Extrinsic reinforcers and intrinsic motivation. In M. Alderman & M. Cohen (Eds.), *Motivation theory and practice for preservice teachers* (pp. 6–15). Washington, DC: American Association of Colleges of Teacher Education.

Combs, A. (1962). Motivation and the growth of self. In *Perceiving, behaving, and becoming. Association for Supervision and Curriculum Development yearbook* (pp. 83–98). Washington, DC: National Education Association.

Cooper, H. (1979). Pygmalion grows up: A model for teacher expectation communication and performance influence. *Review of Educational Research, 49*, 389–410.

Cooper, H. M., & Tom, D. Y. H. (1984). Teacher expectation research: A review with implications for classroom instruction. *Elementary School Journal, 85*, 77–89.

Covington, M. (1984). The self-worth theory of achievement motivation. *Elementary School Journal, 85*, 5–20.

Covington, M. (1985). Strategic thinking and the fear of failure. In J. W. Segal, S. F. Chipman & R. Glaser (Eds.), Thinking and learning skills (Vol. 1). Hillsdale, NJ: Lawrence Erlbaum.

Covington, M., & Beery, R. (1976). *Self-worth and school learning.* New York: Holt, Rinehart & Winston.

Covington, J., & Omelich, C. (1979a). It's best to be able and virtuous too: Student and teacher evaluative responses to successful effort. *Journal of Educational Psychology, 71*, 688–700.

Covington, J., & Omelich, C. (1979b). Effort: The double-edged sword in school achievement. *Journal of Educational Psychology, 71*, 169–182.

Covington, J., & Omelich, C. (1987). "I knew it cold before the exam": A test of the anxiety blockage hypothesis. *Journal of Educational Psychology, 79*, 393–400.

Crooks, T. (1988). The impact of classroom evaluation practices on students. *Review of Educational Research, 58*, 438–481.

deCharms, R. (1972). Personal causation training in the schools. *Journal of Applied Psychology, 2*, 95–113.

deCharms, R. (1976). *Enhancing motivation: Change in the classroom.* New York: Irvington.

deCharms R. (1984). Motivation enhancement in educational settings. In R. Ames & C. Ames (Eds.), *Research on motivation in education. Vol. 1: Student motivation.* San Diego, CA: Academic Press.

Deci, E. (1975). *Intrinsic motivation.* New York: Plenum Press.

Deci, E., & Ryan, R. (1985). *Intrinsic motivation and self-determination in human behavior.* New York: Plenum Press.

Deutch, M. (1979). Education and distributive justice. *American Psychologist, 34(5)*, 391–401.

Eccles, J. (1987). Gender roles and women's achievement-related decisions. *Psychology of Women Quarterly, 11*, 135–172.

Emmer, E., Evertson, C., Sanford, J., Clements, R., & Worsham, M. (1989). *Classroom management for secondary teachers.* Englewood Cliffs, NJ: Prentice Hall.

Eshel, Y., & Klein, Z. (1981). Development of academic self-concept of lower-class and middle-class primary school children. *Journal of Educational Psychology, 73*, 287–293.

Feather, N. (Ed.). (1982). *Expectations and actions.* Hillsdale, NJ: Erlbaum.

Fennema, E. (1987). Sex-related differences in education: Myths, realities and interventions. In V. Richardson-Hoehler (Ed.), *Educators' handbook* (pp. 329–347). White Plains, NY: Longman.

Fiske, S. T., & Taylor, S. E. (1984). *Social Cognition.* Reading, MA: Addison-Wesley.

Frank, J. (1963). *Persuasion and healing.* New York: Shocken Books.

Gagne, E. (1985). *Hard gains in the soft sciences: The case of pedagogy.* Bloomington, IN: Phi Delta Kappa.

Gaudry, E., & Speilberger, C. (1971). *Anxiety and educational achievement.* Sydney: John Wiley and Sons Australasia Pty., Ltd.

Good, T. L. (1987). Two decades of research on teacher expectations: Findings and future directions. *Journal of Teacher Education, 37(4)*, 32–47.

Good, T. L., & Brophy, J. E. (1977). *Looking in classrooms.* New York: HarperCollins.

Gottfried, A. (1985). Academic intrinsic motivation in elementary and junior high students. *Journal of Educational Psychology, 82*, 525–538.

Graham, S., & Weiner, B. (1996). Theories and principles of motivation. In D. Berliner & R. Calfee (Eds.). *Handbook of Educational Psychology* (pp. 63–84). New York: Macmillan.

Harter, S., & Jackson, B. (1992). Trait versus nontrait conceptualizations of intrinsic/extrinsic motivational orientation. Special issue: Perspectives on intrinsic motivation. *Motivation and Emotion, 16*, 29–230.

Hembree, R. (1988). Correlates, causes, effects, and treatment of test anxiety. *Review of Educational Research, 58*, 47–77.

Hill, K., & Wigfield, A. (1984). Test anxiety: A major educational problem and what can be done about it. *Elementary School Journal, 85*, 105–126.

Jagacinski, C. (1977, March). *Effects of goal setting in an ego-involving context.* Paper presented at the Annual Meeting of the American Educational Research Association, Chicago.

Johnson, D., & Johnson, R. (1985). The internal dynamics of cooperative learning groups. In R. Slavin, S. Sharon, S. Kagan, R. Heitz-Lazarowitz, C. Webb, & R. Schmuch (Eds.), *Learning to cooperate, cooperating to learn.* New York: Plenum Press.

Johnson, D., & Johnson, R. (1987). *Learning together and alone: Cooperative, competitive and individualistic learning* (2d ed.). Englewood Cliffs, NJ: Prentice Hall.

Johnson, D. W., Johnson, R. T., & Holubec, E. (1993). *Cooperation in the classroom* (6th ed.). Edina, MN: Interaction Book Company.

Johnson, D. W., Johnson, R. T., & Smith, K. (1991). *Active learning: Cooperation in the college classroom.* Edina, MN: Interaction Book Company.

Klienke, C. L. (1978). *Self-perception: The psychology of personal awareness.* San Francicso: Freeman.

Kohn, A. (1992). No contest: The case against competition. Boston: Houghton Mifflin.

Kohn, A. (1993). Rewards versus learning: A response to Paul Chance. *Phi Delta Kappan, 74*, 783–787.

Kolesnik, W. (1975). *Motivation: Understanding and influencing human behavior.* Boston: Allyn & Bacon.

Kounin, J. (1970). *Discipline and group management in classrooms.* New York: Holt, Rinehart and Winston.

Kukla, A. (1972). Attributional determinants of achievement-related behavior. *Journal of Personality and Social Psychology, 21*, 166–174.

Lepper, M., & Green, D. (Eds.). (1978). *The hidden costs of reward.* Hillsdale, NJ: Erlbaum.

Lepper, M., & Hoddell, M. (1989). Intrinsic motivation in the classroom. In C. Ames & R. Ames (Eds.), *Research in motivation in education. Vol. 3: Goals and cognitions.* San Diego: Academic Press.

Locke, E., & Latham, G. (1990). *A theory of goal setting and performance.* Upper Saddle River, NJ: Prentice Hall.

MacMillan, D., Keogh, B., & Jones, R. (1986). Special educational research on mildly handicapped learners. In M. Wittrock (Ed.), *Handbook of research on teaching* (3d ed.). New York: Macmillan.

Maehr, M. L. & Sjorgen, D. D. (1971). Atkinson's theory of achievement motivation: first step toward a theory of academic motivation, *Review of Educational Research, 41,* 143–161.

Malone, T., & Lepper, M. (1987). Making learning fun: A taxonomy of intrinsic motivation for learning. In R. E. Snow & M. J. Farr (Eds.), *Aptitude, learning and instruction. Vol. III: Conative and affective process analysis.* Hillsdale, NJ: Erlbaum.

Maslow, A. (1954). *Motivation and personality.* New York: Harper & Row.

Maslow, A. (1968). *Toward a psychology of being* (2d ed.). New York: Van Nostrand.

Maslow, A. (1970). *Motivation and personality* (2d ed.). New York: Harper & Row.

McClelland, D. (1973). Testing for competence rather than for intelligence. *American Psychologist, 28,* 1–14.

McClelland, D. (1985). *Human motivation.* Glenview, IL: Scott, Foresman.

McKeachie, W. J. (1986). *Teaching tips: A guide for the beginning college teacher.* Lexington, MA: D. C. Heath.

Michaels, J. W. (1977). Classroom reward structures and academic performance. *Review of Educational Research, 47,* 87–98.

Mitchell, R., & Pietkowska, I. (1974.). Characteristics associated with underachievement. *Australian Psychologist, 9,* 19–41.

Morris, C. (1988). *Psychology: An introduction* (6th ed.). Upper Saddle River, NJ: Prentice Hall.

Murray, H. (1938). *Explorations in personality.* New York: Oxford University Press.

Naveh-Benjamin, M., McKeachie, W. J., & Lin, Y. (1987). Two types of test-anxious students: Support for an information processing model. *Journal of Educational Psychology, 79,* 131–136.

Nicholls, J. (Ed.). (1984). *The development of achievement motivation.* Greenwich, CT: JAI Press.

Paulman, R. G. & Kennelly, K. J. (1984). Test anxiety and ineffective test taking: Different names, same construct, *Journal of Educational Psychology, 76,* 279–288.

Pintrich, P., & Garcia, T. (1991). Student goal orientation and self-regulation in the college classroom. In M. Maehr & P. Pintrich (Eds.), *Advances in motivation and achievement* (Vol. 7, pp. 371–402). Greenwich, CT: JAI Press.

Pintrich, P., & Schunk, D. (1996). *Motivation in education: Theory, research and applications.* Upper Saddle River, NJ: Prentice Hall.

Reeve, J. (1996). *Motivating others: Nurturing inner motivational resources.* Boston: Allyn & Bacon.

Ridley, D., McCombs, B., & Taylor, K. (1994). Walking the talk: fostering self-regulated learning in the classroom. *Middle School Journal, 26(2),* 52–57.

Ringness, T. (1965). Affective differences between successful and non-successful bright ninth grade boys. *Personnel and Guidance Journal, 43,* 600–606.

Rosenshine, B. (1980). How time is spent in elementary classrooms. In C. Denham & A. Lierberman (Eds.), *Time to learn.* Washington, DC: National Institute of Education.

Rotter, J. (1966). Generalized expectancies for internal versus external control of reinforcement. *Psychological Monographs, 80,* 1–28.

Schunk, D. (1990, April). Perceptions of efficacy and classroom motivation. Paper presented at the annual meeting of the American Educational Research Association, Boston.

Schunk, D. H. (1995). Self-efficacy and education and instruction. In J. E. Maddus (Ed.*), Self-efficacy, adaptation, and adjustment.* New York: Plenum Press.

Seligman, D. (1975). *Helplessness: On depression, development and death.* San Francisco, Freeman.

Sharan, S. (1980). Cooperative learning in small groups: Recent methods and effects on achievement, attitudes , and ethnic relations. *Review of Educational Research, 50,* 241–249.

Slavin, R. (1983). *Cooperative learning.* New York: Longman.

Slavin, R. (1990). *Cooperative learning: Theory, research, and practice.* Englewood Cliffs, NJ: Prentice Hall.

Slavin, R. E. (1991). Synthesis of research on cooperative learning. *Educational Leadership, 48(5),* 71–82.

Slavin, R. E. (1995). *Cooperative learning* (2d ed.). Needham Heights, MA: Allyn & Bacon.

Soar, R. S., & Soar, R. M. (1978). *Setting variables, classroom interaction and multiple pupil outcomes.* (Contract No. 60432). Washington, DC: National Institute of Education.

Stipek, D. (1980). A causal analysis of the relationship between locus of control and academic achievement in first grade. *Contemporary Educational Psychology, 5,* 10–137.

Stipek, D. (1988). *Motivation to learn: From theory to practice.* Englewood Cliffs, NJ: Prentice Hall.

Stipek, D. (1996). Motivation and instruction. In D. Berliner & R. Calfee (Eds.), *Handbook of educational psychology* (pp. 85–113). New York: Macmillan

Stipek, D., & Weisz, J. (1981). Perceived personal control and academic achievement. *Review of Educational Research, 51,* 101–137.

Stipek, D. (1984a). The development of achievement motivation. In R. Ames & C. Ames (Eds.), *Research on motivation in education* (Vol. 1). Orlando, FL: Academic Press.

Stipek, D. (1984b). Young children's performance expectations: Logical analysis of wishful thinking? In J. G. Nicholls (Ed.), *The development of achievement motivation.* Greenwich, CT: JAI Press.

Tobias. S. (1985). Test anxiety: Interference, defective skills, and cognitive capacity. *Educational Psychologist, 20,* 135–142.

Tollefson, N., Tracy, D., Johnsen, E., Farmer, W., & Buenning, M. (1984). Goal setting and personal responsibility for LD adolescents. *Psychology in the Schools, 21,* 224–233.

Ugurogulu, M., & Walberg, H. (1979). Motivation and achievement: A quantitative synthesis. *American Educational Research Journal, 16,* 375–389.

Wang, M. Haertal. G., & Walberg, H. (1993, April). Educational resilience: An emerging construct. Paper presented at the Annual Meeting of the American Educational Research Association, San Francisco.

Weiner , B. (1972). *Theories of motivation: From mechanism to cognition.* Chicago: Rand McNally.

Weiner, B. (1979). A theory of motivation for some classroom experiences. *Journal of Educational Psychology, 71,* 3–25.

Weiner, B. (1980). *Human motivation.* New York: Holt, Rinehart & Winston.

Weiner, B. (1984). Principles for a theory of student motivation and their application within an attributional framework. In R. Ames & C. Ames (Eds.), *Research on motivation in education. Vol.1: Student motivation.* San Diego: Academic Press.

Weiner, B. (1986). *An attributional theory of motivation and emotion.* New York: Springer-Verlag.

Weiner, B., Graham, S., Taylor, S., & Meyer, W. (1983). Social cognition in the classroom. *Educational Psychologist, 18,* 109–124.

Weinstein, R. (1998). Promoting positive expectations in schooling. In N. Lambert & B. McCombs (Eds.), *How students learn: Reforming schools through learner-centered education* (pp. 81–111). Washington, DC: American Psychological Association.

Weisz, J. (1979). Perceived control and learned helplessness among mentally retarded and non-retarded children: A developmental analysis. *Developmental Psychology, 15,* 311–319.

Wheeler, R. (1988). Attribution processing. *Middle School Journal, 19(4),* 26–27.

Wittrock, M. (1986). Students' thought processes. In M. Wittrock (Ed.), *Third handbook of research on teaching* (pp. 297–314). New York: Macmillan.

Wlodowski, R. (1984). *Motivation and teaching.* Washington, DC: National Education Association.

CHAPTER 9

Adams, R. S., & Biddle, B. J. (1970). *Realities of teaching: Explorations with video tape.* New York: Holt, Rinehart & Winston.

Arlin, M. (1979). Teacher transitions can disrupt time flow in classrooms. *American Educational Research Journal, 16,* 42–56.

Campbell, D. T. (1958). Common fate, similarity, and other indices of the status of aggregates of persons as social entitities. *Behavioral Science, 3,* 14–25.

Cohen, E. G. (1984). Talking and working together: Status, interaction and learning. In P. Peterson, L. C. Wilkinson & M. Halleman (Eds.), *The social context of instruction: Group organization and group processes.* New York: Academic Press.

Cohen, H. G. (1985). A comparison of the development of spatial conceptual abilities of students from two cultures. *Journal of Research in Science Teaching, 22,* 491–501.

Cohen, E. G. (1986). *Designing groupwork: Strategies for the heterogeneous classroom.* New York: Teachers College Press.

Daum, J. (1972). Proxemics in the classroom: Speaker-subject distance and educational performance. Paper presented at the eighteenth Annual Meeting of the Southeastern Psychological Association. April 6–8, Atlanta, GA.

Delefes, P., & Jackson, B. (1972). Teacher-pupil interaction as a function of location in the classroom. *Psychology in the Schools, 9,* 119–123.

Doyle, W. (1979). Making managerial decisions in classrooms. In D. Duke (Ed.), *78th yearbook of the National Society for the Study of Education: Part 2. Classroom Management.* Chicago: University of Chicago Press.

Doyle, W. (1986). Classroom organization and management. In M. Wittrock (Ed.) *Handbook of research on teaching* (3d ed.) New York: Macmillan.

Dunn, R. (1987). Research on instructional environments: Implication for student achievement and attitudes. *Professional School Psychology, 3,* 43–52.

Dunn, R., Beaudry, J. S., & Klavas, A. (1989). Survey of research on learning styles. *Educational Leadership, 44(6),* 55–63.

Dunn, R., Dunn, K. (1978). *Teaching students through their individual learning styles.* Reston, VA: National Council of Principals.

Dunn, R., Dunn, K., & Price, G. E. (1984). *Learning style inventory.* Lawrence, KS: Price Systems.

Dunn, K. & Dunn, R. (1987). Dispelling outmoded beliefs about student learning styles. *Educational Leadership, 44(6),* 55–63.

Dunn R., & Griggs, S. A. (1988). *Learning styles: Quiet revolution in American secondary schools.* Reston, VA: National Association of Secondary School Principals.

Emmer, E. T., Evertson, C. M., Clements, B. S., & Worsham, M. E. (1994). *Classroom management for secondary teachers* (3d ed.). Needham Heights, MA: Allyn & Bacon.

Evertson, C., & Emmer, E. (1982). Effective management at the beginning of the school year in junior high classes. *Journal of Educational Psychology, 74,* 485–498.

Evertson, C. (1987). *Managing classrooms. A framework for teachers.* In D. Berliner & B. Rosenshine (Eds.), *Talks to teachers* (pp. 54–74). New York: Random House.

Flanders, N. A. (1963). Teacher influence in the classroom. In A. Bellack (Ed.), *Theory and research in teaching* (pp. 37–53). New York: Bureau of Publications, Teachers College.

Flanders, N. (1964). Some relationships among teacher influence, pupil attitudes, and achievement. In B. Biddle & W. Ellena (Eds.), *Contemporary research on teacher effectiveness.* New York: Holt, Rinehart & Winston.

Froyen, L. A. (1993). *Classroom management: The reflective teacher-leader* (2d ed.). New York: Macmillan.

Getzels, J. W. (1969). A social psychology of education. In G. Lindzey & E. Aronsen (Eds.) *The handbook of social psychology* (pp. 459–537). Reading, MA: Addison-Wesley.

Glasser, W. (1990). *The quality school: Managing students without coercion.* New York: Harper & Row.

Good, T. L, & Brophy, J. E. (1990). *Educational Psychology.* (4th ed.). New York: Longman.

Good , T. L. (1983). Classroom research: A decade of progress. *Educational Psychologist, 18,* 127–144.

Griffitt, W. J., & Veitch, R. (1971). Hot and crowded: influence of population density and temperature on interpersonal affective behavior. *Journal of Personality and Social Psychology, 17(1),* 92–98.

Gump, P., & Good, L. (1976). Environments operating in open space and traditionally designed schools. *Journal of Architectural Research, 5,* 20–27.

Johnson, D., & Johnson, R. (1975). *Learning together and alone.* Englewood Cliffs, NJ: Prentice Hall.

Johnson, D., & Johnson, R. (1984). *Learning together and learning alone: Cooperation, competition and individualization.* Englewood Cliffs, NJ: Prentice Hall.

Johnson, D., & Johnson, R. (1987). *Learning together and alone: Cooperative, competitive and individualistic learning* (2d ed.). Englewood Cliffs, NJ: Prentice Hall.

Kuriloff , A., & Atkins, S. (1966). T-Group for a work team. *Journal of Applied Behavioral Science, 2,* 63–94.

Lewis, R., & St. John, N. (1974). Contribution of cross-racial friendship to minority group achievement in desegregated classrooms. *Sociometry, 37(1),* 79–91.

McCown, R., Driscoll, M., & Roop, P. G. (1996). *Educational Psychology: A Learning-centered approach to classroom practice* (3d ed). Needham Heights, MA: Allyn & Bacon.

Musgrave, C. R. (1975). *Individualized instruction: Teaching strategies focusing on the learner.* Boston: Allyn & Bacon.

Putnam, J., & Burke, J. B. (1992). *Organizing and managing classroom learning communities.* New York: McGraw-Hill.

Rosenfield, P., Lambert, S., & Black, R. (1985). Desk arrangement effects on pupil classroom behavior. *Journal of Educational Psychology, 77,* 101–108.

Schmuck, R. (1971). Influence of the peer group. In G. Lesser (Ed.), *Psychology and educational practice* (pp. 502–529). Glenview, IL: Scott, Foresman.

Schmuck, R., & Schmuck, P. (1988). *Group process in the classroom* (5th ed.) Dubuque, IA: William C. Brown.

Schmuck, R., & Schmuck, P. (1992). *Group process in the classroom* (6th ed.). Dubuque, IA: William C. Brown.

Slavin, R. (1984). Students motivating students to excel: Cooperative incentives, cooperative tasks and student achievement. *Elementary School Journal, 85,* 53–64.

Slavin, R. E. (1987). Ability grouping and student achievement in elementary schools. A best-evidence synthesis. *Review of Educational Research, 60,* 471–500.

Slavin, R. (1990). *Cooperative learning.* Englewood Cliffs, NJ: Prentice Hall.

Slavin, R. (1991). Are cooperative learning and untracking harmful to the gifted? *Educational Leadership, 48,* 68–71.

Slavin, R., Sharan, S., Kagan, S., et al. (Eds.). (1985). *Learning to cooperate, cooperating to learn.* New York: Plenum.

Tinker, M. A. (1939). Illumination standards for effective and comfortable vision. *Journal of Consulting Psychology, 3,* 11–19.

Wang, M. (1973). *Teacher's manual for exploratory learning component of LRDC individualized instructional program for the early learning grades.* Pittsburgh: University of Pittsburgh Learning Research and Development Center.

Webb, N. M. (1982). Interaction and learning in small groups. *Review of Educational Research, 52,* 421–450.

Weinstein, C. (1979). The physical environment of the schools: A review of the research. *Review of Educational Research, 49,* 577–610.

Weinstein, C. S., & Mignano, A. (1993). *Organizing the elementary school classroom: Lessons from research and practice.* New York: McGraw-Hill.

Wolfgang, C. H. (1995). *Solving discipline problems: Methods and models for today's teachers* (3d ed.). Needham Heights, MA: Allyn & Bacon.

Zimbardo, P. (1992). *Psychology and life.* New York: HarperCollins.

CHAPTER 10

Abramowitz, A., & O'Leary, S. (1990). Effectiveness of delayed punishment in classroom setting. *Behavior Therapy, 21,* 231–239.

Alberto, P. A., & Troutman, A. C. (1990). *Applied behavior analysis for teachers* (3d ed.). New York: Merrill-Macmillan.

Anderson, L., Evertson, C., & Brophy, J. (1979). An experimental study of effective teaching in first-grade reading groups. *Elementary School Journal, 79,* 193–223.

Bagley, W. C. (1910). *Classroom management.* Norwood, MA: Macmillan Co.

Bellon, J. J., Bellon, E. C., & Blank, M. A. (1992). *Teaching from a research knowledge base: A development and renewal process.* New York: Macmillan.

Berliner, D. (1988). Simple views of effective teaching and a simple theory of classroom instruction. In D. Berliner & B. Rosenshine (Eds.), *Talks to teachers* (pp. 93–110). New York: Random House.

Blechman, E., Kotanchik, N., & Taylor, C. (1981). Families and schools together: Early behavioral intervention with high risk children. *Behavior Therapy, 12,* 308–319.

Boothe, J., et al. (1993). The violence at your door. *Executive Educator, 15(1),* 16–22.

Brophy, J. (1988). Educating teachers about managing classrooms and students. *Teaching and Teacher Education, 4,* 1–8.

Brophy, J., & Evertson, C. (1976). *Learning from teaching: A developmental perspective.* Boston: Allyn & Bacon.

Brophy, J., & Evertson, C. (1978). Context variables in teaching. *Educational Psychologist, 12,* 310–316.

Brophy, J., & Putnam, J. (1979). Classroom management in the elementary grades. In D. Duke (Ed.), *Classroom management, The seventy-eighth yearbook of the National Society for the Study of Education, Part II.* Chicago: University of Chicago Press.

Brophy, J., & Rohrkemper, M. (1981). The influence of problem ownership on teachers' perceptions of and strategies for coping with problem students. *Journal of Educational Psychology, 73,* 295–311.

Bulloch, R. (1987). Planning and the first year of teaching. *Journal of Education for Teaching, 12,* 231–250.

Camp, B. W., Blom, G. E., Herbert, F. & van Doorninck, W. J. (1977). Think aloud: A program for developing self-control in young aggressive boys. *Journal of Abnormal Child Psychology, 5,* 157–189.

Canter, L. (1988). Let the educator beware: A response to Curwin and Mendler. *Educational Leadership, 46(2),* 71–73.

Canter, L., & Canter, M. (1992). *Assertive discipline: Positive behavior management for today's classroom* (2d ed.). Santa Monica, CA: Lee Canter & Associates.

Charles, C. M. (1992). *Building classroom discipline: From models to practice* (2d ed.). New York: Longman.

Charles, C. M. (1996). *Building classroom discipline* (5th ed.). White Plains, NY: Longman.

Corey, G. (1990). *The Skilled Helper.* Belmont, CA: Brooks/Cole.

Curwin, R. L. (1992). *Rediscovering hope: Our greatest teaching strategy.* Bloomington, IN: National Educational Service.

Curwin R. L., & Mendler, A. N. (1988). *Discipline with dignity.* Washington, D.C: ASCD.

Elam, S. (1989). The second Gallup/Phi Delta Kappa Poll of teachers' attitudes toward the public schools. *Phi Delta Kappan, 70(10),* 785–798.

Elam, S., Rose, L., & Gallup, A. (1994). The 26th annual Phi Delta Kappa/Gallup Poll of the public's attitudes toward the public schools. *Phi Delta Kappan, 76(10),* 41–56.

Emmer, E. T. (1987). Classroom management and discipline. In V. Richardson-Koehler (Ed.), *Educators' handbook: A research perspective* (pp. 233–258). New York: Longman.

Emmer, E., Evertson, C., Sanford, J., Clements, B., & Worsham, M. (1989). *Classroom management for secondary teachers* (2d ed.). Englewood Cliffs, NJ: Prentice Hall.

Emmer, E., Evertson, C., Sanford, J., Clements, B., & Worsham, M. (1994). *Classroom management for secondary teachers* (3d ed.). Upper Saddle River, NJ: Prentice Hall.

Emmer, E., Evertson, C., Sanford, J., Clements,. B., & Worsham, M. (1997). *Classroom management for secondary teachers* (4th ed.). Boston: Allyn & Bacon.

Evertson, C. M. (1987). Managing classrooms: A framework for teachers. In D. Berliner & B. Rosenshine (Eds.), *Talks to teachers* (pp. 54–74). New York: Random House.

Evertson, C. M., & Emmer, E. T. (1982). Effective management at the beginning of the school year in junior high classes. *Journal of Educational Psychology, 74,* 485–498.

Evertson, C. M., & Emmer, E., Clements, B., Sandford, J., & Worsham, M. (1989). *Classroom management for elementary teachers* (2d ed.). Englewood Cliffs, NJ: Prentice Hall.

Evertson, C. M., Emmer, E., Clements, B., Sandford, J., & Worsham, M. (1997). *Classroom management for elementary teachers* (4th ed.). Boston: Allyn & Bacon.

Evertson, C. M., & Harris, A. (1992). What we know about managing classrooms. *Educational Leadership, 49,* 74–79.

Evertson, C. M., Emmer, E., Clements, B., Sandford, J., & Worsham, M. (1994). *Classroom management for elementary teachers* (3d ed.). Upper Saddle River, NJ: Prentice Hall.

Evertson, C. M., & Randolph, M. (1995). Classroom management in the learning-centered classroom. In A. Ornstein (Ed.), *Teaching theory and practice.* Needham Heights, MA: Allyn & Bacon.

Feindler, E. L., & Ecton, R. B. (1986). *Adolescent anger control.* New York: Pergammon Press.

Ginott, H. (1971). *Teacher and child.* New York: Macmillan.

Glasser, W. (1990). *The quality school: Managing students without coercion.* New York: Perennial Library.

Good, T. (1979). Teacher effectiveness in the elementary school. *Journal of Teacher Education, 30(2),* 52–64.

Good, T., Brophy, J. E. (1994). *Looking in classrooms* (6th ed.). New York: HarperCollins.

Good, T., & Grouws, D. (1975). Teaching effects: a process-product study in fourth grade mathematics classrooms. *Journal of Teacher Education, 28,* 49–54.

Gordon, T. (1989). *Discipline that works: Promoting self-discipline in children.* New York: Random House.

Hunter, M. (1982). *Mastery teaching.* El Segundo, CA: TIP Publications.

Jones, V. F., & Jones, L. S. (1995). *Comprehensive classroom management: Creating positive learning environments for all students.* Needham Heights, MA: Allyn & Bacon.

Kahn, W. J. (1999). *The A-B-C's of human experience: An intergrative model.* Belmont, CA: Brooks/Cole.

Kohn, A. (1993). *Punished by rewards: The trouble with gold stars, incentive plans, A's, praise and other bribes.* Boston: Hougton Mifflin.

Kounin, J. (1971). *Discipline and group management in classrooms.* New York: Holt, Rinehart & Winston.

Kounin, J. (1977). *Discipline and group management in classrooms* (Rev. Ed.). New York: Holt, Rinehart & Winston.

Kriesberg, S. (1992). *Educating for democracy and community: Toward the transformation of power in our schools.* Cambridge, MA: Education for Social Responsibility.

Lashley, T. J. (1994). Teacher technicians: A "new" metaphor for new teachers. *Action in Teacher Education, 16(1),* 11–19.

Liconia, T. (1991). *Educating for character.* New York: Bantam.

Little, L., & Kelly, M. (1989). The efficacy of response cost procedures for reducing children's noncompliance to parental instructions. *Behavior Therapy, 20,* 525–534

McCaslin, M., & Good, T. (1992). Compliant cognition: The misalliance of management and instructional goals in current school reform. *Educational Researcher, 21(3),* 4–17.

McLaughlin, H. J. (1994). From negation to negotiation: Moving away from the management metaphor. *Action in Teacher Education, 16(1),* 75–84.

Meichenbaum, D. (1977). *Cognitive behavior modification.* New York: Plenum.

Morine-Dershimer, G., & Reeve, P. (1994). Prospective teachers' image of management. *Action in Teacher Education, 16(1),* 29–40.

Moskowitz, G., & Hayman, M. L. (1976). Successful strategies of inner-city teachers: A year long study. *Journal of Educational Research, 69,* 283–289.

Osborn, A. F. (1957). *Applied imagination.* New York: Scribner.

Parsons, R. D. (1995). *The skills of helping.* Needham Heights, MA: Allyn & Bacon.

Parsons, R., & Wicks, R. (1994). *Counseling strategies and intervention techniques for the human services.* Needham Heights, MA: Allyn & Bacon.

Purkey, S., & Smith, M. (1983). Effective schools: A review. *Elementary Journal, 83,* 427–452.

Randolph, C. H., & Evertson, C. M. (1994). Images of management for learner-centered classrooms. *Action in Teacher Education, 16(1),* 55–63.

Rosenshine, B. (1979). Content, time, and direct instruction. In P. Peterson & H. Walberg (Eds.). *Research on teaching: Concepts, findings and implications.* Berkeley, CA: McCutchan.

Rutter, M., Maughan, B., Mortimore, P., Ousten, J. & Smith, A. (1979). *Fifteen thousand hours.* Cambridge, MA: Harvard University Press.

Sardo-Brown, D. (1993). Descriptions of two novice secondary teachers' planning. *Curriculum Inquiry, 23(1),* 63–84.

Sardo-Brown, D. (1994). Middle school teachers' participation in action research. *The AIMS Journal, 9(1),* 13–18.

Schap, E., & Solomon, D. (1990). Schools and classrooms as caring communities. *Educational Leadership, 48(3),* 38–42.

Stratton, C. (1989). Systematic comparison of consumer satisfaction of three cost-effective parent training programs for conduct problem children. *Behavior Therapy, 20,* 103–115.

Sulzer-Azaroff, B., & Mayer, G. (1986). *Achieving educational excellence using behavioral strategies.* New York: Holt, Rinehart & Winston.

Veenman, S. (1984). Perceived problems of beginning teachers. *Review of Educational Research, 54(2),* 143–178.

Weinstein, C. S. (1996). *Secondary classroom management: Lessons from research and practice*. New York: McGraw-Hill.

Weinstein, C. S., & Mignano, A. J., Jr. (1997). *Elementary classroom management: Lessons from research and practice* (2d ed.). New York: McGraw-Hill.

Weinstein, C. S., & Mignano, A. (1993). *Organizing the elementary school classroom: Lessons from research and practice*. New York: McGraw-Hill.

Weinstein, C. S., Woolfolk, A. E., Dittmeier, L., & Shanker, U. (1994). Protector or prison guard? Using metaphors and media to explore student teachers' thinking about classroom management. *Action in Teacher Education, 16(1)*, 41–54.

CHAPTER 11

Bloom, B. S. (1956). *Taxonomy of educational objectives: The classification of educational goals. Handbook I: Cognitive Domain*. New York: McGraw-Hill.

Borko, H., Lalik, R., & Tomchin, E. (1987). Student teachers' understandings of successful and unsuccessful teaching. *Teaching and Teacher Education, 3*, 77–90.

Bullough, R. (1987). Planning and the first year of teaching. *Journal of Education for Teaching, 12*, 231–250.

Calderhead, J. (1984). *Teachers' classroom decision-making*. New York: Holt, Rinehart & Winston.

Calderhead, J. (1993). The contribution of research on teachers' thinking to the professional development of teachers. In C. Day, J. Calderhead & P. Denicolo (Eds.), *Research on teacher thinking: Understanding professional development* (pp. 11–18). London: Falmer Press.

Clark, C. M., & Peterson, P. L. (1986). Teachers' thought processes. In M. C. Wittrock (Ed.), *Handbook of research on teaching* (pp. 255–296). New York: Macmillan.

Clarke, J. H., & Agne, R. M. (1997). *Interdisciplinary high school teaching*. Boston: Allyn & Bacon.

Gagne, R. M. (1985). *The conditions of learning* (4th ed.). New York: Holt, Rinehardt & Winston.

Gagne, R. M., & Driscoll, M. P. (1988). *Essentials of learning for instruction* (2d ed.). Englewood Cliffs, NJ: Prentice Hall.

Gronlund, N. (1995). *How to write and use instructional objectives*. Upper Saddle River, NJ: Merrill/Prentice Hall.

Harrow, A. J. (1972). *A taxonomy of the psychomotor domain*. New York: McKay.

Hunter, M. (1982). *Mastery teaching*. El Segundo, CA: TIP publications.

Kellough, R. D., & Kellough, N. G. (1996). *Middle school teaching: A guide to methods and resources*. Upper Saddle River, NJ: Prentice Hall.

Krathwohl, D. R., Bloom, B. S., & Masia, B. B. (1964). *Taxonomy of educational objectives: The classification of educational goals. Handbook 2. Affective domain*. New York: Longman.

Mager, R. F. (1975). *Preparing instructional objectives* (2d ed.). Belmont, CA: Fearon Publishers.

Marshall, H. (1992). Seeing, redefining, and supporting student learning. In H. Marshall (Ed.), *Redefining student learning: Roots of educational change* (pp. 1–32). Norwood, NJ: Ablex.

McCutcheon, G. (1980). How do elementary school teachers plan? The nature of planning and influences on it. *Elementary School Journal, 81*, 4–23.

Perrone, V. (1994). How to engage students in learning. *Educational Leadership, 51(5)*, 11–13.

Roskos, K., & Neuman, S. B. (1995). Two beginning kindergarten teachers' planning for integrated literacy instruction. *Elementary School Journal, 96*, 195–215.

Sardo-Brown, D. (1988). Twelve middle school teachers' planning. *Elementary School Journal, 89*, 69–87.

Sardo-Brown, D. (1990). A survey of experienced teachers' planning practices. *Journal of Education for Teaching, 16*, 57–59.

Sardo-Brown, D. (1993). Descriptions of two novice secondary teachers' planning. *Curriculum Inquiry, 23*, 63–84.

Sardo-Brown, D. (1996). A longitudinal study of novice secondary teachers' planning: Year two. *Teaching and Teacher Education 12(5)*, pp. 519–530.

Sardo-Brown, D. (1996). A glimpse into the life of one novice second-career teacher using the lens of instructional planning. *Journal of Research in Education, 5(1)*, pp. 20–22.

Sorensen, N. (1993, April). *Stories of teaching and reflections on practice: Year two*. Paper presented at the Annual Meeting of the American Educational Research Association, Atlanta, Georgia.

Zahorik, J. A. (1975). Teachers' planning models. *Educational Leadership, 33*, 134–139.

CHAPTER 12

Ausubel, D. P. (1968). *Educational psychology: A cognitive view*. New York: Holt, Rinehart & Winston, Inc.

Benjafield, J. G. (1992). *Cognition*. Englewood Cliffs, NJ: Prentice Hall, Inc.

Bevevino, M. M., Dengel, J., & Adams, K. (1999). Constructivist theory in the classroom: Internalizing concepts through inquiry learning. *The Clearing House, 72*, 275–278.

Boekaerts, M. (1997). Self-regulated learning: A new concept enhanced by researchers, policy makers, educators, teachers, and students. *Learning and Instruction, 7(2)*, 161–186.

Boone, D., & Boone, C. (1997). Beyond city sidewalks: The blind traveler in a rural environment. *American Rehabilitation, 23(3)*, 2–8.

Brown, D. F., & Rose, T. (1995). Self-reported classroom impact of teachers' theories about learning and obstacles to implementation. *Action in Teacher Education, 17(2)*, 20–29.

Bruner, J. S. (1966). *Toward a Theory of Instruction*. Cambridge, MA: The Belknap Press of Harvard University.

Byrnes, J. P. (1996). *Cognitive development and learning in instructional contexts*. Boston: Allyn & Bacon.

Cardelle-Elaware, M. (1995). Effects of metacognitive instruction on low achievers in mathematics problems. *Teaching and Teacher Education, 11(1)*, 81–95.

Cardellicho, T. L. (1995). Curriculum and the structure of school. *Phi Delta Kappan, 76(8)*, 629–632.

Carr, M., & Jessup, D. L. (1997). Gender differences in first grade mathematics strategy use: Social and metacognitive influences. *Journal of Educational Psychology, 89*, 318–328.

Carter, M., Ensrud, M., & Holden, J. (1997). The Paideia Seminar: A constructivist approach to discussions. *Teaching and Change, 5(1)*, 32–49.

Ciardiello, A. V. (1998). Did you ask a good question today? Alternative cognitive and metacognitive strategies. *Journal of Adolescent and Adult Literacy, 42,* 210–219.

Cole, P. (1993). Learner-generated questions and comments: Tools for improving instruction. ERIC Document Service No.: ED362160.

Deming, M. P., & Valeri-Gold, M. (1994). Portfolio evaluation: Exploring the theoretical base. *Research and Teaching in Developmental Education, 11(1),* 21–29.

Dixon-Krauss, L. (1996). *Vygotsky in the classroom: Mediated literacy instruction and assessment.* White Plains, NY: Longman.

Eggen, P., & Kauchak, D. (1994). *Educational Psychology: Classroom Connections.* New York: Macmillan College Publishing.

Fang, A., & Cox, B. E. (1999). Emergent metacognition: A study of preschoolers' literate behavior. *Journal of Research in Childhood Education,* 13, 175–187.

Feden, P. D. (1994). About instruction: Powerful new strategies worth knowing. *Educational Horizons, 73(1),* 18–24.

Fogarty R., & McTighe, J. (1993). Educating teachers for higher order thinking: The three-story intellect. *Theory into Practice, 32(3),* 161–169.

Fosnot, C. T. (1993). Comments and criticism: Rethinking science education: A defense of Piagetian constructivism. *Journal of Research in Science Thinking, 30(9),* 1189–1201.

Fosnot, C. T. (1996). Construction: A psychological theory of learning. In C. T. Fosnot (Ed.), *Constructivism: Theory, Perspective, and Practice.* New York: Teachers College Press. pp. 8–33.

Frid, S., & Malone, J. (1994). Negotiation of meaning in mathematics classrooms. Science and Mathematics Education Centre. ERIC Document Service No.: ED372944.

Ganz, M. N., & Ganz, B. C. (1990). Linking metacognition to classroom success. *The High School Journal, 73(3),* 180–185.

Garcia, T., & Pintrich, P. R. (1992). Critical thinking and its relationship to motivation: Learning strategies and classroom experience. ERIC Document Service No.: ED351643.

Garnett, P. J., Garnett, P. J., & Hackling, M. W. (1995). Students' alternative conceptions in chemistry: A review of research and implications for teaching and learning. *Studies in Science Teaching,* 25, 69–95.

Good, T., & Brophy, J. (1995). *Contemporary Educational Psychology.* White Plains, NY: Longman Publishers USA.

Gordon, R. (1994). Keeping students at the center: Portfolio assessment at the college level. *Journal of Experiential Education, 17(1),* 23–27.

Gourgey, A. F. (1998). Metacognition in basic skills instruction. *Instructional Science, 26(1–2),* 81–96.

Gregg, D., et al. (1996). Your city as a global field trip. *Social Studies Review, 35(3),* 12–15.

Hartman, H. J., Everson, H. T., & Tobias, S. (1996). Self concept and metacognition in ethnic minorities: Predictions from the BACEIS model. *Urban Education,* 31, 222–238.

Hennessey, M. G. (1993). Students' ideas about their conceptualization: Their elicitation through instruction. ERIC Document Service No.: ED361209

Henson, K. T. (1996). *Methods and Strategies for Teaching in Secondary and Middle Schools.* White Plains, NY: Longman Publishers USA.

Hettich, P. I. (1993). Inducing students to think about their learning: Four approaches. ERIC Document Service No.: ED372039.

Heywood, J., et al. (1992). The training of student-teachers in discovery methods of instruction and learning [and] Comparing guided discovery and expository methods: Teaching the water cycle in geography. ERIC Document Service No.: ED358034.

Higgins, K. M. (1993). An investigation of the effects on students' attitudes, beliefs, and abilities in problem solving and mathematics after one year of a systematic approach to the learning of problem solving. Paper presented at the annual meeting of the American Educational Research Association (Atlanta, Ga, April 12–16, 1993). ERIC Document Service No.: ED365521.

Hwangbo, Y., & Yawkey, T. (1994). Constructivist schooling at early and middle grades: Some key elements that work. *Contemporary Education, 65(4),* 207–210.

Hyde, A. A., Bizar, M. (1989). *Thinking in Context: Teaching Cognitive Processes Across the Elementary School Curriculum.* New York: Longman.

Jones, J. E., & Davenport, M. (1996). Self-regulation in Japanese and American art education. *Art Education, 49(1),* 60–65.

Kamii, C. (1981). Piaget for principals. *Principal, 60(5),* 12–17.

Klein, A. (1991). All about ants: Discovery learning in the primary grades. *Young Children, 46(5),* 23–27.

Lee, O., Fradd, S. H., & Sutman, F. X. (1995). Science knowledge and cognitive strategy use among culturally and linguistically diverse students. *Journal of Research in Science Teaching,* 32, 797–816.

Li, M. F. (1993). Empowering learners through metacognitive thinking, instruction, and design. ERIC Document Service No.: ED362180.

Loranger, A. L. (1994). The study strategies of successful and unsuccessful high school students. *Journal of Reading Behavior, 26(4),* 347–360.

Lord, T. R. (1998). How to build a better mousetrap: Changing the way science is taught through constructivism. *Contemporary Education, 69(3),* 134–136.

Lucangeli, D., et al. (1995). Specific and general transfer effects following metamemory training. *Learning Disabilities Research and Practice, 10(1),* 11–21.

Manning, B., et al. (1996). The self-regulated learning aspect of metacognition: A component of gifted education. *Roeper Review, 18(3),* 217–223.

Mason, L., & Santi, M. (1994). Argumentation structure and metacognition in constructing shared knowledge at school. ERIC Document Service No.: ED371041.

McLain, K. V. M. (1993). Effects of two comprehension monitoring strategies on the metacognitive awareness and reading achievement of third and fifth grade students. ERIC Document Service No: ED364840.

Mokros, J., & Russell, S. J. (1995). Children's concepts of average and representativeness. *Journal for Research in Mathematics Education, 26(1),* 20–29.

Powell, S. D., & Makin, M. (1994). Enabling pupils with learning difficulties to reflect on their own thinking. *British Educational Research Journal, 20(5),* 579–593.

Purdie, N., & Hattie, J. (1996). Cultural differences in the use of strategies for self-regulated learning. *American Educational Research Journal, 33(4),* 845–871.

Reder, L. M., & Schunn, C. D. (1996). Metacognition does not imply awareness: Strategy choice is governed by implicit learning and memory. In L. M. Reder (Ed.), *Implicit Memory and Metacognition.* pp. 45–78. Mahwah, NJ: Lawrence Erlbaum Associates, Publishers.

Reid, D. K., et al. (1994). Special education teachers interpret constructivist teaching. *Remedial and Special Education, 15(5),* 267–280.

Rosenthal-Malek, A. L. (1997). Stop and think: Using metacognitive strategies to teach students social skills. *Teaching Exceptional Children, 29(3),* 29–31.

Schwanenflugel, P. J., Fabricius, W. V., Alexander, J. (1994). Developing theories of mind: Understanding concepts and relations between mental activities. *Child Development, 65,* 1546–1563.

Scruggs, T. E., Mastropieri, M. A., Bakken, J. P., & Brigham, F. J. (1993). Reading versus doing: The relative effects of textbook-based and inquiry-oriented approaches to science learning in special education classrooms. *Journal of Special Education, 27(1),* 1–15.

Smilkstein, R. (1991). A natural teaching method based on learning theory. *Gamut, 36,* 12–15.

Spence, D. J., et al. (1995). Explicit science reading instruction in grade 7: Metacognitive awareness, metacognitive self-management and science reading comprehension. ERIC Document Service No.: ED388500.

Sternberg, R. J. (1998). Metacognition, abilities, and developing expertise: What makes an expert student? *Instructional Science, 26(1),* 127–140.

Thomas, E. L., & Robinson, H. A. (1972). *Improving Reading in Every Class: A Sourcebook for Teachers.* Boston: Allyn & Bacon.

Turner, N. D. (1993). Learning styles and metacognition. *Reading Improvement, 30,* 82–85.

Valsinger, J. (1996). Whose mind? *Human Development, 39,* 295–300.

Vermunt, J. D. (1996). Metacognitive, cognitive, and affective aspects of learning styles and strategies: A phenomenographic analysis. *Higher Education, 31,* 25–50.

Wadsworth, B. J. (1996). *Piaget's Theory of Cognitive and Affective Development.* White Plains, NY: Longman Publishers USA.

Wadsworth, P. (1997). When do I tell them the right answer? *Primary Science Review, 49,* 23–24.

Weber, K. (1989). The case of the walking sweater. In K. Weber, *Five Minute Mysteries* (pp. 151–152). Philadelphia: Running Press.

Wilcox, R. (1987). Rediscovering discovery learning. *The Clearing House, 61,* 53–56.

Wilen, W. W., & Phillips, J. A. (1995). Teaching critical thinking: A metacognitive approach. *Social Education 59(3),* 135–138.

Windschitl, M. (1999). The challenges of sustaining a constructivist classroom culture. *Phi Delta Kappan, 80,* 751–755.

Winemiller, B., Pedersen, B., & Bonnstetter, R. (1991). The rocket project. *Science Scope, 15(2),* 18–22.

Yager, R. E., & Lutz, M. V. (1994). Integrated science: The importance of "how" versus "what." *School Science and Mathematics, 94(7),* 338–345.

Zohar, A. (1999). Teachers' metacognitive knowledge and the instruction of higher order thinking. *Teaching and Teacher Education, 15,* 413–429.

CHAPTER 13

Adams, T. L., & Hsu, J. Y. (1998). Classroom assessment: teachers' conceptions and practices in mathematics. *School Science and Mathematics, 98(4),* 174–180.

Airasian, P. W. (1997). *Classroom Assessment.* McGraw-Hill Companies: New York.

Baxter, G. P., Elder, A., & Glaser, R. (1995). *Cognitive analysis of a science performance assessment (CSE Technical Report 398).* Los Angeles: University of California National Center for Research on Evaluation, Standards, and Student Testing.

Belcher, T., Coates, G. D., & Franco, J. (1997). Assessment and equity. *Yearbook of the National Council of Teachers of Mathematics,* 1997, 195–200.

Berk, R. A. (Ed.). (1986). *Performance assessment.* Baltimore: The Johns Hopkins University Press.

Brophy, J., & Allman, J. (1998). Assessment in a social constructivist classroom. *Social Education, 62(1),* 32–34.

Camp, R. (1992). Assessment in the context of school and school change. In H. Marshall (Ed.), *Redefining student learning: Roots of educational change.* Norwood, NJ: Ablex, pp. 241–263.

Canady, R. L., & Hotchkiss, P. R. (1989). It's a good score! Just a bad grade, *Phi Delta Kappan, 71(1),* 68–71.

Carmichael, H., & Caldwell, M. (1988). Evaluation. In R. McNergney (Ed.) *Guide to classroom teaching* (pp. 263–283). Needham Heights, MA: Allyn & Bacon.

Case, S. (1994). Will mandating portfolios undermine their value? *Educational Leadership, 52(2),* 46–47.

Garner, M., & Englehard, G. (1999). Gender differences in performance on multiple choice and constructed response mathematics items. *Applied Measurement in Education, 12(1),* 29–51.

Gordon, E. W. (1995). Toward an equitable system of educational assessment. *The Journal of Negro Education, 64,* 360–372.

Grady, J. B. (1994). Authentic assessment and tasks: Helping students demonstrate their abilities. *NASSP Bulletin, 78,* 92–98.

Gronlund, N. (1993). *How to make achievement tests and assessments.* Needham Heights, MA: Allyn & Bacon.

Herman, J., Aschbacher, P., & Winters, L. (1992). *A practical guide to alternative assessment.* Alexandria, VA: Association for Supervision and Curriculum Development.

Jovanovic, J., Solano, F. G., & Shavelson, R. J. (1994). Performance-based assessments: Will gender differences in science achievement be eliminated? *Education and Urban Society, 26,* 352–366.

Kamen, M. (1996). A teacher's implementation of authentic assessment in an elementary science classroom. *Journal of Research in Science Teaching, 33(8),* 859–877.

Kindsvatter, R., Wilen, W., & Ishler, M. (1996). *Dynamics of Teaching.* White Plains, NY: Longman Publishers USA.

Klein, S. P., Jovanovic, J., & Stecher, B. M. (1997). Gender and racial/ethnic differences on performance assessments in science. *Educational Evaluation and Policy Analysis, 19,* 83–97.

Krumboltz, J. D., & Yeh, C. J. (1996). Competitive grading sabotages good teaching. *Phi Delta Kappan, 78(4)*, 324–329.

Lensch, J. E. (1996). A sensible approach to assessment. *Principal, 75*, 36–37.

Mackey, J., & Appleman, D. (1988). Questioning skill. In R. McNergney (Ed.), *Guide to Classroom Teaching*, pp. 145–165. Needham Heights, MA: Allyn & Bacon.

Marzano, R. J., Pickering, D., & McTighe, J. (1993). *Assessing student outcomes: Performance assessment using the dimensions of learning model.* Alexandria, VA: Association for Supervision and Curriculum Development.

Mawhinney, T. C. (1999). How standard is standardized testing? *High School Magazine, 6(6)*, 4.

McTighe, J. (1997). What happens between assessments? *Educational Leadership, 54(4)*, 6–12.

Murphy, S. (1995). Revisioning reading assessment: Remembering to learn from the legacy of reading tests. *The Clearing House, 68*, 235–239.

Nitko, A. (1996). *Educational assessment of students* (2d Ed.). Englewood Cliffs, NJ: Prentice Hall.

Sardo-Brown, D. (1990). Middle level teachers' participation in action research. *The Middle School Journal, 22(2)*, 30–32.

Shepard, L. A. (1994). The challenges of assessing young children appropriately. *Phi Delta Kappan, 76(3)*, 206–212.

Stiggins, R. J. (1997). *Student-Centered Classroom Assessment.* Upper Saddle River, NJ: Prentice Hall, Inc.

Tierney, R. J., Carter, M. A., & Desai, L. E. (1991). *Portfolio assessment in the reading-writing classroom.* Norwood, MA: Christopher-Gordon Publishers.

Valencia, S. (1990). The portfolio approach to classroom assessment: The whys, whats, and hows. *The Reading Teaching, 43(4)*, 338–340.

Wolfe, E., & Miller, T. R. (1997). Barriers to implementation of portfolio assessment in secondary education. *Applied Measurement in Education, 10*, 235–251.

Worthen, B. (1993). Critical issues that will determine the future of portfolio assessment. *Phi Delta Kappan 14*, 44–454.

Worthen, B. R., & Spandel, V. (1991). Putting the standardized test debate in perspective. *Educational Leadership, 48*, 65–69.

CREDITS

CHAPTER 1

Page 3, David Young-Wolff / PhotoEdit; page 4, Will Hart / PhotoEdit; page 6, Steve Skjold / PhotoEdit; page 7 *(top left)*, David Young-Wolff / PhotoEdit; *(top right)*, Spencer Grant / Monkmeyer Press; *(bottom right)*, Michael Newman / PhotoEdit; page 9, Tom McCarthy / Index Stock; page 10, Ellen Senisi / The Image Works.

CHAPTER 2

Page 31, Elizabeth Crews / The Image Works; page 34, Michael Newman / PhotoEdit; page 35, Anderson / Monkmeyer Press; page 38, Mary Langenfeld; page 43, Tony Freeman / PhotoEdit; page 52, Bob Daemmrich / The Image Works; page 63, Bob Daemmrich / Stock Boston.

CHAPTER 3

Page 71, David Young-Wolff / PhotoEdit; page 74, Will Hart / PhotoEdit; page 85, Bob Daemmrich Photography; page 86 Richard Hutchings / PhotoEdit; page 88, Michael Newman / PhotoEdit; page 92, Peter Huizdak / The Image Works.

CHAPTER 4

Page 111, Elizabeth Crews / The Image Works; page 117, Bettmann / Corbis; page 119, Courtesy of Jerry Bauer / Harvard University; page 122, Bob Daemmrich / Stock Boston; page 138, Tom Nebbia / Corbis; page 145, Robin Sachs / PhotoEdit.

CHAPTER 5

Page 161, David Young-Wolff / PhotoEdit; page 164, Will Hart / PhotoEdit; page 176, David Young-Wolff / PhotoEdit; page 178, Bob Daemmrich Photography; page 191, David Young-Wolff / PhotoEdit.

CHAPTER 6

Page 203, Tony Freeman / PhotoEdit; page 211, Dean Conger / Corbis; page 218, Christopher Johnson / Stock Boston; page 220, Mary Kate Denny / PhotoEdit; page 230, Mary Kate Denny / PhotoEdit.

CHAPTER 7

Page 245, Bob Daemmrich Photography; page 262, Bill Aron / PhotoEdit.

CHAPTER 8

Page 281, Bob Daemmrich Photography; page 282, Billy E. Barnes / PhotoEdit; page 285, Tony Freeman / PhotoEdit; page 307, Randi Anglin / Syracuse Newspapers / The Image Works; page 308, Bill Aron / PhotoEdit.

CHAPTER 9

Page 317, Spencer Grant / PhotoEdit; page 318, Jeffry W. Myers / Stock Boston; page 321, Mary Kate Denny / PhotoEdit; page 337 Mary Kate Denny / PhotoEdit; page 339, Bob Daemmrich / The Image Works.

CHAPTER 10

Page 349, Bob Daemmrich Photography; page 353, Grantpix / Monkmeyer Press; page 354, Dana White / PhotoEdit; page 358, Jonathan Nourok / PhotoEdit; page 362, David Young-Wolff / PhotoEdit; page 363, Frank Siteman/Index Stock; page 368, Bill Aron / PhotoEdit.

CHAPTER 11

Page 387, Elizabeth Crews / The Image Works; page 390, John Berry/Syracuse Newspapers/The Image Works; page 401, Hunter Freeman / Tony Stone Images; page 405, Adamski Peek / Tony Stone Images; page 412, Will Hart / PhotoEdit.

CHAPTER 12

Page 419, David Young-Wolff / PhotoEdit; page 426, Will Hart / PhotoEdit; page 430, Peter Cade / Tony Stone Images; page 441, Richard B. Levine.

CHAPTER 13

Page 447, Bob Daemmrich / The Image Works; page 450, Will Hart / PhotoEdit; page 464, Bob Daemmrich / Stock Boston; page 467, Ellen Senisi / The Image Works.